The Official CompTIA® A+® Core 2 Study Guide (Exam 220-1002)

The Official CompTIA® A+® Core 2 Study Guide (Exam 220-1002)

COURSE EDITION: 1.01

Acknowledgements

James Pengelly, Author

Pamela J. Taylor, Author

Brian Sullivan, Media Designer

Peter Bauer, Content Editor

Thomas Reilly, Vice President Learning

Katie Hoenicke, Director of Product Management

James Chesterfield, Manager, Learning Content and Design

Becky Mann, Senior Manager, Product Development

Notices

DISCLAIMER

TRADEMARK NOTICES

COPYRIGHT NOTICE

Table of Contents

About This Guide

CompTIA A+ certified professionals are proven problem solvers. They support today's core technologies from security to cloud to data management and more. CompTIA A+ is the industry standard for launching IT careers into today's digital world. It is the only industry recognized credential with performance-based items to prove pros can think on their feet to perform critical IT support tasks in the moment. It is trusted by employers around the world to identify the go-to person in end point management and technical support roles. CompTIA A+ is regularly re-invented by IT experts to ensure that it validates core skills and abilities demanded in the workplace.

The Official CompTIA® A+® Core 2 (Exam 220-1002) guide provides the background knowledge and skills you will require to be a successful A+ technician. It will help you prepare to take the CompTIA A+ Core Series certification examination (exam number 220-1002), in order to become a CompTIA A+ Certified Professional.

Guide Description

Target Student
This guide is designed for individuals who have basic computer user skills and who are interested in obtaining a job as an entry-level IT technician. This guide is also designed for students who are seeking the CompTIA A+ certification and who want to prepare for the CompTIA A+ Core 2 220-1002 Certification Exam.

Prerequisites
To ensure your success, you should have experience with basic computer user skills, be able to complete tasks in a Microsoft® Windows® environment, be able to search for, browse, and access information on the Internet, and have basic knowledge of computing concepts. You can obtain this level of skills and knowledge by taking the following official CompTIA courses:

*   *The Official CompTIA® IT Fundamentals+ (Exam FC0-U61)*

Note: These prerequisites might differ significantly from the prerequisites for the CompTIA certification exams. For the most up-to-date information about the exam prerequisites, complete the form on this page: **https://certification.comptia.org/training/exam-objectives**

Guide Objectives
In this guide, you will install, configure, optimize, troubleshoot, repair, upgrade, and perform preventive maintenance on personal computers, digital devices, and operating systems. You will:

*   Support operating systems.
*   Install, configure, and maintain operating systems.
*   Maintain and troubleshoot Microsoft Windows.
*   Configure and troubleshoot network connections.
*   Manage users, workstations, and shared resources.
*   Implement physical security.
*   Secure workstations and data.
*   Troubleshoot workstation security issues.
*   Support and troubleshoot mobile devices.
*   Implement operational procedures.

How to Use This Book

As You Learn

This book is divided into lessons and topics, covering a subject or a set of related subjects. In most cases, lessons are arranged in order of increasing proficiency.

The results-oriented topics include relevant and supporting information you need to master the content. Each topic has various types of activities designed to enable you to solidify your understanding of the informational material presented in the guide. Information is provided for reference and reflection to facilitate understanding and practice.

At the back of the book, you will find a glossary of the definitions of the terms and concepts used throughout the guide. You will also find an index to assist in locating information within the instructional components of the book. In many electronic versions of the book, you can click links on key words in the content to move to the associated glossary definition, and on page references in the index to move to that term in the content. To return to the previous location in the document after clicking a link, use the appropriate functionality in your PDF viewing software.

As a Reference

The organization and layout of this book make it an easy-to-use resource for future reference. Taking advantage of the glossary, index, and table of contents, you can use this book as a first source of definitions, background information, and summaries.

Guide Icons

Watch throughout the material for the following visual cues.

Student Icon	Student Icon Descriptive Text
	A **Note** provides additional information, guidance, or hints about a topic or task.
	A **Caution** note makes you aware of places where you need to be particularly careful with your actions, settings, or decisions, so that you can be sure to get the desired results of an activity or task.

Lesson 1

Supporting Operating Systems

LESSON INTRODUCTION

As a professional IT support representative or PC service technician, your job will include installing, configuring, maintaining, and troubleshooting personal computer operating systems, applications, hardware, and networks. Before you can perform any of these tasks, you need to understand the basics of what an operating system is, including the various versions, features, components, and technical capabilities. With this knowledge, you can provide effective support for all types of system environments.

The operating system is the software that provides a user interface to the computer hardware and provides an environment in which to run software applications and create computer networks. In this lesson, you will identify the basic types, functions, features, and tools of operating systems, with a particular focus on Microsoft® Windows®.

LESSON OBJECTIVES

In this lesson, you will:

- Compare common OSs and their purposes and features.

- Use administrative tools and system utilities in different versions of Windows.

- Perform file management using Explorer and command prompt tools.

- Use the command-line tools and the Disk Management console to configure disks, volumes, arrays, and mount points.

- Use Device Manager and Control Panel/Settings to configure power management, display and sound devices, and to remove devices.

Topic A

Identify Common Operating Systems

EXAM OBJECTIVES COVERED

1002-1.1 Compare and contrast common operating system types and their purposes.
1002-1.2 Compare and contrast features of Microsoft Windows versions.

In this topic, you will identify the types and functions of personal computer (PC) and mobile device operating systems. The first step is to learn about the various operating systems available today, and to identify those that are commonly used on PCs and those that are used on tablets and smartphones.

Without a user-friendly operating system, most people would not be capable of using their computers or mobile devices to successfully perform the tasks required of them. As an IT professional, being familiar with the different types of operating systems can help you to support a variety of computer and mobile device environments.

WHAT IS AN OPERATING SYSTEM?

A computer requires an **operating system (OS)** in order to function. The operating system provides the interface between the hardware, application programs, and the user. The operating system handles many of the basic system functions, such as interaction with the system hardware and input/output.

An operating system is generally made up of a number of core files—called the **kernel** —with additional **device drivers** and **programs** to provide extended functionality. The earliest operating systems for PCs, such as Microsoft's Disk Operating System (DOS), used a command-line user interface or simple menu systems. Windows and software applications for Windows were marked by the use of a **Graphical User Interface (GUI)**. This helped to make computers easier to use by non-technical staff and home users.

Note: Actually, some DOS applications presented a GUI, of a kind. Windows is sometimes described as a WIMP (Window, Icon, Menu, Pointing device) interface.

The **desktop style** favored by a particular OS or OS version is a powerful factor in determining customer preferences for one OS over another.

OS TYPES

The market for operating systems is divided into four main sections:

- Business client—an OS designed to work as a client in business networks.
- Network Operating System (NOS)—an OS designed to run on servers in business networks.
- Home client—an OS designed to work on standalone or workgroup PCs in a home or small office.
- Cell phone (smartphone)/Tablet—an OS designed to work with a handheld portable device. This type of OS must have a touch-operated interface.

COMPATIBILITY ISSUES

A software application is coded to run on a particular OS. You cannot install an app written for iOS® on an Android™ smartphone. The developer must create a different version of the app. This can be relatively easy for the developer or quite difficult, depending on the way the app is coded and the target platforms. The application or app "ecosystem," or the range of software available for a particular OS, is another big driver of customer acceptance for a particular OS product.

Compatibility also affects version updates to operating system software. There is always a chance that some change in the new OS version will cause software (or hardware device drivers) written for an older version not to work properly. In the business client market, this makes companies very reluctant to update to new OS versions without extensive testing. As extensive testing is very expensive, they are generally reluctant to adopt new versions without a compelling need to do so.

 Note: *These compatibility concerns are being mitigated somewhat by the use of web applications and cloud services. A web application only needs the browser to be compatible, not the whole OS. The main compatibility issue for a web application is supporting a touch interface and a very wide range of display resolutions on the different devices that might connect to it.*

Finally, compatibility also affects the way that computers running different operating systems can communicate on data networks. The computers cannot "talk" to one another directly. The operating systems must support common network protocols that allow data to be exchanged in a standard format.

MICROSOFT WINDOWS

Microsoft Windows is the dominant commercial PC OS, estimated to be installed on 90% of the world's desktop and laptop computers. The **Windows Server** OS is also widely used on private network servers and Internet servers running web, email, and social networking apps.

Like most software, Windows and Windows Server® have been released in a number of versions over the years. Historically, a new version would have to be purchased, though upgrade discounts were usually available. A new version may introduce significant changes in desktop styles and user interface of Windows and add new features and support for new types of hardware. On the downside, a new version may not be compatible with hardware and software applications designed for earlier versions.

One of the main functions of an OS is to provide an interface (or **shell**) between the user and the computer hardware and software. Windows has a number of interface components designed both for general use and for more technical configuration and troubleshooting.

The top level of the user interface is the **desktop**. This is displayed when Windows starts and the user logs on. The desktop contains icons to launch applications and possibly user data files. The desktop also contains the Start Menu or **Start Screen** and taskbar, which are used to launch and control applications.

MICROSOFT WINDOWS VERSIONS

Let's start by taking a look at the most popular versions of Windows currently in use. Other operating systems will be examined more closely later in the course.

WINDOWS 10

Windows 10, first released in 2015, is the current version. Windows 10 aims to provide a consistent user experience across different types of devices, including desktop PCs, laptops, tablets, and smartphones.

When installed to a PC or laptop, Windows 10 retains the user desktop and taskbar familiar from legacy versions but uses a touch-optimized **Start Screen** interface to access apps and programs. This replaces the old Start Menu. As well as shortcuts, the **Start Screen** can display app tiles, which can contain live or actively updated content. These app tiles are fully customizable.

Windows 10 (1803) desktop and Start Screen. (Screenshot used with permission from Microsoft.)

The **Start Screen** is activated by selecting the **Start** button ▦ or by pressing the **Windows** key, which might also be labeled the **Start** key.

 Note: *On a smartphone or tablet, the **Start Screen** replaces the desktop entirely.*

WINDOWS 10 FEATURE UPDATES

With Windows 10, Microsoft indicated that they would no longer release new versions of Windows, but would instead maintain the OS with **feature updates** on a periodic basis. Thus, the current version of Windows, at the time of writing, is still Windows 10. This approach is known as "Windows as a service." Feature updates for Windows 10 are identified with a name and number. For example, in July 2016, Microsoft released a Windows 10 feature update called Windows 10 Anniversary Update. This release was identified with the number 1607, which corresponds to the year (2016) and month (07/ July) of release. The full name of the current version of Windows 10 at the time of writing is Windows 10 Spring Creators Update (1803), replacing the Fall Creators Update (1709).

In addition to feature updates, Windows is updated periodically with **quality updates**. Quality updates do not usually make radical changes to Windows, though some do include new features. Quality updates might sometimes cause compatibility problems with some hardware devices and software applications, but this is less likely than with feature updates.

Windows 10 Mobile

Microsoft has developed versions of Windows for mobile devices, including Windows CE, Windows Phone® 7, and Windows Phone 8. None of these have enjoyed the same sort of success as Windows has in the PC market.

With Windows 10 Mobile, Microsoft has adopted a consistent user interface and code base across all types of devices. Windows 10 Mobile has a very small smartphone market share compared to Android and iOS. Microsoft develops and sells Windows 10 Mobile smartphones and Surface® tablets.

WINDOWS 8 AND WINDOWS 8.1

Compared to earlier versions, Windows 8 (released in 2012) and Windows 8.1 (2013) imposed significant user interface changes to provide better support for touchscreens. One of these changes was the first use of the **Start Screen**. Not all of the changes were popular with users familiar with Windows 7, however. Windows 10 addressed this feedback and was also made available as a free upgrade to Windows 8. Consequently, Windows 10 very quickly replaced Windows 8 and Windows 8 is not that widely used, having about 7% market share at the time of writing.

As well as introducing the **Start Screen** for the first time, in Windows 8, some of the search and configuration settings are accessed as **charms**. The Charms bar is opened by swiping from the right of the screen.

Windows 8.1 showing the Charms bar. (Screenshot used with permission from Microsoft.)

On a desktop PC, you can move the mouse pointer down from the top-right or (more simply) press **Windows+C**. The Charms bar was discontinued in Windows 10.

 Note: *Windows 8 was swiftly updated to Windows 8.1 to address some issues with the interface, principally the lack of a **Start** button and forcing use of the **Start Screen** at boot rather than the desktop. In other respects, references to Windows 8 in this course can be taken to apply to Windows 8.1, too. There was never a Windows 9.*

WINDOWS 7

Prior to Windows 8, there was Windows 7 (2009), Windows Vista (2007), and Windows XP (2001). Of these, Windows 7 is still widely used, with an estimated installation base of around 45% of all PCs. Despite no longer being officially supported by Microsoft, Windows XP is still installed on about 5% of devices. Windows Vista never achieved a significant market share.

Windows 7 uses the "classic" Start Menu user interface. The Start Menu contains icon shortcuts to recently used programs and some of the main folders and utilities. The All Programs submenu contains the shortcuts to all the other desktop applications installed on the computer.

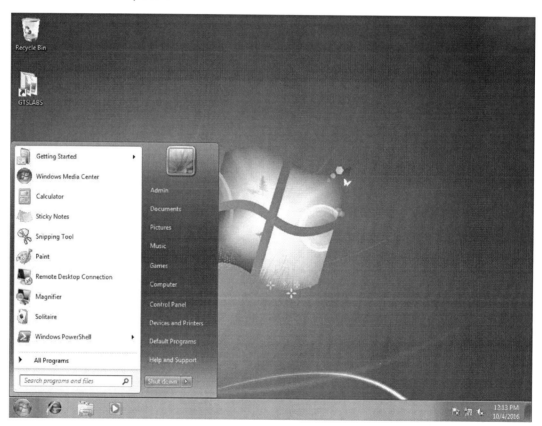

Windows 7 desktop and Start Menu. (Screenshot used with permission from Microsoft.)

 Note: *According to the CompTIA exam objectives, you will not be expected to support Windows Vista or Windows XP.*

WINDOWS EDITIONS

Each version of Windows is available in different editions. Editions are used by Microsoft to create different markets for Windows. Windows 7 editions included

Starter, Home Basic, Home Premium, Professional, Enterprise, and Ultimate. Windows 10 is available in the following editions:

- Windows 10 Home—designed for domestic consumers and Small Office Home Office (SOHO) business use. The Home edition cannot be used to join a Windows domain network.
- Windows 10 Pro—designed for small and medium-sized businesses. The "Professional" edition comes with networking and management features designed to allow network administrators more control over each client device.
- Windows 10 Enterprise/Windows 10 Enterprise (Long Term Servicing Channel)— similar to the Pro edition but designed for volume licensing by medium and large enterprises.
- Windows 10 Education/Pro Education—variants of the Enterprise and Pro editions designed for licensing by schools and colleges.

Note: The Windows 7 Ultimate edition was a "superset" with all the features from other editions. Ultimate editions were discontinued with Windows 8. The distinction between basic and premium home editions was also abandoned. Windows 8 has an unnamed edition—sometimes referred to as "Windows 8 Core"—rather than a "Home" edition.

WINDOWS IN THE CORPORATE WORLD

The principal distinguishing feature of the Professional/Pro, Enterprise, Ultimate, and Education editions (regardless of version) is the ability to join a **domain network**. A personal user or small business owner can just administer each machine they own individually. On a corporate network, it is necessary to manage user accounts and system policies centrally, because there are more machines to manage and security requirements are higher. This centralized management is provided by joining each computer to a domain, where the accounts are configured on Domain Controller (DC) servers. Some other notable corporate features are as follows:

- **BitLocker**—enables the user to encrypt all the information on a disk drive. Encryption means that data on the device is protected even if someone steals it (as long as they cannot crack the user password). BitLocker is included with Windows 7 Enterprise and Ultimate, Windows 8 Pro and Enterprise, and Windows 10 Pro, Enterprise, and Education editions.
- **Encrypting File System (EFS)**—where BitLocker encrypts an entire drive, EFS can be used to apply file- or folder-level encryption. EFS is included with Windows 7 Professional, Enterprise, and Ultimate, Windows 8 Pro and Enterprise, and Windows 10 Pro, Enterprise, and Education editions.
- **BranchCache**—an enterprise might have computers installed at different geographic locations needing to view and update data at a central office. As the Wide Area Network (WAN) links from each location to the office might be quite slow, it can be useful for the remote computers to share access to a single cache of data from shared folders and files or document portals such as SharePoint sites. This reduces the amount of WAN traffic because each client does not have to download its own copy individually. BranchCache is supported on Windows 7 Enterprise and Ultimate, Windows 8 Enterprise, and Windows 10 Pro, Enterprise, and Education editions.

Note: The Pro/Professional editions support a limited type of BranchCache for Background Intelligent Transfer Service (BITS) communications only. Most document and file sharing uses HyperText Transfer Protocol (HTTP) or Server Message Block (SMB), and these types of transfers are only supported by the Enterprise/Ultimate editions. BITS might be used for tasks such as patch deployment or image-based installs.

WINDOWS FOR PERSONAL USE

Windows Media Center is a Microsoft app allowing the computer to be used as a sort of home entertainment appliance, such as playing DVDs (several other functions of the product are no longer supported). Media Center was included in the Windows 7 Home Premium, Professional, Enterprise, and Ultimate editions. It is the principal distinction between the Windows 7 Home Basic and Windows 7 Home Premium editions. It became a paid-for add-on in Windows 8 and was discontinued in Windows 10.

If Media Center is not available, a DVD player is available from Microsoft. Third-party software is required to playback commercial Blu-ray™ discs.

32-BIT AND 64-BIT WINDOWS

Each version and edition of Windows is available as 32-bit or 64-bit (x64) software. 64-bit editions of Windows can run most 32-bit applications software, though there may be some exceptions (you should check with the software vendor). The reverse is not true, however; a 32-bit version of Windows cannot run 64-bit applications software.

64-bit editions of Windows also require 64-bit hardware device drivers authorized ("signed") by Microsoft. If the vendor has not produced a 64-bit driver, the hardware device will not be usable.

WINDOWS SYSTEM LIMITS

The versions and editions of Windows have different restrictions in terms of CPU types and features and memory supported. Windows 10 has the following system limits:

Feature	Home	Pro	Education	Enterprise
SMP (Multiple CPUs)	No	2-way	2-way	2-way
Multicore	Yes	Yes	Yes	Yes
RAM limitations (32-bit)	4 GB	4 GB	4 GB	4 GB
RAM limitations (64-bit)	128 GB	2 TB	2 TB	6 TB

Windows 8 has the following system limits:

Feature	Core	Pro/Enterprise
SMP	No	2-way
Multicore	Yes	Yes
RAM limitations (32-bit)	4 GB	4 GB
RAM limitations (64-bit)	128 GB	512 GB

Windows 7 has the following system limits:

Feature	Home Basic	Home Premium	Professional	Enterprise	Ultimate
64-bit Edition	Yes	Yes	Yes	Yes	Yes
SMP	No	No	2-way	2-way	2-way
Multicore	Yes	Yes	Yes	Yes	Yes
RAM limitations (32-bit)	4 GB	4 GB	4 GB	4 GB	4 GB

Feature	Home Basic	Home Premium	Professional	Enterprise	Ultimate
RAM limitations (64-bit)	8 GB	16 GB	192 GB	192 GB	192 GB

The Windows 7 Starter edition was only available to system builders (OEMs) for installation on netbooks and sub-notebooks. It supports up to 2 GB RAM. There is no 64-bit version of the Starter edition.

OS LIFECYCLES

An **end of life system** is one that is no longer supported by its developer or vendor. End of life systems no longer receive security updates and so represent a critical vulnerability for a company's security systems if any remain in active use.

Microsoft products are subject to a support lifecycle policy. Windows versions are given five years of mainstream support and five years of extended support (during which only security updates are shipped). Support is contingent on the latest Service Pack being applied (non-updated versions of Windows are supported for 24 months following the release of the SP). Windows 10 retirement schedules for feature updates —referred to as "end of service"—are 18 months, except for September updates for Education/Enterprise editions only, which are supported for 30 months.

To find out when Microsoft products will be retired or how long specific products will be supported, visit the Microsoft Product Lifecycle Search tool at **support.microsoft.com/lifecycle/search**.

When you plan to install a new version of an operating system as an upgrade, you must check that your computer meets the hardware requirements for the new version. As operating system software such as Windows 10 moves towards more of a service model, with quite frequent feature updates, it could be the case that an update has its own system requirements that were different from the original. Plus, Microsoft points out that the core hardware requirements for Windows 10 are the same as those for Windows 7. Other factors might impact your ability to apply a feature update, including support for third-party driver or applications software.

APPLE OPERATING SYSTEMS

In 1984, when the IBM PC was the dominant desktop standard, Steve Jobs and Steve Wozniak created a new type of personal computer—the Apple® Macintosh® (or Mac®). It was revolutionary because it came with a graphical user interface at a time when IBM's PC used the command-line/text menu DOS operating system. The Mac has never matched Windows' huge user base, although its current incarnation does have a truly devoted following.

APPLE MAC OS/OS X/macOS

The main difference between Mac OS and other operating systems is that the OS is only supplied with Apple-built computers. You cannot purchase Mac OS and install it on an ordinary PC. This helps to make Mac OS stable but does mean that there is far less choice in terms of buying extra hardware.

macOS desktop. (Screenshot courtesy of Apple.)

The current lines—OS X® and more recently macOS®—were re-developed from the kernel of another type of operating system called UNIX. This kernel is supplemented with additional code to implement the Mac's graphical interface and system utilities and to maintain compatibility with older Mac OS applications. macOS gets periodic "dot" version updates. At the time of writing, the current version is 10.14 or "Mojave," and updates are being released to existing customers free-of-charge.

As there is a tight link between the models of Mac computers and the OS, Apple makes specific update limitations about whether a new version of macOS can be installed to a Mac computer. Check **support.apple.com** for the technical specification for any particular macOS release. Apple does not publish end of life policies.

APPLE iOS

iOS is the operating system for Apple's iPhone® smartphone and iPad® tablet. While also derived from UNIX, iOS is a closed source operating system. This means that the code used to design the software is kept confidential and can only be modified by Apple. macOS and iOS have some similarities but they are not compatible; an app developed for iOS will not run on macOS.

On an iOS device, apart from volume and power, the only external button is the Home key, which returns the user to the home screen "desktop."

The interface is then entirely controlled via touch. Point to icons to open apps, swipe or flick from left-to-right to access the keyboard and search, or flick right-to-left to view more icons. Re-arrange icons by tapping and holding for a few seconds. The icons will then "wobble" and can be dragged to a different page or into the dock taskbar at the bottom. Press the Home key to save.

To view and manage open apps, double-click the Home key to open the Multitasking bar.

iOS 11 running on an iPhone 7. (Screenshot courtesy of Apple.)

Touch can be operated either with your fingers or with a special soft-touch stylus. There are many more gestures in addition to those listed above. For example, shaking the device is often used to activate undo. There are also external keyboards available and most Apple devices support Siri®, a voice recognition system and personal assistant.

New versions are released approximately every year with various .x updates. Version 12 is current at time of writing. Apple makes new versions freely available, though older hardware devices may not support all the features of a new version, or may not be supported at all. As with macOS, update limitations are published at **support.apple.com** but there are no end of life policies.

UNIX-BASED OPERATING SYSTEMS

Windows and macOS dominate the desktop/workstation/laptop market, but a third "family" of operating systems is very widely used on a larger range of devices.

UNIX

UNIX is a trademark for a family of operating systems originally developed at Bell Laboratories beginning in the late 1960s. All UNIX® systems share a kernel/shell architecture, with the kernel providing the core functionality and the interchangeable shells providing the user interface. Unlike Windows and macOS, UNIX is portable to different hardware platforms; versions of UNIX can run on everything from personal computers to mainframes and on many types of computer processors.

LINUX

Originally developed by Linus Torvalds, **Linux** is based on UNIX. UNIX was developed over decades by various commercial, academic, and not-for-profit organizations. This resulted in several versions, not all of which are compatible, and many of which are proprietary or contain copyrighted or patented code or features. Linux® was developed as a fully open source alternative to UNIX (and for that matter, to Windows and macOS and iOS).

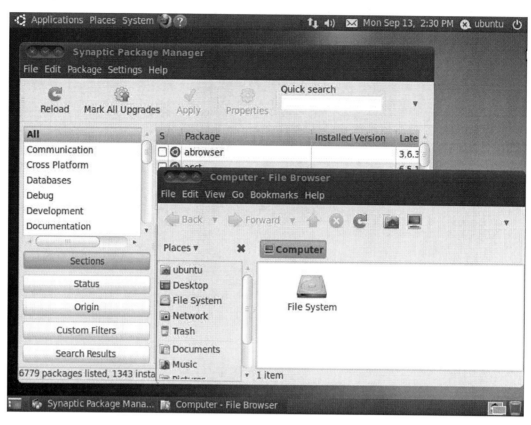

Ubuntu Linux.

Linux can be used as a desktop or server OS. There are many distributions or distros, notably SUSE®, Red Hat®, CentOS, Fedora®, Debian®, Ubuntu®, and Mint®. Each distro adds specific packages and interfaces to the generic Linux kernel and provides different support options. Linux does not require a graphical interface, though many distributions provide one.

IBM®, Sun/Oracle®, and Novell® are among the vendors producing end-user applications for Linux. As a desktop OS it tends to be used in schools and universities more than in business or in the home. As a server OS, it dominates the market for web servers. It is also used very widely as the OS for "smart" appliances and Internet of Things (IoT) devices.

CHROME OS

Chrome OS is derived from Linux, via an open source OS called Chromium™. Chrome OS™ itself is proprietary. Chrome OS is developed by Google to run on specific laptop (Chromebook) and PC (Chromebox) hardware. This hardware is designed for the budget and education markets.

Chrome OS was primarily developed to use web applications. In a web application, the software is hosted on a server on the Internet and the client connects to it using a browser. The client computer does not need to be particularly powerful as the server does most of the processing. Chrome OS provides a minimal environment compared to Windows. This means that there is less chance of some other software application or hardware device driver interfering with the function of the browser.

There are also "packaged" apps available for use offline and Chrome OS can run apps developed for Android.

ANDROID

Android is a smartphone/tablet OS developed by the Open Handset Alliance, primarily driven by Google. Unlike iOS, it is an open-source OS, based on Linux. The software code is made publicly available (**source.android.com**). This means that there is more scope for hardware vendors, such as Acer®, Asus®, HTC®, Huawei®, LG, Motorola®, OnePlus, Oppo™, Samsung®, Sony®, and Xiamoi to produce vendor-specific versions.

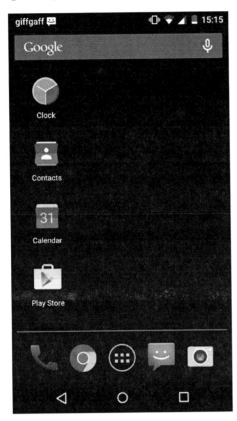

Android lollipop home screen.

Like iOS, Android is updated with new major (1.x) and minor (x.1) versions, each of which is named after some kind of sweet stuff. At the time of writing, current versions include 7.1 (Nougat) and 8.1 (Oreo). Because handset vendors produce their own editions of Android, device compatibility for new versions is more mixed compared with iOS.

End of life policies and update restrictions for particular handsets are determined by the handset vendor rather than any kind of overall Android authority. Companies ordering handsets in bulk as employee devices may be able to obtain their own guarantees.

Topic B
Use Windows Features and Tools

EXAM OBJECTIVES COVERED
1002-1.4 Given a scenario, use appropriate Microsoft command line tools.
1002-1.5 Given a scenario, use Microsoft operating system features and tools.
1002-1.6 Given a scenario, use Microsoft Windows Control Panel utilities.
1002-2.6 Compare and contrast the differences of basic Microsoft Windows OS security settings.

As an administrator, you will manage the computer through a graphic user interface (GUI) for some tasks and through a command line interface for others. In this topic, you will examine some of the administrative tools and utilities for Windows computers.

When you configure or troubleshoot a computer, you need to do so with an account that has sufficient privileges to make major changes to OS settings and files. If misused, these privileges could be a significant threat to the security of the computer system and network. In this topic, you will also learn how to exercise administrative privileges safely.

WINDOWS SETTINGS AND CONTROL PANEL

Many tools are used to configure Windows settings and hardware devices. Some of the tools are accessible to ordinary users; others need administrative privileges to run.

CONTROL PANEL

In Windows 7, the **Control Panel** is the best place to start configuring your system. The icons in the Control Panel represent applets used to configure a part of the system.

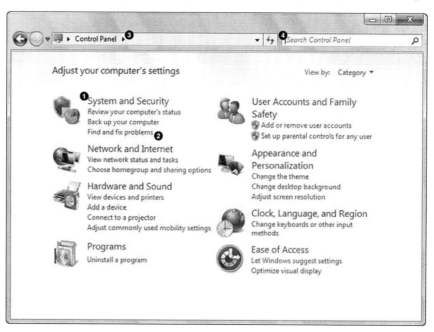

Windows 7 Control Panel showing 1) Task groups; 2) Configuration applets; 3) Navigation breadcrumb; 4) Search box. (Screenshot used with permission from Microsoft.)

Most applets are added by Windows but some software applications, such as antivirus software, add their own applets. Configuration information entered via Control Panel is ultimately stored in the Windows registry database.

You can access Control Panel through the Start Menu. In addition, certain applets are accessible by viewing object properties straight from the desktop or from Explorer.

Control Panel applets are arranged by category by default, although you can display

"All items" via the breadcrumb or the "View by" menu. Note that options with the icon on or next to them will require you to authorize use of the command through User Account Control (UAC).

WINDOWS SETTINGS

Windows Settings is a touchscreen-enabled "app" interface for managing a Windows 10 computer.

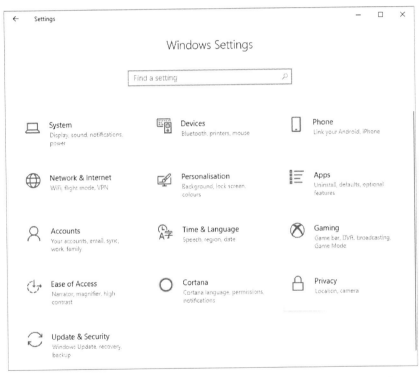

Windows Settings app. (Screenshot used with permission from Microsoft.)

Most of the standard Windows 10 configuration settings can be located within Windows Settings, but not all of them. Some options are still configured via Control Panel. Each Windows 10 feature update tends to move more configuration options from Control Panel to Windows Settings, though.

 Note: In Windows 8, this app is referred to as "PC Settings" and is accessed via the Charms bar.

USER ACCOUNTS

A **user account** is the principal means of controlling access to computer and network resources and rights or privileges. Resources include access to files, folders, or printers; rights or privileges refers to the ability to make configuration changes or read/modify a data file. Each resource is configured with an access list, which is a list of users and their permissions for that resource.

A user account is protected by authenticating the account owner—making them provide some data that is known or held only by them.

Each user account is also associated with a profile, stored in a subfolder of the **Users** folder. The profile contains per-user registry settings (ntuser.dat) and the default document folders. Software applications might also write configuration information to the profile.

ADMINISTRATOR AND STANDARD USER ACCOUNTS

When the OS is first installed, the account created or used during setup is a powerful local administrator account. The account is assigned membership of the local Administrators group. Generally speaking, you should only use this account to manage the computer—install applications and devices, perform troubleshooting, and so on.

You should create ordinary user accounts for day-to-day access to the computer. This is done by putting additional users of the computer in the **Standard users** group. Standard users cannot change the system configuration and are restricted to saving data files within their own user profile folder or the Public profile. For example, a user named David with standard privileges could save files only within C:\Users\David or C:\Users\Public. Administrators can access any folder on the computer.

 *Note: Windows protects system folders from non-root administrative users. These folders are owned by a system account (such as **TrustedInstaller**). This provides more protection against malware and misconfiguration. It is possible for any administrator account to take ownership of a system folder and override these protections, though.*

USER ACCOUNT MANAGEMENT

The **User Accounts** applet in Control Panel allows users to manage their accounts. Users can manage local and network passwords and choose a picture to represent them on the log on screen.

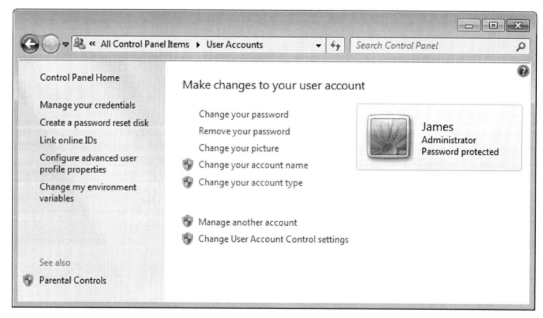

User Accounts applet in Windows 7. (Screenshot used with permission from Microsoft.)

Administrators can create and delete accounts or change the type of account (between administrator and user).

LOCAL AND MICROSOFT ACCOUNTS

In Windows 8 and Windows 10, the **User Accounts** applet is still present and can still be used to change an account name or type, but it cannot be used to create new accounts. That function, plus most other account functions, is performed in the **Accounts** section of Windows Settings. Windows 8/10 accounts can either be local accounts (like Windows 7 user accounts) or linked to a **Microsoft account**, which gives access to Microsoft's cloud services and syncs desktop settings across multiple devices.

Creating a new account. (Screenshot used with permission from Microsoft.)

HOW TO CREATE A USER ACCOUNT IN WINDOWS 10

Here is a general procedure that you can follow to create user accounts in Windows 10.

CREATE A USER ACCOUNT IN WINDOWS 10

To create a user account in Windows 10:

1. Open **Settings**.
2. Select **Accounts**.
3. Select **Family & other people**.
4. Select **Add someone else to this PC**.
5. If you are creating a Microsoft account, enter the email address or phone number associated with their Microsoft account, select **Next**, and then select **Finish**. The user must complete the process of signing in themselves.
6. If you are creating a local account, select **I don't have this person's sign-in information**, and then select **Add a user without a Microsoft account**. Provide a user name, password, and security question information, and then select **Next**. The user must complete the process of signing in themselves.

UAC

User Account Control (UAC) is a solution to the problem of elevated privileges. In order to change important settings on the computer, such as installing drivers or software, administrative privileges are required. Previous versions of Windows make dealing with typical administrative tasks as an ordinary user very difficult, meaning that most users were given administrative privileges as a matter of course. This makes the OS more usable but it also makes it much more vulnerable, as any malicious software infecting the computer would run with the same administrative privileges.

UAC SECURE DESKTOP

Accounts with administrative privileges are mediated by UAC. UAC counters the problem of escalated privileges by first extending some system privileges to ordinary users but then running accounts in a sandbox mode. Tasks that require UAC are shown with a Security Shield icon.

Security Shield icon showing that changing this setting will require UAC authorization. (Screenshot used with permission from Microsoft.)

When a user needs to exercise administrative rights, she or he must explicitly confirm use of those rights:

- If the logged in account has standard privileges, an administrator's credentials must be entered via the authorization dialog box.
- If the logged in account is already an administrator, the user must still click through the authorization dialog box.

The desktop darkens into a special secure desktop mode to prevent third-party software from imitating the authorization dialog box.

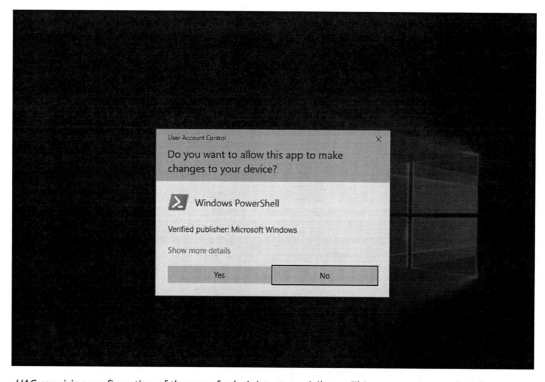

UAC requiring confirmation of the use of administrator privileges. This account is an administrator so only a confirmation is required—no credentials have to be supplied. (Screenshot used with permission from Microsoft.)

CONFIGURING UAC

UAC protects the system from malware running with elevated administrator privileges. This is a good thing, but if you need to perform numerous system administration tasks at the same time, UAC can prove frustrating. You can configure UAC notifications to appear more or less frequently by using the configuration option in the User Accounts applet.

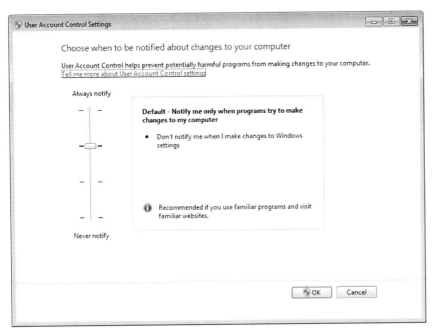

Configuring UAC notifications. (Screenshot used with permission from Microsoft.)

ADMINISTRATIVE TOOLS

One of the options in Control Panel is the **Administrative Tools** shortcut.

Administrative Tools in Windows 7. (Screenshot used with permission from Microsoft.)

Administrative Tools contains several shortcuts, giving you the ability to define and configure various advanced system settings and processes. There are also tools to assist with troubleshooting the system.

DEFAULT MICROSOFT MANAGEMENT CONSOLES

Administrative Tools is a collection of pre-defined Microsoft Management Consoles (MMCs). Each console contains one or more snap-ins that are used to modify various settings. The principal consoles are:

- **Component Services**—enables you to register new server applications or reconfigure security permissions for existing services.
- **Computer Management**—the default management console with multiple snap-ins to configure local users and groups, disks, services, devices, and so on.

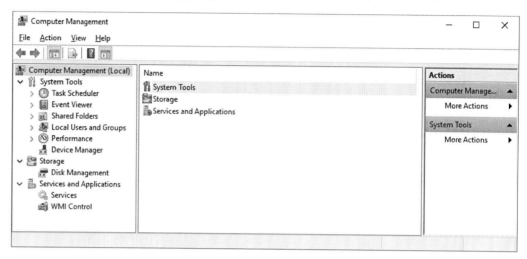

The default Computer Management console in Windows 10 with the configuration snap-ins shown on the left. (Screenshot used with permission from Microsoft.)

- **Data Sources**—control connections to databases set up on the local computer.
- **Event Viewer**—allows monitoring of Windows logs. System, security, and application events are recorded in these logs. There are also application- and service-specific logs.
- **Local Security Policy**—allows you to view and edit the current security policy. A computer that is a member of a domain will have the security settings defined in the domain security policy.
- **Print Management**—set properties and monitor local printers and manage printer sharing on the network.
- **Reliability and Performance Monitoring**—view the performance of the local computer.
- **Services**—start, stop, and pause services.

 Note: Windows 10 adds quite a few more shortcuts under Administrative Tools, including **Disk Cleanup**, **System Configuration**, **System Information**, *and* **Task Scheduler**.

MMC CUSTOMIZATION

As well as using the default consoles, you may find it useful to create your own. Consoles can be configured for each administrator and the details saved as a file with an MSC extension in their Start Menu folders.

 Note: Most MMC snap-ins can be used to manage either the local computer or a remote computer (a computer elsewhere on the network).

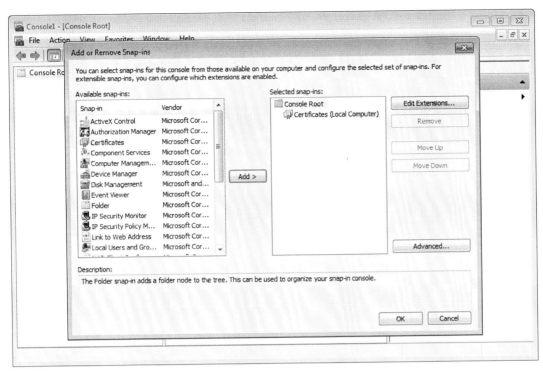

Adding a Snap-in in Windows 7. (Screenshot used with permission from Microsoft.)

HOW TO CREATE CUSTOM MMCs IN WINDOWS

Here is a general procedure that you can follow to create custom MMCs in Windows.

CREATE CUSTOM MMCs IN WINDOWS

To create custom MMCs in Windows:

1. To access the management console, run the `mmc` command.
2. If necessary, in the **User Access Control** message box, select **Yes**.
3. Select **File→Add/Remove Snap-In**.
4. Select a snap-in and select **Add**.
5. If necessary, select a computer to manage and select **OK** or **Finish**.
6. Select and add additional snap-ins as needed.
7. Select **OK**.
8. Select **File→Save As** and save the custom MSC file with a unique name.

ACCESS OPTIONS FOR SYSTEM TOOLS

Control Panel and Administrative Tools contain most of the shortcuts for the system features, but there are other ways of accessing key tools.

COMPUTER/THIS PC

The **Computer** object (renamed **This PC** in Windows 8/10) provides access to your local drives, printers, and any network drives that have been mapped. To browse resources, open **Computer/This PC** then the icon that represents the resource you want to view.

By right-clicking the icon itself and selecting the **Properties** option from the menu, you can access System properties. You can also right-click and select **Manage** to open the default Computer Management console.

WinX/POWER USERS MENU

Pressing **Windows**+**X** or right-clicking the **Start** button shows a shortcut menu including Control Panel, Windows Settings, and File Explorer, but also management utilities such as Device Manager, Computer Management, Command Prompt, and Windows PowerShell®.

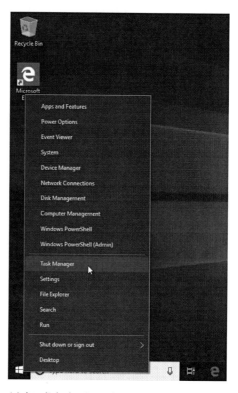

Windows 10 WinX menu (right-click the Start button). (Screenshot used with permission from Microsoft.)

 Note: *Contents of the WinX menu do change frequently. For example, the Control Panel link is no longer included in Windows 10 (1803).*

INSTANT SEARCH BOX AND RUN COMMAND

The **Instant Search** box on the Start Menu/**Start Screen** will execute programs and configuration options using simple names. You can open any file or program by pressing the **Windows** key then typing the path to the file. In the case of registered programs and utilities, you simply need to type the program file name or utility name.

Alternatively, you can access the **Run** dialog box using **Windows**+**R** or entering `run` into the search box.

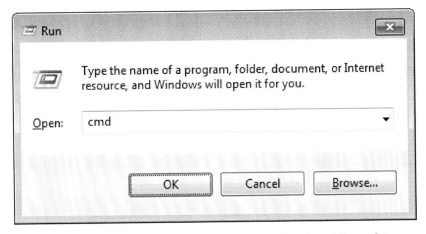

Run dialog box. (Screenshot used with permission from Microsoft.)

Note: *The run command is useful if you want to execute a program with switches that modify the operation of the software. For example, Microsoft Office programs can be executed using safe mode switches for troubleshooting.*

.MSC EXTENSIONS AND THE RUN LINE

There are several management consoles that you can access via the Run line by using the .MSC extension. For example:

- `devmgmt.msc` opens the Device Manager console.
- `diskmgmt.msc` opens the Disk Management console.
- `compmgmt.msc` opens the Computer Management console.

COMMAND LINE TOOLS

Most configuration of Windows can be done via convenient GUI tools, such as the management consoles and Control Panel. In some circumstances, though, it is necessary to use a command prompt to configure or troubleshoot a system. As you learn the commands, you may also find it quicker to use the command shell for actions such as file management. Learning commands is also valuable if you have to write scripts to automate Windows.

COMMAND PROMPT

You can run any command from the **Run** dialog box. However, to input a series of commands or to view output from commands, you need to use the command shell (`cmd.exe`). To open the prompt, type `cmd` in the **Run** dialog box or **Instant Search** box.

Note: *Alternatively, you can type* `command` *to achieve the same thing. This used to be specifically a DOS command interpreter, but now just links to cmd.exe.*

You may need to run the command prompt with elevated privileges in order to execute a command. If a command cannot be run, the error message "The requested operation requires elevation" is displayed.

```
Command Prompt                                              —   □   ×

Microsoft Windows [Version 10.0.17134.285]
(c) 2018 Microsoft Corporation. All rights reserved.

C:\Users\James>netstat -abo
The requested operation requires elevation.

C:\Users\James>
```

Trying to run a command that requires elevation. You must open a new command prompt window as administrator. (Screenshot used with permission from Microsoft.)

You cannot continue within the same window. You need to open a new command prompt as administrator. Right-click the command prompt shortcut and select **Run as administrator** then confirm the UAC prompt. Alternatively, type `cmd` in the Instant Search box then press **Ctrl+Shift+Enter**.

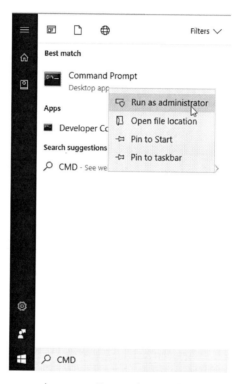

Opening an elevated command prompt. (Screenshot used with permission from Microsoft.)

When run as administrator, the title bar shows "Administrator: Command Prompt" and the default folder is C:\Windows\System32 rather than C:\Users*Username*.

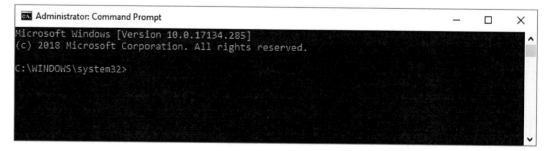

Elevated command prompt. (Screenshot used with permission from Microsoft.)

Note: *You can use this technique to open other utilities, such as Explorer or Notepad, with administrative privileges.*

COMMAND SYNTAX

To run a command, type it at the prompt (>) using the command name and any switches and arguments using the proper syntax. When you have typed the command, press **Enter** to execute it.

The syntax of a command lists which arguments you must use (plus ones that are optional) and the effect of the different switches. Switches are usually preceded by the forward slash escape character.

Note: *If an argument includes a space, it may need to be entered within quotes (."..").*

As you enter commands, the prompt fills up with text. If this is distracting, you can use the `cls` command to clear the screen.

Some commands, such as `nslookup` or `telnet`, can operate in interactive mode. This means that using the command starts that program and from that point, the prompt will only accept input relevant to the program. To exit the program you use the `exit` or `quit` command (or press **Ctrl+C**). The `exit` command will close the cmd window if not used within an interactive command.

GETTING HELP

The command prompt includes a rudimentary help system. If you type `help` at the command prompt then press **Enter**, a list of available commands is displayed. If you enter `help` *CommandName*, help on that command is displayed, listing the syntax and switches used for the command. You can also display help on a particular command by using the `/?` switch (for example, `netstat /?` displays help on the `netstat` command).

```
Administrator: Command Prompt                               —   □   ×

C:\WINDOWS\system32>netstat /?

Displays protocol statistics and current TCP/IP network connections.

NETSTAT [-a] [-b] [-e] [-f] [-n] [-o] [-p proto] [-r] [-s] [-x] [-t] [interval]

  -a            Displays all connections and listening ports.
  -b            Displays the executable involved in creating each connection or
                listening port. In some cases well-known executables host
                multiple independent components, and in these cases the
                sequence of components involved in creating the connection
                or listening port is displayed. In this case the executable
                name is in [] at the bottom, on top is the component it called,
                and so forth until TCP/IP was reached. Note that this option
                can be time-consuming and will fail unless you have sufficient
                permissions.
  -e            Displays Ethernet statistics. This may be combined with the -s
                option.
  -f            Displays Fully Qualified Domain Names (FQDN) for foreign
                addresses.
  -n            Displays addresses and port numbers in numerical form.
  -o            Displays the owning process ID associated with each connection.
  -p proto      Shows connections for the protocol specified by proto; proto
                may be any of: TCP, UDP, TCPv6, or UDPv6. If used with the -s
                option to display per-protocol statistics, proto may be any of:
                IP, IPv6, ICMP, ICMPv6, TCP, TCPv6, UDP, or UDPv6.
  -q            Displays all connections, listening ports, and bound
                nonlistening TCP ports. Bound nonlistening ports may or may not
                be associated with an active connection.
  -r            Displays the routing table.
  -s            Displays per-protocol statistics. By default, statistics are
                shown for IP, IPv6, ICMP, ICMPv6, TCP, TCPv6, UDP, and UDPv6;
```

Help on the netstat command. (Screenshot used with permission from Microsoft.)

TEXT EDITORS

Many files used by the operating system and applications are in a binary file format that can only be interpreted by the application. A plain text file can be modified in any text editor, but if it is saved through an application other than a basic text editor, it could be converted to a binary format and so become unusable. Windows supplies the basic text editor Notepad to modify text files. There are many third-party alternatives with better features, however.

RUN COMMAND

You can also execute commands from **Instant Search** or from the **Run** dialog box. If a command is interactive, it will open a command prompt window for input. If a command is non-interactive, the command prompt window will open briefly and close again as the command executes. If you want to force a command into interactive mode, use the `cmd /k` keyword before the command (for example, `cmd /k ipconfig`).

WINDOWS SHUTDOWN OPTIONS

When the user wants to finish using Windows, simply disconnecting the power runs a risk of losing data or corrupting system files. There are various choices for closing or suspending a session:

- Shut down (`/s`)—close all open programs and services before powering off the computer. The user should save changes in any open files first but will be prompted to save any open files during shut down.
- Standby/Sleep—save the current session to memory and put the computer into a minimal power state.
- Hibernate (`/h`)—save the current session to disk before powering off the computer.
- Log off (`/l`)—close all open programs and services started under the user account but leave the computer running.
- Switch user—log on to another user account, leaving programs and files under the current account open.
- Lock—secure the desktop with a password while leaving programs running.
- Restart (`/r`)—close all open programs and services before rebooting without powering down. This is also called a soft reset.

These options can be selected from the Start Menu/**Start Screen** or by pressing **Ctrl +Alt+Del**.

Options on the Windows 7 power button. (Screenshot used with permission from Microsoft.)

Note: *One of the "quirks" of Windows 8.0 was the lack of an obvious way to select the* **Shut Down** *command. Microsoft expected users to just use the physical power button, which on a modern computer invokes a shut down command (soft power) rather than a hard reset (unless you keep the power button pressed down). Users were reluctant to adopt this method, no doubt following years of IT departments telling them not to turn off a computer that way. The power options in Windows 8.0 are accessed via the Charms bar. The* **Start** *button and a power button on the* **Start Screen** *was returned in 8.1. In Windows 10, it appears right above the* **Start** *button, where no one can miss it.*

The computer can also be shut down at a command prompt by using the `shutdown` command plus the relevant switch (shown in the previous figure). If a shutdown is in progress, `shutdown /a` aborts it (if used quickly enough). The `/t nn` switch can be used to specify delay in seconds before shutdown starts; the default is 30 seconds.

THE WINDOWS REGISTRY

The Windows registry provides a remotely accessible database for storing operating system, device, and software application configuration information. When you boot a Windows machine, the registry is populated with information about hardware detected in your system. During boot, Windows extracts information from the registry, such as which device drivers to load and in what order. Device drivers also send and receive data from the registry. The drivers receive load parameters and configuration data. Finally, whenever you run a setup program or configure the system via Control Panel/Settings or Administrative Tools, it will add or change data in the registry.

The registry does have a dedicated tool called `regedit` for direct editing, but it is not the tool you would use on an everyday basis to modify configuration data. Control Panel/Settings and Administrative Tools are better options for most tasks.

REGISTRY STRUCTURE

The registry is structured as a set of five root keys that contain computer and user databases. The computer database includes information about hardware and software installed on the computer. The user database includes the information in user profiles, such as desktop settings, individual preferences for certain software, and personal printer and network settings.

Root Key Name	Description
HKEY_LOCAL_ MACHINE	Hardware information such as bus type, system memory, device drivers, and startup control data. HKLM also contains the Security Accounts Manager (SAM) password file (not viewable) and system-wide software settings.
HKEY_CLASSES_ROOT	Object Linking And Embedding (OLE) and file association data.
HKEY_CURRENT_USER	Contains the profile for the user who is currently logged on, including environment variables, desktop settings, network connections, printers, and application preferences.
HKEY_USERS	Contains all actively loaded user profiles, including HKEY_CURRENT_ USER, which always refers to a child of HKEY_USERS, and the default profile.
HKEY_CURRENT_CONFIG	Contains system and software configuration information specific to this session.

SUBKEYS AND VALUES

Each root key can contain subkeys and data items called value entries. Subkeys are analogous to folders and the value entries are analogous to files. A value entry has three parts: the name of the value, the data type of the value, and the value itself. The following table lists the different data types.

Data Type	Description
REG_BINARY	Raw binary data. Most hardware component information is stored as binary data and displayed in hex format.
REG_DWORD	Data represented by a 4-byte number. Many parameters for device drivers and services are this type and can be displayed in binary, hex, or decimal format.
REG_SZ	A string or sequence of characters representing human-readable text.
REG_MULTI_SZ	A multiple string. Values that contain lists or multiple text values are usually this type. Entries are separated by NULL characters.
REG_EXPAND_SZ	An expandable data string, which is text that contains a variable to be replaced when called by an application. For example, the string %SystemRoot% would be replaced by the actual location of the folder containing the Windows system files.

REGISTRY DATABASE FILES

The registry database is stored in binary files called **hives**. A hive comprises a single file (with no extension), a .LOG file (containing a transaction log), and a .SAV file (a copy of the key as it was at the end of setup). The system hive also has an .ALT backup file. Most of these files are stored in the %SystemRoot%\System32\Config folder, but hive files for user profiles are stored in the folder holding the user's profile. The following table shows the standard hives.

Hive	Files
HKEY_CURRENT_CONFIG	system, system.alt, system.log, system.sav
HKEY_CURRENT_USER	ntuser.dat, ntuser.dat.log
HKEY_LOCAL_MACHINE \SAM	ssam, sam.log, sam.savv
HKEY_LOCAL_MACHINE\ SECURITY	security, security.log, security.sav
HKEY_LOCAL_MACHINE\ SOFTWARE	software, software.log, software.sav
HKEY_LOCAL_MACHINE\ SYSTEM	system, system.alt, system.log, system.sav
HKEY_USERS\.DEFAULT	default, default.log, default.sav
HKEY_CLASSES_ROOT	Not stored in a hive but built from the \SOFTWARE \CLASSES keys in CURRENT_USER and LOCAL_MACHINE

EDITING THE REGISTRY

You can start the Registry Editor by running `regedit` via **Instant Search**, the **Run** dialog box, or the command prompt. You can use it to view or edit the registry and to back up and restore portions of the registry.

Use the **Find** tool (**Ctrl+F**) to search for a key or value. If you want to copy portions of the registry database and use them on other computers, select **File→Export Registry**

File. The file will be exported in a registry-compatible format and can be merged into another computer's registry by double-clicking the file (or calling it from a script).

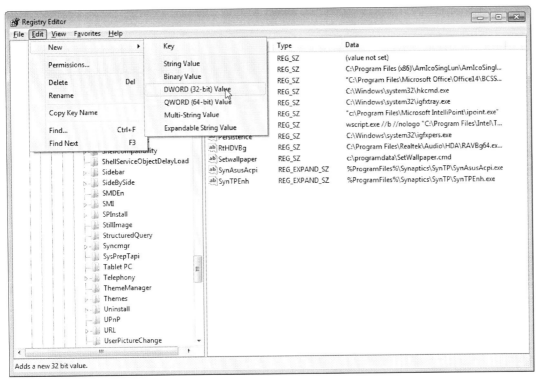

Editing the registry. (Screenshot used with permission from Microsoft.)

A registration file is a plain text file. If you merge changes from a .reg file back to the registry, additions that you have made to the registry will not be overwritten.

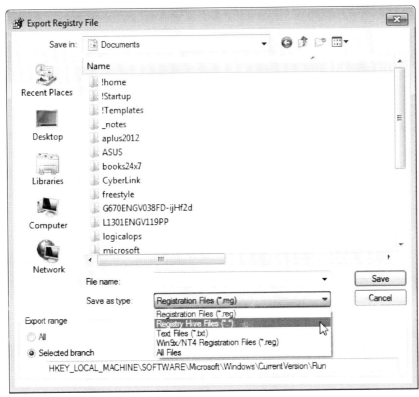

Selecting a file format for exporting a registry key. (Screenshot used with permission from Microsoft.)

Use the **Registry Hive Files** format to create a binary copy of that portion of the registry. Restoring from the binary file will remove any additions you made, as well as reversing the changes.

HOW TO EDIT THE WINDOWS REGISTRY

Here is a general procedure that you can follow to edit the Windows registry.

EDIT THE WINDOWS REGISTRY

To edit the Windows registry:

1. Open **Instant Search**, the **Run** dialog box, or a command prompt.
2. Enter the `regedit` command.
3. If necessary, select **Yes** in the **User Access Control** dialog box.
4. To search for a key or value, select **Edit→Find** or press **Ctrl+F**, type the key or value name, and select **Find Next**.
5. To edit a key or value, double-click it in the right pane to open its dialog box; then change the necessary parameters and select **OK**.
6. To copy portions of the registry database and use them on other computers, select **File→Export**, provide a name for the export file, and select **Save**. The file will be exported in a registry-compatible format and can be merged into another computer's registry by double-clicking the file (or calling it from a script).

Topic C
Manage Files in Windows

EXAM OBJECTIVES COVERED
1002-1.4 Given a scenario, use appropriate Microsoft command line tools.
1002-1.5 Given a scenario, use Microsoft operating system features and tools.
1002-1.6 Given a scenario, use Microsoft Windows Control Panel utilities.
1002-2.6 Compare and contrast the differences of basic Microsoft Windows OS security settings.

File management is a critical part of using a computer. As a computer support professional, you will often have to assist users with locating files. You should also be familiar with the Windows system folders and know how to perform file management at the command prompt as well as the GUI.

WINDOWS FILE AND FOLDER MANAGEMENT TOOLS

File Explorer provides hierarchical access to the system objects, drives, folders, and files stored on the computer. Explorer enables you to open, copy, move, rename, view, and delete files and folders.

Note: File Explorer was previously called "Windows Explorer." It is often just referred to as "Explorer," as the process is run from the file `explorer.exe`*.*

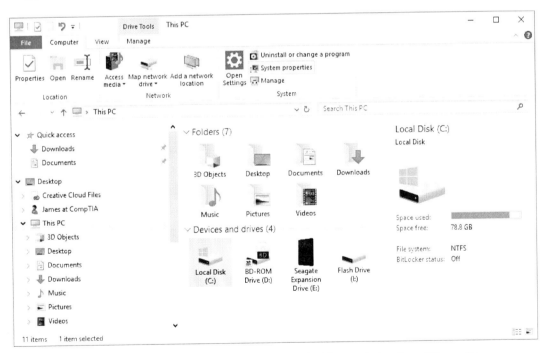

File Explorer in Windows 10. (Screenshot used with permission from Microsoft.)

Explorer appears as a two-paned window showing the hierarchical structure of your system. The left pane shows folders and the right pane shows the contents of the currently selected folder. Arrow symbols are used to indicate parts of the hierarchy that can be expanded or collapsed.

 *Note: You can navigate the whole thing using the keyboard. Use **Tab** and **Shift+Tab** to switch between panes. Use the **Up** and **Down** arrows to move between folders and **Left** and **Right** arrows to expand and collapse trees.*

The basic principle is that ordinary users can write (save data files) only to their profile folders and a special public profile. All other areas of the file system are protected; accessible only to accounts with administrative privileges.

SYSTEM HIERARCHIES IN WINDOWS VERSIONS

In Windows, system objects are organized in a hierarchy. While the system objects themselves remain much the same, their exact name and place in the hierarchy changes from Windows version to Windows version. The basic purpose of the system objects is to mediate user access to personal files stored within their own folder plus local drives and network shares.

WINDOWS 7 SYSTEM HIERARCHY

In Windows 7, each profile folder contains subfolders for different types of files (documents, pictures, music, video, and so on). User access to the profile folder is largely mediated through the Libraries feature. Libraries are virtual folders that can represent content saved in different locations in the file system and on different file systems. For example, a documents library could show the contents of the user's documents folder and a USB drive.

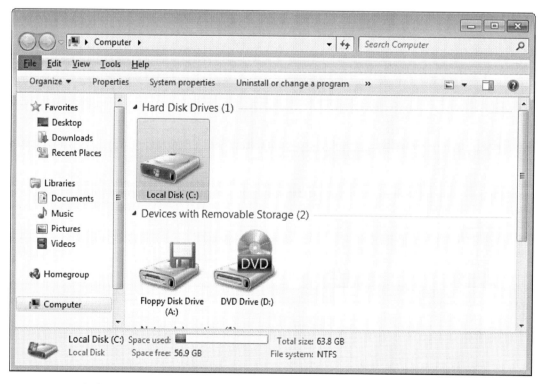

Windows 7 system objects. (Screenshot used with permission from Microsoft.)

The Computer system object allows the user to explore the contents of any local drives attached to the PC. The Network and Homegroup objects show servers and their shared files and printers on the local network. Favorites is a place for users to add shortcuts to other folders or locations in the file system.

WINDOWS 8 SYSTEM HIERARCHY

In Windows 8, the computer object is named This PC and contains the user's desktop, the main document folders (including a downloads folder for files saved via the browser), and any local drives. The Libraries feature is hidden by default. Network, Homegroup, and Favorites work in the same way as Windows 7. The top level may also contain the OneDrive® object, which allows access to a cloud-based storage folder linked to the user's Microsoft account.

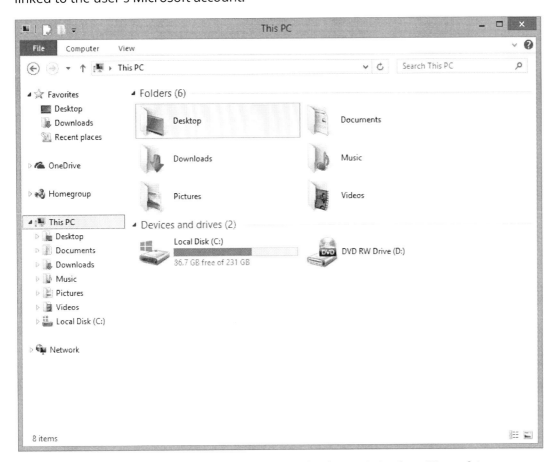

Windows 8 system objects. (Screenshot used with permission from Microsoft.)

WINDOWS 10 SYSTEM HIERARCHY

When browsing the computer using File Explorer in Windows 10, two top-level categories are shown in the navigation pane. Quick access contains shortcuts to folders that are most useful (replacing Favorites). These can be modified by dragging and dropping. By default, it contains shortcuts to your personal Desktop, Downloads, Documents, and Pictures folders.

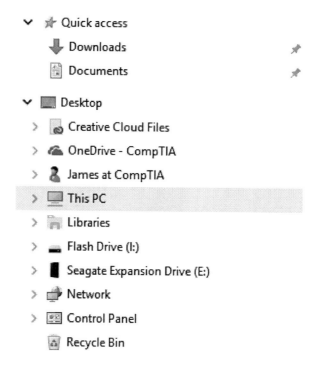

File Explorer navigation pane showing top-level categories in Windows 10. (Screenshot used with permission from Microsoft.)

The second top-level category is the Desktop. Under the "Desktop" object, you can find the following categories:

- **OneDrive**—if you sign into the computer with a Microsoft account, this shows the files and folders saved to your cloud storage service on the Internet. As you can see from the screenshot, other cloud service providers may add links here, too.
- **User account**—the folders belonging to your account profile. For example, in the previous screenshot, the user account is listed as "James at CompTIA."
- **This PC**—access to user-generated files in the user's profile plus the hard drives and removable storage drives available to the PC.
- **Libraries**—these can be used to create views of folders and files stored in different locations and on different disks. As with Windows 8, Libraries may be hidden by default, unless the computer was upgraded from Windows 7.
- **Network**—contains computers, shared folders, and shared printers available over the network.
- **Control Panel**—options for configuring legacy Windows features. Most configuration is now performed via the Settings app rather than Control Panel.
- **Recycle Bin**—provides an option for recovering files and folders that have been recently deleted.

DRIVES, FOLDERS, AND FILES

The top-level categories in the navigation pane show "logical" system objects. Actual data storage is configured on one or more drives. Each drive can have folders and files stored on it.

LOCAL DRIVES

Within the Computer/This PC object, drives are referred to by letters and optional labels. A "drive" can be a single physical disk or a partition on a disk. A drive can also point to a shared network folder "mapped" to a drive letter. By convention, the A: drive is the floppy disk (very rarely seen these days) and the C: drive is the partition on the primary fixed disk holding the Windows installation.

Every drive contains a directory called the **root directory**. The root directory is represented by the backslash (\ ). For example, the root directory of the C: drive is C:\. Below the root directory is a hierarchical structure of directories called subdirectories. A sample directory structure is shown in the diagram.

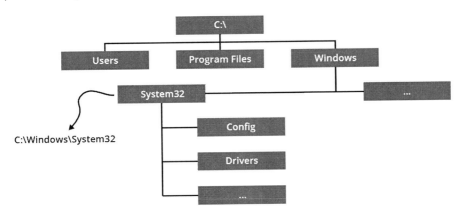

Typical Windows directory structure.

Files may be placed at each level but the root, and certain other folders are designated as system and protected from use by standard users. While it is possible to create subfolders off the root folder, it is much better to keep user data within the profile subfolder within "Users."

FOLDER CREATION

You can use the shortcut or File menus to create a new folder within another object. Windows has various folder naming rules that must be followed when modifying the folder structure:

- No two subfolders within the same folder may have the same name. Subfolders of different folders may have the same name, though.
- Folder names may not contain the following reserved characters: \ / : * ? " < > |
- The full path to an object (including any file name and extension) may not usually exceed 260 characters.

A warning message is displayed if these rules are not followed and the user is prompted to enter a new folder name.

 Note: Folder and file names are case aware, which means that the system preserves case in the name as entered but does not regard the case as significant for operations such as detecting duplicate names or indexing.

FILE CREATION

Files are the containers for the data that is used and modified through the operating system and applications. Files store either text or binary data. Text data is human-readable, while binary data can only be interpreted by a software application compatible with that file type. Most user-generated files are created via the Save command of an application.

Files follow a similar naming convention to folders, except that the last part of the file name represents a **file extension**, which describes what type of file it is. The extension is used by Windows to associate the file with an application. The extension is divided from the rest of the file name by a period. By convention, extensions were three characters, but there are many applications (such as Microsoft Office) that now use four or more characters for the file extension. By default, the extension is not shown to the user.

 Note: You can use a period as part of the main part of the file name, too. It is the last period that delimits the file extension.

SYSTEM FILES

System files are the files that are required for the operating system to function. These files are typically hidden because their deletion can prevent the computer from working properly. For system files, both the file extension and the location of the file in the system hierarchy are important, as they help the computer recognize it as a system file.

The root directory of a typical Windows installation normally contains the following files and subdirectories:

- **Windows**—the system root, containing drivers, logs, add-in applications, system and registry files (notably the System32 subdirectory), fonts, and so on.

 Note: System32 contains most of the applications and utilities used to manage and configure Windows. This is true even of 64-bit versions of Windows. 32-bit Dynamic Link Libraries (DLL) running under 64-bit Windows are stored in the SYSWOW64 folder.

- **Program Files/Program Files (x86)**—subdirectories for installed applications software. In 64-bit versions of Windows, a Program Files (x86) folder is created to store 32-bit applications.
- **Users**—storage for users' profile settings and data. Each user has a folder named after their user account. This subfolder contains NTUSER.DAT (registry data) plus subfolders for "Documents," "Music," "Pictures," "Downloads," "Saved Games," "Searches," and so on. The profile folder also contains hidden subfolders used to store application settings and customizations, favorite links, shortcuts, temporary files, and so on. There is also a "Public" profile, which is used for sharing documents between users on the same computer. The Users folder also contains a subfolder called "Default," which is the template for new user profiles.
- **bootmgr**—this file can present boot options when the computer starts. It reads information from the Boot Configuration Data (BCD) store, which is usually stored in a hidden System Reserved partition.
- **pagefile.sys**—Virtual Memory pagefile. Virtual memory is used to store data used by running applications when there is not enough system memory (RAM).

 Note: In Windows 8 and Windows 10, you will also see a swapfile.sys file. This is used by Windows Store apps.

- **hiberfil.sys**—image of memory contents saved when the computer is put into hibernation.

FILE ATTRIBUTES

A file's name is just one of its **attributes**. Other attributes include the date the file was created, accessed, or modified; its size; its description; and the following markers, which can be enabled or disabled.

Attribute	Usage
Read-only (R)	Prevents changes being saved back to the file. The user will be prompted to create another file containing the modified data.

Attribute	Usage
Hidden (H)	Specifies whether the file is visible in the default view (it is possible to adjust Windows to display hidden files and folders, though).
System (S)	Specifies that the file should not be accessible to ordinary users.
Archive (A)	Shows whether a file has changed since the last backup.

Files stored on a drive formatted using the NTFS file system have extended attributes, including permissions, compression, and encryption.

PERMISSIONS

To view, create, modify, or delete a file in a folder, you need the correct permissions on that folder. Permissions can also be applied to individual files. Administrators can obtain full permissions over any file, but standard users can generally only view and modify files stored either in their profile or in the public profile. If a user attempts to view or save a file with insufficient permissions to do so, Windows displays an Access Denied error message.

Custom permissions can be configured for a file or folder using the **Security** tab in its properties dialog box.

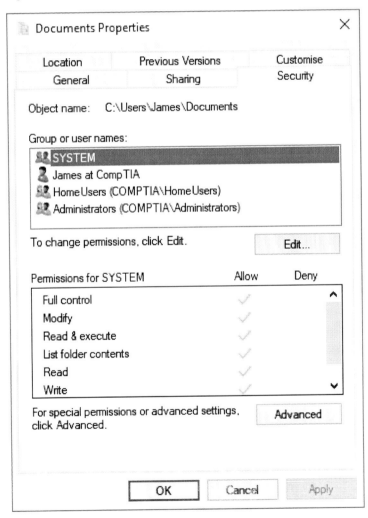

Viewing permissions for a folder object. (Screenshot used with permission from Microsoft.)

To configure permissions, you first select the account to which the permissions apply. You can then set the appropriate permission level. In simple terms, the permissions available are as follows:

Permission	Allows the user to:
Full control	Do anything with the object, including change its permissions and its owner.
Modify	Do most things with an object but not to change its permissions or owner.
Read/list/ execute	View the contents of a file or folder or start a program.
Write	Read a file and change it, or create a file within a folder, but not to delete it.

FOLDER OPTIONS

The **Folder Options** applet in Control Panel (or the **Tools** menu in Explorer or **Options** button in File Explorer) governs how Explorer shows folders and files. On the **General** tab, you can set options for the layout of Explorer windows.

Folder Options dialog box—General tab in Windows 7. (Screenshot used with permission from Microsoft.)

On the **View** tab, you can configure a number of settings for how folders and files are shown.

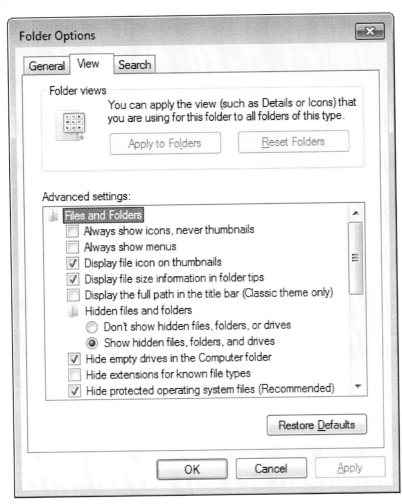

Folder Options dialog box—View tab in Windows 7. (Screenshot used with permission from Microsoft.)

You should pay particular attention to the following settings:

- Hide extensions for known file types—Windows files are identified by a three- or four-character extension following the final period in the file name. The file extension determines which software application is used to open, edit, or print the file by default. Overtyping the file extension (when renaming a file) can make it difficult to open, so extensions are normally hidden from view.
- Hidden files and folders—a file or folder can be marked as "Hidden" through its file attributes. Files marked as hidden are not shown by default but can be revealed by setting the **Show hidden files, folders, and drives** option. Note that this will not show "system" files, unless the following option is also disabled.
- Hide protected operating system files—this configures "system" files as hidden. It is worth noting that in Windows, File/Resource Protection prevents users (even administrative users) from deleting these files anyway.

You can configure file search behavior on the **Search** tab. Search is also governed by how the Indexing Options applet is configured. This allows you to define indexed locations and rebuild the index. A corrupted index is a common cause of search problems.

In Windows 10, you can use the **View** menu ribbon to toggle hidden items and file extensions without going through the **Folder Options** dialog box.

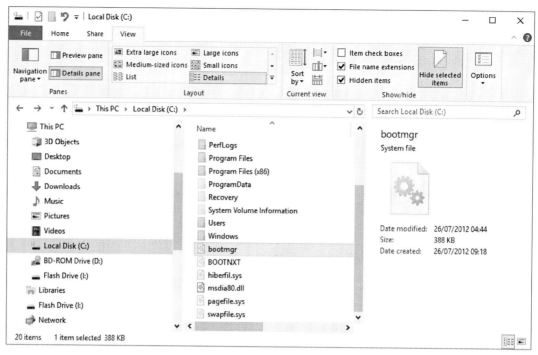

Setting view options in the Windows 10 version of File Explorer. (Screenshot used with permission from Microsoft.)

DIRECTORY NAVIGATION AT THE COMMAND PROMPT

Even under a GUI-operated OS such as Windows, it is important for a PC technician to be able to complete file management and configuration operations using the command prompt. Some actions can be completed more quickly using commands; some commands can only be issued from a command-line; and sometimes the GUI may not be available.

DIRECTORIES AND THE COMMAND PROMPT

If the root directory of the C: drive is selected, the command prompt will display C:\> The greater than sign (>) at the end of the prompt separates the prompt information from your input. If you change from the current directory (in this example, the root directory) to a first-level directory called "Windows," the prompt would become C: \Windows>.

Changing to a second-level directory called "System32" would change the prompt to C: \Windows\System32\>.

A backslash (\ ) is used to separate each directory level.

 Note: *While Windows uses the backslash to delimit directories, if you type a path using forward slashes in Explorer or at the command prompt, it will still be interpreted correctly. The Linux file system uses forward slashes.*

THE DEFAULT DRIVE

Each drive is assigned its own drive letter. When using the command prompt from Windows, the default path will usually be *%HomePath%* (for example, C:\Users\David). If the command prompt is open using **Run as administrator**, the default path will be C: \Windows\System32.

To change the working drive, just enter the drive letter followed by a colon and press **Enter**. For example, E: changes to the "E" drive. The prompt will change to E:\> indicating that the default drive is now drive E.

Note: *If you try to switch to a removable drive when the disk is not in the drive, it will generate an error.*

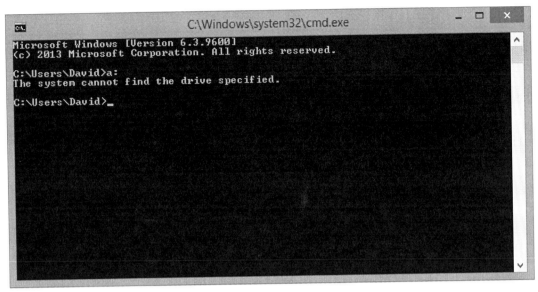

Changing the default drive and dealing with a missing drive. (Screenshot used with permission from Microsoft.)

CHANGING THE CURRENT DIRECTORY (CD)

To find a particular file, it is often necessary to move around the directory structure. The `cd` (chdir) command is used to change the current directory. You can change to any directory by entering the full path, such as: `cd c:\users\david`

There are a number of shortcuts, however. If the current directory is "C:\Users\David" and you want to change to "C:\Users\David\Documents," enter: `cd documents`

If the current directory is "C:\Users\David\Documents" and you want to move up to the parent directory, enter: `cd..`

If the current directory is "C:\Users\David" and you want to change to the root directory of the drive, enter: `cd\`

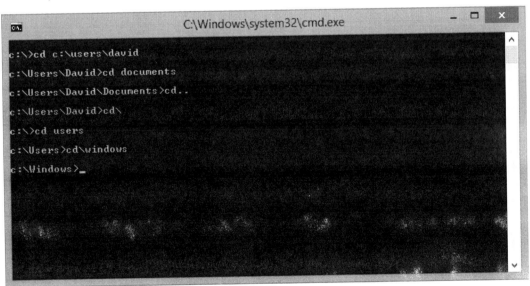

Navigating directories with the cd command. (Screenshot used with permission from Microsoft.)

If the current directory is "C:\Users" and you want to change to "C:\Windows," enter: `cd\windows`

It is not possible to move across from one directory to another at the same level. To reach "C:\Windows" from "C:\Users," the command has to return to the root directory and then select the chosen branch.

Commands such as `cd\` or `cd..` do not require a space. A common error is to use `cd\Directory` when `cd Directory` is required. To move further down the directory structure, use a space. The command `cd\Directory` sends the prompt back to the root directory from where it would then attempt to move into "Directory."

LISTING FILES AND DIRECTORIES (DIR)

Use the `dir` command to list the files and subdirectories from either the current drive and directory or from a specified drive and directory.

dir command. (Screenshot used with permission from Microsoft.)

A subdirectory will be listed with <DIR> next to it in normal view or with square brackets [Windows] around the name if dir/w is used to list in wide view. To view all files and directories within the current directory, enter: `dir`

To view the files and directories in the root directory of the "A:" drive when your current drive is "C:" enter: `dir A:\`

The \ following the A: is important. Typing just `dir A:` or `dir C:` would list the files present in the current directory for that drive (the last one used). To view files in a specific directory on drive A, you must type the full path; for example, `dir A:\backups`

If the current directory has more than one screen of files and directories, type:

- `dir/w` (lists files using wide format with no file details).
- `dir/p` (lists files one screen at a time).
- `dir/w/p` (both of the above).

You can present files in a particular order using the `/o:x` switch, where x could be `n` to list by name, `s` to list by size, `e` to list by extension, or `d` to list by date. The date field can be set by the `/t:x` switch, where x is `c` for created on, `a` for last access, or `w` for last modified.

Another useful switch is /a:x, which displays files with the attribute indicated by x (r for Read-only, h for hidden, s for system, and a for archive).

WILDCARDS (QUESTION MARK [?] AND ASTERISK [*])

A **wildcard** character allows you to use unspecified characters with the command. A question mark (?) means a single unspecified character. For example, the command dir ????????.log will display all .log files with 8 characters in the file name.

The asterisk can be used to indicate a string of unspecified characters. The following examples show possible ways to use the asterisk with the dir command:

- dir *.*—displays all files and directories in the current directory.
- dir *.doc—displays all files with the DOC extension in the current directory.
- dir let*.doc—same as the previous example, but only shows files with LET as the first characters of the name.
- dir let*.doc /s—same as the previous example, but also searches subdirectories.
- dir *.—displays all files without an extension. This is often used to view directories.

FILE MANAGEMENT AT THE COMMAND PROMPT

The move and copy commands provide the ability to transfer files from one disk or directory to another from a command prompt. Both commands use a three-part syntax: COMMAND *Source Destination* where *Source* is the drive name, path, and name of the files to be moved/copied and *Destination* is the drive name and path of the new location. When using copy, you can enter a different filename to create a duplicate in the same directory. For example, you want to copy all the files from the "C:\Documents" directory to the "C:\Backup" directory. You also want to move any files with a "txt" extension from the "C:\Backup" directory to the "C:\Backup\Archive" directory.

COPYING DIRECTORY STRUCTURES

xcopy is a utility that allows you to copy the contents of more than one directory at a time and retain the directory structure. The syntax for xcopy is as follows: xcopy *Source [Destination] [Switches]*.

You can use switches to include or exclude files and folders by their attributes. Check the command help for additional switches and syntax.

robocopy

robocopy (or "robust copy") is another file copy utility. It was previously available in the Windows Resource Kit but is now included as a native command in Windows. Microsoft now recommends using robocopy rather than xcopy.

robocopy is designed to work better with long file names and NTFS attributes. Check the command help for additional switches and syntax.

 Note: Despite the name, you can also use robocopy to move files (/mov switch).

RENAMING A FILE

To change a file name, use the `ren` command. The syntax of this command is: `ren OldName NewName`. For example, to rename the ReadMe.txt file to ReadNow.doc, use the following command: `ren readme.txt readnow.doc`

To rename multiple files, wildcard characters may be used. For example, ren *.txt *.doc will rename all files with an extension of TXT to DOC.

 Note: Changing a file extension is not usually a good idea, as the file will no longer be associated with the application used to open it.

DELETING A FILE

To remove a file from a directory or a disk, use the `del` command. The `erase` command has identical usage. The following switches are available with the `del` command:

Switch	Use
/p	Prompt to delete for each file.
/f	Suppress prompt for read-only files.
/q	Suppress prompt on wildcard delete.
/s	Delete files from subdirectories.
/a:	Delete files with particular attributes (for example, /a:r) or without particular attributes (for example, /a:-r).

CREATING A DIRECTORY

To create a directory, use the `md` or `mkdir` command. For example, to create a directory called "Data" in the current directory, type `md Data`. To create a directory called "Docs" in a directory called "Data" on the A drive, when the current path is "C:\," type `md A:\Data\Docs`

REMOVING A DIRECTORY

To delete an empty directory, type `rd Directory`. If the directory is not empty, you can remove files and subdirectories from it using the `rd /s` command. You can also use the `/q` switch to suppress confirmation messages (quiet mode).

HOW TO COPY FILES AND FOLDERS AT THE COMMAND PROMPT

Here is a general procedure that you can follow to copy files and folders at the Windows command prompt.

COPY FILES AND FOLDERS AT THE COMMAND PROMPT

To copy files and folders at the command prompt:

1. Open a command prompt.
2. If necessary, use the `cd` command to move to the folder containing the files or folders you want to copy.

    Note: You could also use the full path to the files or folders as a source argument.

3. Enter the appropriate command to copy the files and folders to a new folder.

- To copy one file, type `copy` `<filename> <destination_folder>` and press **Enter**.
- To copy all files, type `copy` `*.*` `<destination_folder>` and press **Enter**.
- To copy the contents of multiple folders while retaining the directory structure, type `xcopy` `<source_folder> <destination_folder>` and press **Enter**.
- To copy the contents of multiple folders while retaining the directory structure, type `robocopy` `<source_folder> <destination_folder>` and press **Enter**.

Topic D

Manage Disks in Windows

EXAM OBJECTIVES COVERED
1002-1.3 Summarize general OS installation considerations and upgrade methods.
1002-1.4 Given a scenario, use appropriate Microsoft command line tools.
1002-1.5 Given a scenario, use Microsoft operating system features and tools.

Much of the time the default options for Windows Setup will take care of preparing the computer's fixed disk storage for use. Equally, there will be plenty of occasions in your career when you need to configure custom partitions, use different file systems, or configure software RAID. This topic will teach you how to perform such disk management tasks using the console and command-line tools.

DISK PARTITIONS

A mass storage device or fixed disk, such as Hard Disk Drive (HDD) or Solid State Drive (SSD), requires partitioning and formatting before it can be used. The Disk Management snap-in is used to configure partitions, or you can use `diskpart` from a command line. For a new installation, you can configure and format partitions using the Setup program.

PARTITIONING

Partitioning the physical disk is the act of dividing it into logically separate storage areas, often referred to as "drives." You must create at least one partition on a fixed disk before performing a high-level format to create a file system. Typically, this is done through Windows Setup when building a new PC or through Disk Management when adding an extra disk.

Information about partitions is stored in a Master Boot Record (MBR), which is located in the first 512 byte sector on the disk. The GUI (Globally Unique Identifier) Partition Table (GPT) provides a more up-to-date scheme to address some of the limitations of MBR.

Under Windows, disks can be configured as either basic or dynamic. Configuring dynamic disks enables the use of multiple disks for single "volumes" and is discussed later.

Note: Volume (or drive) is a term used at the OS level to refer to a contiguous storage area formatted with a single file system. This could mean a partition on a hard disk, a CD-ROM, a floppy disk, or a RAID virtual disk spanning multiple hard disks. The term partition is more specific than volume—it refers to an area on a hard disk or SSD.

MBR-STYLE PARTITIONING

With basic storage and MBR-style partitions, a given physical disk can contain up to four primary partitions, any one of which can be marked as active, and therefore made bootable. This allows for four different "drives" on the same physical disk and for multiple operating systems (a **multiboot system**). You might also use partitions to create discrete areas for user data file storage, storing log files, or hosting databases. Each drive can be formatted with a different file system.

Each primary partition contains a boot sector, or Partition Boot Record (PBR)/Volume Boot Record (VBR), at the start of the partition. When a partition is marked as active, its boot sector is populated with a record that points to the Windows boot loader (typically C:\Windows\System32\winload.exe). This active partition is also referred to as the **system partition** or system reserved partition.

The drive containing the operating system files (the system root) is referred to as the **boot partition**. This can be on a logical drive in an extended partition and does not have to be the same as the system drive. The typical installation options for Windows create a "hidden" system reserved partition (with no drive letter) and label the boot partition as drive C:.

If for some reason four drives are insufficient, then three primary partitions can be created and the remaining disk space allocated to an extended partition, which itself can be divided into as many logical drives as needed. Extended partitions do not have boot sectors and cannot be made active.

GPT-STYLE PARTITIONING

A disk with no existing partitions on it can be converted to use the GPT-style partition format. All currently supported versions of Windows have read/write support for GPT disks. GPT is required on the boot device for 64-bit versions of Windows when installed to a computer with Unified Extensible Firmware Interface (UEFI) firmware. A computer with older Basic Input/Output System (BIOS) firmware will normally have to use MBR.

One of the features of GPT is support for more than four primary partitions. Windows allows up to 128 partitions with GPT. GPT also supports larger partitions (2 TB+) and a backup copy of the partition entries. A GPT-style disk includes a Protective MBR for compatibility with systems that do not recognize GPT.

 Note: *For Windows 10 on a UEFI PC, Microsoft's recommendation is to create a number of additional hidden utility partitions, including one for the Recovery Environment (RE). You can read more about Microsoft's recommended partition scheme at* **docs.microsoft.com/en-us/windows-hardware/manufacture/desktop/configure-uefigpt-based-hard-drive-partitions**.

FILE SYSTEMS

High-level formatting prepares a partition for use with an operating system. The format process creates a file system on the disk partition. Each partition can be formatted using a different file system. Drives for use with Windows should generally be formatted using NTFS, which is more efficient and supports advanced features such as permissions, encryption, and quota management. The older FAT/FAT32 system can be used for compatibility with legacy versions of Windows or other operating systems in a dual-boot environment.

CLUSTERS

The smallest unit of storage on a fixed disk has traditionally been the 512 byte **sector**. A file system is not restricted to using a single sector as the basic unit of storage, however. The file system can group sectors into **clusters** (or Allocation Units) of 2, 4, or 8 sectors. Smaller clusters make more efficient use of the disk capacity, but using larger clusters can improve file Input/Output (I/O) performance, especially when working with large files.

As fixed disk sizes have increased, some disk models now use Advanced Format, with 4 kilobyte (4K) sector sizes. If supported by the OS and PC firmware, these can be used in native mode; if not, the drive controller will usually present the disk in 512 emulated (512e) mode.

NEW TECHNOLOGY FILE SYSTEM (NTFS)

The **New Technology File System (NTFS)** is a proprietary file system developed exclusively for use with Windows. It provides a 64-bit addressing scheme, allowing for very large volumes and file sizes. In theory, the maximum volume size is 16 Exabytes, but actual implementations of NTFS are limited to between 137 GB and 256 Terabytes, depending on the version of Windows and the allocation unit size. The key NTFS features are:

- **Recovery**—NTFS utilizes sector sparing and transaction tracking to provide reliable data transfer. When data is written to an NTFS volume, it is re-read and verified. In the event of a problem, the sector concerned is marked as bad and the data relocated. Transaction tracking logs all disk and file system activity, making recovery after power outage a faster and more reliable process.
- **Security**—NTFS has many security features. These include file permissions and ownership, file access audit trails, quota management, and Encrypting File System (EFS).
- **POSIX Compliance**—in efforts to support the UNIX/Linux community, Microsoft engineered the NTFS file system to support case sensitive naming, hard links, and other key features required by UNIX/Linux applications. Although the file system is case-sensitive capable and preserves case, Windows does not insist upon case sensitive naming.
- **Compression**—NTFS allows file- or folder-level compression.
- **Indexing**—the Indexing Service creates a catalog of file and folder locations and properties, speeding up searches.
- **Dynamic Disks**—this is a disk management feature allowing space on multiple physical disks to be combined into volumes.

 Note: Windows Home/Core editions do not support dynamic disks or encryption. There is a cipher.exe tool to allow the user to decrypt files but no option to perform encryption of files or folders.

The only significant drawback of NTFS is that it is not fully supported by operating systems other than Windows. macOS can read NTFS drives but cannot write to them. Linux distributions and utilities may be able to support NTFS to some degree.

FAT

The **FAT** file system is named for its method of organization—the File Allocation Table. This 16-bit table of values provides links from one allocation unit to another.

 Note: FAT was originally designed as a 12-bit file system for floppy disks (FAT12). The 16-bit version (FAT16) was developed for the first PCs to ship with hard drives.

FAT16

A **FAT16** system does not support the recovery or security features of NTFS. The maximum volume size is either 2 GB or 4 GB, depending on the version in use, and the maximum file size is the volume size minus 1 byte. Its only significant feature is that it is compatible with all Microsoft operating systems plus macOS and Linux, and therefore ideal in a multiboot environment or for removable media that must be shared between different operating systems.

FAT32

FAT32 does not differ greatly from FAT16. Because it has a 32-bit allocation table, it supports larger volumes than FAT16—nominally up to 2 TB, though the Windows Setup program will only format partitions up to 32 GB in size. It suffers from the same reliability and security issues as FAT16. The maximum file size is 4 GB minus 1 byte.

Again, it is ideal in a multiboot or removable storage environment with Windows 9x, macOS, or Linux, but it is not supported by DOS.

EXFAT

Another option is a 64-bit version of FAT called **exFAT**. exFAT is designed for use with removable hard drives and flash media. Like NTFS, exFAT supports large volumes (128 petabytes) and file sizes (16 exabytes). Its real use is not for massive drives, however, but for better performance on moderate size volumes (up to 1 TB) than NTFS. There is also support for access permissions but not compression or encryption.

CDFS

The CD File System (CDFS or ISO 9660) is a legacy file system used for CD optical disc media (CD-ROM and CD-R). CDFS supports two main data writing modes: mode 1 has better error correction, whereas mode 2 allows more data to be written to the disc. Joliet is an extension to CDFS that enables long file name support and Unicode characters in file names.

UDF (ISO 13346)

The Universal Disk Format (UDF or ISO 13346) is an updated file system for optical media with support for multisession writing. It is the standard used by Windows, where it is referred to as Live File System, for CD and DVD recordable and rewritable discs.

There are several different versions of UDF, with 2.01 being the default in Windows. Blu-ray reading and writing requires version 2.5 and third-party software.

THE WINDOWS DISK MANAGEMENT CONSOLE

Windows provides the **Disk Management** console to format disks and manage partitions. The utility displays a summary of any fixed and removable drives attached to the system. The top pane lists drives; the bottom pane lists disks, with information about the partitions created on each disk and any unpartitioned space.

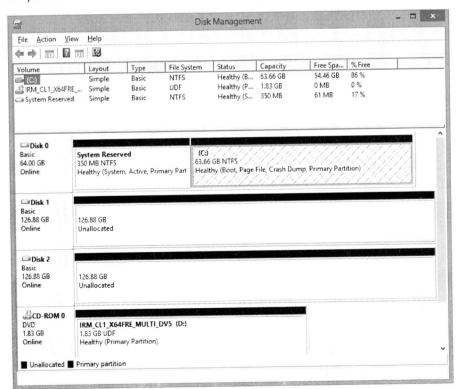

Disk Management utility in Windows 8.1. (Screenshot used with permission from Microsoft.)

To open the tool, right-click **Computer/This PC** and select **Manage** then select the **Disk Management** icon under **Storage**. You can also use the WinX menu (right-click **Start**).

INITIALIZING DISKS

If you add a hard disk to the system, you will be prompted to initialize it when you start Disk Management. You can choose whether to use the MBR or GPT partition style for the new disk.

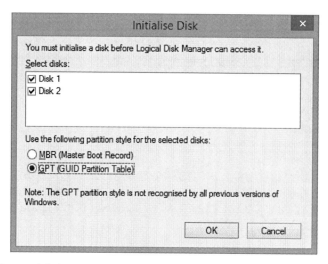

Initializing newly detected disks—note the option to choose between MBR and GPT. (Screenshot used with permission from Microsoft.)

When a disk has been initialized, you can create partitions on it. You can also create a new partition on an existing disk if there is unpartitioned space on the disk.

ADDING DRIVES AND ASSIGNING DRIVE LETTERS

To create a new partition, right-click an area of unallocated space and select **New Simple Volume**. Complete the wizard to select:

- Amount of disk space to use (in megabytes—recall that 1024 MB is 1 GB).

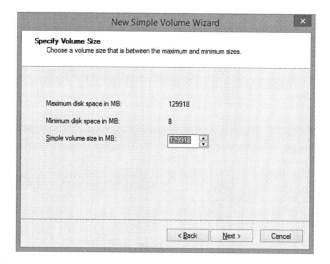

New Simple Volume Wizard—configuring volume size. (Screenshot used with permission from Microsoft.)

- Assign a drive letter or a mount point. You can also choose not to assign a drive or mount point, in which case the volume will be inaccessible via Explorer.

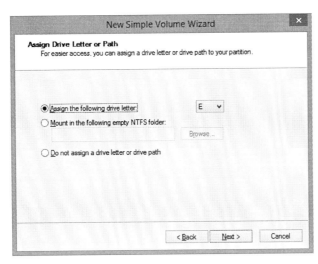

New Simple Volume Wizard—configuring access path. (Screenshot used with permission from Microsoft.)

FORMATTING THE DRIVE

To complete the wizard, you must select a file system to use to format the new partition. You can make the following choices:

- NTFS or FAT for the file system.
- Allocation unit size—default settings are usually best (selects a size based on the volume size). As a rule of thumb, a small allocation unit size is efficient if the disk stores mainly small files or vice versa, but a typical desktop machine will make equal use of small and large files.
- Volume label—shown in Explorer along with the drive letter.
- Quick format—a full format checks the disk for bad sectors; selecting the quick format option skips this check.

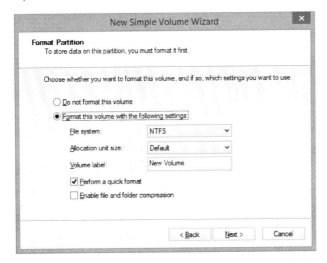

New Simple Volume Wizard—formatting the volume. (Screenshot used with permission from Microsoft.)

 Note: Both types of format remove references to existing files in the volume boot record but the actual sectors are not "scrubbed" or zeroed. Existing files will be overwritten as new files are added to the volume, but in principle data can be recovered from a formatted disk (using third-party tools). A secure format utility prevents this by overwriting each sector with a zero value, sometimes using multiple passes.

Having set up the disk structure, if you want to change it in the future, then partitions can be managed using the shortcut menu, which contains options to mark a partition as active, re-format or delete it, or change its drive letter. You can also access the volume properties sheet, which contains options for the disk performance tools and access permissions and quota management (on NTFS volumes).

 Note: *You cannot format or delete system or boot partitions.*

SPLITTING AND EXTENDING PARTITIONS

You can shrink or extend simple volumes formatted with NTFS and unformatted volumes. Shrinking a volume then creating a new volume on the same disk allows you to "split" the original volume. Shrinking a volume is contingent on the files stored in the volume. If there is an unmovable file, the volume cannot be shrunk past it. Extending a volume is contingent on the amount of space left on the physical disk.

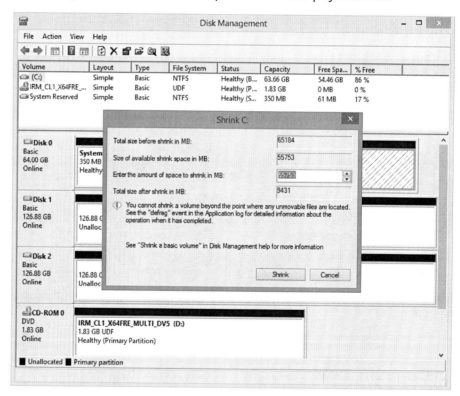

Shrinking a simple volume. (Screenshot used with permission from Microsoft.)

 Note: *Before trying to shrink a volume, disable the hibernation file and pagefile, then clean up and defragment the disk. It may be worth trying a third-party defragmentation utility to try to move files that Windows' built-in Defragmenter cannot.*

DISK ARRAYS

Dynamic storage allows the creation of volumes spanning multiple disks (an **array**). Dynamic disks can only be read by the Professional/Enterprise (and Ultimate) editions of Windows.

Note: *Windows Home/Core editions do not support dynamic disks at all, so if you were to configure dynamic disks under Windows 7 Professional, then move the disks to a computer running Windows 7 Home Premium, the volumes would not be readable. Also, the option to convert from basic to dynamic disks is disabled on laptops.*

Only fixed disks can be used. A fixed disk is one installed within the computer and connected by the SATA or NVMe (PCI Express) bus. Disks connected via USB, Thunderbolt, or eSATA cannot be converted to dynamic.

DYNAMIC VOLUME TYPES

Dynamic volumes can be in the following configurations:

- **Simple**—occupies space on a single disk. There is little difference in practice between this and a basic volume.
- **Spanned**—a volume using space on two or more disks. This arrangement is also referred to as JBOD (Just a Bunch Of Disks).
- **Striped**—a volume using space on two or more disks configured using RAID 0 to improve performance. Basically data is written across all disks, whereas spanned just uses up space on the volume using the standard file access pattern.

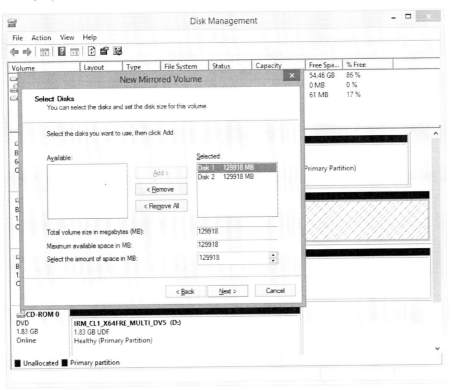

Creating a mirrored volume dynamic disk array. (Screenshot used with permission from Microsoft.)

- **Mirrored**—a volume where one disk stores a copy (mirror) of the other disk. This provides redundancy (RAID 1). Redundancy means that one of the disks can fail, but the volume will still be accessible.
- **RAID 5**—a volume where data is spread across three or more disks. The system writes parity information alongside the data. If one of the disks is damaged, the remaining data can be combined with the remaining parity information to keep the volume functioning. RAID 5 is only supported under Windows 8/10.

MANAGING VOLUMES

When a mirrored volume has been set up, you have two options for converting the mirror set back to a simple volume:

- Breaking the mirror leaves the data in the volumes on both disks intact. You would also use this option to replace one of the disks in the mirror set (install the physical disk then use the **Add Mirror** command on the existing volume).

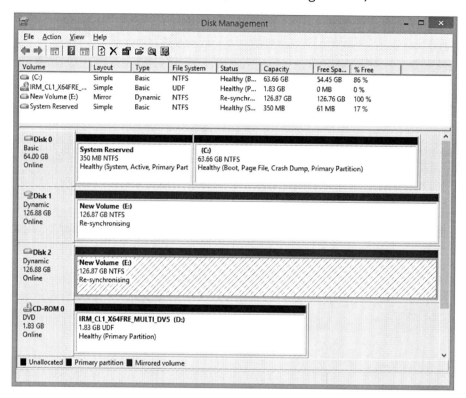

When a physical disk underlying a mirrored volume fails, you can install another disk and add it to the mirror—a resynching process will start to copy data from the first disk to the second.
(Screenshot used with permission from Microsoft.)

- Removing a mirror deletes the volume (and any files it contains) from that disk, leaving the volume on the other disk as a simple volume.

 Note: Spanned and striped volumes offer flexibility, but if any of the disks in the array fail, all data on the volume will be lost. Only mirroring and RAID 5 provide redundancy.

A dynamic disk can be converted back to basic, but the volumes (and any data on them) must be deleted first. As with basic partitions, volumes must be formatted (NTFS or FAT/FAT32) before they can be available to the OS.

DRIVE STATUS INDICATORS

Each disk and drive displays status indicators in the Disk Management program. Disks can have the following status indicators:

- **Online**—The disk is OK.
- **Not Initialized**—When you add a new unpartitioned disk, a wizard runs, prompting you to initialize, partition, and format the disk. If you cancel the wizard, the disk will appear as Not Initialized. Right-click to start the wizard again.
- **Unreadable**—The disk is damaged. This message can be transitory so try right-clicking the **Disk Management** tool and selecting **Rescan Disks**. If the disk is still shown as unreadable, you would have to use third-party tools to try to recover data from it.

- **Foreign**—if you configure a disk as dynamic on one computer, then install the disk in another computer, it will be marked as foreign. Right-click the disk and select **Import Foreign Disk** to make it accessible to the system.
- **Offline/Missing**—a disk configured as dynamic cannot be read. This could be a transitory error but is more likely to indicate that the drive or I/O to the drive is damaged, a cable is unplugged, the disk has been switched off, and so on. There are two options:
  - If the disk can be restored, use the **Reactivate Disk** option to add it back to the array.
  - If the disk cannot be restored, use the **Remove Disk** option.

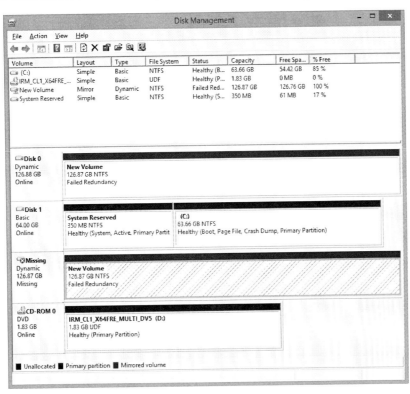

One of the disks underlying the mirrored volume is missing and consequently the volume is marked as failed. (Screenshot used with permission from Microsoft.)

Volumes (or partitions) can have the following status indicators:

- **Healthy**—The volume is formatted and ready to read and write data. Healthy (System) indicates that the volume contains the boot loader, whereas Healthy (Active) represents the system volume used to boot. Healthy (Boot) represents a volume containing an OS, whereas Healthy (Page File) shows one storing a pagefile. A drive may also display as Healthy (At Risk), which means that a number of I/O errors are occurring—a good sign that the disk or controller is failing.
- **Failed/Unknown**—This either indicates a damaged disk (basic) or a dynamic volume where the supporting disk drives are not available. You need to check the status of the devices (if cabling and power are OK, the disk[s] or controller may have been damaged). A volume listed as "Unknown" has an unreadable boot sector.
- **Failed Redundancy**—A RAID volume that is still working but that is no longer fault tolerant. You should identify the failed disk and replace it.
- **Regenerating**—When a disk is brought back into a damaged RAID 5 volume, the controller begins regenerating parity information for the volume. It should be accessible during this period, but performance will be worse.
- **Resynching**—Occurs when a disk is restored to a mirrored volume.

- **Formatting**—A user-initiated format is in progress. Wait for the format to complete before trying to access the volume.

STORAGE SPACES

As mentioned previously, dynamic disks can only be configured on local fixed disks. Windows 8/10 comes with a **Storage Spaces** feature, allowing arrays to be configured across all kinds of storage devices, including USB-connected disks. Also, Storage Spaces is available in the "core" and home editions, unlike dynamic disks.

To configure a storage space, first select the drives that you want to add to the pool. You can then configure what type of redundancy to configure (mirrored or parity), format the volume, and assign a drive letter.

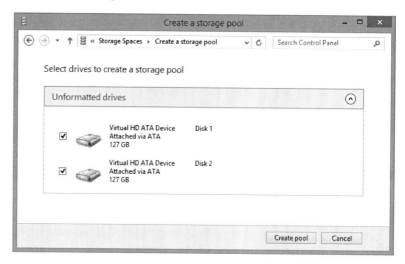

Adding drives to a storage space pool. (Screenshot used with permission from Microsoft.)

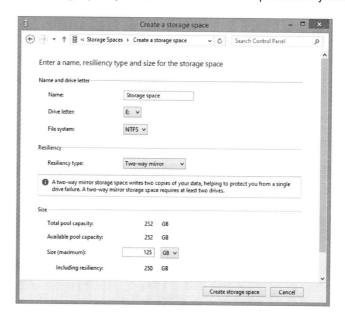

Configuring drive letter, file system, and redundancy options for the pool. (Screenshot used with permission from Microsoft.)

MOUNT POINTS AND DISK IMAGES

A **mount point** means that rather than allocating a drive letter to a volume, it is accessed from a designated folder in the file system. The host file system must be

NTFS but the volume mounted can be formatted with any type of file system. For example, you might partition and format a removable hard disk then mount it as a DATA volume within a user's Documents folder. To assign a volume to a mount point, first create a folder at the point in the file system you want to mount the drive. This folder must be empty. Next, either run the **New Partition/Volume Wizard** or unassign the drive letter from an existing partition and mount it (use the **Change Drive Letter and Paths** shortcut menu to do this).

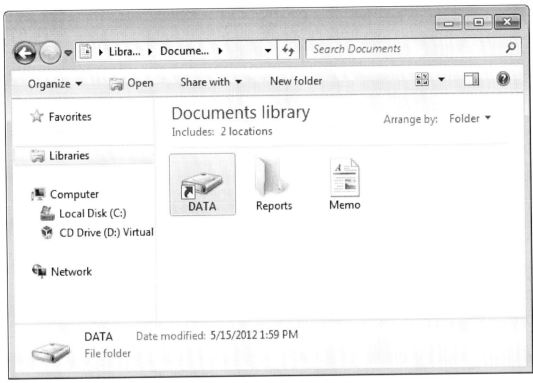

DATA volume mounted within the Documents library—notice that no "DATA" drive appears under any of the drive letters. (Screenshot used with permission from Microsoft.)

Disk images are used with **virtualization** software to store data written to a virtual machine's hard drive. Windows supports mounting Windows Hyper-V disk image files (VHD and VHDX) within the local file system (right-click **Disk Management** and select **Attach VHD**). An ISO image is a file copy of a CD or DVD. Windows 7 cannot mount ISO images natively, though there is third-party software available to do this, but Windows 8/10 can. You can also burn an image to a physical disc through Explorer.

DISK AND VOLUME MANAGEMENT AT THE COMMAND PROMPT

The Disk Management snap-in is easy to use but there are some circumstances where you may need to manage volumes at a command prompt.

THE diskpart COMMAND

The `diskpart` command is the command interface underlying the **Disk Management** tool. It can be run at an elevated Windows command prompt or Windows Recovery Environment/Pre-installation Environment.

*Note: The **Disk Management** tool prevents you from completing certain destructive actions, such as deleting the system or boot volume. diskpart is not restricted in this way, so use it with care.*

There are too many options in `diskpart` to cover here, but the basic process of inspecting disks and partitions is as follows:

1. Run the `diskpart` utility then enter `select disk 0` at the prompt (or the number of the disk you want to check).

2. Type `detail disk` and then press **Enter** to display configuration information for the disk. The utility should report that the partitions (or volumes) are healthy.

    If `diskpart` reports that the hard disk has no partitions, the partition table may have become corrupted by a virus. You may be able to resolve this by partitioning and formatting the drive.

3. Enter either `select partition 0` or `select volume 0` at the prompt (or the number of the partition or volume you want to check).

4. Enter either `detail partition` or `detail volume` to view information about the object. You can now use commands such as `assign` (change the drive letter), `delete` (destroy the volume), or `extend`.

5. Enter `exit` to quit diskpart.

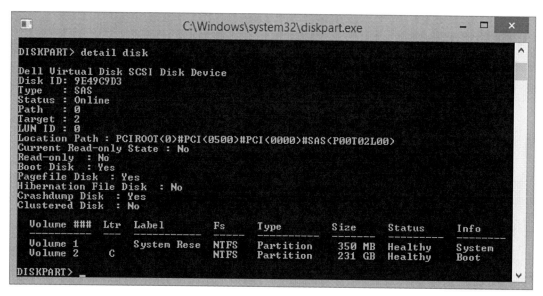

The diskpart program showing a hard disk partition structure. (Screenshot used with permission from Microsoft.)

THE format COMMAND

The `format` command formats (or re-formats) the drive using the specified file system. This process deletes any data existing on the drive.

 Note: You can convert a FAT drive to NTFS without losing data using the command `convert volume /fs:ntfs`. *It is not possible to convert back from NTFS. A full backup of the disk should always be taken before converting.*

The basic command is `format volume`, where volume is a drive letter or volume name. The main switches are as follows.

Switch	Use
`/fs:`	Specify the file system (such as NTFS, exFAT, FAT32, or FAT).
`/v:`	Enter a label for the volume. If you do not include this switch, you are prompted for a label when format is complete.
`/q`	Perform a quick format (does not scan for bad sectors).

Switch	Use
/a:	Specify the size of allocation units (512, 1024, 2048, 4096, 8192, 16K, 32K, 64K). If omitted, the default size depends on the size of the volume.
/x	Force the volume to dismount. This will cause file errors for users with files open on the volume.
/c	Enable file compression if using NTFS. It's not usually a good idea to enable compression on the drive root, especially if the drive contains system files. Use folder properties to enable compression on a case-by-case basis.

Topic E
Manage Devices in Windows

 EXAM OBJECTIVES COVERED
1002-1.5 Given a scenario, use Microsoft operating system features and tools.
1002-1.6 Given a scenario, use Microsoft Windows Control Panel utilities.

In this topic, you will use the Control Panel and Device Manager to install and configure PC peripheral devices and hardware settings under Windows.

POWER OPTIONS

Power management allows Windows to selectively reduce or turn off the power supplied to hardware components. This is important to avoid wasting energy when the computer is on but not being used and to maximize run-time when on battery power. Power management requires three compatible components:

- Hardware—devices that support power management are often labeled Energy Star, after the US Environmental Protection Agency scheme. It is important for the CPU, motherboard, hard disks, and display screen to support power management.
- Firmware—almost all chipsets support the power management standard **Advanced Configuration and Power Interface (ACPI)** but you may need to check that it has been enabled.
- Operating System—current versions of Windows provide full ACPI compatibility.

 Note: *Power management is more important on mobile devices but can be configured on desktops in much the same way.*

One basic feature of ACPI is to support different power-saving modes. The computer can be configured to enter a power saving mode automatically; for example, if there is no use of an input device for a set period. The user can also put the computer into a power-saving state rather than shutting down.

There are several levels of ACPI power mode, starting with S0 (powered on) and ending with S5 (soft power off) and G3 (mechanically powered off). In-between these are different kinds of power-saving modes:

- **Standby/Suspend to RAM**—cuts power to most devices (for example, the CPU, monitor, disk drives, and peripherals) but maintains power to the memory. This is also referred to as ACPI modes S1-S3.
- **Hibernate/Suspend to Disk**—saves any data in memory (open files) to disk (as hiberfil.sys in the root of the boot volume) then turns the computer off. This is also referred to as ACPI mode S4.

In Windows, power management is implemented as the sleep and hybrid sleep modes:

- A laptop goes into the standby state as normal; if running on battery power, it will switch from standby to hibernate before the battery runs down.
- A desktop creates a hibernation file then goes into the standby state. This is referred to as hybrid sleep mode. It can also be configured to switch to the full hibernation state after a defined period.
- Windows 8 supports an alternative mode called Connected Standby or InstantGo, updated to Modern Standby in Windows 10. These utilize a device's ability to

function in an S0 low-power idle mode to maintain network connectivity without consuming too much energy. This option is only available with compatible hardware.

 Note: *You can also set a specific device (such as the display or hard drive) to enter a power-saving state if it goes unused for a defined period (sleep timers). Note that some monitors still consume quite a lot of power in standby mode.*

CONFIGURING POWER OPTIONS

The **Power Options** Control Panel applet lets you configure power management settings via a system of power plans. These enable the user to switch between different sets of preconfigured options easily. Each power plan can be customized, or new plans can be defined and saved.

As well as configuring events for the power button or closing the lid of a laptop, the "shut down" option in Start Menu can be customized; so clicking the button could make the computer sleep while closing the lid could activate the hibernate routine. These settings can be defined for all plans (use the **Choose what the power button does** link in the bar on the left shown in the dialog box in the following figure) or on a per-plan basis (select the plan then configure advanced settings).

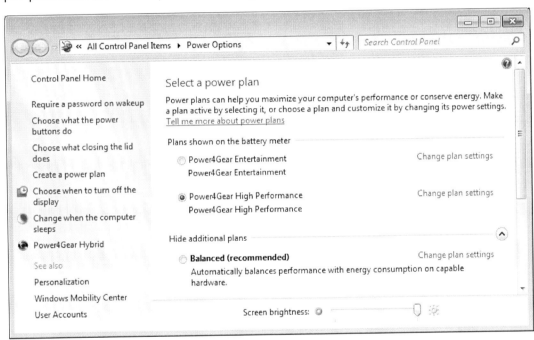

Configuring power management in Windows 7. (Screenshot used with permission from Microsoft.)

Advanced settings allow you to configure a very wide range of options, including CPU states, search and indexing behavior, display brightness, and so on.

There is no GUI option to disable hibernation (and consequently delete hiberfil.sys). This can be done via the command line (`powercfg -h off | on`).

In Windows 10, you can still configure power plans via the Power Options applet but you can also set basic options quickly via the **Power & sleep** page in Windows Settings.

DISPLAY AND SOUND DEVICES

You can configure the way Windows appears through Personalization settings in Control Panel/Settings. This allows you to select and customize themes, which set the appearance of the desktop environment, such as the wallpaper, screen saver, color scheme, and font size used.

CONFIGURING THE DISPLAY RESOLUTION

Most computers are now used with TFT display screens. These screens are really designed to be used only at their native resolution. Windows should detect this and configure itself appropriately. If you do need to adjust the resolution, right-click the desktop and select **Screen resolution** (Windows 7) or **Display settings** (Windows 8/10). Alternatively, you can open the applets via Control Panel/Settings.

COLOR DEPTH AND REFRESH RATE

You might want to change the number of bits used to represent colors at some point; perhaps to make a legacy application work better. From the Screen resolution/Display settings applet, select **Advanced display settings**, and then on the **Adapter** tab for the monitor, select **List All Modes**. Choose an appropriate resolution and color depth mode. Windows 8/10 only supports 32-bit color.

TFTs work at a pre-set refresh rate. If you have a CRT and need to tweak the rate, you can do this on the **Monitor** tab via **Advanced display settings**.

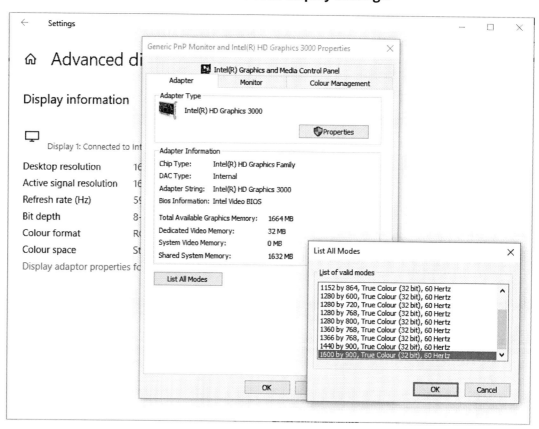

Checking the modes supported by a TFT monitor—various resolutions are available but all at 32-bit color and 60 Hertz refresh rate. (Screenshot used with permission from Microsoft.)

SOUND SETTINGS

Use the **Sound** applet in Control Panel/Settings to test microphone, headset, or speaker hardware and configure settings.

If you have multiple devices, you can choose the defaults on the **Playback** and **Recording** tabs and test levels for audio input and output.

The **Communications** tab lets you set an option to reduce other sounds if the device receives or places a telephone call. The **Sounds** tab lets you configure which noises Windows makes in response to actions and events, such as a calendar reminder or warning dialog box.

Use the icon in the Notification Area to control the volume.

HARDWARE DEVICE CONFIGURATION AND MANAGEMENT

Most hardware devices use **Plug-and-Play**. This means that Windows automatically detects when a new device is connected, locates drivers for it, and installs and configures it, with minimal user input. In some cases, you may need to install the hardware vendor's driver before connecting the device. The vendor usually provides a setup program to accomplish this.

 Note: *When using a 64-bit edition of Windows, you must obtain 64-bit device drivers. 32-bit drivers will not work.*

There may also be circumstances where you need to install a device manually, disable or remove a device, or update a device's driver.

ADD HARDWARE WIZARD

The Add Hardware/Add a Device wizard (in Control Panel) supports the manual addition of devices while Device Manager (in Administrative Tools, the Computer Management snap-in, or Control Panel) is used to configure them.

The precise stages in the **Add Hardware** or **Add a Device** wizards are different between the various versions of Windows, but in all of them—by selecting the appropriate options—you can get to the point where you choose which hardware you want to install manually.

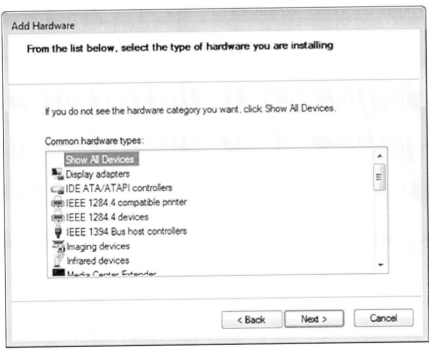

Installing a device manually. (Screenshot used with permission from Microsoft.)

Choose the type of hardware from the list then select from the list of manufacturers and models, and Windows will attempt to allocate it resources.

DEVICES AND PRINTERS

In Windows 7 and Windows 8, **Devices and Printers** is the location for the basic user-configurable settings for peripheral devices attached to the computer. Double-clicking an icon brings up the device's status page and available configuration options (referred to as the Device Stage). The shortcut menu for each device also allows you to set configurable properties, start a troubleshooter (devices with an ⚠ icon are not working properly), or remove the device from the computer.

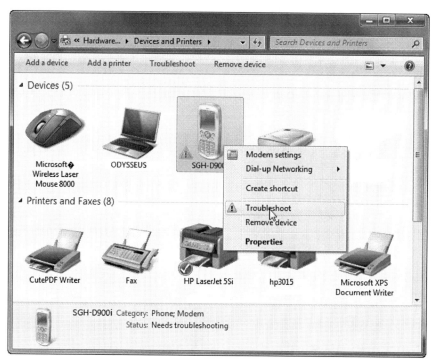

Devices and Printers in Windows 7. (Screenshot used with permission from Microsoft.)

THE DEVICES PAGE

In Windows 10, the **Devices** page in Windows Settings provides options for adding and configuring peripherals.

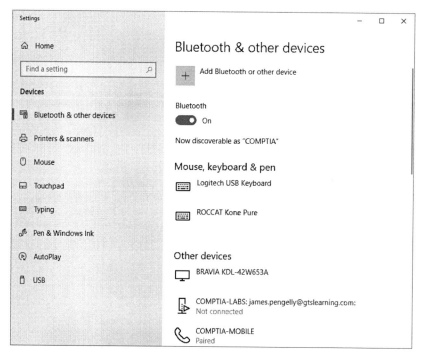

Devices page within the Windows 10 Settings app. (Screenshot used with permission from Microsoft.)

DEVICE MANAGER

When you have installed a device, check that it works. It is a good sign if the device is recognized by Windows, but you should still perform a functional test. For example, print a test page when installing a printer, test file copy when installing removable media, or test audio and video playback when installing multimedia devices.

Device Manager (`devmgmt.msc`) allows you to view and edit the properties of installed hardware. You can change device settings, update drivers, and resolve any known conflicts.

VERIFYING DEVICE INSTALLATION

Beyond installation of its driver, a device's configuration will include an interrupt address (IRQ) and various other properties, including memory addresses and I/O ranges. All hardware devices need a unique configuration so that they can communicate with the processor and other system components. Hopefully, if all your devices are fairly recent, Windows will be able to detect them and install them properly. There may be circumstances where you need to check the system resources assigned to a device, however. You can use the **View** menu in Device Manager to see which resources are assigned to which device.

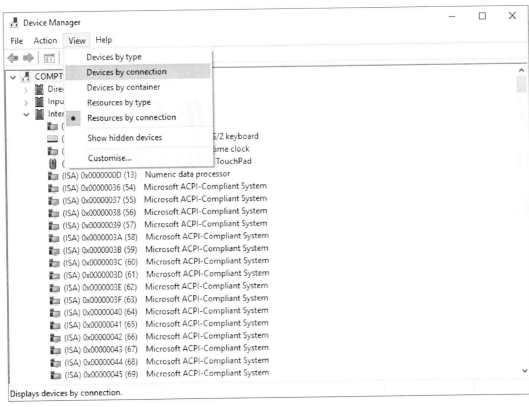

Managing hardware with the Device Manager in Windows 10. (Screenshot used with permission from Microsoft.)

UPDATING AND TROUBLESHOOTING A DEVICE

Sometimes Windows can determine a device's type and function, but cannot locate a driver for the device (perhaps there is no driver included on the Windows setup media or in Windows Update). In this case, you may find an "Unknown Device" or device of a "generic" type listed in the Device Manager with a yellow exclamation mark indicating a problem.

If the device has never worked, check that it (or the driver installed) is compatible with the OS. Manufacturers often release updated drivers to fix known problems. The update can normally be obtained as a download from the support area of the manufacturer's website. Once downloaded, the driver may come with a setup program to install it or may need to be installed manually.

Note: *If a device is not working properly, a warning message is usually displayed in the notification area.*

To update or troubleshoot a device manually, in the Device Manager hardware tree, locate the device, right-click it, and select **Properties** to display the device settings. The **General** tab displays status information for the device. Use the **Update Driver** button on the **Drivers** tab to install a new driver.

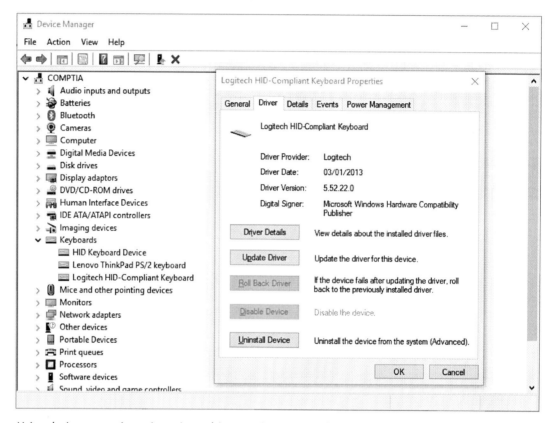

Using device properties to investigate driver version. (Screenshot used with permission from Microsoft.)

Note: *When installing drivers, always check the laptop (or PC) vendor's site for an OEM version of the driver first. Devices used by system builders can be slightly different from retail versions and may need a different driver to work properly with the chipset and firmware. This is more often the case with laptops than desktop PCs.*

If a device supports Plug-and-Play and is hot swappable, you can remove it from the computer without having to uninstall it. Before removing a storage device, close any

applications that might be using it, then select the **Safely Remove Hardware** icon in the notification area on the taskbar and choose the option to stop or eject the device. Otherwise, you can uninstall a device prior to physically removing it by right-clicking in Device Manager and selecting **Uninstall**.

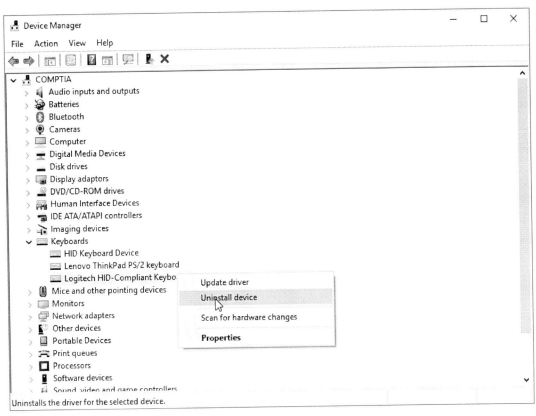

Using Device Manager to uninstall a device. (Screenshot used with permission from Microsoft.)

There is also an option in Device Manager to Disable a device, which you might use if it is not working with the current driver and want to make it inaccessible to users while you find a replacement or to improve system security by disabling unused devices (such as modems). Disabled devices are shown with a down arrow.

HARDWARE DIAGNOSTICS

If you cannot diagnose a hardware driver or configuration problem via Device Manager, there are other tools you can use to get more information.

TROUBLESHOOTING APP

Windows is bundled with a number of automated troubleshooting utilities. These guide you through the process of installing and configuring a device correctly. The troubleshooters are available from Control Panel in Windows 7 or the Settings app in Windows 10.

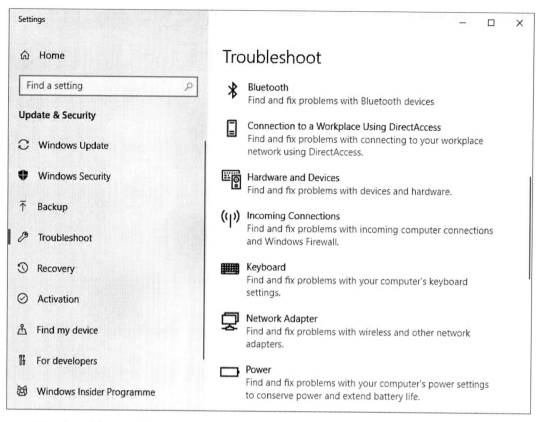

Selection of the troubleshooting tools in Windows 10. (Screenshot used with permission from Microsoft.)

SYSTEM INFORMATION

The System Information (`msinfo32`) application provides a Windows interface to some of the configuration information contained in the registry.

Category	Description
System Summary	Information about operating system and firmware versions and registration details.
Hardware Resources	The I/O, IRQ, and memory address settings used by the CPU to communicate with a component.
Components	A detailed list of all running devices. including configuration information such as IRQ.
Software Environment	Various information including drivers, environment settings, and network connections.

Note: It's `msinfo32` even if you're using a 64-bit version of Windows—there is no such thing as "msinfo64."

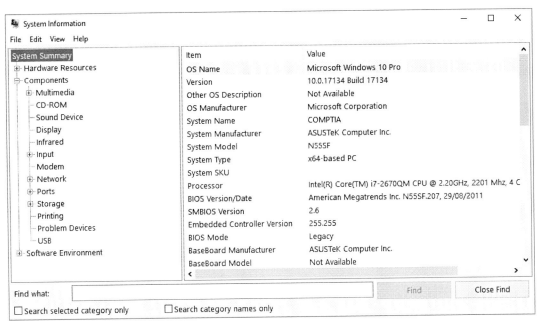

System Information. (Screenshot used with permission from Microsoft.)

DirectX DIAGNOSTIC TOOL

The DirectX Diagnostic Tool (`dxdiag`) displays a report on the system's DirectX configuration, which determines its ability to support 3D graphics and sound.

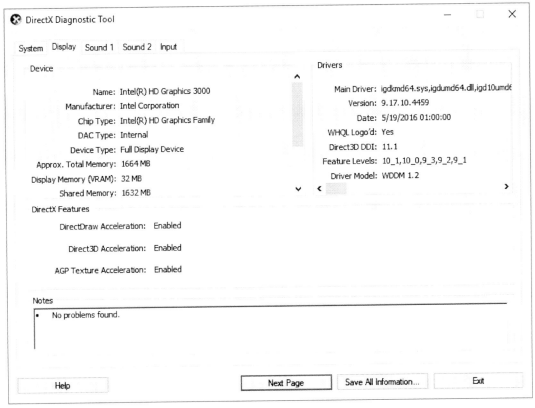

DirectX Diagnostic Tool. (Screenshot used with permission from Microsoft.)

Activity 1-1
Supporting Operating Systems Review

SCENARIO
Answer the following review questions.

1. **Which versions of Windows do you expect to support?**

2. **Which Windows features and tools do you think you will use most often and why?**

Summary

In this lesson, you supported operating systems. By increasing your familiarity with the types of operating systems in use, as well as the tools and capabilities of each, you are well on the way to gaining the knowledge and expertise expected of an A+ technician.

Lesson 2

Installing, Configuring, and Maintaining Operating Systems

LESSON INTRODUCTION

So far in this course, you worked with the Microsoft® Windows® operating system. As you know, a CompTIA® A+® technician will probably also be responsible for setting up, maintaining, and troubleshooting computers and devices that have other operating systems installed. Familiarity with other desktop operating systems, such as Linux® and macOS®, will enable you to support more of your user base.

Since so many computers today come with operating system software installed by the vendor, an ordinary user might never need to install an operating system. As an IT professional, however, you might be called upon to install operating systems for a variety of reasons: if the original installation does not meet a user's needs; if the system needs to be upgraded; if you are redeploying a system from one user to another; or even if you need to complete a brand new build and construct a computer entirely from scratch. In all of these cases, you will need to be able to install, configure, and maintain the computer's operating system.

LESSON OBJECTIVES

In this lesson, you will:

- Configure and use Linux.

- Configure and use macOS.

- Install and upgrade operating systems.

- Perform OS maintenance tasks.

Topic A
Configure and Use Linux

EXAM OBJECTIVES COVERED
1002-1.3 Summarize general OS installation considerations and upgrade methods.
1002-1.9 Given a scenario, use features and tools of the Mac OS and Linux client/desktop operating systems.

The various operating systems you might encounter use different tools, but the functionality of those tools is common across all types of systems. You will need to configure disks and file systems, user accounts, and software applications.

Many individuals and organizations have adopted Linux as a desktop and server OS because of its high security, low cost, and ease of licensing. In this topic, you will examine the basics of Linux so that you can begin to understand and appreciate its benefits.

THE LINUX OPERATING SYSTEM

Like all operating systems, **Linux** enables the most basic common system operations, such as file management, user account management, and so forth. It provides a means for users to interact with their computer's hardware and software.

DISTRIBUTIONS

The core of Linux is called the **kernel** and this is the same on all versions or **distributions** (**distros**). The kernel is the software component that provides the core set of operating system functions. These include features for managing system hardware and for communicating between software and hardware. A Linux distribution is a complete Linux implementation, including kernel, shell, applications, utilities, and installation media, that is packaged, distributed, and supported by a software vendor. Common distributions include:

- **Red Hat/CentOS**—the most commercially successful distribution. Also, the CentOS distribution is a stable, predictable, manageable, and reproducible platform derived from the sources of Red Hat® Enterprise Linux® (RHEL). CentOS is maintained by The CentOS Project, a community-driven free software effort that is modeled on the structure of the Apache® Foundation and has its own governing board. CentOS benefits from Red Hat's ongoing contributions and investment.
- **SUSE®**—originally developed in Germany, the company was bought out by US networking company Novell.
- **Debian/Ubuntu®**—one of the many volunteer-driven distributions. Ubuntu is one of most widely used versions of Debian.
- **Knoppix**—another popular Debian derivative.

These are some of the more popular distributions for PCs. There are a huge number of flavors, many of which have been developed for specialist applications such as running routers, set-top boxes, smart TVs, Internet of Things (IoT) devices, and so on. The smartphone OS, Android™, is based on Linux.

LINUX DESKTOP OPTIONS

Linux was originally developed with a **Command-Line Interface (CLI)** or **shell** very much like **UNIX**.

Today many users of Linux still use the **bash** shell and server-based editions will often only have the command-line environment installed. For this reason, it is important that support technicians are comfortable with using Linux shell commands. Many system tasks still require the use of the command even if a GUI environment is running. Within a GUI, you can open a **terminal window** to run shell commands.

Note: There are other CLI shells, include Bourne (sh), C Shell (csh), and Korn (ksh).

For ease of use, many distributions aimed at end user PCs have a graphical shell loaded. Some popular GUI shells include:

- **Gnome (GNU Object Model Environment)**—the oldest and most widely deployed GUI. Used by default on Fedora® and Debian.

*Note: **GNU** is a recursive acronym standing for "GNU is Not UNIX." Many of the non-kernel bits of software developed under the open source GNU license to replace their proprietary UNIX equivalents can be used with Linux.*

- **KDE® (K Desktop Environment)**—a very popular GUI often used by SUSE.
- **Cinnamon**—based on the MINT GUI.
- **Xfce**—one of the many lightweight GUIs, designed for systems with less RAM and CPU power.

A typical Linux GUI desktop looks like the image in the following figure.

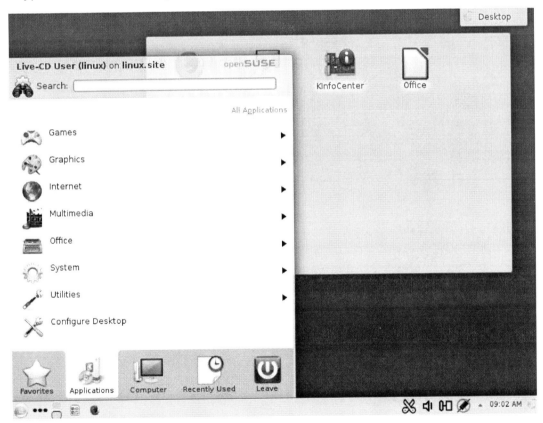

Linux GUI desktop.

It is worth noting that although the desktop can vary from distro to distro, most will have a common theme, with a start menu, taskbar, system tray, and so on, in a similar fashion to Windows and macOS. It should also be noted that unlike Windows and Mac, the default GUI shell can be swapped for a different one. Many GUIs, including **Gnome**, will support features like **virtual desktop** (Mission Control on macOS).

Many distros will come with a range of open source applications pre-installed such as Firefox® Browser and office applications such as Libre.

One thing that does vary from one distro to another is system tools. **SUSE**, for example, comes with a tool called **YaST** which provides a Control Panel style utility for Linux. Other similar tools are **webmin** and **Yumix**. However, it should be noted that all these tools simply update the standard Linux configuration files stored in the **/etc** folder.

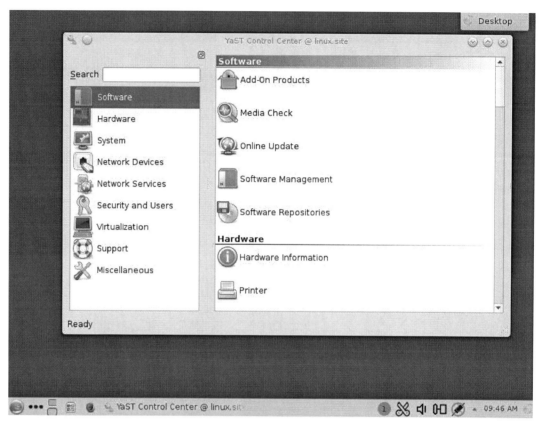

YaST Control Center.

LINUX COMMANDS

Linux commands are entered in a standard format, featuring the command followed by a space then a number of options (or switches) and/or arguments, depending on the function of the command. Wildcards (* and ?) can be used in the same way as at the Windows command line.

- The first "word" input is interpreted as the command. This could be a full or relative path to the executable or just the name of an executable stored in a directory identified by a **PATH** environment variable. The command "word" is completed by the first space character.
- **Options** (or **switches**) are used to change the operation of a command. They can be single letters (preceded by a single hyphen) or words (preceded by a double hyphen). The order the options are placed on the command is not important.
- **Arguments** are values supplied to the command for it to operate on, such as file names. Arguments should be supplied in the correct order for the command's syntax.

You can send or redirect the results of one command to another command. Pipes are used to combine Linux tools on a single command line, enabling you to use the output of one command as the input to another. The **pipe symbol** is a vertical bar (|), which you type between two commands.

You can issue more than one command before pressing **Enter**. Place a semicolon (;) between the commands and they will be issued one after the other.

CASE SENSITIVITY

Commands, parameters, and file and directory names are all case sensitive in Linux. For example, `ls -l file.data` and `ls -L File.data` would produce completely different results. Using capitals in the command name would generate an error message.

GETTING HELP

Any Linux command will generally give a reasonably detailed explanation of its function and syntax when the `--help` parameter is used. The help is often several pages long so use of the `| more` (pipe) at the end of the command is recommended on any command that generates large amounts of output. It shows the results a page at a time. For example: `ls --help | more`

Alternatively, you can use `man` to view the help pages for a particular command. For example, use `man man` to view the help pages for the `man` command.

> **Note:** Also note that Linux terminals support **Tab completion** to help in entering commands. You can use **Shift+Page Up** or **Shift+Page Down** and **Ctrl+Shift+Up Arrow** or **Ctrl+Shift+Down Arrow** to scroll. Use the **Up** and **Down** arrow keys to scroll through previously used commands. Use *q* to quit a command.

LINUX DISK AND FILE MANAGEMENT

In Linux, the directory structure is defined as a **File System Hierarchy**. Unlike Windows, drive letters like C: or D: are not used. The file system starts at the root, represented by /. Directories and subdirectories can be created from the root to store files.

It is important to realize that everything available to the Linux OS is represented as a file in the file system, including devices. This is referred to as the **unified file system**. For example, a single hard drive attached to a SATA port would normally be represented in the file system by /dev/sda. A second storage device—perhaps one attached to a USB port—would be represented as /dev/sdb.

When Linux boots, a system kernel and **virtual file system** are loaded to a RAM drive. The virtual file system identifies the location of the persistent root partition from the appropriate storage device and loads the file system stored on the disk.

MOUNTING PARTITIONS

A file system configured on a partition on a particular storage device is attached to a particular directory (**mount point**) within the unified file system using the `mount` command. For example, the following command mounts partition 1 on the mass storage device **sda** to the directory **/mnt/diskC**.

```
mount /dev/sda1 /mnt/diskC
```

Mountable file systems are listed in the **/etc/fstab** file.

> **Note:** Think of the root file system representing everything on the computer as "THE" file system and a file system for a particular partition as just "A" file system.

LINUX FILE SYSTEMS

Most Linux distributions use some version of the **ext** file system to format partitions on mass storage devices. **ext3** is a 64-bit file system with support for journaling, which means that the file system tracks changes, giving better reliability and less chance of file corruption in the event of crashes or power outages. Support for journaling is the main difference between ext3 and its predecessor (ext2). **ext4** delivers significantly better performance than **ext3** and would usually represent the best choice for new systems.

Linux can also support FAT/FAT32, though it is designated as **VFAT**. Additional protocols, such as the **Network File System (NFS)**, can be used to mount remote storage devices into the local file system.

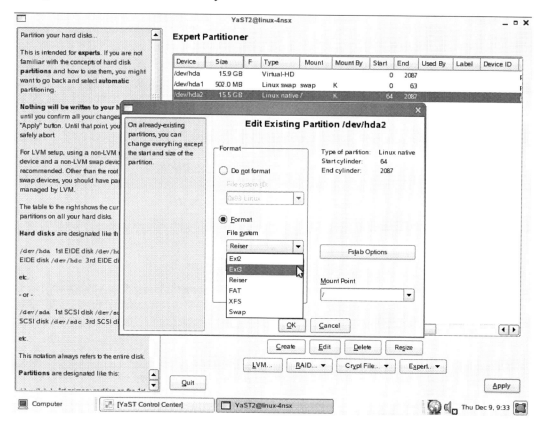

Using YaST to format a partition.

SWAP PARTITION

Virtual memory allows a computer to use disk space to supplement the amount of system RAM installed. If applications or data files use up the available physical memory, "pages" of data from RAM can be written to swap space on a disk to free up some space. If the paged data is required again, it is transferred from the swap space back to RAM.

Most default installations of Linux create a **swap partition** to use as swap space. The swap partition is formatted with a minimal kind of file system. It can only be used by the memory manager and not for storage of ordinary data files.

DISK MANAGEMENT COMMANDS

The file system choice can be made when the disk has been partitioned. Most Linux distros provide GUI tools for managing disks and file systems, but the following represent the main command-line options:

- `fdisk`—used to create and manage partitions on a hard disk.

- `mkfs`—used to format a partition.
- `mkswap`—used to format a swap partition. The `swapon` command is used to activate the partition as swap space.
- `dd`—make a copy of an input file (`if=`) to an output file (`of=`) and apply optional conversions to the file data. One notable use of dd is to clone a disk (in the following, **sda** might be the fixed drive and **sdb** a removable drive): `dd if=/dev/sda of=/dev/sdb`
  - You would need to boot from a live CD so that the file system was not mounted at the time of cloning. You can also clone a disk to a disk image (.img) file: `dd if=/dev/sda of=/mnt/usbstick/backup.img`
  - To restore, you could simply reverse the input and output files: `dd if=/mnt/usbstick/backup.img of=/dev/sda`

NAVIGATION IN THE LINUX DIRECTORY STRUCTURE

The core commands that a technician should know to navigate the Linux file structure include `ls`, `cp`, `mv`, `rm`, and `cd`, along with many more. This table describes these commands and how to use them.

Command	Used to	Description and Examples
`ls`	List files	The `ls` command is used to display a folder in the same way as `dir` at the Windows command prompt. Popular parameters include `-l` to display a detailed (long) list and `-a` to display all files including hidden or system files. The following example shows the entire contents of the **/etc** directory in a detailed format: `ls -l -a /etc`
`pwd`	Print working directory	The `pwd` command simply displays the current directory you are working in. Any commands you use which don't specify a directory will assume your current one. The prompt on some distros will show your **current working directory** or a ~ symbol, which indicates you are in your **home directory**.
`cd`	Change directory	The `cd` command is used to change your working directory. Typical syntax would be: • `cd /etc`—change directory to **/etc**. This is an **absolute path** (begins with /) so will work regardless of your current directory. • `cd documents`—change your directory to a subdirectory called **documents**. This is a **relative path**. The **documents** directory must exist below the current directory. • `cd ..`—change your directory to the **parent directory** of the one you are currently working in.

Command	Used to	Description and Examples
`cp`	Copy files	The `cp` command is used to create a copy of files either in the same or different folder with the same or different name. For example:
		• `cp file1.txt file1.old`—copy **file1.txt** in the current working directory to a new file called **file1.old** in the same directory.
		• `cp /etc/hosts /tmp`—copy the file **hosts** from the directory **/etc** into the directory **/tmp**, keeping the file name the same.
		• `cp -v /var/log/message* /home/usera`—copy all files beginning with the name **message** from the **/var/log** directory into **/home/usera**. The **-v** option displays the files copied.
`mv`	Move files	The `mv` command is used to either move files from one directory to another or rename a file. For example:
		• `mv /home/usera/data.txt /tmp`—move the file **data.txt** from the **/home/usera** directory to the **/tmp** directory, keeping the file name the same.
		• `mv alarm.dat /tmp/alarm.bak`—move and rename the file **alarm.dat** in the current directory to **alarm.bak** in **/tmp**.
		• `mv /var/log/app1.log /var/log/app1.old`—rename the file **app1.dat** in the **/var/log** folder to **app1.old**.
`rm`	Remove files	The `rm` command is potentially very dangerous if used incorrectly. Although its main role is to delete files, with an additional parameter (`-r`) it can also be used to delete directories. For example:
		• `rm data.old`—remove the single file data.old from the current working directory.
		• `rm /var/log/*.bak`—remove all files ending in **.bak** from the **/var/log** directory.
		• `-r /home/usera/data`—remove the contents of the entire directory tree underneath the folder **/home/usera/data**.

Caution: *Use the `-r` switch with caution!*

Note: *Remember that Linux commands operate without prompts, allowing you to cancel.*

Command	Used to	Description and Examples
`grep`	Filter files	The `grep` (Globally search a Regular Expression and Print) command is used to search and filter the contents of files, displaying the lines that match the search string. The search string can be a simple text value to match (a **literal**) or can use a sophisticated pattern-matching system called **regular expressions (regex)**. `grep` is especially useful for searching long files such as system logs. For example, the following command displays only the lines in the Linux system log file for messages that contain the text **uid=1003**, ignoring the case of the text: • `grep -I "uid=1003" /var/log/messages` The `grep` command can also be used to search a directory for a certain file. The `ls -l	grep audit` command returns a long listing of any files in the current directory whose name contains **audit**.

LINUX FILE EDITORS

vi or **vim** is a text file editor derived from a UNIX original. Although this tool is very powerful, it is based on letter- and number-based commands to modify the text. For example, **dd** when pressed will delete the whole line the cursor is on; **5dd** would delete 5 whole lines. When **vi** is in **command mode**, input such as this is interpreted as a command.

To enter text, you need to switch to **insert mode** by pressing an appropriate command key. For example, **i** switches to insert mode at the current cursor position, **a** appends text at the end of the current line, and **o** inserts text on a new line below the current line. The **Esc** key switches from insert mode back to command mode.

To save a file, use **:w** from command mode. To save and quit, use **:wq**. **:q!** quits without saving.

There are other command-line editors, such as **mcedit**, **nano**, **pico**, or **joe**, that are easier to learn to use.

LINUX USER ACCOUNTS

Linux, like most operating systems, supports multiple users. The **root user**, also known as the **superuser**, is the default administrative account on a Linux system. This account can do anything on the system. You should only use this account when absolutely necessary. For most Linux distributions, you create a regular user when you are installing Linux. This is the user you should log on as for day-to-day tasks. Even many administrative tasks can be performed more safely under the regular user account.

User accounts are linked to a **primary group**, which determines many aspects of security in Linux. User settings are stored in the **/etc/passwd** file and group settings are stored in the **/etc/group** file. The user password is typically stored as an encrypted hash in the **/etc/shadow** file, along with other password settings, such as age and expiration date. The command-line utilities `useradd`, `usermod`, and `userdel` can be used to add, modify, and delete user information. The `groupadd`, `groupmod`, and `groupdel` commands can be used to manage groups.

A user can belong to many groups but can only have one **effective group ID** at any one time. The effective group ID is listed for the user account in **etc/passwd** and can be changed using the `newgrp` command.

Many distros have GUI-based utilities that allow user and group management. YaST is an example of one of these.

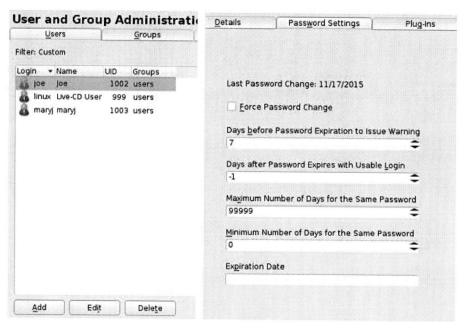

User and group Administration tool in YaST.

su (Superuser)

The `su` command allows a normal Linux user to become superuser (or root). The command will prompt the user for the root user's password. Additionally, it is possible to put a different user name after the `su` command and become that user, assuming the password is known.

Using `su` without an option retains the original user's profile and variables. The switched user also remains in the home directory of the original user. Using `su  -` changes users and launches a new shell under the context of that new user. This is a much better practice.

sudo (Superuser Do)

The `sudo` command allows a normal user to run specified commands with superuser privilege level. The superuser first has to edit the **/etc/sudoers** file listing the commands and users that are allowed to run them. The user enters the `sudo` command followed by the path of the command they wish to run. The user might be asked to confirm his or her password, if it has not been cached recently.

passwd (Password Utility)

The `passwd` command allows a user to change their own password or superuser (root) to change or reset someone else's. When a user runs the command, Linux will prompt first for the existing password then the new one, twice. The superuser can reset another user's password by typing the user name after the command. The existing password is not required in this case. To reset the password for the user **fredb**, the superuser would enter the command `passwd  fredb`

 Note: *Don't confuse* `passwd` *with* `pwd` *(Print Working Directory).*

LINUX FILE SYSTEM PERMISSIONS

The Linux file system has a relatively simple security system compared to Windows NTFS. There are just three different rights, as shown in the following table.

Access Right	Enables You To:
Read (r)	View the contents of a file or directory.
Write (w)	Modify or delete the object (in the case of directories, allows adding, deleting, or renaming files within the directory).
Execute (x)	Run an executable file or script. For directories, execute allows the user to do things like change the focus to the directory and access or search items within it.

For each object, these permissions are set for the **owner**, for the **group** the owner belongs to or that the object has been assigned to, and for **other users** ("the world"). Using symbolic notation, each permission is allowed (**r** or **w** or **x**) or denied (**-**). If you run `ls  -l` to obtain a directory listing, directory or file object permissions will be shown as follows:

- **drwxr-xr-x 2 administrator administrator Desktop**
- **-rw-rw-r-- 1 administrator administrator MEMO.txt**

The leading character designates the file type. For example, **-** represents a regular file and **d** indicates a directory. The permissions for the **Desktop** directory show that the **owner** (administrator) has full (**rwx**) permissions, whereas the **group** (also administrator) and **others** have read and execute (**r-x**). For the **MEMO.txt** file, the **user** and **group** have read/write (**rw-**) permissions, whereas **others** has read permissions only (**r--**).

Permissions can also be expressed numerically, using the octal value format shown in the following table. An octal value can represent up to eight digits (0-7):

Digit	Permission	Binary Value	Rights
0	- - -	0000	Deny all
1	- - x	0001	Execute
2	- w -	0010	Write
3	- w x	0011	Write and execute
4	r - -	0100	Read-only
5	r - x	0101	Read and execute
6	r w -	0110	Read and write
7	r w x	0111	Allow all

So, for example, a file with numeric permission **0775** (the leading zero identifies the value as an octal, but can often be omitted) grants all rights to the owner and the owner's group and Read/Execute rights to everyone else.

 Note: Remember that Execute=1, Write=2, and Read=4—add those values together to get a particular combination of permissions.

From the shell, the `chmod` command can be used to secure files and directories, using either symbolic or octal notation. Only the owner can change permissions. The command `chown` allows the superuser to change the owner of a file or directory, whereas `chgrp` can be used to change the group.

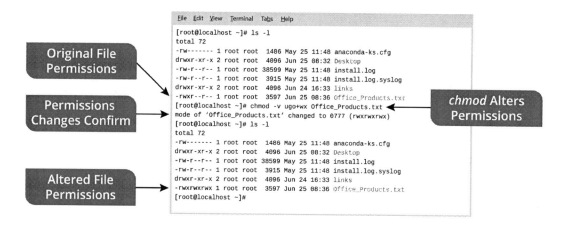

Modifying permissions using the chmod command.

LINUX SOFTWARE MANAGEMENT

A distribution contains any software packages the distribution vendor or sponsor considers appropriate. Copies of these packages (including any updates) will be posted to a software repository. Often the vendor will maintain different repositories. For example, there may be one for officially supported package versions, one for beta/ untested versions, and one for "at own risk" unsupported packages.

The integrity of a package is usually tested by making a cryptographic hash of the compiled package, using a function such as **MD5** or SHA-256. The hash value and function is published on the package vendor's site. When you download a package, you can run the same function on the package file (using a command such as **md5sum** or **sha256sum**) and compare the output with the published value. If they do not match, you should not proceed with the installation.

PACKAGE MANAGERS (APT-GET)

Linux software is made available both as source code and as pre-compiled applications. A source code package needs to be run through the appropriate compiler with the preferred options. Pre-compiled packages can be installed using various tools, such as **rpm** (Red Hat Package Manager), **apt** (Debian), or **yum** (Fedora). Many distributions also provide GUI package manager front-ends to these command-line tools.

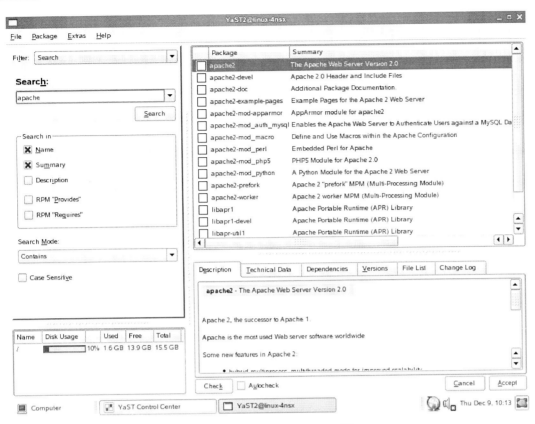

YaST package manager in SUSE.

The following uses of `apt-get` provide some examples of how packages are managed at the command line:

- `apt-get update`—refresh the local database with information about the packages available from the repository.
- `apt-get upgrade`—update all packages with the latest versions.
- `apt-get install` *PackageName*—install a new application.

LINUX SYSTEM COMMANDS

There are many tools and techniques available to troubleshoot issues with applications or update the network configuration. You should also know how to shut down or reboot a Linux PC.

Command	Description
`ps` and `kill`	The `ps` command displays the **Linux processes** (programs) that are currently running. Each process has a system generated **process ID** which can be used with the `kill` command to end the process. The parameter `-ef` displays processes being run by all users along with a more detailed display.
`ifconfig` and `iwconfig`	The `ifconfig` and `iwconfig` tools display the current state of the network interfaces within Linux. `ifconfig` is the original tool designed for cabled Ethernet interfaces, whereas `iwconfig` displays information about the wireless adapters configured within the system.

Command	Description
shutdown	Linux is designed to be a very stable operating system and the server versions often run non-stop for months or even years at a time. However, the desktop versions are likely to be powered on and off much more often. The shutdown command has two main parameters: -h to halt or -r to reboot the system followed by when the event should take place. Examples of this could be now, +10 (+10 meaning ten minutes from now), or 17:30 (to specify an exact time).

HOW TO CONFIGURE AND USE LINUX
Follow these procedures to configure and use Linux.

CREATING A USER IN LINUX
There are many Linux distributions and most of them have some type of GUI for creating users that is specific to that distribution. The following command-line command can be used on any distribution.

1. Logged in as the root user, open a terminal window.
2. Enter useradd *new_user_name* to create a new account, which will remain locked until a password is set for the account.
3. Enter password *new_user_name* to set a password for the account. This also unlocks the account.

ACCESS LINUX
To access Linux systems:

1. If the system boots to a GUI, use the mouse to swipe the screen up to reveal the login screen.
2. Enter the login username and press **Enter**. Unless absolutely necessary that you log in as the **root** user, you should log in with a regular user account.
3. Enter the password associated with the username you previously entered.
4. If you need superuser access, enter the su command, entering the superuser password when prompted.
5. If you want to enter a single command with superuser access, enter sudo *command_name*. This will work with any commands that have been entered in the **/etc/sudoers** file.

ISSUE LINUX COMMANDS
To enter Linux commands that are case-sensitive:

1. At the command prompt, enter the command using the appropriate casing for both the command, arguments, and parameters.
2. If you are in a GUI environment, open a terminal window to access a command prompt.
3. Some commands you will likely need to use include:
   - ls with parameters such as -l, -L, -a to display directory listings.
   - man to display the manual pages for the command identified as an argument to the command.
   - ps to display currently running Linux processes.
   - kill to end a running process.
   - ifconfig to display and manage cabled Ethernet interface settings.

- `iwconfig` to display and manage wireless adapter settings.
- `shutdown -h` *[time]* to halt the system in or at the time indicated (`+10` for in 10 minutes, `now` for do it immediately, or specify an exact time).
- `shutdown -r` *[time]* to restart the system in or at the time indicated.

MANAGE THE LINUX DISK AND FILE SYSTEM

To manage the Linux disk and file system:

1. Log in as root or use `su` or `sudo` to gain superuser access to the file system.
2. Issue the disk or file system command. These include:

   - `mount` followed by the storage device name (for example, /dev/sda1).
   - `fdisk` to create and manage the hard disk partition identified as an argument to the command.
   - `mkfs` to format the partition specified as an argument to the command.
   - `mkswap` to format a swap partition.
   - `swapon` to activate a partition as swap space.
   - `dd if=`*path_of_input* `of=`*path_of_output* to make a copy of the specified input file to the specified output file.

NAVIGATE THE LINUX DIRECTORY STRUCTURE

To navigate the Linux directory structure:

1. Log in as a regular user. You will only be able to navigate to and see the portions of the directory structure to which you have been given access permissions.
2. Issue the appropriate command. These include:

   - `ls` to display directory contents.
   - `ls -l` to display directory contents in a detailed or long-format list.
   - `ls -a` or `ls -la` to include hidden or system files in the list.
   - `pwd` to display the name of the current directory you are working in.
   - `cd` to change the working directory. You can use relative or absolute paths, or change to the parent directory.
   - `cp` to copy files. You can use wildcards to specify multiple files.
   - `mv` to move or rename files. You can use wildcards to specify multiple files.
   - `rm` to remove (delete) files. Using with the **-r** option performs a recursive remove.
   - `grep` to search and filter file contents.

CREATE A FILE AND ENTER TEXT USING THE Vim EDITOR

To create a file and enter text using the Vim editor:

1. Log in as a user.
2. To create a file, at the command prompt, enter `vim` *{file name}*.
3. To switch to insert mode, press **i**.
4. Type the required content.
5. To return to command mode, press **Esc**.
6. To save and close the file, enter `:wq`.

EDIT TEXT FILES IN Vim COMMAND MODE

To edit text files in Vim command mode:

1. Log in as a user.

2. To open a file, enter `vim {file name}`.
3. To make necessary changes, use the appropriate vim shortcuts.
4. To save and close the file, enter `:wq`.

OPEN MULTIPLE WINDOWS USING THE vim COMMAND

To open multiple windows using the vim command:

1. Log in as a user.
2. Open multiple windows.

   - To open different files in multiple windows, enter `vim -o {file name 1} {file name 2} ... {file name n}`.
   - To open a new file in a new window, press **Ctrl+W+N**.
   - To navigate through the windows, hold down **Ctrl+W** and use the arrow keys.
3. To make necessary changes, use the appropriate Vim shortcuts.
4. If necessary, to return to command mode, press **Esc**.
5. Save and close the files.

   - To save and close the files one by one, enter `:wq`.

   - To close all files at the same time, enter `:qa`.

VIEW FILE OR DIRECTORY PERMISSIONS

To view file or directory permissions:

1. Log in as a user.
2. View the permissions of a file or directory.

   - View the permissions of a file or directory, as necessary, from the command line.

     - To view the permissions of a file, enter `ls -l {file name}`.
     - To view the permissions of a directory, enter `ls -ld {directory name}`.
   - View the permissions of a file or folder using the Nautilus browser.

     a. Right-click the file or folder and select **Properties**.
     b. To view the permissions of the file or folder, select the **Permissions** tab.

MODIFY FILE OR DIRECTORY PERMISSIONS

To modify file or directory permissions:

1. Log in as a user or root, depending on what type of files you want to modify.
2. Change the permissions of a file or directory in the CLI or the GUI.

   - To modify permissions in the CLI, enter `chmod [options] {file or directory name}`.
   - Modify permissions in the GUI.

     a. Right-click the file or directory and select **Properties**.
     b. Select the **Permissions** tab.
     c. From the **File Access** or **Folder Access** drop-down list, select the desired permission for owner, owner groups, and other groups.

MANAGE PACKAGES USING RPM

To manage packages using RPM:

1. To install packages:

   a. Download the **rpm** file that you want to install.

b. To install the package, use the `rpm -ivh {package name}` command.

c. If necessary, download the dependency packages.

2. To uninstall packages:

    a. To search for the rpm package that you want to uninstall, use the `rpm -qi {package name}` command.

    b. To uninstall the rpm package, use the `rpm -e {package name}` command.

3. To verify installed packages:

    • To verify all the rpm packages, use the `rpm -Va` command.

    • To verify an individual rpm package, use the `rpm -Vv {package name}` command.

    • To verify a specific file in the package, use the `rpm -V -f {file name}| -p {package name}` command.

4. To upgrade packages:

    a. Download the updated package.

    b. Update the existing package using the `rpm -Uvh {package name}` command.

    c. To verify that the package is updated, use the `rpm -qi {package name}` command.

5. To freshen packages:

    a. Download the updated package.

    b. To freshen the existing package, use the `rpm -Fvh {package name}` command.

    c. To verify that the package is updated, use the `rpm -qi {package name}` command.

MANAGE PACKAGES USING YUM

To manage packages using YUM:

1. Log in as **root**.
2. Manage packages using YUM.

    • To install packages using YUM, enter `yum install {package name}`.

    • To remove packages using YUM, enter `yum remove {package name}`.

    • To display a package's description, enter `yum info {package name}`.

    • To update the system with the specified package, enter `yum update {package name}`.

Topic B
Configure and Use macOS

EXAM OBJECTIVES COVERED
1002-1.3 Summarize general OS installation considerations and upgrade methods.
1002-1.9 Given a scenario, use features and tools of the Mac OS and Linux client/desktop operating systems.

Mac® computers from Apple® use the macOS® operating system. Mac users tend to be found in art, music, graphic design, and education because macOS includes apps geared to those audiences. In this topic, you will examine some of the important features and functions of macOS.

APPLE MACS AND macOS

macOS is the generic name for the operating system that powers Apple Mac computers. It was formerly known as **Mac OS** (from launch until 2001) and then **OS X** (from 2001 through to 2016). All macOS versions are based on UNIX technology, and many "under the hood" commands are shared between the two operating systems.

Whereas Microsoft Windows can be installed and used on any PC with Intel architecture, macOS may only be installed on Apple's own hardware. By creating what has become known as a "walled garden" for their computers and software, Apple has been able to impose strict quality controls on the apps and devices that are available for the Mac. This has ensured that, compared to Windows, there are fewer outbreaks of viruses and malware and fewer system stability issues caused by faulty drivers or application/device conflicts.

Note: You might hear the term "Hackintosh," which refers to installing macOS on non-Apple hardware, often as a virtual machine. Apple's license agreement only permits installation on Apple hardware.

Note that macOS and iOS are separate operating systems. There are several visual and operational similarities between macOS and iOS and there are utilities to exchange information between the two, but it is not possible to run programs built for macOS on iOS and vice versa. iOS® is purely an OS for the iPhone® and iPad®, whereas macOS is only used for desktop and laptop computers.

OS X AND macOS VERSIONS

Since its release in 2001, OS X (and now macOS) has undergone regular 10.x updates and revisions to keep pace with updates to Apple Mac hardware. Updates and new versions are distributed free of charge through the App Store. OS X versions were originally named after big cats and then places in California; something that continues with the latest macOS releases.

Unless the hardware is particularly old and can't be upgraded, most Apple Mac computers will now be running macOS High Sierra (10.13) or macOS Mojave (10.14). OS X 10.7 (Lion) is the earliest release that is still supported by Apple. If your Macintosh computer meets the minimum requirements for OS X installation, the hardware should all be compatible with the latest version of macOS. You can verify that your hardware is supported by examining the technical specifications at **support.apple.com/specs**.

APPLE INPUT DEVICES

You should be aware of some differences between the input devices used for Macs and those used for PCs.

Apple Keyboards and Mice

Although a Windows keyboard can be used on an Apple Mac (and vice versa), there are a number of differences between the keys:

- **Command**—the equivalent of **Ctrl** on a Windows keyboard. For example, **command+C** will copy to the clipboard as **Ctrl+C** does on a Windows computer. If you're using a Windows keyboard on a Mac, use the **Windows** key as the **command** key.
- **Option**—equivalent of the **Alt** key.
- **Control**—*not* the equivalent of **Ctrl** on a Windows keyboard!

Apple mice do not feature obvious buttons. Older mice have five sensors that can be set to different actions via **System Preferences**. The later **Magic Mouse** models have a **touchpad** surface with **gesture** support. The **Magic Trackpad** has a larger working surface.

*Note: You can set up right-click in **System Preferences** or use **Control+click**.*

APPLE MAGIC TRACKPAD AND GESTURE SUPPORT

Like the Magic Mouse®, the Magic Trackpad® supports gestures to control the user interface. Apple introduced gestures as a simple way to control macOS from a Magic Trackpad or built-in trackpad of a MacBook®. To see what gestures are available on the Mac or to change any of the settings, go to **System Preferences→Trackpad**.

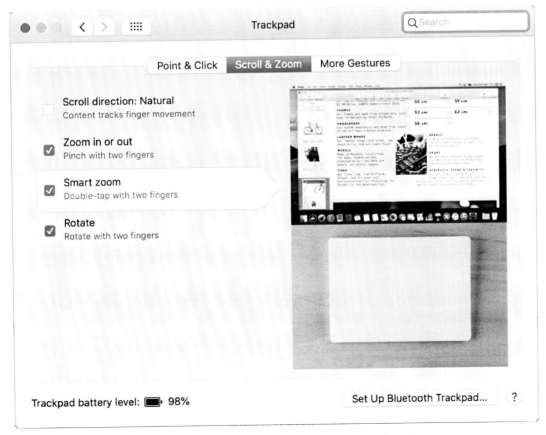

Configuring the trackpad. (Screenshot courtesy of Apple.)

macOS FEATURES

If you are using an Apple Mac computer for the first time, you will notice that the desktop and user interface is similar to a Windows-based PC in some respects but very different in others. As with Windows, a Mac boots to a graphical desktop environment. Any apps that have been installed and configured to launch at boot will also start.

At the top of the screen is the menu bar. This is always present with all apps, but the menu titles shown will vary between different software.

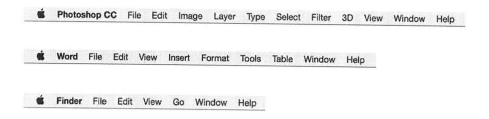

Menu bars with different apps running. (Screenshot courtesy of Apple.)

To the left of the menu bar is the Apple menu, represented by the Apple icon . The items are consistent on this menu for all apps. Some of the key menu items are:

- **About this Mac**: Displays basic support information about the computer.

About this Mac. (Screenshot courtesy of Apple.)

- **Displays**: Shows the current display and its configuration. Click **Displays Preferences** to change the display resolution of the screen, to calibrate the color settings, or to **AirPlay** the display to a device such as an Apple TV.
- **Storage**: Shows the capacity and current usage of the internal hard drive as well as any external drives that are connected to the Mac.
- **Service**: If the computer is under warranty or is protected by the AppleCare Protection Plan, clicking on the relevant links will bring up more information about the available support options. If there is a significant fault with the computer and it is covered by warranty or AppleCare, it is recommended that you follow the

instructions and obtain help and support through an Apple Authorized Service Provider.

In the top-right corner of the menu bar is the **Status** menu. This gives quick access to important key features of the computer.

Status menu options vary according to the software that is installed (from left to right: Dropbox, Adobe Creative Cloud, Google Drive, Wacom Tablet, Evernote, Ring, Todoist, Skype, Arq, Skyfonts, Displays, Bluetooth, Wi-Fi, Drives, Keyboard Preferences and Day/Time). (Screenshot courtesy of Apple.)

THE DOCK

The **dock** at the bottom of the screen gives one-click access to your favorite apps and files, similar to the taskbar in Windows. You can change the way the dock behaves—to configure autohide or position it at another edge of the screen—by right-clicking near the vertical line at the right of the dock.

The dock contains the Finder and Trash icons by default. (Screenshot courtesy of Apple.)

To add a new app or file to the dock, click and drag the icon of the app/file into the dock. The **Finder** and **Trash** icons are always available in the dock. Apps that are open in the dock display a dot below the icon.

Right-click any dock icon to change how that app/file behaves. In the options menu, you can remove that icon from the dock, select **Open at login** to start the app when the computer boots, and **Show in Finder** to find the location of the target file.

SPOTLIGHT SEARCH

Spotlight Search can be used to find almost anything on macOS. To start a new search, click the magnifying glass in the menu bar or press **Command+Space** to bring up the search box. You can change the document types that are searched in **Preferences**. If you wish to specifically exclude locations from **Spotlight** search, click the **Privacy** button to add a folder or drive to the excluded results.

SYSTEM PREFERENCES

The **System Preferences** panel is the equivalent of the Windows **Control Panel**. It is the central "go-to" place for changing settings and network options, and optimizing a macOS configuration.

System Preferences. (Screenshot courtesy of Apple.)

You can access the **System Preferences** panel from the **Apple menu**, from the **System Preferences** icon in the dock, or by entering *system preferences* from **Spotlight Search**.

 Note: If you are not sure where you would change a specific option, just start typing its name in the search box. For example, typing password in the search box will highlight all the options where a password may be set.

MISSION CONTROL AND MULTIPLE DESKTOPS

It is possible to configure macOS with **multiple desktops** (or spaces) using the **Mission Control** feature. This enables the user to set up one or more desktops with different sets of apps, backgrounds, and so on, which is an easy way of managing tasks more effectively.

To set up a new desktop, activate **Mission Control** with the **F3** key. At the top of the screen, it will display a small image of the current desktop with all the open apps below. Move your cursor to the top-right corner of this screen. A tab with a plus symbol will appear from the right. Click on it and a second desktop (Desktop 2; the original will have been renamed Desktop 1) will appear at the top. The open apps shown will still be running on Desktop 1. If you want an app to only run on Desktop 2, click its window and drag it on to the Desktop 2 screen at the top.

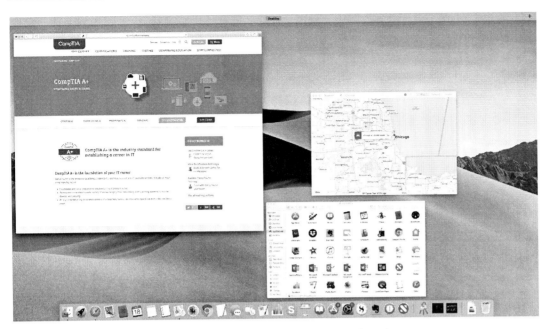

Mission Control. (Screenshot courtesy of Apple.)

It's possible to configure this further from the app menu in the dock. Right-click on an app and you will see the following menu:

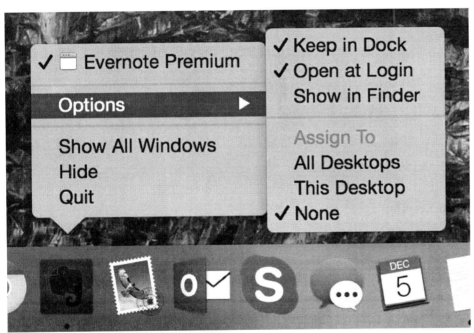

Configuring Mission Control. (Screenshot courtesy of Apple.)

As well as the standard options in the top half of this menu, you can choose to make an app available to all desktops, the currently displayed desktop, or no desktops at all.

To switch between desktops, press the **F3** key and choose a desktop. Alternatively, press **control+left** or **Control+right** to cycle between screens. You can also swipe left or right with three/four fingers on the trackpad, depending on how it is configured.

To remove a desktop, press **F3** and hover the cursor over the desktop to be deleted, then click its **Close** icon. All apps associated with that (now deleted) desktop will revert to the main desktop.

macOS FILE MANAGEMENT

The **Finder** is the **macOS** equivalent of **Explorer** in Windows. It lets the user navigate all the files and folders on a Mac. It is always present and open in the dock.

The Finder icon. (Screenshot courtesy of Apple.)

When you first select **Finder**, it displays your most recently used files under **Recents**. Selecting one of the favorites in the sidebar will change that view. For example, selecting **Applications** will show the apps within that default macOS folder.

Finder with Applications selected. (Screenshot courtesy of Apple.)

HFS PLUS AND APFS

Where Windows uses NTFS and Linux typically uses ext3 or ext4, Apple Mac workstations and laptops use the **Extended Hierarchical File System (HFS Plus)**. HFS Plus supports many of the same features as NTFS but cannot perform native file/folder encryption. The maximum volume and file size is 8 ExaBytes. The only reserved characters are **:** and **/**.

In macOS High Sierra and later, HFS Plus updated to the Apple File System (APFS), which does support native file encryption. It also provides better support for SSDs. Upgrading to High Sierra (or later) automatically converts the startup volume from HFS Plus to APFS if the disk is an SSD. Otherwise, the file system can be converted without data loss using the Disk Utility.

 Note: *While data loss is not expected, always make a backup before performing this type of operation.*

OPTICAL DRIVES AND REMOTE DISC

Since 2016, no Apple Mac has been sold with an internal optical drive. While an external USB drive can be used, another option is the **Remote Disc** app, which lets the user access a CD/DVD drive on another Mac or Windows computer. This isn't suitable for audio CDs, DVD movies, recordable CDs/DVDs, or Windows installation disks, however.

To set up Remote Disc sharing on a Mac, open **System Preferences→Sharing** then make sure the check box is ticked next to **DVD or CD sharing**. To access the optical drive, click **Remote Disc** in **Finder**. The Mac with the drive that has just been configured will be displayed. Click its icon to access the drive.

iCloud

iCloud is Apple's online storage solution for its users. It provides a central, shared location for mail, contacts, calendar, photos, notes, reminders, and so on, across macOS and iOS devices. By default, each user is provided with 5 GB of storage (at the time of writing), although it is possible to upgrade to more space for an additional monthly fee. This space is shared across all iCloud® components and devices.

A **keychain** password cache can also be stored in iCloud to enable easy login to websites across macOS and iOS devices.

To manage iCloud, open **icloud.com** and sign in using an Apple ID. To see usage, click the user name in the top-right of the browser window and select **Settings**. This will show the amount of storage used and the devices that are linked to this account.

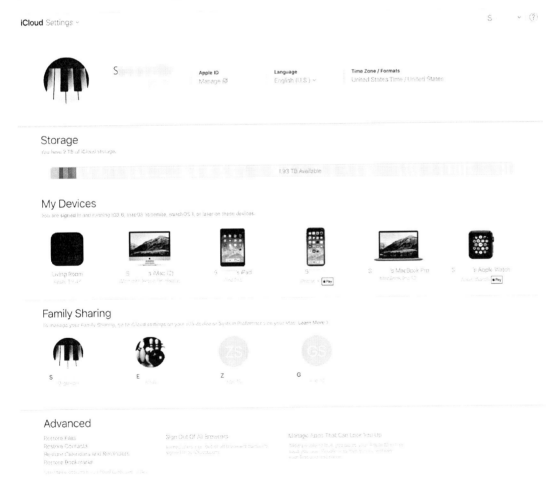

Configuring iCloud. (Screenshot courtesy of Apple.)

macOS USERS AND PASSWORDS

An **Administrator** account and an optional **Guest User** account are created when macOS is installed. To add a new account, open **System Preferences→Users & Groups**. Four types of account are available: **Administrator**, **Standard**, **Managed with Parental Controls**, and **Sharing Only**. The user's password can either be from iCloud or a separate password.

- **Administrator**: This is the user type created when you set up your Mac computer. From this user, additional administrator users or other user types can be created. An administrator user can convert users between standard and administrator user types. This user type should never be configured for automatic login as this could result in someone restarting the computer and gaining access to the user with administrator privileges.
- **Standard**: This type of user can change their own settings, but not those of other users. They can also install apps for their own account. This user cannot create additional users or change the settings of other user accounts.
- **Managed with Parental Controls**: The administrator specifies which apps and other content can be accessed by this user type. The websites that can be accessed can also be restricted by the administrator. In addition, time limits can be implemented for when the user can use the computer.
- **Sharing Only**: This type of user is created to give someone permission to access your shared files or to share your screen. The user cannot log in to the computer and cannot make changes to any settings on the computer. In order to give someone sharing permission, configure settings in the Sharing preferences.

APPLE ID

When first setting up an Apple Mac, the user will be assigned an **Apple ID** that is based on the sign-in email address. This Apple ID is used for purchases from the App Store, accessing iCloud and other functions. A user may already have an Apple ID from previous iTunes purchases or an iOS device.

KEYCHAIN

The Keychain® in macOS helps you to manage passwords for websites and Wi-Fi networks. This feature is also available as **iCloud Keychain**, which makes the same passwords securely available across all macOS and iOS devices. The Keychain makes password management much easier, but occasionally problems can happen. If there are any problems, they will be identified by the **Keychain Access** app (in **Utilities**).

If warning messages are displayed, it's possible to attempt a repair with **Keychain First Aid**. Launch this from the **Keychain Access** menu. After entering an administrator password, select either **Verify** or **Repair**. If the problem persists, try resetting the Keychain itself. Select **Keychain Access→Preferences**. Select **Reset My Default Keychains** to create a new empty keychain.

If you have forgotten a password, search for the website by typing into the search box. From the results, select the password that you want to view or change. Check the box for **Show password** and enter an administrator password to reveal the password for that device or service.

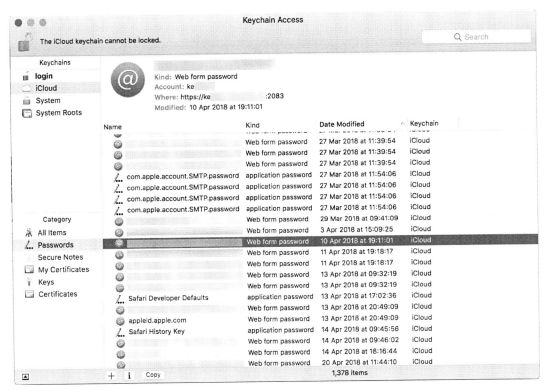

Keychain Access tool. (Screenshot courtesy of Apple.)

If other people have access to the Mac, it is wise to restrict access to the Keychain. To do this, select the Keychain, then under the **Edit** menu, select **Change settings for Keychain *Name***, where *Name* is the Keychain selected.

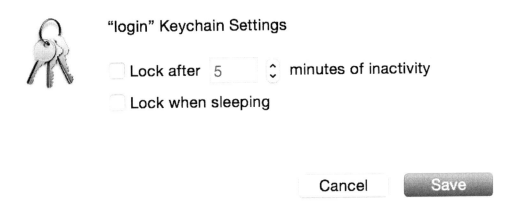

Securing a Keychain. (Screenshot courtesy of Apple.)

macOS SOFTWARE MANAGEMENT

There are two main distribution mechanisms for macOS apps: the App Store and app downloads.

APP STORE

Much like the store for iOS devices, the App Store provides a central portal for Apple and developers to distribute free and paid-for software. It is also used to distribute updates to macOS and new releases of the operating system. The icon for the App Store is ⬡.

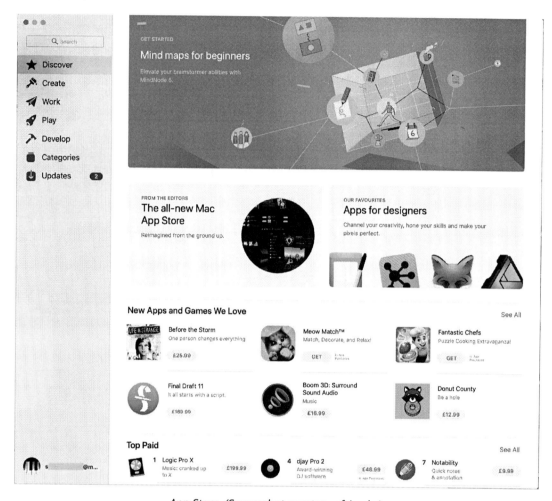

App Store. (Screenshot courtesy of Apple.)

DOWNLOAD APPS

Microsoft Office, Adobe® Creative Cloud®, and Skype® are just three examples of apps that are not available in the App Store. To install any of these apps, it is necessary to download them from the vendor site, ensuring that you select the macOS version. macOS download apps are normally distributed as **.DMG** (disk image) installer files. Follow the on-screen instructions to install the app. The last step will almost certainly ask you to copy the file to the **Applications** folder.

Skype_7.17.377.dmg
41.5 MB

Disk Image file. (Screenshot courtesy of Apple.)

By default, macOS will only allow apps to be installed that have been downloaded from the Mac App Store. To allow the installation of download apps, go to **System Preferences→Security & Privacy**. Click the padlock to make changes to the settings—you will need to enter the Administrator password to continue.

Always use the installer package to remove apps that are no longer required.

Updates for apps that have been downloaded outside of the App Store are usually managed within the app itself. For example, Microsoft Office runs a regular auto-update to check for new versions and security updates.

APPLICATION COMPATIBILITY

If you need to use Mac OS 9 applications on an OS X/macOS system, you can do so in the Classic environment. To use the Classic environment, you must have a Mac OS 9 System Folder installed on your computer, either on the same hard disk as macOS, or on another disk or disk partition.

BOOT CAMP AND WINDOWS

Boot Camp is a utility supplied with macOS that allows a full Windows installation to be made on a Mac. Once installed and Windows set up, the user has a choice of either operating system when booting the computer. In summary, the installation process for Windows on macOS is as follows:

1. Ensure that the Apple Mac meets the system requirements for the version of Windows that is to be installed.
2. Obtain an ISO disk image of Microsoft Windows.
3. Run **Boot Camp Assistant** from the **Applications→Utilities** folder.

 Note: *More comprehensive information about running Boot Camp Assistant can be found at* **support.apple.com/HT201468**.

4. Follow the on-screen instructions to repartition the hard drive on the Mac.
5. Format the new Windows partition and install Windows on it.

To boot into the Windows partition, press and hold the **OPTION** key as the Mac boots. Select the Windows partition from the **Startup Manager**.

APP CRASHES AND FORCE QUIT

When an app is busy or processing a complex request, the spinning wait cursor will appear and usually disappear again within a few seconds. Should it remain visible for longer, it is possible that the app has gone into an endless loop or entered a state where it is not possible to complete its process.

 Note: *The spinning wait cursor is also known as the spinning wheel, spinning pinwheel, and the spinning beach ball of death!*

If a macOS app stops responding, it should be possible to close it down and restart without having to restart the computer. Run **Force Quit** from the **Apple menu** (always available in the Menu Bar) or press **command+option+esc**. You will probably need to switch into another app or window to be able to do this.

Select the app that isn't responding—Mail in the example shown in the following figure—then click **Force Quit** to close it down.

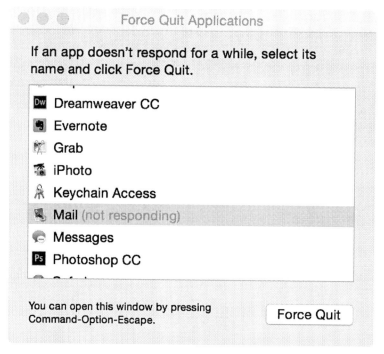

Using Force Quit to stop an app that is not responding. (Screenshot courtesy of Apple.)

It will prompt for a confirmation that you really want to force the app to quit, then show a dialog box enabling you to send a troubleshooting report to Apple.

Clicking **Report** will produce diagnostic information and a crash dump. It is always useful to report errors as they may point to an **undocumented feature** in macOS that needs to be addressed in a future update.

TROUBLESHOOTING AN APP

If an app constantly crashes, take the following steps:

- Ensure the latest version of the app is installed.
- If the crash only happens with a specific document or file, try recreating that file from scratch in case it is corrupt.
- Uninstall the app by dragging it to **Trash** and reinstall from either the App Store or the third-party vendor's site.

macOS DIAGNOSTIC UTILITIES

macOS has several utilities that are provided as part of a default installation. You can find these utility apps in the **Other** folder in **Launchpad**, and in the **Utilities** folder under **Applications**.

SYSTEM INFORMATION

The **System Information** app provides detailed diagnostic information about your Mac.

SCREEN SHARING

Screen Sharing allows another user to view your macOS desktop and operate the computer from another Apple Mac or a computer or device installed with **VNC Viewer**. Configure **Screen Sharing** via **System Preferences→Sharing**. Enable screen sharing, then choose how users are authorized to connect. You can restrict access to specific Mac accounts or groups or a subset of those users as well as allow users to connect by requesting permission. **VNC** users can be configured to access the computer using a password. Connect to another macOS computer with screen sharing enabled by opening it via the **Shared** folder in **Finder**.

ACTIVITY MONITOR

Activity Monitor is used to watch CPU, memory, energy, disk, and network usage. Use this app if you want to track unusual activity or patterns on the Mac and to try and establish if a specific app or process is causing overload of resources.

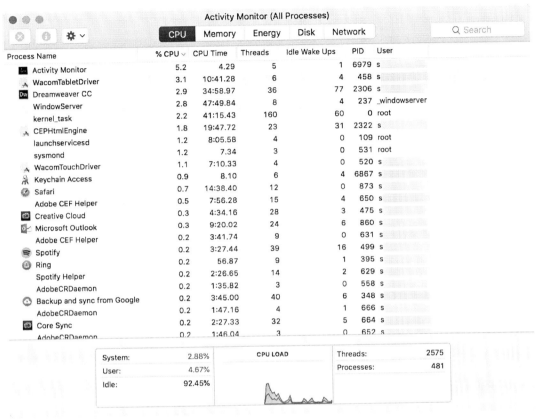

Activity Monitor. (Screenshot courtesy of Apple.)

CONSOLE

The console records error and log messages and helps you to diagnose problems within macOS.

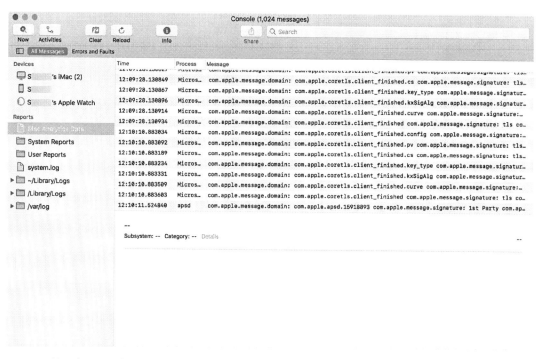

Use the console to view the log and diagnostic reports. (Screenshot courtesy of Apple.)

TERMINAL

The **Terminal** is the equivalent to the Windows **Command Prompt** window. Use **Terminal** to run network troubleshooting utilities such as the ping command, or enter advanced commands to modify the macOS environment—with care!

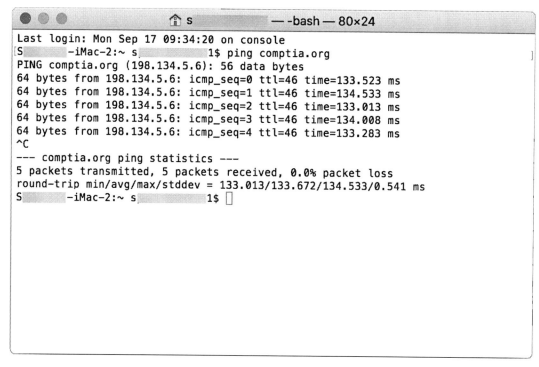

Terminal. (Screenshot courtesy of Apple.)

macOS RECOVERY

macOS includes a set of utilities that you can use to restore a Mac from the **Time Machine** backup program, to reinstall macOS from a system image, or to reformat or repair the system disk.

To access the **Recovery** menu, as you power up the Apple Mac hold down the **command+R** keys until you see the Apple logo. After selecting your language, it will boot into macOS Recovery, enabling you to select from the options shown in the following figure.

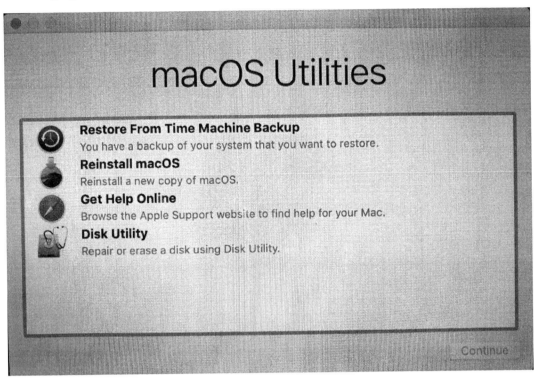

macOS Recovery menu. (Screenshot courtesy of Apple.)

When you reboot an Apple Mac, if the startup drive is not available for any reason and it's connected to the Internet, the computer will try to boot from a web-based drive.

Use a **Time Machine** snapshot backup if you want to restore the Mac to a specific point in time; for example, if you have replaced or reformatted the hard drive. Alternatively, if you have created a disk image (**.DMG**) as a restore point, use the **Disk Utility** option to restore from that file. It's also possible to restore disk images from a web link.

HOW TO CONFIGURE AND USE macOS

Follow these procedures to configure and use macOS.

CREATING USERS IN macOS

To create users in macOS:

1. Log in as a user that is set up as an administrator user. The first user created when first setting up the Mac will be an administrator.
2. From the **Apple menu**, select **System Preferences→Users & Groups**.
3. Select the **Add** button located under the user list.
4. Select the **New Account** pop-up menu, and select the desired type of user.
   - Administrator

- Standard
- Managed with Parental Controls
- Sharing Only
  - To share files and folders:
    a. From the **Apple menu**, select **System Preferences→Sharing**.
    b. Check **File Sharing**.
    c. Click the **Add** button to select a folder to share, then navigate to and select the folder and select **Add**.
    d. If desired, select a person from your Contacts list, from **Network Users** or **Network Groups**, to add a user who can share the file or folder.
    e. If desired, specify the level of access the user has to the shared folder: Read & Write, Read Only, Write Only (Drop Box), or No Access.

USE macOS FEATURES

To use macOS features:

1. Select the **Apple menu** to:
   - Display basic information about the computer through **About this Mac**.
   - Show the current display and its configuration through **Displays**.
   - Show the capacity and current internal hard drive usage through **Storage**.
   - Show available support options through **Service**.
2. Select the **Status menu** to:
   - Get quick access to key features of installed software.
   - Access the **Keyboard Preferences** and **Day/Time** apps.
   - Access the **Spotlight Search**.
   - Access the **Notification Center**.
3. Use the **dock** to quickly access apps, **Finder**, and **Trash**.
4. Use the **Spotlight Search** to find items on macOS. It can be accessed by:
   - Selecting the magnifying glass icon in the menu bar.
   - Pressing **command+space**
5. From the **Apple menu** select **System Preferences** to change settings and network options, and optimize macOS configuration.
6. Manage multiple desktops through **Mission Control**.
   a. Press **F3** to access **Mission Control**.
   b. At the top of the screen, a small image of the current desktop with all the open apps is displayed.
   c. Move the cursor to the top-right corner of this screen.
   d. Click the tab with the plus symbol to add another desktop.
   e. Right-click an app in the dock and select either **All Desktops**, **This Desktop**, or **None** to assign an app to a particular desktop.
   f. Press **F3** to switch between desktops. Alternatively, press **control+left** or **control+right** to cycle between screens. You can also swipe left or right with three/four fingers on the trackpad, depending on how it is configured.
   g. To remove a desktop, press **F3** and hover the cursor over the desktop to be deleted, then click its **Close** icon.

MANAGE FILES IN macOS

To manage files in macOS:

1. From the dock, select the **Finder** icon.
2. In **Finder**, the most recently used files are listed under **Recents**.

3. To access an optical drive located on another system, use the **Remote Disc** app.
    a. If necessary, on the system containing the optical drive, open **System Preferences→Sharing** and check **DVD or CD sharing**.
    b. On the system that will remotely access the drive, open **Finder** and select **Remote Disc**.
    c. Locate the Mac with the drive that was configured, then click its icon to access the drive.
4. To access **iCloud**, open **Finder** then select the **iCloud Drive** in the navigation pane of **Finder**.

MANAGE macOS USERS AND PASSWORDS

To manage macOS users and passwords:

1. Add a new account by selecting **System Preferences→Users & Groups**, select the account type to set up, and follow the prompts to finish setting up the account.
2. To manage passwords:
    a. Select **Utilities→Keychain Access**.
    b. If you have forgotten a password, search for the website by typing into the search box. From the results, select the password that you want to view or change. Check the box for **Show password** and enter an administrator password to reveal the password for that device or service.
    c. To restrict access to the keychain, from the **Edit** menu, select **Change settings for Keychain *Name*** then configure keychain settings as needed.

MANAGE SOFTWARE ON macOS

To manage software on macOS systems:

1. Use the **App Store** to get macOS updates and both free and paid-for software.
2. To allow installation of downloaded apps:
    a. Select **System Preferences→Security & Privacy**.
    b. Click the padlock and make changes to the settings that allow installation of download apps.
    c. Install third-party apps using the **.DMG** installer files.
3. If you need to use Mac OS 9 applications on an OS X/macOS system, use the Classic environment, which requires a Mac OS 9 System Folder installed on hard disk.
4. If you need to run Windows on a macOS system, use **Boot Camp**.
    *   From the **Applications→Utilities** folder, run **Boot Camp Assistant** and follow the on-screen instructions to repartition the hard drive. Format the new partition for Windows and then install a valid copy of **Windows**.
    *   To boot into Windows, hold down the **option** key as the Mac boots and select **Windows** partition from the **Startup Manager**.
5. If an app is unresponsive, from the **Apple menu**, select **Force Quit** or press **command+option+esc**. Select the unresponsive app, and select **Force Quit**.
6. If an app constantly crashes, take the following steps:
    *   Ensure the latest version of the app is installed.
    *   If the crash only happens with a specific document or file, try recreating that file from scratch in case it is corrupt.
    *   Uninstall the app by dragging it to **Trash** and reinstall from either the App Store or the third-party vendor's site.

USE macOS DIAGNOSTIC UTILITIES

To use macOS diagnostic utilities:

1. Locate utilities in the **Other** folder in **Launchpad**, and in the **Utilities** folder under **Applications**.
2. To get detailed information about the Mac computer, select **System Information.**
3. To allow another person to view and operate the Mac computer remotely through the **VNC Viewer**:
    a. Select **Screen Sharing**.
    b. Configure **Screen Sharing** via **System Preferences→Sharing**.
    c. Enable screen sharing, then choose how users are authorized to connect.
    d. Connect to another macOS computer with screen sharing enabled by opening it via the **Shared** folder in **Finder**.
4. To watch CPU, memory, energy, disk, and network usage, select **Activity Monitor**.
5. Use the **Console** to view error and log messages to help you diagnose problems within macOS.
6. Use the **Terminal** to open a command prompt window where you can issue command-line commands.

ACCESS macOS RECOVERY

To access macOS Recovery:

1. As the computer is powering up, hold down **command+R** until the Apple logo is displayed.
2. Select the desired language.
3. Select the desired option.
    - Select **Restore From Time Machine Backup** if you have a system backup you want to restore.
    - Select **Reinstall macOS** to reinstall a new copy of macOS.
    - Select **Get Help Online** to browse the Apple Support website.
    - Select **Disk Utility** to repair or erase a disk.
4. Use a **Time Machine** snapshot to restore the system to a specific point in time.
5. If you created a disk image (.DMG) file as a restore point, use the **Disk Utility** option to restore from your .DMG file.

Topic C

Install and Upgrade Operating Systems

EXAM OBJECTIVES COVERED
1002-1.3 Summarize general OS installation considerations and upgrade methods.
1002-1.4 Given a scenario, use appropriate Microsoft command-line tools.

Being able to install or upgrade an operating system can be important if you have built a custom computer system from scratch, if the system you purchased from a vendor did not have the correct system installed, or if you are completely redeploying existing hardware from one system to another.

The skills and information in this topic will help you plan and perform an OS installation properly, for whatever your technical and business requirements might be.

OS INSTALLATION TYPES

An operating system installation copies the OS system and bundled application files from the installation media to a partition on the target computer's fixed disk. OS setup scans the computer for hardware devices and loads appropriate drivers. The user may be prompted for information about the computer name, network settings, and the primary user account.

OS INSTALLATION OVERVIEW

The installation of an operating system should be carefully planned. It will consist of the following phases:

1. Select an installation method—attended or unattended, and clean install or in-place upgrade, for example.
2. Check compatibility—that the core components of the computer are sufficient to run the OS and that peripheral devices have drivers suitable for use with the OS. If upgrading, you also need to check application compatibility and establish the upgrade path.
3. If upgrading, back up any existing user data or settings.

   This is obviously not necessary if installing to a new computer, but is a vital step if you are replacing (rather than upgrading) an existing installation. While it takes more time, performance and reliability can be improved by performing a clean install.

    Note: If you are performing an in-place upgrade, you should also make a full system backup before proceeding so that the upgrade can be rolled back should anything go wrong.

4. Choose a boot method to use to load the OS setup files.
5. Prepare the fixed disk and copy setup files to the target.
6. Configure installation options.
7. Verify installation—check logs and complete tests to confirm that installation has succeeded.

ATTENDED AND UNATTENDED INSTALLATIONS

An installation where the installer inputs the configuration information in response to prompts from a setup program is called an **attended installation**, whereas an installation that derives configuration information from a file designed for that purpose is called an **unattended installation**.

CLEAN INSTALL OR IN-PLACE UPGRADE

There are two main approaches to performing an attended installation:

- **Clean install**—means installing the OS to a new computer or completely replacing the OS software on an old one. Any existing user data or settings would be deleted during the setup process.
- **In-place upgrade**—means installing on top of an existing version of the OS, retaining applications, user settings, and data files.

A clean install is generally seen as more reliable than upgrading. In a corporate network environment, installations are completed using **images** (a template containing the OS and required software) so that machines use a consistent set of software and configuration options. PC vendors also use images to install new systems for sale.

Upgrades are generally designed for home users. Upgrade software can be purchased at a discount.

HOW TO BACK UP DATA AND SETTINGS

Here is a general procedure for backing up data and settings.

BACK UP DATA AND SETTINGS

This is obviously not necessary if installing to a new computer, but is a vital step if you are replacing (rather than upgrading) an existing installation. Although it takes more time, performance and reliability can be improved by performing a clean install. The general process will be as follows:

1. Back up data from the existing target system. You can use a backup program supplied with the OS or a third-party backup program.

    Note: If you are performing an in-place upgrade, you should also make a full system backup before proceeding so that the upgrade can be rolled back should anything go wrong.

2. Install the new OS, overwriting the existing target and optionally reconfiguring the disk partition and file system structure, too.
3. Reinstall software applications and utilities.
4. Restore data from the previous system using the backup you made.

COMPATIBILITY CONSIDERATIONS

Before you install or upgrade the OS on a computer, you must make sure that the computer hardware supports the new OS version. You may also need to check that any existing software applications will run under the new version.

OS COMPATIBILITY/UPGRADE PATH

If you are considering upgrading, you must check that the current OS version is supported as an upgrade path to the intended version. The OS vendor should publish supported upgrade paths on their website. For example, the upgrade paths for Windows 10 are published here: **docs.microsoft.com/en-us/windows/deployment/upgrade/windows-10-upgrade-paths** while the upgrade support documents for macOS are here: **support.apple.com/macos/high-sierra**.

With Windows, you also have to consider the edition when upgrading. You can usually upgrade to the same or higher edition (Windows 7 Home Premium to Windows 10 Home or Professional or Windows 10 Home to Windows 10 Professional, for instance), but you cannot upgrade from a home to an enterprise edition. Downgrading the edition is supported in some circumstances (Windows 7 Professional to Windows 10 Home, for instance) but this only retains documents and other data, not apps and settings. Downgrading from an Enterprise edition is not supported.

Note that you can only upgrade the same type of operating system. You cannot "upgrade" from Windows to Linux, for instance.

HARDWARE COMPATIBILITY AND APPLICATION COMPATIBILITY

The first step in checking hardware compatibility is to verify that the system exceeds the recommended requirements or prerequisites. The minimum requirements will not usually deliver adequate performance.

The second step is to verify that peripheral devices and expansion cards will work under the OS. Effectively this means, "Has the manufacturer released a stable driver for the OS?" Microsoft maintains a **Windows Logo'd Product List (LPL) catalog**, previously called the **Hardware Compatibility List (HCL)**. This is a catalog of tested devices and drivers. If a device has not passed Windows logo testing, you should check the device vendor's website to confirm whether there is a driver available.

If you are performing an in-place upgrade or if you are planning a clean install and need to know whether you will be able to reinstall a particular app, you also need to check with each application vendor whether the new OS version is supported. In some cases, you may need to purchase an application upgrade, too.

> **Note:** *You can sometimes use automated **Upgrade Advisor** software to check whether the existing computer hardware (and software applications) will be compatible with a new version of Windows. An **Upgrade Advisor** might be bundled with the setup program or available from the vendor website.*

Unsupported hardware or software can cause problems during an in-place upgrade and should be physically uninstalled from the PC. It is also worth obtaining the latest drivers for various devices from the vendor's website. The Windows setup media ships with default drivers for a number of products, but these are often not up-to-date nor are they comprehensive.

> **Note:** *Store the latest drivers for your hardware on a USB drive or network location so that you can update hardware efficiently.*

LINUX INSTALLATION AND COMPATIBILITY

The hardware requirements for installing Linux will depend upon the distribution of Linux you choose. Linux is a portable operating system, which means it can run on a variety of hardware platforms. There are versions available for many different processor types, including Intel x86, Itanium, DEC Alpha, Sun Sparc, Motorola, and others. In general, a basic installation of Linux on a workstation might require as little as 16 or 32 MB of memory and 250 MB of disk space, but you might need several gigabytes of disk space for a complete installation, including all utilities.

Because Linux is a portable operating system, it is compatible with a wide range of hardware. You will need to check with the vendor or provider of your Linux distribution to verify if your particular system hardware is supported by that distribution.

A site that works well for this is **linux.com**. They have a yearly comparison of the Linux distributions and what they feel are the best distributions for various purposes.

Some web resources you can use to research general Linux hardware support include:

- The Linux Hardware Compatibility HOWTO website at **tldp.org/HOWTO/Hardware-HOWTO/index.html**.
- The Linux Questions website's hardware compatibility list at **linuxquestions.org/hcl**.

- Linux hardware and driver support lists at **linux-drivers.org**.

Check your Linux vendor's website and read the technical documentation for the distribution of Linux you plan to install or upgrade to in order to determine if your existing applications will be supported under the new version.

HOW TO CHECK COMPATIBILITY FOR OS INSTALLATION OR UPGRADE

Follow these procedures to check compatibility when you are installing or upgrading an OS.

CHECK COMPATIBILITY

To check compatibility when installing or upgrading the OS on a computer:

1. If upgrading, verify that the current OS version is supported as an upgrade path.
2. Verify that the hardware meets the requirements of the OS.
3. Verify that applications are compatible with the OS and with the hardware.

INSTALLATION BOOT METHODS

The **installation boot method** refers to the way in which the installation program and settings are loaded onto the PC. You may need to access the computer's firmware setup program to ensure that a particular boot method is available, enabled, and set to the highest priority.

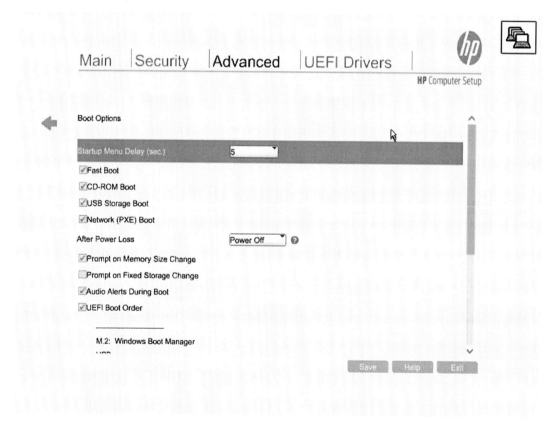

Configuring boot devices and priority in a computer's firmware setup program. (Screenshot courtesy of Hewlett-Packard, Inc.)

OPTICAL DISC (CD-ROM/DVD/BLU-RAY)

Most attended installations and upgrades are run by booting from the setup CD-ROM or DVD. This might be listed as Optical Drive in the firmware setup program. You can also run a clean install or upgrade from an existing Windows installation.

An **ISO file** contains all of the contents from an optical disc in a single file. ISO files stored on removable media or a host system are often used to install virtual machine operating systems. An ISO file can be mounted to the file system as though it were a physical optical drive.

EXTERNAL DRIVE/FLASH DRIVE (USB/ESATA)

One problem with disc-based installs is that the setup disc quickly becomes out-of-date and post-installation tasks for installing drivers, updates, and service packs can take longer than the original installation. One way around this is to build **slipstreamed media**, with all the various patches and drivers already applied. The media could be CD-ROM, DVD, or USB-attached flash drive or external drive connected by USB or by eSATA. The computer firmware must also support USB or eSATA as a boot method.

 Note: *Microsoft provides a tool to create installation media from an ISO of the product setup files (**support.microsoft.com/en-us/help/15088/windows-create-installation-media**).*

NETWORK BOOT (PXE)

A remote network installation means connecting to a shared folder containing the installation files (which could be slipstreamed). The target PC must have a usable partition on the hard disk in which to store temporary files. There also needs to be some means of booting with networking software. Most computers now come with a **Preboot eXecution Environment (PXE)** compliant firmware and network adapter, which supports booting from a network with a suitably configured server.

 Note: *macOS supports a similar network boot method to **PXE** called **NetBoot**.*

INTERNAL FIXED DISK (HDD/SSD)/INTERNAL HARD DRIVE (PARTITION)

Once the OS has been installed, you will usually want to set the internal fixed disk (or the boot partition on the internal fixed disk) as the default (highest priority) boot device and disable any other boot devices. This ensures the system doesn't try to boot to the setup media again. If access to the firmware setup program is secured, it also prevents someone from trying to install a new OS without authorization.

An OS can be installed to a Hard Disk Drive (HDD) or Solid State Drive (SSD). Note that in the firmware setup program, the HDD will probably be on a SATA port while an SSD might be on a SATA, M.2, or PCIe port.

There may be some circumstances where you have to copy the installation media to the computer's fixed disk. To do this, you would remove the disk from the target PC and attach it to another machine. Use the other machine to partition the disk as appropriate and copy the setup files to it. Use the **diskpart** tool to set the partition as active. Use the **bootsect** tool to copy code to make the partition bootable. Finally, reinstall the disk to the target computer and boot to the partition containing your setup files.

SECURE BOOT

Motherboards now use a type of system firmware called **Unified Extensible Firmware Interface (UEFI)**. In UEFI, there is an option called **secure boot**, which restricts OS installation to trusted software. This will prevent installation of Windows 7 and some distributions of Linux if enabled because the setup files for these operating systems are not digitally signed in a way that the firmware is able to trust.

Configuring the Secure Boot option in the system firmware setup program. (Screenshot courtesy of Hewlett-Packard, Inc.)

Also, a 32-bit edition of Windows needs to be installed in legacy BIOS mode. You can also choose to install using legacy BIOS mode if you do not want to use EFI boot for some reason.

HOW TO SELECT AN INSTALLATION BOOT METHOD
Follow these procedures to select the boot method for an OS installation.

SELECT A BOOT METHOD
To select a boot method:

1. Determine the boot method you plan to use to install the operating system.
2. Configure the UEFI or BIOS to allow the system to boot to the selected method.
3. If necessary, configure **Secure Boot** options in the system firmware.

DISK FORMATTING AND PARTITIONING
The operating system must be installed to a partition that is of a suitable size and formatted with an appropriate file system. In Windows, the **boot partition** and **system partition** cannot be changed (except by using third-party tools), so it is important to plan the disk partition scheme in accordance with the way the computer will be used:

- Will the computer have multiple operating systems installed (multiboot)? If so, it is best practice to create a partition for each OS.
- Does the boot partition have spare capacity for growth? Running out of space will cause serious problems, so leave plenty of overhead.

Windows must be installed to a boot partition formatted with NTFS.

- Is some sort of hardware RAID being used? If so, the RAID utility must be used to configure the RAID level and create volumes before the OS can be installed. A RAID configuration utility is invoked by pressing a key combo such as **Ctrl+F** during startup (when the RAID firmware BIOS is processed).
- Is an SSD or hybrid SSD being used? The SSD should be used for the boot partition as this will improve performance.

 Note: *Remember that in Microsoft's terminology, the system partition is where the boot files are and the boot partition is where the operating system is installed.*

MULTIBOOT

If a user needs multiple operating systems, they can be set up on the same computer in a **multiboot** environment. Most operating systems can be run in this way, with the following caveats:

- Each OS should be installed to a separate boot partition.
- The system partition must be accessible to each OS. This means that, typically, it must be formatted using FAT or FAT32).
- New operating systems should not overwrite the boot manager. The general principle is to install the older operating system first, as an older OS is less likely to recognize a multiboot environment. Alternatively, the boot manager may need to be reconfigured manually following installation of an OS.

Multiboot is seldom used anymore as virtualization represents a simpler way of achieving the same aim, with the major advantage that the different operating systems can be used concurrently.

DISK FORMATTING

The easiest way to ensure a properly formatted boot drive with the correct partitions and format is to install to a blank hard disk. If you are using a disk with existing data that you do not want to keep, you can choose to delete existing partitions using the disk setup tool.

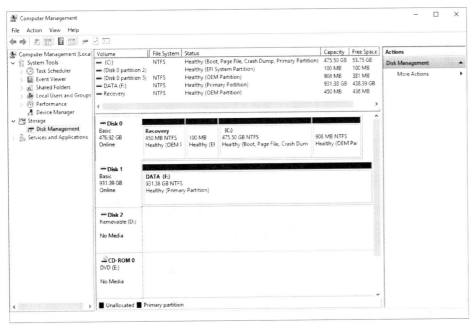

Partition layout for a GPT-style disk and Windows 10. (Screenshot used with permission from Microsoft.)

The previous figure shows the typical partition layout for an OEM-formatted PC with UEFI-type firmware:

- Disk 0 is a Solid State Drive (SSD) hosting the boot and system partitions. There are also two OEM partitions used for OS recovery and vendor diagnostic tools. The boot partition has been assigned drive letter C: and the other partitions have no drive letter.
- Disk 1 is a second fixed disk. More accurately, it is a RAID volume comprising two mirrored HDDs, but because this is hardware RAID, it appears as a single disk to the OS.
- Disk 2 is a flash memory card reader and you can also see the optical disc drive.
- All the partitions except the EFI system partition are formatted using NTFS. The Extensible Firmware Interface (EFI) system partition uses a type of FAT but isn't listed as such in the drive management tool.

By contrast, the following screenshot shows the partitions created by the CentOS Linux setup tool if automatic partitioning is selected.

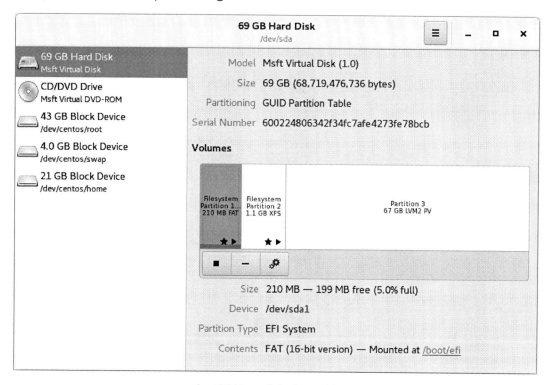

CentOS Linux default partitions.

The fixed disk is divided into three partitions: an EFI system partition, one for the Linux boot loader, and a Logical Volume Manager (LVM) partition. The LVM software is used to divide this last partition into three volumes (block devices)—one for the OS system files (root), one for a swap partition, and one for user data (home).

OS SETUP DISK FORMATTING TOOLS

While you can inspect and configure disks, partitions, and file systems using the Disk Management console once Windows is installed, a different tool is used from the Setup program to prepare the disk.

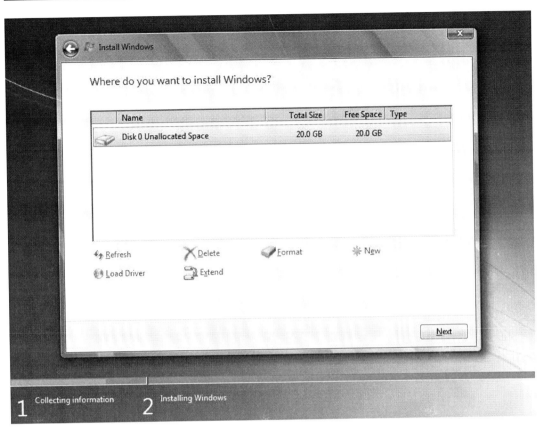

Windows disk setup options. (Screenshot used with permission from Microsoft.)

If you are performing a clean install but the target disk already has a partition structure, you can use the setup tool to delete the existing partitions. You can use the **New** button to create a custom partition structure or just select a disk with enough unallocated space and allow setup to create the required partitions automatically.

LOADING DISK DRIVERS

In order to manage the hard disk, the setup program must have an appropriate driver for it. Most of the time the setup media will include a suitable driver. If you are installing to a RAID volume or to a computer with legacy firmware, it is possible that the disk or volume may not be recognized. If this is the case, you will have to load the disk or RAID vendor's driver via the **Load Driver** option on the **Where do you want to install Windows** dialog box in setup.

LOCALE SETTINGS AND SOFTWARE SELECTION

When you perform an attended installation, you need to manually configure setup at various points in the process. Windows setup is much better streamlined than in the past, with all the configuration options at the beginning and end of the process.

 Note: You are focusing on the Windows setup program here, but other operating systems present similar choices.

The first step in a Windows attended installation is to choose the language, regional format settings, time zone, and keyboard type. You should also check that the date and time are displayed correctly.

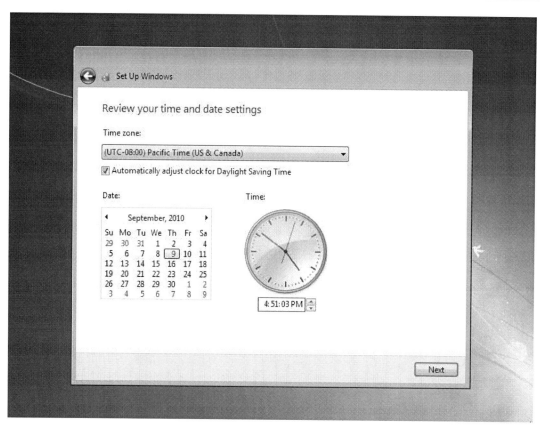

Configuring the time zone during Windows 7 setup. (Screenshot used with permission from Microsoft.)

Having done that, you can initialize setup by entering the product key, accepting the End User License Agreement (EULA), choosing the install type—upgrade or custom (clean install)—and partitioning and formatting the disk. Setup then proceeds without requiring any intervention. During this time, setup copies the OS files to the system folder, detects hardware devices, and loads appropriate drivers. Once this process is complete, the PC will restart.

SOFTWARE SELECTIONS

In Windows setup, there is no opportunity to install additional software as such, though you can choose options such as linking the installation to a Microsoft user account and syncing files to OneDrive. When you install Linux, however, there is typically a setup option prompting you to select the type of installation and choose specific software packages to use.

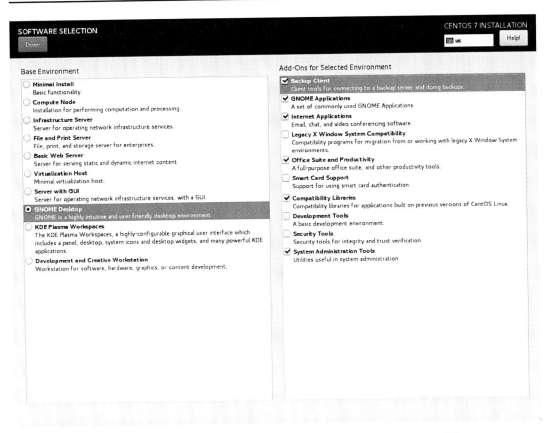

Selecting a computer environment/role and software add-ons during CentOS setup.

NETWORKING CONSIDERATIONS

There are some network-related things you will want to consider during installation.

WINDOWS UPDATE

If the setup program detects that a network connection is present, it may present an option to use **Windows Update** to download the latest installation files from the Internet. If no Internet connection is available or you want to skip this step, you can use **Windows Update** after setup is complete.

> *Note: In Windows 7, you could disable **Windows Update** automatic updating during setup if desired. This option is not available when installing Windows 10.*

WORKGROUP VS. DOMAIN SETUP

A **workgroup** is a Microsoft peer-to-peer network model in which computers are grouped together with access to shared resources for organizational purposes. A **domain** is a Microsoft client/server network model that groups computers together for security and to centralize administration. Computers that are members of a domain have access to a shared central user account database, which means that an individual can use a single user account to log on at any computer within the domain.

Windows does not support joining a domain during an attended installation. The computer can be joined by reconfiguring **System** properties in **Control Panel**, via the **Settings** interface, or can be joined during an unattended installation by using an answer file or script.

There is no option to change the default workgroup name (**WORKGROUP**) either. In Windows networking, the workgroup name is now entirely cosmetic.

In Windows 7, you are prompted to configure the computer's host name and choose a user name and password for the local administrator account. In Windows 8/10, you can choose to use a **Microsoft account** rather than creating a **local account**.

If the computer is not connected to the Internet, you will just be prompted to create a local account. You can convert a local account to a Microsoft account (or vice versa) using Windows **Settings**.

HOW TO SELECT A NETWORK TYPE DURING WINDOWS INSTALLATION

Follow these procedures to select a network type during Windows installation.

SELECT A NETWORK TYPE

During Windows installation, you will be joined to a workgroup. If you want to join a domain:

1. Connect the computer to the domain network using a wired connection.
2. Sign in to the computer using a local administrator account.
3. From the **Start** menu, select **Settings**.
4. Select **Accounts**.
5. Select **Access work or school**.
6. Under **Connect to work or school**, select **Connect**.
7. On the **Set up a work or school account** page, select **Join this device to a local Active Directory domain**.
8. In the **Join a domain** window, enter the full domain name, then select **Next**.
9. Type the domain user name and password, then select **OK**.
10. In the **User account** window, type your user name. From the **Account type** drop-down list, select **Administrator**, and then select **Next**.
11. In the **Restart your PC** window, select **Restart now**.

POST-INSTALLATION TASKS

Windows should detect all supported hardware and load the appropriate drivers during setup. When you have gotten to the final configuration screens, it is a good sign that the installation has succeeded. You might want to check the log files, check Device Manager to confirm all hardware has been recognized, and test each hardware device to verify functionality. You can use Programs and Features (in Control Panel) or the Microsoft Store to install any optional Windows components or third-party software applications.

Update the system documentation with details of the installation. Keeping up-to-date documentation is important for system maintenance and troubleshooting.

MICROSOFT PRODUCT ACTIVATION

Microsoft Product Activation or **Volume Activation for Windows** operating system is an antipiracy technology that verifies that software products are legitimately purchased. Product activation reduces a form of piracy known as casual copying. For example, you must activate the Windows operating systems within a given number of days after installation. After the grace period, users cannot access the system until they activate Windows. Volume Activation automates the activation process.

For individual installations of Windows, you can activate the installation over the Internet. If you do not have an Internet connection, you can activate over the phone, although this takes a little longer. If you wish, you can postpone product activation and activate later in the activation grace period.

In large organizations, you can use a Volume License Product Key, which eliminates the need to individually activate each installation of Windows. You can also activate Windows as part of an automated installation.

REPAIR INSTALLATIONS

If a Windows computer will not boot or if you are troubleshooting a problem such as slow performance and cannot find a single cause, it may be necessary to perform some sort of "repair installation." There are several means of accomplishing this.

> **Note:** *A repair install will only work if you are replacing the same version of the operating system; you cannot upgrade in this manner.*

FACTORY RECOVERY PARTITION

A **recovery disc** or **factory recovery partition** (also called a **Rescue Disk**) is a tool used by OEMs to restore the OS environment to the same state on which it was shipped. The disc or recovery partition is used to boot the system, then a simple wizard-driven process replaces the damaged installation with an image stored on a separate partition on the hard disk. The recovery process can be started by pressing a key during startup (**F11** or **Ctrl+F11** are often used; a message is usually shown on-screen).

OEM media will not usually recover user data or settings or applications installed—everything gets set back to the state in which the PC was shipped from the factory. User data should be recovered from backup, which obviously has to be made before the computer becomes unbootable.

You could also create recovery media manually or using backup software or drive imaging. In this scenario, you can create images that reflect all the software and service packs that a typical machine should include. Most backup suites have a simple wizard-driven routine for creating recovery media.

The advantages of using a recovery partition are that less time is required to re-build the machine and from a technical support point-of-view, recovery is much easier for end-users than re-installing Windows.

The main disadvantages with OEM recovery media are that the tool only works if the original hard disk is still installed in the machine and will not include patches or service packs applied between the ship date and recovery date. The recovery image also takes up quite a lot of space and users may not feel that they are getting the hard disk capacity that they have paid for!

> **Note:** *A recovery partition is not usually allocated a drive letter so will not be obvious to the user. You can make the partition visible to Explorer through the Disk Management program.*

REFRESH/RESTORE INSTALLATION

An in-place upgrade repair install is a "last gasp" method of restoring a Windows 7 installation that will not boot. The install process is run over the top of an existing installation. This can preserve some settings, application software installation, and data files while restoring system files. In Windows 8 and Windows 10, there are officially supported refresh and reset options to try to repair the installation. Using refresh (called **Just remove my files** in Windows 10) recopies the system files and reverts most system settings to the default, but can preserve user personalization settings, data files, and apps installed via Windows Store. Desktop applications are removed.

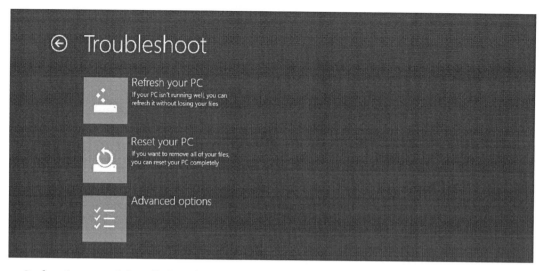

Performing a repair installation of Windows 8. (Screenshot used with permission from Microsoft.)

Using the **Reset** option (called **Fully clean the drive**) deletes the existing OS plus apps, settings, and data ready for the OS to be reinstalled.

UNATTENDED INSTALLATIONS

Performing an attended installation is time-consuming. Although the setup process has been streamlined since the early versions of Windows, an attended installation still requires the installer to monitor the setup program and input information. When it comes to deploying large numbers of installations (whether at the same time or over a period of months), there are several options for completing fully or partially unattended installations. As with ordinary installs, these can be completed using a variety of media but most would be based on the remote network installation boot method (PXE).

IMAGE DEPLOYMENT

Any installation involving more than a few PCs makes using imaging technology worthwhile. An image is a clone of an existing installation stored in one file. The image can contain the base OS and configuration settings, service packs and updates, applications software, and whatever else is required. An image can be stored on DVD or USB media or can be accessed over a network.

Windows supports the use of **answer files**, allowing for fully or partially unattended installations. An answer file is an **eXtensible Markup Language (XML)** text file that contains all of the instructions that the Windows **Setup** program will need to install and configure the OS without any administrator intervention.

Using unattended installation allows for multiple installations to occur simultaneously, can prevent errors during installation, and creates more consistency between installations in a large-scale rollout, all while lowering overhead costs and decreasing installation time and effort.

WINDOWS SYSTEM IMAGE MANAGER

The **Windows System Image Manager** is used to configure answer files. An answer file contains the information input during setup, such as product key, disk partitions, computer name, language and network settings (including whether to join a domain or workgroup), and so on. This file is accessed automatically during setup, meaning that an installer does not have to be present. The **System Image Manager** is packaged with the **Windows Assessment and Deployment Kit (ADK)**, formerly the **Windows Automated Installation Kit (WAIK)**, available from Microsoft's website.

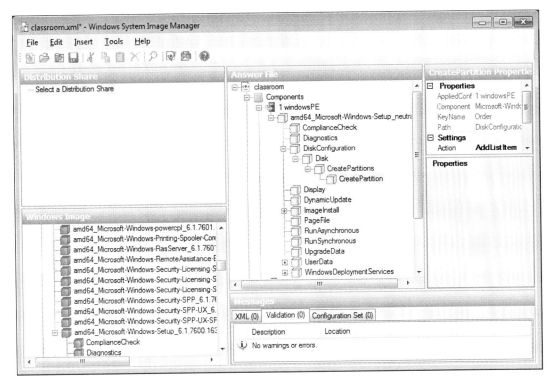

Windows System Image Manager. (Screenshot used with permission from Microsoft.)

DRIVE CLONING AND SYSPREP

If Windows is to be deployed to multiple machines with similar hardware specifications, the most common method of deployment is to use disk imaging software to clone an installation from one PC (the **reference machine**) to the rest. This has the advantage that a full system can be built, including applications, service packs and patches, and default user settings.

 Note: *You need different images for 32- and 64-bit platforms.*

Microsoft's **Deployment Image Servicing and Management** tool (**dism**, part of the ADK) is used to duplicate the disk contents. **Dism** reads the contents of a drive and writes the output to a **.WIM** (Windows Image File) format file.

However, duplicating an existing installation exactly can cause problems, as it repeats the **Security ID** (**SID**; a unique identifier for each machine) and assumes that the machines have exactly the same hardware configuration, which may not be the case.

Microsoft's **System Preparation Tool (Sysprep)** utility should be run before imaging the disk to side-step these problems. You can run the tool from **%SystemRoot% \System32\Sysprep\sysprep.exe**.

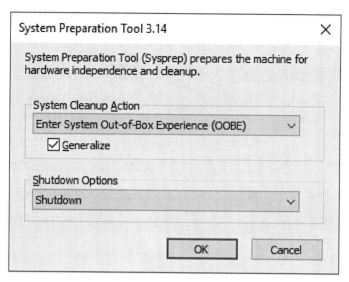

Resealing your computer using sysprep. (Screenshot used with permission from Microsoft.)

*Note: The **Sysprep** utility has gone through several updates with different Windows versions and service packs.*

WINDOWS DEPLOYMENT SERVICES

A basic network installation can be set up by putting the installation files in a network share, booting the machine to the network, then accessing the installation program from the share.

Windows Deployment Services is a Windows Server component used to implement network installs more effectively for **.WIM** images and answer files.

To support network deployments, clients must have a PXE compatible firmware and network adapter.

Topic D

Maintain OSs

EXAM OBJECTIVES COVERED
1002-1.3 Summarize general OS installation considerations and upgrade methods.
1002-1.4 Given a scenario, use appropriate Microsoft command-line tools.
1002-1.5 Given a scenario, use Microsoft operating system features and tools.
1002-1.9 Given a scenario, use features and tools of the Mac OS and Linux client/desktop operating systems.

Once you have installed the OS, you need to maintain it on an ongoing basis and set up some basic preventive maintenance procedures to keep the computer working well. Maintaining an OS might not seem as exciting or interesting as performing a new installation or replacing a hard disk, but it is actually one of the most crucial tasks for a support technician. System maintenance is important for two reasons: first, proper maintenance can prevent system problems from arising. Second, proper maintenance of the system, including the creation of appropriate backups, can make recovery or troubleshooting operations much easier. As a CompTIA A+ technician, you can use the skills and information in this lesson to perform preventive maintenance as part of your ongoing job tasks.

DISK MAINTENANCE

Of all the computer's subsystems, disk drives and the file system probably require the most attention to keep in optimum working order. They are subject to three main problems:

- **Fragmentation**—ideally, each file would be saved in contiguous clusters on the disk. In practice, over time as files grow, they become fragmented (written to non-contiguous clusters), reducing read performance.
- **Capacity**—typically, much more file creation occurs on a computer than file deletion. This means that capacity can reduce over time, often quite quickly. If the system disk has less than 20% free space, performance can be impaired. When space drops below 200 MB, a **Low Disk Space** warning is generated.
- **Damage**—hard disk operations are physically intensive and the platters of the disk are easy to damage, especially if there is a power cut. If the disk does not recognize that a sector is damaged, files can become corrupted.

These problems can be addressed by the systematic use of disk performance tools. These tools should be run regularly—at least every month and before installing software applications.

In Windows, you can access tools to maintain and optimize a drive through the drive's properties dialog box (right-click the drive icon and select **Properties**).

WINDOWS DISK MAINTENANCE TOOLS

There are several tools that you will find helpful when it comes to performing disk maintenance in Windows.

CHECK DISK

The Check Disk (**chkdsk**) Windows utility checks the integrity of disks and can repair any problems detected. Scheduling a check disk to run regularly will keep errors from accumulating on the hard disk. It is recommended that you run the Check Disk utility weekly.

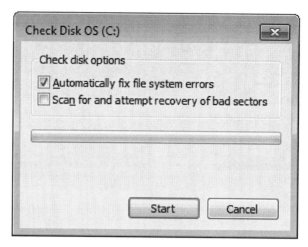

The Check Disk utility in Windows 7. (Screenshot used with permission from Microsoft.)

There are three ways to run the tool:

- No option selected—runs in Read-Only mode.
- Automatically fix file system errors—file system errors are caused by crashes, power loss, and the like. At a command line, use `chkdsk volume: /f`, where *volume* is the drive letter.
- Scan for and attempt recovery of bad sectors—bad sectors are damage to the actual drive. If a drive has many bad sectors, it is probably nearing the end of its useful life. You are prompted to save any recoverable data, which is copied to the root directory as filennnn.chk files. At a command line, use `chkdsk volume: /r`, where *volume* is the drive letter.

 Note: *Note that* `/r` *implies* `/f` *so you do not need to use both switches.*

Check Disk cannot fix open files, so you may be prompted to schedule the scan for the next system restart. A version of Check Disk (**autochk**) will also run automatically if the system detects file system errors. The other main parameters and switches for the command-line version are as follows:

Switch	Use
`path`	Specify a path (and optionally file name) to check.
`/x`	Force the volume to dismount. This will cause file errors for users with files open on the volume. If the volume is in use and you use the `/f` or `/r` switches without `/x`, you are prompted to schedule `chkdsk` for the next system restart.
`/i /c`	On NTFS volumes only, skips parts of the checking process.

 Note: chkdsk *can take a long time to scan and fix errors on a large disk. You cannot cancel once started. Run a Read-Only scan first.*

DISK DEFRAGMENTER

In Windows, the **Disk Defragmenter** reorganizes a drive to store information relating to each file in contiguous sectors of the disk. This improves performance by reducing the time required to load a file. The **Disk Defragmenter** can also move data to the start of the disk, leaving a single free area of disk for use by new files.

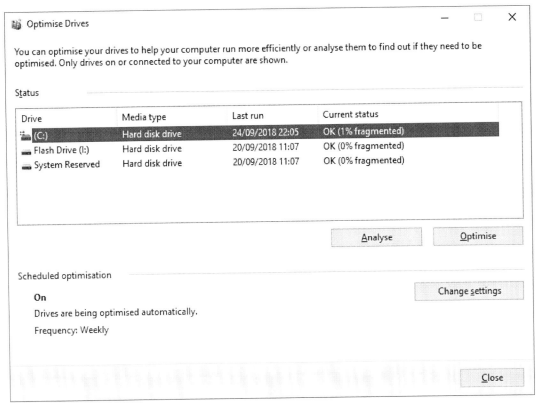

Optimize Drives (Defragmenter) in Windows 10. (Screenshot used with permission from Microsoft.)

In Windows 8/10, the GUI tool is named **Optimize Drives**. It performs additional disk and file system improvements compared to the basic utility.

You can **defragment** local and external hard disks. You cannot defragment an optical disc or a network drive.

> **Note:** *With flash drives and SSDs, while seek time is not a performance factor, the file system does still benefit from defragmentation. You can read more about the technical considerations in optimizing SSDs at* **hanselman.com/blog/ TheRealAndCompleteStoryDoesWindowsDefragmentYourSSD.aspx**.

Although it is possible to run this utility in the background while you work, it will slow your machine and prevent defragmentation of open files. It is usually better to run **defragmenter** when your computer is not being used.

> **Note:** *The **Defragmenter** requires above 15% of free disk space to work effectively. If insufficient free disk space is available, some files may not be defragmented.*

Windows automatically schedules **Defragmenter** to run using **Task Scheduler**.

> **Note:** *Windows Task Scheduler is discussed in greater detail later in this topic.*

LINUX AND macOS DISK MAINTENANCE TOOLS

The file systems used by Linux and macOS (ext and HFS Plus/APFS) are less prone to fragmentation than NTFS. Regular use of disk maintenance utilities is still considered best practice, however.

LINUX DISK MANAGEMENT TOOLS

Linux file systems do not ordinarily require defragmenting. Linux leaves gaps between each file, allowing the files to grow or shrink within their own "space," avoiding the worst effects of fragmentation. Performance will suffer if the disk is more than 80% full, however. You can use the following tools to check the health of the disk and file system:

- `df` and `du`—check free space and report usage by directories and files.
- `fsck`—check a partition for errors. Note that the partition should be unmounted before running this tool.

 Note: *Most systems automatically run the fsck command at boot time so that errors, if any, are detected and corrected before the system is used.*

macOS DISK UTILITY

In macOS, the **Disk Utility** app can be used to verify or repair a disk or file system. It can also be used to erase a disk with security options in case you are selling or passing on a Mac.

Disk Utility. (Screenshot courtesy of Apple.)

As with Linux, there is no need to regularly defragment a Mac hard drive. It's possible to run a defragmentation, but it should only be needed very rarely.

PATCH MANAGEMENT

Patch management is an important maintenance task to ensure that PCs operate reliably and securely. A **patch** or **update** is a file containing replacement system or application code. The replacement file fixes some sort of coding problem in the original file. The fix could be made to improve reliability, security, or performance.

Patch management is the practice of monitoring, obtaining, evaluating, testing, and deploying fixes and updates. As the number of computer systems in use has grown over recent years, so has the volume of vulnerabilities and corresponding patches and updates intended to address those vulnerabilities. However, not every computer within an organization will necessarily be compatible with a certain patch, whether because of outdated hardware, different software versions, or application dependencies.

Because of the inconsistencies that may be present within the various systems, the task of managing and applying patches can become very time-consuming and inefficient without an organized patch management system. In typical patch management, software updates are evaluated for their applicability to an environment and then tested in a safe way on non-production systems. If the patch is validated on all possible configurations without causing more problems, only then will the valid patch be rolled out to all computers throughout the entire organization.

A patch management program might include:

- An individual responsible for subscribing to and reviewing vendor and security patches and updating newsletters.
- A review and triage of the updates into urgent, important, and non-critical categories.
- An offline patch test environment where urgent and important patches can be installed and tested for functionality and impact.
- Immediate administrative push delivery of approved urgent patches.
- Weekly administrative push delivery of approved important patches.
- A periodic evaluation phase and full rollout for non-critical patches.

Many organizations have taken to creating official patch management policies that define the who, what, where, when, why, and how of patch management for that organization.

OS UPDATES

While working within patch management procedures, you also need to know the processes involved in performing updates in different operating systems.

WINDOWS UPDATE

Windows Update is a website (**update.microsoft.com**) hosting maintenance updates for different versions of Microsoft Windows. A control installed on the computer enables it to browse the site and select updates for download and installation, using the **Background Intelligent Transfer Services (BITS)** protocol.

 Note: Unless they address a critical issue, updates are released on **Patch Tuesday** *(the second Tuesday of every month).*

Windows Update hosts critical updates and security patches (code to fix security vulnerabilities in Windows and its associated software) plus optional software and hardware updates to add or change features or drivers. There is also a complementary program, called **Microsoft Update**, which can be used to keep **Microsoft Office** software patched at the same time.

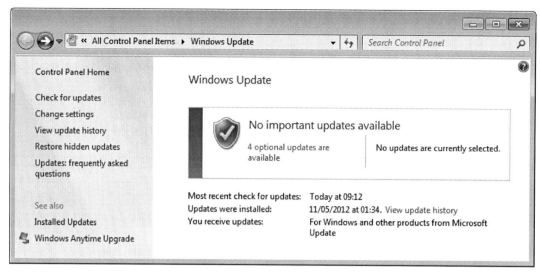

Windows Update (Windows 7). (Screenshot used with permission from Microsoft.)

Note: **Hotfixes** *are released to fix problems being experienced in specific circumstances. They are not always available through* **Windows Update** *but can be requested via the Microsoft Knowledge Base article describing the problem.*

During setup, Windows can be configured to check for system updates (via the Internet) and download them as needed. Update settings can be reconfigured via the **Windows Update** applet in **Control Panel**.

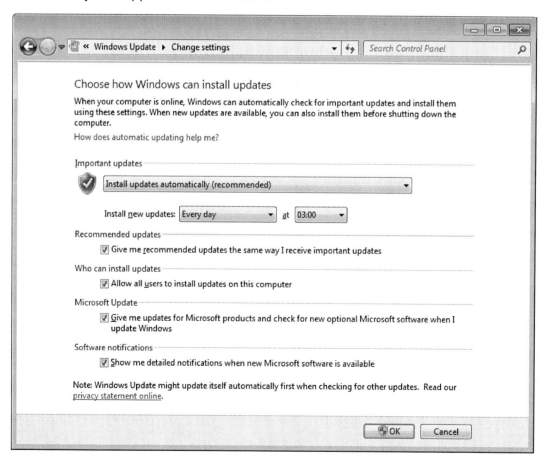

Changing update settings in Windows 7. (Screenshot used with permission from Microsoft.)

In Windows 10, you can also check for updates via Windows **Settings→Update & Security**. Note that, in the basic interface, **Windows Update** can only be disabled temporarily in Windows 10.

You can choose which updates to apply and also configure update settings.

The **WindowsUpdate.txt** log (stored in the **%SystemRoot%** folder) records update activity. If an update fails to install, you should check the log to find the cause; the update will fail with an error code that you can look up on the Microsoft Knowledge Base.

If an update causes problems, you can use the **Programs and Features** applet to uninstall it. Note, however, that **%SystemRoot%** also contains **KB??????.txt** log files listing which updates have been installed and hidden uninstall folders for the updates (**$NtUninstallKB??????$**). If these folders are deleted, the updates cannot be uninstalled.

 Note: *To check the current build of Windows, run **winver**. To check the version number of a particular file, right-click and select **Properties**.*

On a corporate network, updates can also be served using a **Windows Server Update Services (WSUS)** server. This allows the network administrator to approve updates for selected computer groups.

APPLICATION UPDATES

Software applications (especially those with browser plug-ins) may also need updating with the latest patches. Applications can contain security vulnerabilities in the same way as the OS; in fact, applications are targeted more aggressively than Windows itself as attackers recognize that they are less likely to be patched than the OS.

Microsoft software (such as MS Office) can be updated via the same update interface by selecting **Give me updates for other Microsoft products when I update Windows**. Most third-party vendors install autoupdate software with their applications.

LINUX PACKAGE MANAGEMENT

To manage updates and software in Linux, the package manager (such as **yum** or **apt-get**) needs to be configured with the web address of the software repository (or repositories) that you want to use. It can then be used to install, uninstall, or update the software.

Configuring package manager sources in Ubuntu Linux.

Most Linux software is configured by editing one or more text files with the required parameters, though some software may provide a GUI front-end.

Updates to the Linux kernel and drivers and a distribution's software tools and applications can be obtained via the package manager.

For example, you can edit a configuration file in the unattended-packages package to allow **apt** to obtain different types of updates. In the following example, only security updates are being obtained—the other types are commented out.

Configuring update types.

Having configured automatic updates, another configuration file sets options for the frequency of updates, cleaning out temporary files, and so on. Finally, you would use an executable update task for scheduling by the cron tool.

```
# Unlike any other crontab you don't have to run the `crontab`
# command to install the new version when you edit this file
# and files in /etc/cron.d. These files also have username fields,
# that none of the other crontabs do.

SHELL=/bin/sh
PATH=/usr/local/sbin:/usr/local/bin:/sbin:/bin:/usr/sbin:/usr/bin

# m h dom mon dow user  command
17 *    * * *   root    cd / && run-parts --report /etc/cron.hourly
25 6    * * *   root    test -x /usr/sbin/anacron || ( cd / && run-parts --repo$
47 6    * * 7   root    test -x /usr/sbin/anacron || ( cd / && run-parts --repo$
52 6    1 * *   root    test -x /usr/sbin/anacron || ( cd / && run-parts --repo$
#

                        [ Read 17 lines ]

lms-admin@lms:/etc/cron.daily$ ls
apache2  apt        bsdmainutils  logrotate  mlocate  popularity-contest
apport   aptitude   dpkg          man-db     passwd   standard
lms-admin@lms:/etc/cron.daily$
```

The apt script runs as a daily task to install updates as per the configuration files.

macOS PATCH MANAGEMENT

In macOS, the App Store checks daily for new updates and releases of installed apps. If a new version is available, a notification will be shown against the App Store icon in the dock. Also when you open the App Store, it will highlight that updates are available against the **Updates** button in the App Store window menu bar. To update the app, run **App Store** and click the **Updates** button in the top bar of the window.

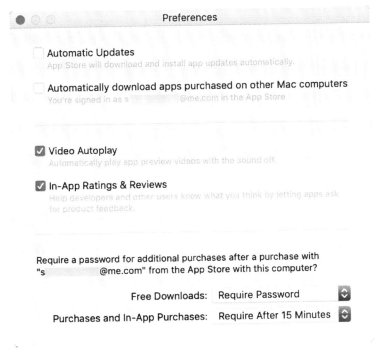

Configuring automatic updates. (Screenshot courtesy of Apple.)

You will have a choice to either update the apps individually or update all from the button at the top. It is recommended to choose **Update All** so that the latest versions of your apps and updates to macOS (not necessarily new versions) are on the Mac. It is also possible to automatically update apps to the latest version. To do this, go to **App Store→Preferences** and configure the appropriate settings:

Most apps that are downloaded and installed from a third-party developer will automatically check if updates are available each time they are run. A prompt will be displayed to update or to cancel. It's also possible to manually check for updates using the **Check for Updates** menu option in the app itself.

ANTI-MALWARE UPDATES

On any Windows system, it is particularly important that anti-virus software (or any other type of malware-blocking software) be updated regularly. Two types of update are generally necessary:

- Virus definitions/patterns—this is information about new viruses. These updates may be made available daily or even hourly.
- Scan engine/components—this fixes problems or makes improvements to the scan software itself.

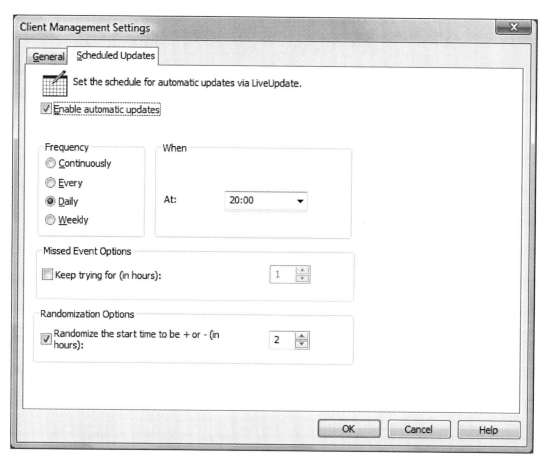

Schedule regular virus definition and scan engine updates. (Screenshot used with permission from Microsoft.)

There is usually an option within the software program to download and install these updates automatically. In the example in the previous figure, note the options to retry and randomize the start time—this helps to ensure that an update will take place.

LINUX AND VIRUSES/MALWARE

Some people feel that virus detection is unnecessary for Linux when used as a desktop PC OS. The way the Linux operating system is built (and the fact that there are many distributions) means that unlike Windows, it is harder to write a virus that will affect every Linux system. Different command-line/graphical shells, a simpler security system, and software package managers with authorized software repositories all mean that a virus writer has a harder job to infect a Linux system.

This does not mean that Linux is risk-free, however, and each installation should be assessed for security controls to suit the use to which it is put. Any high value target could be subject to specific, targeted attacks against it. Where Linux is used as the platform for a web server, for instance, it is imperative to configure appropriate security controls. Products such as Clam Anti-Virus (ClamAV) and the Snort Intrusion Prevention System (IPS) can be used to block varied malware threats and attempts to counteract security systems. Though now owned by Cisco, both ClamAV and Snort are open source products made freely available under the General Public License (GPL).

Another scenario for installing Linux anti-malware software is to detect infected files and prevent onward transmission via email or file transfer to Windows-based systems.

macOS AND VIRUSES/MALWARE

Like any other software, macOS is subject to numerous vulnerabilities and security advisories, some of which can be exploited and are serious enough to an unprivileged user to obtain root access. It is imperative to patch macOS systems against known vulnerabilities. There are relatively few instances of the infection of macOS systems by conventional computer viruses or worms. However, this does not mean that new threats will not appear in the future. Also, macOS is vulnerable to different kinds of malware, such as fake A/V and Trojans. Also, a macOS host could pass on Windows viruses to other users via email or file transfer. If a Windows boot partition is installed on macOS, it's possible for the Windows installation to become infected with a virus.

The following steps can help to protect a macOS computer from infection:

- Only download trusted apps—by default, macOS will only allow apps to be installed that have been downloaded from the App Store. If this setting is changed, ensure that you only download apps and content from trusted websites.
- Only download trusted content—again, make sure that you only download media or other content from reliable, trusted sources.
- Use anti-virus software—a number of free A-V packages are available for the Mac (from Avira, Avast, and Sophos for instance) that will detect malware directed at macOS—and Windows viruses too—and prevent redistribution via email or file sharing.
- If you have a bootable Windows partition on your macOS installation (Boot Camp), it is essential to treat it as if you were running and managing a Windows computer. Any anti-virus package can be used; make sure you follow the same processes and procedures to protect Windows as if it were a standalone computer.

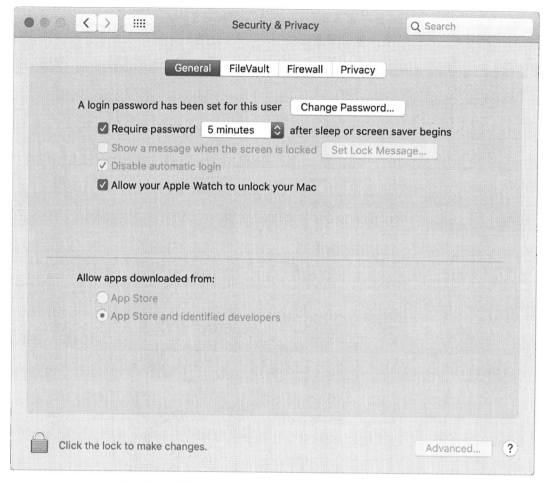

Security and Privacy settings. (Screenshot courtesy of Apple.)

DRIVER AND FIRMWARE UPDATES

Windows ships with a number of core and third-party device drivers for system components and peripheral hardware. Updates for these devices can be obtained via Windows Update, though they will be listed as optional updates and might not install automatically.

You might need to use the device vendor's website to obtain a driver. To update, you download the driver files and install them using the supplied setup program or extract them manually and save them to a local folder. You can then use the device's property dialog box in Device Manager to update the driver. You can either scan for the update automatically or point the tool to the updated version you saved locally.

FIRMWARE UPGRADES

Motherboard manufacturers may update their system firmware in order to fix bugs, solve incompatibilities with operating systems, or to add new features. You should visit your motherboard manufacturer's website regularly to check if and when upgrades are available.

As well as the chipset firmware, you may need to update the firmware on other devices, such as drive units, printers, and networking equipment. Devices directly attached to the PC (via USB) can normally be updated from Windows using a setup utility provided by the vendor. A network device would typically be updated using its management software or web configuration interface.

Caution: *Interrupting a firmware update can damage a device beyond repair. Try to ensure a stable power supply during the update process, using an Uninterruptible Power Supply (UPS) if possible.*

macOS DRIVER UPDATES

Unlike Windows-based PCs, where desktops are made from various hardware components from different manufacturers, each requiring its own driver, Apple's integrated approach to system building means that drivers are easier to manage. All drivers for display, network interfaces, drives, and so on, are integral to macOS and will be updated (where necessary) either through software updates through the App Store or even new releases of macOS itself.

Where third-party devices are installed, always make sure that the latest version of the driver is installed. Use the **About** button from the device's page in **System Preferences** to verify the current driver version.

Driver information for this Wacom graphics tablet is accessed via the About option in System Preferences.

Check the manufacturer's website to see if this is the latest version. If installing a new driver, first remove the old driver from macOS. In the example in the previous figure, you would use the **Wacom Utility** under **Applications**, then click **Remove** under **Tablet Software** to delete the driver and utilities. You may be prompted to enter an administrator password to do this.

Next, download the latest version from the manufacturer website. This will almost certainly take the form of a .dmg disk image. Double-click the package and follow the instructions to install the driver. Complete the process by verifying the updated version number is shown via System Preferences.

 Note: *Always remember to remove the old version of a third-party driver before updating.*

SCHEDULED BACKUPS

One of the most important operations in computing is the creation of a secure backup of data files. Typically, network backups take place using a tape system, which has the advantages of high capacity, relatively low cost, and portability. For this type of backup, advanced backup software capable of backing up online databases and remote systems is required. Most large organizations will implement a structured backup scheme that includes a backup schedule and specifications for which files are backed up, where the backup is stored, and how it can be retrieved. The backup scheme will specify the media rotation method, which determines how many backup tapes or other media sets are needed, and the sequence in which they are used and reused. Designated administrators will have the responsibility for designing and managing the backup scheme and for restoring data when needed.

Note: *When a computer is connected to a network, it is bad practice for a user to store data locally (on the client PC's hard drive). Network home folders and the use of scripts to copy data can help users to transfer data to a file server, where it can be backed up safely.*

Personal backups are necessary for home users or on workgroups, where no central file server is available. In this scenario, the backup software supplied with Windows is serviceable. Most home users will backup to external hard drives or use some sort of cloud-based storage.

WINDOWS BACKUP

The backup tool included with Windows 7 has the ability to back up selected locations. The home editions are restricted to backing up to local drives or removable media, whereas the business/Ultimate editions can back up to a network share.

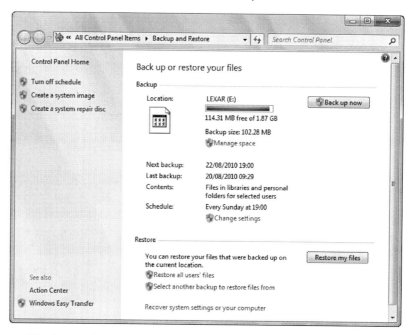

Windows 7 Backup and Restore Center. (Screenshot used with permission from Microsoft.)

In Windows 8 and Windows 10, user data backup options are implemented via File History. To configure the backup device and select folders to back up, select **Settings→Update & security→Backup**.

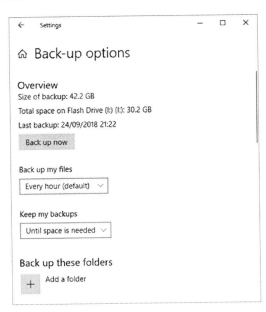

Configuring backup options via Windows Settings. (Screenshot used with permission from Microsoft.)

If you need to restore a file or folder, you can either check the **Previous Versions** tab in the object's **Properties** dialog box or use the **File History** applet.

Redirecting file output for a restore operation. (Screenshot used with permission from Microsoft.)

macOS TIME MACHINE BACKUP

In macOS, the **Time Machine** utility enables data to be backed up to an external, attached drive. To enable **Time Machine**, go to **System Preferences→Time Machine** and slide the switch to **On**. Select the disk where the backups are to be stored. Under

Options it is possible to unselect certain files, folders, or even drives from a backup plan. By default, **Time Machine** keeps hourly backups for the past 24 hours, daily backups for a month, and weekly backups for all previous months. When the drive used to store backups becomes full, **Time Machine** removes older backups to free up space.

Configuring Time Machine. (Screenshot courtesy of Apple.)

To restore files from **Time Machine**, a timeline on the right-hand side of the screen will show the available backups. Using the **Finder** window in **Time Machine**, find the folder with file (or files) that you want to restore. Then slide the timeline back to the date/time of the previous version.

 *Note: **Time Machine** stores backups on the local drive as snapshots as well as any available backup drive. If the backup drive is not attached, you may still be able to restore a file or version from the local snapshot. If the tick mark next to an item in the timeline is dimmed, the backup drive needs to be attached to restore that item.*

LINUX BACKUP TOOLS

Linux does not have an "official" backup tool. You could create a custom backup solution using the **cron** task scheduler (see the following section) and file copy scripts. There are plenty of commercial and open source backup products for Linux, however. Some examples include Amanda, Bacula, Fwbackups, and Rsync.

TASK SCHEDULERS

While you might establish procedures for performing the maintenance tasks discussed previously, you might also want the tasks to run automatically within the OS. To accomplish this, you can use a task scheduler.

WINDOWS TASK SCHEDULER

Task Scheduler, as its name suggests, is a Windows tool that sets tasks to run at a particular time. Tasks can be run once at a future date or time or according to a recurring schedule. A task can be a simple application process (including switches, if necessary) or a batch file or script. **Task Scheduler** is accessed via **Administrative Tools**. Apart from defining the path to the file or script you want to execute and setting the schedule, you should also enter the credentials that the task will run under—if the selected user account does not have sufficient permissions, the task will not run.

Many of Windows' processes come with predefined task schedules. **Disk Defragmenter/Optimize Drives**, for instance, is configured to run automatically by default. Other features include:

- You can define triggers other than a simple schedule—running a task when the machine wakes from sleep or hibernation, for instance.
- You can add multiple actions under a single task.
- You can view a log of events connected to the task.
- You can organize tasks in folders and there are more tools for managing them.

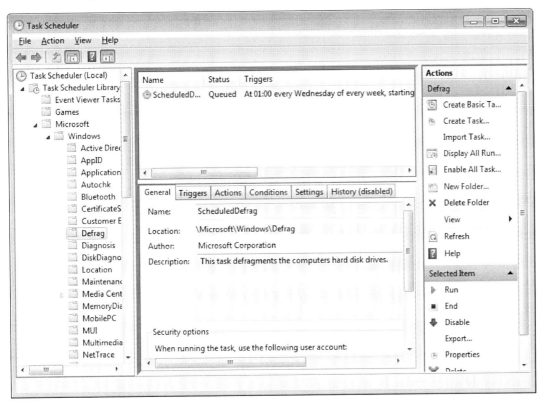

Windows 7 Task Scheduler. (Screenshot used with permission from Microsoft.)

cron

In Linux, if you want to run a batch of commands or a script to perform a backup or other maintenance task, there is a scheduling service called **cron**. Every user of the system is allowed to schedule programs or tasks in their own personal **crontab** (**cron table**). These tables are merged together by **cron** to create an overall system schedule. Every minute, the **cron** service checks the schedule and executes the programs for that time period.

To add or delete a scheduled job, use the **crontab editor**. To review a user's **crontab** jobs, enter the command: `crontab -l`.

To remove jobs from the scheduled list, use the command: `crontab -r`.

To enter the editor, run the command `crontab -e`. `crontab` uses the **vi** editor by default. To add a new job, press the **Insert** key then type a new job using the appropriate syntax. After the job syntax has been typed, press the **Esc** key to return to command mode. To save the job and exit, type `:wq`; to abandon changes, type `:q!`

The basic syntax for scheduling a job using crontab can include the following:

- `mm`—specifies the minutes past the hour when the task is to initiate (0-59).
- `hh`—specifies the hour (0-23).
- `dd`—can be used to specify the date within the month (0-31).
- `MM`—specifies the month in either numerical or text format (1-12 or jan, feb, mar).
- `weekday`—sets the day of the week (1-7 or mon, tue, wed).
- `command`—the command or script to run. This should include the full path to the file.

It is important to note that any of the time/date related parameters can be replaced by wildcards:

- `*` specifies any or other characters.
- `,` allows multiple values.
- `-` allows a range of values.
- `/2` indicates every other.

For example, consider the following crontab entry:

- ```
  15 02 * * 5 /usr/bin/rsync -av --delete /home/fred /
  mount/rsync
  ```

This would cause the system to run the **rsync** backup program at 2:15am on a Friday (day 5), synchronizing the **/home/fred** directory with the **/mount/sync** folder (which could be a mount point to an external backup device).

macOS also supports **cron** but Apple's own **launchd** scheduler is preferred.

HOW TO MAINTAIN OPERATING SYSTEMS
Follow these procedures to maintain operating systems.

MAINTAIN OPERATING SYSTEMS
To maintain operating systems:

1. Use a scheduler to perform routine maintenance tasks on a regular basis.
2. Check for, test, and install operating system updates as they become available.
3. Check for, test, and install patches to applications and operating systems as they become available.
4. Check for and determine whether driver or firmware updates are appropriate to any issues you are having with your system, applications, or components.

     Note: If power is lost during a system firmware update, the machine might become unusable. Connect the system to a UPS when performing a system firmware update.

5. Keep virus definitions and the scan engine up-to-date. This is most important on Windows systems.
  ```

Activity 2-1

Installing, Configuring, and Maintaining Operating Systems Review

SCENARIO

Answer the following review questions.

1. Do you have experience installing operating systems? Do you feel you will be able to perform installations more efficiently as a result of the information presented in this lesson?

2. How often do you expect to be able to perform in-place upgrades instead of clean installs at your workplace?

Summary

In this lesson, you installed, configured, and maintained OSs. Whether you are upgrading, installing from scratch, or redeploying a system, you will need the skills that enable you to install, configure, and optimize computer operating systems to meet your organization's business needs.

Lesson 3

Maintaining and Troubleshooting Microsoft Windows

LESSON INTRODUCTION

You have learned to use tools and features to install and configure devices and manage disks and file systems. These tasks are important but they are not the reason people and companies use computers. Computers are useful devices because they run different kinds of software applications. In this lesson, you will learn how to install and configure software in Windows.

Using the computer effectively also brings up the issues of performance and availability. If the computer is slow or unresponsive, users cannot work efficiently. This lesson will also show you how to monitor system performance and troubleshoot Windows OS problems.

LESSON OBJECTIVES

In this lesson, you will:

- Install and manage Windows applications.
- Manage Windows performance.
- Troubleshoot Windows issues.

Topic A

Install and Manage Windows Applications

 EXAM OBJECTIVES COVERED
1002-1.4 Given a scenario, use appropriate Microsoft command-line tools.
1002-1.5 Given a scenario, use Microsoft operating system features and tools.
1002-1.6 Given a scenario, use Microsoft Windows Control Panel utilities.
1002-1.7 Summarize application installation and configuration concepts.

Installing and configuring software applications is a crucial part of the IT support role. In this topic, you will learn the tools and features used in Windows® to follow best practices for software management. You will also use Task Manager to examine processes and performance of the operating system and applications.

APPLICATION INSTALLATION AND CONFIGURATION

When you are selecting, installing, and configuring software applications, you need to consider both compatibility and security concepts.

OS REQUIREMENTS (COMPATIBILITY)

Every software application is designed to run under a specific operating system. When purchasing, you need to make sure you select the version for your OS. You cannot purchase software for macOS® and then run it on Windows. Additionally, a software application might not be supported for use under newer operating systems. For example, if you have been using version 1 of the Widget App on Windows 7 and you subsequently upgrade to Windows 10, the Widget App might need to be upgraded to version 2 for full compatibility.

SYSTEM REQUIREMENTS

System requirements refers to the PC specification required to run the application. Some applications, such as 3D games, may have high requirements for CPU and GPU (graphics). There will also be specific RAM and disk space requirements:

- Random Access Memory (RAM)—most applications will require at least 2 GB of system memory.
- Drive space—applications can have quite high disk space requirements. For example, Microsoft Office needs at least 3 GB of disk space.

The application's documentation may specify additional requirements, such as a microphone, speakers, or headset.

INSTALLATION AND DEPLOYMENT OPTIONS

Most applications are installed from a setup file. The setup file packs the application's executable(s), configuration files, and media files within it. During setup, the files are extracted and installed to the program directory. A setup file can be distributed on CD/DVD, it could be run from a USB drive, or it could be downloaded from the Internet.

When an organization wants to deploy an application to a number of desktops, they are likely to use a network-based installer. In this scenario, the setup file is simply copied to a shared folder on the network and client computers run the setup file from the network folder. In Windows, you can use policies—**Group Policy Objects (GPO)**—to set a computer to remotely install an application from a network folder without any manual intervention from an administrator. Products such as centrally managed anti-virus suites often support "push" deployment tools to remotely install the client or security sensor on each desktop.

PERMISSIONS AND OTHER SECURITY CONSIDERATIONS

One advantage of using a tool such as GPO to deploy applications is that a user does not have to log on to the local client with administrator privileges. Write/modify permissions over folders to which the application executable files are installed are restricted to administrator-level accounts. This prevents unauthorized modification of the computer or the installation of programs that could threaten security policies. The setup file for a deployed application can run using a service account.

To run an application, the user needs to be granted read/execute permission over the application's installation directory. Any files created using the application or custom settings/preferences specific to a particular user should be saved to the user's home folder/profile rather than the application directory.

When selecting applications for installation on desktops, proper security considerations need to be made in respect of potential impacts to the device (computer) and to the network. The principal threat is that of a Trojan Horse; that is, software whose true (malicious) purpose is concealed. Such malware is likely to be configured to try to steal data or provide covert remote access to the host or network once installed. A setup file could also be wittingly or unwittingly infected with a computer virus. These security issues can be mitigated by ensuring that software is only installed from trusted sources and that the installer code is digitally signed by a reputable software publisher.

As well as overt malware threats, software could impact the stability and performance of a computer or network. The software might consume more CPU and memory resource than anticipated or use an excessive amount of network bandwidth. There could be compatibility problems with other local or network applications. The software could contain unpatched vulnerabilities that could allow worm malware to propagate and crash the network. Ideally, applications should be tested in a lab environment before being deployed more widely. Research any security advisories associated with the software, and ensure that the developer has a robust approach to identifying and resolving security issues.

WINDOWS PROGRAMS AND FEATURES

In Windows, local applications are installed to the **Program Files** directory on the boot partition (for example, **C:\Program Files**). Most applications will also write configuration data to the registry and may add folders and files to the user's home directory (or to the **All Users** directory for settings shared by all users). To ensure that all these folders, files, and registry settings are created correctly, applications should be installed and removed using the supplied Setup program.

 Note: Application installation and removal under legacy versions of Windows could cause problems if an application changed or removed DLL (Dynamic Link Library) files used by other applications, causing them to malfunction. Microsoft introduced the Windows Installer Service to mitigate these problems. Most application vendors use setup programs that are compliant with Windows Installer (Windows Installer packages have .MSI extensions). System Restore can also be configured to create a Restore Point automatically upon application installation, adding a further measure of protection.

64-BIT WINDOWS AND 32-BIT APPLICATIONS

Many of the software applications available for Windows are still 32-bit. These applications can usually be installed under 64-bit versions of Windows. They run within a special application environment called WOW64 (Windows on Windows 64-bit). This environment replicates the 32-bit environment expected by the application and translates its requests into ones that can be processed by the 64-bit CPU, memory, and file subsystems.

In a 64-bit Windows environment, 32-bit application files are installed to the **Program Files (x86)** folder while 64-bit applications are stored in **Program Files** (unless the user chooses custom installation options). Windows' 64-bit shared system files (DLLs and EXEs) are stored in **%SystemRoot%\system32**; that is, the same system folder as 32-bit versions of Windows. Files for the 32-bit versions are stored in **%SystemRoot% \syswow64**.

 Note: *A 32-bit version of Windows cannot run 64-bit applications.*

INSTALLING A DESKTOP APPLICATION

Launch the program's setup application and complete the setup wizard to install it. In order to install a program successfully, you should exit any other applications or files. You may also need to disable anti-virus software.

USING PROGRAMS AND FEATURES

Programs and Features allows you to uninstall a program or add or remove component features of software such as Microsoft Office. There is also usually a repair option, which will reinstall the components of the program.

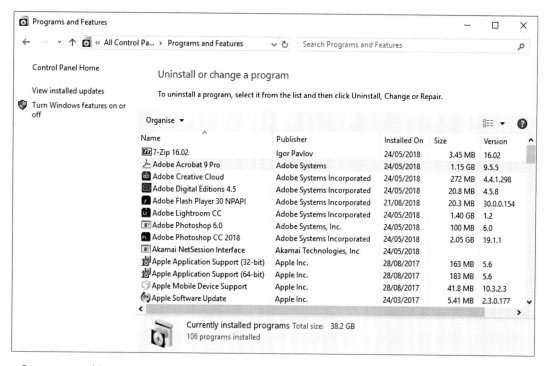

Programs and Features—select a program icon then use the options to uninstall, change, or repair.
(Screenshot used with permission from Microsoft.)

Note: *In order to uninstall a program successfully, you should exit any applications or files that might lock files installed by the application or the PC will need to be restarted. You may also need to disable anti-virus software. If the uninstall program cannot remove locked files, it will normally prompt you to check its log file for details (the files and directories can then be deleted manually).*

ENABLING WINDOWS FEATURES

You can use **Programs and Features** to enable or disable optional Windows components. Click the **Turn Windows features on or off** link then check the boxes for the features you want to enable (or uncheck boxes to remove those features).

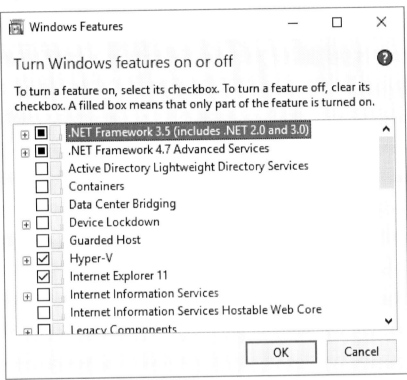

Enabling and disabling Windows Features. (Screenshot used with permission from Microsoft.)

SOFTWARE CONFIGURATION

Most configuration options for software are quite specific to each program. You can use menus such as **File→Options**, **Edit→Preferences**, or the **Help** menu to change the configuration settings.

DEFAULT PROGRAMS

Use the **Default Programs** applet to set the programs you wish to use for particular tasks or to configure individual file associations (choosing which application is used to open files with a particular extension).

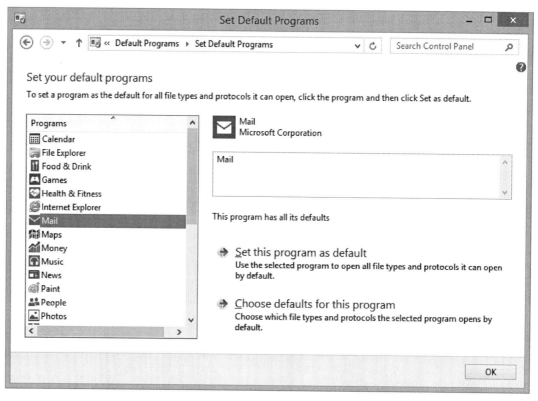

Default Programs applet in Windows 8.1. (Screenshot used with permission from Microsoft.)

 Note: *In Windows 10, select* **Windows Settings→Apps→Default apps**.

COMPATIBILITY MODE

One of the challenges for Microsoft in releasing a new version of Windows is to provide compatibility for hardware and software developed for previous versions.

Windows provides a degree of support for legacy DOS and Windows 9x programs, and each version provides support for earlier 2000/XP/Vista/7/8 versions. The **Properties** dialog box for executable files and the shortcuts to such programs have a **Compatibility** tab. It allows you to configure the program's original operating system environment and force it to use compatible display settings.

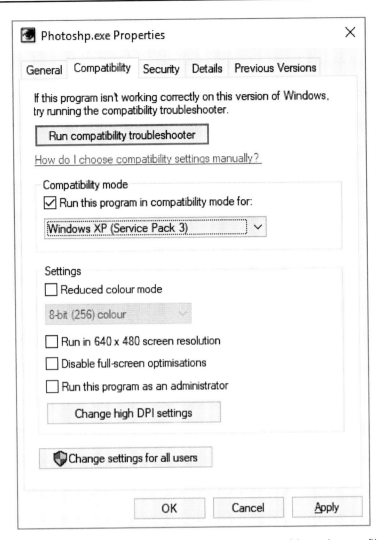

Access program compatibility options via the application's executable or shortcut file properties.
(Screenshot used with permission from Microsoft.)

Features such as User Account Control and its greater protection for system folders (Program Files and the system root), the Aero desktop compositing engine, and 64-bit Windows versions have made application compatibility even more challenging. UAC problems can be solved by running the program as an administrator, and there is an option to turn off advanced desktop compositing effects. There is a **Program Compatibility Troubleshooter** wizard (right-click the shortcut or executable) to help.

MICROSOFT STORE APPS

Windows 8 introduces support for a different kind of program, referred to variously as a Windows app, Store app, Universal app, or Modern/Metro app. These apps run across any kind of Windows device, including Windows-based smartphones and tablets. Windows apps are not installed via **Programs and Features** but via the **Microsoft Store**.

Users must sign into the Microsoft Store using a Microsoft account. Apps can be transferred between any Windows device where the user signs in with that Microsoft account.

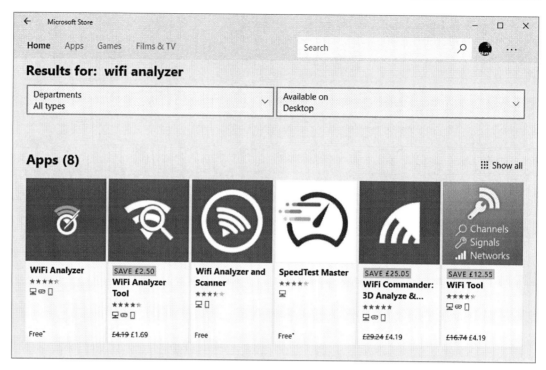

Microsoft Store. (Screenshot used with permission from Microsoft.)

Unlike desktop applications, store apps run in a restrictive sandbox. This sandbox is designed to prevent a store app from making system-wide changes and prevent a faulty store app from "crashing" the whole OS or interfering with other apps and applications. This extra level of protection means that users with only standard permissions are allowed to install store apps. Installing a store app does not require confirmation with UAC or computer administrator-level privileges.

Apps can be uninstalled via the app's shortcut menu on the **Start Screen**. You can choose to uninstall an app from that device only or from all devices, wiping any data stored by the app in your account in the process.

APPLICATION AND PRINT SERVICES

A **service** is a Windows process that does not require any sort of user interaction and so runs in the **background** (without a window). Services provide functionality for many parts of the Windows OS, such as allowing logon, browsing the network, or indexing file details to optimize searches. Services may be installed by Windows and by other applications, such as antivirus, database, or backup software.

SERVICES CONSOLE

You might want to disable non-essential services to improve performance or security. You can prevent a service from running at startup by setting it to **Manual** or prevent it from running completely by setting it to **Disabled**. Note that this may cause problems if other services depend upon it. If something is not working properly, you should check that any services it depends upon are started.

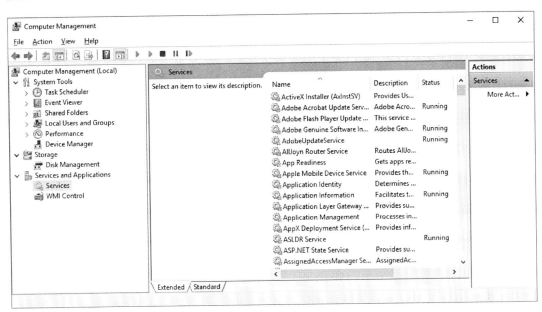

Managing services using the Computer Management console. (Screenshot used with permission from Microsoft.)

To configure services, open the **Computer Management** console, then expand **Services and Applications** from the tree and click the **Services** icon. Alternatively, you can run the **services.msc** command. The services snap-in displays a list of installed services in the right-hand panel. Clicking a service displays information about it in the left-hand panel. The shortcut menu for a service allows you to start, stop, pause/resume, or restart (stop then start).

PRINT MANAGEMENT

If you use Windows to host a printer (acting as a print server), you need to make drivers available for the different client operating systems that may be connecting to the printer. Windows comes with a **Print Management** snap-in (in **Administrative Tools**), where you can manage drivers and monitor the status of printers.

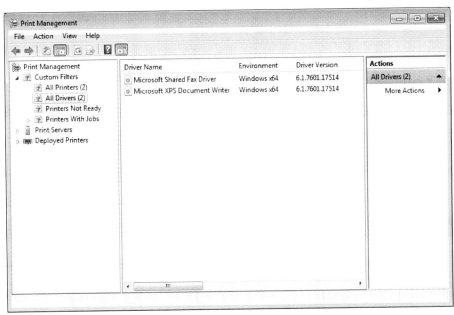

Print Management (Windows 7). (Screenshot used with permission from Microsoft.)

Note: *Note that* **Print Management** *is not available in the Home editions.*

COMPONENT SERVICES

The **Component Object Model** (**COM+, Distributed COM [DCOM]**, and **ActiveX**) is a means for developers to link software applications and leverage Windows services. For example, **COM OLE** (Object Linking and Embedding) allows an Excel® spreadsheet to be saved within a Word document or a custom software application could use COM to write to the event log. The **Component Services** snap-in (accessed via **Administrative Tools**) enables you to register new server applications or reconfigure security permissions for existing services.

DATA SOURCES

The **Data Sources** or **ODBC Data Sources** snap-in (from **Administrative Tools**) enables you to control data connections set up on the local computer. A data source allows a client application to share data from a server application. For example, an Excel spreadsheet could be set up with a data connection to an SQL Server®.

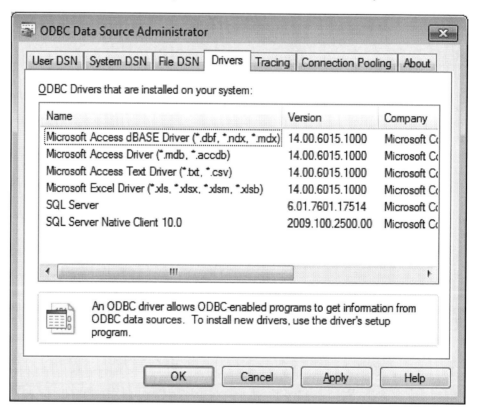

Checking available drivers using the Data Sources snap-in. (Screenshot used with permission from Microsoft.)

An Open Database Connectivity (ODBC) data source consists of a driver for the server application plus the location of the data (a file or a server). You may also need to supply the table name and logon credentials. Typically, drivers get added when an application is installed.

Users can set up new data sources using the **My Data Sources** folder that gets added within their **Documents** folder in their profile.

TASK MANAGER

The **Task Manager** utility (`taskmgr.exe`) allows the user to shut down applications that are not responding. An ordinary user can end an unresponsive application that they ran initially, but administrative rights are required to end processes that were not started by the user. This protects the system by ensuring malware cannot disable antivirus software or other protections. In addition to this functionality, **Task Manager** can be used to monitor the PC's key resources. The quickest way to open **Task Manager** is to press **Ctrl+Shift+Esc**.

> *Note: Other ways to open **Task Manager** include pressing **Ctrl+Alt+Del** and selecting **Task Manager**, right-clicking the taskbar, and running `taskmgr.exe`.*

Task Manager has been significantly overhauled in Windows 8 and Windows 10. First we examine the Windows 7 version and the Windows 10 version follows after.

APPLICATIONS TAB

The **Applications** tab shows applications currently running in a desktop window. The shortcut menu for each allows you to force the application to close (**End Task**), manage its window, and show the process associated with the application.

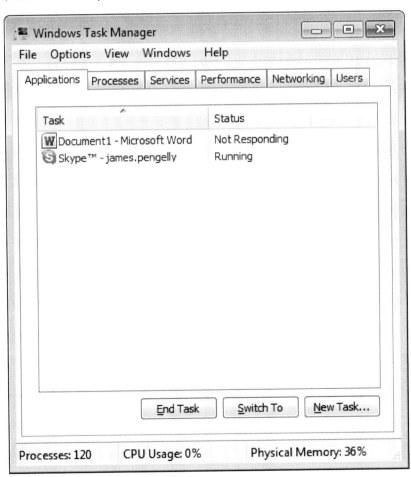

Windows 7 Task Manager—Applications tab. (Screenshot used with permission from Microsoft.)

If an application is not responding, forcing it to close may result in the loss of any unsaved data. You are prompted to confirm what you want to do.

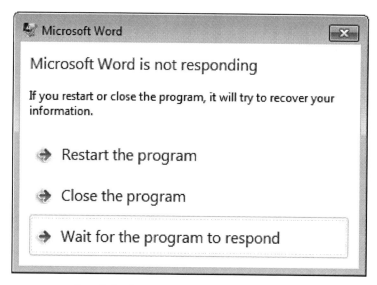

Program not responding dialog box. (Screenshot used with permission from Microsoft.)

Some applications, including Microsoft Office ones, can try to recover unsaved information from autosave and temp files.

PROCESSES TAB

The **Processes** tab shows CPU utilization and memory usage for each process.

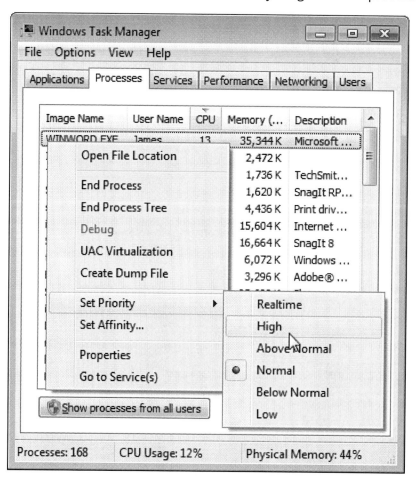

Windows 7 Task Manager—Processes tab. (Screenshot used with permission from Microsoft.)

To view system-level processes (those not running under the logged-on user account), you must select the **Show processes from all users** option.

You would examine these values to discover whether a particular application was misbehaving. For example, an application may "leak" memory by not freeing it up when it has finished using it. To show more than the default CPU and Memory Usage, select **View**→**Select Columns** and check the items that you want to look at.

If a process is not responding or if you suspect it is faulty, you can right-click and select **End Process** to terminate it.

In some circumstances, you may want to privilege one task over another, or conversely, set one task to have fewer resources than others. You can do this by right-clicking the process and choosing an option from the **Set Priority** submenu. For example, if you had a Voice over IP application and its priority was not already set to **Above normal**, changing its priority might improve call quality as the CPU would privilege that process over ones set to any other level.

Note: *As with other administrative tools, some settings in **Task Manager** (such as showing system level processes) are not available unless you run the tool with administrative privileges.*

You can choose to open the folder containing the process and inspect its file properties. This can be useful if you suspect a malware infection—you should check that the process is installed to a valid location. Sometimes a single process (such as svchost.exe) will "host" multiple services; conversely, there may be multiple versions of the process running. You can use the **Go to Service(s)** option in the process's shortcut menu to view them.

Note: *Use the **File** menu to launch a new process. You can choose to launch the process with administrative privileges by checking the box.*

SERVICES TAB

You can use the **Services** tab to show which services are running, start and stop services, or open the services management console. Each running service is associated with a host process through its **Process ID (PID)**. You can use the **Go to Process** option in the process's shortcut menu to view it.

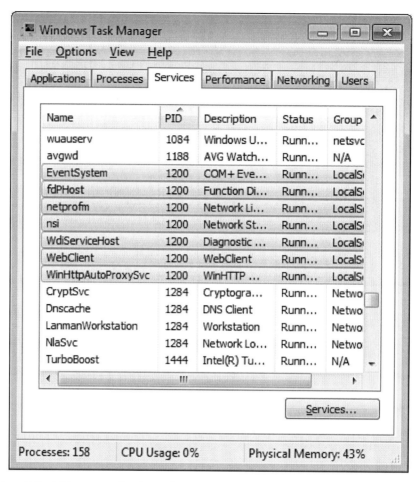

Windows 7 Task Manager—Services tab. (Screenshot used with permission from Microsoft.)

PERFORMANCE TAB

The **Processes** tab shows which applications might be using (or over-using) system resources. You can also use Task Manager to get a snapshot of overall system performance. Select the **Performance** tab to view resource usage. On a system with multiple processors, you should see multiple graphs for CPU Usage (one for each CPU). If this is not the case, select **View→CPU History→One Graph per CPU**. Note that physical, multicore, and HyperThreaded processors are all represented.

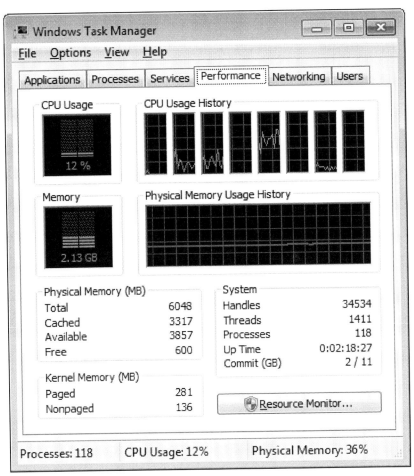

Windows 7 Task Manager—Performance tab. (Screenshot used with permission from Microsoft.)

The following memory usage is displayed:

- **Physical Memory**—usage of system RAM (not including the pagefile).
- **Kernel Memory**—physical and paged memory used by Windows core files.
- **System summary**—showing handles, threads, and processes (software objects being managed by the CPU), system uptime, and the commit charge (overall memory usage, including physical memory and pagefile).

High peak values are nothing to worry about, but consistently high utilization means that you should consider adding more resources to the system (or run fewer processes!). CPU and physical memory obviously require physical upgrades. Windows will normally change the **pagefile** dynamically if it is running out of space. If it has been set manually, you should increase it using the **Performance Settings** button on the **Advanced** page of **System Properties**.

Note: If the commit charge exceeds total physical memory, then performance will suffer as the system will be using the disk-based pagefile extensively. You need to multiply the commit charge (measured here in gigabytes) by 1024 to compare to physical memory (measured in megabytes).

There is also a link to **Resource Monitor**, which shows additional live performance information.

NETWORKING TAB

The **Networking** tab shows the status and utilization of the network adapter(s). Utilization is expressed as a percentage, so if the link is 10 Gbps (as shown), 10% utilization shows that the computer is transferring about 1 Gbps currently.

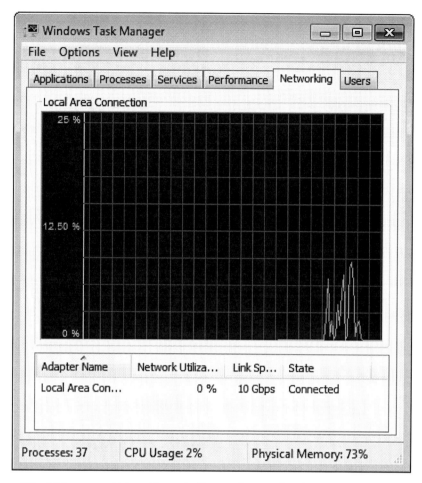

Windows 7 Task Manager—Networking tab. (Screenshot used with permission from Microsoft.)

USERS TAB

The **Users** tab shows who is logged on to the machine. An administrator can disconnect or log off other users or send them a notification (to inform them that the computer will be shut down, for instance).

WINDOWS 10 TASK MANAGER

In Windows 10, you can open **Task Manager** via the **Ctrl+Shift+Esc** key combo, by right-clicking the taskbar, or by using the **Windows+X** menu. **Task Manager** may start in a "compact" mode; click the **Show details** button to expand it.

 Note: Task Manager in Windows 8 is essentially the same as in Windows 10.

In Windows 10, the functions of the **Applications** and **Processes** tabs are consolidated across the **Processes** and **Details** tabs. On the **Processes** tab, you can expand each app or background process to view its sub-processes and view more clearly what resources each is taking up.

The shortcut menu allows you to end a task. There is also an option to search for information about the process online. Another option is to view more information about a process via the **Details** tab. You can identify services associated with a process via the shortcut menu on the **Details** tab.

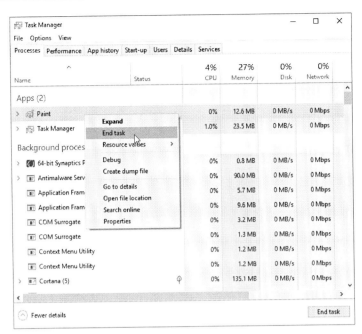

Windows 10 Task Manager—Processes tab. (Screenshot used with permission from Microsoft.)

The **Performance** tab provides more information about the CPU, memory, disk, and network subsystems, while the **App History** tab shows usage information for Windows Store apps.

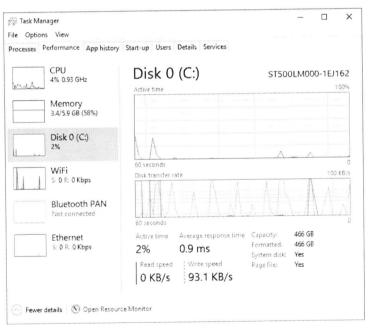

Windows 10 Task Manager—Performance tab. (Screenshot used with permission from Microsoft.)

The **Users** tab lets you see who is logged on (and allows you to send them a message or sign them out) plus information about the processes they are running and the resource utilization associated with their account.

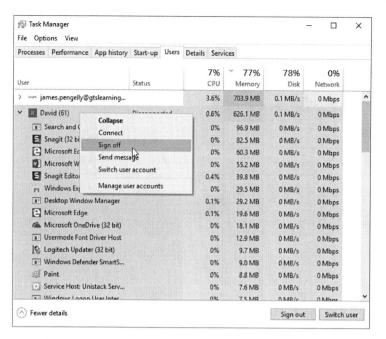

Windows 10 Task Manager—Users tab. (Screenshot used with permission from Microsoft.)

The **Startup** tab lets you disable programs added to the Startup folder (type `shell:startup` at the **Run** dialog box to access this) or set to run using the registry. Right-click the headers and select **Startup type** to show how the program is launched. It also shows how much impact each item has on boot times.

The tasklist and taskkill Commands

You can also identify which service is running in which process (and vice versa) at a command line using the `tasklist` command. `tasklist` shows a list of processes (images) along with a PID, session name and number, and memory usage (in kilobytes). You can run the command with the `/fi` switch to apply various filters (for example, `tasklist /fi "memusage gt 150000"` shows processes using more than 150 MB)—check the online help for details. Using `tasklist /svc` shows a list of services within each process.

The `taskkill` command can be used to end processes and services. Use `taskkill /pid processid` or `taskkill /im ImageName` to end a task by PID or image name respectively. Use the **/t** switch to also halt any child processes.

The `/f` switch terminates the process without any user notification (for the user to save changes, for instance) and will also terminate it even if it is currently displaying a dialog box. You can run the command with an appropriate filter (`/fi "Criteria"`). You can use a PID, image name, service name, or window title or target multiple images using a filter for CPU time, memory usage, or status ("Not Responding," for instance).

 *Note: There may be circumstances when you need to run Explorer with administrative privileges. To do this, open a command prompt using **Run as administrator**. Use `taskkill /f /im explorer.exe` to terminate the existing **Explorer** process, then run `explorer.exe` again from the same command prompt.*

Note: *On a network, you can use* `taskkill` *and* `tasklist` *to manage processes on a remote computer using the* `/s` *switch to identify the remote host (by IP address or host name) and the* `/u` *and* `/p` *switches to specify credentials (user name and password).*

HOW TO INSTALL AND MANAGE WINDOWS APPLICATIONS

Follow these procedures to install and manage Windows applications.

CONFIGURE DEFAULT PROGRAMS IN WINDOWS

To configure default programs:

1. Open **Control Panel**.
2. Select **Programs**.
3. Select **Default Programs**.
4. Select **Set your default programs**.
5. Under **Choose default apps**, select an app name then select the app to use for the app category.
6. If desired, in **Control Panel→Programs→Default Programs**, select **Associate a file type or protocol with a program** or on the **Default apps** page in **Windows Settings**, select **Choose default apps by file type** or **Choose default apps by protocol** or **Set defaults by app**. Select the current app to display a list of choices or select **Choose a default** if no app is currently associated with a file type.

CONFIGURE COMPATIBILITY MODE IN WINDOWS

To configure compatibility mode:

1. In **File Explorer**, right-click a program executable file and select **Properties**.
2. In the properties dialog box for the program file, select the **Compatibility** tab.
3. Check **Run this program in compatibility mode for** and then select the OS version to make the program compatible with.
4. If necessary, check options under **Settings**.
5. If desired, select the **Run compatibility troubleshooter** to be guided through configuring compatibility settings.
6. Select **OK** after making changes.
7. Test the application to verify that the compatibility configuration works with the program. If necessary, try other settings.

MANAGE SERVICES IN COMPUTER MANAGEMENT CONSOLE

To manage services in the Computer Management console:

1. Right-click the **Start** menu and select **Computer Management**.
2. Expand **Services and Applications** in the left pane, then select **Services**.

 Note: *Alternatively, you can run the* **services.msc** *command.*

3. Double-click the desired service.
4. If necessary, change the **Startup type**.
5. If necessary, select one of the buttons:
   - **Start**
   - **Stop**
   - **Pause**
   - **Resume**

6. Select **OK**.

USE WINDOWS MANAGEMENT TOOLS

To use Windows management tools:

1. Use Task Manager to:
- Manage applications.
- Manage processes.
- Manage services.
- Manage performance.
- Manage networking.
- Manage users.

2. To end an unresponsive task:

  a. Open **Task Manager**.
  b. Select the **Processes** tab.
  c. Right-click the unresponsive application.
  d. Select **End task**.

3. Use `tasklist` to show running processes and related information.

4. Use `taskkill` with information gathered from `tasklist` to end a process.

Topic B

Manage Windows Performance

EXAM OBJECTIVES COVERED
1002-1.5 Given a scenario, use Microsoft operating system features and tools.
1002-1.6 Given a scenario, use Microsoft Windows Control Panel utilities.

Diagnosing the cause of slow performance can be a difficult and frustrating task. You need to be able to use the system configuration and monitoring/logging tools to capture utilization of system components over time.

SYSTEM PROPERTIES

You can obtain a brief overview of some key system information from the **System Properties** applet. You can access this via **Control Panel** or by right-clicking the **Computer/This PC** object and selecting **Properties**. The **System Properties** home page displays summary information about the computer, including the processor type and installed RAM, plus the Windows edition, product key, and activation status. The system settings include network identification and domain membership, hardware settings and configuration, user profiles, and performance and recovery options. Select the **Tasks** or **Advanced system settings** links to access the configuration dialog boxes.

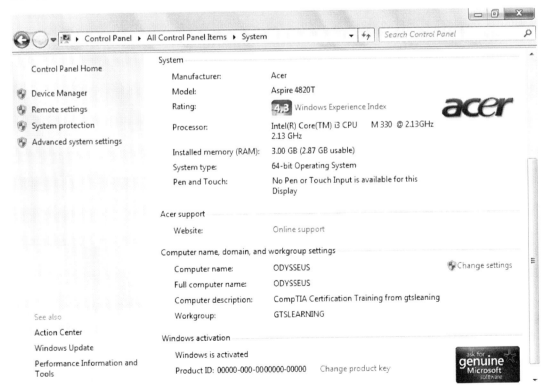

Windows 7 system properties. (Screenshot used with permission from Microsoft.)

In Windows 10, the **System** applet shown in the previous graphic is still available, though the **Performance Information** tool has been discontinued, but there is also a system category within Windows **Settings**. Some of the system information is available on the **About** page.

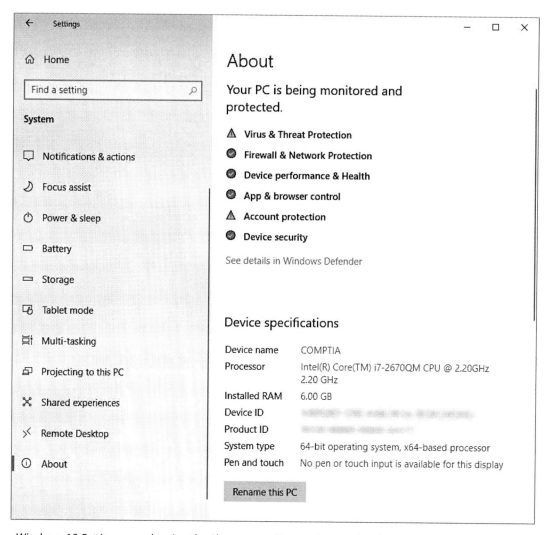

Windows 10 Settings app showing the About page. (Screenshot used with permission from Microsoft.)

ADVANCED SYSTEM PROPERTIES

From the **System** applet, clicking **Advanced system settings** opens the **System Properties** dialog box. This allows you to configure remote settings, system protection, and advanced settings.

REMOTE SETTINGS

The **Remote Settings** tab enables (or disables) connections to the local PC from another PC on the network. There are two types of remote connection:

- **Remote Assistance** means that the local user sends a request to another user on a remote computer inviting them to view or control their desktop.
- **Remote Desktop** means that the remote user can initiate a connection at any time. The remote user needs to sign on to the local machine using an authorized account (configured via this dialog box).

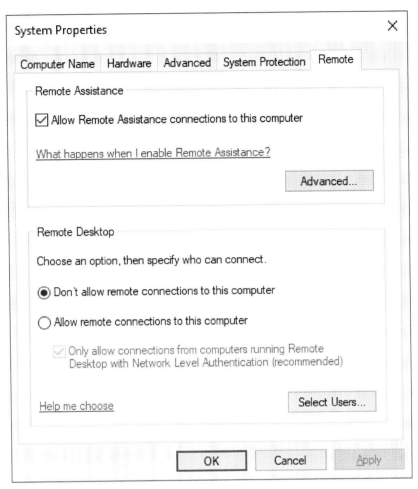

System Properties dialog box—Remote Settings tab in Windows 10. (Screenshot used with permission from Microsoft.)

SYSTEM PROTECTION

The **System Protection** tab provides options for configuring the **System Restore** feature. **System Restore** creates configuration backups. If there are changes or file corruptions that damage information in the registry or you want to reverse changes made when installing an application or device driver, you can use **System Restore** to reset the system configuration to an earlier point in time. Click **Configure** to enable or disable **System Protection** and set how much disk space the tool is allowed to use.

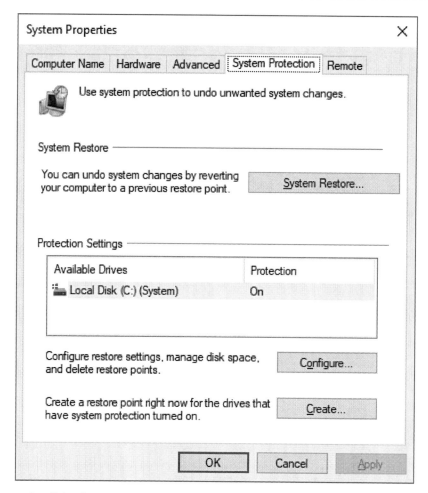

System Properties dialog box—System Protection tab in Windows 10. (Screenshot used with permission from Microsoft.)

ADVANCED SETTINGS

Upgrading the hardware resources on a system is fine if you have the budget and you can find compatible parts, but the rapid changes in computer technology mean that PCs and laptops can be very quickly left behind in terms of upgrade potential. There are various tweaks that can be made to improve the performance of an older system without specifying new hardware. The options on the **Advanced** tab include the following:

- Performance options, including:
    - Configure desktop visual effects for best appearance or best performance.
    - Virtual Memory (paging).
    - Foreground/Background processing priority (a desktop PC should always be left optimized for programs).
- Startup and recovery options.
- Environment variables.
- User Profiles.

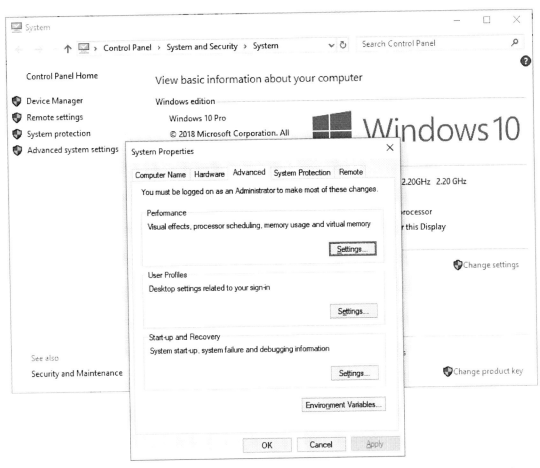

System Properties dialog box—Advanced tab in Windows 10. (Screenshot used with permission from Microsoft.)

VIRTUAL MEMORY

Using **virtual memory** is a way for the computer to accomplish more than the limits of what its physical memory can perform. The computer system uses a portion of the hard disk as if it was physical RAM. When all physical memory is filled, the OS can transfer some of the least-recently used data from memory to a file on the hard disk called the **pagefile**, thereby freeing up an equivalent amount of space in the memory chips for other purposes. When the original data is needed again, the next least-recently used data is moved out of RAM onto the hard drive to make room to reimport the needed data.

In Windows systems, the **Virtual Memory Manager (VMM)** manages the memory mappings and assignments .Running out of memory would mean that a process might not be able to start or could crash.

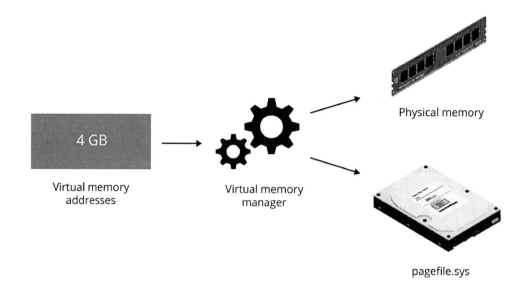

Virtual memory. (Image © 123RF.com.)

Virtual memory is not nearly as fast as actual memory. Modern DDRx SDRAM DIMMs read/write speeds are measured in nanoseconds, whereas hard drive seek, read, and write times are measured in milliseconds. If your computer is frequently exceeding its physical RAM and having to resort to using a pagefile on disk, adding more physical RAM may be the most economical way of effecting a noticeable change in performance.

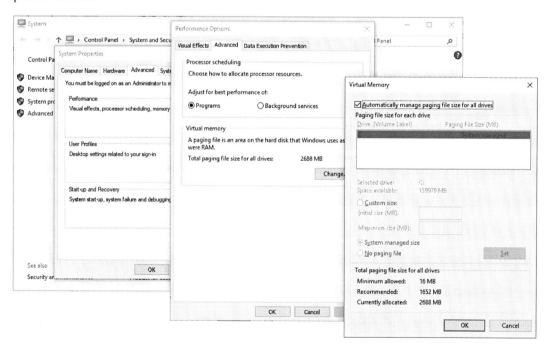

Configuring virtual memory in Windows 10. (Screenshot used with permission from Microsoft.)

When tuning the pagefile, keep the following in mind:

- Windows can manage the pagefile and set an appropriate level. There is very little point in setting custom values unless you have a specific performance goal or requirement in mind.

- Each physical disk can have a pagefile of its own. This will allow Windows, depending on hardware, to concurrently access the paging files and, therefore, increase performance.
- The pagefile does not have to use contiguous disk space, although performance can be further enhanced if it does. To ensure that the pagefile uses contiguous space, you will need to defragment your disk then set the maximum and minimum sizes of the pagefile to the same value.

 Note: *If the pagefile is a fixed size but too small, Windows might run out of memory, which could cause programs to crash. Also, if the pagefile is too small, the system may not be able to generate a complete crash dump of the memory contents, which will hamper efforts to troubleshoot system errors.*

For more information on pagefile tuning considerations, view Microsoft's Knowledge Base article (**support.microsoft.com/en-us/help/2860880/how-to-determine-the-appropriate-page-file-size-for-64-bit-versions-of**).

WINDOWS PERFORMANCE MANAGEMENT TOOLS

Windows provides numerous Administrative Tools to monitor system performance.

- **Task Manager**—as you have seen, you can use the **Performance** tab in **Task Manager** to monitor utilization statistics in real time.
- **Resource Monitor**—shows an enhanced version of the sort of snapshot monitoring provided by **Task Manager**. You can see graphs of resource performance along with key statistics, such as threads started by a process or hard page faults/second. Continually rising numbers of either of these can indicate a problem.
- **Reliability Monitor**—displays a log of "system stability" events, so you can see at a glance whether a particular application has stopped responding frequently.
- **Performance Monitor**—configure detailed reports on different system statistics and log performance over time.

PERFORMANCE MONITOR

Windows **Performance Monitor** can be used to provide real-time charts of system resources or can be used to log information to a file for long-term analysis. You can run the tool from the **Administrative Tools** folder or **Computer Management**; you can also run `perfmon.exe`.

By monitoring different resources at different times of the day, you can detect bottlenecks in a system that are causing problems. It may be that a particular application starts freezing for longer and longer periods. This could be caused by a number of things. Perhaps it is that the processor is too slow, which would cause the requests to take longer; perhaps the hard disk is too slow, which would mean that it takes too long for the computer to open and save files; perhaps the application uses a network link that has become faulty or congested.

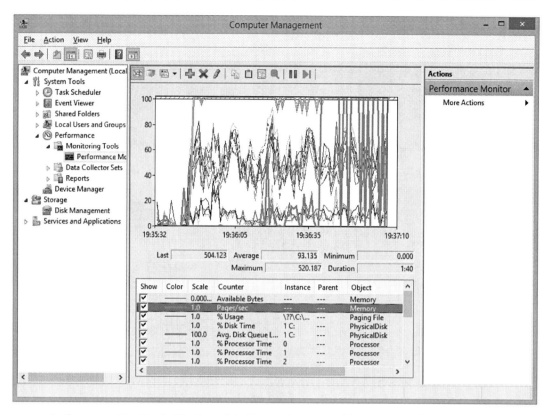

Performance Monitor in Windows 8.1. (Screenshot used with permission from Microsoft.)

The performance of the computer could be increased by upgrading any or all of these components, but **Performance Monitor** will help you decide which is critical.

ADDING OBJECTS, COUNTERS, AND INSTANCES

Resources, such as memory and disk, are collected into **objects**. Objects have counters, representing different performance statistics, and there can be multiple instances of the same type of object. For example, disk performance can be measured using the **Physical Disk Object**, and a useful counter is the **Average Queue Length**. If there are two disks, three instances of this object can be viewed: disk 0, disk 1, and disks Total.

Some of the most commonly used counters are listed here:

Object	Counter	Description
Processor	% Processor Time	The percentage of time that the processor is executing a non-idle thread. In general terms, this should be low. If it is greater than 85% for a sustained period, you may have a processor bottleneck.

Object	Counter	Description
	% Privileged Time % User Time	If overall processor time is very high (over 85% for sustained periods), it can be helpful to compare these. Privileged time represents system processes, whereas user time is software applications. If privileged time is much higher, it is likely that the CPU is underpowered (it can barely run Windows core processes efficiently).
Physical Disk	% Disk Time	The percentage of elapsed time that the selected disk drive is busy servicing read or write requests. This is a good overall indicator of how busy the disk is. Again, if the average exceeds 85% for a sustained period, you may have a disk problem.
	Average Disk Queue Length	The number of requests outstanding on the disk at the time the performance data is collected. Taken with the preceding counter, this gives a better indicator of disk problems. For example, if the disk queue length is increasing and disk time is high, then you have a disk problem.
Memory	Available Bytes	The amount of memory available—this should not be below about 10% of total system RAM. If available bytes falls continuously, there could be a memory leak (that is, a process that allocates memory but does not release it again).

Object	Counter	Description
	Pages/sec	The number of pages read from or written to disk to resolve hard page faults. This means your system is using the paging file. Nothing wrong as long as this is not excessive (averaging above about 50). You probably also want to check the paging file's usage by viewing the paging object itself.
Paging File	% Usage	The amount of the pagefile instance in use in percent. If your paging file is currently 1000 MB on the disk and this figure averages 50%, then it means you might benefit from adding memory (about 500 MB, in fact). Don't forget that if your system pages excessively, then disk performance will suffer—paging is disk intensive.

Notice that it is not always immediately apparent which component is causing a problem. Many counters are interrelated and must be viewed with other counters in mind. For instance, if your system memory is low, then the disk will likely be slow because of excessive paging.

LOGGING PERFORMANCE

In **Performance Monitor**, you can create log files, referred to as **Data Collector Sets**, to record information for viewing at a later date. You can generate a library of performance measurements taken at different times of the day, week, or even year. This information can provide a system baseline and then be used to give a longer-term view of system performance. There are two types of logs: counter and trace:

- **Counter logs** allow you to collect statistics about resources, such as memory, disk, and processor. These can be used to determine system health and performance.
- **Trace logs** can collect statistics about services, providing you with detailed reports about resource behavior. In essence, trace logs provide extensions to the Event Viewer, logging data that would otherwise be inaccessible.

Saved log files can be loaded into **Performance Monitor** from the **Reports** folder for analysis or exported to other programs.

HOW TO MANAGE WINDOWS PERFORMANCE

Follow these procedures to manage Windows performance.

MANAGE VIRTUAL MEMORY

To manage virtual memory

1. Open the **System Properties** dialog box.

2. Select the **Advanced** tab.
3. In the **Performance** panel, select the **Settings** button.
4. From the **Performance** dialog box, select the **Advanced** tab and then select the **Change** button.

USING PERFORMANCE MONITOR

To use **Performance Monitor** to monitor Windows performance:

1. Open **Performance Monitor** using one of these methods:
   - **Administrative Tools** folder on the **Start** menu.
   - **Computer Management**.
   - Run `perfmon.exe`.
2. Add counters for monitoring.
   a. Select the **Add** button to open the **Add Counters** dialog box.
   b. Specify the computer you want to monitor.
   c. In the list of counter categories, select the expand button to show the available counters. For instance, the **Processor Performance** category has three counters available.
   d. Select a counter and select the **Add** button.
   e. If necessary, in the **Instances of selected object** list box, select an instance and select **Add**.
   f. When you have selected all the counters you want, select **OK**.

Topic C
Troubleshoot Windows

EXAM OBJECTIVES COVERED
1002-1.4 Given a scenario, use appropriate Microsoft command-line tools.
1002-1.5 Given a scenario, use Microsoft operating system features and tools.
1002-3.1 Given a scenario, troubleshoot Microsoft Windows OS problems.

An operating system like Windows provides a lot of information to assist troubleshooting, through configuration utilities and event logs. Plenty of tools are available to diagnose and recover from different kinds of problems. In this topic, you will learn which tools and techniques can help to resolve some of the common Windows OS problem symptoms.

EVENT VIEWER

When a problem is related to Windows or a software application rather than the computer hardware, there will often be an error message associated with the problem. This makes troubleshooting simpler as you may only need to find out what the error message means using product documentation, the Microsoft Knowledge Base, or useful websites and newsgroups.

The **Event Viewer** (`eventvwr.msc`) is a management console snap-in for viewing and managing system logs. It can also be accessed via **Computer Management** or **Administrative Tools**. The default page shows a summary of system status, with recent error and warning events collected for viewing.

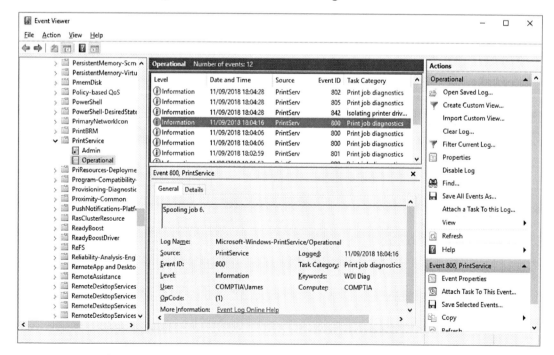

Windows 10 Event Viewer. (Screenshot used with permission from Microsoft.)

The three-part pane view lets you see the details of the selected event in the bottom pane without having to open a separate dialog box. The third pane contains useful tools for opening log files, filtering, creating a task from an event, and so on.

DEFAULT LOG FILES

The principal Windows log files are shown in this table.

Log File	Description
System Log	Contains information about service load failures, hardware conflicts, driver load failures, and so on.
Security Log	This log holds the audit data for the system.
Application Log	Contains information regarding application errors.
Setup	Records events generated during installation.

The files (**application.evtx**, **security.evtx**, **system.evtx**, and **setup.evtx**) are stored (by default) in the **%SystemRoot%\System32\Winevt\Logs** folder.

 Note: You can also log boot events by using `msconfig`*. This boot log file is saved to* **%SystemRoot%\ntbtlog.txt***. It is not shown in* **Event Viewer***, though.*

Each log file has a default maximum size (usually about 20 MB), but you can change this by selecting **Properties** on the appropriate log. This option also allows the overwrite option to be set either as overwrite, do not overwrite, or archive (close the current file and start a new one).

 Note: Be careful about preserving logs. Many computers have ample free disk space, but archive logs can grow very large if left unmonitored.

There are many other logs, stored under the **Applications and Services Logs** node. You would investigate these when troubleshooting a particular Windows service or third-party application.

EVENT TYPES

The **Event Viewer** displays each line or item in the source log file as an event and categorizes each event. The types of events are shown here.

Event	Description
Information	Significant events that describe successful operations, such as a driver or service starting or a document printing.
Warning	Events that may indicate future problems, such as when the system runs low on disk space.
Error	Significant problems, such as service failures and device conflicts.
Critical	An unrecoverable error that made the application or Windows close unexpectedly.

Event	Description
Successful Audit	Security access attempts that were successful.
Failure Audit	Security access attempts that were unsuccessful. This may indicate a possible security breach or simply a user mistyping a password.

More information for each event can be displayed by double-clicking the event in question. This displays a screen that contains the date and time of the event, the user and computer name, an event ID, source, type, and category, and a description of the event and the data in bytes and words.

THE SYSTEM CONFIGURATION UTILITY

The **System Configuration Utility** (`msconfig`) is used to modify various settings and files that affect the way the computer boots and loads Windows.

 Note: *The* `msconfig` *tool is frequently used to test various configurations for diagnostic purposes, rather than to permanently make configuration changes. Following diagnostic testing, permanent changes would typically be made with more appropriate tools, such as* **Services**, *to change the startup settings of various system services.*

GENERAL TAB
The **General** tab allows you to configure the startup mode, choosing between **Normal**, **Diagnostic**, and a **Selective** startup, where each portion of the boot sequence can be selected.

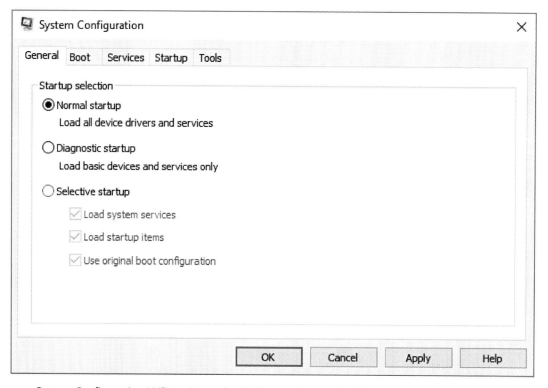

System Configuration Utility—General tab. (Screenshot used with permission from Microsoft.)

BOOT TAB

The **Boot** tab lets you configure basic settings in the **Boot Configuration Data (BCD)** store.

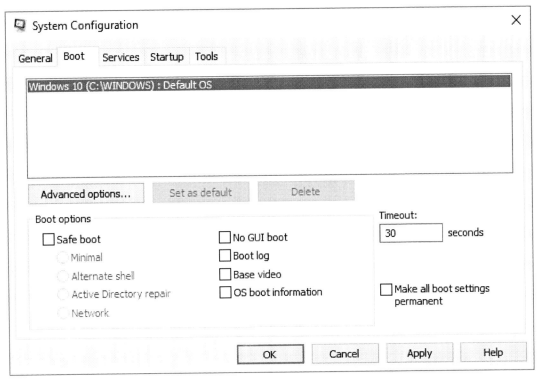

System Configuration Utility—Boot tab. (Screenshot used with permission from Microsoft.)

You can change the default OS, add boot options, such as Safe boot, with minimal drivers and services, and set the timeout value—the duration for which the boot options menu is displayed. To add boot paths you have to use the `bcdedit` command.

 *Note: If you are troubleshooting a system that keeps using Safe boot or boots to a command prompt, check that one of the previous options has not been made permanent in **System Configuration**.*

SERVICES TAB

The **Services** tab lets you choose specifically which services are configured to run at startup. The date that a service was disabled is also shown, to make troubleshooting easier.

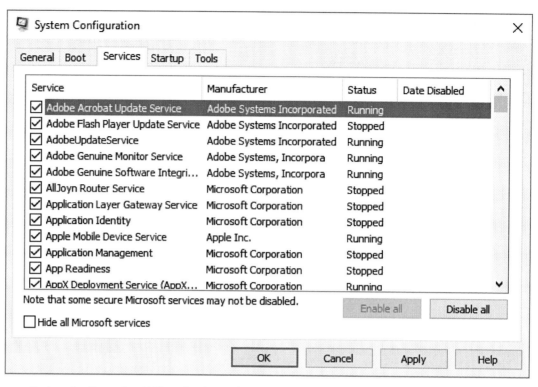

System Configuration Utility—Services tab. (Screenshot used with permission from Microsoft.)

STARTUP TAB

In Windows 7, the **Startup** tab controls the shortcuts that have been placed in the **Startup** folder of the **Start Menu** and startup items that have been written to the registry.

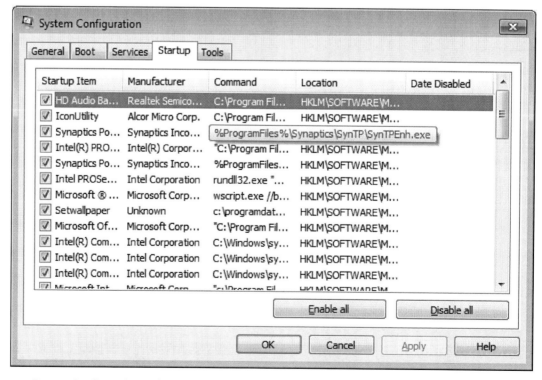

System Configuration Utility—Startup tab (Windows 7). (Screenshot used with permission from Microsoft.)

The **Start Menu** is built from a template containing settings for all users plus shortcuts customized for the current user profile. The template is stored in **C:\ProgramData \Microsoft\Windows\Start Menu\Programs** and the user-specific shortcuts are in **C: \Users\UserName\AppData\Roaming\Microsoft\Windows\Start Menu**.

 Note: If the computer's performance is sluggish, try disabling startup items, as long as they are not providing key services, such as virus protection.

Windows 8 and Windows 10 use **Task Manager** as the means of disabling startup items.

TOOLS TAB

The **Tools** tab contains shortcuts to various administrative utilities including System Information, Configuring UAC, Registry Editor, and so on.

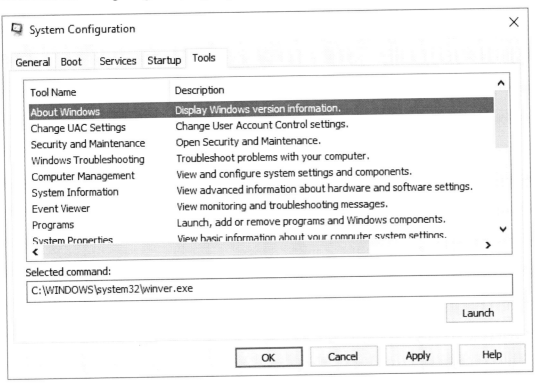

System Configuration Utility—Tools tab. (Screenshot used with permission from Microsoft.)

TROUBLESHOOTING TIPS FOR WINDOWS SYSTEM ISSUES

This section discusses some typical Windows error messages and conditions.

SLOW SYSTEM PERFORMANCE

Slow system performance can have many causes. Use **Task Manager** to determine if any resources are at 90-100% utilization and then note which process is most active. You may need to identify a particular Windows service running within a `svchost.exe` process (use the PID). **Windows Update/Installer**, the Superfetch/Prefetch caching engine, and **Windows Defender** (or third-party security software) are often the culprits.

1. Wait for these processes to complete—if there is a mix of CPU, memory, and disk activity, then the process is probably operating normally, if slowly. If there is no disk activity or conversely if disk activity does not drop from 100%, the process could have stalled.

2. If the process or system continues to be unresponsive, you can either restart the service or kill the task process.
3. If killing the process doesn't restore system performance, try restarting the computer (reboot). The problem could be transitory and might not reoccur.
4. If the service or process becomes unresponsive again after restarting, disable it and check with the software vendor for any known problems.

If you can't identify any overutilization, consider the following troubleshooting techniques and solutions:

- Apply updates—check for any missing Windows and application updates and install the latest drivers for hardware devices.
- Defragment the hard drive—running defrag regularly on a Hard Disk Drive (HDD) improves file I/O by putting files into contiguous clusters. Also make sure there is sufficient free disk space.
- Power management issues—if the user has been closing sessions using sleep or hibernate, try restarting the computer. Verify that the system is not operating in a power-saving mode (CPU throttling).
- Check for underpowered components—check resource utilization using **Task Manager**, **Resource Monitor**, or (for more extended periods) **Performance Monitor**. If CPU, system memory, disk, or network resources are continually stretched then the system will have to be upgraded.
- Disable application startup—use the **System Configuration Utility** (`msconfig`) or **Task Manager** to prevent unnecessary services and programs from running at startup. If you need to run the services, consider setting them to delayed startup or manual startup to avoid slowing down boot times too much.
- Disable Windows services/applications—if a service is not required and is causing problems, you can set it to Disabled to prevent it from being started. Note that some security-critical services (such as Windows Update) can be re-enabled automatically by the OS.
- Security scan—scan the computer for viruses and other malware.
- Check the configuration of anti-virus software—while necessary to keep users as safe as possible from malware, A-V software can have a very harmful effect on performance. Try disabling scanning temporarily to test whether performance improves. Make sure the software is configured to exclude Windows system files it shouldn't scan and configure any exceptions for software applications recommended by the vendor. These typically include database files and the image files used for virtual hard disks.

SERVICE FAILS TO START

If you see a message such as **One or more services failed to start** during the Windows load sequence, check **Event Viewer** and/or the **Services** snap-in to identify which service has failed. Troubleshooting services can be complex, but bear the following general advice in mind:

- Try to start the service manually—as most computers run a lot of services at startup, some can sometimes become "stuck." If a service is not required "immediately," it may help to set it to delayed start.
- Services depend on account permissions to run—make sure that the service has sufficient privileges. Check that the service is associated with a valid user or system account and that the password configured for the account is correct.
- Some services depend on other services to run—verify that disabling one service has not inadvertently affected others.
- If a core Windows service is affected, check system files and scan the disk for errors and malware.
- If an application service is affected, try reinstalling the application.

- You may be able to use **regsvr32** to re-register the software component (Dynamic Link Library [DLL]) that the service relies upon. In 64-bit versions of Windows, there are two versions of **regsvr32**. The 64-bit version (located in **%SystemRoot% \System32\regsvr32.exe**) is called by default and used with 64-bit DLLs. The 32-bit version is in **%SystemRoot%\SysWOW64\regsvr32**. Run this version to re-register 32-bit DLLs.
- Check whether the service is supposed to run—faulty software uninstall routines can leave "orphan" registry entries and startup shortcuts. Use the **System Configuration Utility** (**msconfig**) or **Registry Editor** (`regedit`) to look for orphaned items.

TROUBLESHOOTING TIPS FOR APPLICATION ISSUES

As well as system-wide issues, some errors may be isolated to a particular application or file type.

APPLICATION CRASHES

If an application crashes, the first priority is to try to preserve any data that was being processed. Users should be trained to save regularly, but modern suites such as Microsoft Office are configured to save recovery files regularly, minimizing the chance of data loss.

Try to give the process time to become responsive again and try to establish if you need to try to recover data from temporary files or folders. When you have done all you can to preserve data, kill the task process. If the application crashes continually, check the event logs for any possible causes. Try to identify whether the cause lies in processing a particular data file or not.

If you cannot identify a specific cause of a problem, the generic solution to this type of problem is to uninstall then reinstall. Sometimes the Windows installer fails to remove every file and registry setting; if this is the case, then following manual uninstall instructions might help.

An uninstall followed by a reinstall can be a lengthy process. Many installers offer a **Repair** option (accessed via **Programs and Features**).

PRINTING ISSUES

Printing issues can involve the printer hardware, network connectivity, or Windows settings. If you can discount hardware and network problems, make the following checks in Windows:

1. Use the printer's property dialog box to try printing a test page. If this is successful, there must be an application or file-specific problem.
2. Open the print queue and check for stalled print jobs.
3. Restart the print spooler service.
4. Check for any driver updates or known issues.
5. Check permissions configured on the printer.
6. Check for disk problems on the partition hosting the spool folder.

BLUE SCREENS AND SPONTANEOUS SHUTDOWNS

A **Blue Screen of Death (BSoD)** displays a Windows **STOP** error. A **STOP** error is one that causes Windows to halt. **STOP** errors can occur when Windows loads or while it is running. Most BSoDs, especially those that occur during startup, are caused by faulty hardware or hardware drivers.

- Use **System Restore**, or (if you can boot to **Safe Mode**), **Rollback Driver** to restore the system to a working state.

- Remove a recently added hardware device or uninstall a recently installed program.
- Check seating of hardware components and cables.
- Run hardware diagnostics, `chkdsk`, and scan for malware.
- Make a note of the stop error code (which will be in the form: Stop: 0x0...) and search the Microsoft Knowledge Base (**support.microsoft.com/search**) for known fixes and troubleshooting tips. The various newsgroups accessible from this site offer another valuable source of assistance.

```
A problem has been detected and windows has been shut down to prevent damage
to your computer.

A process or thread crucial to system operation has unexpectedly exited or been
terminated.

If this is the first time you've seen this stop error screen,
restart your computer. If this screen appears again, follow
these steps:

Check to make sure any new hardware or software is properly installed.
If this is a new installation, ask your hardware or software manufacturer
for any windows updates you might need.

If problems continue, disable or remove any newly installed hardware
or software. Disable BIOS memory options such as caching or shadowing.
If you need to use Safe Mode to remove or disable components, restart
your computer, press F8 to select Advanced Startup Options, and then
select Safe Mode.

Technical information:

*** STOP: 0x000000F4 (0x0000000000000003,0xFFFFFA800275F060,0xFFFFFA800275F340,0
xFFFFF80002984DB0)



Collecting data for crash dump ...
Initializing disk for crash dump ...
Beginning dump of physical memory.
Dumping physical memory to disk:  10
```

Blue Screen (of Death or BSoD). (Screenshot used with permission from Microsoft.)

 Note: *If the system autorestarts after a blue screen and you cannot read the error, press* **F8** *after POST to open the* **Advanced Options** *menu and select the* **Disable automatic restarts** *option. This option can also be set from* **Advanced System Properties→Startup and Recovery Settings***.*

If a system halts without any sort of error message, there is likely to be a power problem or a problem with the CPU.

TROUBLESHOOTING TIPS FOR FILE AND MEMORY CORRUPTION

Problems with slow performance, application crashes, and blue screens could be caused by some sort of file corruption occurring on the disk or in system memory. You can use the following tools to verify the integrity of system files and memory hardware.

SYSTEM FILE CHECKER

Windows comes with a **Windows Resource Protection** mechanism to prevent damage to or malicious use of system files and registry keys and files.

The **System File Checker** utility (sfc) provides a manual interface for verifying system files and restoring them from cache if they are found to be corrupt or damaged. System files (and shared program files) are maintained and version controlled in the **WINSxS** system folder. This means that the product media is not called upon, but the **WINSxS** folder can consume quite a lot of disk space.

The program can be used from a command line (as Administrator) in the following modes:

- sfc /scannow—runs a scan immediately.
- sfc /scanonce—schedules a scan when the computer is next restarted.
- sfc /scanboot—schedules scans whenever the PC boots.

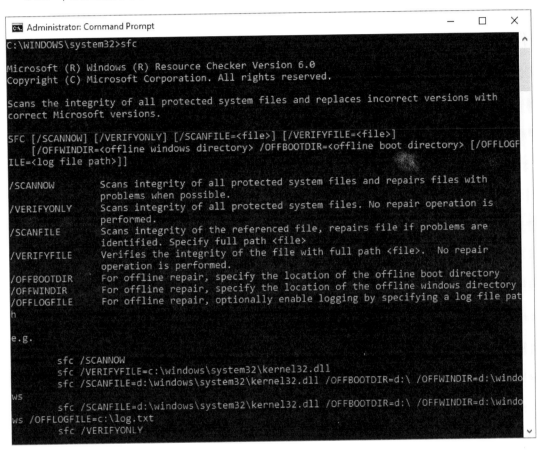

System File Checker utility. (Screenshot used with permission from Microsoft.)

WINDOWS MEMORY DIAGNOSTICS

Windows includes a **Windows Memory Diagnostics** tool to test memory chips for errors. You can either run the tool from **Administrative Tools** or boot to **Windows Preinstallation/Recovery Environment** and select **Windows Memory Diagnostic**. Select **Restart now** and check for problems. The computer will restart and run the test. Press **F1** if you want to configure test options.

If errors are found, first check that all the memory modules are correctly seated. Remove all the memory modules but one and retest. You should be able to identify the faulty board by a process of elimination. If a known-good board is reported faulty, the problem is likely to lie in the motherboard.

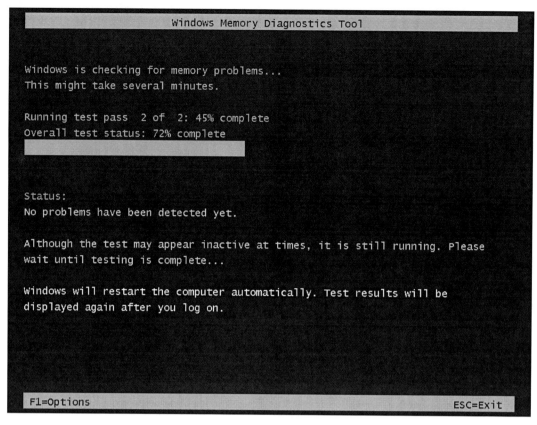

Windows Memory Diagnostics. (Screenshot used with permission from Microsoft.)

TROUBLESHOOTING TIPS FOR BOOT PROBLEMS

Assuming there is no underlying hardware issue, the general technique for troubleshooting boot problems is to determine the failure point, and therefore the missing or corrupt file. This can then be replaced, either from the source files or using some sort of recovery disk.

BOOT PROCESS

When a computer starts, the firmware runs a **Power On Self Test (POST)** to verify that the system components are present and functioning correctly. It then identifies a boot device and passes control to the operating system's boot loader process.

With a legacy BIOS, the firmware scans the disk identified as the boot device and reads the **Master Boot Record (MBR)** in the first sector of the disk. The MBR identifies the **boot sector** or **Volume Boot Record (VBR)** for the partition marked as active. The VBR loads the boot manager, which for Windows is **bootmgr.exe**. The boot manager reads information from the **Boot Configuration Data (BCD)** file, which identifies operating systems installed on the computer. bootmgr and the BCD are normally installed to a hidden **System Reserved** partition. This partition can be formatted as either FAT32 or NTFS.

Assuming there is only a single Windows installation, the boot manager loads the Windows boot loader **winload.exe** in the system root folder.

 Note: If there is more than one OS installation, the boot manager shows a boot menu allowing the user to select the installation to boot.

winload then continues the Windows boot process by loading the kernel (**ntoskrnl.exe**), the Hardware Abstraction Layer (**hal.dll**), and boot device drivers.

Control is then passed to the kernel, which initializes and starts loading the required processes. When complete, the **winlogon** process waits for the user to authenticate.

With an EFI boot, the initial part of the boot process is different. Following POST, the firmware reads the **GUID Partition Table (GPT)** on the boot device.

The GPT identifies the EFI System Partition, which is always formatted with FAT. The EFI system partition contains the **bootmgr.efi** boot manager and the BCD. In point-of-fact, Windows uses its own implementation of the boot manager called **bootmgfw.efi** (**bootmgr.efi** is configured to time out quickly and **bootmgfw.efi** loads instead). Each Windows installation has a subfolder under **\EFI\Microsoft** that contains a BCD and **bootmgfw.efi**.

bootmgfw.efi reads the BCD to identify whether to show a boot menu and for the location of **winload.efi**. From this point, the Windows boot loader continues the boot process by loading the kernel, as described previously.

FAILURE TO BOOT/INVALID BOOT DISK

If the system firmware returns an error message such as **No boot device found** or **Invalid boot disk**, then the system has completely failed to boot. The most common cause of this error used to be leaving a floppy disk in the drive on a restart. A modern cause is for the system firmware to be set to use USB for boot. Check for any removable disks and change the boot device priority/boot order if necessary. If this message occurs when booting from a hard disk or SSD, check the connections to the drive. If the error is transitory (for example, if the message occurs a few times then the PC starts to boot OK), it could be a sign that the hard disk is failing. On an older system, it could be that the system firmware is having trouble detecting the drive.

NO OS FOUND

An **OS missing** type message can appear when a disk drive is identified as the boot device but does not report the location of the OS loader. This could indicate a faulty disk, so try running disk diagnostics (if available) then use a recovery option to run `chkdsk`.

If the disk cannot be detected, enter system setup and try modifying settings (or even resetting the default settings). If the disk's presence is reported by the system firmware but Windows still will not boot, use a startup repair tool to open a recovery mode command prompt and use the `bootrec` tool to try to repair the drive's boot information.

1. Enter `bootrec /fixmbr` to attempt repair of the MBR.
2. Enter `bootrec /fixboot` to attempt repair of the boot sector.
3. Enter `bootrec /rebuildbcd` to add missing Windows installations to the Boot Configuration Database (BCD).

You could also use `diskpart` to ensure that the system partition is marked as active and that no other partitions have been marked as active.

GRAPHICAL INTERFACE FAILS TO LOAD/BLACK SCREEN

If Windows appears to boot but does not display the logon dialog box or does not load the desktop following logon, the likely causes are malware infection or corruption of drivers or other system files. If the system will boot to a GUI in Safe Mode, then replace the graphics adapter driver. If the system will not boot to a GUI at all, then the Windows installation will probably have to be repaired or recovered from backup. It is also possible that the boot configuration has been changed through `msconfig` and just needs to be set back.

Windows is also sporadically prone to black screen issues, where nothing appears on the screen. This will often occur during update installs, where the best course of action is to give the system time to complete the update. Look for signs of continuing disk activity and spinning dots appearing on the screen. If the system does not recover from a black screen, then try searching for any currently known issues on support and troubleshooting sites (**support.microsoft.com/en-ph/help/14106/windows-10-troubleshoot-black-screen-problems**). You can use the key sequence **Windows+Ctrl+Shift+B** to test whether the system is responsive. There should be a beep and the display may reinitialize.

If the problem occurs frequently, use `sfc` to verify system file integrity and check video drivers.

SLOW BOOT/SLOW PROFILE LOAD

If Windows does boot, but only very slowly, you need to try to identify what is happening to slow the process down. You can enable verbose status messages during the Windows load sequence by configuring a system policy or applying a registry setting. In Windows 7, enable **Verbose vs normal status messages** or in Windows 8/10, enable **Display highly detailed status messages**.

Delays affecting the system prior to logon are caused by loading drivers and services. Quite often the culprit will be some type of network service or configuration not working optimally, but there could be some sort of file corruption, too.

If the system is slow to load the desktop following logon, the issue could be a corrupt user profile. The registry settings file **ntuser.dat** is particularly prone to this. Rebuilding a local user profile means creating a new account and then copying files from the old, corrupt profile to the new one, but excluding the following files:

- **Ntuser.dat**
- **Ntuser.dat.log**
- **Ntuser.ini**

SAFE BOOT

Safe Mode loads only basic drivers and services required to start the system. This is a useful troubleshooting mode as it isolates reliability or performance problems to add-in drivers or application services and rules out having to fully reinstall Windows. It may also be a means of running analysis and recovery tools, such as `chkdsk`, **System Restore**, or anti-virus utilities.

Safe Mode defaults to SVGA resolution (800x600). Higher resolutions may be available if the basic driver supports them.

You can boot to Safe Mode using the System Configuration utility, but this option is only useful if you can sign in to Windows anyway. If you cannot sign in, there are different startup repair options for Windows 7 and Windows 8/10.

WINDOWS 7 ADVANCED BOOT OPTIONS

In Windows 7, the **Advanced Boot Options** menu allows the selection of different startup modes for troubleshooting. To show the menu, press **F8** during startup—after the memory count; try tapping repeatedly if the menu doesn't get displayed.

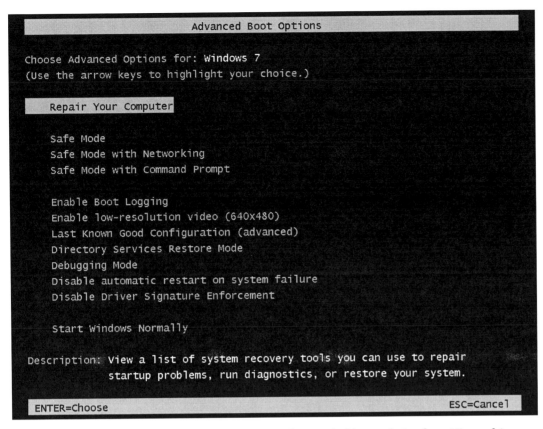

```
                    Advanced Boot Options

Choose Advanced Options for: Windows 7
(Use the arrow keys to highlight your choice.)

   Repair Your Computer

   Safe Mode
   Safe Mode with Networking
   Safe Mode with Command Prompt

   Enable Boot Logging
   Enable low-resolution video (640x480)
   Last Known Good Configuration (advanced)
   Directory Services Restore Mode
   Debugging Mode
   Disable automatic restart on system failure
   Disable Driver Signature Enforcement

   Start Windows Normally

Description: View a list of system recovery tools you can use to repair
            startup problems, run diagnostics, or restore your system.

ENTER=Choose                                          ESC=Cancel
```

Advanced Boot Options in Windows 7. (Screenshot used with permission from Microsoft.)

Apart from Safe Mode, some of the other options include:

- **Safe Mode with Networking**—includes drivers and services required to access the network.
- **Safe Mode with Command Prompt**—runs the command shell rather than Explorer.
- **Last Known Good**—boots with the last registry configuration that was used to log on successfully.

WINDOWS 8/10 STARTUP SETTINGS

In Windows 8 and Windows 10, the boot process happens too quickly to use **F8**. You can hold the **Shift** key when selecting the **Restart** option from the **Power** menu to display troubleshooting options—note that you don't have to sign in to view the power menu.

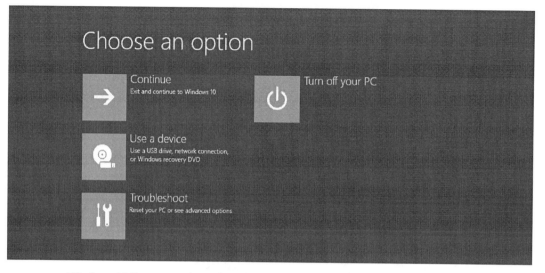

Windows 10 Startup options. (Screenshot used with permission from Microsoft.)

From the first **Choose an option** screen, select **Troubleshoot**. From the next screen, select **Advanced options**. Select **Startup Settings**, then on the next screen, select **Restart**.

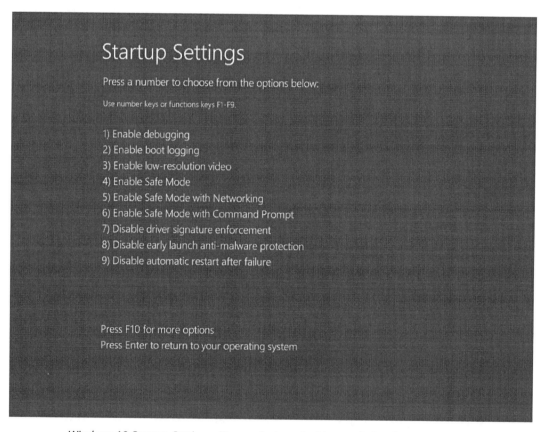

Windows 10 Startup Settings. (Screenshot used with permission from Microsoft.)

Press **F4** to select **Safe Mode**, or choose another option as necessary.

WinRE AND STARTUP REPAIR

If you cannot boot the computer from the local installation, you can try booting from the product media, a repair disk, or a recovery partition. You may have to access BIOS or UEFI setup to configure the boot device to the recovery media.

If you don't have the product media, you can make a system repair disk from Windows using the `recdisc` tool. Obviously, you need to have done this before the computer starts failing to boot or create one using a working Windows installation.

Once in the recovery environment, if the boot files are damaged, you can use the **Startup Repair** option to try to fix them. You can also launch **System Restore** or restore from an image backup from here. The last two options are to run a memory diagnostic and to drop into the **Recovery Environment** command prompt, where you could run startup recovery commands such as `diskpart`, `sfc`, `chkdsk`, `bootrec`, `bcdedit`, or `regedit` manually.

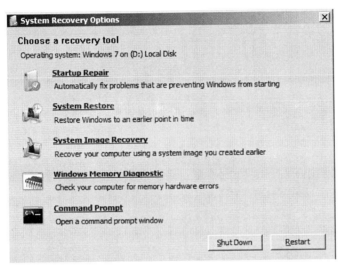

Windows 7 System Recovery Options. (Screenshot used with permission from Microsoft.)

> **Note:** *The Recovery Environment is an extended version of the Preinstallation Environment (PE) used to set up Windows in the first place.*

In Windows 8/10, as well as `recdisc`, you can use the **Recovery Media Creator** to create a USB-based repair disk and optionally include any recovery partition from the local disk. Boot using the recovery media, then from the first **Choose an option** screen, select **Troubleshoot**. From the next screen, select **Advanced options**.

Advanced options let you run system restore, reinstall from a system image backup, run the automated startup repair tool, or drop to a command prompt. On a UEFI-based install, there is also an option to reboot to the system firmware setup program. In Windows 10, you may also be able to use **See more recovery options** to revert to a previous build, following a feature update.

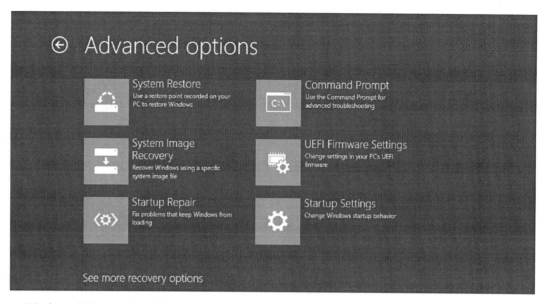

Windows 10 Startup Troubleshooting—Advanced options. (Screenshot used with permission from Microsoft.)

SYSTEM RESTORE

System Restore allows you to roll back from system configuration changes. **System Restore** allows for multiple restore points to be maintained (some are created automatically) and to roll back from changes to the whole registry and reverse program installations and updates.

 *Note: **System Restore** does not restore (or delete) user data files. Files stored in users' **Documents** folders will be preserved. Also, the contents of settings folders such as **Recent** and **Favorite** links and **Temporary Internet Files** will not be rolled back.*

CONFIGURING SYSTEM PROTECTION

The **System Protection** tab (opened via the **System Properties** applet) lets you select which disk(s) to enable for system restore and configure how much disk capacity is used. The disk must be formatted with NTFS, have a minimum of 300 MB free space, and be over 1 GB in size.

Restore points are created automatically in response to application and update installs. They are also created periodically by the **Scheduled Tasks** applet. Windows will try to create one when it detects the PC is idle if no other restore points have been created in the last 7 days. You can also create a restore point manually from this dialog box.

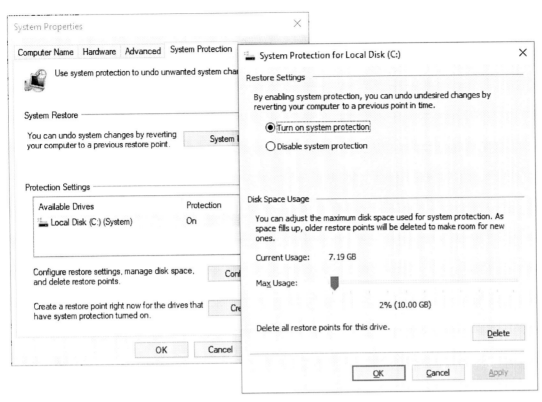

Configuring System Protection in Windows 10. (Screenshot used with permission from Microsoft.)

USING SYSTEM RESTORE

To restore the system, open the **System Restore** tool (`rstrui`), or run it by booting from the product disk or selecting the **Repair Your Computer** from the **Advanced Options** boot menu (Windows 7) or the Startup Recovery tools in Windows 8/10.

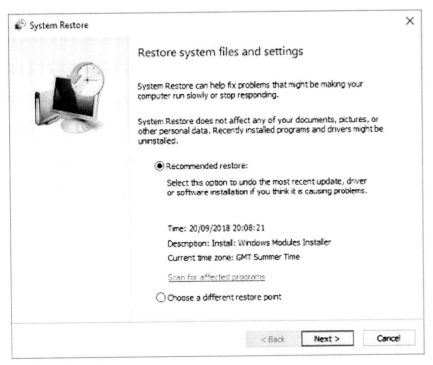

Using System Restore to apply a previous system configuration. (Screenshot used with permission from Microsoft.)

*Note: **System Restore** does not usually reset passwords (that is, passwords will remain as they were before you ran the restore tool), but **System Restore** does reset passwords to what they were at the time the restore point was created if you run it from the product disk. This can be used to recover from a forgotten administrator password (refer to **https://support.microsoft.com/en-us/help/940765/how-to-use-system-restore-to-log-on-to-windows-7-or-windows-vista-when** for more details).*

ROLL BACK UPDATES

If an update causes problems, you can try to uninstall it. You might be able to use **System Restore** to do this. Otherwise, open the **Programs and Features** applet and click **View installed updates**. Select the update then click the **Uninstall** button.

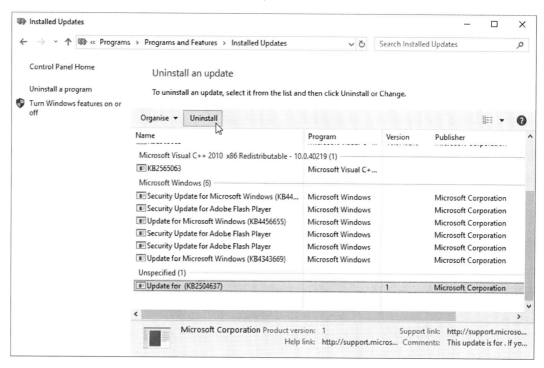

Using Programs and Features to uninstall an update. (Screenshot used with permission from Microsoft.)

ROLL BACK DEVICE DRIVERS

If you are experiencing problems with a device and you have recently updated the driver, Windows also provides a **Roll Back Driver** feature. A new driver may not work properly because it has not been fully tested or it may not work on your particular system. Driver roll back can recover a system speedily and easily where this has occurred. You can use **Device Manager** to revert to the previous driver. Right-click the device and select **Properties**. Click the **Driver** tab then click the **Roll Back Driver** button.

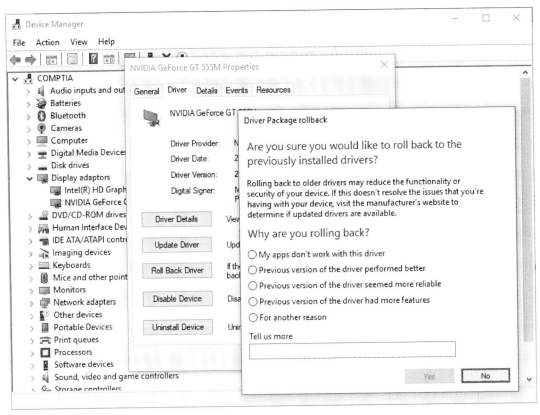

Using driver rollback via Device Manager. (Screenshot used with permission from Microsoft.)

SYSTEM REPAIR AND REINSTALL

If **System Restore** or **Startup Repair** do not work and you cannot boot to a log on, try to boot in **Safe Mode**. If this works, you should then be able to pinpoint the problem to a particular driver or service. **Safe Mode** loads Windows with a minimal set of drivers and services, so if this works it tells you that something is going wrong later on in the OS load. If the computer will not boot at all, you will have to resort to a system repair tool or possibly a reinstall option and restore from data backup (presuming you have made one). The various versions of Windows use different system recovery tools and backup processes.

CREATING AND USING A RECOVERY IMAGE

You can make a complete backup of the system configuration and data files. This is called an **image**. This method is simple, but you do need a backup device with large capacity. The best option is usually a removable hard drive. The best compression ratio you can hope for is 2:1—so a 20 GB system will create a 10 GB image—but if the system contains a lot of files that are already heavily compressed, the ratio could be a lot lower. You do have to keep the image up-to-date or make a separate data backup.

You create a system image using the **Backup and Restore** applet in **Control Panel**. Click the **Create a system image** link in the tasks pane. Select a backup device and give the image a suitable name.

To recover the system using the backup image, use the **Advanced Boot Option** or the **System Image Recovery** option off a repair disk or recovery environment.

REINSTALLING WINDOWS

If you do not have an up-to-date image, the last option is to reinstall Windows. You can try reinstalling Windows 7 over the top of an existing installation. This will preserve the previous data in a **Windows.old** folder and might allow you to recover data files, if you do not have a data backup. You will need to reinstall software applications and reconfigure user accounts and settings.

In Windows 8 and Windows 10, there is a **reset** option to try to repair the installation. This recopies the system files and reverts all PC settings to the default, but can preserve user personalization settings, data files, and apps installed via Windows Store. Desktop applications are removed.

Restart to the recovery environment (or use a repair disk). From the first **Choose an option** screen, select **Troubleshoot**. Select **Reset this PC**.

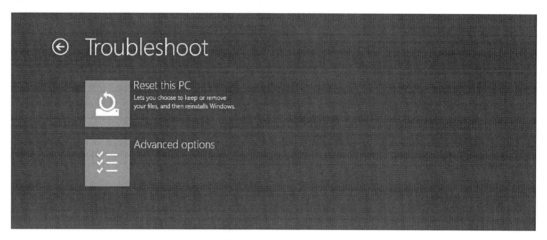

Windows 10 startup recovery. (Screenshot used with permission from Microsoft.)

Reset this PC options. (Screenshot used with permission from Microsoft.)

Select **Keep my files** or **Remove everything** as appropriate. The computer will restart and you will be prompted to sign on using an administrator account to authorize the reinstallation. Select **Reset** to continue (or **Cancel** if you have changed your mind).

If you choose to remove everything, there is a further option to securely delete information from the drive. This will take several hours but is recommended if you are giving up ownership of the PC.

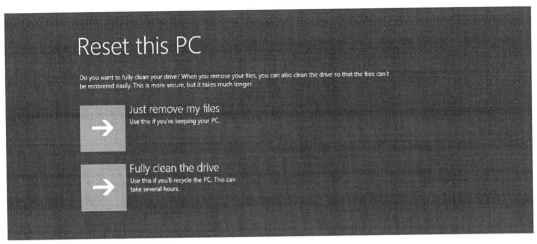

Choosing whether to securely erase the drive. (Screenshot used with permission from Microsoft.)

GUIDELINES FOR TROUBLESHOOTING WINDOWS ISSUES

Consider the following guidelines when troubleshooting issues on a Windows machine.

TROUBLESHOOT WINDOWS ISSUES

Follow these guidelines for troubleshooting Windows issues.

- Examine log files and **Event Viewer** to get information about what has happened on the system.
- Use the **System Configuration Utility** to modify system settings and files that affect the way the computer boots and loads Windows.
- Use **Task Manager** to attempt to locate a reason for slow system performance.
- Use **Event Viewer** to attempt to determine why a service fails to start.
- If an application crashes:
  - Try to preserve any data that was being processed.
  - See if the process will become responsive again or if you need to kill the process.
  - Attempt to recover data from temporary files or folders if the process was killed.
  - Examine **Event Viewer** logs.
  - If the application repeatedly crashes, uninstall then reinstall the application, or if available, use the **Repair** option in **Programs and Features**.
- If there are printing issues, determine whether the issue is with the printer hardware or network connectivity. If it isn't those issues, examine Windows settings and check the following:
  1. Use the printer's property dialog box to try printing a test page. If this is successful, there must be an application or file-specific problem.
  2. Open the print queue and check for stalled print jobs.
  3. Restart the print spooler service.
  4. Check for any driver updates or known issues.
  5. Check permissions configured on the printer.
  6. Check for disk problems on the partition hosting the spool folder.
- If the user experiences frequent BSoDs:
  - Use **System Restore**, or (if you can boot to **Safe Mode**), **Rollback Driver** to restore the system to a working state.
  - Remove a recently added hardware device or uninstall a recently installed program.
  - Check seating of hardware components and cables.

- Run hardware diagnostics, **chkdsk**, and scan for malware.
- Make a note of the stop error code (which will be in the form: Stop: 0x0...) and search the Microsoft Knowledge Base (**support.microsoft.com/search**) for known fixes and troubleshooting tips. The various newsgroups accessible from this site offer another valuable source of assistance.
- If the user experiences file or memory corruption:
  - Use **sfc** to verify system files and restore them from cache if corrupt or damaged.
  - Use the **Windows Memory Diagnostics** tool to test memory chips for errors.
- If the user is experiencing boot problems, determine the failure point, and therefore the missing or corrupt file. This can then be replaced, either from the source files or using some sort of recovery disk.
- Try booting into **Safe Mode** to troubleshoot by loading only minimal required components.
- If you cannot boot the computer from the local installation, you can try booting from the product media, a repair disk, or a recovery partition. You may have to access BIOS or UEFI setup to configure the boot device to the recovery media.
- Use **System Restore** to rollback system configuration changes.
- Rollback updates that are causing issues by uninstalling them.
  1. Open **Programs and Features**.
  2. Select **View installed updates**.
  3. Select the update that is causing the problem, then select the **Uninstall** button.
- Rollback troublesome device drivers:
  1. Open **Device Manager**.
  2. Right-click the device having the problem and select **Properties**.
  3. Select the **Driver** tab.
  4. Select the **Roll Back Driver** button.
- If all else fails, determine whether you need to perform a system restore or reinstall Windows.

Activity 3-1

Maintaining and Troubleshooting Microsoft Windows Review

SCENARIO

Answer the following review questions.

1. **Which Windows performance management tools would you expect to use most in your workplace?**

2. **Have you ever recovered a severely compromised Windows system? If so, then describe your experience.**

Summary

In this lesson, you maintained and performed troubleshooting on Windows PCs. In your role as an A+ technician, you will be advising and supporting users in a number of areas surrounding computing devices, so using the guidelines and procedures provided in this lesson will enable you to provide the required level of support to users.

Lesson 4
Configuring and Troubleshooting Networks

LESSON INTRODUCTION

In a previous lesson, you identified networking technologies. With that knowledge, you are now prepared to implement those technologies. In this lesson, you will install and configure networking capabilities.

As a CompTIA® A+® technician, your duties will include setting up and configuring computers so that they can connect to a network. By installing, configuring, and troubleshooting networking capabilities, you will be able to provide users with the connectivity they need to be able to perform their job duties.

LESSON OBJECTIVES

In this lesson, you will:

- Configure Windows settings for different types of Internet and VPN connections.

- Install and configure SOHO router/modems and set up secure wireless access.

- Configure firewall settings and browser options to ensure safe Internet use on a SOHO network.

- Use remote access technologies to connect to hosts over a network.

- Troubleshoot wired and wireless problems plus IP configuration issues using command-line tools.

Topic A

Configure Network Connection Settings

EXAM OBJECTIVES COVERED
1001-2.3 Given a scenario, install and configure a basic wired/wireless SOHO network.
1002-1.8 Given a scenario, configure Microsoft Windows networking on a client/desktop.
1002-1.6 Given a scenario, use Microsoft Windows Control Panel utilities.

Once all the hardware connections are made in a networking environment, you will need to make sure that the operating system is configured to use the hardware successfully. It is important to fully understand not only the hardware and the connections within a network, but also how Windows will need to be setup and configured to accomplish connectivity with the resources of a network.

NIC PROPERTIES

A computer joins a network by connecting the network adapter—or Network Interface Card (NIC)—to a switch or wireless access point. For proper end user device configuration, the card settings should be configured to match the capabilities of the network appliance.

WIRED NETWORK CARDS

Almost all wired network adapters are based on some type of Ethernet. The adapter's media type must match that of the switch it is connected to. Most use copper wire cable (RJ-45 connectors), though installations in some corporate networks may use fiber optic connections. The adapter and switch must also use the same Ethernet settings. The main parameters are:

- **Signaling speed**—most devices you will see will support Gigabit Ethernet, working at a nominal data rate of 1 Gbps. Older standards include Fast Ethernet (100 Mbps) and "plain" Ethernet (10 Mbps). Most network adapters will work at all three speeds. There is also a 10 Gbps standard, though this is not often used for desktop machines as the adapters and switches are expensive.
- **Half or full duplex**—this determines whether the connection transfers data in both directions simultaneously (full duplex) or not (half duplex). The overwhelming majority of devices use full duplex. Gigabit Ethernet requires full duplex to work.

Most wired network adapters will autonegotiate network settings such as signaling speed and half- or full duplex operation with the switch. For this to work, both the port on the switch and the network adapter should be configured to use the "Autonegotiate" setting, which should be the default.

If these settings do need to be configured manually, locate the adapter in **Device Manager**, right-click and select **Properties**, then update settings using the **Advanced** tab.

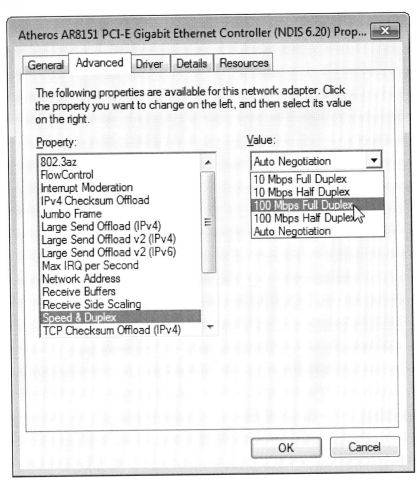

Ethernet adapter properties in Device Manager. (Screenshot used with permission from Microsoft.)

Most of the other settings can be left to the default. In some circumstances, you may be able to improve performance or troubleshoot connectivity problems by enabling or disabling or tweaking the parameters for settings such as jumbo frames, buffers, scaling, and offloads.

QOS

Quality of Service (QoS) means using a network protocol to prioritize certain types of traffic over others. Enterprise networks can use QoS protocols to make sure traffic such as Voice over IP calling or video conferencing is given higher priority than traffic where the timing of packets is less important, such as ordinary file downloads.

QoS parameters are usually configured on a managed switch. In the network adapter properties, you may need to enable the QoS protocol ("802.1p" or "QoS Packet Tagging," for instance). It is possible that QoS may also be controlled by a higher level protocol, which would be configured via the QoS Packet Scheduler client software installed by default on the OS's logical adapter.

ONBOARD NETWORK CARDS

Most computers come with an onboard Gigabit Ethernet network adapter as part of the system chipset. The port will be an RJ-45 type for use with twisted-pair cabling. If there is any issue with the onboard NIC, the first step should be to use the BIOS/UEFI system setup program to find out whether it is enabled (look in the "Integrated Peripherals" or "Onboard Devices" section). You might disable the onboard adapter if installing a plug-in card.

WIRELESS NETWORK CARDS

The most important setting on a wireless card is support for the 802.11 standard supported by the access point. Most cards are set to support any standard available. This means that a card that supports 802.11n will also be able to connect to 802.11g and 802.11b networks.

With the card shown in the following figure, for instance, you can enable or disable 802.11n Mode and select either mixed support for 802.11b/g or force use of either. For 802.11.n, you can also configure whether to use channel bonding.

 Note: *Making a network work in compatibility mode can reduce the performance of the whole network.*

A couple of other settings are of interest:

- **Roaming Aggressiveness**—when the adapter starts to move out of range of one access point, it might try to connect to another one with a better signal. Roaming aggressiveness determines how tolerant the adapter is of weak signals. If you use multiple APs, tweaking this setting up or down might result in better performance.
- **Transmit Power**—this sets the radio power level. It is typically set to the highest possible by default.

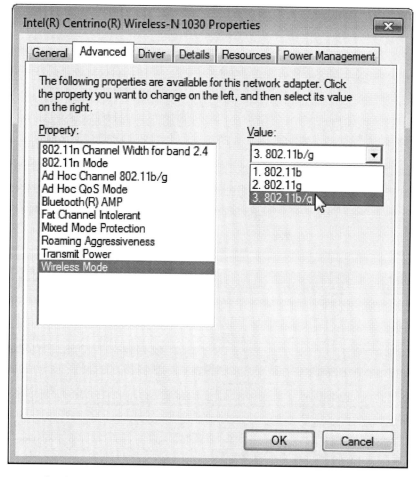

Wireless network adapter properties in Device Manager. (Screenshot used with permission from Microsoft.)

Note: *You might see a setting for "Ad hoc QoS Mode" on a wireless adapter. This enables Wireless Multimedia (WMM), which is a Wi-Fi specification for delivering QoS over wireless networks.*

WAKE ON LAN

Wake on LAN (WoL) allows you to start up a computer remotely. When the computer is switched off (but not unplugged), the network card can be kept active using standby power. The administrator would use network software to broadcast a "magic packet" to the NIC; when it receives it, the NIC initiates the computer's boot process.

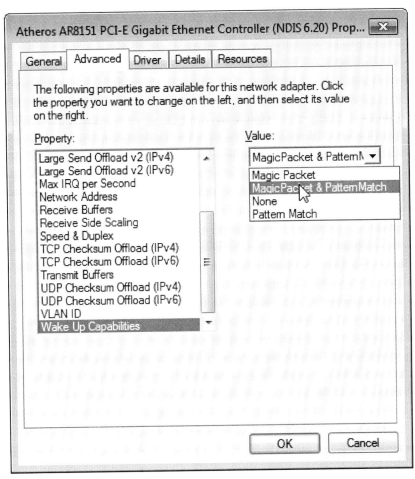

WoL settings for a network adapter. (Screenshot used with permission from Microsoft.)

Some devices with wireless chipsets come with **Wake-on-Wireless LAN (WoWLAN)**, but the technology is not so widely supported.

HOW TO SET UP WAKE ON LAN

Here are some general steps for setting up WoL.

SET UP WoL

To set up Wake on LAN:

1. Enable WoL in system setup. Any motherboard released in the last few years should support WoL.
2. Open the adapter's **Properties** dialog in **Device Manager**. Select the **Advanced** tab then enable the option for WoL. This option may be described as many different things: WoL, power management, wake up, and so on. Check the vendor

documentation. Again, older NICs might not support WoL but these would be the exception rather than the rule now.

3. Configure the network software to send magic packets. This type of software is often provided with systems and network management suites or you can obtain standalone utilities.

NETWORK CONNECTIONS IN WINDOWS 7 AND WINDOWS 8

Having verified connection properties of the Ethernet or Wi-Fi interface, you must also configure the card with the appropriate network client software and protocol, including addressing information relevant to the protocol.

Most Ethernet and Wi-Fi networks use the Internet Protocol (IP) with a DHCP server, which means that the card receives address parameters automatically.

NETWORK AND SHARING CENTER

In Windows® 7 and Windows 8, the Network and Sharing Center is used to provide an overview of network availability and configuration. Right-click the network status icon in the notification area and select **Open Network and Sharing Center** or open the applet via Control Panel.

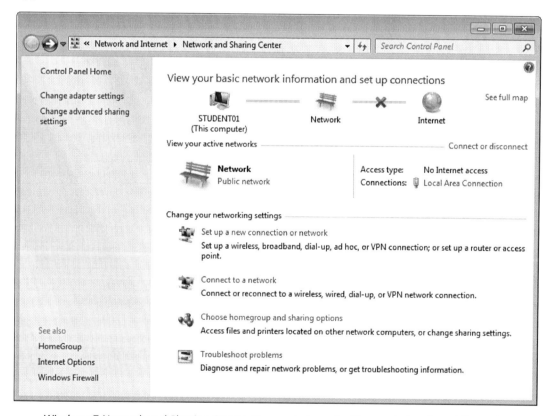

Windows 7 Network and Sharing Center. (Screenshot used with permission from Microsoft.)

WIRED NETWORK CONNECTIONS

To access the adapter property sheets, select **Change adapter settings**. In Windows 8, the option is labeled **Manage network connections**.

> **Note:** *Alternatively, run* `ncpa.cpl` *from the* **Instant Search** *box or* **Run** *dialog box.*

In Windows 7, the wired network adapter will be listed as **Local Area Connection** (though you can rename it if you prefer), whereas a wireless adapter will be listed as **Wireless Network Connection**. In Windows 8, the adapters are named **Ethernet** and **WiFi**.

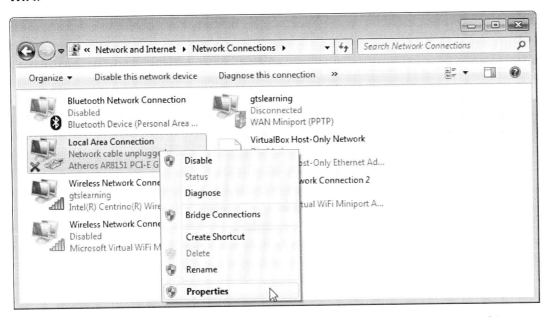

Network Connections in Windows 7. (Screenshot used with permission from Microsoft.)

ADAPTER PROPERTIES

Right-click an adapter and select **Properties** to configure settings or **Status** to view information about the connection. From the **Properties** dialog box, you can add or configure the appropriate service, protocol, or client.

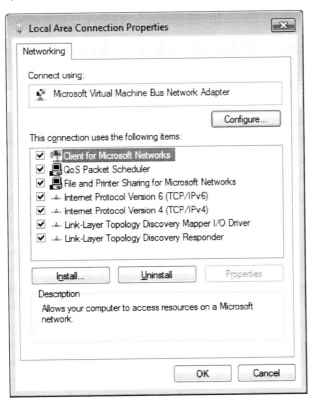

Local Area Network Adapter properties. (Screenshot used with permission from Microsoft.)

- **Clients** provide connections to types of file servers, such as Linux/UNIX or Windows.
- **Protocols** provide the format for addressing and delivering data messages between systems, the most widely adopted being TCP/IP.
- **Services** allow your machine to provide network functionality to other machines.

By default, the following clients, protocols, and services are installed on the default Ethernet adapter:

- Client for Microsoft Networks.
- File and Print Sharing for Microsoft Networks.
- Internet Protocol—both IP version 4 and IP version 6 will be installed. The network adapter automatically uses the appropriate version of the protocol depending on the network it is connected to.
- Link-layer Topology Discovery—provides the network mapping and discovery functions in the Network and Sharing Center.

Checked items are described as being "bound" to an adapter. When installing a new protocol or service, check that it is only bound to adapters that should be using that protocol or service.

WIRELESS NETWORK CONNECTIONS

To join a WLAN, click the network status icon in the notification area and select from the list of displayed networks. If the access point is set to broadcast the network name or Service Set ID (SSID), then the network will appear in the list of available networks. The bars show the strength of the signal and the lock icon indicates whether the network uses encryption. To connect, select the network then enter the pre-shared key (or log on in the specified way if using a network authentication server).

If you choose the **Connect automatically** option, Windows will use the network without prompting whenever it is in range.

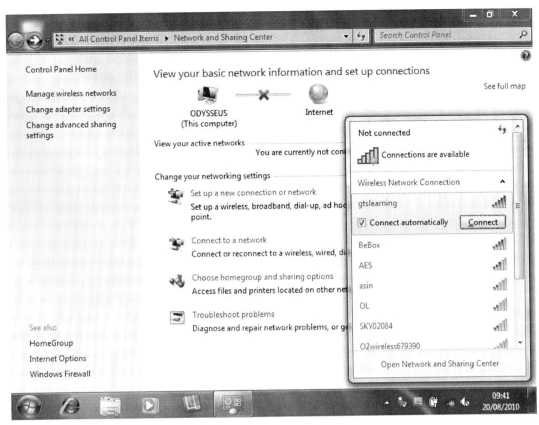

Connecting to a network using Windows 7. (Screenshot used with permission from Microsoft.)

If the WLAN is not shown (if SSID broadcast is disabled), click **Open Network and Sharing Center** then **Set up a new connection or network** and proceed by entering the network SSID, security information, and network location type.

NETWORK CONNECTIONS IN WINDOWS 10

Windows 10 manages network settings via the **Network & Internet** section in the Settings app. Use the **Status** page to monitor the current network connection. There are links to the **Network and Sharing Center** and **Network Connections** applets (via **Change adapter options**) from there.

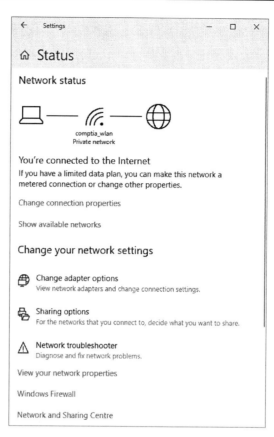

Windows 10 Network & Internet Settings app. (Screenshot used with permission from Microsoft.)

You can join a wireless network using the network status icon in the notification area. If you need to input WLAN settings manually, from the **Network & internet** page, select **WiFi →Manage known networks→Add a new network**.

IP ADDRESS CONFIGURATION

IP address properties can be configured through the network connection's **Properties** dialog box. Both wired and wireless adapters are configured in the same way. By default, Windows machines obtain an IP address dynamically, but you can configure a static IP address and other settings, such as DNS servers.

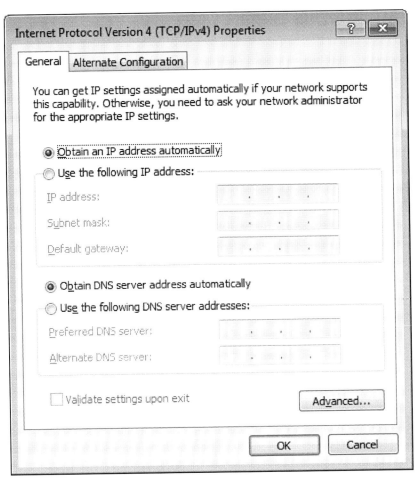

Internet Protocol version 4 (TCP/IP/v4) Properties dialog box. (Screenshot used with permission from Microsoft.)

Note: *A machine can communicate with local hosts with a valid IP address and subnet mask but cannot communicate with other networks unless a default gateway is specified.*

Note: *A machine that cannot access a DNS server will not be able to resolve host names or web addresses. As DNS is a critical service, two server addresses are usually specified for redundancy.*

Note: *In Windows 10, you can also configure IP via the Settings interface. Select **Network & Internet** then **Ethernet** or **WiFi** as appropriate. Click the adapter or WLAN SSID. Under "IP Settings," click the **Edit** button.*

AUTOMATIC IP CONFIGURATION AND DHCP

Configuring IP addresses and other TCP/IP network information manually raises many difficult administrative issues and makes misconfiguration of one or more hosts more likely. A Dynamic Host Configuration Protocol (DHCP) service can be provided by a Windows Server or by a device such as a switch or router. DHCP can allocate an IP address to a new machine joining the network. To use DHCP, select the **Obtain an IP address automatically** option. If a Windows machine fails to obtain an IP address dynamically, it will utilize an Automatic Private IP Addressing (APIPA) address from a reserved range (169.254.x.y).

ALTERNATE CONFIGURATION

Windows allows you to define an alternative IP address configuration for a machine if it cannot contact a DHCP server and using APIPA is unsuitable. This is useful in the scenario where you have a laptop computer connecting to DHCP in a corporate network but that requires a static IP address on the user's home network.

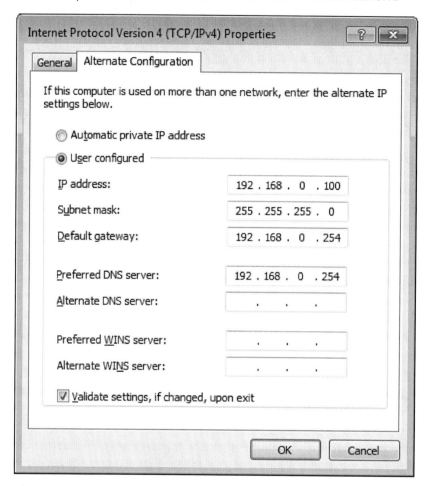

TCP/IP Alternate Configuration dialog box. (Screenshot used with permission from Microsoft.)

*Note: The **Alternate Configuration** tab is not displayed unless the **Obtain an IP address automatically** option is selected.*

HOW TO CONFIGURE IP ADDRESSES

Here are some general procedures you can use to configure IP addresses.

CONFIGURE IPv4 ADDRESSES MANUALLY

To manually configure an IPv4 address:

1. From **Network Connections** (`ncpa.cpl`), open the adapter's Properties and from the **Networking** tab, double-click **Internet Protocol version 4 (TCP/IP/v4)**.
2. To enter an IP address manually, check **Use the Following IP address**. Type in an appropriate IP address and Subnet mask for your network.
3. Enter the IP address of your router in the **Default Gateway** box, if appropriate.
4. Enter the IP addresses of DNS servers (check with your ISP or network administrator for these addresses).

CONFIGURE ALTERNATE IP CONFIGURATIONS

To set up an alternate IP configuration:

1. From **Network Connections** (`ncpa.cpl`), open the adapter's Properties.
2. On the **General** tab, select **Obtain an IP address automatically**.
3. On the **Alternate Configuration** tab, provide the applicable details. For instance, select **User configured** and enter a static IP address.
4. Select **OK.**

OTHER NETWORK CONNECTIONS

Most residential and small office networks connect to the Internet via a SOHO "router." These Internet appliances combine a 4-port switch and wireless access point with a router/modem that can connect to the ISP's network over DSL or Hybrid Fiber Coax (HFC) lines. The computers connect to the router by using the switch ports or access point and are assigned an IP configuration by a DHCP server running in the appliance. Correctly configuring the Ethernet or WiFi adapter in Network Connections will allow the computer to join this type of network.

There are a number of other ways of connecting to the Internet and other remote networks, however.

DIAL-UP

A **dial-up connection** uses an analog modem to dial another modem on the ISP's remote access server, which then transfers the data onto the ISP's network and to and from the wider Internet. The call is placed in the same way as a voice call and may incur connection charges. The maximum link speed is just 56 Kbps.

 Note: *Given perfect line conditions, modems can work at up to 56 Kbps downlink and 48 Kbps uplink. Line conditions are rarely perfect, however, and actual speeds may be a lot lower.*

To create a dial-up connection, a modem must be installed in the computer or an external modem can be connected via USB. The dial-up port on the modem should then be connected to the phone socket. This is typically done using a silver satin cable with an RJ-11 connector for the modem and a suitable connector for the phone point, depending on region. For example, in the US an RJ-11 connector is used, but in the UK, a BT connector is often required. Regardless of the physical interface, the modem must be installed to one of the computer's software COM ports. The modem must also be configured with the local dialing properties, such as access prefix for an outside line, area code, and so on.

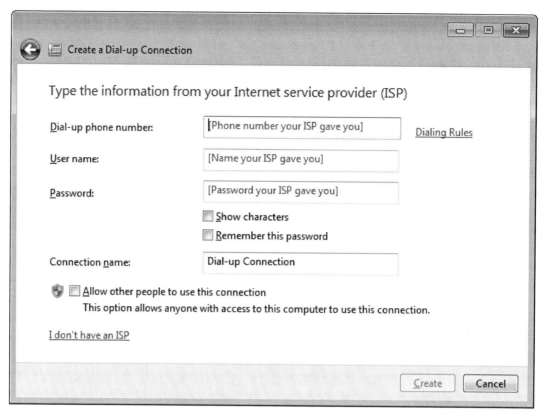

Configuring a dial-up connection in Windows 7. (Screenshot used with permission from Microsoft.)

You can use the **Set Up a Connection or Network** wizard to configure a link to the ISP's server.

You can connect or disconnect the link or reconfigure it using the network status icon.

WIRELESS WAN (CELLULAR)

Wireless Wide Area Network (WWAN or cellular) Internet access refers to using an adapter to link to a cellular phone provider's network via the nearest available transmitter (base station). The bandwidth depends on the technologies supported by the adapter and by the transmitter (3G or 4G, for instance).

The WWAN adapter can be fitted as a USB device or (on laptops) as an internal adapter. The advantage of the latter is that they do not protrude from the chassis; USB adapters are quite unwieldy.

Once the vendor's software has been installed, plug in the adapter and it will be detected and configured automatically. You can then use the software to open a connection, check signal strength, view usage, and so on.

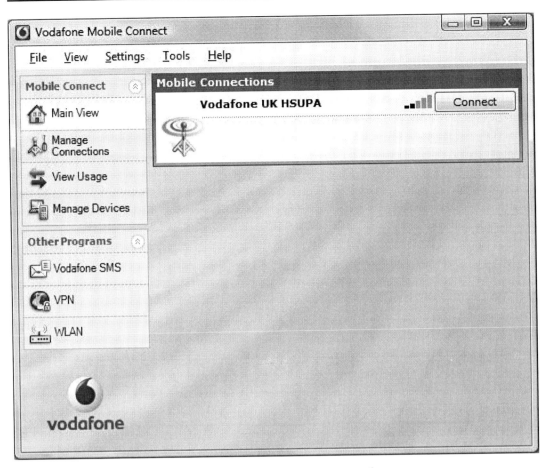

Vodafone Mobile Connect management software.

VIRTUAL PRIVATE NETWORK (VPN)

A Virtual Private Network (VPN) is a "tunnel" through the Internet. It allows a remote computer to join the local network securely. Windows supports a number of VPN types but you may need to obtain third-party software.

If the VPN type is supported, you can configure a connection using the Windows client from Network Connections.

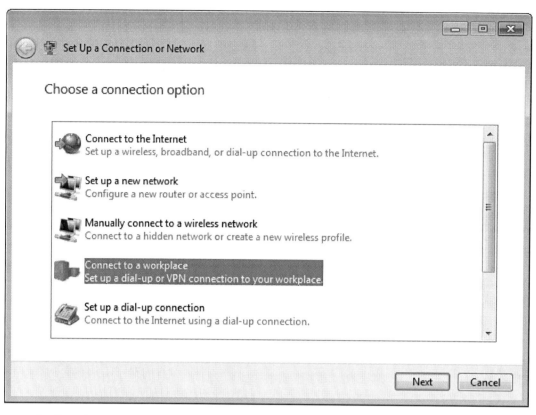

Set Up a Connection or Network wizard. (Screenshot used with permission from Microsoft.)

Subsequently, the network connection will be available by clicking the network status icon. Right-click the icon under "Dial-up and VPN" to **Connect** or **Disconnect** or modify the connection's Properties.

Accessing a VPN connection from the network status icon in Windows 7. (Screenshot used with permission from Microsoft.)

HOW TO CONFIGURE OTHER NETWORK CONNECTION SETTINGS

Here are some general procedures for configuring other network connection settings.

CREATE A DIAL-UP CONNECTION

To create a dial-up connection:

1. Verify that a modem is installed or connected to the computer, and that it is connected to a working telephone connection.
2. Open the **Network and Sharing Center** and select **Set up a dial-up connection**. In Windows 10, select **Settings→Network & Internet→Dial-up→Set up a dial-up connection**.
3. Select **Connect to the Internet** and select **Next**.
4. Type the telephone number of the computer you are calling and your username and password, plus a descriptive name for the link.
5. Optionally, select **Dialing Rules** to configure features of your phone line (such as a number to access an outside line).
6. Select **Create**.

SET UP A VPN CONNECTION IN WINDOWS 7

To set up a VPN connection in Windows 7:

1. Ensure the computer is connected to the Internet. You can use any Internet access method.
2. Open the **Network and Sharing Center** and select **Set up a new connection or network**.
3. Select **Connect to a workplace** and select **Next**.
4. For a VPN, choose to use your Internet connection.

 Note: *Old remote access networks used servers equipped with modems to receive incoming dial-up connections; the bandwidth is very low but these are sometimes still used as a backup connection method.*

5. Select **Next**. Enter the IP address or Fully Qualified Domain Name of the remote access server plus a descriptive name for the link. Select **Next**.
6. Enter the username and password (plus the domain name if appropriate) to connect to the remote network then select **Connect** to verify that the link works.

SET UP A VPN CONNECTION IN WINDOWS 10

To set up a VPN connection in Windows 10:

1. Select **Settings→Network & Internet→VPN→Add a VPN connection**.
2. In the **Add a VPN connection** dialog box, enter the **VPN provider** and **Connection name**, and then select **Save**.

Topic B
Install and Configure SOHO Networks

 EXAM OBJECTIVES COVERED
1001-2.3 Given a scenario, install and configure a basic wired/wireless SOHO network.
1002-2.3 Compare and contrast wireless security protocols and authentication methods.
1002-2.10 Given a scenario, configure security on SOHO wireless and wired networks.

Previously in this course, you covered basic networking concepts, the Transmission Control Protocol/Internet Protocol (TCP/IP) addressing scheme, and how networks are connected. In this topic, you will use that knowledge to install and configure a SOHO network.

No matter what the size or location of the network, you are still responsible for understanding how it is structured and configured. A+ technicians must understand the needs and complexities of SOHO wired and wireless networks.

SOHO NETWORKS

A Small Office Home Office (SOHO) LAN is a business-oriented network, possibly using a centralized server in addition to client devices and printers, but often using a single Internet appliance to provide connectivity. Home and residential networks may also be classed as SOHO.

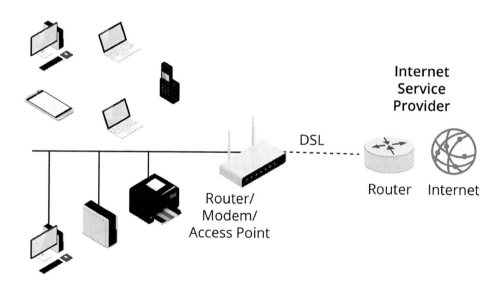

A typical SOHO network layout.

COMMON SOHO NETWORK HARDWARE

A DSL/cable modem is installed as Customer Premises Equipment (CPE), typically as some sort of combined router/modem. Make sure you understand the functions of the separate device types bundled within these appliances:

- **Modem**—connects to the service provider cabling and transfers frames over the link. The modem type must be matched to the network type (ADSL, VDSL, or cable).
- **Router**—forwards packets over the WAN (Internet) interface if they do not have a local destination IP address. Some appliances may provide the ability to configure local subnets, though this is not typical of the device's supplied by the service providers.
- **Switch**—allows local computers and other host types to connect to the network via RJ-45 ports. This will be an unmanaged switch so no configuration is necessary.
- **Access point**—allows hosts to connect to the network over Wi-Fi.

On a DSL modem, the RJ-11 port on the modem connects to the phone point. A microfilter (splitter) must be installed to separate voice and data signals. These can be self-installed on each phone point by the customer. Modern sockets are likely to feature a built-in splitter.

A self-installed DSL splitter.

 Note: *The modem might be provided as a separate device. If this is the case, it will provide an RJ-45 port to connect to the RJ-45 WAN port on the router.*

 Note: *The steps for most cable modems are the same except that you will be connecting to the provider network using a coax cable. Make sure the coax connector is secure (but do not overtighten it).*

SOHO NETWORK CONFIGURATION

You need to connect a computer (PC or laptop) to the device's built-in unmanaged switch so that you can configure the appliance. Make sure the computer is set to obtain an IP address automatically. Connect the computer to one of the RJ-45 LAN ports on the router/modem. These are usually color-coded yellow. Wait for the Dynamic Host Configuration Protocol (DHCP) server running on the router/modem to allocate a valid IP address to the computer.

Use a browser to open the device's management URL, as listed in the documentation. This could be an IP address or a host/domain name:

```
http://192.168.0.1
http://www.routerlogin.com
```

It might use HTTPS rather than unencrypted HTTP: If you cannot connect, check that the computer's IP address is in the same range as the device IP.

The management software will prompt you to choose a new administrator password. Enter the default password (as listed in the documentation or printed on a sticker accompanying the router/modem). Choose a long password (12 characters or more) with a mix of alphanumeric and symbol characters. If there is also an option to change the default username of the administrator account, this is also a little bit more secure than leaving the default configured.

CONFIGURING INTERNET ACCESS

Most appliances will use a wizard-based setup to connect to the Internet via the service provider's network. The DSL/cable link parameters are normally self-configuring. You might need to supply a username and password. If manual configuration is required, obtain the settings from your ISP.

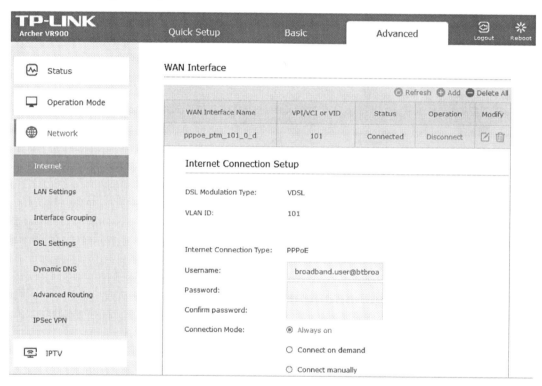

Configuring DSL modem settings. Note that this VDSL modem is connecting to a Fiber to the Curb (FTTC) service. The DSL segment only runs between the premises and the service provider's cabinet, located in a nearby street. From the cabinet, there is a fiber optic cable running back to the local exchange. (Screenshot courtesy of TP-Link.)

You can also use the management console to view line status and the system log. These might be required by the ISP to troubleshoot any issues with the connection.

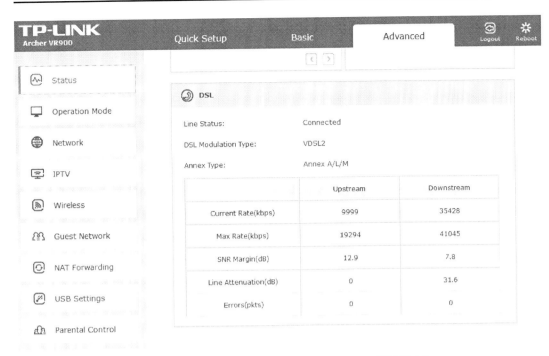

Viewing DSL line status. (Screenshot courtesy of TP-Link.)

WIRELESS SETTINGS

Having set up Internet access, the next step is to configure wireless settings. The majority of hosts will connect to the network wirelessly. Initial configuration is likely to be part of the device's setup wizard, but if you skipped that or need to reconfigure settings, the management software will have a separate page or section for wireless configuration.

Having checked the box to enable wireless communications, you can adjust the following settings from the default.

- Frequency band (2.4 GHz or 5 GHz)—on an 802.11ac access point, you can use the same network settings over both bands. Clients will connect to any supported frequency. Alternatively, you can configure different network names for each frequency. You might want to use one frequency but not the other, depending on the range of devices you have using the wireless network.

> **Note:** *It is best practice not to enable services you do not need, especially on a multifunction device such as this. Most devices are now shipped in "security-enabled" configurations, meaning that you explicitly have to choose to enable services that you want to run.*

- SSID (Service Set ID)—a name for the WLAN. This can be up to 32 characters and must be different to any other networks nearby.
- Security version and encryption type—always choose the highest mode supported by your wireless clients (WPA2 with AES). Note that WEP provides very weak security and should not be relied upon for confidentiality.
- Password (Pre-Shared Key)—on a SOHO network you will choose a password for use by all client devices to connect to the network. The password generates the encryption key. The same key must be configured on client adapters to enable them to connect.

> **Note:** *Choose a strong passphrase and keep it secret. In order to generate a strong key, use a longer phrase than you would for a normal password.*

- Mode—enable compatibility for different 802.11 devices. Performance may be improved if you disable support for unnecessary legacy standards. The typical configuration is to use the 2.4 GHz band for legacy b/g/n stations and the 5 GHz band for ac stations.
- Channel and channel width—the access point will try to auto-detect the best channel at boot time. You might adjust the settings manually if you subsequently experience a weak connection caused by interference from other devices. For 802.11n/ac access points, you may be able to configure the use of wide channels (bonding) for more bandwidth. This may only be practical in the 5 GHz band, depending on the wireless site design.

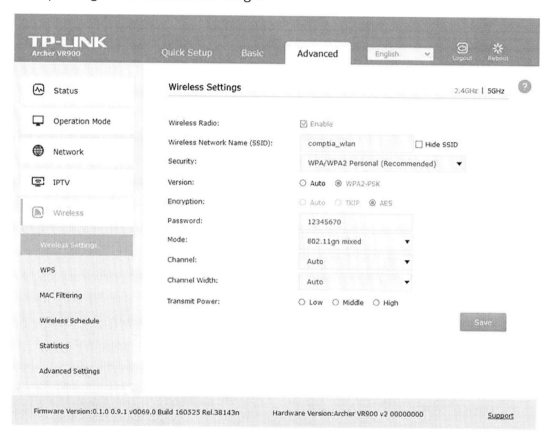

Configuring an access point. (Screenshot courtesy of TP-Link.)

DHCP AND IP ADDRESS CONFIGURATION

You may want to adjust the settings for the DHCP server. This assigns wired and wireless clients an appropriate IP addressing configuration. It is always enabled "out of the box" to allow users to connect to the configuration page easily. If you disable DHCP, IP settings have to be allocated and configured manually on client devices. This adds a lot of administrative overhead and introduces the possibility of configuration errors. Also, it is not difficult for a determined attacker to identify the IP scope in use.

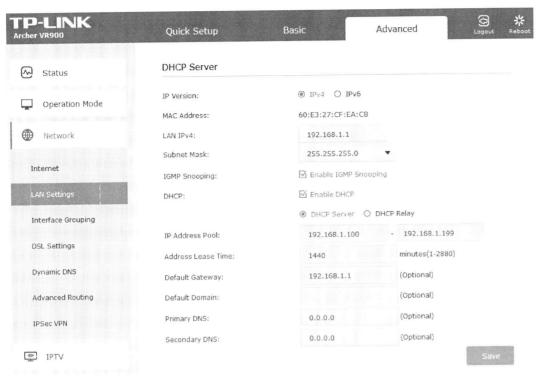

Configuring the DHCP server. (Screenshot courtesy of TP-Link.)

WPS

As setting up an access point securely is relatively complex, vendors have developed a system to automate the process called **Wi-Fi Protected Setup (WPS)**. To use WPS, all the wireless devices (access point and wireless adapters) must be WPS-capable. Typically, the devices will have a pushbutton. Activating this on the access point and the adapter simultaneously will associate the device with the access point using WPA2. The system generates a random SSID and passphrase.

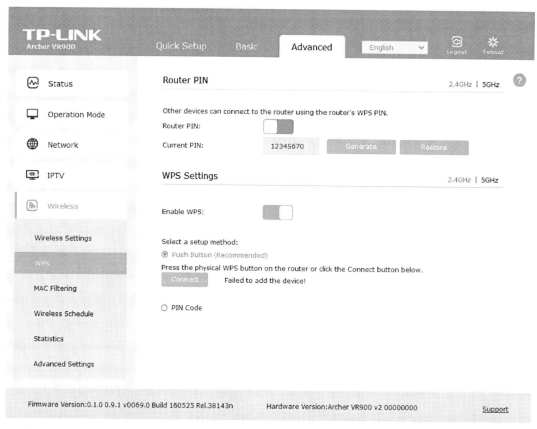

If you use WPS, disable the PIN configuration method if possible. (Screenshot courtesy of TP-Link.)

 Note: *There is a WPS PIN method too but this is vulnerable to "brute force" attacks, where someone tries to guess the passphrase to get access to the networks. It is advisable to disable this method if possible.*

ACCESS POINT PLACEMENT

Antenna and access point placement is important for ensuring a robust network—one that clients can connect to wherever they are in the building. In a SOHO network, with an integrated router/modem/access point, placement of the access point is likely to be constrained by the location of the service provider's cabling. If this does not provide sufficient coverage, the typical solution is to use extenders to repeat and boost the wireless signal in locations where it is not strong enough.

A site survey can be performed with wireless signal measuring software (such as inSSIDer) to identify "dead zones."

CHANNEL SELECTION

The 2.4 GHz band for 802.11b/g/n is subdivided into 11 channels (in the US), spaced at 5 MHz intervals. However, the recommendation is to allow 25 MHz spacing between channels in active use. In practice, therefore, no more than three nearby 802.11b/g/n access points can have non-overlapping channels. This could be implemented, for example, by selecting channel 1 for AP1, channel 6 for AP2, and channel 11 for AP3. When using the 5 GHz band, more non-overlapping channels are available.

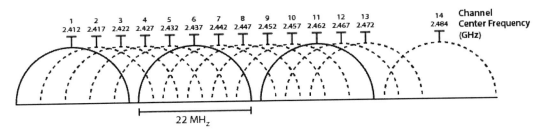

Frequencies and overlap of wireless channels.

Newer access points will auto-detect the channel that seems least congested at boot time. As the environment changes, you may find that this channel selection is not the optimum one. You can use a wireless spectrum analyzer to find which channels in your area are actually the least busy.

RADIO POWER LEVELS

You may want to turn the power output on an AP down to prevent "war driving." War driving is the practice of driving around with a wireless-enabled laptop scanning for unsecure WLANs. The main problem with this approach is that it requires careful configuration to ensure that there is acceptable coverage for legitimate users. You also expose yourself slightly to "evil twin" attacks, as users may expect to find the network at a given location and assume that a rogue AP is legitimate.

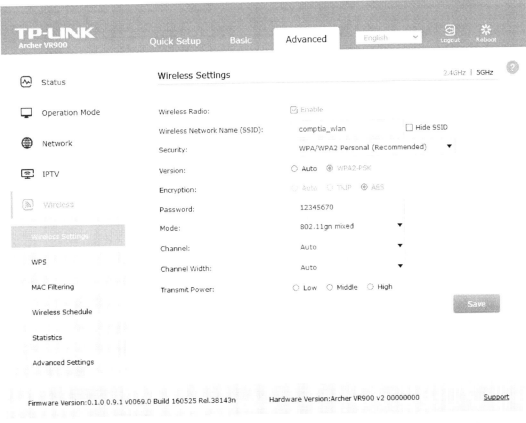

You have the option to set the Transmit Power level when configuring wireless settings on this access point. (Screenshot courtesy of TP-Link.)

Increasing power output to boost a signal is not always reliable. As you increase power, you also increase the chance of the signal bouncing, causing more interference, especially if there are multiple access points. Also, the client radio power levels should match those of the access point or they may be able to receive signals but not transmit back. Consequently, power levels are best set to autonegotiate. You should also be aware of legal restrictions on power output—these vary from country-to-country.

WI-FI SECURITY PROTOCOLS

Wireless LANs require careful configuration to make the connection and transmissions over the connection secure. The main problem with wireless is that because it is "unguided," there is no way to contain the signal. Anyone with a suitably equipped laptop or RF (Radio Frequency) scanner can intercept the signals. If the proper security has not been put in place, this could allow the interception of data or the unauthorized use of the network.

The crucial step in enforcing wireless security is to enable encryption. Encryption scrambles the messages being sent over the WLAN so that anyone intercepting them is not able to capture any valuable information. An encryption system consists of a cipher, which is the process used to scramble the message, and a key. The key is a unique value that allows the recipient to decrypt a message that has been encrypted using the same cipher and key. Obviously, the key must be known only to valid recipients or the encryption system will offer no protection.

WIRED EQUIVALENT PRIVACY (WEP)

The **Wired Equivalent Privacy (WEP)** encryption system is based on the RC4 cipher. RC stands for Ron's Cipher, after its inventor, Ron Rivest. Under WEP version 1, you can select from different key sizes (64-bit or 128-bit). A larger key makes it more difficult to attack the security system.

Although WEP might sound like a good solution at first, it is not as secure as it should be. The problem stems from the way WEP produces keys. Because of a flaw in the method, attackers can quite easily generate their own keys by using a wireless network capture tool to analyze network data and crack WEP in a short period of time.

Consequently, WEP is deprecated and should not be used to secure a wireless network.

WI-FI PROTECTED ACCESS (WPA)

Wi-Fi Protected Access (WPA) fixes most of the security problems with WEP. WPA still uses the RC4 cipher but adds a mechanism called **Temporal Key Integrity Protocol (TKIP)** to fix the issues with key generation.

The original version of WPA was introduced as an upgrade for equipment supporting WEP. The continued reliance on WEP meant that the protocol did not meet the requirements of the IEEE 802.11i security standard. An update, known as WPA2, was developed as a fully compliant 802.11i security protocol. The main difference to WPA is the use of the **Advanced Encryption Standard (AES)** cipher for encryption. AES is much stronger than RC4/TKIP.

The only reason not to use WPA2 is if it is not supported by adapters, APs, or operating systems on the network. WPA2 is very well-established now and most devices should support it. WPA is an acceptable fallback, especially on home networks, where the risk of intrusion is quite low.

 Note: WPA/WPA2 can still depend on the use of a passphrase to generate the key. If the passphrase is an easy-to-guess word or phrase, the key can be discovered and the encryption system cracked.

WI-FI AUTHENTICATION

It is possible to configure a WLAN as open, meaning that anyone can connect to it. In order to secure the WLAN, however, you need to be able to confirm that only valid users are connecting to it by authenticating them. WLAN authentication comes in two types.

PERSONAL

The personal authentication mode is based on a **Pre-shared Key (PSK)**. This is the key that is used to encrypt communications. A PSK is generated from a passphrase, which is like a long password. In WPA-PSK, the router administrator defines a passphrase of between 8 and 63 ASCII characters. This is converted into a 256-bit cryptographic hash, expressed as a 64-digit hex value where each hex digit represents 4 bits.

> *Note: It is critical that PSK passphrases be long (12 characters or more) and complex. This means that it should contain a mixture of upper- and lower-case letters and digits and no dictionary words or common names.*

The main problem is that distribution of the key or passphrase cannot be secured properly, and on a home network, the user acting as the administrator may choose an unsecure phrase. It also fails to provide accounting, as all users share the same key. The advantage is that it is simple to set up. Conversely, changing the key periodically (as would be good security practice) is difficult as the new key must be communicated to all users and updated on all their devices.

PSK is the only type of authentication available for WLANs that use WEP encryption technology. It is also suitable for SOHO networks and workgroups that use WPA or WPA2 encryption.

ENTERPRISE

WPA and WPA2 can implement enterprise mode authentication, where the access point passes authentication information to a **Remote Authentication Dial-in User Service (RADIUS)** server for validation. This type of authentication is suitable for server-/domain-based networks.

COMMON SOHO SECURITY ISSUES

Although encryption and setting a strong passphrase are the most important factors in configuring effective Wi-Fi security, there are other configuration changes you may want to make. Here are some additional security problems and solutions.

SERVICE SET ID (SSID)

The **Service Set ID (SSID)** is a simple name (case sensitive 32-bit alphanumeric string) for users to identify the WLAN by. Vendors use default SSIDs for their products based on the device brand or model. You should change it to something that your users will recognize and will not get confused between nearby networks. Given that, on a residential network, you should not use an SSID that reveals personal information, such as an address or surname. Similarly, on a business network, you may not want to use a meaningful name. For example, an SSID like "Accounts" could prove tempting to would-be attackers.

Disabling broadcast of the SSID prevents any adapters not manually configured to connect to the name you specify from finding the network. This provides a margin of privacy.

> *Note: Hiding the SSID does not secure the network; you must enable encryption. Even when broadcast is disabled, the SSID can still be detected using packet sniffing tools.*

PHYSICAL SECURITY

On a business network, physical access to important network infrastructure like switches and routers should be restricted to administrators and technicians. Most devices are stored in a locked equipment room and may also be protected by lockable cabinets. Many devices can be reset to the factory configuration with physical access. This could allow someone to disrupt the network or gain access to administrative settings (though probably not without being noticed).

UPDATING FIRMWARE

You should keep the firmware and driver for the Internet appliance up-to-date with the latest patches. This is important to fix security holes and to support the latest security standards, such as WPA2. To perform a firmware update, download the update from the vendor's website, taking care to select the correct patch for your device make and model. Select the **Firmware Upgrade** option and browse for the firmware file you downloaded.

Make sure that power to the device is not interrupted during the update process.

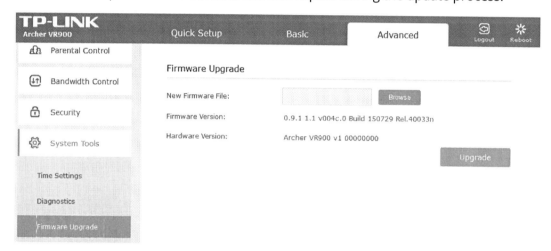

Upgrading device firmware. (Screenshot courtesy of TP-Link.)

ASSIGNING STATIC IP ADDRESSES

Assigning static IP addresses means that the DHCP server is disabled and clients must be configured manually to join the network properly. It would be trivial for an attacker to identify the appropriate subnet so this is not something that would deter a determined attack.

Note that devices such as the router/modem must be configured with a static address because it acts as a DHCP server, and client devices need to use it as the default gateway.

LATENCY AND JITTER

Quality of Service (QoS) means using a network protocol to prioritize certain types of traffic over others.

Many networks are now being pressed into service to provide two-way communications, with applications such as Voice over IP (VoIP), video conferencing, and multiplayer gaming. Applications such as voice and video that carry real-time data have different network requirements to the sort of data represented by file transfer. With "ordinary" data, it might be beneficial to transfer a file as quickly as possible, but the sequence in which the packets are delivered and variable intervals between packets arriving do not materially affect the application. This type of data transfer is described as "bursty." Network protocols such as HTTP, FTP, or email are very sensitive to packet loss but are tolerant to delays in delivery. The reverse is applicable to real-time applications; they can compensate for some amount of packet loss, but are very sensitive toward delays in data delivery.

Problems with the timing and sequence of packet delivery are defined as latency and jitter:

- **Latency** (Delay)—the time it takes for a signal to reach the recipient. A video application can support a latency of about 80 ms, while typical latency on the Internet can reach 1000 ms at peak times. Latency is a particular problem for 2-way applications, such as VoIP (telephone), online conferencing, and multiplayer gaming.
- **Jitter**—variation in the delay; often caused by congestion at routers and other internetwork devices or by configuration errors.

Real-time applications are sensitive to the effects of latency and jitter because they manifest as echo, delay, and video slow down. End users are generally very intolerant of these kinds of errors.

It is difficult to guarantee Quality of Service (QoS) over a public network such as the Internet. Enterprise networks can deploy sophisticated QoS and traffic engineering protocols on managed switches and routers. On a SOHO network, you may be able to configure a QoS or bandwidth control feature on the router/modem to prioritize the port used by a VoIP application over any other type of protocol. This will help to mitigate issues if, for example, one computer is trying to download a Windows 10 feature update at the same time as another set of computers are trying to host a video conference.

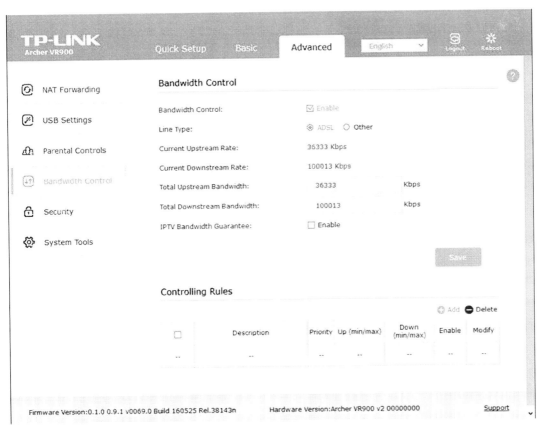

The Bandwidth Control feature on this router/modem provides a basic QoS mechanism. (Screenshot courtesy of TP-Link.)

Topic C
Configure SOHO Network Security

EXAM OBJECTIVES COVERED
1001-2.2 Compare and contrast common networking hardware devices.
1001-2.3 Given a scenario, install and configure a basic wired/wireless SOHO network.
1002-1.5 Given a scenario, use Microsoft operating system features and tools.
1002-1.6 Given a scenario, use Microsoft Windows Control Panel utilities.
1002-1.8 Given a scenario, configure Microsoft Windows networking on a client/desktop.
1002-2.10 Given a scenario, configure security on SOHO wireless and wired networks.

Although security models stress the importance of defense in depth, the network edge must still be closely guarded. As a CompTIA A+ technician, you must be able to configure firewall settings and other types of access controls to ensure safe Internet use. In this topic, you will learn how to configure common security features of SOHO router/modems, use the Windows Firewall, and set browser options.

FIREWALLS

There are many types of **firewalls** and many ways of implementing them. One distinction can be made between network and host firewalls:

- **Network firewall**—placed inline in the network and inspects all traffic that passes through it.
- **Host firewall**—installed on the host and only inspects traffic addressed to that host.

Another distinction is what parts of a packet a firewall can inspect and operate on.

PACKET FILTERING FIREWALL

Packet filtering describes the earliest type of firewall. All firewalls can still perform this basic function. A **packet filtering** firewall can inspect the headers of IP packets. This means that rules can be based on the information found in those headers:

- IP filtering—accepting or blocking traffic on the basis of its source and/or destination IP address.
- Protocol ID/type—TCP, UDP, ICMP, and so on.
- Port filtering/security—accepting or blocking a packet on the basis of source and destination port numbers (TCP or UDP application type).

This configuration is referred to as an **Access Control List (ACL)**. The firewall may provide the option to accept all packets except for those on the reject list or, alternatively, it may provide the option to reject all packets except for those on the accept list. Generally, the latter is the best choice, since it is more secure and involves less configuration.

HOST FIREWALL

A host (or software or personal) firewall is one that is implemented as software on the individual host PC or server. This might be deployed instead of or in addition to the network firewall. As well as being able to filter traffic based on data in network packets (IP address and port number, for instance), a host-based firewall can be defined with rules for whether particular software programs and services (processes) or user accounts are allowed or denied access.

Having two firewalls is more secure; if one firewall is not working or is misconfigured, the other firewall might prevent an intrusion. The downside is complexity; you must configure rules in two places, and there are two things that could be blocking communications when you come to troubleshoot connections.

 Note: *Using both a network firewall to secure the "perimeter" and a host firewall provides defense in depth. This is the concept that multiple, well-coordinated layers of defensive controls make a system harder to compromise than a single defensive barrier.*

FIREWALL SETTINGS

Most Internet router/modems come with a basic firewall product; some come with quite sophisticated firewalls. On a SOHO network, it is more typical to filter incoming traffic than outgoing traffic. Some router/modems may not support outbound filtering at all.

DISABLING PORTS

One of the basic principles of secure configuration is only to enable services that must be enabled. If a service is unused, then it should not be accessible in any way. The most secure way of doing this is to remove the service on each host. There may be circumstances in which you want a service port to be available on the local network but not on the Internet. This is where a firewall is useful. If you configure an ACL to block the port, or if the port is blocked by the default rule, then Internet hosts will not be able to access it.

MAC FILTERING

The MAC is the hardware address of a network card, in the format aa:bb:cc:dd:ee:ff. Firewalls, switches, and access points can be configured either with whitelists of allowed MACs or blacklists of prohibited MACs. This can be time-consuming to set up and it is easy for malicious actors to spoof a MAC address. On a SOHO network, the security advantages are unlikely to outweigh configuration and troubleshooting issues.

CONTENT FILTERING/PARENTAL CONTROLS

Most Internet appliances also support the configuration of filters to block websites and services on the basis of keywords or site rating and classification services. Another option is to restrict the times at which the Internet is accessible. These are configured in conjunction with services offered by the ISP.

One issue for ISP-enforced parental controls is that the filters are not usually able to distinguish account types, so the filters apply to all Internet access unless the filtering is manually disabled, which requires the ISP account holder's password. Parental controls can also be enforced at the OS level in Windows 10, where different filters can be applied based on the account type.

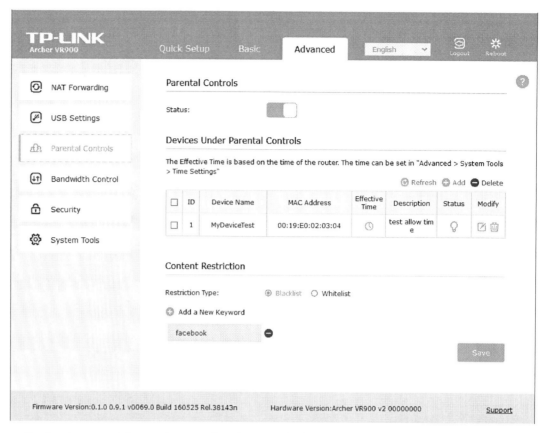

Configuring parental controls to restrict when certain devices can access the network. (Screenshot courtesy of TP-Link.)

WHITELISTS/BLACKLISTS

Content filtering works on the basis of **blacklists** of URLs that are known to harbor a particular type of content. There will be separate blacklists for different types of content that users might want to block. There are also blacklists of sites known to host malware. The firewall will block any IP address or domain name appearing on a blacklist for which a filter has been configured.

Conversely, **whitelisting** a site means that it will be accessible even if a filter is applied. If you want to lock down Internet usage very tightly, it should be possible to configure a filter so that only whitelisted sites are accessible.

NAT

All router/modems implement **Network Address Translation (NAT)**. More specifically, they implement **Network Address Port Translation (NAPT)**, which is also referred to as NAT overloading or **Port Address Translation (PAT)**. The router/modem is issued with a single public IP address by the ISP. Some ISPs might allocate a static address, but it is more common for it to be dynamic (issued by the ISP's DHCP server).

Hosts connected to the router/modem's switch or access point are configured with local (private) addresses, typically in the range 192.168.0.0/24 or 192.168.1.0/24. When one of these devices tries to contact a host on the Internet, the router identifies the connection using an ephemeral port number, adds the original private IP address and port number to a NAT table, and sends the transmission to the Internet host, using its public IP address and the new port number. When (or if) an Internet host replies to that port, the router looks up the port number in the NAT table, locates the original IP address and port, and forwards the response to the local device.

NAT overloading on a SOHO router/modem generally works without any configuration. There might be an option to configure an Application Layer Gateway (ALG) for one or more protocols. NAT can pose problems for some types of protocol. ALG mitigates these problems by opening ports dynamically to allow connections.

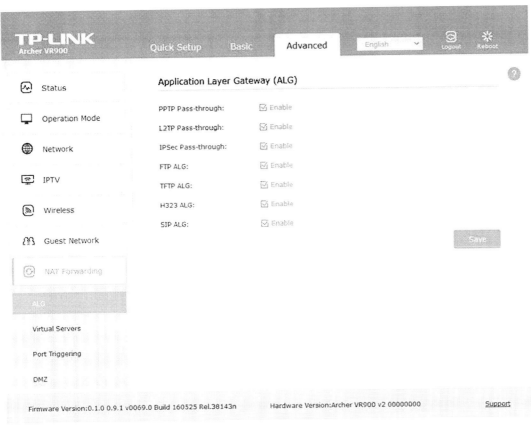

Configuring ALGs for NAT. (Screenshot courtesy of TP-Link.)

PORT FORWARDING AND PORT TRIGGERING

When NAT overloading is deployed, hosts on the Internet can only "see" the router and its public IP address. If you want to run some sort of server application from your network and make it accessible to the Internet, you need to set up port forwarding or Destination NAT (DNAT).

Port forwarding means that the router takes requests from the Internet for a particular protocol (say, HTTP/port 80) and sends them to a designated host on the LAN. The request could also be sent to a different port, so this feature is often also called port mapping. For example, the Internet host could request HTTP on port 80, but the LAN server might run its HTTP server on port 8080 instead.

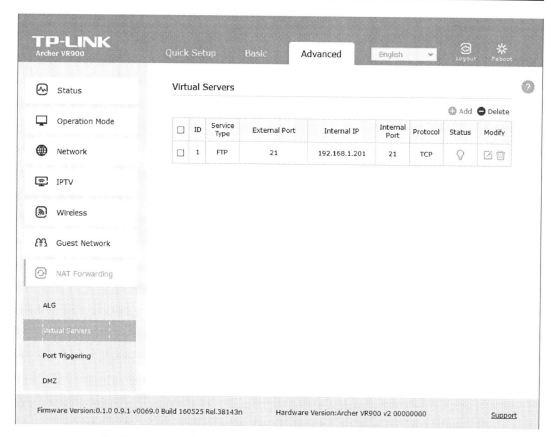

Configuring port forwarding for FTP. (Screenshot courtesy of TP-Link.)

Port triggering is used to set up applications that require more than one port. Basically, when the firewall detects activity on outbound port A destined for a given external IP address, it opens inbound access for the external IP address on port B for a set period.

DMZ

When making a server accessible on the Internet, careful thought needs to be given to the security of the local network. A simple firewall with port forwarding will only support servers on the local network. There can only be one set of access rules. If a server is compromised, because it is on the local network there is the possibility that other LAN hosts can be attacked from it or that the attacker could examine traffic passing over the LAN.

In an enterprise network, a **Demilitarized Zone (DMZ)** is a means of establishing a more secure configuration. The idea of a DMZ is that hosts placed within it are untrusted by the local network zone. Some traffic may be allowed to pass between the DMZ and the local network, but no traffic is allowed to pass from the Internet to the local network through the DMZ.

Most SOHO routers come with only basic firewall functionality. The firewall in a typical SOHO router screens the local network, rather than establishing a DMZ.

However, you should note that many SOHO router/modem vendors use the term "DMZ" or "DMZ host" to refer to a computer on the LAN that is configured to receive communications for any ports that have not been forwarded to other hosts. When DMZ is used in this sense, it means "not protected by the firewall" as the host is fully accessible to other Internet hosts (though it could be installed with a host firewall instead). This also means that the LAN is still exposed to the risks described previously.

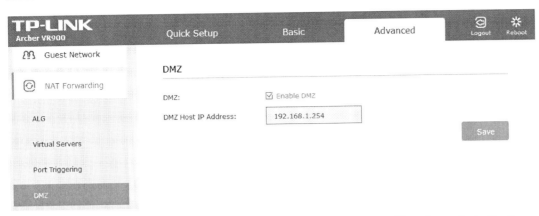

Configuring a SOHO router version of a DMZ—the host 192.168.1.254 will not be protected by the firewall. (Screenshot courtesy of TP-Link.)

UNIVERSAL PLUG-AND-PLAY

ACLs and port forwarding/port triggering are challenging for end users to configure correctly. Many users would simply resort to turning the firewall off in order to get a particular application to work. As a means of mitigating this attitude, services that require complex firewall configuration can use the **Universal Plug-and-Play (UPnP)** framework to send instructions to the firewall with the correct configuration parameters.

On the firewall, check the box to enable UPnP. A client UPnP device, such as an Xbox, PlayStation, or Voice-over-IP handset, will be able to configure the firewall automatically to open the IP addresses and ports necessary to play an online game or place and receive VoIP calls.

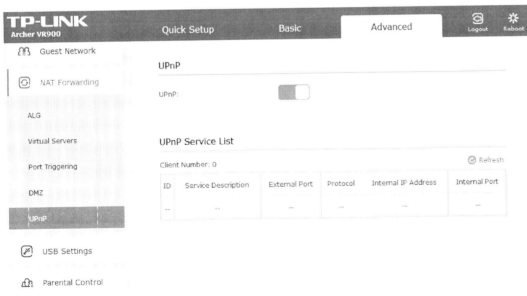

Enabling UPnP—there is nothing to configure, but when client devices use the service, the rules they have configured on the firewall are shown in the service list. (Screenshot courtesy of TP-Link.)

UPnP is associated with a number of security vulnerabilities and is best disabled if not required. You should ensure that the router does not accept UPnP configuration requests from the external (Internet) interface. If using UPnP, keep up-to-date with any security advisories or firmware updates from the router manufacturer.

Note: *Also make sure that UPnP is disabled on client devices, unless you have confirmed that the implementation is secure. As well as game consoles, vulnerabilities have been found in UPnP running on devices such as printers and web cams.*

WINDOWS FIREWALL

As well as configuring the network firewall, you may want to configure a personal firewall on each host. Windows ships with bundled firewall software.

Note: *There are also third-party firewalls. If you install another firewall product, it should disable Windows Firewall. Do not try to run two host firewalls at the same time. The products may interfere with one another and attempting to keep the ACLs synchronized between them will be extremely challenging.*

CONFIGURING WINDOWS FIREWALL

To configure the firewall in Windows 7, open **Windows Firewall** in Control Panel to view a status page, then click **Turn Windows Firewall on or off**. The Windows Firewall can be turned on or off depending on whether the network location is private (home/work) or public or domain. For example, you could have an Internet connection through an open access point set to public with a VPN to your corporate network running over the link, but set to domain.

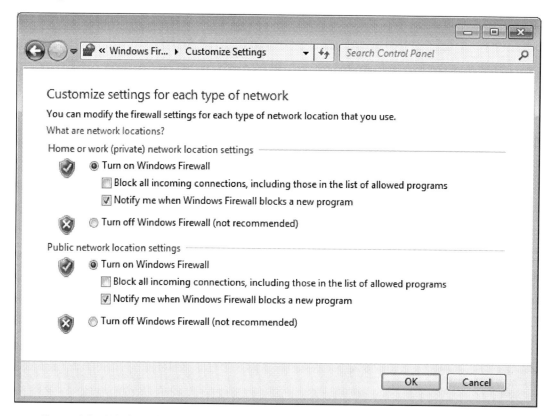

Customizing Windows Firewall settings in Windows 7. (Screenshot used with permission from Microsoft.)

CONFIGURING EXCEPTIONS

To allow or block programs (configure exceptions), from the **Windows Firewall** status page, click **Allow a program or feature through the Windows Firewall**. Check the box for either or both network type or use **Allow another program** to locate its executable file and add it to the list.

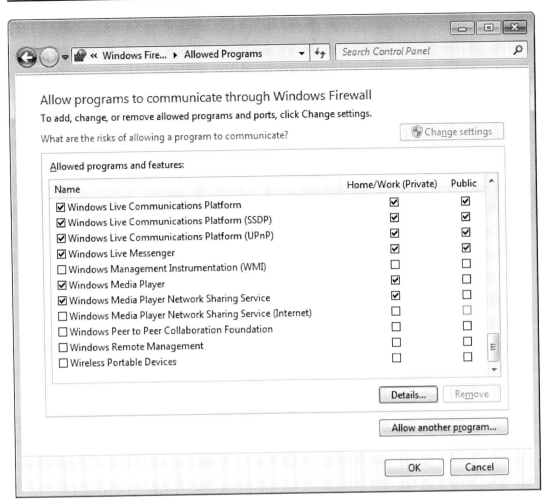

Windows Firewall Allowed Programs. (Screenshot used with permission from Microsoft.)

WINDOWS DEFENDER SECURITY CENTER

In Windows 10, you can turn the firewall on or off and access the configuration applets shown previously via the **Firewall & network protection** page in the Windows Defender Security Center.

WINDOWS FIREWALL WITH ADVANCED SECURITY

An add-in to the basic firewall (Windows Firewall with Advanced Security) allows configuration of outbound filtering, as well as IPsec connection security and additional monitoring tools.

The Advanced Firewall can be configured through group policy on a domain; on a standalone PC or workgroup, open the `wf.msc` management console (or enter "firewall" at the Search box or use the **Advanced settings** link in the Windows Firewall Control Panel applet). On the status page, you can click **Windows Firewall properties** to configure each profile. The firewall can be turned on or off and you can switch the default rule for inbound and outbound traffic between **Block** and **Allow**.

You can also set which network adapters are linked to a profile and configure logging.

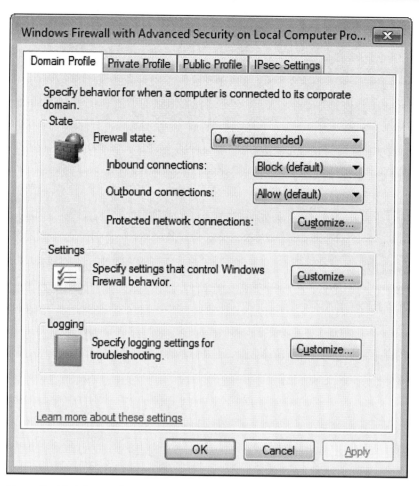

Windows Firewall with Advanced Security—Profile Settings. (Screenshot used with permission from Microsoft.)

*Note: **Block** stops traffic unless a specific rule allows it. Conversely, **Allow** accepts all traffic unless a specific rule blocks it. You can also use **Block all connections** to stop inbound connections regardless of the rules set up.*

Back in the main Advanced Firewall console, you enable, disable, and configure rules by clicking in the **Inbound Rules** or **Outbound Rules** folder as appropriate. Rules can be based on a number of triggers, including program, Windows Feature, service, protocol type, network port, and IP address range.

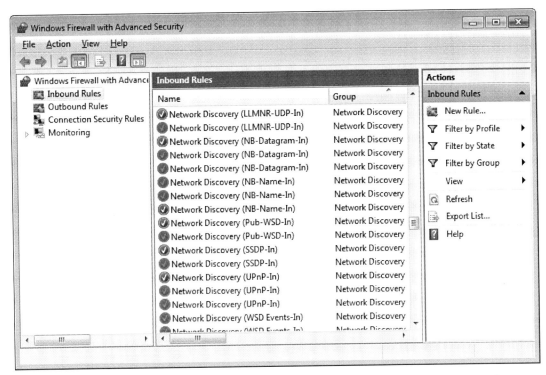

Configuring Windows Firewall with Advanced Security. (Screenshot used with permission from Microsoft.)

LOCATION AWARENESS

Different Windows Firewall settings can be applied depending on the network to which the PC is connected. When Windows 7 detects a new network (wired, wireless, dial-up, or VPN), the **Set Network Location** dialog box is displayed.

You can make the following choices:

- **Home**—enables network discovery (the ability to contact other computers on the network) and the use of homegroups.
- **Work**—enables network discovery.
- **Public**—disables network discovery and file sharing.
- **Domain**—you cannot choose this option, but if the computer is joined to a domain, then the firewall policy will be configured via Group Policy.

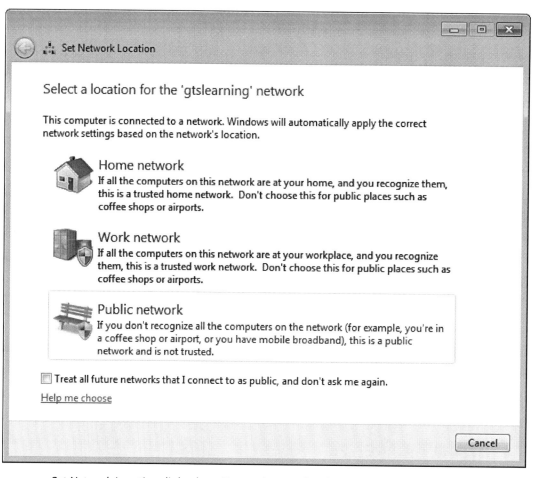

Set Network Location dialog box. (Screenshot used with permission from Microsoft.)

To change the location defined for a network, open the **Network and Sharing Center**. Click the network location label under the network name.

In Windows 8 and Windows 10, the concept of home and work networks has been discarded. Networks are either public or private depending on whether you choose to enable discovery and file sharing or not. If the computer is joined to a domain, then the network type will be set to domain.

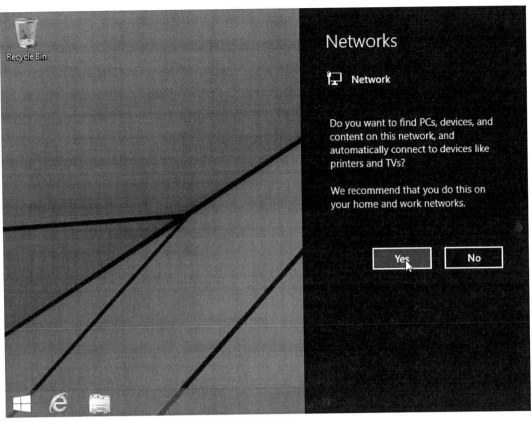

Setting network location type in Windows 8. (Screenshot used with permission from Microsoft.)

You can subsequently change the setting via the **Settings** app.

BROWSER CONFIGURATION

The browser has become one of the most important bits of software on a computer. As well as actual web browsing, it is frequently used as the interface for many types of web applications. The basic browser is also often extended by plug-ins that run other types of content. Internet Explorer (IE) used to be completely dominant in the browser market, but alternatives such as Google's Chrome™ and Mozilla's Firefox® now have substantial market share. This section describes the **Internet Options** applet for Internet Explorer®, but similar settings can be configured for other versions and browsers.

Note: *In fact, in Windows 10, the Internet Explorer browser is replaced by the Edge browser. IE is still available in Windows 10, but its use is deprecated.*

GENERAL TAB

The main functions of the **General** tab are to configure home pages (pages that load when the browser is started) and manage browsing history. On a public computer, it is best practice to clear the browsing history at the end of a session. You can configure the browser to do this automatically.

Internet Options—General tab. (Screenshot used with permission from Microsoft.)

 Note: *You can also start an "In Private" mode session by pressing **Ctrl+Shift+P**. This mode disables browsing history, cookies, and browser toolbars and extensions.*

CONNECTIONS TAB AND PROXY SETTINGS

The **Connections** tab sets the method Internet Explorer uses to connect to the Internet.

- To use a dial-up connection, select either **Dial whenever a network connection is not present** or **Always dial my default connection**. You would typically select the former option for a laptop computer that connects via the LAN in the office but a modem elsewhere. If the connection selected in the **Dial-up Settings** box is not the default, click **Set Default**.

- To use a router, you simply need to configure the Default gateway and DNS server parameters in TCP/IP properties for the local network adapter (though more typically, this would be configured automatically using DHCP). The browser will use this connection when you select **Never dial a connection** or **Dial whenever a network connection is not present**.

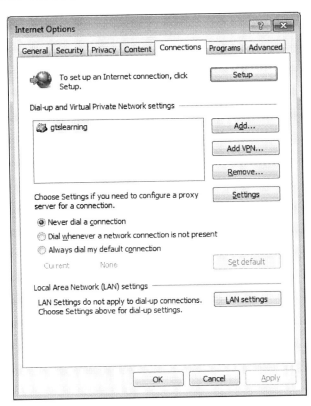

Internet Options—Connections tab. (Screenshot used with permission from Microsoft.)

On some networks, a proxy may be used to provide network connectivity. A proxy server can be used to improve both performance and security. User machines pass Internet requests to the proxy server, which forwards them to the Internet. The proxy may also cache pages and content that is requested by multiple clients, reducing bandwidth. The proxy may be able to autoconfigure the browser but if not, its address must be configured manually. Select the **LAN Settings** button to do this.

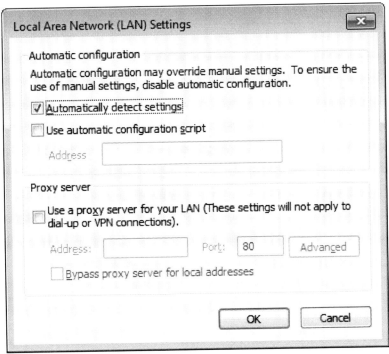

Local Area Network (LAN) Settings dialog box. (Screenshot used with permission from Microsoft.)

Note: *In Windows 10, use the* **Settings→Network & Internet→Proxy** *configuration page.*

SECURITY TAB

The **Security** tab is designed to prevent malicious content hosted on web pages from infecting the computer or stealing personal information.

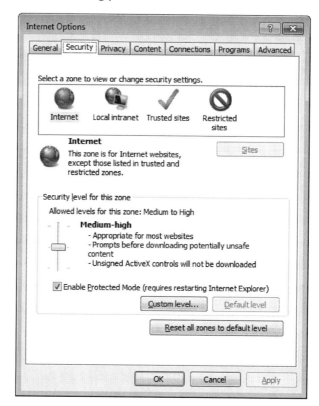

Internet Options—Security tab. (Screenshot used with permission from Microsoft.)

There are lots of security settings, configuring things such as whether scripts and plug-ins are allowed to run or install, files to download, and so on.

Internet Explorer operates a system of zones, each with different security settings. Everything off the local subnet is in the Internet zone by default; the user (or a domain's group policy) can add particular sites to the **Trusted** and **Restricted** zones as appropriate. The settings for a particular zone can also be changed using the **Custom Level** button.

PRIVACY TAB

The main function of the **Privacy** tab is to control sites' use of cookies. A cookie is a text file used to store session data. For example, if you log on to a site, the site might use a cookie to remember who you are. If the site is prevented from setting these cookies, it may not work correctly. On the other hand, a modern website might host components from many different domains. These components might try to set third-party cookies, most often to track pages you have been visiting and display relevant advertising at you.

You can use the slider to set the default policy for the Internet zone and use the **Sites** button to always block or allow cookies from particular domains.

The **Privacy** tab also allows you to configure the Pop-up Blocker, which prevents sites from spawning new windows through scripting.

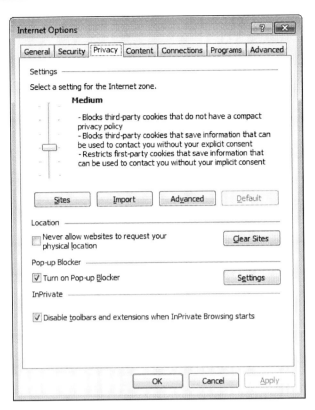

Internet Options—Privacy tab. (Screenshot used with permission from Microsoft.)

PROGRAMS TAB

You can use the **Programs** tab to check whether IE is the default browser.

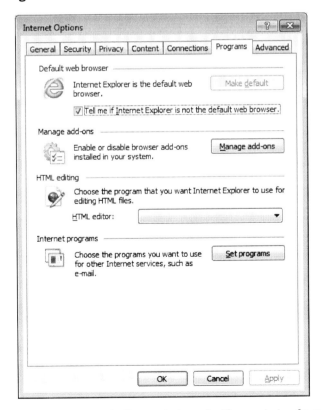

Internet Options—Programs tab. (Screenshot used with permission from Microsoft.)

Click **Set programs** to open the **Default Programs** applet to make another browser the default. You can also manage add-ons from here. Add-ons are code objects that extend the functionality of the browser. Examples include toolbars, malware scanners, content players (such as Adobe® Flash® player), and document readers (such as PDF viewers). **Manage add-ons** lets you disable or uninstall these objects.

ADVANCED TAB

The **Advanced** tab contains settings that do not fit under any of the other tabs.

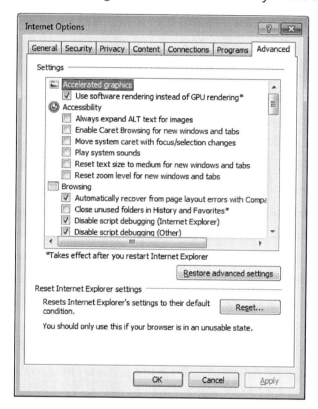

Internet Options—Advanced tab. (Screenshot used with permission from Microsoft.)

Some notable options include:

*   Disable certain types of content (pictures,for instance).
*   Enable a script debugger.
*   Enable or disable passive FTP.
*   Allow or prevent active content from running on local computer drives.

You can also use this tab to completely reset the browser.

Topic D
Configure Remote Access

EXAM OBJECTIVES COVERED
1001-2.1 Compare and contrast TCP and UDP ports, protocols, and their purposes.
1002-1.5 Given a scenario, use Microsoft operating system features and tools.
1002-1.8 Given a scenario, configure Microsoft Windows networking on a client/desktop.
1002-4.9 Given a scenario, use remote access technologies.

A remote access utility allows you to establish a session on another computer on the network. There are command-line and GUI remote access tools. These are very useful for technical support and troubleshooting. The fact that remote access is so useful shows how important it is that such tools be used securely. In this topic, you will learn about the features of different remote access tools and security considerations of using each one.

WINDOWS REMOTE ACCESS TOOLS

Windows comes with several remote access features. Two of the GUI remote tools are Remote Desktop and Remote Assistance. These use some of the same underlying technologies but suit different purposes.

REMOTE DESKTOP

Remote Desktop allows a remote user to connect to their desktop machine. The desktop machine functions as a terminal server and the dial-in machine as a Windows terminal. This allows the user to work as if physically connected to their workstation.

This would ideally suit laptop users working from home with a slow link. Having gained access to the corporate network (via the Internet using a VPN, for example) they could then establish a remote desktop connection to their own office-based system. A technician can also use Remote Desktop to configure or troubleshoot a computer.

Remote Desktop runs on TCP port 3389.

> **Note:** *Windows Home editions do not include the Remote Desktop server so you cannot connect to them, but they do include the client so you can connect to other computers from them.*

REMOTE ASSISTANCE

Remote Assistance allows a user to ask for help from a technician or co-worker. The "helper" can then connect and join the session with the user. This session can include an interactive desktop, whereby the helper can control the system of the user.

Remote Assistance assigns a port dynamically from the ephemeral range (49152 to 65535). This makes it difficult to configure through firewalls, but remote assistance is designed more for local network support anyway.

REMOTE SETTINGS CONFIGURATION

By default, Remote Assistance connections are allowed but Remote Desktop ones are not. To change these settings, open **System Properties** then click **Remote settings**.

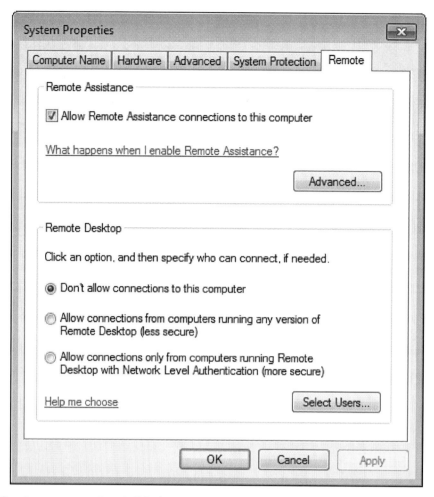

Configuring remote settings in Windows 7. (Screenshot used with permission from Microsoft.)

You can choose between allowing older RDP clients to connect and requiring RDP clients that support **Network Level Authentication (NLA)**. NLA protects the computer against Denial of Service attacks. Without NLA, the system configures a desktop before the user logs on. A malicious user can create multiple pending connections in an attempt to crash the system. NLA authenticates the user before committing any resources to the session.

RDP authentication and session data is always encrypted. This means that a malicious user with access to the same network cannot intercept credentials or interfere or capture anything transmitted during the session.

Click the **Select (Remote) Users** button to define which users can connect remotely. Users in the local administrators group already have this property. You can select from members of the local accounts database or from the domain of which your machine is a member.

 Note: The biggest limitation of Remote Desktop on Windows is that only one person can be logged in to the machine at once, so once you log in using Remote Desktop, the monitor at the local computer will go to the login screen. If a local user logs in, the remote user will be disconnected. Remote Desktop is not really a remote diagnostic and troubleshooting tool as much as a management tool.

REMOTE CREDENTIAL GUARD

If Remote Desktop is used to connect to a machine that has been compromised by malware, the credentials of the user account used to make the connection become highly vulnerable. **RDP Restricted Admin (RDPRA) Mode** and **Remote Credential Guard** are means of mitigating this risk. You can read more about these technologies at **docs.microsoft.com/en-us/windows/security/identity-protection/remote-credential-guard**.

THE REMOTE ASSISTANCE PROCESS

A request for remote assistance is made using the **Windows Remote Assistance** tool. You can send an invitation as a file, via email, or using Easy Connect. The tool will generate a password and a connection file for you to transmit to the helper.

To provide assistance, open the invitation file and enter the password and wait for the user to accept the offer of assistance. When the offer is accepted, a remote desktop window is opened with an additional chat tool that you can use to communicate with the user.

Remote Assistance sessions are encrypted using the same technologies as RDP.

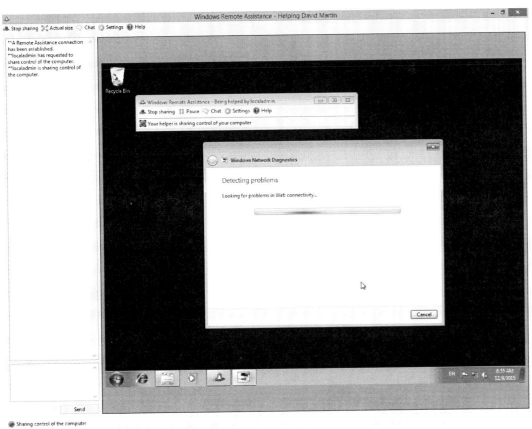

Using Remote Assistance. (Screenshot used with permission from Microsoft.)

REMOTE DESKTOP

To connect to a server via Remote Desktop, from the **Communications** menu in **Accessories**, open the **Remote Desktop Connection** shortcut, or run `mstsc` at a command prompt or the **Run** dialog box or **Instant Search** box. Enter the server's computer name or IP address to connect. The server can be installed with a certificate to identify it securely.

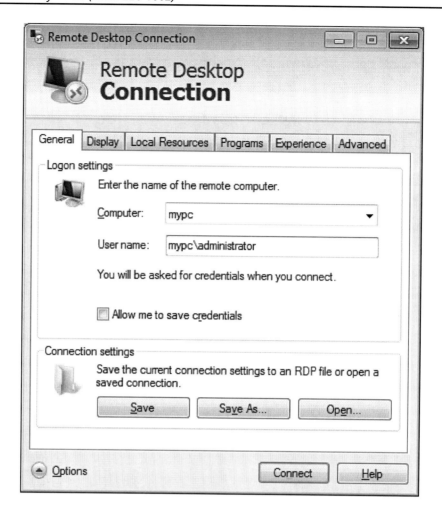

Remote Desktop Connection client. (Screenshot used with permission from Microsoft.)

You will need to define logon credentials. To specify a domain or computer account, use the format *ComputerOrDomainName\UserName*. In addition, you might need to define display properties. You can use either full screen or some windowed display. Also, you can configure the quality of the color scheme. The **Local Resources** tab allows you to define how key combinations (such as **Alt+Tab**) function—that is, will they affect the local computer, the remote computer, or the remote computer in full screen mode. Because the connection may be over a slow link, such as dial-up, you can configure optimization based on the line speeds (modem, LAN, and so on). This affects bitmap caching and video options.

Once you have your remote desktop connection established, you can work quite normally, as if physically adjacent to the target machine—but be aware that no one else can use the target system while in remote mode. The system becomes locked and can be unlocked by the administrator or the remotely connected user only.

REMOTE ACCESS TECHNOLOGIES

Remote Desktop and Remote Assistance are technologies for Windows networks.

There are versions of the `mstsc` client software for Linux®, macOS®, iOS®, and Android™ so you can use devices running those operating systems to connect to an RDP server running on a Windows machine.

Other protocols and software tools are available for accepting incoming connections to non-Windows devices.

TELNET

Telnet is a command-line terminal emulation protocol and program. The host server runs a Telnet daemon listening for connections on TCP port 23. The client system runs a Telnet program to send commands to the daemon. When you connect, your computer acts as if your keyboard is attached to the remote computer and you can use the same commands as a local user.

> **Note:** *Telnet sends all messages in clear text. Anyone able to intercept ("sniff") network traffic would be able to see the passwords for accounts.*

If you enter `telnet` at a command prompt, some of the basic commands you can use are listed in the following table.

Command	Use
`open HostPort`	Starts a session with the host on that port. Host can be a host name, FQDN, or IP address.
`?`	Displays help.
`status`	Check session status.
`close`	Ends the current session.
`quit`	Exits the telnet prompt.

Telnet is sometimes still used for troubleshooting services such as SMTP or HTTP. For example, to connect to an SMTP server at the IP address 192.168.1.2, you would enter `telnet 192.168.1.2 25`.

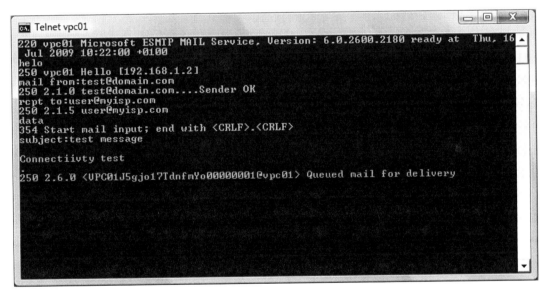

Telnet session with an SMTP server. (Screenshot used with permission from Microsoft.)

Another application of Telnet is router or switch configuration. The Telnet application is used to connect to the Telnet Daemon on the router and then command-line instructions can be issued to configure it.

> **Note:** *Telnet is not installed by default in Windows. You can add it using Programs and Features. On a Windows network, you are more likely to use Windows Remote Shell (WinRS), which has better functionality and security features.*

SSH

Secure Shell (SSH) is designed to replace unsecure administration and file copy programs such as Telnet and FTP. SSH uses TCP port 22 (by default). SSH uses encryption to protect each session. There are numerous commercial and open source SSH products available for all the major OS platforms (UNIX, Linux, Windows, and macOS).

SSH servers are identified by a public/private key pair (the host key). A mapping of host names to public keys can be kept manually by each SSH client or there are various enterprise software products designed for SSH key management.

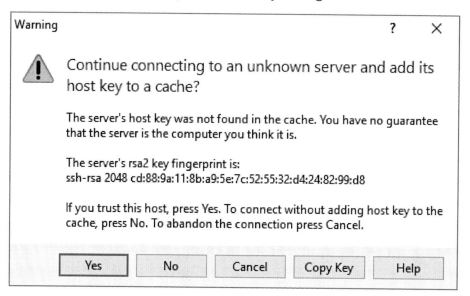

Confirming the SSH server's host key. (Screenshot used with permission from Microsoft.)

SSH CLIENT AUTHENTICATION

The server's host key is used to set up a secure channel to use for the client to submit authentication credentials. SSH allows various methods for the client to authenticate to the SSH server. Each of these methods can be enabled or disabled as required on the server:

- Username/password—the client submits credentials that are verified by the SSH server either against a local user database or using an authentication server.
- Kerberos—this allows Single Sign On (SSO) on a network that runs the Kerberos authentication protocol. Windows Active Directory domain networks use Kerberos.
- Host-based authentication—the server is configured with a list of authorized client public keys. The client requests authentication using one of these keys and the server generates a challenge with the public key. The client must use the matching private key it holds to decrypt the challenge and complete the authentication process. This provides non-interactive login but there is considerable risk from intrusion if a client host's private key is compromised.

 Note: With host-based authentication, managing valid client public keys is a critical security task. Many recent attacks on web servers have exploited poor key management.

- Public key authentication—host-based authentication cannot be used with fine-grained access controls as the access is granted to a single user account. The same sort of public key authentication method can be used for each user account. The user's private key can be configured with a passphrase that must be input to access the key, providing an additional measure of protection compared to host-based authentication.

SCREEN SHARING AND VNC

In macOS, you can use the Screen Sharing feature for remote desktop functionality. Screen Sharing is based on **Virtual Network Computing (VNC)**. You can use any VNC client to connect to a Screen Sharing server.

VNC itself is a freeware product with similar functionality to RDP. It works over TCP port 5900. Freeware versions of VNC provide no connection security and so should only be used over a secure connection, such as a VPN. However, there are commercial products packaged with encryption solutions. macOS Screen Sharing is encrypted.

FILE SHARE

Setting up a network file share can be relatively complex. You need to select a file sharing protocol that all the connecting hosts can use, configure permissions on the share, and provision user accounts that both the server and client recognize. Consequently OS vendors have developed other mechanisms for simple file sharing between devices.

- AirDrop®—supported by Apple iOS and macOS, this uses Bluetooth® to establish a Wi-Fi Direct connection between the devices for the duration of the file transfer. The connection is secured by the Bluetooth pairing mechanism and Wi-Fi encryption.
- Near Share—Microsoft's version of AirDrop. Near Share was introduced in Windows 10 (1803), partly replacing the previous Homegroup feature.

There are plenty of third-party and open source alternatives to AirDrop.

Although the products have security mechanisms, there is the potential for misuse of features such as this. Users accepting connections from any source could receive unsolicited transfer requests. It is best only to accept requests from known contacts. The products can be subject to security vulnerabilities that allow unsolicited transfers.

Topic E
Troubleshoot Network Connections

 EXAM OBJECTIVES COVERED
1001-2.8 Given a scenario, use appropriate networking tools.
1001-5.7 Given a scenario, troubleshoot common wired and wireless network problems.
1002-1.4 Given a scenario, use appropriate Microsoft command line tools.
1002-3.1 Given a scenario, troubleshoot Microsoft Windows OS problems.

As a CompTIA A+ technician, you will be expected to be able to troubleshoot basic network connectivity issues. At this support level, you will be focusing on client issues. As you have learned, networks are complex and involve many different hardware devices, protocols, and applications, meaning that there are lots of things that can go wrong! In this topic you will learn how to identify and diagnose the causes of some common wired and wireless network issues.

COMMON WIRED NETWORK CONNECTIVITY ISSUES

When troubleshooting a network issue, it is often a good idea to rule out any problem with connectivity at the hardware layer. If a single host is unable to connect to the network, the first thing you should check is whether the network cable is properly connected. If the problem is not that obvious, then there are a few other tools you can use to diagnose a problem with network hardware (adapters and cabling).

TROUBLESHOOTING WIRED CONNECTIVITY

To diagnose a cable problem, perform a basic local connectivity test using the `ping` utility (discussed later) with a known working system on the local subnet. If you can ping another local system, the problem is not in the cabling (at least, not this cable).

If you can't ping anything then, assuming you've physically checked the back of the machine for the cable's presence, verify that the patch cord is good. The easiest thing to do is swap the patch cord to the wall socket with another—known working—cable.

Can you ping anything now? If not, verify the patch cord between the patch panel and the switch. Swap with another known good cable and test again. If this still fails, try connecting a different host to the network port. If the other host connects, suspect a problem with network adapter in the original host. Use Device Manager to verify that the adapter's link properties are set correctly (typically to autonegotiate). If there is no configuration issue, swap the network adapter with a known good one and re-test.

 Note: The link LEDs on network adapter and switch ports will indicate whether the link is active and possibly at what speed the link is working. The LEDs typically flicker to show network activity.

If you still haven't isolated the problem, try plugging the problem computer into a different network port. By testing from different ports, you should be able to establish the scope of the problem and the likely location of the fault. Eventually, through the process of substituting working components for suspect components, you should resolve the cable problem. Remember that if several users have the problem, you should check the switch in this way too.

Note: *If you have suitable tools, you can use them in place of substituting and transposing devices. For example, a loopback plug can be used to test whether a port is working (and therefore indicate that the problem is with the cable).*

Problems with patch cords are simple as you can just throw the broken one away and plug in a new one. If the problem is in the structured cabling, however, you will want to use cable testing tools to determine its cause, especially if the problem is intermittent (that is, if the problem comes and goes). The solution may involve installing a new permanent link, but there could also be a termination or external interference problem.

TROUBLESHOOTING SLOW TRANSFER SPEEDS

The transfer speed of a cabled link could be reduced if the network equipment is not all working to the highest available standard. Check the configuration of the network adapter driver (via Device Manager) and the setting for the switch port (via the switch's management software). Slow transfer speeds can be caused by a variety of other problems and can be very difficult to diagnose.

- There may be congestion at a switch or router or some other network-wide problem. This might be caused by a fault or by user behavior, such as transferring a very large amount of data over the network.
- There could be a problem with the network adapter driver.
- The computer could be infected with malware.
- The network cabling could be affected by interference. This could be from an external source but check the ends of cables for excessive untwisting of the wire pairs as poor termination is a common cause of problems.

COMMON WIRELESS NETWORK CONNECTIVITY ISSUES

When troubleshooting wireless networks, as with cabled links, you need to consider problems with the physical media, such as interference and configuration issues.

The **Radio Frequency (RF)** signal from radio-based devices weakens considerably as the distance between the devices increases. If you experience slow transfer speeds or you cannot establish a connection, try moving the devices closer together. If you still cannot obtain a connection, check that the security and authentication parameters are correctly configured on both devices.

TROUBLESHOOTING WIRELESS CONFIGURATION ISSUES

If a user is looking for a network name that is not shown in the list of available wireless networks (**SSID not found**), the user could be out of range or broadcast of the SSID name might be suppressed. In the latter scenario, the connection to the network name must be configured manually.

Another factor to consider is **standards mismatch**. Choosing a compatibility mode for an access point will reduce the features available (no WPA for 802.11b compatibility, for instance). If an access point is not operating in compatibility mode, it will not be able to communicate with devices that only support older standards. Also, when an older device joins the network, the performance of the whole network can be affected. To support 802.11b clients, an 802.11b/n access point must transmit legacy frame preamble and collision avoidance frames, adding overhead. If at all possible, upgrade 802.11b devices rather than letting them join the WLAN. 802.11g and 802.11n are more compatible in terms of negotiating collision avoidance. In a mixed 802.11g/n WLAN, performance of the 802.11n devices operating in the 2.4 GHz band is only likely to be severely impacted when 802.11g devices perform large file transfers. As these take longer to complete, there is less "airtime" available for the 802.11n clients.

Note: *With 802.11n dual-band APs operating in mixed mode or with 802.11ac, it is typical to assign the 2.4 GHz band to support legacy clients. The 5 GHz band can be reserved for 802.11n or 802.11ac clients and bonded channels can be configured.*

Also consider that not all clients supporting 802.11n have dual band radios. If a client cannot connect to a network operating on the 5 GHz band, check whether its radio is 2.4 GHz-capable only.

LOW RF SIGNAL/RSSI

A wireless adapter will be configured to drop the connection speed if the **Received Signal Strength Indicator (RSSI)** is not at a minimum required level. The RSSI is an index level calculated from the signal strength level. For example, an 802.11n adapter might be capable of a 144 Mbps data rate with an optimum signal, but if the signal is weak it might drop to a 54 Mbps or 11 Mbps rate to make the connection more reliable. If the RSSI is too low, the adapter will drop the connection entirely and try to use a different network. If there are two fairly weak networks, the adapter might "flap" between them. Try moving to a location with better reception.

TROUBLESHOOTING WIRELESS SIGNAL ISSUES

If a device is within the supported range but the signal is very weak or you can only get an **intermittent connection**, there is likely to be interference from another radio source broadcasting at the same frequency. If this is the case, try adjusting the channel that the devices use. Another possibility is interference from a powerful electromagnetic source, such as a motor or microwave oven. Finally, there might be something blocking the signal. Radio waves do not pass easily through metal or dense objects. Construction materials such as wire mesh, foil-backed plasterboard, concrete, and mirrors can block or degrade signals. Try angling or repositioning the device or antenna to try to get better reception.

Note: *The ideal position for an access point is high up and in the center of the area it is supposed to serve.*

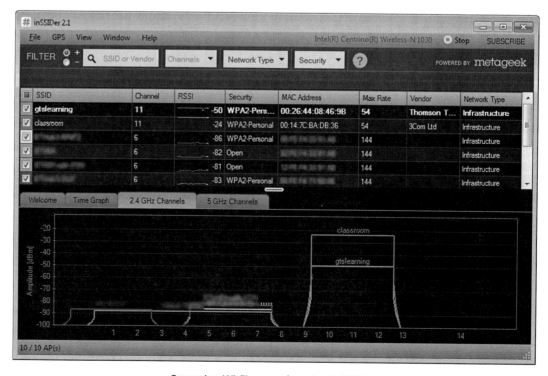

Surveying Wi-Fi networks using inSSIDer.

Wi-Fi Analyzer software, such as inSSIDer, is designed to support a site survey, to identify nearby networks that may be causing interference problems, and to measure signal strength. You can use a Wi-Fi Analyzer for troubleshooting, too. It shows the signal strength, measured in dBm. This can also be expressed as a percentage; for example, -35 dBm or better would represent the best possible signal at 100%, -90 dBm or worse would represent 1%, and -65 dBm would represent 50% signal strength.

The analyzer will also show how many networks are utilizing each channel. Setting the network to use a less congested channel can improve performance.

IP CONFIGURATION ISSUES

If a host does not have an appropriate IP configuration for the network that it is connected to, it will not be able to communicate with other hosts, even if the physical connection is sound. There are a number of command-line tools for testing and troubleshooting the IP configuration.

VIEWING IP CONFIGURATION (ipconfig)

In Windows, IP configuration information is displayed through the adapter's status dialog (Windows 7/8) or Windows Settings (Windows 10). You can also view this information at a command line using the `ipconfig` tool. Used without switches, `ipconfig` displays the IP address, subnet mask, and default gateway (router) for all network adapters to which TCP/IP is bound. Typical ipconfig switches and arguments are as follows.

Switch	Description
`ipconfig /all`	Displays detailed configuration, including DHCP and DNS servers, MAC address, and NetBIOS status.
`ipconfig /release AdapterName`	Releases the IP address obtained from a DHCP server so that the network adapter(s) will no longer have an IP address.
`ipconfig /renew AdapterName`	Forces a DHCP client to renew the lease it has for an IP address.
`ipconfig /displaydns`	Displays the DNS resolver cache. This contains host and domain names that have been queried recently. Caching the name-to-IP mappings reduces network traffic.
`ipconfig /flushdns`	Clears the DNS resolver cache.

Note that omitting the *AdapterName* argument releases or renews all adapters. If *AdapterName* contains spaces, use quotes around it (for example, `ipconfig / renew "Local Area Connection"`).

TROUBLESHOOTING WITH ipconfig

You would use `ipconfig` to determine whether the adapter has been correctly configured. `ipconfig` can resolve the following questions:

- Is the adapter configured with a static address? Are the parameters (IP address, subnet mask, default gateway, and DNS server correct)?
- Is the adapter configured by DHCP? If so:
  - An address in the range 169.254.x.y indicates that the client could not contact a DHCP server and is using Automatic Private IP Addressing (APIPA). If this is the

case, Windows will display a yellow alert icon and a notification that the adapter has only **Limited connectivity**. 🖳

- A DHCP lease can be static (always assigns the same IP address to the computer) or dynamic (assigns an IP address from a pool)—has the computer obtained a suitable address and subnet mask?
- Are other parameters assigned by DHCP correct (default gateway, DNS servers, and so on)?

```
C:\Users\Admin>ipconfig /all

Windows IP Configuration

    Host Name . . . . . . . . . . . . : ROGUE
    Primary Dns Suffix  . . . . . . . :
    Node Type . . . . . . . . . . . . : Hybrid
    IP Routing Enabled. . . . . . . . : No
    WINS Proxy Enabled. . . . . . . . : No
    DNS Suffix Search List. . . . . . : classroom.local

Ethernet adapter Ethernet:

    Connection-specific DNS Suffix  . : classroom.local
    Description . . . . . . . . . . . : Microsoft Hyper-V Network Adapter
    Physical Address. . . . . . . . . : 00-15-5D-01-CA-0E
    DHCP Enabled. . . . . . . . . . . : Yes
    Autoconfiguration Enabled . . . . : Yes
    IPv4 Address. . . . . . . . . . . : 10.1.0.131(Preferred)
    Subnet Mask . . . . . . . . . . . : 255.255.255.0
    Lease Obtained. . . . . . . . . . : Wednesday, January 4, 2017 2:40:05 AM
    Lease Expires . . . . . . . . . . : Thursday, January 12, 2017 2:40:03 AM
    Default Gateway . . . . . . . . . : 10.1.0.254
    DHCP Server . . . . . . . . . . . : 10.1.0.1
    DNS Servers . . . . . . . . . . . : 10.1.0.1
    NetBIOS over Tcpip. . . . . . . . : Enabled
```

Using ipconfig. (Screenshot used with permission from Microsoft.)

If any of these results are negative, you should investigate either communications between the client and the DHCP server, the configuration of the DHCP server, or whether multiple DHCP servers are running on the network (and the client has obtained the wrong configuration from one).

ifconfig

UNIX and Linux hosts provide a command called `ifconfig`, which provides similar output to Windows' ipconfig program. Note some differences between the Windows and Linux commands:

- `ifconfig` can also be used to bind an address to an adapter interface, set up communication parameters, and enable or disable the adapter.
- The Windows switches for configuring the adapter with DHCP and DNS are not supported by `ifconfig`.
- The `ifconfig` command output does not show the default gateway (use `route` instead). It does show traffic statistics, though.

```
administrator@lamp:~$ ifconfig
eth0      Link encap:Ethernet  HWaddr 00:15:5d:01:c0:9f
          inet addr:192.168.1.1  Bcast:192.168.1.255  Mask:255.255.255.0
          inet6 addr: fe80::215:5dff:fe01:c09f/64 Scope:Link
          UP BROADCAST RUNNING MULTICAST  MTU:1500  Metric:1
          RX packets:0 errors:0 dropped:0 overruns:0 frame:0
          TX packets:36 errors:0 dropped:0 overruns:0 carrier:0
          collisions:0 txqueuelen:1000
          RX bytes:0 (0.0 B)  TX bytes:1728 (1.7 KB)

lo        Link encap:Local Loopback
          inet addr:127.0.0.1  Mask:255.0.0.0
          inet6 addr: ::1/128 Scope:Host
          UP LOOPBACK RUNNING  MTU:16436  Metric:1
          RX packets:57 errors:0 dropped:0 overruns:0 frame:0
          TX packets:57 errors:0 dropped:0 overruns:0 carrier:0
          collisions:0 txqueuelen:0
          RX bytes:4153 (4.1 KB)  TX bytes:4153 (4.1 KB)

administrator@lamp:~$ _
```

Using ifconfig. (Screenshot used with permission from Microsoft.)

Note: *Additionally, a separate command (`iwconfig`) is used to manage wireless interfaces. Note that both these commands are deprecated in favor of the newer `ip` and `iw` utilities.*

IP CONNECTIVITY ISSUES

If the link and IP configuration both seem to be correct, the problem may not lie with the local machine but somewhere in the overall network topology. You can test connections to servers such as files shares, printers, or email by trying to use them. One drawback of this method is that there could be some sort of application fault rather than a network fault. Therefore, it is useful to have a low-level test of basic connectivity that does not have any dependencies other than a working link and IP configuration.

ping

The `ping` utility is a command-line diagnostic tool used to test whether a host can communicate with another host on the same network or on a remote network. It is the basic tool to use to establish that a link is working. `ping` uses the **Internet Control Message Protocol (ICMP)** to request status messages from hosts. The following steps outline the procedures for verifying a computer's configuration and for testing router connections:

1. Ping the loopback address to verify TCP/IP is installed and loaded correctly (`ping 127.0.0.1`)—the loopback address is a reserved IP address used for testing purposes.
2. Ping the IP address of your workstation to verify it was added correctly and to check for possible duplicate IP addresses.
3. Ping the IP address of the default gateway to verify it is up and running and that you can communicate with a host on the local network.
4. Ping the IP address of a remote host to verify you can communicate through the router. If no router is available, Windows will display a yellow alert icon and a notification that the adapter has **No Internet access**.

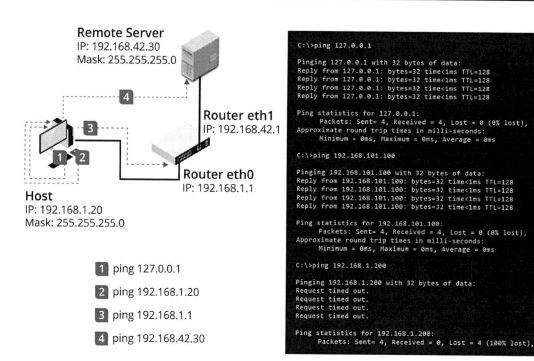

Troubleshooting with ping.

If `ping` is successful, it responds with the message **Reply from IP Address** and the time it takes for the server's response to arrive. The millisecond measures of Round Trip Time (RTT) can be used to diagnose latency problems on a link.

If `ping` is unsuccessful, one of two messages are commonly received:

- **Destination unreachable**—there is no routing information (that is, the local computer or an intermediate router does not know how to get to that IP address). If the host is on the same network, check the local IP configuration—IP address, subnet mask, and so on. If you can discount any configuration error, then there may be a hardware or cabling problem. If the host is on another network, check the IP configuration and router.

- **No reply (Request timed out)**—the host is unavailable or cannot route a reply back to your computer. Check physical cabling and infrastructure devices such as the switch. If the host is on a remote network, try using `tracert` (described shortly).

 Note: Be aware that ICMP traffic is often blocked by firewalls, making a response such as request timed out or destination unreachable inevitable. As well as network firewalls, consider that a host firewall, such as Windows Firewall, might be blocking ICMP.

TESTING DNS

You can also ping DNS names (`ping comptia.org`, for example) or FQDNs (`ping sales.comptia.org`, for instance). This will not work if a DNS server is unavailable. Use the `-a` switch to perform a reverse lookup on an IP address to try to get the host name. For example, `ping -a 192.168.1.1` should return the message "Pinging *HostName* [192.168.1.1]."

TROUBLESHOOTING AN IP CONFLICT

Two systems could end up with the same IP address because of a configuration error; perhaps both addresses were statically assigned or one was assigned an address that was part of a DHCP scope by mistake. If Windows detects a duplicate IP address, it will display a warning and disable IP. If there are two systems with duplicate IPs, a sort of "race condition" will determine which receives traffic. Obviously, this is not a good way for the network to be configured and you should identify the machines and set them to use unique addresses.

ROUTING ISSUES

The `tracert` command-line utility is used to trace the route a packet of information takes to get to its target. Like `ping`, it uses ICMP status messages. For example, a user might type the following: `tracert 10.0.0.1`. This command would return details of the route taken to find the machine or device with the IP address of 10.0.0.1. `tracert` can also be used with a domain name or FQDN, such as: `tracert comptia.org`.

```
C:\Users\localadmin>tracert 10.0.0.1

Tracing route to 10.0.0.1 over a maximum of 30 hops

  1  HOST [192.168.1.110]  reports: Destination host unreachable.

Trace complete.

C:\Users\localadmin>tracert gtslearning.com

Tracing route to gtslearning.com [185.41.10.123]
over a maximum of 30 hops:

  1    <1 ms    <1 ms    <1 ms  ARCHER_VR900 [192.168.1.1]
  2     *        *        *     Request timed out.
  3     *       11 ms    11 ms  31.55.187.181
  4    11 ms    11 ms    11 ms  31.55.187.188
  5    12 ms    11 ms    11 ms  core2-hu0-17-0-1.southbank.ukcore.bt.net [195.99
.127.188]
  6    12 ms    12 ms    12 ms  195.99.127.70
  7    13 ms    13 ms    13 ms  peer2-et-9-1-0.redbus.ukcore.bt.net [62.172.103.
43]
  8    13 ms    13 ms    18 ms  linx2.ixreach.com [195.66.236.217]
  9    20 ms    20 ms    20 ms  r1.tcw.man.ixreach.com [91.196.184.181]
 10    19 ms    23 ms    20 ms  rt1-tjh-ixr.as200083.net [46.18.174.222]
 11    20 ms    20 ms    20 ms  server1.gtslearning.com [185.41.10.123]

Trace complete.

C:\Users\localadmin>_
```

Using tracert—the first trace to a local private network has failed but the trace over the Internet to gtslearning.com's web server has succeeded, passing first through the SOHO router then through the routers belonging to the user's ISP, then the routers belonging to the web host. (Screenshot used with permission from Microsoft.)

If the host cannot be located, the command will eventually timeout but it will return every router that was attempted. The output shows the number of hops (when a packet is transferred from one router to another), the ingress interface of the router or host (that is, the interface from which the router receives the ICMP packet), and the time taken to respond to each probe in milliseconds (ms). If no acknowledgement is received within the timeout period, an asterisk is shown against the probe.

Note: `ping` and `tracert` use Internet Control Message Protocol (ICMP) traffic. A firewall may be configured to block this traffic to prevent network snooping.

UNAVAILABLE RESOURCES

If you cannot identify a problem with the cabling, switches/routers, or the IP configuration, you should start to suspect a problem at a higher layer of processing. There are three main additional "layers" where network services fail:

- Security—a firewall or other security software or hardware might be blocking the connection.
- Name resolution—if a service such as DNS is not working, you will be able to connect to file/print/email services by IP address but not by name.
- Application/OS—the software underpinning the service might have failed. If the OS has failed, there might not be any sort of connectivity to the host server. If the server can be contacted, but not a specific service, the service process might have crashed.

When troubleshooting Internet access or unavailable local network resources, such as file shares, network printers, and email, try to establish the scope of the problem. If you can connect to these services using a different host, the problem should lie with the first client. If other hosts cannot connect, the problem lies with the application server or print device or with network infrastructure between the client and the server.

TROUBLESHOOTING INTERNET AVAILABILITY

When Windows reports that a network adapter has "No Internet access," it means that the IP configuration is valid but that Windows cannot identify a working Internet connection. Windows tests Internet access by attempting a connection to `www.msftncsi.com` and checking that DNS resolves the IP address correctly.

If the local PC settings are correct, locate your ISP's service status page or support helpline to verify that there are no wider network issues or DNS problems that might make your Internet connection unavailable. If there are no ISP-wide issues, try restarting the router/modem.

 Note: *Do not restart a router without considering the impact on other users!*

If these measures don't help, also consider that there might be some sort of security issue, such as a proxy configuration not working or a firewall blocking the host.

PERFORMING A NETWORK RESET

If there are persistent network problems with either a client or a server, one "stock" response is to try restarting the computer hardware. You can also try restarting just the application service.

 Note: *As before, do not restart a server without considering the impact on other users. A restart is probably only warranted if the problem is widespread.*

In Windows, you can try running the network troubleshooter app to automatically diagnose and fix problems. Another option is to reset the network stack on the device. In Windows, this will clear any custom adapter configurations and network connections, including VPN connections. These will have to be reconfigured after the reset.

In Windows 10, there is a **Network reset** command on the **Settings→Network & Internet→Status** page. In Windows 7/8, you can use the Network Adapter troubleshooter or run the following commands (as administrator):

```
ipconfig /flushdns
netsh int ip reset resetlog.txt
netsh winsock reset
```

Use Device Manager to remove any network adapters. Reboot the computer and allow Windows to detect and install the adapter(s) again. Update network settings on all adapters to the appropriate configuration.

netstat

`netstat` can be used to investigate open ports and connections on the local host. In a troubleshooting context, you can use this tool to verify whether file sharing or email ports are open on a server and whether other clients are connecting to them.

```
C:\Windows\system32>netstat -b -n

Active Connections

  Proto  Local Address          Foreign Address        State
  TCP    192.168.1.110:5806     185.41.10.123:80       CLOSE_WAIT
[IEXPLORE.EXE]
  TCP    192.168.1.110:5807     185.41.10.123:80       CLOSE_WAIT
[IEXPLORE.EXE]
  TCP    192.168.1.110:5808     216.58.208.40:443      ESTABLISHED
[IEXPLORE.EXE]
  TCP    192.168.1.110:5809     216.58.208.40:443      ESTABLISHED
[IEXPLORE.EXE]
  TCP    192.168.1.110:5810     104.27.151.216:80      CLOSE_WAIT
[IEXPLORE.EXE]
  TCP    192.168.1.110:5811     104.27.151.216:80      CLOSE_WAIT
[IEXPLORE.EXE]
  TCP    192.168.1.110:5812     104.27.151.216:80      CLOSE_WAIT
[IEXPLORE.EXE]
  TCP    192.168.1.110:5813     104.27.151.216:80      CLOSE_WAIT
[IEXPLORE.EXE]
  TCP    192.168.1.110:5814     104.27.151.216:80      CLOSE_WAIT
[IEXPLORE.EXE]
  TCP    192.168.1.110:5815     104.27.151.216:80      CLOSE_WAIT
[IEXPLORE.EXE]
  TCP    192.168.1.110:5816     52.28.192.217:443      ESTABLISHED
[IEXPLORE.EXE]
  TCP    [fe80::5c9e:8be5:bb3e:f341%4]:2179  [fe80::5c9e:8be5:bb3e:f341%4]:5519
ESTABLISHED
[vmms.exe]
  TCP    [fe80::5c9e:8be5:bb3e:f341%4]:3587  [fe80::5cf0:94fe:4f4:a8a%4]:57395
ESTABLISHED
  p2psvc
[svchost.exe]
  TCP    [fe80::5c9e:8be5:bb3e:f341%4]:5519  [fe80::5c9e:8be5:bb3e:f341%4]:2179
ESTABLISHED
[VmConnect.exe]

C:\Windows\system32>_
```

Displaying open connections with netstat. (Screenshot used with permission from Microsoft.)

The following represent some of the main switches that can be used:

- `-a` displays all the connections and listening ports.
- `-b` shows the process that has opened the port.
- `-n` displays ports and addresses in numerical format. Skipping name resolution speeds up each query.

Linux supports a similar utility with slightly different switches.

nslookup

If you identify or suspect a problem with name resolution, you can troubleshoot DNS with the `nslookup` command, either interactively or from the command prompt:

```
nslookup -Option Host Server
```

`Host` can be either a host name/FQDN or an IP address. Server is the DNS server to query; the default DNS server is used if this argument is omitted. `-Option` specifies an nslookup subcommand. Typically, a subcommand is used to query a particular DNS record type.

For example, the following command queries Google's public DNS servers (8.8.8.8) for information about comptia.org's mail records:

```
nslookup -type=mx comptia.org 8.8.8.8
```

```
C:\Users\James>nslookup -type=mx comptia.org 8.8.8.8
Server:  google-public-dns-a.google.com
Address:  8.8.8.8

Non-authoritative answer:
comptia.org     MX preference = 10, mail exchanger = comptia-org.mail.protection.outlook.c
om
```

Using nslookup to query the mail server configured for the comptia.org domain name using Google's public DNS servers (8.8.8.8). (Screenshot used with permission from Microsoft.)

If you query a different name server, you can compare the results to those returned by your own name server. This might highlight configuration problems.

Note: The *dig* utility is often used as a more up-to-date and flexible alternative to *nslookup*. *dig* allows you to query a name server directly and retrieve any of the information known about the domain name. It is helpful in determining if the server is running correctly and if the domain record is properly configured.

Activity 4-1
Configuring and Troubleshooting Networks Review

SCENARIO
Answer the following review questions.

1. **What experiences do you have in working with the networking technologies discussed in this lesson?**

2. **Do you have any experience working with SOHO networks? What do you expect to support in future job functions?**

Summary

In this lesson, you configured and performed troubleshooting on SOHO and other networks. Ensuring consistent access to network resources is often an integral part of an A+ technician's day-to-day duties.

Lesson 5

Managing Users, Workstations, and Shared Resources

LESSON INTRODUCTION

Once you have the computer network up and running, you can start to configure it to provide useful services. File and print sharing are key uses of almost every network. When configuring these resources, you have to be aware of potential security issues and understand how to set permissions correctly, to ensure that data is only accessible to those users who really should have been authorized to see it.

Along with permissions, you will also need to manage user accounts on networks. Windows® networks can use local accounts within workgroups or centralized Active Directory® accounts on a domain network. In this lesson, you will learn some basic principles for managing users in both types of environment.

LESSON OBJECTIVES

In this lesson, you will:

- Manage Windows local user and group accounts.
- Configure network shares and permissions.
- Configure accounts and policies in Active Directory domains.

Topic A
Manage Users

 EXAM OBJECTIVES COVERED
1002-1.4 Given a scenario, use appropriate Microsoft command line tools.
1002-1.5 Given a scenario, use Microsoft operating system features and tools.
1002-1.6 Given a scenario, use Microsoft Windows Control Panel utilities.
1002-2.6 Compare and contrast the differences of basic Microsoft Windows OS security settings.

Managing user accounts and permissions is an important task on any type of network. In this topic, you will learn how group accounts can be used to allocate permissions more easily and use consoles to configure system policies that can improve the security of the computer and network.

USER AND GROUP ACCOUNTS

A user account is the principal means of controlling access to computer and network resources and rights or privileges. The **User Accounts** applet in Control Panel is adequate for creating accounts on a family computer. If you are configuring computers for business use, you might want to use more advanced tools to create group accounts as well as user accounts.

SECURITY GROUPS

A **security group** is a collection of user accounts that can be assigned permissions in the same way as a single user object. Security groups are used when assigning permissions and rights, as it is more efficient to assign permissions to a group than to assign them individually to each user. You can assign permissions to a user simply by adding the user to the appropriate group(s).

Group	Description
Built-in Local Groups	Built-in groups are given a standard set of rights that allow them to perform appropriate system tasks. Starter and Home editions of Windows allow the use of two groups only: • Limited/standard user. • Computer administrator. For Windows Professional/Business, the principal built-in local groups include Administrators, Users, Guests, and Power Users.

Group	Description
Administrators	An Administrator account can perform all management tasks and generally has very high access to all files and other objects in the system. The user created at installation is automatically added to this group. You should restrict use of this type of account, using a regular user account when appropriate, and only log in with administrative privileges for specific tasks.
	When Windows is installed to a new computer, the account actually named "Administrator" is disabled by default. The setup procedure creates an account with administrative privileges in its place.
	Note: *If the computer is not part of a domain, the "Administrator" account is re-enabled in Safe Mode if all other administrative accounts have been deleted or disabled (as a disaster recovery mechanism). Note that the "Administrator" account is not subject to UAC and so should be left disabled if the computer is to be used securely.*
Users	When a new user is created, they are typically added to the standard Users group. The group is able to perform most common tasks, such as shutting down the computer, running applications, and using printers. Ordinary users can also change the time zone and install a local printer, provided there is a suitable driver already installed.
Guests	The Guests group has only limited rights; for example, members can browse the network and Internet and shut down the computer but cannot save changes made to the desktop environment. Generally, you should disable the Guest account (its default condition) and establish a proper user account for each user accessing your system. If the account is enabled, then any user attempting to access your computer who does not hold their own user account, will be connected using the Guest account credentials.
	Note: *The default Guest account is the only member of the Guests group. While the Guest user account is usually disabled, the Guests group is not.*
Power Users	The Power Users group still appears to support legacy applications, but its use is strongly deprecated. The rights allocated to this account type can be abused to allow the user to obtain more powerful Administrator or System privileges. You can read more about issues with using Power Users at **support.microsoft.com/en-us/help/825069/a-member-of-the-power-users-group-may-be-able-to-gain-administrator-ri**.

Group	Description
System Groups	There are a number of other default groups, providing a means to easily configure things like privileges to access remote desktop, backup, event logs, and so on. Windows also includes built-in system groups. Their membership cannot be changed manually, as it is dependent on what users are doing at the time.
	• **Everyone**—All users who access the computer are members of the group Everyone. This includes users who have not been authenticated and who are accessing the computer as a guest.
	• **Authenticated Users**—All users who access the computer and have a valid user account.
	• **Creator Owner**—The Creator Owner group includes the account of the resource owner. Normally, the creator of a resource is the owner, but administrators (and other users who have been allowed to do so) are able to take ownership.
	• **Interactive**—This group contains the user account of the person currently working locally at the computer.
	• **Network**—This group contains the user account(s) of any users currently connected to the computer over a network.
System and Service Accounts	There are also some non-interactive accounts that you should be aware of. Users cannot sign in to these accounts. They are "owned" by the OS (NT_AUTHORITY). They are used to run Windows processes and services:
	• **LocalSystem**—An account with the same, or in some ways better, privileges as the default Administrator account. A process executed using the system account is unrestricted in terms of making changes to the system configuration and file system.
	• **LocalService**—A limited account used to run services that cannot make system-wide changes. LocalService can access the network anonymously.
	• **NetworkService**—An account that has the same privileges as LocalService but can access the network using the computer's machine account's credentials.

LOCAL USERS AND GROUPS

In Pro, Professional, and Enterprise editions of Windows, the **Local Users and Groups** management console provides an interface for managing both user and group accounts. It is not available in Starter or Home editions.

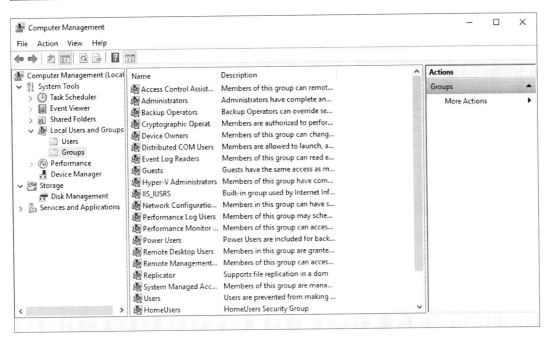

Local Users and Groups management console. (Screenshot used with permission from Microsoft.)

CREATING A NEW USER

To create a user, right-click on or in the **Users** folder and select **New User**. The account can be configured with the following properties:

Setting	Use
Username (required)	The username may be up to 20 characters and cannot contain the characters "∧ [ ] : ; | = , + * ? < > The username must be unique. Usernames are not case sensitive.
Full name (optional)	This should include the first and last name, and any middle initials if required.
Description (optional)	May be used to describe the user's job role.
Password (optional but recommended	Passwords can be up to 128 characters (at least 8 is recommended). Passwords are case sensitive. Avoid passwords that simply use words; include upper and lower case letters, punctuation, and numbers.
User must change password at next logon	A useful way to ensure that an administrator-assigned password is reset by the user when they first access the account.
User cannot change password	Generally, users control their own passwords, but for some user accounts it is preferable for the administrator to control the password.
Password never expires	A useful option which overrides the local security policy to expire passwords after a fixed number of days. This option should be selected for system accounts, such as those used for replication and application services.
Account is disabled	Prevents use of the account. Acts as an alternative to deleting an account.

RENAMING AND DELETING USER ACCOUNTS

To rename a user account, select the account name, then right-click and choose the **Rename** option. A renamed account retains all the properties of the original account and also retains access to system resources.

To delete an account, select the account name and either press the **Delete** key or choose **Delete** from the context menu.

Windows uses a Security ID (SID) to uniquely identify each user and group. A warning message is displayed to remind you that this account identifier is unique. Even if you recreate another account with exactly the same username, the identifier created is still different. The new account cannot assume any access to resources that were assigned to the original.

Disabling an account prevents it from being used, but allows the account to be reactivated if required.

ADDING A USER TO A GROUP

When a user is made a member of a group, the user obtains all the permissions allocated to that group. A user account can be a member of more than one group account. To add a user to a group or remove a user from a group, right-click the group account and select **Properties**.

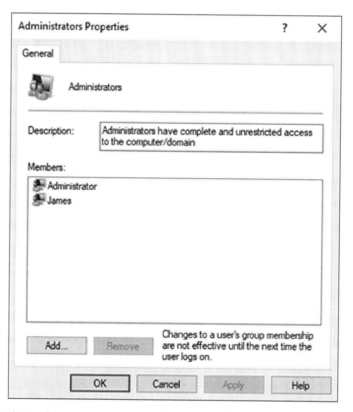

Configuring members of the Administrators built-in group. (Screenshot used with permission from Microsoft.)

THE net user COMMANDS

You can also manage accounts at the command line using the `net user` command. You need to execute these commands in an administrative command prompt:

- `net user dmartin Pa$$w0rd /add /fullname:"David Martin" /logonpasswordchg:yes`

This example adds a new user account and forces the user to choose a new password at first login.

- `net user dmartin /active:no`

    Disables the `dmartin` account.

- `net user dmartin`

    Show the properties of the `dmartin` account.

- `net localgroup Administrators dmartin /add`

    Add the `dmartin` account to the Administrators local group.

 Note: *Don't confuse* `net user` *commands with* `net use`, *which is for configuring file shares.*

HOW TO MANAGE WINDOWS LOCAL USERS AND GROUPS

Follow these procedures to manage Windows local users and groups.

MANAGE LOCAL USERS AND GROUPS

To manage users and groups stored on the local computer:

1. Right-click the **Start** menu and select **Run** (or press **Windows+R)** to open the **Run** dialog box.
2. In the **Run** dialog box, type *lusrmgr.msc* then select **OK**.
3. In the **lusrmgr - [Local Users and Groups (Local)\Users]** window, select the **Users** container to manage users or the **Groups** container to manage groups.
4. To create a new user:
    a. With the **Users** container selected from the **Actions** menu, select **New User**.
    b. Enter information in the text fields and check the desired options for the new user, then select **Create**.
    c. Create another user or select **Close**.
5. To create a new group:
    a. With the **Groups** container selected from the **Actions** menu, select **New Group**.
    b. Enter a group name.
    c. Select **Add**.
    d. In the **Enter the object names to select** text box, type a user name, then select **Check Names** and select **OK**.

     Note: *Alternatively, select **Advanced**, then select **Find Now** and select names from the list and select **OK**.*

    e. Select **Create**.
    f. Create another group or select **Close**.
6. To manage an existing user:
    a. Right-click the user and select the desired action or select **Properties**.
    b. In the *Username* **Properties** dialog box, select the tab needed to change the user properties, then select **Apply** before moving to another tab if needed.
    c. Select **OK**.
7. To manage an existing group:
    a. Right-click the group and select the desired action or select **Properties**.
    b. To remove a group member, select the username, then select **Remove**.

   c.   To add a group member, select the **Add** button, then follow the procedure to
           add a group member.

   d.   When done making changes to the group, select **OK**.

LOCAL SECURITY POLICY

Policies are the most fine-grained means of adjusting registry settings outside of
editing the registry directly. Policies can be used to configure almost any aspect of
Windows, from the color of the desktop to the number of characters required in a user
password.

On a standalone workstation, password and account policies can be configured via the
Local Security Policy snap-in (`secpol.msc`) located in **Administrative Tools**. You
would use this to force users to choose more complex or longer passwords or to
prevent users from re-using old passwords.

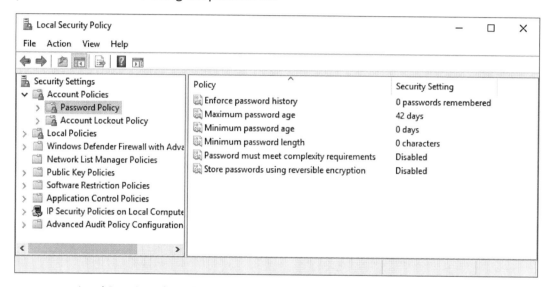

Local Security Policy editor. (Screenshot used with permission from Microsoft.)

A wider range of settings can be configured via the **Local Group Policy** snap-in
(`gpedit.msc`). Group policy exposes pretty much the whole of the registry to
configuration via a dialog-based interface, rather than editing individual keys through
regedit. Policies can be applied to the computer object or to user accounts.

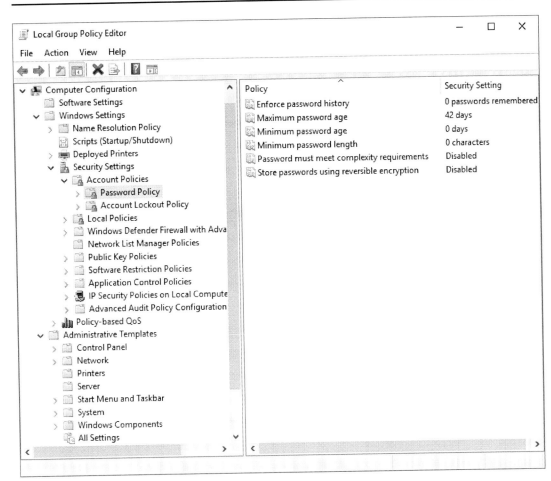

The Local Group Policy editor. You can edit the same security policies here but any other number of computer and user account settings can also be configured. (Screenshot used with permission from Microsoft.)

Note: *The policy editors are not included in the Starter or Home editions of Windows.*

SSO AND CREDENTIAL MANAGER

Single Sign On (SSO) means that a user only has to authenticate to a system once to gain access to all its resources (that is, all the resources to which the user has been granted rights). An example is the Kerberos authentication and authorization model for Active Directory domain networks. This means, for instance, that a user who has authenticated with Windows is also authenticated with the Windows domain's SQL Server® and Exchange Server services. Another example is the use of a Microsoft account to sign in to Windows and also be signed in to web applications such as OneDrive® and Office365®.

The advantage of single sign-on is that each user does not have to manage multiple user accounts and passwords. The disadvantage is that compromising the account also compromises multiple services.

Note: *It is critical that users do not re-use work passwords or authentication information on third-party sites. Of course, this is almost impossible to enforce, so security managers have to rely on effective user training.*

CREDENTIAL MANAGER

SSO is not available for many services. Most users do not try to remember each password for every website or network they use. Instead, they use the OS to save (or cache) the password. You can view cached passwords for websites and Windows/network accounts using the Control Panel app **Credential Manager**.

You can remove any credentials that you no longer want to store. Removing a credential may also resolve an authentication or service problem. You can view the plaintext of a web credential but not of a Windows credential.

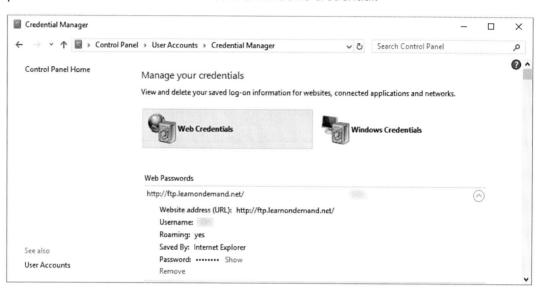

Credential Manager. (Screenshot used with permission from Microsoft.)

Topic B

Configure Shared Resources

EXAM OBJECTIVES COVERED
1002-1.4 Given a scenario, use appropriate Microsoft command line tools.
1002-1.8 Given a scenario, configure Microsoft Windows networking on a client/desktop.
1002-1.6 Given a scenario, use Microsoft Windows Control Panel utilities.
1002-2.6 Compare and contrast the differences of basic Microsoft Windows OS security settings

One of the main uses of networks is for file and printer sharing. As a CompTIA A+ technician, you will often need to configure network shares. It is important that you configure the correct permissions on shares, understanding how share and NTFS permissions interact.

WORKGROUPS

In a **peer-to-peer network**, each computer can be both a server and a client. Each user administers his or her PC and the resources on it. The user can decide to give others access to files on his or her PC or to printers that are attached to it. Under Windows, this type of network is described as a workgroup.

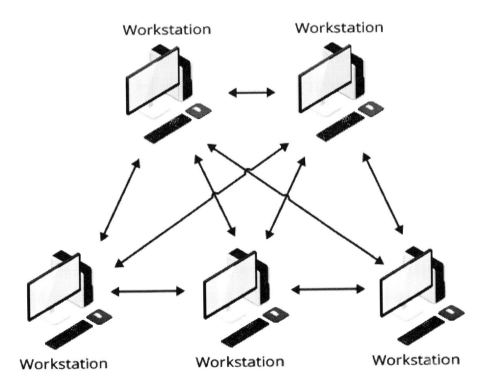

Peer-to-peer network. (Image © 123RF.com.)

A workgroup is quite simple to set up initially, but unreliable and difficult to organize. For example, a user could switch off their machine while someone else was accessing it. There is no good means of deciding who should have access to the network. It is difficult to grow the network, as when a machine or new user is added, all the other machines have to be "informed" about it.

Workgroups are designed to support small groups of users. There is no centralized management of user accounts or of resources, and each machine requires a separate administrator. Desktop operating systems such as Windows can act as servers in a workgroup, but they are restricted in terms of the number of inbound connections they can support.

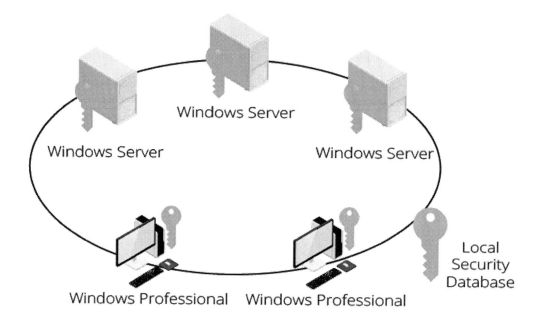

Workgroup security accounts are all stored locally. (Image © 123RF.com.)

Note: *Not all real-world networks are completely peer-to-peer or completely client-server. Some networks use a mixture of both approaches.*

As different versions of Windows have been released, Microsoft has implemented different ways for users to set up home networks simply.

Note: *The workgroup name can be changed using the* **Computer Name** *dialog box from* **System** *properties. The workgroup name is cosmetic, however. It is almost always left set to "WORKGROUP."*

HOMEGROUPS

A **homegroup** is a feature introduced in Windows 7, and continued in Windows 8, to simplify secure access to shared folders and printers on a home network.

The problem with a workgroup network is that there is no centralized database of users. Sharing folders would either require the local user's password to be shared, identical user accounts to be set up and maintained on each machine, or facilitated via the Guest account with no authentication.

Homegroups are secured via a simple password. A computer can only belong to one homegroup at a time. Homegroups can contain a mix of Windows 7 and Windows 8 computers.

To set up a homegroup, open the Network and Sharing Center and select **Choose homegroup and sharing options**.

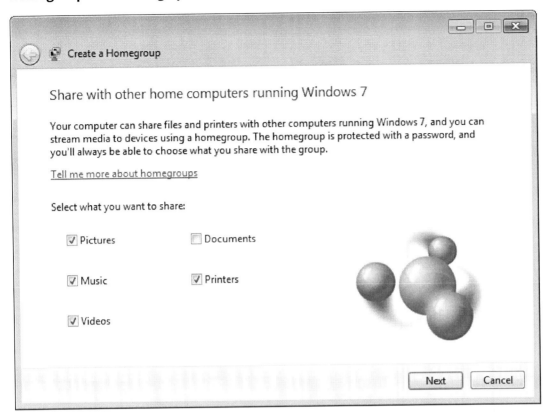

Configuring a homegroup—choosing which resources to share. (Screenshot used with permission from Microsoft.)

 *Note: The network type must be defined as **Home** (Windows 7) or **Private** (Windows 8) or Windows will not allow the creation of a homegroup. Also, IPv6 must be enabled for homegroups to work.*

JOINING A HOMEGROUP

When a homegroup has been configured on a network, you will see a **Join now** button when you are browsing the **Homegroup** object in Explorer. Having joined a group, network users can access shared libraries and folders and choose whether to share their own libraries. Shared homegroup folders are shown via the **Homegroup** object in Explorer, which shows all the user accounts participating in the homegroup.

WINDOWS 10 AND HOMEGROUPS

The early versions of Windows 10 continued to support the homegroup feature. With the release of Windows 10 (1803), support for homegroups was discontinued. Windows 10 (1803) computers cannot create or join a homegroup.

 *Note: At the time of writing, a bug means that homegroup options can still appear in a folder's **Give Access To** shortcut menu. These options do not do anything.*

NETWORK AND SHARING CENTER

Whenever a new network link is detected, Windows prompts you to define it as **Public** or **Private** (Home or Work). The former option disables file and printer sharing and network discovery on the link. On a private network, you can customize the sharing options to include printers, disable password-protected sharing, and so on. These options are configured via the **Network and Sharing Center**.

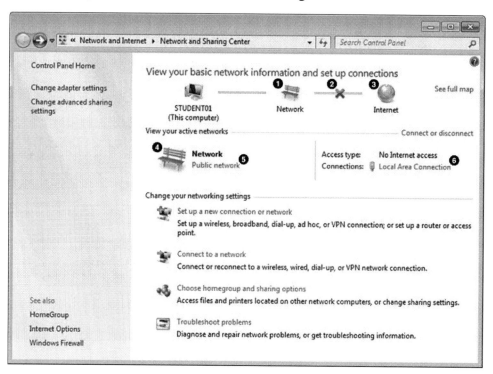

Navigating the Windows 7 Network and Sharing Center—1) Select to view computers on the network; 2) Select a cross to start the troubleshooter; 3) Select to open the web browser; 4) Select the network icon to manage names and locations; 5) Select the link to change the network type; 6) Select the adapter link to view status and configure properties. (Screenshot used with permission from Microsoft.)

In Windows 8 and Windows 10, the network map feature has been dropped and there is no option to change the network location type. This is done via Windows Settings instead. Select **Network & Internet** and then **Ethernet** or **WiFi** as appropriate. Under **Network profile**, select **Public** or **Private**.

 Note: *Note that the "Network profile" options do not appear if UAC is set to the highest "Always notify" level.*

ADVANCED SHARING SETTINGS

From the Network and Sharing Center, select **Advanced sharing settings** to configure the options for each profile. To share files on the network, **Turn on network discovery** and **Turn on file and printer sharing** must both be selected.

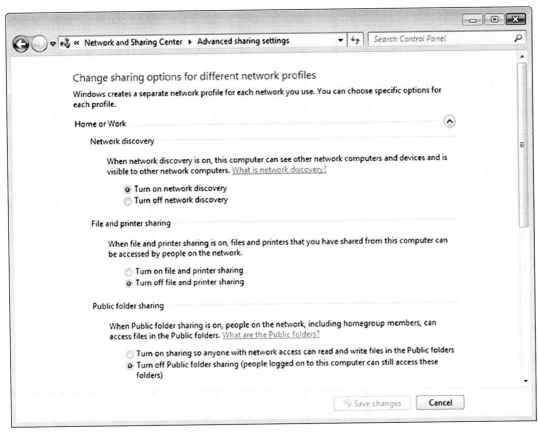

Advanced sharing settings. (Screenshot used with permission from Microsoft.)

Windows has a pre-defined folder for sharing files (the Public folder), which is available to all users of the PC and to network users, if enabled here.

Under **All networks**, you can select **Turn off password-protected sharing** to allow anyone to access any file share configured on the local computer without entering any credentials. This enables the Guest user account, which is normally disabled.

Note: For password-protected sharing, network users must have an account configured on the local machine. This is one of the drawbacks of workgroups compared to domains. Either you configure accounts for all users on all machines, use a single account for network access (again, configured on all machines), or you disable security entirely.

NETWORK SHARE CONFIGURATION

You can share other folders by right-clicking and selecting **Share with** (Windows 7) or **Give access to** (Windows 10). Select an account, then set the **Permission level** to **Read** or **Read/write** as appropriate.

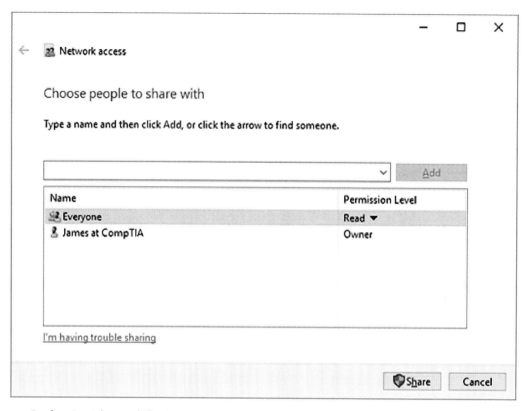

Configuring Advanced Sharing properties. (Screenshot used with permission from Microsoft.)

ADVANCED SHARING

In the folder's property dialog box, you can use the **Share** tab to configure advanced share properties:

- **Share name and optional comment**—the share name identifies the share on the network while the comment can describe the purpose of the share. You can share the same folder multiple times with different names and permissions.
- **Maximum number of users allowed to connect at any one time**—Windows desktop versions are limited to 20 inbound connections. Only Windows Server systems support more connections.
- **Permissions**—choose the groups or users allowed to access the folder and what type of access they have.

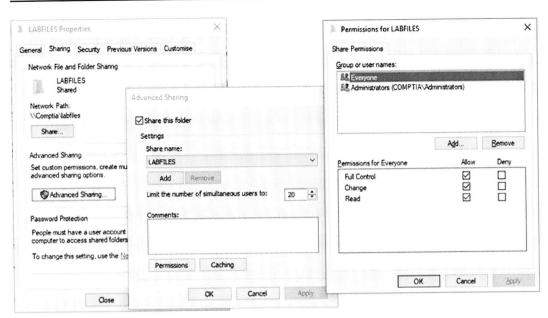

Configuring Advanced Sharing properties—Notice that while Everyone has "Read" permission, the share permissions for Everyone are "Full Control." The "Read" permission is enforced by NTFS security. (Screenshot used with permission from Microsoft.)

Windows provides three levels of share permissions:

- **Full Control**—allows users to read, edit, create, and delete files and subdirectories, and to assign permissions to other users and groups.
- **Change**—this is similar to full control but does not allow the user to set permissions for others.
- **Read**—users are permitted to connect to the resource, run programs, and view files. They are not allowed to edit, delete, or create files.

Most of the time, the shared folder permission is set to **Full Control**. The effective permissions are managed using NTFS security.

MANAGING SHARED FOLDERS

The **Shared Folders** snap-in (available through the Computer Management console) lets you view all the shares configured on the local machine as well as any current user sessions and open files.

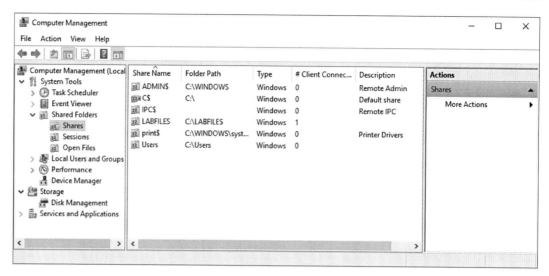

Viewing the Shared Folders snap-in via the Computer Management console. (Screenshot used with permission from Microsoft.)

ADMINISTRATIVE SHARES

You can think of the shares configured manually on a computer using the process described previously as local shares. In addition to any local shares created by a user, Windows automatically creates a number of hidden administrative shares, including the root folder of any local drives (C$), the system folder (ADMIN$), and the folder storing printer drivers (PRINT$). Administrative shares can only be accessed by members of the local Administrators group.

> **Note:** *Note that if you disable password-protected sharing, the administrative shares remain password-protected.*

In fact, if you add a $ sign at the end of a local share name, it will be hidden from general browsing too. It can still be accessed via the command-line or by mapping a drive to the share name.

BROWSING SHARES AND MAPPING DRIVES

In File Explorer, network shares are listed by the server computer under the system object Network. Any network-enabled devices such as wireless displays, printers, smartphones, and router/modems are also listed here. The shortcut menu for Network allows you to open the Network and Sharing Center (via the Properties option) and map or disconnect network drives.

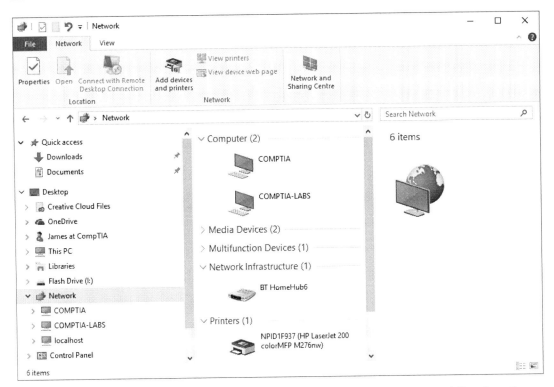

Viewing devices on the network—the LaserJet 200 printer listed here is connected directly to the network. (Screenshot used with permission from Microsoft.)

You can also access a shared folder using Universal Naming Convention (UNC) syntax (***ComputerName*\Path**), where *ComputerName* is the host name, FQDN, or IP address of the server and Path is the folder and/or file path. Remember that you can view an administrative share this way (if you have the relevant permissions). For example, the path **\\COMPTIA\Admin$** connects to the "Windows" folder on the "COMPTIA" computer.

A **network drive** is a local share that has been assigned a drive letter. To map a share as a drive, right-click it and select **Map Network Drive**. Select a drive letter and keep **Reconnect at sign-in** checked, unless you want to map the drive temporarily. The drive will now show up under Computer or This PC. To remove a mapped drive, right-click it and select **Disconnect**.

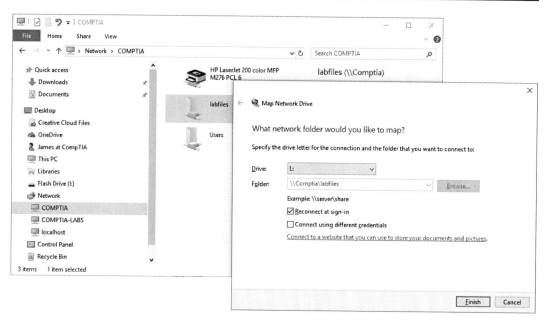

Mapping a network drive. (Screenshot used with permission from Microsoft.)

PRINTER SHARING VERSUS NETWORK PRINTER MAPPING

Many print devices come with an integrated Ethernet and/or Wi-Fi adapter. This means that they can communicate directly on the network. Such a printer can be mapped using the **Add Printer** wizard (from **Devices** and **Printers**). Just enter the IP address or host name of the printer to connect to it.

Any printer directly connected to a computer (whether via USB or direct network connection) can also be shared so that other network users can access it. A local printer is shared on the network via the **Sharing** tab on its **Printer Properties** sheet. To connect to a shared printer, open the server object from **Network** and the printer will be listed. Right-click it and select **Connect**.

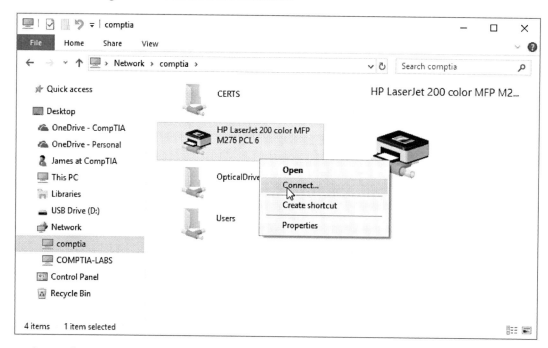

Connecting to a printer shared via the COMPTIA PC—Note that this is the same LaserJet 200 print device as shown earlier but it is being connected to as a shared device, rather than mapped directly. (Screenshot used with permission from Microsoft.)

OFFLINE FILES AND SYNC CENTER

One of the issues with a workgroup is that a computer may get turned off by its user without the user consulting the rest of the workgroup first. There is no centralized control or administration over access to resources. If you need to use files on a network share where the connection is unreliable for any reason, you can use Windows' offline files feature to cache the files in the share on your local computer. To enable this, just right-click the share or mapped drive and select **Always available offline**.

When the connection is restored, any changes between the local cache and the network share are synchronized automatically. If there are any conflicts, these are reported in the **Sync Center** Control Panel applet. You can use the **Resolve** button to choose whether to keep one or both versions.

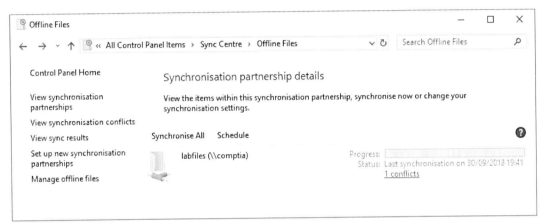

Using Sync Center to resolve file conflicts in an offline folder cache. (Screenshot used with permission from Microsoft.)

THE net COMMANDS

There are several `net` command utilities that you can use to view and configure shared resources on a Windows network. A few of the commands are provided here, but you can view the full list by entering `net /?` You can view help on a specific command by entering `net use /?`

- `net use DeviceName \\ComputerName\ShareName`

  This command will connect to a network resource, such as a folder or printer. For example, to map the DATA folder on MYSERVER to the M: drive, you would enter:
  `net use M: \\MYSERVER\DATA /persistent:yes`

- `net use DeviceName /delete`

  This command removes a connection (`net use * /delete` removes all connections).

- `net view`

  Used without switches, this displays a list of servers on the local network. Use `net view \\Host` to view the shares available on a particular server (where *Host* is an IP address or computer name).

NTFS FILE AND FOLDER PERMISSIONS

When you configure a network share, you can set share permissions for the accounts allowed to access the share. Share permissions have a number of limitations:

- The resource is only protected when a user connects over the network. Someone gaining access to the local machine would not have the same restrictions.
- The permissions set apply from the root of the share and all subdirectories and files within the share inherit the same permissions.

Systems that use the FAT file system are only able to support share permissions, but with NTFS it is possible to implement a much more comprehensive and flexible system of permissions. NTFS security protects the resource even when it is accessed locally and has a configurable system of propagation and inheritance.

Windows enforces local security on an NTFS volume by holding an Access Control List (ACL) as part of the record for each file and folder stored in the volume's Master File Table (MFT). When a user attempts to access a file or directory, the security system checks which users and groups are listed in the ACL. A list of permissions is then obtained for that user.

Security can be applied to individual files or (more commonly) to folders. When folders are secured, the matter of inheritance needs to be considered.

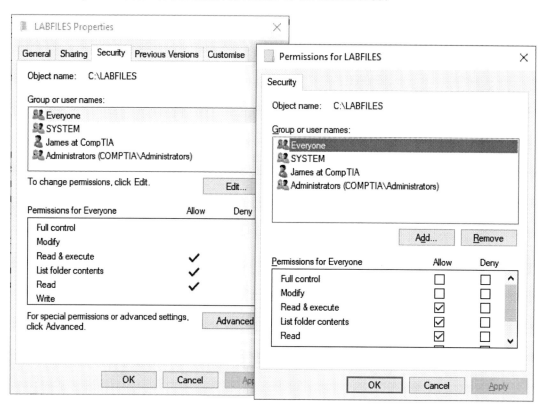

Configuring NTFS permissions via the Security tab for a folder. (Screenshot used with permission from Microsoft.)

CONFIGURING NTFS PERMISSIONS

To configure the NTFS security settings of a file or folder, right-click the object and select **Properties**, then select the **Security** tab. Users that may set permissions are restricted to administrators, users with full control permissions, and the owner of the file or folder.

Permissions that may be applied to folders differ from those that apply to files. The differences are summarized in the following tables. Note that each permission may either be allowed or denied.

Folder Permission	Allows
Read	View files and subfolders including their attributes, permissions, and ownership.
Write	Create new folders and files, change attributes, view permissions and ownership.
List	View the names of files and subfolders.
Read & Execute	Pass-through folders for which no permissions are assigned, plus read and list permissions.
Modify	Read/Execute and Write permissions, as well as the ability to rename and delete the folder.
Full Control	All the above, plus changing permissions, taking ownership, and deleting subfolders and files.

File Permission	Allows
Read	Read the contents of the file and view attributes, ownership, and permissions.
Write	Overwrite the file and view attributes, ownership, and permissions.
Read & Execute	Read permissions, plus the ability to run applications.
Modify	Read/Execute and Write permissions, as well as the ability to rename and delete the file.
Full Control	All the above, plus changing permissions and taking ownership.

Note: These are available via the basic interface. There are in fact 12 individual permissions that could be applied to a file or folder (select Advanced), but the combinations listed are usually sufficient.

EFFECTIVE PERMISSIONS AND ALLOW VERSUS DENY

Permissions are usually applied at one of three levels:

- For application folders, the read/execute permission is granted to the appropriate group.
- For data areas, the modify or read permission is assigned as appropriate.
- To home directories (personal storage areas on a network), full control is assigned to the relevant user.

A user may obtain multiple permissions from membership of different groups or by having permissions allocated directly to his or her account. Windows analyzes the permissions obtained from different accounts to determine the effective permissions. In this process, it is important to understand that "deny" overrides anything else (in most cases). If an account is not granted an "allow" permission, an implicit deny is applied. This is usually sufficient for most purposes. Explicit deny permissions are only used in quite specific circumstances.

Putting explicit deny permissions to one side, the user obtains the most effective "allow" permissions obtained from any source. For example, if one group gives the user "Read" permission and another group gives the user "Modify" permission, the user will have "Modify" permission.

PERMISSION PROPAGATION AND INHERITANCE

NTFS permissions that are assigned to a folder are automatically inherited by the files and subfolders created under the folder. To prevent this from happening, open the

Security page and select **Advanced**, then select the **Permission** tab. In Windows 7, select the **Change permissions** button to proceed.

Select the **Disable inheritance** button. In Windows 7, there is an **Include inheritable permissions** check box to uncheck rather than a button. Then, choose whether to **Convert inheritable permissions into explicit permissions** (in Windows 7, this is the **Copy** option) or **Remove** inherited permissions. You can then modify the permissions on this folder independently of its parent.

To apply security settings for the current folder to all child objects (permission propagation), check the **Replace all child object permissions with inheritable permissions** box.

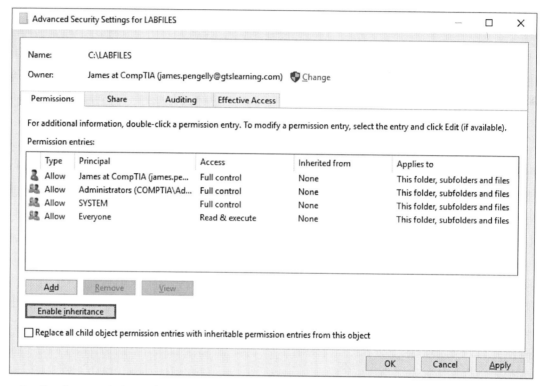

Configuring permissions inheritance on a folder. (Screenshot used with permission from Microsoft.)

 Note: Directly assigned permissions (explicit permissions) always override inherited permissions, including "deny" inherited permissions. For example, if a parent folder specifies deny write permissions but an account is granted allow write permissions directly on a child file object, the effective permission will be to allow write access on the file object.

OWNERSHIP

The owner of a resource can manage that resource in terms of permissions and other attributes. Generally speaking, if a user creates a file, they will own the file. Administrators can assign ownership to some other user (or group). This might be done because the current owner of a resource has been deleted from the user accounts database.

When a folder's ownership details are modified, the administrator can choose to propagate the changes down the tree to subfolders and their contents.

MOVING AND COPYING NTFS FILES AND FOLDERS

The behavior of NTFS permissions when moving and copying files under Windows is summarized in the following table.

Action	Effect
Moving files and folders on the same NTFS volume	Write permission is required for the destination folder and Modify for the source folder. NTFS permissions are retained.
Moving files and folders to a different NTFS volume	Write permission is required for the destination folder and Modify for the source folder. NTFS permissions are inherited from the destination folder and the user becomes the Creator/Owner.
Copying files and folders on the same NTFS volume or different NTFS volumes	Write permission is required for the destination folder and Read for the source folder. NTFS permissions are inherited from the destination folder and the user becomes the Creator/Owner.
Moving files and folders to a FAT or FAT32 partition	Modify permission is required for the source folder. All permissions and NTFS attributes (such as encryption) are lost, as FAT does not support permissions or special attributes.

COMBINING NTFS AND SHARE PERMISSIONS

It is possible to use a combination of share and NTFS permissions to secure resources. The factors to consider include:

- Share permissions only protect the resource when it is accessed across the network.
- NTFS permissions are used to protect the resource from unauthorized local access.
- Disk partitions using the FAT file system can only be protected using share permissions.
- Share permissions are set at the root of the share and all files and subdirectories inherit the same permissions.
- NTFS permissions are used in combination with the share permissions to provide greater flexibility; for example, to place more restrictive permissions at lower levels in the directory structure.
- If both share and NTFS permissions are applied to the same resource, the most restrictive applies (when the file or folder is accessed over the network). For example, if the group "Everyone" has Read permission to a share and the "Users" group is given Modify permission through NTFS permissions, the effective permissions for a member of the "Users" group will be Read.

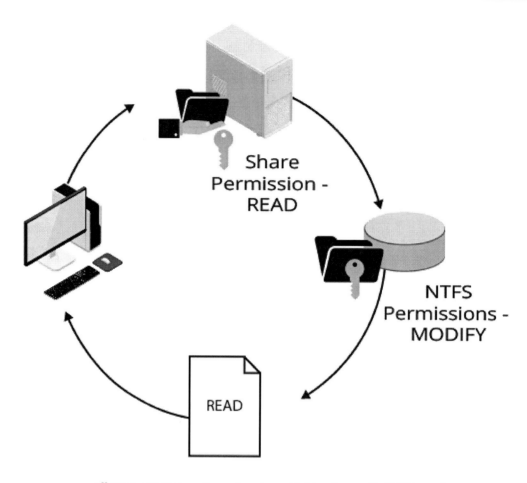

Effective permissions through a shared folder. (Image © 123RF.com.)

In practice, share permissions are always configured as Full Control and the NTFS permissions are used to configure the actual rights.

 Note: *If you do not have sufficient permissions to access or modify a resource, you will see an "Access denied" error message.*

Topic C

Configure Active Directory Accounts and Policies

EXAM OBJECTIVES COVERED
1002-1.4 Given a scenario, use appropriate Microsoft command line tools.
1002-1.8 Given a scenario, configure Microsoft Windows networking on a client/desktop.
1002-2.2 Explain logical security concepts.
1002-2.7 Given a scenario, implement security best practices to secure a workstation.

So far in this lesson, you have managed users and shared resources from a single computer. If you are part of a large organization, you would quickly find that this is a very inefficient way to configure resources. On a network, you can use something called directory-based tools to manage users, groups, and folders.

WINDOWS ACTIVE DIRECTORY DOMAINS

Windows networking provides two kinds of user account: local and domain. **Local accounts** are stored in the **Local Security Accounts database** known as the **Security Account Manager (SAM)**, stored in the registry, as a subkey of HKEY_LOCAL_MACHINE. These accounts are local to the machine and cannot be accessed from other computers. If a user needs access to multiple computers in a workgroup environment, then each computer will need to hold a relevant user account.

Domain accounts are stored in the Active Directory (AD) on a **Windows Server Domain Controller (DC)**. These accounts can be accessed from any computer joined to the domain. Only domain administrators can create these accounts.

ACTIVE DIRECTORY COMPONENTS

Active Directory is a complex service, with many components. Some of the components that you will encounter as an A+ technician include domain controllers, member servers, and organizational units.

DOMAIN CONTROLLERS

A **domain** is the basic administrative building block in Windows client/server networking. To create a domain, you need one or more Windows servers configured as **domain controllers**.

The domain controllers store a database of network information called **Active Directory**. This database stores user, group, and computer objects. The domain controllers are responsible for providing authentication services to users as they attempt to logon to the network.

The servers are controlled by network administrators, who also define client computers and users permitted to access resources. This network model is centralized, robust, scalable, and secure.

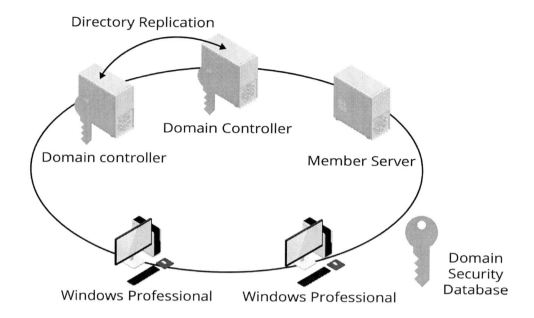

Active Directory security accounts are stored and managed from a domain controller. (Image © 123RF.com.)

MEMBER SERVERS

Member servers are any server-based systems that have been configured into the domain, but do not maintain a copy of the Active Directory database and are, therefore, unable to provide logon services. Because the user validation process consumes resources, most servers are configured as member servers rather than domain controllers. They will provide file and print and application server services (such as Exchange for email or SQL Server for database or line-of-business applications).

ORGANIZATIONAL UNITS

Organizational Units (OUs) provide a way of dividing a domain up into different administrative realms. You might create OUs to delegate responsibility for administering different company departments or locations. For example, a "Sales" department manager could be delegated control with rights to add, delete, and modify user accounts but no rights to change account policies, such as requiring complex passwords or managing users in the "Accounts" OU.

DOMAIN MEMBERSHIP

To fully participate in the benefits of an Active Directory domain, client computers must become members of the domain. Domain membership means:

- The computer has a computer account object within the directory database.
- Computer users can log on to the domain with domain user accounts.
- The computer and its users are subject to centralized domain security, configuration, and policy settings.
- Certain domain accounts automatically become members of local groups on the computer.
- Client computers within the domain allow users to access the network's services.

In Windows 7, Windows 8/8.1, and Windows 10, you can use the **System Properties** dialog box to join a domain. On a Windows 10 PC, you can also use the **Settings** app to join a domain.

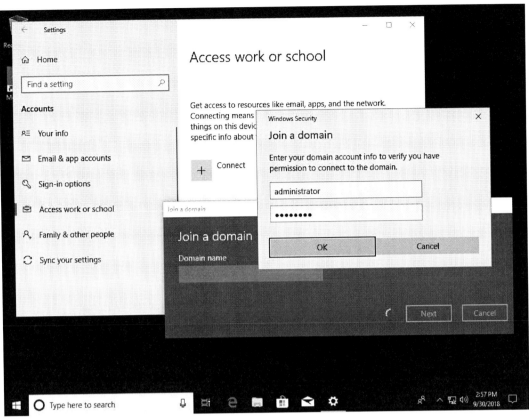

Joining a domain using the Settings app in Windows 10. (Screenshot used with permission from Microsoft.)

 Note: *The other option is to join an Azure Active Directory. Azure is essentially a cloud-hosted version of AD.*

HOW TO JOIN A DOMAIN
Follow these procedures to join a domain.

JOINING A DOMAIN VIA SYSTEM PROPERTIES
To add a Windows 7, Window 8/8.1, or Windows 10 computer to a domain by using the **System Properties** dialog box:

1. Ensure the computer is configured with an appropriate IP address and the address of a suitably configured DNS server. These settings would normally be configured automatically using a DHCP server on the domain network.
2. Open **System properties**, then under **Computer name, domain, and workgroup settings**, select **Change settings**.
3. Select the **Change** button.
4. Select the **Domain** option button and type the name of the domain in the box. Optionally, you can change the computer name too. Select **OK**.
5. Enter the credentials of an account with permission to join the domain. This would usually be a domain administrator account.
6. If the operation is successful, some confirmation dialog boxes are displayed. Click through these to restart the PC.

JOINING A DOMAIN IN WINDOWS 10 VIA THE WINDOWS SETTINGS APP

To join a Windows 10 PC to a domain by using Windows **Settings**:

1. Ensure the computer is configured with an appropriate IP address and the address of a suitably configured DNS server. These settings would normally be configured automatically using a DHCP server on the domain network.
2. Open the **Settings** app.
3. Select **Accounts→Access work or school** and then select the **Connect** button.
4. In the dialog box, select **Join this device to a local Active Directory domain**.
5. Provide a domain administrator account name and password, and select **OK**.

DOMAIN SIGN-IN

To use services in the domain, the user must sign into the PC using a domain account. The **Other user** option in the sign in screen will provide a domain option if it is not the default. You can also enter a username in the format ***Domain\UserName*** to specify a domain login.

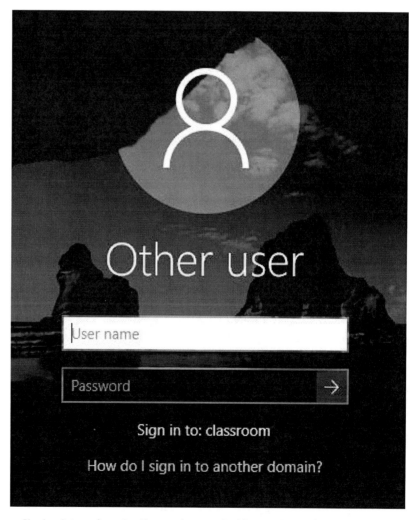

Signing into a domain. (Screenshot used with permission from Microsoft.)

GROUP POLICY OBJECTS

On a standalone workstation, security policies for the local machine and for local accounts are configured via the **Local Security Policy** or **Local Group Policy** snap-in. In an AD domain, they can be configured via **Group Policy Objects (GPOs)**. GPOs are a means of applying security settings (as well as other administrative settings) across a range of computers and users. GPOs are linked to network administrative boundaries in Active Directory, such as domains and OUs.

GPOs can be used to configure software deployment, Windows settings, and, through the use of **Administrative Templates**, custom Registry settings. Settings can also be configured on a per-user or per-computer basis.

A system of inheritance determines the **Resultant Set of Policies (RSoPs)** that apply to a particular computer or user. GPOs can be set to override or block policy inheritance where necessary.

Windows ships with default **security templates** to provide the basis for GPOs (**configuration baselines**). These can be modified using the **Group Policy Editor** or **Group Policy Management Console (GPMC)**. GPOs can be linked to objects in Active Directory using the object's property sheet.

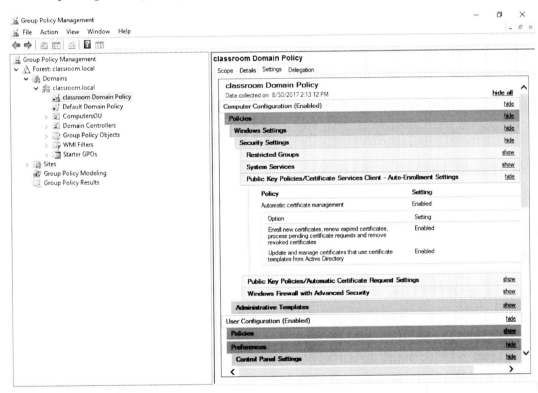

Group Policy Management. (Screenshot used with permission from Microsoft.)

SECURITY POLICY UPDATES

When updating local or group security policies, it is important to be familiar with the use of two command-line tools:

- `gpupdate`—policies are applied at log on and refreshed periodically (normally every 90 minutes). The `gpupdate` command is used to apply a new or changed policy to a computer immediately whereas `gpupdate /force` causes all policies (new and old) to be reapplied. The `gpupdate` command can be used with `/logoff` or `/boot` to allow a sign-out or reboot if the policy setting requires it.

- `gpresult`—displays the RSoP for a computer and user account. When run without switches, the current computer and user account policies are shown. The `/s`, `/u`, and `/p` switches can be used to specify a host (by name or IP address), user account, and password.

BASIC AD FUNCTIONS

Windows Server versions are quite similar to their desktop equivalent, so Windows Server 2016 shares many of the features of Windows 10. In Windows Server, the **Server Manager** app provides a single location where you can access server management tools. When you install Active Directory on a server, several management consoles are added to the **Tools** menu in **Server Manager**.

Accessing the AD management consoles via Server Manager. (Screenshot used with permission from Microsoft.)

*Note: Logging in locally to the server is burdensome and an increased security risk. More typically, you will install the **Remote Server Administration Tools** (RSATs) to your local computer to connect to the server to make changes.*

ACCOUNT CREATION AND DELETION

The **Active Directory Users and Computers** console allows you to manage users, groups, and Organizational Units. By default, there are some existing containers and OUs to store some of the default accounts created when AD is installed. You can create more OUs to store accounts in. You can use OUs to store accounts that have a similar security or administrative profile.

To create a new user account, right-click in the container or OU where you want to store the account and select **New→User**.

Complete the username fields then in the next dialog box, choose an initial password. The default option is to force the user to select a new password at first sign in.

You can delete a user account by right-clicking the object and selecting **Delete**. Deleting an account is not easy to reverse, though AD does now support a **Recycle Bin** feature. In many circumstances, it may be more appropriate to disable an account.

Once an account is disabled, the user is denied access to the network until the administrator re-enables the account.

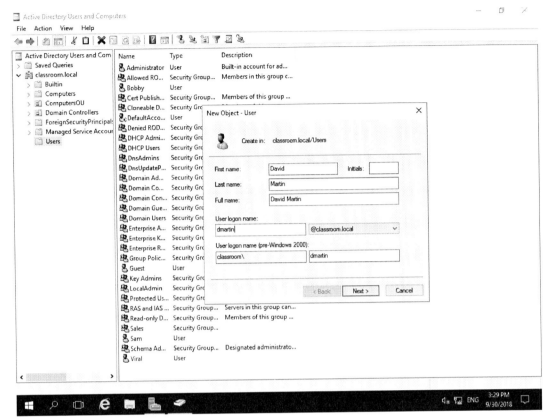

Creating a new user account in AD. (Screenshot used with permission from Microsoft.)

HOW TO CREATE AND DELETE DOMAIN ACCOUNTS
Follow these procedures to create and delete domain accounts.

CREATE A DOMAIN ACCOUNT
To create a domain account:
1. Open the **Active Directory Users and Computers** console.
2. Navigate to the OU where the new user will be created.
3. Right-click the container or OU where you want to store the account.
4. Select **New→User**.
5. Complete the username fields in the next dialog box.
6. Choose an initial password. The default option is to force the user to select a new password at first sign in.
7. Select **Finish**.

DELETE A DOMAIN ACCOUNT
To delete a domain account:
1. Open the **Active Directory Users and Computers** console.
2. Navigate to the OU where the user is stored.
3. Right-click the object and select **Delete**.

 Note: If you accidentally deleted an object, you can use the AD recycle bin to retrieve the object.

Note: Consider disabling rather than deleting accounts.

LOGON SCRIPTS

Logon scripts, also known as login scripts or sign-in scripts, run when a user logs on to a computer. User logon scripts can be assigned to users as part of a **group policy**. Logon scripts can be used to configure the environment for the user—setting environmental variables, setting a home folder, mapping drives to specific server-based folders, and mapping to printers or other resources, for example. A logon script can also be used to ensure that the client meets the security requirements for signing on to the network. For example, if the client has out-of-date software, logon can be denied until the software is updated.

If possible, assign logon scripts to the largest number of users that need the same configuration. A script can be assigned at the domain level, the OU level, or security group level. If a user requires additional or different settings, a logon script can be created for individual users, but that is one more item to maintain.

HOW TO MANAGE LOGON SCRIPTS

Follow these procedures to manage logon scripts.

MANAGE A LOGON OR LOGOFF SCRIPT THROUGH GROUP POLICY

To manage a logon or logoff script in a group policy:

1. In the **User\Scripts\Logon** or the **User\Scripts\Logoff** folder for the related policy, create the scripts you want to run. Policies are stored in the **%SystemRoot%\Sysvol\Domain\Policies** folder on domain controllers.
2. In the **GPMC**, right-click the GPO for the site, domain, or organizational unit you want to work with and then select **Edit**. The policy editor for the GPO opens.
3. In the **User Configuration** node, select the **Windows Settings** folder, and then select **Scripts**.
4. To edit **logon scripts**, right-click **Logon** and then select **Properties**. To edit **logoff scripts**, right-click **Logoff** and then select **Properties**.
5. Select **Show Files**. If you copied the user script to the correct location in the **Policies** folder, you should see the script.
6. Select **Add** to open the **Add A Script** dialog box so that you can assign a script.
7. In the **Script Name** field, type the name of the script you created or copied to the **User\Scripts\Logon** or the **User\Scripts\Logoff** folder for the related policy.
8. In the **Script Parameter** field, enter any command-line arguments to pass to the command-line script or parameters to pass to the scripting host for a WSH script. Repeat this step to add other scripts. During logon or logoff, scripts are executed in the order in which they're listed in the **Properties** dialog box.
9. Use the **Up** and **Down** buttons to reposition scripts as necessary.
10. If you want to edit the script name or parameters later, select the script in the **Script For** list and then select **Edit**.
11. To delete a script, select the script in the **Script For** list, and then select **Remove**.

HOME FOLDER

A **home folder** is a private network storage area located in a shared network server folder in which users can store personal files. The home folder can be created for domain users through the **Active Directory Users and Computers** tool. Using home folders, administrators can more easily create backups of user files because all of the files are located in one place on a file server. If the administrator doesn't assign a home folder location, the computer will automatically use the **Documents** folder location as the default home folder.

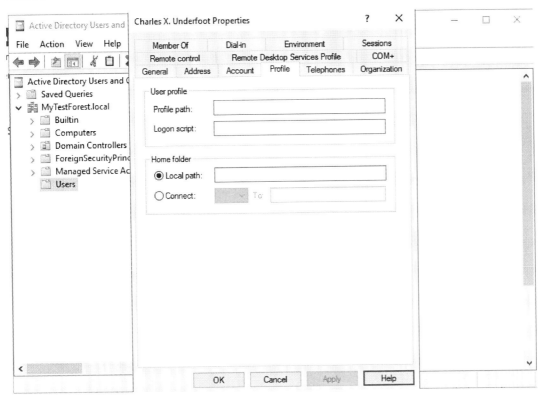

The home folder is configured as a Profile property for a user. (Screenshot used with permission from Microsoft.)

HOW TO CREATE HOME FOLDERS
Follow these procedures to create home folders.

CREATE A HOME FOLDER THROUGH ACTIVE DIRECTORY USERS AND GROUPS
To assign a home folder to a domain user through Active Directory Users and Groups:

1. Verify that there is a shared network folder that can be used to house the users' home folders.
2. Logged in as an administrative user, open **Active Directory Users and Computers**.
   - From the **Start** menu, open **Windows Administrative Tools**, then select **Active Directory Users and Computers**.
   - From the **Server Manager** window, select the **Tools** menu, then select **Active Directory Users and Computers**.
3. In the navigation pane on the left, select the **Users** node.
4. In the **Details** pane in the center of the window, select the desired user. Right-click the user and select **Properties**.
5. In the **Properties** dialog box, select the **Profile** tab.
6. In the **Home folder** section, select **Connect**, select a drive letter, then in the **To** text box, enter the path to the shared folder in the format ***server_name**shared_folder**folder***.
7. Select **OK**.

FOLDER REDIRECTION

By default, user settings and data files are stored in a local user profile located in the **Users** folder. For users that work on more than one computer, they will have separate profiles on each computer and the data files stored on the first computer are not available on the second computer. Microsoft created a couple of technologies to deal with this issue. One is **folder redirection** and the second is **roaming profiles**. Folder redirection allows an administrative user to redirect the path of a local folder (such as the user's home folder) to a folder on a network share. Roaming profiles redirect user profiles to a network share as well. By using both folder redirection and roaming profiles, the user's data and profile information is available when the user logs into any computer on the network where the network share is located.

BENEFITS OF USING FOLDER REDIRECTION

By having folders redirected from local storage to network storage, administrators can back up user data while backing up network data folders. This ensures that user data is being backed up without relying on users to back up their data.

Another benefit is, by using folder redirection with roaming profiles and the **offline files** feature, users can access network files even if the network is unavailable, if network access is slow, or users are working offline.

HOW TO CONFIGURE FOLDER REDIRECTION

Follow these procedures to configure folder redirection.

MANAGE FOLDER REDIRECTION

Logged in as an administrative user, follow these steps to manage folder redirection:

1. Create a security group for folder redirection and add group members.

    a. In **Server Manager**, from the **Tools** menu, select **Active Directory Administration Center**.

    b. Select a Domain or OU and in the **Tasks** pane, select **New→Group**.

    c. In the **Create Group** dialog box, with **Group** selected, enter a name for the security group and then verify **Group type** is set to **Security** and **Group scope** is set to **Global**, and select **OK**.

    d. In the left pane, select **Members**. Select **Add**, then in the **Select Users, Contacts, Computers, Service Accounts, or Groups** dialog box, use the **Enter the object names to select** field to locate members to add. You can use the **Check Names** button to ensure the user name was properly entered, then select **OK**.

2. Create a network file share to use for folder redirection.

    a. In **Server Manager**, from the left pane, select **File and Storage Services**.

    b. Select **Shares**.

    c. From the **Share** section **Tasks** drop-down menu, select **New Share**.

    d. Work through the **New Share Wizard** to create the share. When specifying the share name, add a **$** after the name to hide it from view. Configure the permissions using **Customize permissions** and select **Disable inheritance**, select **Convert inherited permissions into explicit permission on this object**, and give the group you created for folder redirection **Special** permissions by selecting **Show advanced permissions** and then selecting the appropriate permissions. At the end of the wizard, select **Create**.

3. Create a folder redirection group policy object.

    a. In **Server Manager**, from the **Tools** menu, select **Group Policy Management**.

    b. Right-click the domain or OU and select **Create a GPO in this domain, and Link it here.**

    c. In the **New GPO** dialog box, enter the GPO name and select **OK**.

    d. If desired, right-click the new GPO and uncheck **Link Enabled** to keep it from being used before folder redirection configuration has been completed. Be sure to check this box again after you have finished creating the GPO.

    e. With the new GPO selected, on the **Scope** tab, in the **Security Filtering** section, select **Authenticated Users** then select **Remove**. This will prevent the GPO from being applied to Everyone.

    f. Select **Add** and add the group you created for folder redirection.

    g. On the **Delegation** tab, select **Add** and type *Authenticated Users*. Select **OK** as needed to complete the action and accept Read permissions.

4. Configure Offline Files for folder redirection.

    a. In **Group Policy Management**, select the GPO created for folder redirection.

    b. Right-click the GPO and select **Edit**.

    c. Navigate to **User Configuration→Policies→Windows Settings→Folder Redirection**.

    d. Right-click the folder that will be redirected and select **Properties**.

    e. In the **Properties** dialog box, in the **Setting** section, select **Basic - Redirect everyone's folder to the same location**.

    f. In the **Target folder location** section, select **Create a folder for each user under the root path** and then in the **Root Path** box, type the path to the file share where redirected folders will be stored.

    g. If desired, on the **Settings** tab, in the **Policy Removal** section, select **Redirect the folder back to the local user profile location when the policy is removed** and select **OK**. In the **Warning** dialog box, select **Yes**.

5. In **Group Policy Management**, right-click the folder redirection GPO and select **Link Enabled**.

6. Test at a computer with a user account that has been configured for folder redirection.

    a. If necessary, at an elevated command prompt or PowerShell prompt, enter *gpupdate /force* to apply the updated Group Policy settings.

    b. In File Explorer, display properties for a redirected folder.

    c. In the **Properties** dialog box, on the **Location** tab, verify that the path shows the file share that was specified rather than the local file path.

ACCOUNT LOCKS AND PASSWORD RESETS

If a user account violates a security policy, such as an incorrect password being entered repeatedly, it may be locked against further use. The account will be inaccessible until it is unlocked by setting the option in the **Properties** dialog box on the **Account** tab.

Using the Properties dialog box to unlock a user account. (Screenshot used with permission from Microsoft.)

If a user forgets a password, you can reset it by right-clicking the account and selecting **Reset Password**. You can use this dialog as another way to unlock an account too.

HOW TO UNLOCK DOMAIN ACCOUNTS AND RESET PASSWORDS

Follow these procedures to unlock accounts and reset passwords in Active Directory.

UNLOCK A WINDOWS DOMAIN USER ACCOUNT

To unlock an account through **Active Directory Users and Computers**:

1. In Server Manager select **Tools→Active Directory Users and Computers**.
2. Navigate to the container or OU where the account is stored.
3. Right-click the locked account and select **Properties**.
4. On the **Account** tab, check **Unlock account**.
5. Select **Apply**.
6. If the account was locked because the user forgot their password, or the account was compromised by an attacker and then locked, reset the password.
7. Select **OK**.

RESET A WINDOWS DOMAIN USER PASSWORD

To reset a Windows domain user password:

1. In Server Manager select **Tools→Active Directory Users and Computers**.
2. Navigate to the container or OU where the account is stored.
3. Right-click the account and select **Reset Password**.
4. If the account is locked, check **Unlock account**.
5. In the **New password** and **Confirm password** text boxes, type a password that meets the complexity requirements of the organization.
6. If desired, check **User must change password at next logon**.
7. Select **OK**.
8. Communicate the new password to the user over a secure communication method.

Activity 5-1

Managing Users, Workstations, and Shared Resources Review

SCENARIO
Answer the following review questions.

1. **What experiences do you have in working with any of the technologies discussed in this lesson?**

2. **Which AD configuration task do you expect to perform most often in your workplace?**

Summary

In this lesson, you managed user accounts, workstations, and shared resources. These administrative tasks are critical knowledge for any A+ technician.

Lesson 6

Security Concepts

LESSON INTRODUCTION

So far in this course, you have installed and configured PC hardware and software and network devices. Another facet of a CompTIA® A+® technician's duties involves protecting organizational computing assets from attacks. In this lesson, you will identify security threats and vulnerabilities, plus some of the logical and physical controls used to mitigate them.

In today's work environment, cybersecurity is everyone's responsibility. As an A+ technician, you are in the position to identify potential security issues before they become big problems. By identifying security threats and vulnerabilities, as well as some of the controls that can counteract them, you can help keep your organization's computing resources safe from unauthorized access.

LESSON OBJECTIVES

In this lesson, you will:

- Describe logical security concepts.
- Describe physical security threats and vulnerabilities.
- Describe physical security controls.

Topic A
Logical Security Concepts

EXAM OBJECTIVES COVERED
1002-2.2 Explain logical security concepts.
1002-2.7 Given a scenario, implement security best practices to secure a workstation.

Logical security refers to the idea that any information or data that is created, stored, and transmitted in digital form is secured to the desired level. This concept applies to many components of the digital world, such as the Internet, cloud-based computing, networks, mobile devices, tablets, laptops, and standard desktop computers.

SECURITY BASICS

Security is the practice of controlling access to something (a resource). Security is always balanced against accessibility; restricting access makes a resource better protected but also less usable. Secure information has three properties, often referred to as the CIA triad:

- **Confidentiality**—this means that certain information should only be known to certain people.
- **Integrity**—this means that the data is stored and transferred as intended and that any modification is authorized.
- **Availability**—this means that information is accessible to those authorized to view or modify it.

Security policies ensure that an organization has evaluated the risks it faces and has put in place controls to mitigate those risks. Making a system more secure is also referred to as **hardening** it. Different security policies should cover every aspect of an organization's use of computer and network technologies, from procurement and change control to acceptable use.

SECURITY CONTROLS

Security controls are safeguards or prevention methods to avoid, counteract, or minimize security risks relating to personal or company property. For example, a firewall is a type of security control because it controls network communications by allowing only traffic that has specifically been permitted by a system administrator. Security controls can be classified by several criteria, such as by the time that they act relative to a security incident, according to their nature, or by people, technology, and operations/processes. There are different classification schemes, but one way to understand the types of security controls is to consider the following classes:

- Physical controls such as fences, doors, locks, and fire extinguishers.
- Procedural controls such as incident response processes, management oversight, security awareness, and training.
- Logical controls such as user authentication (login) and software-based access controls, anti-virus software, and firewalls.
- Legal and regulatory or compliance controls such as privacy laws, policies, and clauses.

LOGICAL SECURITY CONTROLS

Logical security refers to controls implemented in software to create an access control system. The overall operation of an access control system is usually described in terms of three functions, referred to as the AAA triad:

- **Authentication** means one or more methods of proving that a user is who she/he says she/he is.
- **Authorization** means creating one or more barriers around the resource such that only authenticated users can gain access. Each resource has an access control list specifying what users can do. Resources often have different access levels; for example, being able to read a file or being able to read and edit it.
- **Accounting** means recording when and by whom a resource was accessed.

IMPLICIT DENY AND LEAST PRIVILEGE

Logical security is founded on the principle of implicit deny. **Implicit deny** means that unless there is a rule specifying that access should be granted, any request for access is denied. This level of minimal access includes facilities, computing hardware, software, and information.

This principle can be seen clearly in firewall policies. A firewall filters access requests using a set of rules. The rules are processed in order from top-to-bottom. If a request does not fit any of the rules, it is handled by the last (default) rule, which is to refuse the request.

A complementary principle is that of **least privilege**. This means that a user should be granted rights necessary to perform their job and no more.

Note: These principles apply equally to users (people) and software processes. Much software is written without regard to the principles of implicit deny and least privilege, making it less secure than it should be.

ENCRYPTION

Many logical security controls depend to some extent on the use of encryption technologies. **Encryption** is an ancient technique for hiding information. Someone obtaining an encrypted document cannot understand that information unless they possesses a key. The use of encryption allows sensitive data to travel across a public network, such as the Internet, and remain private. If the data packets were intercepted and examined, the content would be unreadable.

The use of encryption and other digital security techniques provides users with three important security requirements on computer networks: confidentiality, integrity, and authentication. There are three principal types of cryptographic technology: symmetric encryption, asymmetric encryption, and cryptographic hashing. These all have different roles in achieving the goals of confidentiality, integrity, and/or authentication. Often two or more of these three different types are used together in the same product or technology.

SYMMETRIC ENCRYPTION

In symmetric encryption, a single secret key is used to both encrypt and decrypt data. The secret key is so-called because it must be kept secret. If the key is lost or stolen, the security is breached.

Note: Symmetric encryption is also referred to as single-key or private-key. Note that "private key" is also used to refer to part of the PKI process (discussed shortly), so take care not to confuse the two uses.

The main problem with symmetric encryption is secure distribution and storage of the key. This problem becomes exponentially greater the more widespread the key's distribution needs to be. The main advantage is speed, as symmetric key encryption is less processor intensive than asymmetric encryption.

Symmetric encryption is used to encode data for storage or transmission over a network. The most widely used symmetric encryption technology (or cipher) is the Advanced Encryption Standard (AES). Older ciphers such as Data Encryptions Standard (DES/3DES) and Rivest Cipher (RC) have known weaknesses that make them less suitable for use in modern security systems.

One of the principal measures of the security of an encryption cipher is the size of the key. Early ciphers used between 32- and 64-bit keys. Currently, 1024-bit keys would be selected for general use, with larger keys required for highly sensitive data. The larger the key, however, the more processing is required to perform encryption and decryption.

ASYMMETRIC ENCRYPTION

In asymmetric encryption, if a public key is used to encrypt data, only a mathematically related private key can be used to decrypt it. The private key must be kept a secret known only to a single subject (user or computer). The public key can be widely and safely distributed to anyone with whom the subject wants to communicate, because the private key cannot be derived from the public key. Also, the public key cannot be used to decrypt a message that it has just encrypted.

 Note: A key pair can be used the other way around. If the private key is used to encrypt something, only the public key can then decrypt it. The point is that one type of key cannot reverse the operation it has just performed.

Asymmetric encryption is mostly used for authentication technologies, such as digital certificates and digital signatures, and key exchange. **Key exchange** is where two hosts need to know the same symmetric encryption key without any other host finding out what it is. Symmetric encryption is much faster than asymmetric, so it is often used to protect the actual data exchange in a session. Asymmetric encryption is more complex, taking longer for a computer to process, and so typically only used on small amounts of data, such as the authentication process to set up the session.

Most asymmetric encryption technologies use the **RSA cipher**, named after its designers Ron Rivest, Adi Shamir, and Leonard Adleman.

CRYPTOGRAPHIC HASHES

A **hash** is a short representation of data. A **hash function** takes a variable-length string (text) as input and produces a fixed-length value (32-bit, for instance) as output. A **cryptographic hash** makes it impossible to recover the original string from the hash value. This technique can be used to prove that a message has not been tampered with (integrity). For example, when creating a digital signature, the sender computes a cryptographic hash of the message and then encrypts the hash with his or her private key. When the recipient receives the message and decrypts the hash, the recipient computes its own hash of the message and compares the two values to confirm they match. Cryptographic hashes are also used for secure storage of data where the original meaning does not have to be recovered (passwords for instance).

Two of the most commonly used cryptographic hash algorithms are **Secure Hash Algorithm** (SHA-1 and SHA-2) and **Message Digest** (MD5). MD5 is the older algorithm and is gradually being phased out of use.

PKI AND CERTIFICATES

Asymmetric encryption is an important part of **Public Key Infrastructure (PKI)**. PKI is a solution to the problem of authenticating subjects on public networks. Under PKI, users or server computers are validated by a **Certificate Authority (CA)**, which issues the subject a digital certificate. The **digital certificate** contains a public key associated with the subject embedded in it. The certificate has also been signed by the CA, guaranteeing its validity. Therefore, if a client trusts the signing CA, they can also trust the user or server presenting the certificate.

The client can then send the server (comptia.org, for example) data (their credit card details, for example) encrypted using the public key, safe in the knowledge that only that particular server will be able to decrypt it (using its private key). A similar technique can be used to encrypt the contents of emails. The sender uses the recipient's public key to encrypt the data with the assurance that only the linked private key can be used to decrypt the data again. PKI can also be used by mobile applications to encrypt any data sent between the client and the server.

Digital certificates are also used for secure authentication to computer networks. The certificate is stored with the private key on a smart card hardware token. To authenticate, the card provides the certificate to the authentication server, which checks that it is valid and trusted. It then uses the public key in the certificate to issue an encrypted challenge to the user. The smart card should be able to decrypt this challenge using the private key and send an appropriate response.

EXECUTION CONTROL

Authentication and authorization gives subjects the right to sign on to a computer and network and (potentially) to make changes to the system configuration. This places a certain amount of trust in the user to exercise those rights responsibly. Users can act maliciously, though, or could be tricked into an adverse action. **Execution control** refers to logical security technologies designed to prevent malicious software from running on a host. Execution control can establish a security system that does not entirely depend on the good behavior of individual users.

TRUSTED/UNTRUSTED SOFTWARE SOURCES

To prevent the spread of malware such as Trojans, it is necessary to restrict the ability of users to run unapproved program code, especially code that can modify the OS, such as an application installer. Windows uses the system of Administrator and Standard user accounts, along with User Account Control (UAC) and system policies, to enforce these restrictions.

Developers of Windows applications can use digital certificates to perform code signing and prove the authenticity and integrity of an installer package. Linux® also prompts when you attempt to install untrusted software. Software is signed with a cryptographic key. Packages need the public key for the repository in order to install the software. When prompted that you are installing untrusted software, you can either respond that you want to install it anyway or cancel the installation.

Mobile OS vendors use this "walled garden" model of software distribution as well. Apps are distributed from an approved store, such as Apple's App Store or the Windows Store. The vendor's store policies and procedures are supposed to prevent any Trojan-like apps from being published.

There are also third-party network management suites to enforce application control. This means configuring blacklists of unapproved software (allowing anything else) or whitelists of approved software (denying anything else).

DISABLE AutoRun

One of the problems with legacy versions of Windows is that when an optical disk is inserted or USB or network drive is attached, Windows would automatically run commands defined in an **autorun.inf** file stored in the root of the drive. A typical autorun.inf would define an icon for a disk and the path to a setup file. This could lead to malware being able to install itself automatically.

In modern versions of Windows®, an **AutoPlay** dialog box is shown prompting the user to take a particular action. AutoPlay settings can be configured via a drive's property dialog box. Also, UAC will require the user to explicitly allow any executable code to run. There is a Control Panel applet to configure default AutoPlay actions.

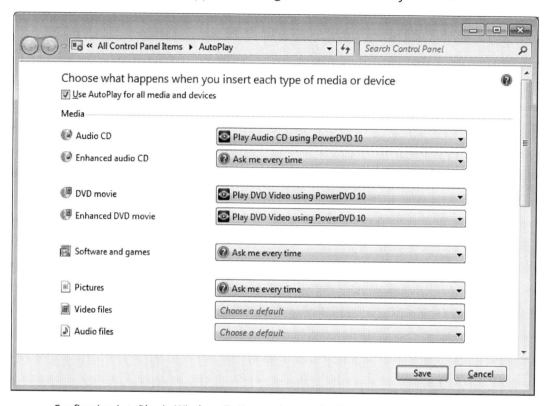

Configuring AutoPlay in Windows 7. (Screenshot used with permission from Microsoft.)

ANTI-VIRUS/ANTI-MALWARE

Anti-virus (A-V) is software that can detect malware and prevent it from executing. The primary means of detection is to use a database of known virus patterns, called definitions, signatures, or patterns. Another technique is to use **heuristic** identification. "Heuristic" means that the software uses knowledge of the sort of things that viruses do to try to spot (and block) virus-like behavior. Most anti-virus software is better described as **anti-malware**, as it can detect software threats that are not technically virus-like, including spyware, Trojans, rootkits, and ransomware. It is critical to ensure that the security software is updated regularly.

PATCH MANAGEMENT

It is important to apply critical and security updates for OS and application software. Failing to keep operating systems and software applications up-to-date can cause anything from graphical corruptions when using new video drivers to complete system crashes and vulnerability to malware. That said, there are two approaches to applying updates:

*   Apply all the latest patches to ensure the system is as secure as possible against attacks against flaws in the software.

- Only apply a patch if it solves a particular problem being experienced.

The second approach obviously requires more work, as you need to keep up-to-date with security bulletins. However, it is well recognized that updates can cause problems, especially with software application compatibility. Best practice is to test updates on a non-production system before rolling them out.

 Note: *To check the current build of Windows, run* `winver`. *To check the version number of a particular file, right-click and select* **Properties**.

NAC

Firewalls are principally deployed to manage access between networks. They control communications by blocking packets based on access rules permitting or denying certain combinations of IP addresses and network ports, or other filtering criteria.

Firewalls cannot control whether a device can connect to a network in the first place. **Defense in depth**, or endpoint security, refers to controls that monitor the security of a network "behind" the perimeter firewall. **Network Access Control (NAC)** allows administrators to devise policies or profiles describing a minimum security configuration that devices must meet to be granted network access. This is called a **health policy**. Typical policies check things such as malware infection, firmware and OS patch level, personal firewall status, and the presence of up-to-date virus definitions. A solution may also be to scan the registry or perform file signature verification. The health policy is defined on a NAC management server along with reporting and configuration tools.

PHYSICAL PORT SECURITY

With wired ports, access to the physical switch ports and switch hardware should be restricted to authorized staff, using a secure server room and/or lockable hardware cabinets. To prevent the attachment of unauthorized client devices, a switch port can be disabled using the management software or the patch cable can be physically removed from the port. Completely disabling ports in this way can introduce a lot of administrative overhead and scope for error. Also, it doesn't provide complete protection as an attacker could unplug a device from an enabled port and connect their own laptop. Consequently, more sophisticated methods of ensuring port security have been developed.

MAC ADDRESS FILTERING

Configuring **MAC filtering** on a switch means defining which MAC addresses are allowed to connect to a particular port. This can be done by creating a list of valid MAC addresses or by specifying a limit to the number of permitted addresses. For example, if port security is enabled with a maximum of two MAC addresses, the switch will record the first two MACs to connect to that port but then drop any traffic from machines with different network adapter IDs that try to connect.

Many devices also support **whitelisting** and/or **blacklisting** of MAC addresses. A MAC address added to a whitelist is permitted to connect to any port, whereas a MAC address on a blacklist is prohibited from connecting to any port.

PORT SECURITY / IEEE 802.1X

The IEEE 802.1X standard defines a **Port-based Network Access Control (PNAC)** mechanism. PNAC means that the switch (or router) performs some sort of authentication of the attached device before activating the port.

Under 802.1X, the device requesting access is the **supplicant**. The switch, referred to as the authenticator, enables the **Extensible Authentication Protocol over LAN (EAPoL)** protocol only and waits for the device to supply authentication data. Using

EAP, this data could be a simple username/password (EAP-MD5) or could involve using a digital certificate or token. The authenticator passes this data to an authenticating server, which checks the credentials and grants or denies access.

MDM

Mobile Device Management (MDM) is a class of management software designed to apply security policies to the use of mobile devices in the enterprise. This software can be used to manage enterprise-owned devices as well as **Bring Your Own Device (BYOD)**.

The core functionality of these suites is similar to Network Access Control (NAC) solutions. The management software logs the use of a device on the network and determines whether to allow it to connect or not, based on administrator-set parameters. When the device is enrolled with the management software, it can be configured with policies to allow or restrict use of apps, corporate data, and built-in functions, such as a video camera or microphone.

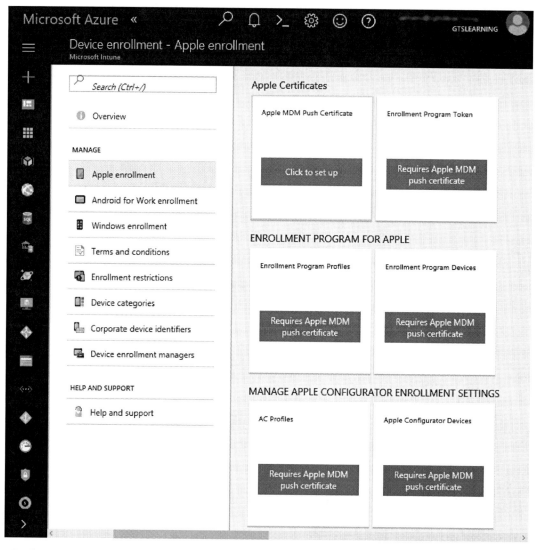

Configuring iOS device enrollment in Microsoft's Intune Enterprise Mobility Management (EMM) suite. Used with permission from Microsoft.

VPN

As well as allowing hosts to connect over wired or wireless local connections, most networks have to allow devices to connect remotely, to support home workers, field workers, branch offices, partners, suppliers, and customers. A remote connection is obviously easier for external attackers to try to exploit than a local one, so remote access must be subject to stringent security policies and controls.

A Virtual Private Network (VPN) connects the components and resources of two (private) networks over another (public) network. A VPN is a "tunnel" through the Internet (or any other public network). It uses special connection protocols and encryption technology to ensure that the tunnel is secure and the user is properly authenticated. Once the connection has been established, to all intents and purposes, the remote computer becomes part of the local network (though it is still restricted by the bandwidth available over the WAN link).

With a VPN, TCP/IP communications are encrypted and then packaged within another TCP/IP packet stream. The VPN hardware or software can encrypt just the underlying data in a packet or the entire packet itself before wrapping it in another IP packet for delivery. If a packet on the public network is intercepted along the way, the encrypted contents cannot be read by a hacker. Such encryption of data or packets is typically implemented by using a protocol suite called **Internet Protocol Security** (IPSec).

A remote access request is only granted if the user authenticates correctly and the account has been given remote (or "dial-in") permission. The client device could also be subject to NAC policy checks before it is allowed to fully join the VPN.

Topic B
Threats and Vulnerabilities

 EXAM OBJECTIVES COVERED
1002-2.5 Compare and contrast social engineering, threats, and vulnerabilities.

In this topic, you will distinguish the concepts of threats, vulnerabilities, and controls. By identifying common security threats and vulnerabilities, you will be better equipped to suggest or implement the most effective counteractive measures.

VULNERABILITIES, THREATS, AND RISKS

In IT security, it is important to distinguish between the concepts of vulnerability, threat, and risk:

- **Vulnerability**—a weakness that could be triggered accidentally or exploited intentionally to cause a security breach.
- **Threat**—the potential for a **threat agent** or **threat actor** (something or someone that may trigger a vulnerability accidentally or exploit it intentionally) to "exercise" a vulnerability (that is, to breach security). The path or tool used by the threat actor can be referred to as the threat vector.
- **Risk**—the likelihood and impact (or consequence) of a threat actor exercising a vulnerability.

To understand network security, you need to understand the types of threats that a network is exposed to and how vulnerabilities can be exploited to launch actual attacks.

SOCIAL ENGINEERING THREATS

Much of the focus in computer security is in deterring malicious external and insider threats. Attackers can use a diverse range of techniques to compromise a security system. A prerequisite of many types of attack is to obtain information about the security system. **Social engineering** refers to means of getting users to reveal this kind of confidential information or allowing some sort of access to the organization that should not have been authorized. A social engineering attack uses deception and trickery to convince unsuspecting users to provide sensitive data or to violate security guidelines. Social engineering is often a precursor to another type of attack.

It is also important to note that gaining access to a network is often based on a series of small steps rather than a single large step. That is, knowing the email address of an employee allows an attacker to search for facts about that user online. This might help target the user with fake messages. A message might be convincing enough to persuade the user to reveal some confidential information or install some malware. The malware allows the attacker to access the network and try to discover the ID of a more privileged account or the location of important data files.

Because these attacks depend on human factors rather than on technology, their symptoms can be vague and hard to identify. Social engineering attacks can come in a variety of methods: in person, through email, or over the phone. Social engineering typically takes advantage of users who are not technically knowledgeable, but it can also be directed against technical support staff if the attacker pretends to be a user who needs help.

COMMON SOCIAL ENGINEERING EXPLOITS

Preventing social engineering attacks requires an awareness of the most common forms of social engineering exploits.

IMPERSONATION

Impersonation (pretending to be someone else) is one of the basic social engineering techniques. The classic impersonation attack is for an attacker to phone into a department, claim they have to adjust something on the user's system remotely, and get the user to reveal their password.

Attackers will generally try one of the following methods to make an impersonation attack convincing:

- Intimidate their target by pretending to be someone senior in rank.
- Intimidate the target by using spurious technical arguments and jargon or alarm them with a hoax.
- Coax the target by engaging with them in and putting them at their ease.

Do you really know who's on the other end of the line? (Photo by Uros Jovicic on Unsplash.)

PHISHING AND SPEAR PHISHING

Phishing is a combination of social engineering and **spoofing** (disguising one computer resource as another). The attacker sets up a spoof website to imitate a target bank or ecommerce provider's secure website. The attacker then emails users of the genuine website informing them that their account must be updated, supplying a disguised link that actually leads to their spoofed site. When the user authenticates with the spoofed site, their log on details are captured. Another technique is to spawn a "pop-up" window when a user visits a genuine site to try to trick them into entering their credentials through the pop-up.

Spear phishing refers to a phishing scam where the attacker has some information that makes the target more likely to be fooled by the attack. The attacker might know the name of a document that the target is editing, for instance, and send a malicious copy, or the phishing email might show that the attacker knows the recipient's full name, job title, telephone number, or other details that help to convince the target that the communication is genuine.

PHARMING

Pharming is another means of redirecting users from a legitimate website to a malicious one. Rather than using social engineering techniques to trick the user, however, pharming relies on corrupting the way the victim's computer performs Internet name resolution, so that they are redirected from the genuine site to the malicious one. For example, if mybank.com should point to the IP address w.x.y.z, a pharming attack would corrupt the name resolution process to make it point to IP address a.b.c.d.

TRUST AND DUMPSTER DIVING

Being convincing or establishing trust usually depends on the attacker obtaining privileged information about the organization or about an individual. For example, an impersonation attack is much more effective if the attacker knows the user's name. As most companies are set up toward customer service rather than security, this information is typically easy to come by. Information that might seem innocuous, such as department employee lists, job titles, phone numbers, diary appointments, invoices, or purchase orders, can help an attacker penetrate an organization through impersonation.

Another way to obtain information that will help to make a social engineering attack credible is by obtaining documents that the company has thrown away. **Dumpster diving** refers to combing through an organization's (or individual's) garbage to try to find useful documents. Attackers may even find files stored on discarded removable media.

 Note: Remember that attacks may be staged over a long period of time. Initial attacks may only aim at compromising low-level information and user accounts, but this low-level information can be used to attack more sensitive and confidential data and better protected management and administrative accounts.

SHOULDER SURFING

Shoulder surfing refers to stealing a password or PIN, or other secure information, by watching the user type it. Despite the name, the attacker may not have to be in close proximity to the target. They could use high-power binoculars or CCTV to directly observe the target from a remote location.

TAILGATING

Tailgating (or piggybacking) is a means of entering a secure area without authorization by following close behind the person that has been allowed to open the door or checkpoint. This might be done without the target's knowledge or may be a means for an insider to allow access to someone without recording it in the building's entry log. Another technique is to persuade someone to hold a door open, using an excuse such as "I've forgotten my badge/key."

MITIGATION OF SOCIAL ENGINEERING ATTACKS

Social engineering is best defeated by training users to recognize and respond to such situations.

- Train employees to release information or make privileged use of the system only according to standard procedures.
- Establish a reporting system for suspected attacks—though the obvious risk here is that a large number of false negatives will be reported.
- Train employees to identify phishing-style attacks plus new styles of attack as they develop in the future.
- Train employees not to release any work-related information on third-party sites or social networks (and especially not to reuse passwords used for accounts at work).

Other measures include ensuring documents and information is destroyed before disposal, using multifactor access control, to put more than one or two barriers between an attacker and his or her target, and restricting use of administrative accounts as far as possible.

NETWORK FOOTPRINTING THREATS

Footprinting is another information-gathering threat, in which the attacker attempts to learn about the configuration of the network and security systems. Footprinting can be accomplished by social engineering attacks. There are also many software-based tools and techniques for gathering information.

 Note: Footprinting describes investigating the overall network and security topology, whereas fingerprinting describes probes that attempt to discover how a particular host is configured.

OPEN PORTS

Network mapping refers to tools that gather information about the way the network is built and configured and the current status of hosts. One approach to protecting a network from unwanted footprinting or fingerprinting is to prevent unauthorized hosts from connecting at all. An "open port" in this sense is an Ethernet port that allows any computer to connect to the switch. Ethernet ports can be physically or administratively disabled to prevent this, though that would not stop an attacker from unplugging an authorized machine and connecting a different one. There are various Network Access Control (NAC) or endpoint security solutions that can require devices to authenticate before network access is granted.

As well as the physical Ethernet port, an "open port" can also refer to a TCP or UDP network application port. **Port scanning** aims to enumerate the TCP or UDP application ports on a host that are accepting connections. The `netstat` tool can be used on Windows and Linux to investigate open connections on the local computer. More advanced probes, such as `nmap`, can discover a good deal more information about a host.

```
C:\Windows\system32>netstat -b -n

Active Connections

  Proto  Local Address          Foreign Address        State
  TCP    192.168.1.110:5806     185.41.10.123:80       CLOSE_WAIT
 [IEXPLORE.EXE]
  TCP    192.168.1.110:5807     185.41.10.123:80       CLOSE_WAIT
 [IEXPLORE.EXE]
  TCP    192.168.1.110:5808     216.58.208.40:443      ESTABLISHED
 [IEXPLORE.EXE]
  TCP    192.168.1.110:5809     216.58.208.40:443      ESTABLISHED
 [IEXPLORE.EXE]
  TCP    192.168.1.110:5810     104.27.151.216:80      CLOSE_WAIT
 [IEXPLORE.EXE]
  TCP    192.168.1.110:5811     104.27.151.216:80      CLOSE_WAIT
 [IEXPLORE.EXE]
  TCP    192.168.1.110:5812     104.27.151.216:80      CLOSE_WAIT
 [IEXPLORE.EXE]
  TCP    192.168.1.110:5813     104.27.151.216:80      CLOSE_WAIT
 [IEXPLORE.EXE]
  TCP    192.168.1.110:5814     104.27.151.216:80      CLOSE_WAIT
 [IEXPLORE.EXE]
  TCP    192.168.1.110:5815     104.27.151.216:80      CLOSE_WAIT
 [IEXPLORE.EXE]
  TCP    192.168.1.110:5816     52.28.192.217:443      ESTABLISHED
 [IEXPLORE.EXE]
  TCP    [fe80::5c9e:8be5:bb3e:f341%4]:2179  [fe80::5c9e:8be5:bb3e:f341%4]:5519
 ESTABLISHED
 [vmms.exe]
  TCP    [fe80::5c9e:8be5:bb3e:f341%4]:3587  [fe80::5cf0:94fe:4f4:a8a%4]:57395
 ESTABLISHED
  p2psvc
 [svchost.exe]
  TCP    [fe80::5c9e:8be5:bb3e:f341%4]:5519  [fe80::5c9e:8be5:bb3e:f341%4]:2179
 ESTABLISHED
 [VmConnect.exe]

C:\Windows\system32>_
```

Displaying open connections with netstat. (Screenshot used with permission from Microsoft.)

When a host running a particular operating system responds to a port scan, the syntax of the response might identify the specific operating system. This fact is also true of application servers, such as web servers, FTP servers, and mail servers. The responses these servers make often include several headers or banners that can reveal a great deal of information about the server.

Ports can be closed by disabling unnecessary or unused protocols, services, and applications. If a service must be run, a port can be blocked on a particular interface or restricted to certain hosts using an Access Control List (ACL) enforced by a firewall.

Port scanning tools are also useful defensive tools because a network administrator needs to ensure that unauthorized ports are not open on the network. These could be a sign of some sort of Trojan or backdoor server. Such tools often try to hide themselves from diagnostic port scans.

EAVESDROPPING THREATS

Eavesdropping (or sniffing) refers to capturing and reading data packets as they move over the network. When an attacker (for example, a malicious user) has gained access to the network, they can use a packet sniffer such as Wireshark® to capture live network traffic. Unless the packets are encrypted, the attacker can gain a lot of information about the way the network is designed as well as intercepting any data transmitted in plaintext.

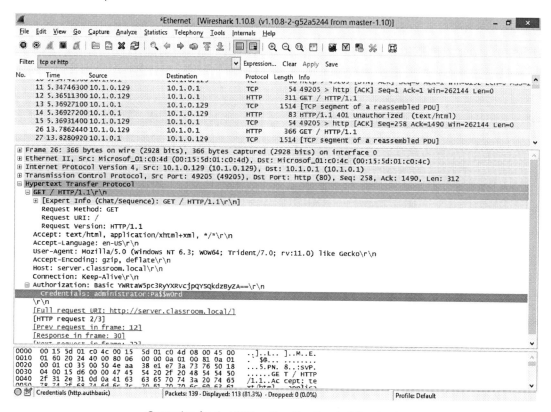

Capturing basic HTTP authentication in Wireshark.

In the first instance, an attack would be limited to data traffic to and from the individual user's computer (as well as broadcast traffic) as network switches will prevent all other traffic from being directed to that computer. However, switches can be subverted by various different types of attack:

- **MAC flooding**—overloading the switch's MAC cache, referred to as the **Content Addressable Memory (CAM) table**, using a tool such as Dsniff or Ettercap to prevent genuine devices from connecting and potentially forcing the switch into "hub" or "flooding" mode.

- **ARP poisoning**—the attacker poisons the switch's ARP table with a false MAC-IP address mapping, typically allowing the attacker to masquerade as the subnet's default gateway.

 Note: *A packet sniffer is a defensive as well as an offensive tool. It can be used to try to detect network intrusions and unauthorized and malicious traffic.*

SPOOFING AND MITM THREATS

Having gathered information about a network, an attacker may be able to probe or damage it by launching further attacks. Many of the network, transport, and application protocols in use on private networks and the Internet were designed without any regard for security. Protocols such as TCP or UDP are vulnerable to packet sniffing because they were designed to transmit information in plain text. Devices communicating using these protocols do not typically authenticate with one another, making them vulnerable to spoofing, Denial of Service, and Man-in-the-Middle attacks.

SPOOFING AND PACKET/PROTOCOL ABUSE

The term spoofing (or impersonation or masquerade) covers a very wide range of different attacks. Social engineering and techniques such as phishing and pharming are types of spoofing attack. It also possible to abuse the way a protocol works or network packets are constructed to inject false or modified data onto a network. The ARP poisoning attack described earlier is a good example of this. The ARP and DNS protocols are often used as vectors for spoofing attacks.

Spoofing can also be performed by obtaining a logical token or software token. A logical token is assigned to a user or computer when they authenticate to some service. A token might be implemented as a web cookie, for instance. If an attacker can steal the token and the authorization system has not been designed well, the attacker may be able to present the token again and impersonate the original user. This type of spoofing is also called a **replay attack**.

MAN-IN-THE-MIDDLE ATTACK

A **Man-in-the-Middle (MITM)** attack is another specific type of spoofing attack where the attacker sits between two communicating hosts and transparently monitors, captures, and relays all communication between them. Man-in-the-middle attacks are used to gain access to authentication and network infrastructure information for future attacks, or to gain direct access to packet contents.

For example, in an ARP poisoning attack, the attacker sends spoofed ARP messages onto the network to associate his IP address with another host, typically the subnet's default gateway. The rest of the network hosts will then start communicating with the attacker, who will be able to sniff the packets and either send them on to the genuine host (to try to keep the attack covert), send modified versions of the packets, or drop them (performing a Denial of Service attack).

MitM attacks can be defeated using **mutual authentication**, where both server and client exchange secure credentials.

PASSWORD ATTACKS

Computer systems are protected by accounts and accounts are protected by credentials, typically passwords. Passwords can be discovered via social engineering or because a user has written one down. Packet sniffing attacks are often launched with the purpose of obtaining credentials for one or more accounts. If a network protocol uses cleartext credentials, then the attacker's job is done. Most passwords are only sent over the network or stored on a device using some sort of cryptographic protection, however.

 Note: *A password might be sent in an encoded form, such as Base64, which is simply an ASCII representation of binary data. This is not the same as cryptography. The password value can easily be derived from the Base64 string.*

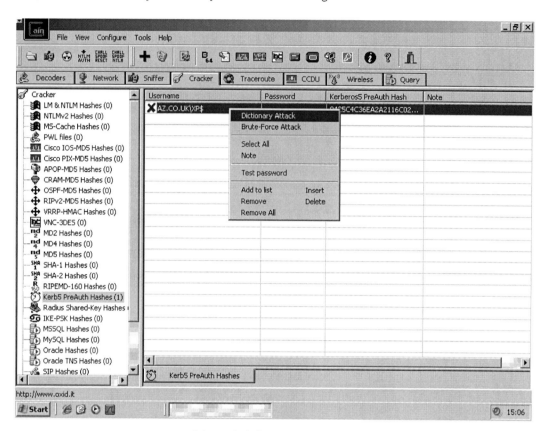

Cain and Abel password cracker.

Either the channel can be protected or the password can be protected (or both). If the channel is encrypted, the attacker has to compromise the encryption keys stored on the server. If the password is protected by a cryptographic hash, the attacker might be able to use password cracking software to decipher it.

TYPES OF PASSWORD ATTACKS

A cryptographic hash scrambles the data in a way that the original plaintext password is normally unrecoverable. However, the cryptographic hash function might be vulnerable to these types of attacks:

- **Dictionary**—the password cracker matches the hash to those produced by ordinary words found in a dictionary. This could also include information such as user and company names or pet names or any other data that people might naively use as passwords.
- **Brute force**—the software tries to match the hash against one of every possible combination it could be. If the password is short (under 7 characters) and non-complex (using only letters, for instance), a password might be cracked in minutes. Longer and more complex passwords increase the amount of time the attack takes to run.

RAINBOW TABLE ATTACKS

A dictionary attack can be used where there is a good chance of guessing the likely value of the plaintext. **Rainbow tables** refine the dictionary approach. The technique was developed by Phillipe Oechsli and used in his Ophcrack Windows password cracker. The attacker uses a precomputed lookup table of all probable plaintext passwords (derived from the dictionary) and their matching hashes. Not all possible hash values are stored, as this would require too much memory. Values are computed in "chains" and only the first and last values need to be stored. The hash value of a stored password can then be looked up in the table and the corresponding plaintext discovered.

The hash functions used to store passwords can be made more secure by adding salt. Salt is a random value added to the plaintext. This helps to slow down rainbow table attacks against a hashed password database, as the table cannot be created in advance and must be recreated for each combination of password and salt value. Rainbow tables are also impractical when trying to discover long passwords (over about 14 characters). UNIX and Linux password storage mechanisms use salt, but Windows does not. Consequently, in a Windows environment it is even more important to enforce password policies, such as selecting a strong password and changing it periodically.

DENIAL OF SERVICE ATTACKS

A **Denial of Service (DoS)** attack causes a service at a given host to fail or to become unavailable to legitimate users. Typically, DoS attacks focus on overloading a service. It is also possible for DoS attacks to exploit design failures or other vulnerabilities in application software. An example of a physical DoS attack would be cutting telephone lines or network cabling. DoS attacks may simply be motivated by the malicious desire to cause trouble. They may also be part of a wider attack, such as a precursor to a DNS spoofing attack.

DISTRIBUTED DoS (DDoS) ATTACKS/BOTNETS

Network-based DoS attacks are normally accomplished by flooding the server with bogus requests. They rely on the attacker having access to greater bandwidth than the target or on the target being required to devote more resources to each connection than the attacker. There are many different methods of achieving this, often exploiting weaknesses in protocols.

Most bandwidth-directed DoS attacks are **Distributed DoS (DDoS)**. This means that the attacks are launched from multiple compromised systems, referred to as a **botnet**. To establish a botnet, an attacker will first compromise one or two machines to use as "handlers" or "masters." The handlers are used to compromise multiple **zombie** devices with DoS tools (bots). In this way, the attacker can conceal his or her activities. This is also referred to as an asymmetric threat, because the attacker's resources can be far less than those of the victim.

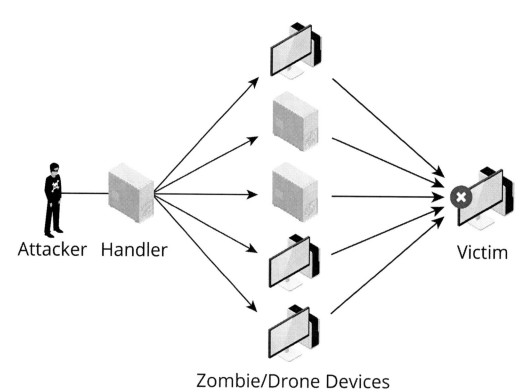

DDoS attacks using zombies/drones. (Image © 123RF.com.)

Large botnets are necessary to overcome the high bandwidth of targets. The increasing use of "always-on" broadband connections means that attackers can target a large base of naïve home users with the aim of compromising their PCs. Also, any Internet-connected device can potentially be infected and used as a bot. Devices such as webcams that can be configured over the Internet are often vulnerable.

Once the bot is installed, the attacker has a backdoor that gives them access to the device. They can then use the backdoor to install DDoS tools and trigger the zombies to launch the attack at the same time. As well as a single attacker using a botnet, DDoS attacks might be coordinated between groups of attackers. There is growing evidence that nation states are engaging in **cyber warfare** and terrorist groups have also been implicated in DDoS attacks on well-known companies and government institutions. There are also **hacker collectives** who might target an organization as part of a campaign.

VULNERABILITIES AND ZERO-DAY EXPLOITS

Software exploitation means an attack that targets a vulnerability in OS or application software or device firmware. A vulnerability is a design flaw that can cause the application security system to be circumvented or that will cause the application to crash. The most serious vulnerabilities allow the attacker to execute arbitrary code on the system, which could allow the installation of malware. Malicious code that can successfully use a vulnerability to compromise a host is called an "exploit."

 Note: This issue does not just affect PCs. Any type of network appliance or device can also be vulnerable to exploits. The risks to embedded systems have become more obvious and the risks posed by unpatched mobile devices and the "Internet of Things" is likely to grow.

Typically, vulnerabilities can only be exploited in quite specific circumstances, but because of the complexity of modern software and the speed with which new versions must be released to market, almost no software is free from vulnerabilities. Most vulnerabilities are discovered by software and security researchers, who notify the vendor to give them time to patch the vulnerability before releasing details to the wider public. A vulnerability that is exploited before the developer knows about it or can release a patch is called a **zero-day** exploit. It is called "zero-day" because the developer has had zero days to fix the flaw. These can be extremely destructive, as it can take the vendor a lot of time to develop a patch, leaving systems vulnerable for days, weeks, or even years.

While some zero-day attacks can be extremely destructive, they are relatively rare. A greater risk is the large number of unpatched or legacy systems in use. An unpatched or non-compliant system is one that its owner has not updated with OS and application patches or installed with A-V and firewall security software. A **legacy** system is one where the software vendor no longer provides support or fixes for problems.

 Note: *There is a class of network security software described as Network Access Control (NAC) that scans devices as they attempt to join and use the network and denies access if they are non-compliant with regard to a "system health" or Standard Operating Environment (SOE) policy.*

Topic C
Physical Security Measures

EXAM OBJECTIVES COVERED
1002-2.1 Summarize the importance of physical security measures.
1002-2.9 Given a scenario, implement appropriate data destruction and disposal methods.

Physical security refers to the implementation and practice of control methods that are intended to restrict physical access to facilities. One case where physical security is important is when there is a need to control access to physical documents, password records, and sensitive documents and equipment. One successful unauthorized access attempt can lead to financial losses, credibility issues, and legalities. In addition, physical security involves increasing or assuring the reliability of certain critical infrastructure elements such as switches, routers, and servers.

PHYSICAL SECURITY CONTROLS

Physical security measures means controlling who can access a building or a secure area of a building, such as a server room. One of the oldest types of security is a wall with a door in it (or a fence with a gate). In order to secure such a gateway, it must be fitted with a lock or door access system.

LOCK TYPES

Door locks can be categorized as follows:

- **Conventional**—a conventional lock prevents the door handle from being operated without the use of a key. More expensive types offer greater resistance against lock picking.
- **Deadbolt**—this is a bolt on the frame of the door, separate to the handle mechanism.
- **Electronic**—rather than a key, the lock is operated by entering a PIN on an electronic keypad. This type of lock is also referred to as cipher, combination, or keyless.
- **Token-based**—a smart lock may be opened using a magnetic swipe card or feature a proximity reader to detect the presence of a wireless key fob or one-time password generator (physical tokens) or smart card.
- **Biometric**—a lock may be integrated with a biometric scanner, so that the lock can be activated by biometric features, such as a fingerprint, voice print, or retina scan. Biometric locks make it more difficult for someone to counterfeit the key used to open the lock.
- **Multifactor**—a lock may combine different methods, such as smart card with PIN.

A secure gateway will normally be self-closing and self-locking, rather than depending on the user to close and lock it.

TURNSTILES AND MANTRAPS

Tailgating is a means of entering a secure area without authorization by following close behind the person who has been allowed to open the door or checkpoint. Training and a strict policy can mitigate the sort of instinctive politeness that causes employees to "co-operate" with this type of attack. Effective training should also ensure that employees keep doors locked to protect secure areas, such as server and equipment rooms. Gateways can also have improved physical security, such as CCTV monitoring or the presence of a security guard.

Another option is a turnstile or a mantrap. A **mantrap** is two sets of interlocking doors inside a small space, where the first set of doors must close before the second set opens. If the mantrap is manual, a guard locks and unlocks each door in sequence. In this case, an intercom or video camera is typically used to allow the guard to control the trap from a remote location. If the mantrap is automatic, identification or a key of some kind may be required for each door, and sometimes different measures may be required for each door. Metal detectors are often built in to prevent entrance of people carrying weapons. Such use is particularly frequent in banks and jewelry shops.

SECURITY GUARDS

Human security guards, armed or unarmed, can be placed in front of and around a location to protect it. They can monitor critical checkpoints and verify identification, allow or disallow access, and log physical entry occurrences. They also provide a visual deterrent and can apply their own knowledge and intuition to potential security breaches.

ID BADGES AND SMART CARDS

A photographic ID badge showing name and (perhaps) access details is one of the cornerstones of building security. Anyone moving through secure areas of a building should be wearing an ID badge; anyone without an ID badge should be challenged.

Radio Frequency ID (RFID) badges can be used with proximity badge readers to monitor the location of the subject. When the RFID badge passes a reader (with a range up to about 5 m), it registers a signal and transmits its ID to the management software.

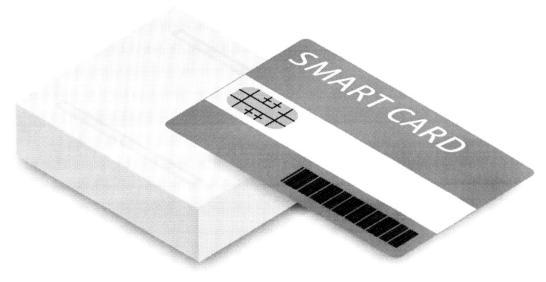

A contactless smart card reader. (Image © 123RF.com.)

As well as using RFID tracking, smart card badges and key fobs can be programmed with biometric authentication or with some sort of token-generating or certificate-based authentication. This type of badge could be used to open smart locks, as described earlier.

ENTRY CONTROL ROSTERS

An electronic lock may be able to log access attempts but if no technological solution is available, a security guard can manually log movement using a sign-in and sign-out sheet. An **entry control roster** requires all visitors to sign in and out when entering and leaving the building. Logging requirements will vary depending on the organization, but should include the following:

- Name and company being represented.
- Date, time of entry, and time of departure.
- Reason for visiting.
- Contact within the organization.

When possible, one single entry point should be used for all incoming visitors. This decreases the risk of unauthorized individuals gaining access to the building and tailgating.

PHYSICAL SECURITY CONTROLS FOR DEVICES

The most vulnerable point of the network infrastructure will be the communications room. This should be subject to the most stringent access and surveillance controls that can be afforded.

CABLE LOCKS AND LOCKING CABINETS

Another layer of security can be provided by installing equipment within lockable rack cabinets. These can be supplied with key-operated or electronic locks.

Rack cabinet with key-operated lock. (Image by Bunlue Nantaprom © 123RF.com.)

Server-class hardware often features physical chassis security (server locks). The chassis can be locked, preventing access to the power switch, removable drives, and USB ports. An attacker with access to these might be able to boot the machine with a different operating system to try to steal data or install malware. If there is no chassis protection and the computer cannot be located in a secure room, another tool is a USB lock. This device engages springs to make it difficult to remove from a USB port unless the key is used. Although they can deter and delay, they are unlikely to prevent a determined attacker.

If installing equipment within a cabinet is not an option, it is also possible to obtain cable hardware locks for use with portable devices such as laptops.

PRIVACY SCREENS

A **privacy screen** prevents anyone but the user from reading the screen. Modern TFTs are designed to be viewed from wide angles. This is fine for home entertainment use but raises the risk that someone would be able to observe confidential information shown on a user's monitor. A privacy filter restricts the viewing angle to only the person directly in front of the screen.

DATA DISPOSAL METHODS

As well as the security of premises, equipment rooms, and devices, physical security measures also need to account for the media on which data is stored. **Remnant removal** refers to decommissioning data storage media, including hard disks, flash drives, tape media, and CDs/DVDs. The problem has become particularly prominent as organizations recycle their old computers, either by donating them to charities or by sending them to a recycling company, who may recover and sell parts. There are at least three reasons that make remnant removal critical:

- An organization's own confidential data could be compromised.
- Third-party data that the organization processes could be compromised, leaving it liable under Data Protection legislation, in addition to any contracts or Service Level Agreements signed.
- Software licensing could be compromised.

The main issue is understanding the degree to which data on different media types may be recoverable. Data "deleted" from a magnetic-type disk such as a hard disk is not erased. Rather, the sectors are marked as available for writing and the data they contain will only be removed as new files are added. Similarly, using the standard Windows format tool will only remove references to files and mark all sectors as useable. In the right circumstances and with the proper tools, any deleted information from a drive could be recoverable.

There are several approaches to the problem of data remnants on magnetic disks.

PHYSICAL DESTRUCTION

A magnetic disk can be mechanically shredded, incinerated, or degaussed in specialist machinery:

- **Shredding**—the disk is ground into little pieces. A mechanical shredder works in much the same way as a paper shredder.
- **Incineration**—exposing the disk to high heat melts its components.
- **Degaussing**—exposing the disk to a powerful electromagnet disrupts the magnetic pattern that stores the data on the disk surface.

These types of machinery are costly and will render the disk unusable, so it cannot be recycled or repurposed.

 Note: There are many companies specializing in secure disposal. They should provide a certificate of destruction, showing the make, model, and serial number of each drive they have handled plus date of destruction and the means by which it was destroyed.

A less expensive method is to destroy the disk with a drill or hammer—do be sure to wear protective goggles. This method is not appropriate for the most highly confidential data as it will leave fragments that could be analyzed using specialist tools.

Optical media cannot be reformatted. Discs should be destroyed before discarding them. Shredders are available for destroying CD and DVD discs.

OVERWRITING/DISK WIPING

If a disk can be recycled or repurposed, destruction is obviously not an option. **Disk wiping** software ensures that old data is destroyed by writing to each location on the media, either using zeroes or in a random pattern. This leaves the disk in a "clean" state ready to be passed to the new owner. This overwriting method is suitable for all but the most confidential data, but is time consuming and requires special software.

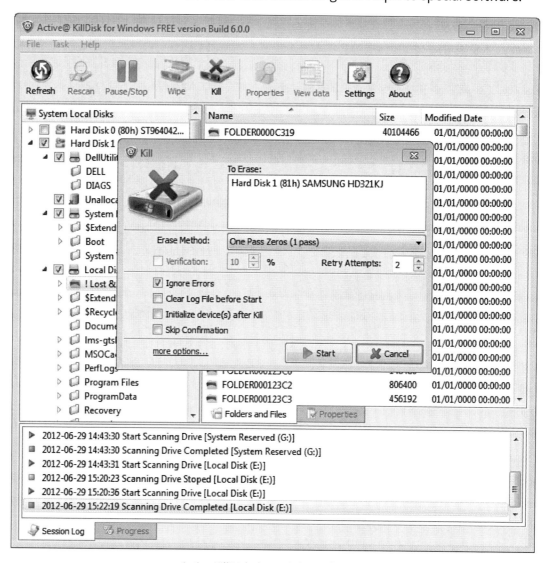

Active KillDisk data wiping software.

LOW LEVEL FORMAT

Most disk vendors supply tools to reset a disk to its factory condition. These are often described as **low level format** tools and will have the same sort of effect as disk wiping software. A "proper" low level format creates **cylinders** and **sectors** on the disk. This can generally only be done at the factory. The disk utilities just clean data from each sector; they don't re-create the sector layout.

 Note: *Check with the drive vendor for more information. For example, Seagate describe the tools available at knowledge.seagate.com/articles/en_US/FAQ/203931en.*

Activity 6-1
Security Concepts Review

SCENARIO
Answer the following review questions.

1. **What physical security controls have been employed at organizations where you have worked?**

2. **What steps has your organization taken to ensure the security of mobile devices? Have you planned ahead in case the devices are lost or stolen? If so, how?**

Summary

In this lesson, you explored general security concepts. Every organization will have different security requirements based on the type of business they conduct. It is your job to understand those requirements and know how security controls should be implemented to directly support those needs.

Lesson 7
Securing Workstations and Data

LESSON INTRODUCTION

Ensuring the security of information processing systems isn't an easy job. Sources of vulnerabilities and weaknesses can seem as limitless as the range of threats and attackers poised to try to take advantage of them. As a CompTIA® A+® PC technician, you need to make yourself aware of the latest developments and best practices to use to secure systems.

In thinking about securing those systems, you also need to be aware that your focus cannot just be on the devices or even the users. The data processed by those devices and users is typically the asset that an attacker will be after. Being able to classify and identify data types and know why certain types pose high risks is essential to implementing effective security measures.

LESSON OBJECTIVES

In this lesson, you will:

- Use security best practices to secure a workstation.
- Implement data protection policies.
- Describe data protection processes during incidents.

Topic A

Implement Security Best Practices

EXAM OBJECTIVES COVERED
1002-2.2 Explain logical security concepts.
1002-2.3 Compare and contrast wireless security protocols and authentication methods.
1002-2.7 Given a scenario, implement security best practices to secure a workstation.

You have seen how logical and physical security controls can be deployed together in an access control system. In this topic, we will focus on best practices regarding authentication and authorization. You need to make sure that the devices attached to your network are only being operated by authorized users. To ensure that, you have to use policies and technologies effectively to protect their account credentials.

AUTHENTICATION

Workstation security is ensured by following best practices. As you have seen, best practices can include things like using anti-virus software, configuring a firewall, configuring execution control, and using patch management procedures. These controls are very important but the cornerstone of effective security is an access control system. Accounts on the computer system are configured with permissions to access resources and (for privileged accounts) rights to change the system configuration. To access an account, the user must authenticate by supplying the correct credentials, proving that he or she is the valid account holder.

The validity of the whole access control system depends on the credentials for an account being known to the account holder only. The format of the credentials is called an **authentication factor**. There are many different authentication factors. They can be categorized as something you *know* (such as a password), something you *have* (such as a smart card), or something you *are* (such as a fingerprint). Each has advantages and drawbacks.

SOMETHING YOU KNOW: STRONG PASSWORDS

The typical "something you know" factor is the logon, which comprises a username and a password. The username is typically not a secret (though it's wise to share it as little as possible), but the password must be known only by a single user.

For a system to be secure against attack, strong passwords are required. Hackers often use dictionary files containing popular words and phrases, or they may investigate the background of their target to look for likely passwords. Once a hacker obtains a password, she or he can gain access to a system posing as that person.

The following rules make passwords difficult to guess:

- A longer password is more secure—between 8 and 14 characters is suitable for an ordinary user account. Administrative accounts should have longer passwords.
- No single words—better to use word and number/punctuation combinations.
- No obvious phrases in a simple form—birthday, username, job title, and so on.
- Mix upper and lowercase.
- Use an easily memorized phrase—underscored characters or hyphens can be used to represent spaces if the operating system does not support these in passwords.
- Do not write down a password or share it with other users.

• Change the password periodically.

The main problem with passwords is that they are prone to user error; selecting weak passwords, writing them down, and so on. Some types of behavior can be improved by system policies.

Another concern is password management. A typical user might be faced with having to remember dozens of logons for different services and resort to using the same password for each. This is unsecure, as your security becomes dependent on the security of these other (unknown) organizations. In a Windows domain, password management can be mitigated by applications that are compatible with the Kerberos authentication mechanism used by the domain. This is referred to as single sign on. Users must also be trained to practice good password management—at the least not to re-use work passwords on websites they access in a personal capacity.

Another instance of "something you know" authentication is a password reset mechanism, where to authorize the reset you have to answer with some personal information (childhood friend, city or town of birth, and so on).

BIOS/UEFI PASSWORDS

A system user password is one that is required before any operating system can boot. The system password can be configured by the BIOS or UEFI firmware setup program. A BIOS user password is shared by all users and consequently very rarely configured. It might be used to provide extra security on a standalone computer that does not often require user logon, such as a computer used to manage embedded systems. A PC with UEFI firmware may support pre-boot authentication. This means that the system loads an authentication application to contact an authentication server on the network and allow the user to submit the credentials for a particular user account.

 Note: *The system user password just allows the computer to proceed with the boot process. A system/supervisor password protects access to the firmware system setup program. Configuring a user password requires a supervisor password to be set, too.*

SOMETHING YOU HAVE: SMART CARDS AND TOKENS

There are various ways to authenticate a user based on something they *have* (a token). A smart card contains a chip that stores the user's account details in a digital certificate. The logon provider uses the certificate to decide if it should trust the card and ensure secure transmission of the credentials. The card must be presented to a card reader before the user can be authenticated. The user must typically also input a PIN or biometric scan. This prevents misuse of lost or stolen cards. It is also possible for the data to be read wirelessly (contactless cards), via **Radio Frequency Identification (RFID)**.

Another token-based technology is the SecurID token, from RSA. A **key fob** generates a random number code synchronized to a code on the server. The code changes every 60 seconds or so. This is an example of a one-time password.

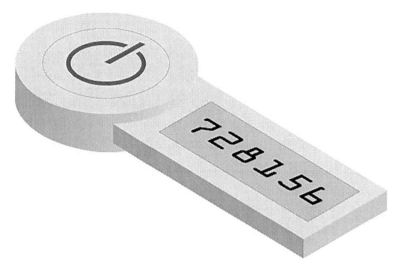

Key fob token generator. (Image © 123RF.com.)

The main concerns with token-based technologies are loss and theft and the chance that the device can be faked. There are also equipment and maintenance costs.

SOMETHING YOU ARE: BIOMETRICS

Something you *are* means employing some sort of biometric recognition system. Many types of biometric information can be recorded, including fingerprint patterns, signature recognition, iris or retina recognition, or facial recognition.

The chosen biometric information (the template) is scanned and recorded in a database. When the user wants to access a resource, he or she is re-scanned and the scan compared to the template. If they match, access is granted.

The main problems with biometric technology are that users find it intrusive and threatening to privacy, setup and maintenance costs, and the chance that the confirmation scan could be spoofed. For example, a facial recognition scan could be fooled by using a photo of the subject. Biometrics can also be prone to false negative and false positives. A **false negative** occurs when the system denies entry when it should allow it. A **false positive** occurs when the system grants entry when it should deny it.

MULTIFACTOR AUTHENTICATION

An authentication technology is considered "strong" if it combines the use of more than one type of factor (multifactor). Single factor authentication systems can quite easily be compromised: a password could be written down or shared, a smart card could be lost or stolen, and a biometric system could be subject to high error rates.

Two-factor authentication combines something like a smart card or biometric mechanism with "something you know," such as a password or PIN. **Three-factor authentication** combines all three technologies. An example of this would be a smart card with integrated thumb- or fingerprint reader. This means that to authenticate, the user must possess the card, the user's fingerprint must match the template stored on the card, and the user must input a PIN.

 Note: *Multifactor authentication requires a combination of different technologies. For example, requiring a PIN along with Date of Birth may be stronger than entering a PIN alone, but it is not multifactor.*

SOFTWARE TOKENS

Most networks and services require users to authenticate before providing access. The problem is that the user does not want to have to submit his or her credentials every time he or she performs an action. The user expects the system to remember that they have authenticated already. To accommodate this, the system grants a software token to the device or app that the user used to authenticate with. Whenever the user submits a request, the app submits the authorization token as proof that the user is authenticated.

If the token system is not designed securely, any third-party that is able to obtain the token from the user's device or capture it as it is transmitted over the network will be able to act as that user. This is called a **replay attack**.

Token-based authorization is used on Single Sign On (SSO) networks. One example is the Kerberos authentication and authorization system used for Windows domain logon. On the web, tokens can be implemented using cookies, but JavaScript Object Notation (JSON) Web Tokens (JWT) are now more popular. Software tokens can use digital signing to prove the identity of the issuing server. Tokens should also be designed with mechanisms to prevent replay. This could mean issuing them as "use once" or time-limiting them.

REMOTE AUTHENTICATION

Enterprise networks and ISPs potentially need to support hundreds or thousands of users and numerous different remote and wireless access technologies and devices. The problem arises that each access device needs to be configured with authentication information, and this information needs to be synchronized between them.

RADIUS

A scalable authentication architecture can be developed using RADIUS. **RADIUS** stands for Remote Authentication Dial-in User Service. Under this protocol, Authentication, Authorization, and Accounting are performed by a separate server (the AAA server). Network access devices, such as routers, switches, wireless access points, or VPN servers, function as client devices of the AAA server. Rather than storing and validating user credentials directly, they pass this data between the AAA server and the user.

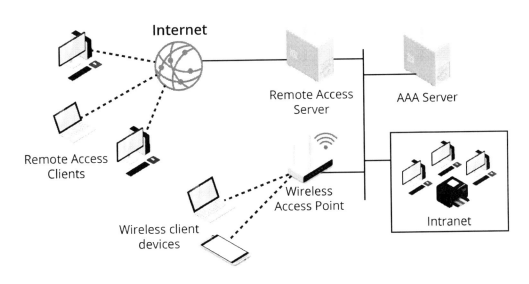

RADIUS. (Image © 123RF.com.)

TACACS+

Terminal Access Controller Access Control System Plus (TACACS+) is a similar protocol to RADIUS but designed to be more flexible and reliable. TACACS+ was developed by Cisco® but is also supported on many of the other third-party and open source RADIUS server implementations. Where RADIUS is often used to authenticate connections by wireless and VPN users, TACACS+ is often used in authenticating administrative access to routers and switches.

PASSWORD AND ACCOUNT POLICIES

Despite the availability of multifactor methods, many authentication systems are still based on passwords. This means that good password management is a critical element of network security. Users can be made to choose strong passwords by configuring account policies. There are also more general account policies that can be applied to improve security.

ACCESS CONTROL POLICIES

Most resources in a computer or network environment are protected from unauthorized use by an **Access Control List (ACL)**. An ACL is basically a list of subjects (users or computers) and the privileges they have on the object (or resource). ACLs can be defined for resources such as files and directories or for network connections (a firewall ACL).

The following policies enforce the use of ACLs and ensure that they are effective:

- Requiring passwords (mandatory logon)—when Windows is used for home computers, local user accounts are allowed to be configured without passwords. In a business environment, the security policy will default to requiring the user to sign in with a password.
- Change default admin user—rename default accounts so attackers cannot use known account names to access the system. It can make it harder to "hack" a computer if the identity of the default administrator or root account is concealed. In Windows, this account is disabled by default and replaced with a named account created during setup.
- Change default user passwords—as well as default usernames, appliances ship with a default password, such as "admin" or "password." To secure the device, you must change this when first setting it up.
- Disable guest account—the guest account allows limited access to Windows but is disabled by default. Keep it disabled to prevent unauthorized access to any shared files and folders on the device or system. File permissions can be allocated to the Everyone group account and the guest account is a member of Everyone. This might be overlooked when configuring permissions as the guest account is not typically enabled.
- Restricting user permissions (least privilege)—least privilege is a basic principle of security stating that someone (or something) should be allocated the minimum necessary rights, privileges, or information to perform their role. Users can be configured either as administrators or standard users. Additionally, User Account Control mitigates against exploitation of administrative privileges.

LOCAL SECURITY POLICY AND GROUP POLICY

On a standalone workstation, password and account policies can be configured via the Local Security Policy snap-in (`secpol.msc`) or the Group Policy snap-in (`gpedit.msc`).

 Note: These tools are not available on the Basic/Home/Core editions of Windows.

On a Windows domain network, Group Policy Objects (GPO) can be saved as collections of group policy settings.

PASSWORD PROTECTION POLICIES

System policies can help to enforce credential management principles by stipulating particular requirements for users. Password protection policies mitigate against the risk of attackers being able to compromise an account and use it to launch other attacks on the network.

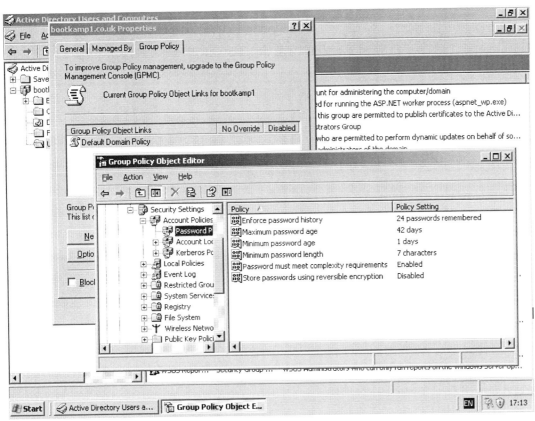

Configuring domain password policy using Group Policy. (Screenshot used with permission from Microsoft.)

The following table provides some examples used by Windows.

Policy	Description
Minimum password length	A minimum acceptable password length is specified.
Password must meet complexity requirements	Enforce password complexity rules—that is, no use of username within password and combination of at least six upper/lower case alpha-numeric and non-alpha-numeric characters. Note that this only applies when passwords are created or changed. Existing passwords are not tested against the policy.
Maximum password age	This configures a password expiration policy. When the time limit is reached, the user is forced to change the password.

Policy	Description
Enforce password history/ Minimum password age	This specifies that a unique password must be used when the user changes the password. The system remembers up to 24 previously used passwords so the minimum password age must be set to a value of 1 or greater to make the policy effective (otherwise users can quickly cycle through a number of passwords to get back to choosing an old favorite).
User cannot change password	This user account setting stops the user from changing his or her account password.
Password never expires	This user account setting can override a system policy set to force a regular password change.

 Note: *"Password reuse" can also mean using a work password elsewhere (on a website, for instance). Obviously, this sort of behavior can only be policed by "soft" policies.*

ACCOUNT RESTRICTIONS

To make the task of compromising the user security system harder, account restrictions can also be used. These may be specific to a particular user or applied globally.

Policy	Description
Logon Time Restrictions	For each account on the system, access to the server may be restricted to particular times. Periodically, the server checks whether the user has the right to continue using the network. If the user does not have the right, then an automatic logout procedure commences.
Station Restrictions	User access to the server can be restricted to a particular workstation or a group of workstations.
Concurrent Logons	By default, any user can log on to the domain from multiple workstations. If required, concurrent logons may be restricted to a specific number of connections.
Account Expiration Date	Setting an expiration date means that an account cannot be used beyond a certain date. This option is useful for accounts for temporary and contract staff.
Disable Account	Once an account is disabled, the user is denied access to the server until the network administrator re-enables the account.
Failed Attempts Lockout	The network administrator may specify a maximum number of incorrect logon attempts within a certain period. Once the maximum number of incorrect logons has been reached, the server disables the account. This prevents hackers from trying to gain system access using lists of possible passwords.

DESKTOP LOCK AND TIMEOUT

One problem with the logon system is that once logged on, the system trusts the workstation implicitly. If a user leaves the workstation unattended, someone else could perform actions as though they were that user (a so-called "lunchtime attack"). To prevent the possibility of this happening, users should be trained to lock the workstation whenever they leave it. The simple means of doing this is to press

Windows+L (every version of Windows puts the menu option for lock screen in a different place). Another way of locking the computer is to set a screensaver-required password. The screensaver can be set to timeout and lock the desktop after a set period of inactivity (no mouse or keyboard input). The user must then input their credentials to resume the session.

 Note: *On a domain, a GPO can be configured to enforce the use of password-protected screensavers.*

GUIDELINES FOR IMPLEMENTING SECURITY BEST PRACTICES

Here are some best practices to follow for implementing security on workstations and data.

IMPLEMENT SECURITY BEST PRACTICES

Follow these guidelines for implementing security best practices:

- Consider using multifactor authentication.
- Create secure passwords.
- Consider password protecting BIOS/UEFI.
- Take measures to prevent software tokens from being used in replay attacks.
- Consider using RADIUS in VPN implementations and TACACS+ for authenticating administrative access to routers and switches.
- Enforce use of ACLs through Local Security Policy or Group Policy Objects.
- Enforce the use of strong passwords through GPOs.
- Implement account restrictions to make compromising user security harder.
- Require users to lock unattended systems.
- Implement timeouts for unattended systems.

Topic B

Implement Data Protection Policies

EXAM OBJECTIVES COVERED
1002-1.6 Given a scenario, use Microsoft Windows Control Panel utilities.
1002-2.2 Explain logical security concepts.
1002-2.6 Compare and contrast the differences of basic Microsoft Windows OS security settings.
1002-2.7 Given a scenario, implement security best practices to secure a workstation.
1002-4.6 Explain the processes for addressing prohibited content/activity, and privacy, licensing, and policy concepts.

An access control system designates which accounts are authorized to view and modify which data files or records. In designing security, however, you always have to think about what might go wrong. What if an attacker can circumvent the access control system somehow? When data that should be kept private is breached, it is almost impossible to recover and re-secure. As a CompTIA A+ technician, it is imperative that you be able to recognize confidential and sensitive data types and understand the mechanisms that can be deployed to keep data secure.

DATA POLICIES

Most organizations process private, confidential, and secret information, recorded in different kinds of documents or data stores. Document management, or more generally **Information Content Management (ICM)**, is the process of managing information over its lifecycle, from creation to destruction. At each stage of the lifecycle, security considerations are vital. All employees must be trained to identify different types of confidential, private, and regulated data and follow all policies and security best practices when handling it.

Most documents go through one or more draft stages before they are published and subsequently may be revised and re-published. As a draft or revision, a document will be subject to a workflow, which describes how editorial changes are made and approved. The workflow will specify who are the authors, editors, and reviewers of the document.

As part of the creation process, the document must be classified depending on how sensitive it is. Classification restricts who may see the document contents. Classification is generally divided into several levels, following military usage:

- **Unclassified**—there are no restrictions on viewing the document.
- **Classified (internal use only/official use only)**—viewing is restricted to the owner organization or to third-parties under a Non-disclosure Agreement (NDA).
- **Confidential**—the information is highly sensitive, for viewing only by approved persons within the organization (and possibly by trusted third-parties under NDA).
- **Secret**—the information is too valuable to permit any risk of its capture. Viewing is severely restricted.
- **Top Secret**—this is the highest level of classification.

Confidential, secret, and top-secret information should be securely protected (encrypted) for storage and transmission.

Over its lifecycle, information may change in sensitivity, typically (but not always) becoming less sensitive over time. A document may be downgraded to a lower security level or eventually declassified. In this circumstance, there needs to be a clear process of authorization and notification so that confidentiality is not breached.

Corporate documents such as accounts information, product designs, and sales plans are relatively simple to identify and classify. Companies must also take regard of other types of sensitive information, such as Personally Identifiable Information (PII), software licenses, and Digital Rights Management (DRM) content.

 Note: *While we have discussed documents, the same principles hold for other types of information store, such as records in a database.*

PII

The rise in consciousness of identity theft as a serious crime and growing threat means that there is an increasing impetus on government, educational, and commercial organizations to take steps to obtain, store, and process **Personally Identifiable Information (PII)** more sensitively and securely.

PII is data that can be used to identify, contact, or locate an individual or, in the case of identity theft, to impersonate them. A social security number is a good example of PII. Others include names, date of birth, email address, telephone number, street address, biometric data, and so on.

Some types of information may be PII depending on the context. For example, when someone browses the web using a static IP address, the IP address is PII. An address that is dynamically assigned by the ISP may not be considered PII. These are the sort of complexities that must be considered when laws are introduced to control the collection and storage of personal data.

Employees should be trained to identify PII and to handle personal or sensitive data appropriately. This means not making unauthorized copies or allowing the data to be seen or captured by any unauthorized persons. Examples of treating sensitive data carelessly include leaving order forms with customers' credit card details on view on a desk, putting a credit card number in an unencrypted notes field in a customer database, or forwarding an email with personal details somewhere in the thread.

 Note: *In the European Union (EU), personal data is subject to Data Protection laws, recently updated by the General Data Protection Regulation (GDPR) framework, which make data handlers responsible for compliant collection and storage of personal information. The US does not have comparable legislation though it does operate a "Privacy Shield" scheme for US companies exchanging data with EU ones. While there is no single "data protection" law in the US, there are various Federal and state-level statutes that impact privacy and data collection/processing.*

PII may also be defined as responses to challenge questions, such as "What is your favorite color/pet/movie?" PII is often used for password reset mechanisms and to confirm identity over the telephone. Consequently, disclosing PII inadvertently can lead to identity theft.

PROTECTED HEALTH INFORMATION (PHI)

Protected Health Information (PHI) refers to medical and insurance records, plus associated hospital and laboratory test results. PHI may be associated with a specific person or used as an anonymized or de-identified data set for analysis and research. An anonymized data set is one where the identifying data is removed completely. A de-identified data set contains codes that allow the subject information to be reconstructed by the data provider. PHI trades at high values on the black market, making it an attractive target. Criminals would seek to exploit the data for insurance fraud or possibly to blackmail victims. PHI data is highly sensitive and unrecoverable. Unlike a credit card number or bank account number, it cannot be changed.

Consequently, the reputational damage that would be caused by a PHI data breach is huge.

PAYMENT CARD INDUSTRY DATA SECURITY STANDARD (PCI DSS)

There are also industry-enforced regulations mandating data security. A good example is the **Payment Card Industry Data Security Standard (PCI DSS)** governing processing of credit card and other bank card payments. It sets out protections that must be provided if cardholder data—names, addresses, account numbers, and card numbers and expiry dates—is stored. It also sets out sensitive authentication data, such as the CV2 confirmation number or the PIN used for the card (not that the cardholder should ever divulge that to a third party).

Regulations such as PCI DSS have specific cybersecurity control requirements; others simply mandate "best practice," as represented by a particular industry or international framework. Frameworks for security controls are established by organizations such as the National Institute of Standards and Technology (NIST).

ACLs AND DIRECTORY PERMISSIONS

It's easy to overlook the fact that the most important part of a computer system is the data stored on it. A computer is just a tool and is relatively easy to replace. Data could represent days, months, or years of work. Data can be protected against unauthorized access, modification, or deletion by several mechanisms.

A **permission** is a security setting that determines the level of access a user or group account has to a particular resource. Permissions can be associated with a variety of resources, such as files, printers, shared folders, and network directory databases. Permissions can typically be configured to allow different levels of privileges, or to deny privileges to users who should not access a resource.

A permission is usually implemented as an **Access Control List (ACL)** attached to each resource. The ACL contains a number of **Access Control Entries (ACE)**, which are records of subjects and the permissions they hold on the resource. A subject could be identified in a number of ways. On a network firewall, subjects might be identified by MAC address, IP address, and/or port number. In the case of directory permissions in Windows, each user and security group account has a unique Security ID (SID).

Recall that in Windows, there are two systems of permissions:

- File-system permissions enforced by NTFS allow the object owner to set access control to individual files and folders. File-level permissions will prevent any unauthorized access to a file or folder both across the network and locally by prompting all users, including the user who created the file, to enter the correct user name and password for access.
- Share-level permissions only apply when a folder is accessed over a network connection. They offer no protection against a user who's logged on locally to the computer or server containing the shared resource.

Separate permissions at the share level and file level is unique to Windows environments. In Linux, the same set of read, write, and delete permissions are valid at both the local level and across the network.

DATA ENCRYPTION

When data is hosted on a file system, it can be protected by the operating system's security model. Each file or folder can be configured with an Access Control List (ACL), describing the permissions that different users (or user groups) have on the file. These permissions are enforced only when the OS mediates access to the device. If the disk is exposed to a different OS, the permissions could be overridden. To protect data at-rest against these risks, the information stored on a disk can be encrypted.

FILE/FOLDER ENCRYPTION (EFS)

One approach to encrypting file system data is to apply encryption to individual files or folders. The **Encrypting File System (EFS)** feature of NTFS supports file and folder encryption. EFS is only available to use with professional/enterprise editions of Windows.

Without strong authentication, encrypted data is only as secure as the user account. If the password can be compromised, then so can the data. The user's password grants access to the key that performs the file encryption and decryption.

There is also the chance of data loss if the key is lost or damaged. This can happen if the user's profile is damaged, if the user's password is reset by an administrator, or if Windows is reinstalled. It is possible to back up the key or (on a Windows domain) to set up recovery agents with the ability to decrypt data.

To apply encryption, open the file's or folder's property sheet and select the **Advanced** button. Check the **Encrypt contents** box, then confirm the dialog boxes.

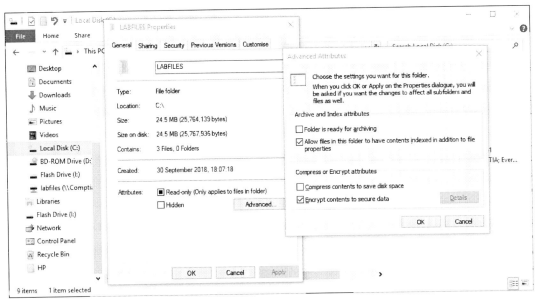

Applying encryption to a folder using EFS. (Screenshot used with permission from Microsoft.)

Folders and files that have been encrypted can be shown with green color coding in Explorer. Any user other than the one that encrypted the file will receive an "Access Denied" error when trying to browse, copy, or print the file.

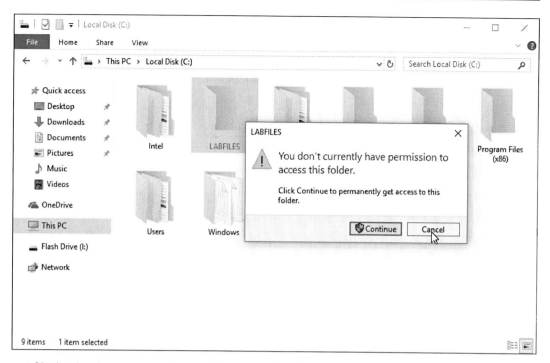

A file that has been encrypted cannot be opened by other users—even administrators. (Screenshot used with permission from Microsoft.)

FULL DISK ENCRYPTION

An alternative to file encryption is to use a **Full Disk Encryption (FDE)** product. The **BitLocker** disk encryption product is built into Windows Enterprise editions and is available with Windows 7 Ultimate, Windows 8 Pro, and Windows 10 Professional.

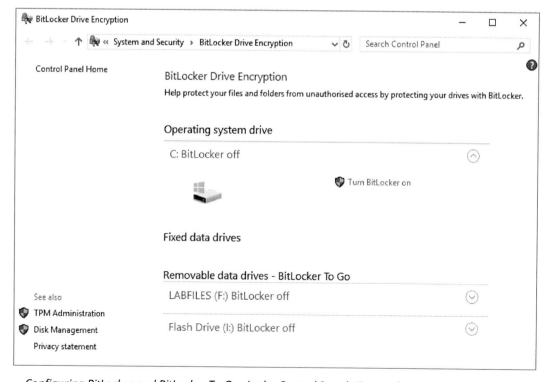

Configuring BitLocker and BitLocker To Go via the Control Panel. (Screenshot used with permission from Microsoft.)

Disk encryption carries a processing overhead but modern computers usually have processing capacity to spare. It is particularly useful for mobile devices, such as laptops, and removable drives. The main advantage is that it does not depend on the user to remember to encrypt data so mitigates the risk of data loss in the case of the theft or loss of the device. Disk encryption also encrypts the swap file, print queues, temporary files, and so on.

BitLocker® can be used with any volumes on fixed (internal) drives. It can also be used with removable drives in its **BitLocker To Go** form.

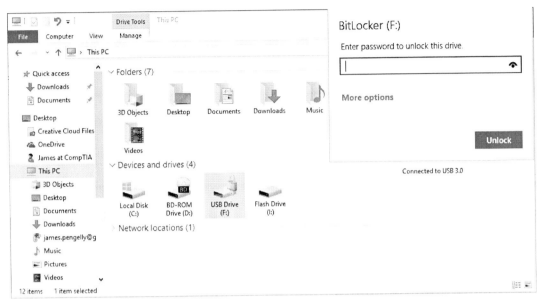

Removable drive protected with BitLocker To Go. (Screenshot used with permission from Microsoft.)

Note: *In older Windows versions (Vista and XP), there was no support for encrypting removable drives. BitLocker To Go Reader is a standalone application that allows USB drives encrypted in Windows 7 or later to be read in Windows XP or Windows Vista. This gives the user read-only access to the files on the drive. They can be copied but this removes the encryption from the copies.*

When the data is encrypted, the user must have access to the encryption key to access it. Some disk encryption products, including BitLocker, can make use of a **Trusted Platform Module (TPM)** chip in the computer to tie use of a hard disk to a particular motherboard. The TPM is used as a secure means of storing the encryption key and to ensure the integrity of the OS used to boot the machine. Alternatively, the key could be stored on a removable smart card or on a USB stick. The computer's firmware must support booting from USB for the last option to work.

Note: *The TPM must be configured with an owner password (often the system password set in firmware). You can manage TPM settings from Windows using the TPM Management snap-in (select **TPM Administration** from the BitLocker applet).*

During BitLocker setup, a recovery key is also generated. This should be stored on removable media (or written down) and stored securely (and separately from the computer). This key can be used to recover the encrypted drive if the startup key is lost.

DATA LOSS PREVENTION (DLP)

In a workplace where mobile devices with huge storage capacity proliferate and high bandwidth network links are readily available, attempting to prevent the loss of data by controlling the types of storage device allowed to connect to PCs and networks can be impractical. Another option is to use policies or software to prevent data "leakage" or loss by focusing on the data files.

Users must of course be trained about document confidentiality and make sure that they are aware of the insecurity of unencrypted communications. This should also be backed up by Human Resources (HR) and auditing policies that ensure staff are trustworthy. "Soft" measures such as these do not protect against user error or insider threats, however.

Data Loss Prevention (DLP) products scan content in structured formats, such as a database with a formal access control model, or unstructured formats, such as email or word processing documents. DLP software uses some sort of dictionary database or algorithm (regular expression matching) to identify confidential data. The transfer of content to removable media, such as USB devices, or by email, IM, or even social media, can then be blocked if it does not conform to a predefined policy.

Such solutions will usually consist of the following components:

- Policy server—to configure confidentiality rules and policies, log incidents, and compile reports.
- Endpoint agents—to enforce policy on client computers, even when they are not connected to the network.
- Network agents—to scan communications at network borders and interface with web and messaging servers to enforce policy.

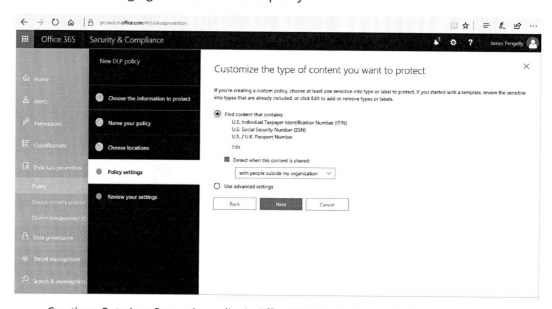

Creating a Data Loss Prevention policy in Office 365. Used with permission from Microsoft.

SOFTWARE LICENSING AND DRM

As well as managing use of confidential and sensitive data, you need to consider methods for identifying and removing prohibited content. The acceptable use policies built into most employee contracts will prohibit the abuse of Internet services to download games or obscene content. Employees should also avoid using work accounts for personal communications.

Prohibited content also extends to the installation and use of software. When you buy software, you must accept the license governing its use, often called the **End User License Agreement (EULA)**. The terms of the license will vary according to the type of software, but the basic restriction is usually that the software may only be installed on one computer.

The software is often activated using a product key, which will be a long string of characters and numbers printed on the box or disk case. The product key will generate a different product ID, which is often used to obtain technical support. The product ID is displayed when the application starts and can be accessed using the About option on the Help menu.

A company may have hundreds of employees who need the same software on their computers. Software manufacturers do not expect such companies to buy individual copies of the software for each employee. Instead, they will issue a license for multiple users, which means that the company can install the software on an agreed number of computers for their employees to use.

If a site has a large number of computers, these computers are often networked. This means that software bought under license can be installed onto a network server so that all authorized users can access it without it being installed on each individual computer.

Consider the example of Microsoft Windows. Windows is commercial software, meaning it must be paid for. A condition of installing Windows is accepting the EULA. Microsoft requires you to activate Windows when you install it, which helps them to verify that you are not breaking the terms of the license. There are several different types of license, summarized here:

- **Original Equipment Manufacturer (OEM)**—this is for pre-installed versions of Windows sold with new PCs. The license is not transferable and the software may not be installed on a different PC.
- **Retail**—these personal licenses are subdivided into Full and Upgrade versions of software. The software may be transferred between computers but may only be installed on one computer at any one time. Upgrade versions require a valid license and setup media for a qualifying upgrade product.
- **Volume**—these enterprise licenses are schemes to simplify license administration in larger organizations and businesses.
- **Server**—licensing for servers is different from licensing desktop software. As well as a license for the software installed on the server, **Client Access Licenses (CAL)** are required, based on the number of clients accessing the software services. CALs can be sold per server (limiting the number of simultaneous accesses) or per seat (specifying each unique device or user).

It is illegal to use or distribute unauthorized copies of software (pirate copies). Pirated software often contains errors and viruses as well. Enterprises need monitoring systems to ensure that their computers are not hosting unlicensed or pirated software.

SHAREWARE, FREEWARE, AND OPEN SOURCE APPLICATIONS

Shareware, freeware, and open source licenses are different ways of distributing applications to commercial software:

- **Shareware** is software that you can install free of charge so that you can evaluate it for a limited period. If you decide to continue using the software after this period, you must register it, usually for a fee. When you register the software you often become entitled to extra features and support.
- **Freeware** is software that is available free of charge.

 Note: Even if software is distributed as shareware or freeware, the copyright is still held by the publisher or designer. Both shareware and freeware may still be governed by a license, which may restrict its use (for example, to prevent commercial use of the product or to redistribute or resell it).

- **Open source** is software that also makes the program code used to design it available. The idea is that other programmers can investigate the program and make it more stable and useful. An open source license does not forbid commercial use of applications derived from the original, but it is likely to impose the same conditions on further redistributions.

DIGITAL RIGHTS MANAGEMENT (DRM)

Digital music and video is often subject to copy protection and **Digital Rights Management (DRM)**. When you purchase music or video online, the vendor may license the file for use on a restricted number of devices. You generally need to use your account with the vendor to authorize and deauthorize devices when they change. Most DRM systems have been defeated by determined attackers and consequently there is plenty of content with DRM security removed circulating. From an enterprise's point-of-view, this is prohibited content and they need monitoring systems to ensure that their computers are not hosting pirated content files.

GUIDELINES FOR IMPLEMENTING DATA PROTECTION POLICIES

Here are some guidelines to follow regarding data protection policies.

IMPLEMENT DATA PROTECTION POLICIES

Follow these guidelines for implementing data protection policies:

- Classify documents based on how sensitive it is.
- Protect PII, PHI, and PCI data.
- Implement permissions as ACLs attached to resources.
- Use full disk, folder, and file encryption.
- Implement a data loss prevention policy.
- Follow all software licensing agreements and DRM.

Topic C
Protect Data During Incident Response

EXAM OBJECTIVES COVERED
1002-4.6 Explain the processes for addressing prohibited content/activity, and privacy, licensing, and policy concepts.

While you hope that security and data handling policies will be sufficient to protect your computer systems and networks, you also need to consider the situations where those protections fail. To cope with failures of security policy, or attempted breaches of policy, organizations need well-rehearsed incident response procedures to investigate and remediate the breach.

As an IT technician, you will often be involved in identifying and reporting security incidents and potentially in assisting with investigations and evidence gathering. It is important that you understand some of the general principles of effective incident response and forensic investigation procedures.

INCIDENT RESPONSE POLICIES

In the course of performing technical support, you may have to report or respond to security incidents. A **security incident** could be one of a wide range of different scenarios, such as:

- A computer or network infected with viruses, worms, or Trojans.
- An attempt to break into a computer system or network through phishing or an "evil twin" Wi-Fi access point.
- An attempt to damage a network through a Denial of Service (DoS) attack.
- Users with unlicensed software.
- Finding prohibited material on a PC—illegal copies of copyrighted material, obscene content, or confidential documents that the user should not have access to.

An **incident response policy** sets out procedures and guidelines for dealing with security incidents. The actions of staff immediately following detection of an incident can have a critical impact on these aims, so an effective policy and well-trained employees are crucial. Incident response is also likely to require coordinated action and authorization from several different departments or managers, which adds a further level of complexity.

SECURITY INCIDENT HANDLING LIFECYCLE

The NIST Computer Security Incident Handling Guide special publication SP800-61 identifies the following stages in an incident response lifecycle:

- **Preparation**—making the system resilient to attack in the first place. This includes hardening systems, writing procedures, and establishing confidential lines of communication. It also implies creating incident response resources and procedures.
- **Detection and Analysis**—determining whether an incident has taken place and assessing how severe it might be, followed by notification of the incident to stakeholders.
- **Containment, Eradication, and Recovery**—limiting the scope and magnitude of the incident. The typical response is to "pull the plug" on the affected system, but

this is not always appropriate. Once the incident is contained, the cause can then be removed and the system brought back to a secure state.

- **Post-incident Activity**—analyzing the incident and responses to identify whether procedures or systems could be improved. It is also imperative to document the incident.

INCIDENT RESPONSE DOCUMENTATION

A serious incident will be a highly pressured scenario. Without adequate preparation, staff will not be able to respond effectively. Without clear policies and guidelines, staff discovering and investigating the incident are more likely to make bad decisions. Without an incident log, different employees will find it harder to coordinate their efforts. If there are no contact lists and lines of communication, information about the incident might be disclosed inappropriately, whether that means senior personnel not being informed or knowledge of the incident becoming public too early.

Preparing for incident response means establishing documented policies and procedures for dealing with security breaches and the personnel and resources to implement those policies. Incident response documentation should also establish clear lines of communication, both for reporting incidents and for notifying affected parties as the management of an incident progresses. It is vital to have essential contact information readily available. Also consider that the incident response personnel might require secure, out-of-band communication methods, in case standard network communication channels have been compromised.

As with any type of procedural documentation, this must also be kept up to date with changes. The procedures should be reviewed periodically (every few months) but events such as staff changes, the deployment of new network or security systems, or changes in the legal/regulatory environment should trigger an immediate review of incident response documents.

FIRST RESPONDERS

An **incident** is any event that breaches security policy. Of course, this covers a huge number and variety of different scenarios. In order to prioritize and manage incidents, an organization should develop some method of categorizing and prioritizing them (triage), in the same way that troubleshooting support incidents can be logged and managed.

Larger organizations will provide a dedicated **Computer Security Incident Response Team (CSIRT)** as a single point-of-contact for security incidents so that they can be reported through the proper channels.

The members of this team should be able to provide the range of decision making and technical skills required to deal with different types of incidents. The team needs a mixture of senior decision makers (up to director level) who can authorize actions following the most serious incidents, managers, and technicians (who can deal with minor incidents on their own initiative).

When an incident is detected, it is critical that the appropriate person on the CSIRT be notified so that they can take charge of the situation and formulate the appropriate response (first responder). This means that employees at all levels of the organization must be trained to recognize and respond appropriately to actual or suspected security incidents.

It is also wise to provide for confidential reporting so that employees are not afraid to report insider threats, such as fraud or misconduct. It may also be necessary to use an "out-of-band" method of communication so as not to alert the intruder that his or her attack has been detected.

Note: *An employee (or ex-employee) who reports misconduct is referred to as a whistleblower.*

When notification has taken place, the CSIRT or other responsible person(s) can formulate the response.

DATA AND DEVICE PRESERVATION

Computer **forensics** is the science of collecting evidence from computer systems to a standard that will be accepted in a court of law. It is highly unlikely that a computer forensic professional will be retained by an organization, so such investigations are normally handled by law enforcement agencies. Like DNA or fingerprints, digital evidence is mostly **latent**. Latent means that the evidence cannot be seen with the naked eye; rather, it must be interpreted using a machine or process.

If a forensic investigation is launched (or if one is a possibility), it is important that technicians and managers are aware of the processes that the investigation will use. It is vital that they are able to assist the investigator and that they not do anything to compromise the investigation. In a trial, the defense will try to exploit any uncertainty or mistake regarding the integrity of evidence or the process of collecting it.

COLLECTION OF EVIDENCE

The first phase of a forensic investigation is collection of evidence. The two principal questions here are:

- What evidence must be collected?
- How should the evidence be collected?

Neither question is trivial. A computer system may contain multiple gigabytes (or even terabytes) of data, most of which will not be relevant to the incident. Evidence may only exist in volatile storage (system or cache RAM). If the computer system is not owned by the organization, there is the question of whether search or seizure is legally valid. This may also make it difficult for law enforcement agents to begin an investigation. For example, if an employee is accused of fraud, you must verify that the employee's equipment and data can be legally seized and searched. Any mistake may make evidence gained from the search inadmissible.

The question of "how" is complicated because it is much more difficult to capture evidence from a digital "crime scene" than it is from a physical one. As mentioned, some evidence will be lost if the computer system is powered off; on the other hand, some evidence may be unobtainable until the system *is* powered off. Additionally, evidence may be lost depending on whether the system is shut down or "frozen" by suddenly disconnecting the power.

The general procedure will be as follows:

1. The crime scene must be thoroughly documented using photographs and ideally video and audio. Investigators must record every action they take in identifying, collecting, and handling evidence.

   Note: *Remember that if the matter comes to trial, the trial could take place months or years after the event. It is vital to record impressions and actions in notes.*

2. The investigator should then interview witnesses to establish what they were doing at the scene and also to gather information about the computer system.
3. If possible, evidence is gathered from the live system, including screenshots of display screens and the contents of cache and system memory, using forensic software tools. It is vital that these tools do nothing to modify the digital data that they capture.

4. Forensic tools are used to make a copy of data on the hard drive(s). This is performed using drive imaging rather than file copy methods, so that the copy is made at sector level.

5. A cryptographic hash is made of the collected data. This can be used to prove that the digital evidence collected has not been modified subsequently to its collection.

6. The system is either shut down or powered off.

7. Depending on the strength of evidence required, the physical drives are then identified, bagged, sealed, and labeled using tamper-proof bags. It is also appropriate to ensure that the bags have anti-static shielding to reduce the possibility that data will be damaged or corrupted on the electronic media by Electrostatic Discharge (ESD). Any other physical evidence deemed necessary is also "Bagged and Tagged."

CHAIN OF CUSTODY

It is vital that the evidence collected at the crime scene conform to a valid timeline. Digital information is susceptible to tampering, so access to the evidence must be tightly controlled.

A crucial element of the investigation is that each step is documented and (ideally) recorded. This proves that the evidence has been handled correctly and has not been tampered with. Once evidence has been bagged, it must not subsequently be handled or inspected, except in controlled circumstances.

A **Chain of Custody** form records where, when, and who collected the evidence, who has handled it subsequently, and where it was stored. The chain of custody must show access to, plus storage and transportation of, the evidence at every point from the crime scene to the court room. Anyone handling the evidence must sign the chain of custody and indicate what they were doing with it.

Activity 7-1

Securing Workstations and Data Review

SCENARIO

Answer the following review questions.

1. **Which security best practices do you feel are the most important? Which are the minimum measures that should be taken? Does your organization implement good security practices?**

2. **Have you had experience with security incidents such as data breaches? What might have been done differently to further protect the data that was put at risk?**

Summary

In this lesson, you implemented and described many concepts and techniques that can be used to establish the desired level of security for data and workstations within an organization. Every organization will have different security requirements based on the type of business they conduct. It is your job to understand those requirements and know how security controls should be implemented to directly support those needs.

Lesson 8
Troubleshooting Workstation Security Issues

LESSON INTRODUCTION

For all that you try to configure workstation security according to best practices—securing user accounts, installing antivirus software, updating with patches, and encrypting data—there will be times when those procedures fail to work properly and you have to deal with malware infection. As a CompTIA® A+® PC technician, it is essential that you be able to identify types of malware, the symptoms of malware infections, and the steps to take to remove malicious code and prevent it from re-infecting computers and networks.

LESSON OBJECTIVES

In this lesson, you will:

- Detect, remove, and prevent malware infections.

- Troubleshoot common workstation security issues.

Topic A

Detect, Remove, and Prevent Malware

 EXAM OBJECTIVES COVERED
1002-2.4 Given a scenario, detect, remove, and prevent malware using appropriate tools and methods.
1002-3.3 Given a scenario, use best practice procedures for malware removal.

Malware is a catch-all term to describe malicious software threats and social engineering tools designed to vandalize or compromise computer systems. In this topic, you will learn to describe different malware threats and operate antivirus software to protect the computer against infection and remediate infections.

COMPUTER VIRUSES AND WORMS

Computer **viruses** are programs designed to replicate and spread amongst computers. They produce a wide variety of symptoms on a PC and, in extreme cases, can cause permanent damage or loss of files. There are several different types of viruses, and they are generally classified by the different ways they can infect the computer (the vector). For example:

- **Boot sector viruses**—these attack the boot sector information, the partition table, and sometimes the file system.
- **Firmware viruses**—these are targeted against the firmware of a specific component, such as the drive controller. Such viruses are often only used in highly directed attacks, as the firmware is specific to particular models of drive, the firmware code is difficult to obtain and compromise, and executing the firmware update without the user realizing it is tricky.
- **Program viruses**—these are sequences of code that insert themselves into another executable program. When the application is executed, the virus code becomes active.
- **Script viruses**—scripts are powerful languages used to automate OS functions and add interactivity to web pages. Scripts are executed by an interpreter rather than self-executing. Most script viruses target vulnerabilities in the interpreter.
- **Macro viruses**—these viruses affect Office documents by using the programming code that underpins macro functionality maliciously.

What these types of viruses have in common is that they must infect a host file. That file can be distributed through any normal means—on a disk, on a network, or as an attachment through an email or instant messaging system.

Email attachment viruses—usually program or macro viruses in an attached file—often use the infected host's electronic address book to spoof the sender's address when replicating. For example, Alice's computer is infected with a virus and has Bob's email address in her address book. When Carlos gets an infected email apparently sent by Bob, it is the virus on Alice's computer that has sent the message.

Viruses are also categorized by their virulence. Some viruses are virulent because they exploit a previously unknown system vulnerability—a "zero-day" exploit. Others employ particularly effective social engineering techniques to persuade users to open the infected file. An infected email attachment with the subject "I Love You" is one of the best examples of the breed.

While the distinguishing feature of a virus is its ability to replicate by infecting other computer files, a virus can also be configured with a payload that executes when the virus is activated. The payload can perform any action available to the host process. For example, a boot sector virus might be able to overwrite the existing boot sector, an application might be able to delete, corrupt, or install files, and a script might be able to change system settings or delete or install files.

WORMS

Worms are memory-resident malware that replicate over network resources. Unlike a virus, a worm is self-contained; that is, it does not need to attach itself to another executable file. They typically target some sort of vulnerability in a network application, such as a database server. The primary effect of a worm infestation is to rapidly consume network bandwidth as the worm replicates. A worm may also be able to crash an operating system or server application (performing a Denial of Service attack). Also, like viruses, worms can carry a payload that may perform some other malicious action (such as installing a backdoor).

TROJAN HORSES AND SPYWARE

Other types of malware are not classed as viruses as they do not necessarily try to make copies of themselves within another "host" process. They can be just as much of a security threat as viruses, however. A **Trojan Horse**—or, more simply, just "Trojan"—is a program (usually harmful) that is packaged as something else. For example, you might download what you think is a new game, but when you run it, it also installs a keylogger and starts sending a transcript of whatever you type to a host on the Internet. There is also the case of rogueware or scareware fake anti-virus, where a web pop-up displays a security alert and claims to have detected viruses on the computer and prompts the user to initiate a full scan, which installs the attacker's Trojan.

Many Trojans function as **backdoor** applications. Once the Trojan backdoor is installed, it allows the attacker to access the PC, upload files, and install software on it. This could allow the attacker to use the computer in a botnet, to launch Denial of Service (DoS) attacks or mass-mail spam. Trojans are also used by attackers to conceal their actions. Attacks or spam appear to come from the corrupted computer system.

SPYWARE AND KEYLOGGERS

Spyware is a program that monitors user activity and sends the information to someone else. It may be installed with or without the user's knowledge. Aggressive spyware or Trojans known as "keyloggers" actively attempt to steal confidential information by capturing a credit card number by recording key strokes entered into a web form, for example. Another spyware technique is to spawn browser pop-up windows to try to direct the user to other websites, often of dubious origin.

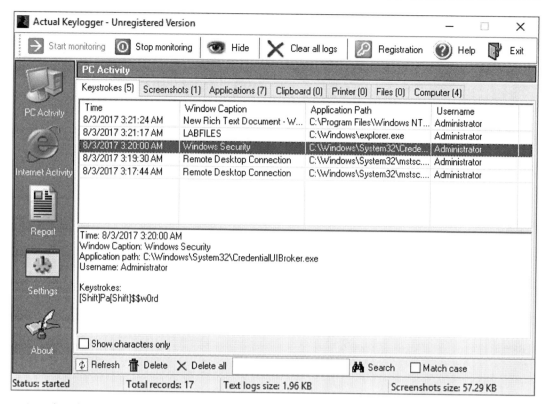

Actual Keylogger—Windows software that can run in the background to monitor different kinds of computer activity (opening and closing programs, browsing websites, recording keystrokes, and capturing screenshots). (actualkeylogger.com)

Note: *Spyware doesn't have to depend on executable programs installed locally. Script and server-side programs on websites can be used to track a user's Internet history through use of cookies and information reported to the site by the browser.*

ROOTKITS

Many Trojans cannot conceal their presence entirely and will show up as a running service. Often the service name is configured to be similar to a genuine process to avoid detection. For example, a Trojan may use the filename `run32dll` to masquerade as `run32dll`. One class of backdoor that is harder to detect is the **rootkit**. A rootkit is a set of tools designed to gain control of a computer without revealing its presence. They are so-called because they execute with root or system-level privileges. The general functions of a rootkit will be as follows:

- Replace key system files and utilities to prevent detection and eradication of the rootkit itself.
- Provide a backdoor channel for the rootkit handler to reconfigure the PC, steal information, or install additional spyware or other malware remotely.
- Evade anti-virus software by infecting firmware code.

Rootkits may also be deployed as part of Digital Rights Management (DRM) and copy protection mechanisms. Infamously, Sony released a music player for its Extended Copy Protection CDs that also installed a rootkit.

RANSOMWARE

Ransomware is a type of malware that tries to extort money from the victim. One class of ransomware will display threatening messages, such as requiring Windows® to be reactivated or suggesting that the computer has been locked by the police because it was used to view child pornography or for terrorism. This may block access to the computer by installing a different shell program but this sort of attack is usually relatively trivial to fix. Another class of ransomware attempts to encrypt data files on any fixed, removable, and network drives. If the attack is successful, the user will be unable to access the files without obtaining the private encryption key, which is held by the attacker. If successful, this sort of attack is extremely difficult to mitigate, unless the user has up-to-date backups of the encrypted files.

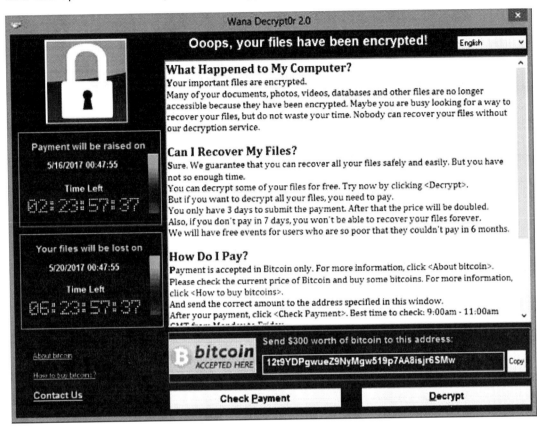

WannaCry ransomware. Wikimedia Public Domain image.

Note: *Most ransomware will be capable of encrypting removable drives too so backup devices should not be left attached routinely. A cloud-based backup might offer a better alternative, but if the credentials for the cloud file server are cached, the ransomware is likely to be able to encrypt those, too.*

Ransomware uses payment methods such as wire transfer, Bitcoin, or premium rate phone lines to allow the attacker to extort money without revealing his or her identity or being traced by local law enforcement.

SOURCES OF MALWARE INFECTION

There are numerous sources of malware infection, but the main ones are:

- Visiting "unsavory" websites with an unpatched browser, low security settings, and no anti-virus software.
- Opening links in unsolicited email.
- Infection from another compromised machine on the same network.
- Executing a file of unknown origin—email attachments are still the most popular vector, but others include file sharing sites, websites generally, attachments sent via chat/Instant Messaging, AutoRun USB sticks and CDs, and so on.
- Becoming victim to a "zero-day" exploit (that is, some infection mechanism that is unknown to software and anti-virus vendors).

ANTIVIRUS SOFTWARE

Antivirus software (A-V) uses a database of known virus patterns (definitions) plus **heuristic** malware identification techniques to try to identify infected files and prevent viruses from spreading. "Heuristic" means that the software uses knowledge of the sort of things that viruses do to try to spot (and block) virus-like behavior.

Typically, the software is configured to run automatically when a user or system process accesses a file. The antivirus software scans the file first and blocks access if it detects anything suspicious.

The user can then decide either to try to disinfect the file, quarantine it (block further access), or delete it. Another option might be for the user to ignore the alert (if it is deemed a false positive, for instance) and exclude the file from future scans.

The A-V scanner also runs at boot-time to prevent boot sector viruses from infecting the computer. Most types of software can also scan system memory (to detect worms), email file attachments, removable drives, and network drives.

The latest "antivirus" software is usually "anti-malware" software, and includes routines and signatures to detect and block Trojans, rootkits, ransomware, and spyware.

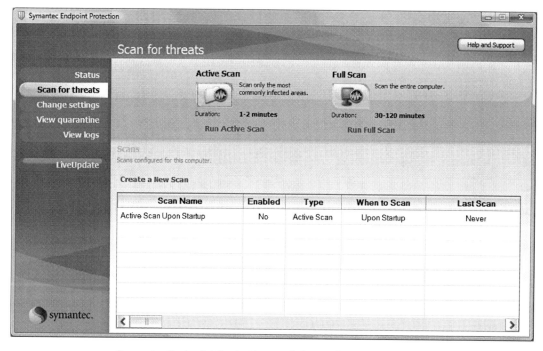

Symantec Endpoint Protection malicious software protection.

Antivirus software can be purchased either as personal security suites, designed to protect a single host, or network security suites, designed to be centrally managed from a server console. Most antivirus software is designed for Windows PCs and networks, as these are the systems targeted by most virus writers, but software is available for Linux® and macOS® as well.

Some of the major vendors are Symantec™ (including the Norton™ brand), McAfee®, Trend Micro™, Kaspersky™, ESET® (NOD32®), and Bitdefender™.

Antivirus updates must be managed as they are made available. Antivirus engine updates can include enhancements, bug fixes, or new features being added to the software engine, improving the manner in which the software operates. Updates can be implemented automatically or manually depending on the software. Automatic updating refers to software that periodically downloads and applies updates without any user intervention, whereas manual updating means that a user must be involved to either initiate the update, download the update, or at least approve installation of the update.

BEST PRACTICES FOR MALWARE REMOVAL

CompTIA has identified a seven-step best practice procedure for malware removal:

1. Identify and research malware symptoms.
2. Quarantine infected systems.
3. Disable **System Restore** (in Windows).
4. Remediate infected systems:
   - Update anti-malware software.
   - Scan and use removal techniques (Safe Mode, Pre-installation environment).
5. Schedule scans and run updates.
6. Enable **System Restore** and create restore point (in Windows).
7. Educate end user.

These steps are explained in more detail in the remainder of this topic.

MALWARE RESEARCH

There are several websites dedicated to investigating the various new attacks that are developed against computer systems. Apart from the regular IT magazines, some good examples include **cert.org**, **sans.org**, **schneier.com**, and **grc.com**. The SANS "Top 20" critical security controls is one of the most useful starting points (**sans.org/top20/**). Antivirus vendors also maintain malware encyclopedias ("bestiaries") with complete information about the type, symptoms, purpose, and removal of viruses, worms, Trojans, and rootkits.

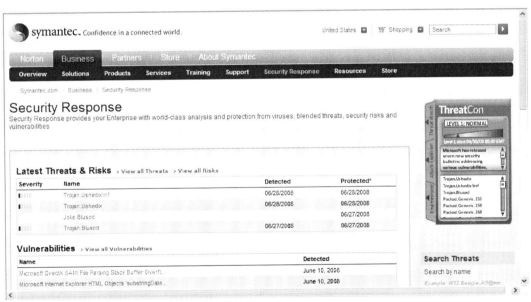

Symantec's Security Response portal showing current threat status, recent viruses and vulnerabilities, and search options for the malware database.

QUARANTINE AND REMEDIATION OF INFECTED SYSTEMS

Following the seven-step procedure, if symptoms of a malware infection are detected, the next steps should be to apply a quarantine, disable **System Restore**, and then remediate the infected system.

QUARANTINING INFECTED SYSTEMS

Malware such as worms propagate over networks. This means that one of the first actions should be to disconnect the network link. Infected files could have been uploaded to network servers or cloud services, though these systems should have server-side scanning software to block infected files.

Move the infected system to a physically or logically secure work area. To remediate the system, you might need network access to tools and resources but you cannot risk infecting the production network. You should also ensure that the infected computer is not used until it has been cleaned up.

Once the infected system is isolated, the next step is to disable System Restore and other automated backup systems, such as File History. If you are relying on a backup to recover files infected by malware, you have to consider the possibility that the backups are infected, too. The safest option is to delete old system restore points and backup copies, but if you need to retain them, try to use antivirus software to determine whether they are infected.

Also consider identifying and scanning any removable media that has been attached to the computer. If the virus was introduced via USB stick, you need to find it and remove it from use. Viruses could also have infected files on any removable media attached to the system while it was infected.

The main tool to use to try to remediate an infected system will be antivirus software, though if the software has not detected the virus in the first place, you are likely to have to use a different suite. Make sure the antivirus software is fully updated before proceeding. This may be difficult if the system is infected, however. It may be necessary to remove the disk and scan it from a different system.

REMEDIATING INFECTED SYSTEMS

If a file is infected with a virus, you can (hopefully) use antivirus software to try to remove the infection (cleaning), quarantine the file (the antivirus software blocks any attempt to open it), or erase the file. You might also choose to ignore a reported threat, if it is a false positive, for instance. You can configure the action that software should attempt when it discovers malware as part of a scan.

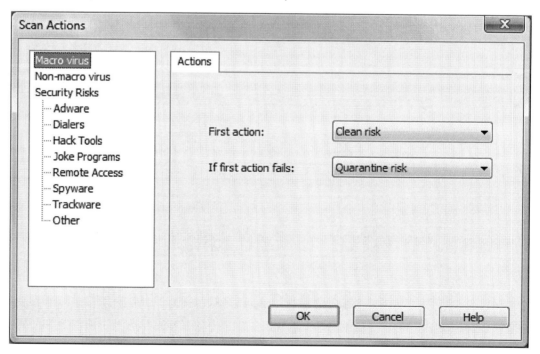

Configuring scan remediation options.

Most of the time the software will detect the virus and take the appropriate action. If you cannot clean a file, and have a backup copy, use it to restore the file. Check the files you restore to make sure that your backups are not infected.

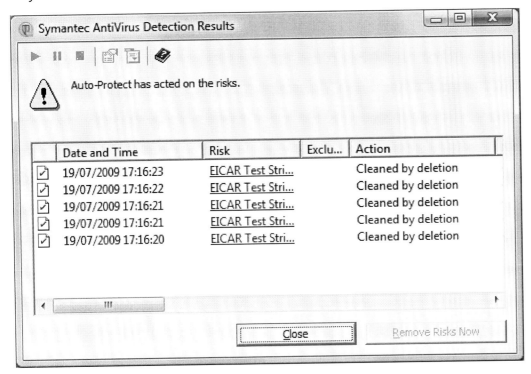

Detecting and remediating a virus infection.

Another option is to remove the virus manually. For assistance, check the website and support services for your anti-virus software. In some cases, you may have to follow a further procedure to remove the virus or Trojan Horse:

- Use Task Manager or `taskkill` to terminate suspicious processes.
- Execute commands at a command prompt terminal and/or manually remove registry items using `regedit`.
- Use `msconfig` to perform a safe boot or boot into Safe Mode, hopefully preventing any infected code from running at startup.
- Boot the computer using the product disk and use the Windows Recovery Environment (WinRE) to run commands from a "clean" command environment. Another option, as mentioned previously, is to remove the disk from the infected system and scan it from another system, taking care not to allow cross-infection.

 Note: *The CompTIA exam objectives mention the recovery console. This is a precursor to WinRE, used by the Windows 2000 and Windows XP versions. Recovery console presents a limited subset of the commands normally available at a Windows command prompt and does not provide as many tools as WinRE.*

Antivirus software will not necessarily be able to recover data from infected files. Also, if a virus does disrupt the computer system, you might not be able to run antivirus software anyway and would have to perform a complete system restore. This involves reformatting the disk, reinstalling the OS and software (possibly from a system image snapshot backup), and restoring data files from a (clean) backup.

 Note: *Windows 8 and Windows 10 support a "refresh" reinstallation mode that wipes desktop applications but preserves user data files, personalization settings, and Windows Store apps. This might be of use in removing malware.*

MALWARE INFECTION PREVENTION

Once a system has been cleaned, you need to take the appropriate steps to prevent re-infection.

CONFIGURING ON-ACCESS SCANNING

Almost all security software is now configured to scan on-access. **On-access** means that the A-V software intercepts an OS call to open a file and scans the file before allowing or preventing it from being opened. This reduces performance somewhat but is essential to maintaining effective protection against malware.

 Note: When configuring antivirus software, it is vital to configure the proper exceptions. Real-time scanning of some system files and folders (notably those used by Windows Update) can cause serious performance problems.

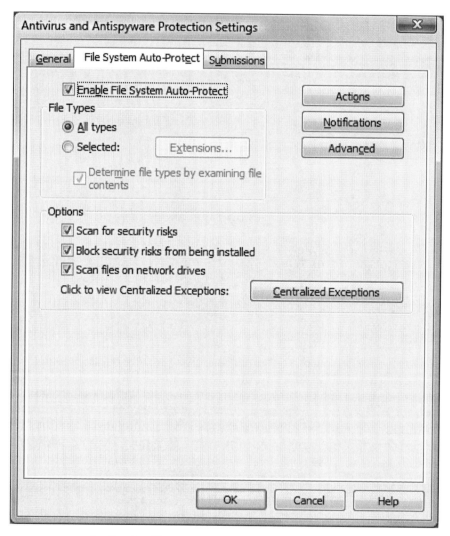

Configuring File System Auto-Protect on-access scans.

 Note: Antivirus software depends on services to run properly—make sure that these are not disabled.

CONFIGURING SCHEDULED SCANS

All security software supports scheduled scans. These scans can impact performance, however, so it is best to run them when the computer is otherwise unused. Symantec

Endpoint Protection performs an "Active Scan" at startup, but the user can define any type of scan to run to a schedule of their own choosing.

You also need to configure the security software to perform malware pattern and antivirus engine updates regularly.

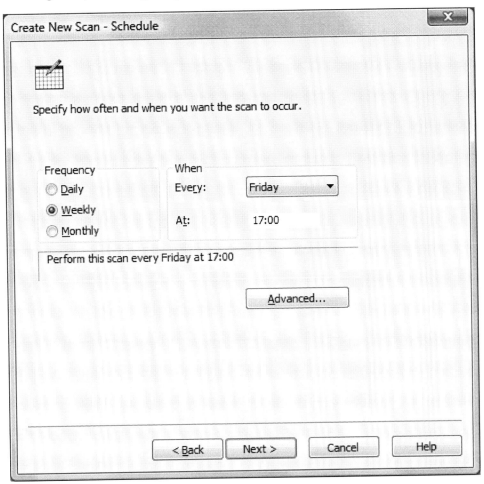

Configuring a scheduled scan.

DNS CONFIGURATION

DNS spoofing allows attackers to direct victims away from the legitimate sites they were intending to visit and towards fake sites. As part of preventing reinfection, you should inspect and re-secure the DNS configuration.

- Flush the local DNS cache to clear out any potentially malicious entries. In Windows, you can use `ipconfig /flushdns` to do this.
- Check the HOSTS file for spoofed entries—mappings in the HOSTS file are loaded into the DNS cache and can override other name resolution methods, depending on how the system is configured. Malware often tries to corrupt the file to insert malicious entries. In Windows, the file is stored in **%SYSTEMROOT% \System32\drivers\etc\hosts**. In Linux, it is located in **/etc/hosts**. These files should generally be empty, though there may be commented (#) text.
- In Windows, check the priority order for name resolution services is set as per network policies. The priority order is set in the registry key **HKLM→SYSTEM→CurrentControlSet→Services→Tcpip→ServiceProvider**.
- Validate the DNS resolvers set as primary and secondary in the client's IP configuration (use `ipconfig /all`).

- Check these local DNS resolver services to make sure they are operating normally and are configured according to policy. You may also want to flush the cache on these servers. You could also test name resolution with `nslookup` to compare results of queries performed by your local DNS infrastructure with results obtained from a trusted Internet DNS provider. Google's public DNS servers (8.8.8.8 and 8.8.4.4) are quite widely used, for instance. Another option is Quad9, sponsored by IBM. Quad9 has a special focus on blocking domains known to host malicious content. There is a filtered service (9.9.9.9 and 149.112.112.112) and a non-secured service (9.9.9.10 and 149.112.112.10).
- Check that where you are forwarding queries, these queries are being sent to legitimate DNS servers on the Internet. Most organizations use their ISP's servers. Ensure that queries are reaching the intended servers and are not being redirected to a rogue DNS.

SOFTWARE FIREWALLS

If malware was able to run with administrative privileges, it may have made changes to the software (host) firewall configuration. An unauthorized port could potentially facilitate reinfection of the machine. You should inspect the firewall policy to see if there are any unauthorized changes. Consider resetting the policy to the default.

ENABLING SYSTEM RESTORE

If you disabled **System Restore** and automatic backups, you should re-enable them as part of the recommissioning process. Create a fresh restore point or system image and a clean data backup. As a final step, complete another antivirus scan; if the system is clean, then remove the quarantine and return it to service.

GUIDELINES FOR REDUCING MALWARE EFFECTS

Consider the following guidelines to help reduce the effects of malware.

REDUCE THE RISK AND IMPACT OF MALWARE

Several steps can be taken to reduce the risk and impact of malware:

- Carry out regular backups that allow data to be recovered, in case of loss due to a virus infection. Do not leave the backup device attached to the host. This minimizes the risk of the backup files becoming infected.
- Apply operating system and application security patches.
- Do not allow users to bring in their own software programs. If necessary, measures such as removing (or disabling) removable drives can be used. Windows-based systems also allow the administrator to determine who can run new programs, install new software, or download files from the web. Use these rights effectively.
- Install and use an anti-virus package. The virus package must be kept up-to-date with updated signatures (or definitions), since viruses are continually being developed and the latest signatures offer the most protection.
- Select antivirus software that scans automatically (on-access). This provides much more reliable protection against web and email attachment threats.
- Configure filtering on the messaging server—this will prevent most of the unsolicited messages (spam) arriving at the server from getting to the users' mailboxes.
- Do not log on with administrative privileges except where necessary. Limit administrative privileges to a few, selected accounts. Keep passwords for these accounts secure.
- Educate users about not running attachments—and supplement this with procedures that will prevent files, such as executables and Office macros, from being allowed to run. This could be accomplished (for instance) by only allowing digitally signed code to be executed.

- Audit system events (such as logons) and review logs for unusual activity.
- Establish a procedure for recovery following virus infection to minimize the spread and effect of a virus.

Routine procedures, such as applying critical and security patches to the OS and applications and updating virus definitions and malware threats in antivirus software, should be automated where possible or performed according to a strict schedule. Try to find time to monitor security developments so that you are aware of new threat types and strategies or "zero-day" vulnerabilities (flaws that have not been fixed by a patch).

Training and educating users can be more problematic. You may well have to overcome resistance to end users accepting responsibility for security. The efforts of a single support technician are unlikely to make much difference. An organization needs to develop and enforce effective policies, backed up by disciplinary procedures to supplement training and education programs.

Topic B
Troubleshoot Common Workstation Security Issues

EXAM OBJECTIVES COVERED
1002-2.2 Explain logical security concepts.
1002-3.2 Given a scenario, troubleshoot and resolve PC security issues.

As with many areas of computer support, your responsibility for computer security does not end as soon as the security measures are implemented. As with printing, networking, hardware, and software, it is your responsibility to your users and clients to ensure proper security functions on an ongoing basis as well as to correct security problems that might compromise your systems or prevent users from accessing the resources that they need. The information and skills in this topic should help you troubleshoot any security issues that arise and restore your organization's security functions.

COMMON SYMPTOMS OF MALWARE INFECTION

A virus's payload can be programmed to perform many different actions and there are, besides, many different types of malware. Consequently, there can be very many different symptoms of malware infection.

PERFORMANCE SYMPTOMS

When the computer is slow or "behaving oddly," one of the things you should suspect is malware infection. Some specific symptoms associated with malware include:

- The computer fails to boot or experiences lock ups.
- Unexpected or threatening messages or graphics appear on the screen.
- Performance at startup or generally is very slow.
- Network performance is slow or Internet connections are disrupted.

Any sort of activity or configuration change that was not initiated by the user is a good reason to suspect malware infection. Of course, all these things can have other causes, too. If you identify these symptoms, run an antivirus scan. If this is negative but you cannot diagnose another cause, consider quarantining the system or at least putting it under close monitoring.

> *Note: If a system is "under suspicion," do not allow users with administrative privileges to sign in to it, either locally or remotely. This reduces the risk that malware could compromise a privileged account.*

APPLICATION CRASHES AND SERVICE PROBLEMS

One of the key indicators of malware infection is that security-related applications, such as antivirus, firewall, and Windows Update, stop working. You might also notice that applications or Windows tools (Notepad for instance) stop working or crash frequently.

Software other than Windows is often equally attractive for malware writers as not all companies are diligent in terms of secure coding. Software that uses browser plug-ins is often targeted; examples include Adobe's Reader® software for PDFs and Flash®

Player. If software from a reputable vendor starts crashing (faulting) repeatedly, suspect malware infection and apply the quarantining/monitoring procedures described earlier.

FILE SYSTEM ERRORS AND ANOMALIES

Another "red flag" for malware infection is changes to system files and/or file permissions.

- The file system or individual files are corrupted or deleted.
- Date stamps and file sizes of infected files change.
- Permissions attributes of files change, resulting in "Access Denied" errors.
- New executable files (EXEs and DLLs) appear in system folders. They may have file names that are very close to valid programs (notpad.exe).

These sorts of issues are less likely to have other causes so you should quarantine the system and investigate it closely.

EVENT VIEWER

The system, application, and security logs may be of use in detecting malware that is attempting to remain concealed. You can inspect these log files using Event Viewer. High numbers of audit failures in the security log or unexpected Windows Installer events are the types of thing that warrant further investigation. The log will also list application and service crash events, which may reveal some sort of malware infection.

WEB BROWSER SECURITY ISSUES

Malware often targets the web browser. Remember that malware is not always destructive. Malware such as adware and spyware is designed with commercial or criminal intent rather than to vandalize the computer system.

Common symptoms of infection by spyware or adware are pop-ups or additional toolbars, the home page or search provider changing suddenly, searches returning results that are different to other computers, slow performance, and excessive crashing (faults). Viruses and Trojans may spawn pop-ups without the user opening the browser.

 Note: The lines between useful utilities, adware, and spyware are not completely clear-cut, but if something is there that the user (or IT department) did not explicitly sanction, then it's best to get rid of it.

Another symptom is **redirection**. This is where the user tries to open one page but gets sent to another. Often this may imitate the target page. In adware, this is just a blunt means of driving traffic through a site, but spyware may exploit it to capture authentication details.

 Note: If a user experiences redirection, check the HOSTS file for malicious entries. HOSTS is a legacy means of mapping domain names to IP addresses and is a popular target for malware. Also verify which DNS servers the client is configured to use.

TROJANS, ROOTKITS, AND BOTNETS

Malware that tries to compromise the PC will try to create a communications channel with its "handler." If the firewall is still working, you may see unfamiliar processes or ports trying to connect to the Internet.

 Note: Remember that the most powerful malware can disguise its presence. For example, the `netstat` *utility shows ports open on the PC. A rootkit may replace* `netstat` *with a modified version that does not show the ports in use by the rootkit.*

One use of Trojans and rootkits is to scan other hosts for weaknesses and launch Denial of Service (DoS) attacks against networks. Most ISPs monitor the use of scanning tools and will warn you if they detect their use coming from your IP address.

 Note: Trojans and rootkits are likely to try to disguise their presence. New breeds of rootkit try to occupy firmware, for instance, so that not even disinfecting the file system or re-formatting the hard drive will remove them. Sometimes the only way to diagnose such infections is to examine network traffic from the infected PC from a different machine.

VIRUS ALERT HOAXES AND ROGUE ANTIVIRUS

Hoax virus alerts are quite common. They are often sent as mass emails as a prank. Most advise you to forward the "alert" to everyone in your address book. Some hoax virus alerts describe a number of steps that you "must take" to remove the virus—following these steps may cause damage to your computer. Use legitimate portals to research malware.

Rogue antivirus is a particularly popular way to disguise a Trojan. In the early versions of this attack, a website would display a pop-up disguised as a normal Windows dialog box with a fake security alert, warning the user that viruses have been detected. As browsers and security software have moved to block this vector, cold calling vulnerable users claiming to represent Microsoft support has become a popular attack.

DIGITAL CERTIFICATE ISSUES

Websites and program code are very often made trustworthy by proving the site or code author's identity using a **digital certificate**. The certificate is a wrapper for the public key in a public/private key pair. The public key enables a client to read the certificate holder's signature, created using an encryption mechanism. As that signature could only have been made with the linked private key, and the private key should be known only to the holder, if the user trusts the certificate, then the user can trust the website or program code.

The issue then is how the user is able to trust the certificate. Most certificates are issued and vouched for by a third-party called a **Certificate Authority (CA)**. The CA adds its own signature to the site certificate. The user can validate the CA's signature, because the CA's root certificate is installed on the computer.

Root certificates have to be trusted implicitly, so it would obviously be highly advantageous if a malicious user could install a bogus root certificate and become a trusted root CA. Installing a trusted root certificate usually requires administrative privileges. On a Windows PC, most root certificate updates are performed as part of Windows Update or installed by domain controllers or administrators as part of running Active Directory. There have been instances of stolen certificates and root certificates from CAs being exploited because of weaknesses in the key used in the certificate.

When you browse a site using a certificate, the browser displays the information about the certificate in the address bar:

- If the certificate is valid and trusted, a padlock icon is shown. Click the icon to view information about the certificate and the Certificate Authority guaranteeing it.

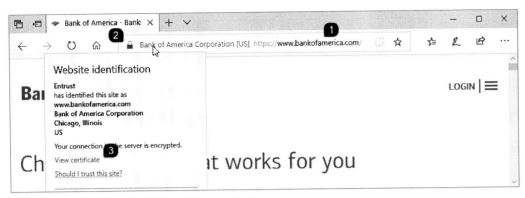

Browsing a secure site: 1) Check the domain name as highlighted in the address bar; 2) Only enter confidential data into a site using a trusted certificate; 3) Click the padlock to view information about the certificate holder and the CA that issued it and optionally to view the certificate itself.

- If the certificate is highly trusted, the address bar is colored green. High assurance certificates make the website owner go through an even more rigorous identity validation procedure.
- If the certificate is untrusted or otherwise invalid, the address bar might show a color-coded alert and the site is blocked by a warning message. If you want to trust the site anyway, click through the warning.

 There is a problem with this website's security certificate.

The security certificate presented by this website was not issued by a trusted certificate authority.
The security certificate presented by this website has expired or is not yet valid.

Security certificate problems may indicate an attempt to trick you or intercept any data you send to the server.

We recommend that you close this webpage and do not continue to this website.

✅ Click here to close this webpage.

❌ Continue to this website (not recommended).

⌄ More information

Untrusted certificate warning. (Screenshot used with permission from Microsoft.)

 Note: Digital certificates are also used to verify the identity of software publishers. If a certificate has not been issued by a one of the trusted root CAs, Windows will warn you that the publisher cannot be verified when you try to install an add-on or other type of application.

EMAIL ISSUES

Spam is unsolicited email messages, the content of which is usually advertising pornography, miracle cures for various personal conditions, or bogus stock market tips and investments. Spam is also used to launch phishing attacks and spread viruses and worms. Spam needs to be filtered before it reaches the user's inbox. Most email applications now ship with junk mail filters or you can install a filter at the organization's mail gateway. These filters need to be kept up-to-date in order to protect against the latest spamming techniques.

Note: *Host-based spam filters are fine for home users but enterprise networks will usually deploy a mail gateway to filter spam and scan message for malware before it reaches the company's internal mail servers.*

If the filter tags a message as spam, it posts it to a "Junk" email folder and no notification is displayed to the user. The user can inspect the junk folder manually to retrieve any legitimate messages that have been blocked by accident (false positives).

The main problem with **email filtering** is that it can block genuine messages too, leading to missed communications. Some filters may support detection levels so that where the scan is not certain the message is spam, it may hold it and send a blocked notification to the user's inbox.

As well as detecting spam automatically, these tools allow the user to blacklist known spammer domains or to whitelist known safe senders.

Email file attachments are frequently used as a vector for malware. As well as deploying filtering to detect such messages as spam, most A-V software can scan message attachments for malware before they can be opened.

In addition to being a vector for infection, spam may be a symptom of malware infection. One of the main criminal uses of Trojans is to install spamming software on the "zombie" PC. The software starts sending out spam emails. The software may do this surreptitiously to avoid detection; that is, it does not try to send thousands of messages at a time, but a few messages every hour. Because the Trojan may have infected thousands or millions of PCs (a botnet), it is capable of delivering huge quantities of spam.

If a computer's email is hijacked in this way, the user is likely to receive bounces, non-deliverable messages, automated replies from unknown recipients, or messages from users regarding the spam that has been sent. This does not always indicate malware infection, however; it could simply be that the spammer has spoofed the user's email address. If the volume is large, they may receive complaints from other networks and from their ISP. You can use various websites—**mxtoolbox.com** is one example—to check whether your organization's public IP address appears on any blacklist.

GUIDELINES FOR TROUBLESHOOTING COMMON WORKSTATION SECURITY ISSUES

Consider the following guidelines when troubleshooting common workstation security issues.

TROUBLESHOOT COMMON WORKSTATION SECURITY ISSUES

Follow these guidelines for troubleshooting common workstation security issues.

- Symptoms of malware infection might include:
  - Performance issues such as failure to boot, lock ups, slow performance, or strange messages or images on screen.
  - Frequent application crashes and service problems.
  - Changes to system files or changes to file permissions.
  - Event log entries showing a high number of audit failures or application and service crash events.
- Web browsers are frequent targets for malware delivery.
  - May be adware or spyware.
  - Might redirect users to a site that imitates the site the user attempted to access.
  - As compromised PC attempts to communicate with handler, unfamiliar processes or ports show up in firewall log files.
  - Hoax virus alerts requesting users to forward the message, or messages including steps to remove the virus with the steps doing the actual damage.

- • Rogue antivirus disguises Trojans.
- Check for compromised CAs.
- Verify the padlock icon is shown in browsers for secure sites and that the address bar is not maroon, which would indicate an untrusted, insecure site.
- Check the Junk email folder to ensure legitimate emails are not improperly flagged.
- Make sure users understand the potential issues in running email file attachments.

Activity 8-1
Troubleshooting Workstation Security Issues Review

SCENARIO
Answer the following review questions.

1. **Which best practice for minimizing the effect of malware do you think is most important?**

2. **How might you recognize a possible spyware or adware infection on a workstation?**

Summary

In this lesson, you performed troubleshooting on workstation security issues such as malware, web browser and digital certificate issues, and email issues. In your role as an A+ technician, you will be advising and supporting users in multiple areas surrounding computing devices, so using the guidelines and procedures provided in this lesson will enable you to provide the required level of support to users.

Lesson 9

Supporting and Troubleshooting Mobile Devices

LESSON INTRODUCTION

Mobile devices are everywhere today. Because of their portability and powerful computing capabilities, they are prominent in most workplaces. So, as a certified CompTIA® A+® technician, you will be expected to configure, maintain, and troubleshoot mobile computing devices. With the proper information and the right skills, you will be ready to support these devices as efficiently as you support their desktop counterparts.

LESSON OBJECTIVES

In this lesson, you will:

- Secure mobile devices.
- Troubleshoot mobile device issues.

Topic A
Secure Mobile Devices

EXAM OBJECTIVES COVERED
1002-2.8 Given a scenario, implement methods for securing mobile devices.

Mobile devices can be used for multiple functions within the professional workplace. Knowing that, you must be able to provide basic level support to your users, including configuring security settings.

POPULAR SECURITY CONTROLS FOR MOBILE DEVICES

It is critical that the organization's mobile device security practices be specified via policies, procedures, and training. Although you always want your practices specified via policies and procedures, it is particularly important with respect to mobile devices, because these devices tend to be forgotten or overlooked. They don't reside, or "live," in the workplace in the same way as, for example, a desktop computer, and they won't necessarily be there when virus databases are being updated, patches are being installed, files are backed up, and so on. Procedural and technical controls to manage these mobile devices mitigate the risk that they may introduce vulnerabilities in the company's network security.

There are two principal challenges when it comes to mobile device security: portability and capacity:

- **Portability**—devices that are portable are easy to lose or to steal or to sneak into somewhere they should not be allowed.
- **Capacity**—while great for consumers, the capacity and ease of portability of flash media, removable hard drives, smartphones, and tablets is a big problem for information security. A typical removable hard drive or Network Attached Storage (NAS) device or even a smartphone can copy down the contents of a workstation or even a server in a few minutes. Because they use USB or network ports, it is difficult to prevent the attachment of such devices.

The problems, therefore, surround the fact that because of their portability and capacity, mobile devices can be both targets of attack and the means by which an attack can be accomplished. You have to protect the data on your mobile devices from being compromised, and you have to protect the data in any of your systems from being removed by mobile devices.

Note: One of the most important steps you can take to maintain security of mobile devices is to not leave the devices unattended.

MOBILE DEVICE ACCESS CONTROL

The majority of smartphones and tablets are single-user devices. Access control can be implemented by configuring a password or PIN and screen lock. iOS does not support multiple user accounts at all. Later versions of Android support multiple user accounts on both tablets and smartphones.

SCREEN LOCKS AND BIOMETRIC AUTHENTICATION

If an attacker is able to gain access to a smartphone or tablet, they can obtain a huge amount of information and the tools with which to launch further attacks. Apart from confidential data files that might be stored on the device, it is highly likely that the user has cached passwords for services such as email or remote access VPN and websites. In addition to this, access to contacts and message history (SMS, text messaging, email, and IM) greatly assists social engineering attacks.

Consequently, it is imperative that data stored on the device be encrypted and access to the device protected by a **screen lock**.

Configuring a screen lock means that a password/passcode (or at the very least a PIN) is required to use the device. There are also "join-the-dots" **pattern locks**, which are also referred as **swipe locks**.

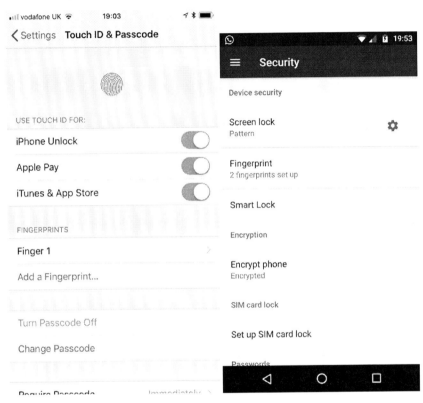

Configuring screen lock options in iOS (left) and Android (right).

 Note: *Pattern passcodes have several drawbacks. The smudge pattern may remain visible on the surface, making it much easier to guess or copy. Swipe patterns are also quite easy to observe over someone's shoulder.*

All but the cheapest device models now include a **fingerprint sensor** to provide a **biometric authentication** method. Apple refers to this feature as **Touch ID**. The user sets up a template fingerprint scan, which is converted to a unique hash and stored within a secure cache on the device (enrollment). To authenticate, the user touches the reader and the device re-computes the hash; if it matches the stored value, then access is granted.

Another biometric mechanism is the **face lock**, with the hash being computed from a picture of the user's face rather than a scan of their fingerprint. This has the advantage of being able to use a standard device (the camera) rather than a special sensor. Apple refers to their system as **Face ID**.

Note: *Biometric methods tend to suffer from high error rates, including false negatives (where the sensor does not identify the scan as valid) and false positives (where the sensor validates a scan it should not have). A passcode is also configured as a backup authentication method.*

LOCKOUT POLICY AND REMOTE WIPING

The screen lock can also be configured with a **lockout policy** or (put another way) a policy to restrict **failed login attempts**. This means that if an incorrect passcode is entered, the device locks for a set period. This could be configured to escalate—so the first incorrect attempt locks the device for 30 seconds while the third locks it for 10 minutes, for instance. This deters attempts to guess the passcode.

Another option on some phones is the support for **remote wipe** or a **kill switch**. This means that if the handset is stolen, it can be set to the factory defaults, disabled, and/or cleared of any personal data. Some utilities may also be able to wipe any plug-in memory cards, too. The remote wipe could be triggered by a number of incorrect passcode attempts or by enterprise management software.

Other features include backing up data from the phone to a server first and displaying a "Lost/stolen phone—return to XX" message on the handset.

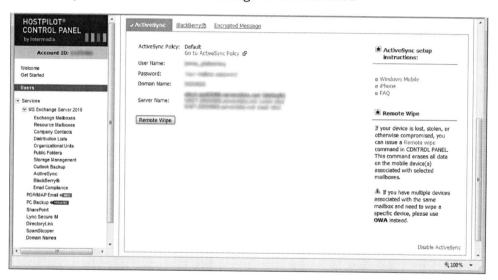

Most corporate messaging systems come with a Remote Wipe feature, allowing mail, calendar, and contacts information to be deleted from mobile devices.

The OS vendors now often supply the same services, such as Apple's **Activation Lock** or Google's **Device Protection**.

A thief can (in theory) prevent a remote wipe by ensuring the phone cannot connect to the network, then hacking the phone and disabling the security, but this requires some expertise. Even in those cases, services such as **Activation Lock** work in the device firmware, preventing restores or the disabling of location services.

MOBILE DEVICE AND DATA RECOVERY

If a mobile device is lost or stolen, there are mechanisms to use to try to effect its recovery and to prevent any misuse or loss of data stored on the device.

GPS, GEOTRACKING, AND LOCATOR APPLICATIONS

Most smartphones and many tablets are now fitted with Global Positioning System (GPS) receivers. GPS is a means of determining a receiver's position on the Earth based on information received from GPS satellites. The receiver must have line-of-sight to the

GPS satellites. As GPS requires line-of-sight, it does not work indoors. **Indoor Positioning Systems (IPS)** work out a device's location by triangulating its proximity to other radio sources, such as Wi-Fi access points or Bluetooth beacons.

Knowing the device's position (**geotracking**) also allows app vendors and websites to offer location-specific services (relating to search or local weather, for instance) and (inevitably) advertising. You can use **Location Services** settings to determine how visible your phone is to these services.

As well as supporting maps and turn-by-turn instructions, **Location Services** can be used for security to locate a lost or stolen device. Such **Find My Phone** or **locator applications** are now a standard service for all the major mobile OSes. Once set up, the location of the phone (as long as it is powered on) can be tracked from any web browser.

You can use the iCloud and Find My Phone apps to locate an iOS device and remotely lock or wipe it (or send the current holder a polite message to please return it ASAP).

Note: If a mobile device has a locator app installed and the device is lost or stolen, some apps allow the user to remotely enable features in the app. One feature that can be quite useful is enabling the camera on the phone. It has been reported that sometimes the thief has been captured using the photos taken in this manner.

FULL DEVICE ENCRYPTION

All but the earliest versions of mobile device OSes for smartphones and tablets provide **full device encryption**. The purpose of device encryption is to prevent anyone in possession of the device being able to circumvent the mobile OS's access controls and read the raw data stored on the flash memory components. If that raw data is encrypted (and the attacker cannot retrieve the encryption key from the device), then the information remains inaccessible.

In iOS, there are various levels of encryption.

- All user data on the device is always encrypted but the key is stored on the device. This is primarily used as a means of wiping the device. The OS just needs to delete the key to make the data inaccessible rather than wiping each storage location.
- Email data and any apps using the **Data Protection** option are also encrypted using a key derived from the user's passcode. This provides security for data in the event that the device is stolen. Not all user data is encrypted; contacts, SMS messages, and pictures are not, for example.

In iOS, Data Protection encryption is enabled automatically when configuring a password lock on the device.

In Android, encryption is enabled via **Settings→Security**. Android uses full-disk encryption with a passcode-derived key. When encryption is enabled, it can take some time to encrypt the device.

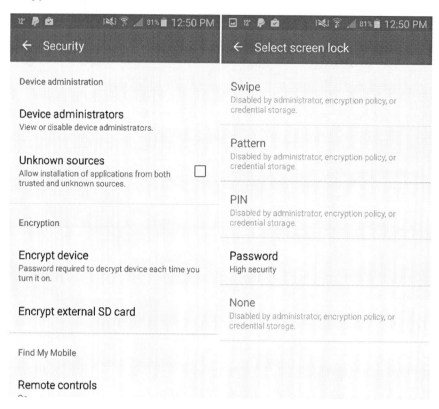

Encryption options in Android OS.

 Note: *The encryption key is derived from the PIN or password. In order to generate a strong key, you should use a strong password. Of course, this makes accessing the device each time the screen locks more difficult.*

 Note: *With the release of Android Nougat, full device encryption is being deprecated in favor of file-level encryption.*

REMOTE BACKUP APPLICATIONS

Most mobile OS devices are configured with a user account linked to the vendor's cloud services (iCloud for iOS, Google Sync for stock Android, and OneDrive for Microsoft). The user can then choose to automatically back up data, apps, and settings to the cloud. A user may choose to use a different backup provider (OneDrive on an Android phone, for instance) or a third-party provider, such as Dropbox.

As well as cloud services, a device can be backed up to a PC. For example, iOS supports making backups via the iTunes program. A third option is for Mobile Device Management (MDM) software to be configured to back up user devices automatically.

MULTIFACTOR AUTHENTICATION AND AUTHENTICATOR APPLICATIONS

Authentication methods are stronger when they are combined. There are four main types of "factor" describing different authentication methods:

- **Something you know**—such as a password or pass code or swipe pattern.

- **Something you are**—such as your fingerprint or face.
- **Something you have**—such as a unique digital token or smart card.
- **Somewhere you are**—use of a device or service might be tied to your geolocation.

Multifactor authentication means using two different methods. Requiring a user to enter a password and then a PIN is not multifactor.

Mobile device unlock methods are almost always single factor because no one wants to go through the bother of multifactor authentication every time the device is used. A user might configure two alternative methods of unlocking the device, such as configuring face lock and a pattern lock, but this is not multifactor authentication.

Multifactor authentication is often used with online services. For example, when using a new device with a web service or app such as email or online storage, many vendors encourage the use of **2-step verification**. 2-step verification means that as well as a password for the service, you register a phone or alternative email address. When you use a new computer or device to access the service, the **authenticator application** sends a code in the form of a **One Time Password (OTP)** to your phone. You must then supply the account user name and password and the OTP code to authenticate.

This reduces the risk that someone who has discovered your password could access your account, because the computer they are using is not one recognized by the service.

 Note: The OTP is computed in such a way that it can only be used once (and often has to be used within a limited time frame).

MOBILE DEVICE POLICIES

Mobile Device Management (MDM) is a class of enterprise software designed to apply security policies to the use of smartphones and tablets in business networks. This software can be used to manage corporate-owned devices as well as **Bring Your Own Device (BYOD)**. BYOD means allowing employees to use their private smartphones and tablet devices to access corporate data.

A key feature of MDM is the ability to support multiple operating systems, such as iOS, Android, and the various iterations of Windows and Windows Mobile. A few MDM suites are OS-specific (such as Apple Configurator) but the major ones, such as AirWatch (**www.air-watch.com**), Symantec (**www.symantec.com**), and Citrix Endpoint Management (**www.citrix.com**), support multiple device vendors.

PROFILING SECURITY REQUIREMENTS

The MDM software logs use of a device on the network and determines whether to allow it to connect or not, based on administrator-set parameters. This process can be described as **onboarding**.

When the device is enrolled with the management software, it can be configured with policies to allow or restrict use of apps, corporate data, and built-in functions such as a video camera or microphone. Policies can also be set to ensure the device patch status is up-to-date, that anti-virus software is present and updated, and that a device firewall has been applied and configured correctly.

Policy has disabled swipe, pattern, and PIN access, forcing use of a complex password.

A company needs to create a **profile of security requirements** and policies to apply for different employees and different sites are areas within a site. For example, it might be more secure to disable the camera function of any smartphone while onsite but users might complain that they cannot use their phones for video calls. A sophisticated security system might be able to apply a more selective policy and disable the camera only when the device is within an area deemed high risk from a data confidentiality point-of-view. Some policies can be implemented with a technical solution; others require "soft" measures, such as training and disciplinary action.

TRUSTED AND UNTRUSTED APP SOURCES

A **trusted app source** is one that is managed by a service provider. The service provider authenticates and authorizes valid developers, issuing them with a certificate to use to sign their apps and warrant them as trusted. It may also analyze code submitted to ensure that it does not pose a security or privacy risk to its customers (or remove apps that are discovered to pose such a risk). It may apply other policies that developers must meet, such as not allowing apps with adult content or apps that duplicate the function of core OS apps.

The mobile OS defaults to restricting app installations to the linked store (App Store for iOS and Play for Android). Most consumers are happy with this model but it does not work so well for enterprises. It might not be appropriate to deliver a custom corporate app via a public store, where anyone could download it.

Apple operates an enterprise developer program to solve this problem. The enterprise developer can install a profile with their security credentials along with the app. This is normally handled by an MDM suite. The user then chooses to trust the app via **Settings→General→Profiles**. It is also possible to sideload enterprise apps via iTunes and a desktop PC.

The Play store has a private channel option and Google runs an Android for Work program for enterprise developers.

Android allows for selection of different stores and installation of untrusted apps from any third party, if the user chooses the third party or unknown sources option. This allows a greater degree of customization but also makes the device vulnerable to attacks. With unknown sources enabled, untrusted apps can be downloaded from a website and installed using the **.apk** file format.

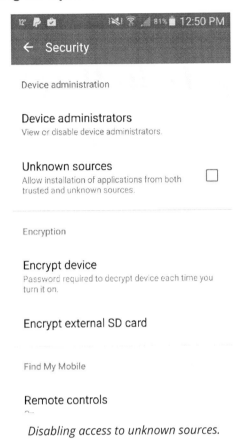

Disabling access to unknown sources.

MOBILE DEVICE SECURITY SOFTWARE

Mobile devices can use the same classes of security software as PCs and laptops to harden against malware, software exploits, or network exploits.

ANTI-VIRUS/ANTI-MALWARE AND FIREWALLS

Modern smartphones are computers in their own right and as such are vulnerable to software exploits as well as being targets of malware and viruses, especially if an untrusted app source has been configured. **Anti-virus apps** have become popular in the Android app market especially after some publicized cases of viral infection on Android devices. Some mobile anti-virus software scans only installed apps and ignores plug-in flash memory cards. There is also a problem with the limited user base and the emerging natures of mobile OS threats and vulnerabilities. This makes it difficult to create pattern databases of known threats and use heuristics (machine learning) to identify new threats.

Another class of security software is the **app scanner**. These are designed to monitor the permissions allocated to apps and how they are using (or abusing) them. There are also **firewall apps** for mobile devices. These can be used to monitor app activity and prevent connections to particular ports or IP addresses. One issue for firewalls is that they must be able to control other apps and therefore logically work at a higher permission level (root). Installing an app with root access is challenging, however. "No-root" firewalls work by creating a Virtual Private Network (VPN) and then controlling app access to the VPN.

Apple has traditionally been relaxed about the need for third-party security solutions, such as anti-virus or firewalls. Consequently, there are few iOS security apps.

PATCHING/OS UPDATES

Keeping a mobile OS and its apps up-to-date with patches (and ideally new OS versions) is as critical as it is for a desktop computer. The install base of iOS is generally better at applying updates because of the consistent hardware and software platform. Updates for iOS are notified by an alert on wake and delivered via **Settings→General→Software Update**. App updates are indicated via red notifications on the app icon and delivered via the **Updates** page in the app store.

Android patches are more reliant on the device vendor as they have to deliver the patch for their own "flavor" of Android. Support for new OS versions can also be mixed. Android uses the notification shade to deliver updates. You can also go to **Settings→About→System updates**.

Topic B

Troubleshoot Mobile Device Issues

 EXAM OBJECTIVES COVERED
1002-3.4 Given a scenario, troubleshoot mobile OS and application issues.
1002-3.5 Given a scenario, troubleshoot mobile OS and application security issues.

You can use similar troubleshooting techniques as for PCs and laptops to resolve issues on mobile device operating systems and applications. One difference is that apps, operating system, and hardware are tightly integrated in mobile devices such as smartphones and tablets. You may need to troubleshoot all three components in order to determine which one is actually causing the issue.

MOBILE OS TROUBLESHOOTING TOOLS

When you are troubleshooting a mobile OS, you need to know how to find configuration options and perform different types of device resets.

ADJUSTING SETTINGS

In iOS, configuration settings are stored under the **Settings** app. There are settings for both the core OS and for individual apps. In Android, the **Settings** app can be added to the home screen or accessed via the **Cog** icon in the notification shade.

CLOSING RUNNING APPS

A mobile OS performs sophisticated memory management to be able to run multiple applications while allowing each app to have sufficient resources and preventing an app from consuming excessive amounts of power and draining the battery. The memory management routines shift apps between foreground (in active use), background (potentially accessing the network and other resources), and suspended (not using any resources).

Both iOS and Android show a "multitasking" list of apps that the user has opened. This multitasking list doesn't actually mean that the app is loaded into memory, however. In Android, you can remove an app from the list by pressing the multitasking button (a square or rectangle) then swiping the app left or right off the screen. Doing this won't have any impact on performance.

If an app is actually unresponsive, it can be closed via the **force stop** option.

- In Android, open **Settings→Apps**. Tap an app, then select the **Force Stop** option to close it or the **Disable** option to make it unavailable.
- In iOS, clearing an app from the multitasking list also force stops it. Double tap the **Home** button then swipe the app up off the screen.

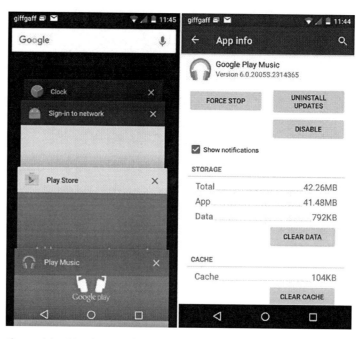

In Android, tap the multitasking button (bottom-right) to view open apps, then swipe left or right to remove them; use the Force Stop option in app settings to fully close an app.

UNINSTALL/REINSTALL APPS

Another stock response to an app issue is to uninstall then reinstall it.

- To uninstall an iOS app, tap-and-hold it until it wiggles, then press the **X** icon and confirm by pressing **Delete**. You cannot uninstall default apps. To return the screen to normal, press the **Home** button. You can also delete apps from **Settings** or from **iTunes**.

- In Android, use **Settings→Apps** to uninstall (completely remove) or disable (prevent from running) apps. You can also long-press an icon on the home screen then drag it to the **Uninstall** icon (dragging it to **Remove** just hides the app icon).

Apps can be reinstalled via the store (without having to pay for them again!).

REBOOTING A MOBILE DEVICE

Just as turning it off and on again is the tried and trusted method of "fixing" a computer, a reboot can resolve many software-related issues on a mobile device. Users generally leave their mobile devices in a sleep state. Powering the device off closes all applications and clears any data from RAM. Data and settings stored in the device are not affected. This kind of **soft reset** is usually effective in restoring unresponsive or frozen systems and is one of the first things to try when faced with a malfunctioning app or slow performance. It is also used after the installation of some apps.

- On iOS, holding the **Sleep/Wake** button down for a few seconds brings up a menu prompting the user to swipe so the device can be shut down. When you are troubleshooting, leave the device powered off for a minute, and then restart by holding the **Sleep** button again. If the touchscreen is unresponsive, you can perform a forced restart by pressing the **Sleep/Wake** and **Home** buttons for 10 seconds. The screen will go black then the device will restart. When performing a forced restart, unsaved data in current use may be lost.

- On Android, to power off, hold the **Power** button for a few seconds to bring up the **Power Off** prompt. If the touchscreen is unresponsive, a forced restart can often be performed by holding the **Power** button for 10 seconds, though some Android devices use a different key combination for this. You can also boot an Android device to Safe Mode by tap-and-holding the **Power Off** message. Safe Mode disables third-party apps, but leaves core services running.

FACTORY DEFAULT RESET

A **factory default reset** removes all user data, apps, and settings. The device will either have to be manually reconfigured with a new user account and apps reloaded, or restored from a backup configuration. When you are performing a factory reset, ensure that the device has a full battery charge or is connected to an external power source.

- To factory reset an iOS device, connect it to a PC or Mac running **iTunes**. You can use the **Update** button on the device's summary page to try to reinstall iOS without removing user data. If this does not work, use the **Restore** button to perform a factory reset. If the **Update** or **Restore** buttons are not available, use the force soft restart method described earlier while the device is connected to **iTunes**.
- For Android, you should check for specific instructions for each particular device. On stock Android, you can initiate a reset from the **Backup and Reset** section of **Settings**. If the device will not boot normally, you can enter recovery mode using some combination of the power and volume buttons.

Note: Some vendors may use the term "hard reset" to mean a factory reset.

Note: You might be required to sign in immediately after performing a factory restore to protect against theft of the device or your account information. Make sure you have the account credentials available and do not attempt a factory reset within 72 hours of changing your account password.

GUIDELINES FOR USING MOBILE TROUBLESHOOTING TOOLS

Here are some guidelines to help you use mobile troubleshooting tools.

USE MOBILE TROUBLESHOOTING TOOLS

Consider these guidelines for using mobile troubleshooting tools:

- Adjust settings for the core OS and for apps.
- Close running apps that are consuming too much power and draining the battery or those that are unresponsive.
- Uninstall apps that are no longer needed or reinstall apps after replacing a device or after previously uninstalling an app.
- Try a soft reset for devices that are frozen or unresponsive. If that doesn't work, use a forced restart.
- Perform a factory default reset when reissuing the mobile device to another user or preparing it for disposal.

MOBILE OS ISSUE TROUBLESHOOTING

Like any other computer, mobile devices can have their own issues that need diagnosing and fixing.

DIM DISPLAY

One of the common issues is a **dim display**. This usually happens when the user has set the **backlight** to its lowest setting (and disabled automatic light adjustment) or the phone is set to conserve power by auto dimming the light. To adjust, open **Display** settings and select the automatic brightness option or adjust the slider.

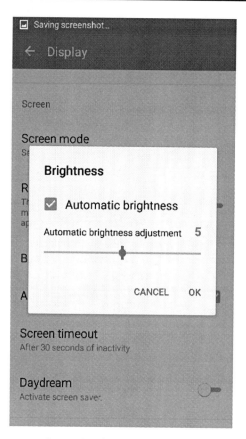

Screen Brightness adjustment.

It is also worth checking for third-party power management apps or the use of a battery-saver mode or profile that automatically dims the backlight to conserve power.

TOUCHSCREEN UNRESPONSIVE OR INACCURATE

If the touchscreen is unresponsive or does not register touches at the correct coordinates, first check for obvious hardware issues (dirt, grease, or cracks). If a screen protector is fitted, check that it is securely adhered to the surface and that there are no bubbles or lifts.

If you can rule out simple hardware causes, unresponsive touch input can be an indication of resources being inadequate (too many open apps) or badly written apps that hog memory or other resources. A soft reset will usually fix the problem in the short term. If the problem is persistent, either try to identify whether the problem is linked to running a particular app or try freeing space by removing data or apps. Windows devices and some versions of Android support re-calibration utilities, but if you cannot identify another cause, then you are likely to have to look at warranty repair.

EXTERNAL MONITOR ISSUES

Screen sharing can be enabled via an adapter cable. If there is a problem, you should try to rule out a bad cable first.

Mobiles can also connect to wireless displays or reception dongles. The principal issue here is that the various wireless standards (Miracast/Wi-Fi Direct, Intel WiDi, Apple AirPlay, Google Chromecast, and Amazon Fire TV) are not interoperable so you need to ensure both the broadcast and reception devices are using the same technology. You also need to rule out the usual potential sources of wireless interference.

Note: *Miracast is based on Wi-Fi Direct, which is less proprietary than the other standards but there are lots of interoperability problems between "Miracast-compatible" devices. The TV vendors all have different names for it (SmartShare, Screen Mirroring, Display Mirroring, and so on).*

SOUND ISSUES

If no sound is playing from the device speakers, first check that the volume controls are not turned all the way down and that the mute switch is not activated. Next verify that the device is not in a silent/no interruptions mode. If the problem is restricted to a particular app, check whether it has its own volume controls. If you cannot identify a software issue, check that the device is not configured to use external speakers. These could be connected via a cable or by Bluetooth.

OVERHEATING

Devices have protective circuitry that will initiate a shut down if the internal temperature is at the maximum safe limit.

Handheld devices use passive cooling and so can become quite warm when used intensively. Also make sure that the device is not left sitting in direct sunlight. If a handheld device becomes unusually hot, suspect a problem with the battery. There may be a utility that you can use to access battery status information. You can also use an app to monitor the battery temperature and then compare that to the operating limits. Generally speaking, approaching 40°C is getting too warm.

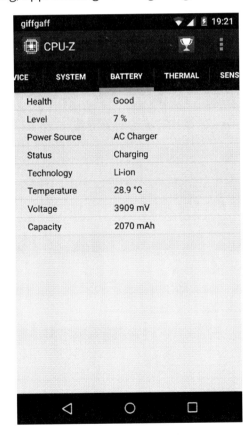

CPU-Z app showing the device's battery status.

If a device overheats repeatedly, check for apps with consistently high CPU utilization. If the device is a few years old, consider the possibility that the battery is failing. Monitor the device during charging cycles; if it overheats, then discontinue use and have it inspected at a repair center.

Note: *If you have any reason to suspect that a device is prone to overheating, do not leave it to charge unattended.*

GUIDELINES FOR TROUBLESHOOTING MOBILE OS ISSUES

Here are some guidelines to help you troubleshoot mobile OS issues.

TROUBLESHOOT MOBILE OS ISSUES

Consider these guidelines as you troubleshoot the following mobile OS issues:

- **Dim display**. Open the **Display** settings and adjust the automatic brightness option or adjust the brightness slider. Check for apps that dim the backlight to conserve power.
- **Unresponsive or inaccurate touchscreen**. Check for issues with the screen, that any screen protectors are not damaged or incorrectly applied. Check that there are adequate resources available. Use a re-calibration utility if no other cause for the issue is found.
- **Issues with external monitor**. Verify that the cable is good. Verify that a casting dongle (Google Chromecast, Miracast, AirPlay, Amazon Fire, etc) is configured correctly between the device and the mobile device.
- **Sound issues**. Verify volume controls are set correctly. Verify silent mode is not enabled. Check volume controls within the app. Verify it is not configured to use external speakers through a cable or Bluetooth.
- **Overheating**. Determine if the device is being used intensively. Use a battery monitor to view battery status information. Keep device away from direct sunlight or other heat sources.

MOBILE APP ISSUE TROUBLESHOOTING

As noted previously, with a mobile device it can be difficult to identify when a problem might be caused by the hardware, the OS, or a particular app.

APPS NOT LOADING

Sometimes the user cannot open a series of apps. This is common when apps have been moved or installed to a flash memory card. If the card is removed, malfunctions, or has been wiped, it will cause the user to lose access to that app. Apps can usually be reinstalled from the preferred app store without having to repurchase again.

Missing apps on an Android phone.

Other issues could be some sort of file corruption. Try uninstalling and reinstalling the app; if the problems persist, consider a factory reset.

> **Note:** *Also consider that Mobile Device Management (MDM) software might prevent an app or function from running in a certain context. Security policies might prevent use of the camera within the corporate office, for instance, and any app that requires the camera might then fail to start.*

APP LOG ERRORS

As consumer-level devices, iOS and Android do not support simple log viewing tools. An app could choose to display its own logs to the user if required, but an app requires root-level permissions to view system logs or the logs of other apps.

Android supports a developer mode, enabled via **Settings** (access **System→About phone** and tap **Build number** seven times), which can show additional diagnostic information when using apps or making network connections. You can also output debugging information over USB. You can use this in conjunction with the SDK to retrieve system logs. Also, on most Android handsets, you can dial ***#*#4636#*#*** to open the status page.

You can view an iOS device's logs from a macOS computer with the Xcode developer tools installed.

SLOW PERFORMANCE

As phones get older, their performance naturally degrades as apps are updated to provide more functionality and features. In order to enable these extra features, they require more memory, space, and CPU power. This results in greater battery utilization and a decrease in performance. As space is reduced and the phone is used more intensively, this can lead to an increase in the amount of errors and corruptions.

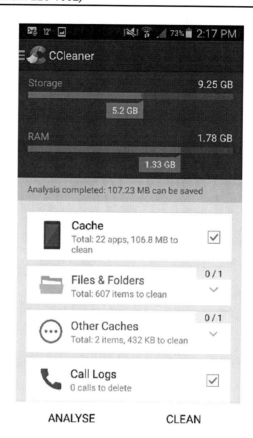

Regular clean with CCleaner.

If soft resets are not working, consider performing a factory reset. When restoring apps and data from backup, try to be selective in choosing what is restored. There are also various apps dedicated to performance optimization and maintenance.

You should also consider any recently installed apps. Having many apps that run some sort of monitoring or connectivity check in the background or apps that display real-time content in a home screen widget will impact performance. You should also check that there is sufficient space left on the flash memory storage.

 Note: *Vendors try to support device models for as long as possible, but it is frequently the case that major (or sometimes minor) version updates can quite severely impact performance if applied to older devices. Unfortunately, vendors tend not to provide a rollback option for version updates. You can only report the issue and hope the vendor supplies a fix.*

BATTERY LIFE

Smartphone batteries degrade over time with each charge and recharge cycle so some decrease in performance is to be expected. Some mobile devices have replaceable batteries but for most models this will be a warranty service operation.

CPU and GPU intensive apps such as games and video playback will drain the battery quickly. A battery charge might be degraded by a faulty or malicious app utilizing high powered peripherals such as GPS, network connections, or even the microphone and camera. You can get information about battery usage via **Settings→More→Battery** in Android or **Settings→Battery** in iOS.

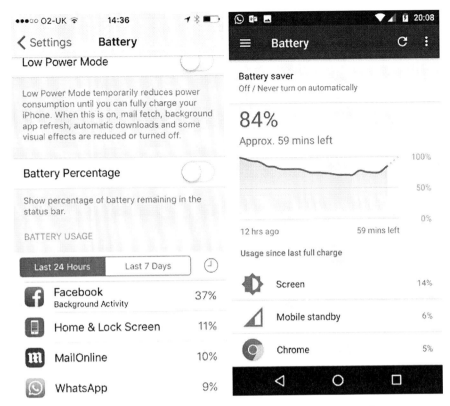

Battery Analyzers for iOS and Android with option to conserve battery.

It might be appropriate to uninstall the app. Alternatively you might be able to restrict the app from running in the background. In iOS, configure this via **Settings→General→Background App Refresh**. In Android, a battery saver mode can be applied automatically when the charge level drops to a certain percentage or you can apply it manually. To configure it, select **Settings→Battery**. Tap the top-right ellipse button for the settings menu and select **Battery saver**.

Keeping your device up-to-date with the latest patches and OS version also ensures optimum operation and battery life conservation.

GUIDELINES FOR TROUBLESHOOTING MOBILE APP ISSUES

Here are some guidelines to help you troubleshoot mobile app issues.

TROUBLESHOOT MOBILE APP ISSUES

Consider these guidelines as you troubleshoot the following mobile app issues:

- If an app is not loading, verify that it wasn't installed on a memory card that is not in the mobile device. Verify that the app is not corrupted; uninstall and reinstall the app.
- Examine app log files to determine if the issue can be tracked down in the log file.
- Put the device in developer mode to access log files:
  - Android devices: **System→About phone** and tap **Build number** seven times or dial ***#*#4636#*#***.
  - iOS devices: Connect the device to a macOS computer with the Xcode developer tools installed.
- Slow performance can be caused by newer apps requiring more resources than are available, reduced battery life, and lack of free storage space. Check that recently installed apps are functioning correctly and are not running in the background.

- Battery life degrades over time. Keep the OS up-to-date to ensure optimum operations and battery life conservation.

MOBILE WIRELESS ISSUE TROUBLESHOOTING

Networking is another area where problems occur frequently. On a mobile device, that means troubleshooting wireless connections of different types (Wi-Fi, Bluetooth, or cellular radio). To approach these problems, try to establish whether there is a configuration error or some sort of hardware/interference problem.

TROUBLESHOOTING INTERFERENCE ISSUES

Radio signals can be affected by the distance between the broadcast and reception antennas and by interference from other devices or by barriers such as thick walls or metal. On a mobile, you should also consider that a low battery charge will weaken the signal strength.

You can troubleshoot issues with Wi-Fi signal strength using a Wi-Fi Analyzer app installed on the device. Most apps can record the settings in a particular location so that you have a baseline reading to compare to. If the signal varies from the baseline, check what interference sources might have been introduced.

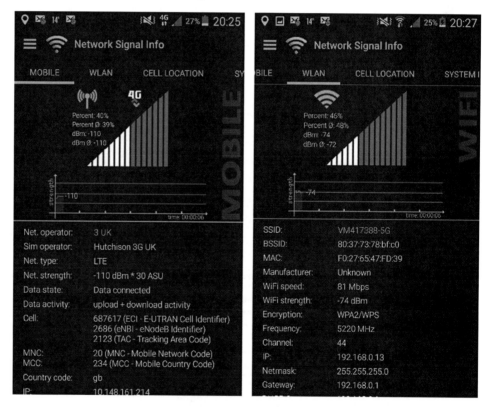

Cell Tower Analyzer (left) and Wi-Fi Analyzer (right).

A similar utility (**Cell Tower Analyzer** or **GSM Signal Monitor**) can be used to analyze cellular radio signals, which use different frequencies to Wi-Fi. An app might combine both functions.

TROUBLESHOOTING WIRELESS CONFIGURATION ISSUES

If there is no Wi-Fi, cellular, or Bluetooth connectivity, first check that the device is not in airplane mode or that the particular radio has not been disabled. Next use **Settings** to verify that the network parameters or Bluetooth pairing information is correct. Try removing the network or Bluetooth pair and reconnecting.

With Wi-Fi, verify that the access point supports the same 802.11 standard as the device. For example, an access point configured to use 802.11ac only will not be accessible to a smartphone with an 802.11n adapter. The access point must be put into compatibility mode.

If you can rule out any other configuration errors, consider obtaining an OS or firmware update for the device or for the access point. Research any known issues between the access point and the model of device.

GUIDELINES FOR TROUBLESHOOTING MOBILE WIRELESS ISSUES

Here are some guidelines to help you troubleshoot mobile wireless issues.

TROUBLESHOOT MOBILE WIRELESS ISSUES

Consider these guidelines as you troubleshoot the following mobile wireless issues:

- **Interference issues**. Use a Wi-Fi Analyzer app to check for interference and signal strength.
- **Configuration issues**.
  - Verify that the device is not in airplane mode.
  - Verify that a particular radio service has not been disabled.
  - Use **Settings** to verify that configuration parameters are correctly configured.
  - Verify that the Wi-Fi access point supports the same standard as the mobile device.

  If none of these are the issue, determine if an OS or firmware update is needed.

MOBILE DEVICE SECURITY TROUBLESHOOTING

As mentioned previously, antivirus software for mobile OS is available but not always that reliable, as new threats and exploits are emerging all the time. You should be alert to general symptoms of malware.

UTILIZATION SYMPTOMS

Malware or rogue apps are likely to try to collect data in the background. They can become unresponsive and might not shut down when closed. Such apps might cause excessive **power drain** and **high resource utilization**. Another telltale sign of a hacked device is reaching the **data transmission overlimit** unexpectedly. Most devices have an option to monitor data usage and have limit triggers to notify the user if the limit has been reached. This protects from large data bills but should also prompt the user to check the amount of data used by each application in order to monitor their legitimacy.

Unauthorized location tracking can give away too much sensitive information to third parties. Many apps collect location data; not many explain clearly what they do with it. Most app developers will just want information they can use for targeted advertising, but a rogue app could use location data to facilitate other crimes, such as domestic burglary.

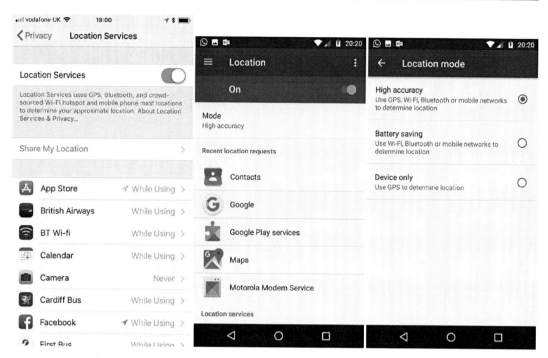

Location services in iOS (left) and Android. Note the option to configure location mode/accuracy.

 Note: *Criminals don't necessarily need to hack a device to get location information. If someone posts pictures online, most will be tagged with location information. A criminal can quite easily get information about where someone lives and then identify when they are on vacation from social media. Users should be trained to strip* **geotagging** *information (or all* **metadata***) from images before posting them online.*

Location Services can be turned off completely but this will stop many apps from working. You can disable location services on an app-by-app basis, too.

Mobile OSes, like other operating systems, potentially have vulnerabilities that can be exploited to allow an attacker **unauthorized root access**. Root is an account with system-level access to every process running in the OS. If an attacker has this type of access, they can even remotely activate the camera and microphone. With corporate and government installations, this could cause a security breach of sensitive data. The recommendation is to disable and cover cameras and microphones when in sensitive areas. Some companies and government buildings prevent usage of mobile devices in such areas to avoid **unauthorized camera and microphone usage**.

Good patch and upgrade management is required to keep the OS current and up to date.

USER BEHAVIOR ISSUES

System security is not just compromised by malware and hackers. Careless use and failure to follow security best practices cause users to put themselves and the data stored on their devices at risk.

When a user needs to connect to the Internet, it can be tempting to use any available open hotspot, especially if the hotspot has the name of a major brand. An open hotspot set up with malicious intent can harvest a huge amount of information. Any data passing over the access point can be intercepted, unless it is protected by encryption (an HTTPS website, an SSL-enabled mail server, or a Virtual Private Network, for instance). There have also been instances where attackers have been able to exploit faults in the certificate-handling processes of the OS and gained the ability to intercept encrypted traffic too.

There are apps and OS settings that autoconnect to service providers' hotspots. These should be secure, if you trust the service provider to operate a secure network. If the user notices unintentional behavior, however, such as connecting to a Wi-Fi network without prompting or the Wi-Fi radio turning itself on, suspect a rogue app.

 Note: *In the context of troubleshooting security issues, if the signal from wireless equipment drops unexpectedly or users experience slow data speeds, you might also suspect some sort of* **jamming** *or* **Denial of Service (DoS)** *attack. An attacker might try to block the signal from a legitimate access point to try to trick users into connecting to a* **rogue access point** *or* **evil twin**.

Unintended Bluetooth pairing is when anonymous devices are allowed to pair with Bluetooth-enabled devices. Once paired, a rogue device could access most of the data and functions on the target device. Bluebugging, for instance, exploited a firmware flaw to allow an attacker to monitor and place telephone calls. Most devices only turn Bluetooth discoverable mode on for a limited amount of time to minimize the risk of rogue pairing events. Bluetooth should be disabled completely when not in use. Also consider the possibility that a rogue app could be changing Bluetooth settings.

SYSTEM LOCKOUT AND UNAUTHORIZED ACCOUNT ACCESS

A user can be **locked out** if the device has been disabled either by means of the user forgetting the passcode or remotely by **Find My Phone** type software if the device is reported stolen. There are a number of ways to re-enable the device. Usually the user has to wait a certain amount of time to try again or use the recovery tool in iTunes (iOS devices) to restore the device.

 Note: *Lost and stolen devices can expose sensitive corporate data. Data containers mitigate this issue by isolating business data from personal data. A data container creates a virtual environment when the app is launched. Using this virtual environment, the user accesses corporate emails and other corporate data. The app creates an encrypted data store, and the user is not permitted to copy data from outside the container or to move data from within the container. This keeps the business data isolated and secure.*

If an online account becomes locked and the user has not been making the logon attempts, suspect attempted **unauthorized account access**. Various data breaches have provided hackers with mountains of authentication credentials and personal information to use to try to access email accounts. Once an email account is compromised, the hacker can typically access any other online account that is not protected by secondary authentication, such as 2-step verification.

Whenever a website or service suffers a data breach and leaks personal files/data, it should notify users immediately. Users need to be alert to the possibility of the theft of their personal information and deploy good security practices, such as not using the same password for two different websites and changing passwords regularly.

TROUBLESHOOTING EMAIL PROBLEMS

When you are troubleshooting an email problem, verify that the user's credentials and the email server parameters are set correctly (server type, location (IP or URL), port number, and SSL enable/disable). One typical problem with corporate email is where a password change is enforced on the enterprise network but the mobile device has not been updated with the new password.

Users often want to send confidential email with the assurance that only the recipient can read it. To do this, the recipient sends the sender a digital certificate and the sender uses the public key in that certificate to encrypt the message. The recipient then uses another part of the certificate (the private key) to decrypt the message.

If the certificate is missing or not recognized, the device will be unable to decrypt the email. Use the email client or encryption program's support documentation to find out how to install or locate the appropriate certificate.

GUIDELINES FOR TROUBLESHOOTING MOBILE DEVICE SECURITY ISSUES

Here are some guidelines to help you troubleshoot mobile device security issues.

TROUBLESHOOT MOBILE DEVICE SECURITY ISSUES

Consider these guidelines as you troubleshoot the following mobile device security issues:

- If there is a huge power drain or high resource utilization, check for malware or rogue apps.
- Check for unauthorized location tracking.
- Remove geotagging information or metadata from images posted online.
- Ensure users are not engaging in behavior that makes their devices vulnerable to attack.
- If using settings that allow automatic connection to service provider hotspots, verify that the hotspot and device are using trusted, secure connections.
- Ensure unintended Bluetooth pairing is not allowed.
- Ensure users are locking the device when unattended.
- Install apps or enable OS features that allow the phone to be locked and/or wiped if it is lost or stolen.
- Verify that email passwords changed on the enterprise network are replicated to the mobile device.
- When sending and receiving encrypted emails with a digital certificate, use the email client or encryption program's support documentation to install or locate the appropriate certificate.

Activity 9-1
Supporting and Troubleshooting Mobile Devices Review

SCENARIO
Answer the following review questions.

1. In your professional experience, have you supported mobile devices? If not, what kind of experience do you have with them?

2. What type of technical support do you think will be expected of an A+ technician as mobile devices become even more prominent within the workplace?

Summary

In this lesson, you worked with mobile computing devices. You examined mobile device technologies, including smartphones, tablets, wearable devices, and more. As an A+ technician, you will need to be able to expertly support and troubleshoot mobile devices.

Lesson 10

Implementing Operational Procedures

LESSON INTRODUCTION

As a CompTIA® A+® technician, you will be asked to install, configure, maintain, and correct problems with a variety of computer components and software. You will usually be performing this work within the context of a company's operational procedures. You have already explored procedures governing safe working practices, regulated data and content, incident response, and ways of using remote access to handle problems more efficiently.

Other types of operational procedures are designed to ensure the secure and efficient functioning of the IT system. Companies need documentation and change management procedures to keep the use of systems under control, potentially using scripting to ensure standardized configuration changes. They need plans to cope with disasters so that data loss and system downtime is minimized. They need to ensure the physical environment is optimized and does not present any health hazards. This lesson will help you to identify the technologies that underpin these important procedures.

LESSON OBJECTIVES

In this lesson, you will:

- Use appropriate safety procedures for avoiding hazards associated with PC support and minimize the risk of damage from ESD.

- Describe environmental impacts and controls.

- Create and maintain documentation.

- Use change management best practices.

- Implement disaster prevention and recovery methods.

- Describe basic scripting concepts.

- Use proper communication techniques and general professional attitude.

Topic A

Use Appropriate Safety Procedures

 EXAM OBJECTIVES COVERED
1002-4.4 Explain common safety procedures.

To complete PC support tasks without damaging the equipment that you are servicing or causing physical injury to yourself or others, there are several tools to use and operational procedures to follow in order to get the job done quickly, safely, and correctly. In this topic, you will identify the best practices for PC technicians to follow to promote electrical and environmental safety.

LOCAL GOVERNMENT REGULATIONS

When performing PC maintenance work, you may need to take account of compliance with government regulations. Regulations that typically affect PC maintenance or the installation of new equipment are:

- Health and safety laws: Keeping the workplace free from hazards.
- Building codes: Ensuring that fire prevention and electrical systems are intact and safe.
- Environmental regulations: Disposing of waste correctly.

For example, in the United States, the most common safety regulations are those issued by the federal government, such as the Occupational Safety and Health Administration (OSHA), and state standards regarding employee safety. OSHA-compliant employers must provide:

- A workplace that is free from recognized hazards that could cause serious physical harm.
- Personal protective equipment designed to protect employees from certain hazards.
- Communication—in the form of labeling, Material Safety Data Sheets (MSDSs), and training about hazardous materials.

While specific regulations may vary from country to country and state to state, in general employers are responsible for providing a safe and healthy working environment for their employees. Employees have a responsibility to use equipment in the workplace in accordance with the guidelines given to them and to report any hazards. Employees should also not interfere with any safety systems, including signs or warnings or devices such as firefighting equipment. Employees should not introduce or install devices, equipment, or materials to the workplace without authorization or without making an assessment of the installation.

HEALTH AND SAFETY PROCEDURES

A company's health and safety procedures should be set out in a handbook, possibly as part of an employee's induction handbook. Health and safety procedures should:

- Identify what to do in the event of a fire or other emergency.
- Identify responsible persons (for example, for overall health and safety, nominated first aiders, fire marshals, and so on).

- Identify hazardous areas in the workspace and precautions to take when entering them.
- Describe best practice for use and care of the workspace and equipment within it.
- Establish an incident reporting procedure for detecting and eliminating workplace hazards and accidents.

GENERAL EMERGENCY PROCEDURES

Here is a general procedure for emergency situations:

1. Raise the alarm and contact the emergency services, giving them a description of the emergency and your location.
2. If possible, make the scene safe. For example, if you are faced with a fire, establish that you have an escape route, or if faced with electrical shock, disconnect the power (if it is safe for you to do so).
3. If you have training and it is safe to do so, do what you can to tackle the emergency (for example, give first aid or use firefighting equipment).

Of course, circumstances might dictate that you do something differently. It is vital that you keep calm and do not act rashly.

ELECTRICAL HAZARDS

The most prevalent physical hazards that computer technicians face are electrical hazards. Electricity is necessary to run a computer, but it can also damage sensitive computer equipment, and in some cases, pose a danger to humans. Following established best practices for promoting electrical safety will protect not only the computer equipment that you work on, but also your personal safety and the safety of others.

Electrical equipment can give an electric shock if it is broken, faulty, or installed incorrectly. An electric shock can cause muscle spasms, severe burns, or even kill (electrocution).

Electrical currents can pass through metal and most liquids, so neither should be allowed to come into contact with any electrical device installations. Damaged components or cables are also a risk and should be replaced or isolated immediately. It is important to test electrical devices regularly. The frequency will depend on the environment in which the device is used. In some countries, **portable appliance testing (PAT)** carried out by a qualified electrician or technician ensures that a device is safe to use.

The human body is an electrical conductor and a resistor, so a current will pass through it and make it heat up, manifesting as a burn if the current is strong enough. A current can interfere with the body's nervous system, which also uses electrical signals. This might manifest as spasm or paralysis or in a severe case cause a heart attack. Collateral injuries occur when involuntary muscle contractions caused by the shock cause the body to fall or come in contact with sharp edges or electrically live parts.

Electricity can hurt you even if you are careful and avoid becoming part of an electrical ground circuit. The heat generated by an electric arc or electrical equipment can burn your skin or set your clothes on fire.

> **Note:** *High voltages (over about 30V) are more dangerous because they have the power to push more current through you (skin's resistance drops at higher voltages), but it is the current that causes the actual damage. This is why static electricity is not dangerous to you, despite the high voltages. More current will flow if a larger area of your body is exposed.*

FUSES

An electrical device must be fitted with a **fuse** appropriate to its power output. A fuse blows if there is a problem with the electrical supply, breaking the circuit to the power source. Fuses come in different ratings, such as 3A, 5A, and 13A. A device's instructions will indicate what rating of fuse to use, but most computer equipment is rated at 3A or 5A. If the fuse fitted is rated too low, it will blow too easily; if the rating is too high, it may not blow when it should (it will allow too much current to pass through the device).

If multiple devices need to be attached to a single power point, a power strip of sockets should be used. If too many devices are attached to a single point, there is a risk that they will overheat and cause a fire. "Daisy-chaining" one power strip to another is dangerous. The total amperage of devices connected to the strip must not exceed the strip's maximum load (typically 12 amps).

EQUIPMENT GROUNDING

Electrical equipment must also be **grounded** (or earthed). If there is a fault that causes metal parts in the equipment to become live, a ground provides a path of least resistance for the electrical current to flow away harmlessly. Most computer products (PCs, printers, and so on) are connected to the building ground via the power plug. However, the large metal equipment racks often used to house servers and network equipment must also be grounded. Do not disconnect the ground wire. If it has to be removed, make sure it is replaced by a competent electrician.

Grounding terminals and wires. (Image by phadventure © 123RF.com.)

HIGH VOLTAGE DEVICE SAFETY

Most of the internal circuitry in a computer is low voltage (12 V or less) and low current, so there is not much of a threat to your personal safety. However, there are exceptions to this, and these exceptions can be very dangerous. Power supplies, CRT monitors, the inverter card in an LCD display's fluorescent backlight, and laser printers can carry dangerously high levels of voltage. Charges held in capacitors can persist for hours after the power supply is turned off. You should not open these units unless you have been specifically trained to do so. Adhere to all printed warnings, and never remove or break open any safety devices that carry such a warning.

 Caution: Never insert anything into the power supply fan to get it to rotate. This approach does not work, and it is dangerous.

ELECTRICAL FIRE SAFETY

Faulty electrical equipment can pose a fire risk. If the equipment allows more current to flow through a cable than the cable is rated for, the cable will heat up. This could ignite flammable material close to the cable. If an electrical wire does start a fire, it is important to use the correct type of extinguisher to put it out. Many extinguishers use water or foam, which can be dangerous if used near live electrical equipment. The best type to use is a Carbon Dioxide (CO_2) gas extinguisher. CO_2 extinguishers have a black label. Dry powder extinguishers can also be used, though these can damage electronic equipment.

 Caution: Care must be taken in confined spaces as the CO_2 plus smoke from the fire will quickly replace the available oxygen, making it hard to breathe.

You should also ensure that the electricity supply is turned off. This should happen automatically (the fuses for the circuit should trip), but make sure you know the location of the power master switches for a building.

GUIDELINES FOR WORKING SAFELY WITH ELECTRICAL SYSTEMS

Consider these guidelines as you prepare to work with electrical equipment.

ELECTRICAL SAFETY

Follow these guidelines to work safely with electrical systems:

- Do not work on electrical systems unless you have a good understanding of the risks and appropriate safety procedures.
- Do not attempt repair work when you are tired; you may make careless mistakes, and your primary diagnostic tool, deductive reasoning, will not be operating at full capacity.
- Do not assume anything without checking it out for yourself. A ground wire might have been disconnected or never properly installed, for example.
- Disconnect the power to a circuit if you must handle it.
- Hold down the power button on the device to ensure the circuits are drained of residual power.
- Test live parts with a multimeter to ensure that no voltage is present.
- Always use properly insulated tools and never grip a tool by its metal parts.

 Note: It is especially important not to touch the live parts of multimeter probes, as these may be connected to an energized circuit. Handle the probes by the insulated sheaths only.

- Take care not to touch any part of a circuit with both hands to reduce the risk of a serious shock. This is called the "hand in pocket" rule. It reduces the chance that the current will pass through your chest and cause a heart attack.
- Make sure your hands and the surrounding area are dry. Sweat can make your hands more conductive.

- Do not leave any spill hazards in the vicinity and ensure you are not standing on a wet floor.
- Do not wear jewelry or a wrist watch or other items such as name badges that may dangle from your neck or wrist and cause a short circuit or become trapped by moving parts.

ENVIRONMENTAL SAFETY

In addition to electrical hazards, there are other environmental issues that computer technicians must deal with on a regular basis. The health and safety of you and those around you should always be your highest priority. Recognizing potential environmental hazards and properly dealing with them in a safe manner is a critical responsibility for a CompTIA® A+® technician.

Category	Description
Trip hazards	A **trip hazard** is caused by putting any object in pathways where people walk.
Lifting and carrying risks	Lifting a heavy object in the wrong way can damage your back or cause muscle strains and ligament damage. You may also drop the object and injure yourself or damage the object. Lifting and manual handling risks are not limited to particularly heavy objects. An object that is large or awkward to carry could cause you to trip over or walk into something else. An object that has sharp or rough edges or contains a hot or corrosive liquid could cause you to cut or hurt yourself.

TOXIC WASTE HANDLING

The conditions surrounding computer equipment can be an issue when there is a large number of airborne particles flowing in and around various devices. Contaminants can be either gaseous, such as ozone; particles, such as dust; or organic, which comes from industrial processing of fossil fuels or plastics. There is also a risk of poisonous or corrosive chemicals leaking from faulty equipment. Special care must be taken in respect of the following device types:

- **CRT monitors**: A cathode ray tube (CRT) is an older type of computer monitor. These are very heavy and bulky and can contain substantial amounts of hazardous materials, notably lead. They also contain a glass vacuum tube and high-voltage capacitors. While the tube is designed to be shatter resistant, it is still potentially very hazardous if dropped. The capacitors represent a high risk of electric shock.
- **Batteries**: Swollen or leaking batteries from laptop computers or within cell phones and tablets must be handled very carefully and stored within appropriate containers. Use gloves and safety goggles to minimize any risk of burns from corrosive material.
- **Electronic devices (PCs, cell phones, and tablets)**: Many components in electronic devices contain toxins and heavy metals, such as lead, mercury, and arsenic. These toxins may be present in batteries, in circuit boards, and in plastics used in the case. These toxins are harmful to human health if ingested and damaging to the environment. This means that you must not dispose of electronic devices as general waste in landfill or incinerators. If an electronic device cannot be donated for reuse, it must be disposed of through an approved waste management and recycling facility.
- **Toner kits and cartridges**: Photocopier and laser printer toner is an extremely fine powder. The products in toner powder are not classed as hazardous to health but

any dust in substantial concentration is a nuisance as it may cause respiratory tract irritation.

GUIDELINES FOR WORKING SAFELY AMONG ENVIRONMENTAL HAZARDS

Here are some guidelines to help you work safely when environmental hazards are present.

ENVIRONMENTAL SAFETY

Follow these guidelines to work safely among environmental hazards:

- When installing equipment, ensure that cabling is secured, using cable ties or cable management products if necessary. Check that cables running under a desk cannot be kicked out by a user's feet. Do not run cabling across walkways or, if there is no option but to do so, use a cord protector to cover the cabling.
- When servicing equipment, do not leave devices (PC cases for instance) in walkways or near the edge of a desk (where it could be knocked off). Be careful about putting down heavy or bulky equipment (ensure that it cannot topple).
- When you need to lift or carry items, be aware of what your weight limitations are, as well as any restrictions and guidance set forth in your job description or site safety handbook. Weight limitations will vary depending on context. For example, a 50 pound limitation for lifting and carrying an object while holding it close to your body is not the same as lifting an object from a shelf above your head.
- If necessary, you should obtain protective clothing (gloves and possibly goggles) for handling equipment and materials that can be hazardous.
- To lift a heavy object safely:
  1. Plant your feet around the object with one foot slightly toward the direction in which you are going to move.
  2. Bend your knees to reach the object while keeping your back as straight as is possible and comfortable and your chin up.
  3. Find a firm grip on the object then lift smoothly by straightening your legs—do not jerk the object up.
  4. Carry the object while keeping your back straight.
- To lower an object, reverse the lifting process; keep your chin up and bend at the knees. Take care not to trap your fingers or to lower the object onto your feet.
- If you cannot lift an object because it is too awkward or heavy, then get help from a coworker, or use a cart to relocate the equipment. If you use a cart, make sure the equipment is tightly secured during transport. Do not stack loose items on a cart. If you need to carry an object for some distance, make sure that the route is unobstructed and that the pathway (including stairs or doorways) is wide and tall enough.
- Follow these guidelines when working with toxic materials.
  - Never disassemble a CRT and never try to stack old units on top of one another.
  - Use gloves and safety goggles to minimize any risk of burns from corrosive materials from batteries, cell phones, and tablets.
  - Use an air filter mask that fits over your mouth and nose when servicing toner kits and cartridges to avoid breathing in the particles. People who suffer from asthma or bronchitis should avoid changing toner cartridges where possible. Loose toner must be collected carefully using an approved toner vacuum and sealed within a strong plastic waste container. Get the manufacturer's advice about disposing of loose toner safely. It must not be sent directly to a landfill.

ESD

Static electricity is a high voltage (potential difference) stored in an insulated body. **Electrostatic discharge (ESD)** occurs when a path is created that allows electrons to rush from a statically charged body to another with an unequal charge. The electricity is released with a spark. The charge follows the path of least resistance, so it can occur between an electrical ground, such as a doorknob or a computer chassis, and a charged body, such as a human hand.

Although the voltage is high, the amount of ESD current sustained is very low, so static electricity is not that harmful. It can, however, be slightly painful. You might have felt a small shock when reaching for a metal door handle for instance. You can feel a discharge of over about 2500V. A discharge of 20,000V or more could produce a visible spark. Walking over an untreated carpet in dry conditions could create a charge of around 35,000V.

The human body is mostly water and so does not generate or store static electricity very well. Unfortunately, our clothes are often made of synthetic materials, such as nylon and polyester, which act as good generators of static electricity and provide insulating layers that allow charges to accumulate. Humidity and climate also affect the likelihood of ESD. The risk increases during dry, cool conditions when humidity is low. In humid conditions, such as before or during a storm, the residual charge can bleed into the environment before it can increase sufficiently to be harmful to electrical components.

An electronic component, such as a memory or logic chip, is composed of fine, conductive metal oxides deposited on a small piece of silicon. Its dimensions are measured in fractions of a micron (one millionth of a meter). Any static electricity discharged into this structure will flash-over (spark) between the conductive tracks, damaging or even vaporizing them. A transistor designed to work with 1-3V can be damaged by a charge of under 100V, though most have ESD protection circuits that improve this tolerance.

A static discharge may make a chip completely unusable. If not, it is likely to fail at some later time. Damage occurring in this way can be hidden for many months and might only manifest itself in occasional failures.

COMPONENT HANDLING

By eliminating unnecessary activities that create static charges and by removing unnecessary materials that are known charge generators, you can protect against ESD-related damage and injuries. There are several other prevention techniques that you can use to protect yourself and equipment when you are working with computer components.

- **Self-grounding**, or manual dissipation of static buildup by touching a grounded object prior to touching any electronic equipment. You can accomplish this by touching an unpainted part of a metal computer chassis or other component.
- Using an anti-ESD wrist strap or leg strap can dissipate static charges more effectively than self-grounding. The band should fit snugly around your wrist or ankle to maximize contact with the skin. Do not wear it over clothing. The strap ground is made either using a grounding plug that plugs into a wall socket or a crocodile clip that attaches to a grounded point or an unpainted part of the computer's metal chassis.

Electrostatic Discharge ESD wrist strap on ESD mat. (Image by Audrius Merfeldas © 123RF.com.)

- An anti-ESD service mat is also useful. Sensitive components can be placed on the mat safely. The mats contain a snap that you connect to the wrist or leg strap. If the technician's clothing has the potential to produce static charges, an ESD smock, which covers from the waist up, can be helpful.

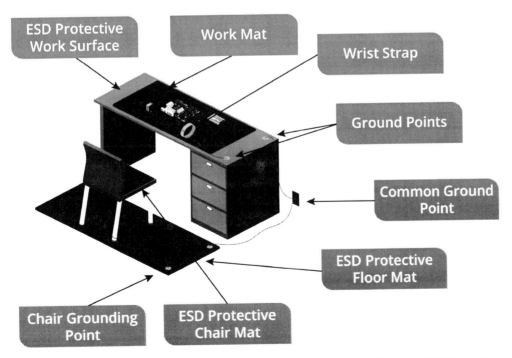

An example of a basic electrostatic discharge (ESD) workstation. (Image © 123RF.com.)

- Electronic components, assemblies, and spare parts, known as **field replaceable units (FRUs)** are often shipped in **antistatic bags** to protect them from ESD damage.

ANTISTATIC BAG TYPES

Antistatic packaging includes either anti-ESD shielding or dissipative material.

- Anti-ESD Shielding—this packaging reduces the risk of ESD because it is coated with a conductive material (such as a nickel compound). This material prevents static electricity from discharging through the inside of the bag. These bags are usually a shiny grey metallic color. To protect the contents of the bag fully, you should seal it, or at least fold the top over and seal that down.
- Dissipative Packaging—this light pink or blue packaging reduces the build-up of static in the general vicinity of the contents by being slightly more conductive than normal. A plastic bag or foam packaging may be sprayed with an anti-static coating or have anti-static materials added to the plastic compound. This is used to package non-static-sensitive components packed in proximity to static-sensitive components.

GUIDELINES FOR PROTECTING COMPONENTS FROM ESD DAMAGE

Here are some guidelines to help you protect your electronic components from ESD damage.

ESD PROTECTION

Follow these guidelines to protect electronic components from damage due to ESD:

- Use proper component handling and storage procedures whenever you are performing PC maintenance work.
- To protect components and equipment from ESD damage:
  - Make sure that your body and clothing are drained of static electricity before starting work.
  - If possible, work in an uncarpeted area.
  - The simplest (but least effective) means of self-grounding is to touch an unpainted metal part of the PC, such as the power supply unit, before you handle a sensitive component. This is only a temporary solution and a static charge could build up again.

 Caution: Do not leave the PC plugged in if you open the case for servicing. Your safety is more important than the risk of damaging some PC components.

  - Where possible, handle vulnerable components by holding the edges of the plastic mounting card, and avoid touching the surfaces of the chips themselves.
- Use ESD wrist or ankle straps and dissipative floor mats.

 Note: Ensure that the strap has a working current-limiting resistor for safety (straps should be tested daily). Do not use a grounding plug if there is any suspicion of a fault in the socket or in the building's electrical wiring, or if the wiring is not regularly inspected and tested.

Topic B
Environmental Impacts and Controls

 EXAM OBJECTIVES COVERED
1002-4.5 Explain environmental impacts and appropriate controls.
1002-4.3 Given a scenario, implement basic disaster prevention and recovery methods.

While you explored personal safety previously, there is also the issue of environmental impacts on computer systems to consider. Computers need stable power supplies and are sensitive to excessive heat. As a CompTIA A+ technician, you must understand the use of controls to ensure the proper environmental conditions for IT systems.

POWER ISSUES

Environmental power problems such as surges, brownouts, and blackouts are caused by failures in the building power supply, rather than failures in the computer's power supply unit, AC adapter, or battery pack.

SURGES

A **surge** is an abrupt but brief change in the value of the voltage. It can last from a few billionths of a second (a transient) to a few thousandths of a second. A **spike** is a powerful surge, such as that caused by a lightning storm. A surge or spike can be caused by high power devices, such as machinery, being turned on or off. Many surges are very small and of too short a duration to cause problems, but some can take the supply several hundred volts over its normal value and cause sufficient interference to a computer's power supply to crash, reboot, or even damage it.

SAGS/BROWNOUTS

Some electrically powered devices require very high starting, or inrush, current. These include items with large motors, such as lifts, washing machines, or power tools, and transformers. When this kind of device is turned on, the large current surge into the device may cause the available voltage within the locality to dip for a brief period, causing a **sag**. Sags may also be caused by the switching of power distribution circuits by the generating companies. A power sag may only last for a few milliseconds but sags of longer than about 10 to 20 milliseconds can cause computer equipment to malfunction. If a sag lasts for longer than a second, it is often called a **brownout**. Overloaded or faulty building power distribution circuits sometimes cause brownouts.

BLACKOUTS

A complete power failure is called a **blackout**. A blackout may be caused by a disruption to the power distribution grid—an equipment failure or the accidental cutting of a cable during construction work, for example—or may simply happen because a fuse has blown or a circuit breaker has tripped.

POWER PROTECTION CONTROLS

Computing devices of all types, including client systems, network appliances, and servers, require a stable power supply to operate. Electrical events such as voltage spikes or surges can crash computers and network appliances, while loss of power from brownouts or blackouts will cause equipment to fail. A range of power protection devices is available to mitigate these issues.

SURGE PROTECTOR

Passive protection devices can be used to filter out the effects of spikes and surges. The simplest **surge protector** or suppression devices come in the form of adapters, trailing sockets, or filter plugs, with the protection circuitry built into the unit. These devices offer low-cost protection to one or two pieces of equipment. Surge protectors are rated according to various national and international standards, including Underwriters Laboratory (UL) 1449. There are three important characteristics:

- **Clamping voltage**—defines the level at which the protection circuitry will activate, with lower voltages (400 V or 300 V) offering better protection.
- **Joules rating**—the amount of energy the surge protector can absorb, with 600 joules or more offering better protection. Each surge event will degrade the capability of the suppressor.
- **Amperage**—the maximum current that can be carried, or basically the number of devices you can attach. As a general rule of thumb, you should only use 80% of the rated capacity. For example, the devices connected to a 15 A protector should be drawing no more than 12 A. Of course, for domestic wiring, you should take care not to overload the building's power circuits in any case.

LINE CONDITIONERS

Larger industrial power filter units called **line conditioners** or **Power Distribution Units (PDUs)** can be used to protect entire power circuits from the effects of surges or brownouts, but they are unable to remove or reduce the effects of blackouts.

BATTERY BACKUPS AND UPS

Power redundancy means deploying systems to ensure that equipment is protected against blackout events so that both system and network operations can either continue uninterrupted or be recovered quickly. If there is loss of power, system operation can be sustained for a few minutes or hours, depending on load, by using **battery backup**. Battery backup can be provisioned at the component level for disk drives, RAID arrays, and memory modules. The battery protects any read or write operations cached at the time of power loss.

At the system level, an **Uninterruptible Power Supply (UPS)** will provide a temporary power source in the event of complete power loss. The time allowed by a UPS is sufficient to activate an alternative power source, such as a standby generator. If there is no alternative power source, a UPS will at least allow you to shut down the server or appliance properly. Users can save files and the operating system can complete the proper shutdown routines.

Example of a UPS. (Image by magraphics© 123RF.com.)

UPS SIZING

In its simplest form, a UPS comprises a bank of batteries and their charging circuit, plus an inverter to generate AC voltage from the DC voltage supplied by the batteries. The capacity of the battery cells determines the amount of run-time a UPS can supply to any given load. This may range from a few minutes for a desktop-rated model to hours for an enterprise system. The power supplies in the computer equipment are connected to the ports on the UPS, then the UPS is connected to building power. There may also be a USB connection to facilitate monitoring and automated shutdown.

Factors to consider when purchasing a UPS include reliability, cost, uptime, maintenance, and system performance and features. Different UPS models support different power outputs and form factors, such as desktop or rack mounted, depending upon your needs. Determining an appropriate UPS to protect the load from a given system is called **UPS sizing**.

The maximum power rating (and hence cost) of a UPS is determined by the battery specification and the power handling of the inverter and other circuitry. Each UPS is rated according to the maximum VA (power) it can supply without overloading.

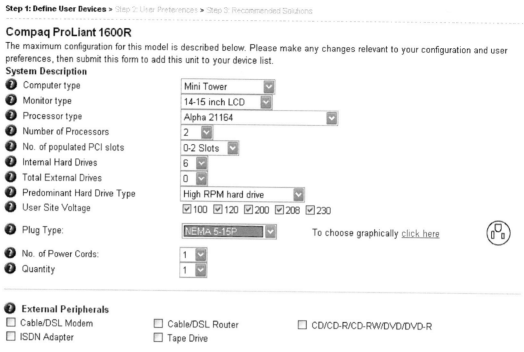

Choosing the UPS—defining the computer and peripherals.

To calculate the required VA rating for a UPS, simply add up the VA ratings of all the equipment to be connected to the unit. These may be calculated by taking the number of watts used by each device and multiplying by 1.67.

Note: The 1.67 conversion factor is required because the power drawn by a component in a DC circuit is not the same as the power required from the AC circuit. This is caused by the operation of the capacitors in the PC power supply unit.

Most UPS vendor websites have a configuration wizard, which you can complete to determine what the power output you require is and the UPS models that would suit. You can also specify the maximum duration of battery power (10 minutes, for instance), which enables you to determine how much charge the unit must be able to hold to supply your needs.

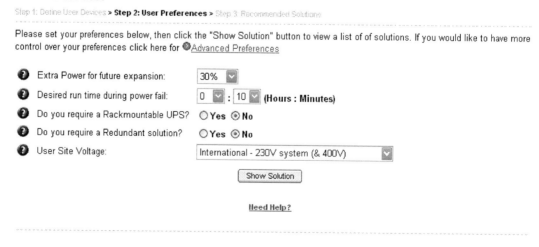

Defining the power requirements.

ENVIRONMENTAL IMPACTS

The environment in which computer equipment is kept can affect its proper operation and lifespan. All electronic equipment should be kept away from extremes of temperature and damp or dusty conditions. Regular inspection and cleaning of a PC's components and inspection of its surroundings may increase the Mean Time Between Failure (**MTBF**) of many components.

DUST AND DEBRIS

Dust (**airborne particles**) is drawn into the computer via ventilation holes. Over time, the dust can form a thick layer over components and ventilation slots, preventing effective heat dissipation. It can clog up peripherals such as keyboards and mice. Dust and smears can make the display hard to read.

Dust can be controlled by cleaning, but you can also deploy controls to ensure that the surrounding environment is clean. Many buildings have environmental control systems with filters that can reduce the amount of dust in the air.

The PC chassis may be designed to protect internal components from airborne particles. For example, fan inlets can be protected by **air or dust filters**. These polyester sheets trap dust on their surface. If using filters, make sure they are cleaned or replaced periodically or they will clog up and prevent air circulating in the PC.

If the environment is particularly dusty, the whole PC can be placed within an **enclosure** with its own air filters and fans.

TEMPERATURE, HUMIDITY, AND VENTILATION

Excessive heat can make a computer unreliable. Computers generate plenty of heat just by running. Obviously a personal computer will be situated in an environment where the temperature is comfortable for humans (around 20°C/68°F). Do check the precise location of the PC though—direct sunlight or proximity to a radiator can cause heat to build up too easily. You must ensure that there is space for air to flow around the case, especially around the ventilation slots.

High humidity—the amount of water vapor in the air—can cause condensation to form. On the other hand, low humidity allows static charges to build up more easily and increases the risk of Electrostatic Discharge (ESD). The ideal level is around 50%.

Condensation can form as a result of sudden warming. When installing new equipment that has just been delivered, it is important to leave it in its packaging for a few hours—depending on the outside temperature—to allow it to adjust to room temperature gradually.

A **Heating, Ventilation, Air Conditioning (HVAC)** system ensures adequate cooling and humidity and dust control within a room or other enclosed space. All air flow into and out of the room is run through ducts, fans, and filters and warmed or cooled to the correct temperature and humidity.

GENERAL PREVENTIVE MAINTENANCE

Regular maintenance can increase the lifespan of equipment, but can also be time-consuming. You may want to consider providing cleaning materials and procedures to users and training them to perform these tasks themselves. To ensure that these tasks are performed regularly, you can also provide them with a schedule as suggested in the following table.

Frequency	Checks
Daily	• Check that nothing is obstructing the ventilation slots of the system unit. • Check that the equipment is installed securely—for example, not positioned near desk edges, no cable trip hazards, no overloaded power points, no damaged cabling, and so on. • Also ensure that there are no liquid hazards (chance of spills).
Weekly	• Clean the exterior of the monitor and system unit. • Clean the keyboard and mouse.
Monthly	• Check that fans are functioning correctly. • Check that all cables are correctly seated and secured to the system unit and peripherals.

It is important to control the build-up of dust (and clean up spills), but it is also important not to use household cleaning products for PC maintenance. Do not blow away dust with your mouth, as moisture may land on electronic components!

 Note: Always power off the computer and disconnect any devices before cleaning them.

MASK AND GLOVES

A **mask** that fits over your mouth and nose should be worn when you are using a compressed air canister, working around toner spills, or working in an otherwise dusty environment. A mask minimizes the risk of inhaling damaging airborne particles. You should also wear latex **gloves** when cleaning up a toner spill.

COMPRESSED AIR

Use a **compressed air blaster** to dislodge dust from difficult to reach areas. Take care with use, however, as you risk contaminating the environment with dust. Ideally, perform this sort of maintenance within a controlled work area and wear an appropriate air filter mask. Also consider wearing safety goggles to minimize the risk of irritating your eyes with dust.

 Note: Do not use compressed air blasters to clean up a toner spill or a laser printer within an office-type area. You will blow fine toner dust into the atmosphere and create a health hazard.

Use caution when working with compressed air. Read the instructions on the can and follow them carefully. Tipping the can too much can cause the propellant to leave the can in liquid form and at sub-freezing temperatures. The freezing could easily damage components, particularly those that may still be hot from use. There is also the issue of the corrosiveness of the chemical damaging components later on. Also, some delicate components on the motherboard can be damaged—literally blown off the board—if compressed air is used too close to a component.

VACUUMS

Use a PC vacuum cleaner or natural bristle brush to remove dust from inside the system unit, especially from the motherboard, adapter cards, and fan assemblies. Home appliances should not be used, as they can produce high levels of static electricity. PC-safe vacuums can often be used to blow air as well as for suction, so they can replace the need for compressed air canisters for blowing dust out of machines.

Sucking the dust up is usually better, though, since blowing the dust can cause it to get onto or into other components.

> **Note:** *A PC vacuum can be used to deal with toner spills if the filter and bag are fine enough to contain toner particles. Such vacuums should be labeled "toner safe." Ideally, move the printer to a maintenance room with filters to contain airborne particles. Alternatively, a toner cloth is a special cloth that you stretch that picks up toner particles that are either in the printer or around the printer. Be careful if you are using it inside the printer so that the cloth does not get caught on any components and leave fibers behind.*

PERIPHERAL DEVICE AND LAPTOP MAINTENANCE

Peripheral and mobile devices receive the most wear and tear and require the most regular cleaning to keep them working properly.

There are several types of wipes and cloths that you can use to clean displays, keyboards, and other equipment. These use an appropriate cleaning solution for the type of plastic or surface coating that you are cleaning. They should also be non-abrasive and lint-free so that cleaning does not cause scratches or leave behind stray fibers.

MOUSE

Mice suffer from build-up of grease and dust around the buttons and scroll wheel and need regular cleaning. To ensure that the mouse functions correctly, you should use it on a clean, flat surface, such as that provided by a proper mouse mat.

KEYBOARD

Ensure that keyboards are not used in an environment where food and beverages are present, as spillage of these substances can cause the keyboard to malfunction and make it difficult to clean. You can use a compressed air canister, PC vacuum cleaner, or natural bristle brush to clean debris from a keyboard then wipe down the surfaces with a lint-free cloth and approved cleaner. Tightly wound cotton swabs or toothpicks are useful when trying to get dust and debris out from between keys and around buttons or other tight areas.

DISPLAY

The display screen should be kept clean and free of smears to avoid eyestrain when using the computer for prolonged periods. If the screen requires more than dusting, use an approved display screen cleaner, spraying the cleaner onto the cloth or pad, not onto the screen. You can also obtain pre-moistened wipes. You must use approved cleaning products and a non-abrasive cloth to avoid damaging the screen's anti-glare coating. The products are also formulated to provide anti-static protection against further dust buildup. When cleaning the screen, wipe horizontally across the screen and then vertically. Do not forget to clean into the screen corners.

LAPTOP MAINTENANCE ISSUES

Laptops are typically used in dirtier environments than desktops. Despite the name, it is important to encourage users to put the laptop on a firm, flat surface during use, to allow the cooling fan and vent on the bottom to work properly. These vents should be cleaned regularly using a PC-approved vacuum cleaner or compressed air. For actual "laptop" use, it is best to provide a chiller pad or mat to provide air flow and (with active chiller pads) extra USB-powered fans for cooling.

Compressed air can also be used to clean the keyboard. The screen, touchpad, and case can be cleaned using a soft cloth and approved cleaning solution.

DISPOSAL, RECYCLING, AND COMPLIANCE

Even with procedures in place to properly maintain IT equipment, eventually it will need to be decommissioned and either disposed of or recycled. IT equipment contains numerous components and materials that can cause environmental damage if they are disposed of as ordinary refuse.

COMPLIANCE AND GOVERNMENTAL REGULATIONS

In the United States and many other nations, your employer is obligated to comply with governmental regulations that apply to its specific business. The most common regulations are those issued by the federal government, such as the Occupational Safety and Health Administration (OSHA), and state standards regarding employee safety. OSHA-compliant employers must provide:

- A workplace that is free from recognized hazards that could cause serious physical harm.
- Personal protective equipment designed to protect employees from certain hazards.
- Communication—in the form of labeling, Material Safety Data Sheets (MSDSs), and training about hazardous materials.

Your responsibility—to yourself, your employer, your coworkers, and your customers—is to be informed of potential hazards and to always use safe practices.

Protection of the environment is another area that is regulated by the federal and local governments in the United States and many other nations. Many municipalities have regulations that control the disposal of certain types of computer equipment. Your responsibility is to be aware of any environmental controls that are applicable to your workplace, and to be in compliance with those regulations.

Materials safety and environmental legislation require that environmental hazards be disposed of correctly. In the US, environmental matters are the responsibility of the Environmental Protection Agency (EPA).

MSDS DOCUMENTATION

Employers are obliged to assess the risk to their workforce from hazardous substances at work and to take steps to eliminate or control that risk. No work with hazardous substances should take place unless an assessment has been made. Employees are within their rights to refuse to work with hazardous substances that have not been assessed.

Suppliers of chemicals are required to identify the hazards associated with the substances they supply. Some hazard information will be provided on labels, but the supplier must also provide more detailed information on a **Material Safety Data Sheet (MSDS)**.

An MSDS will contain information about:

- Ingredients.
- Health hazards, precautions, and first aid information.
- What to do if the material is spilled or leaks.
- How to recycle any waste product or dispose of it safely.

You may need to refer to an MSDS in the course of handling monitors, power supplies, batteries, laser printer toner, and cleaning products. If handling devices that are broken or leaking, use appropriate protective gear, such as gloves, safety goggles, and an air filter mask.

SAFETY DATA SHEET

Date of issue/Date of revision   **16 July 2018**
Version 9.01

Section 1. Identification

Product name	: Metal Cleaner
Product code	: DX579
Other means of identification	: Not available.
Product type	: Liquid.

Relevant identified uses of the substance or mixture and uses advised against

Product use	: Industrial applications.
Use of the substance/ mixture	: Coating. Paints. Painting-related materials.

An example of MSDS documentation.

Topic C

Create and Maintain Documentation

 EXAM OBJECTIVES COVERED
1002-4.1 Compare and contrast best practices associated with types of documentation.

There are many reasons for creating and maintaining documentation. A big reason is so that in case of a disaster, you already have critical documentation in place that will help you rebuild as quickly as possible. Without detailed documentation, you would have to rely on memory to determine your network layout, which would likely be very time consuming, costly, and ultimately inaccurate. A complete set of configuration documentation will give you a solid base from which you can begin rebuilding individual workstations, servers, and your network.

You should also document organizational policies. By identifying common organizational policies and procedures that deal with computer use, you will be more capable of dealing with compliance issues as they arise and protecting organizational resources.

EQUIPMENT INVENTORY

It is crucial for an organization to have a well-documented inventory of its tangible and intangible assets and resources. This should include all hardware that is currently deployed as well as spare systems and components kept on hand in case of component or system failure. In terms of network management, these will include network appliances (routers, switches, threat management devices, access points), servers, workstations, and passive network infrastructure (cabling and cross-connects).

There are many software suites and associated hardware solutions available for tracking and managing **assets** (or inventory). An asset management database can be configured to store as much or as little information as is deemed necessary, though typical data would be type, model, serial number, asset ID, location, user(s), value, and service information. Tangible assets can be identified using a **barcode label** or **Radio Frequency ID (RFID) tag** attached to the device (or more simply using an identification number). An RFID tag is a chip programmed with asset data. When in range of a scanner, the chip powers up and signals the scanner. The scanner alerts management software to update the device's location. As well as asset tracking, this allows the management software to track the location of the device, making theft more difficult.

For each asset record there should also be a copy of or link to the appropriate vendor documentation. This would include both an invoice and warranty/support contract and support and troubleshooting guidance.

IT **asset management** is the set of management policies that include information about the financial and contractual specifications of all the hardware and software components present in an organization's inventory. Some organizations have exclusive asset management for hardware and software components. As part of inventory management, use the system life cycle to determine whether the items in the inventory need to be retired or replaced. Use proper asset disposal methods when removing assets from inventory. Critical hardware and software inventory provides insurance documentation and helps determine what you need to rebuild the network.

Inventory Entry	Hardware/ Software	Information to Include
Standard workstation	Hardware	A basic description of a standard client workstation. Include minimum requirements and the installed operating system as well as how many workstations of this type are deployed. For workstations that deviate from the norm, be sure to document the deviations.
Specialty workstation	Hardware	A description of any specialty workstations deployed. Include a brief description of their roles and special configurations implemented on them.
Server	Hardware	A list of the basic server hardware configuration and the role of these servers. List their internal hardware and any special configuration settings and software. Include a configuration list for the operating system.
Connectivity hardware	Hardware	A list of all connectivity hardware in as much detail as possible. This includes the device brand and model numbers, but a description of each feature ensures that replacements can be made without research.
Backup hardware	Hardware	Document critical information about backup hardware, such as the vendor and model number of a tape drive, backup hard drives, DVD drives, and network attached storage, if applicable.
Operating system software	Software	All operating system software, including desktop and server operating systems. Include documentation on licensing and copies of the bulk licenses, if possible. Many vendors retain records of software licenses sold to their customers. If this is the case, include this fact in your documentation.
Productivity and application software	Software	Off-the-shelf productivity software, including any applications installed on client devices and servers.
Maintenance utilities	Software	The utilities used to maintain a network, especially backup software and software configuration.
Backup documentation	Software	Records of when backups were made, how frequently to make them, what backups contain, where backups are stored, and credentials needed to restore backups. Document the backup software and version. Special setup and configuration considerations need to be documented, too.

Inventory Entry	Hardware/ Software	Information to Include
Overall asset inventory	Software	If your company maintains an overall asset inventory, attach a copy. Many companies use the inventory as a base to track hardware and maintenance. This usually includes most of the information needed.

NETWORK TOPOLOGY DIAGRAMS

Diagrams are the best way to capture the complex relationships between network elements. They are also the most effective means of locating particular items within the network. Diagrams can be used to model physical and logical relationships at different levels of scale and detail. These relationships are described as the **network topology**.

SCHEMATIC BLOCK DIAGRAM

A **schematic** is a simplified representation of the network topology. In terms of the **physical** network topology, it can show the general placement of equipment and telecommunications rooms plus device and port IDs without trying to capture the exact position or relative size of any one element. Schematics can also be used to represent the **logical** structure of the network in terms of security zones, VLANs, and subnets.

Schematics can either be drawn manually using a tool such as Microsoft® Visio® or compiled automatically from network mapping software.

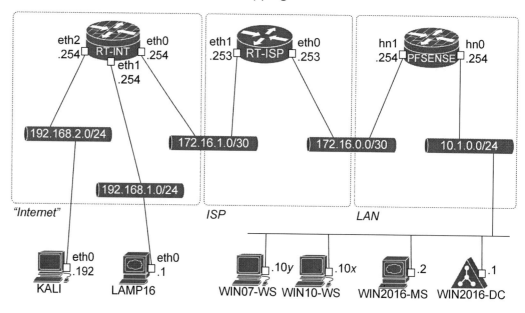

Use a tool such as Visio to create network diagrams.

REFERENCE DOCUMENTATION

There are several types of documentation and resources that you might find helpful when you are dealing with common hardware and operating system problems. You can also share documentation and resources with users as a means of assisting and educating them.

Resource	Description
User/installation manuals	User and installation manuals can provide you with basic guidance for installing, configuring, and troubleshooting hardware and software.
	By providing users with various user and installation manuals, users can fix minor issues and problems before requesting additional assistance from a technician. Examples include installing company-specific applications, installing network printers, and mapping drives.
Internet/web-based resources	Internet and web-based resources can provide a wealth of information on installing, configuring, and troubleshooting hardware and software. Many hardware and software manufacturers maintain **knowledge bases (KBs)** and **wikis** to share information about both common and unusual issues that can arise with PC hardware and software.
	Articles written by industry leaders, by support professionals, and by vendors can be a good source of information. Be sure to take into consideration who wrote the article and any verifiable credentials so you can determine the legitimacy of the article content.
	Internet and web-based materials can also provide users with quick reference materials for dealing with everyday issues on their own. Some organizations provide a web page or wiki with user-specific information and reference materials.
Training materials	Most major hardware and software manufacturers provide training materials on how to install and use their products. These materials can be helpful for both new and experienced technicians.
	You can provide training materials for various tasks that users may need to complete on their own, such as virus scans, computer maintenance tasks, and PC clean-up tasks. By providing training materials, you empower users to be proactive in maintaining their systems.

INCIDENT DOCUMENTATION

A piece of software that can be considered part of your support toolkit is a tracking database where incidents that occur can be documented. There are different kinds of incidents, with different reporting requirements. One type of incident is for troubleshooting or support requests. Each support incident will be logged as a job or ticket within the incident management system. The following information will form the core of a job ticket:

Information	Notes
Job ID	Job IDs are often referred to as tickets.
Contact	Name, organization, department, email address, telephone number. In a database, the job could be linked to a contact record.
Priority	Assessed from caller's description and customer's service level.

Information	Notes
Problem description	Including information about platform (hardware, OS, application [including version and update number]), and what the user was doing.
Asset	Hardware component or software application associated with the problem, linked to an asset management database.
Details	What was attempted during the first contact.
Follow up	Date and description of follow up actions.
Dates	Dates when the ticket was opened, updated, and closed.

Security incident reporting needs to capture some of the same information but will normally be handled by a dedicated security response team. Reports of actual or suspected security policy violations will initially be processed by a first responder. The report will log the location and time of the incident plus systems affected and the actors and methods used to perform the intrusion. It is important to identify whether any data breach has occurred and what sort of notification must be made for regulatory or compliance purposes. The contents of security incident reports must be kept confidential and access granted on a need-to-know basis only.

Sample incident report.

Accidents represent another type of incident reporting requirement. An **accident** is any instance where a person is injured or computer equipment is damaged due to environmental issues. The report is also used for accidents involving hazardous materials, such as chemical spills, that could have an impact on the environment. Any time an accident occurs at a work site, you should submit an incident report. Reporting these occurrences is often part of company policy and can help provide protection against liability.

Incident documentation might use a simple spreadsheet or database, or it might be a complex help desk management tracking application; it all depends on the needs of your organization. **Incident management** includes the practices and procedures that govern how an organization will respond to an incident in progress.

ORGANIZATIONAL POLICIES

As a vital component of a company's IT infrastructure, employees must understand how to use computers and networked services securely and safely and be aware of their responsibilities. To support this, the organization needs to create written policies and procedures to help staff understand and fulfill their responsibilities and follow best practice.

STANDARDS, PROCEDURES, AND GUIDANCE

A **policy** is an overall statement of intent. In order to establish the correct working practices, three different mechanisms can be put in place.

Policy Type	Description
Standard	A standard is a measure by which to evaluate compliance with the policy.
Procedure	A procedure, often referred to as a **Standard Operating Procedure (SOP)**, is an inflexible, step-by-step listing of the actions that must be completed for any given task. Most critical tasks should be governed by SOPs.
Guidelines	Guidelines exist for areas of policy where there are no procedures, either because the situation has not been fully assessed or because the decision making process is too complex and subject to variables to be able to capture it in a procedure. Guidelines may also describe circumstances where it is appropriate to deviate from a specified procedure.

POLICY ENFORCEMENT

It is not enough to just have standards and policies. Your organization and its employees and contractors need to adhere to them as well. For employees and contractors, this requires that they read the standards and policies, and understand that they need to follow them. For the organization, it also needs to follow the standards and policies, regardless of who is acting on the organization's behalf. In addition, the organization may also have regulatory compliance and additional adherence to laws, regulations, guidelines, and specifications relevant to its business. Violations of regulatory compliance regulations often result in legal punishment, including federal fines.

PERSONNEL MANAGEMENT POLICIES

Human Resources (HR) is the department tasked with recruiting and managing the organization's most valuable and critical resource: people. Personnel management policies can be conceived as applying in three phases.

Phase	Description
Recruitment or hiring	Recruitment involves locating then selecting and hiring people to work in particular job roles. Security issues here include screening candidates and performing background checks.
Operation or working	It is often the HR department that manages the communication of policy and training to employees, though there may be a separate training and personal development department within larger organizations. As such, it is critical that HR managers devise training programs that communicate the importance of security to employees.
Termination or separation	Whether an employee leaves voluntarily or involuntarily, termination is a difficult process, with numerous security implications. An employee might be fired, retired, or simply be moving on to another job at another organization.

Operational policies include privilege management, data/information handling, incident response, and use of company devices and services such as Internet access. One function of HR is to draft and communicate these written policies to employees, including any updates to the policies. Another function is to enforce disciplinary measures, perhaps in conjunction with departmental managers.

PASSWORD POLICIES

A **password policy** defines standards for creating password complexity. It also defines what an organization considers weak passwords and the guidelines for protecting password safety. It specifies standards such as avoiding common passwords, how to create strong passwords, and rules for not using work-related passwords for other sites or services.

ACCEPTABLE USE POLICIES

An **Acceptable Use Policy (AUP)**, or **Fair Use Policy**, sets out what someone is allowed to use a particular service or resource for. Such a policy might be used in different contexts. For example, an AUP could be enforced by a business to govern how employees use equipment and services such as telephone or Internet access provided to them at work. Another example might be an ISP enforcing a fair use policy governing usage of its Internet access services. Enforcing an acceptable use policy is important to protect the organization from the security and legal implications of employees (or customers) misusing its equipment. Typically, the policy will forbid the use of equipment to defraud, defame, or to obtain illegal material. It is also likely to prohibit the installation of unauthorized hardware or software and to explicitly forbid actual or attempted intrusion (snooping). An organization's acceptable use policy may forbid use of Internet tools outside of work-related duties or restrict such use to break times.

AUPs often include policies for the items listed in the following table.

An AUP Policy for	Covers
Rules of Behavior	The equipment used to access the Internet in the workplace is owned by the employer. Many employees expect relatively unrestricted access to Internet facilities for personal use. In fact, employees' use of social networking and file sharing poses substantial risks to the organization, including threat of virus infection or systems intrusion, lost work time, copyright infringement, and defamation. If an employee breaks copyright laws or libels someone using an organization's equipment, the organization itself could be held liable.
	To avoid confusion, an employee's handbook should set out the terms under which use of web browser/email/social networking/P2P software is permitted for personal use, and what penalties infringements could incur. Employers are within their rights to prohibit all private use of Internet services.
	Users should be aware that any data communications, such as email, made through an organization's computer system are liable to be stored within the system, on servers, backup devices, and so on. Consequently, employees should not use computers at work to send personal information, for their own security and privacy if nothing else.
Use of Personally Owned Devices in the Workplace	Portable devices such as smartphones, USB thumb drives, media players, and so on pose a considerable threat to data security as they facilitate file copying. Camera and voice recording functions are other obvious security issues.
	Network access control/endpoint security and data loss prevention solutions can be of some use in preventing the attachment of such devices to corporate networks. Some companies may try to prevent staff from bringing such devices on site. This is quite difficult to enforce, though.

GUIDELINES FOR CREATING AND MAINTAINING DOCUMENTATION

Here are some guidelines to follow when creating and maintaining your documentation.

CREATE AND MAINTAIN DOCUMENTATION

Consider the following guidelines for creating and maintaining documentation.

- Keep an accurate record of the equipment and software within the organization, including:
  - Deployed hardware, both complete systems and components.
  - Deployed software, both applications and operating systems.
  - Spare hardware, both complete systems and components.
  - Software that is not currently installed, both applications and operating systems.
- Use asset tags, either printed barcodes or RFID tags, to track equipment.
- Each asset record should include a copy of or link to the appropriate vendor documentation.
- Document network components through the use of schematic block diagrams showing physical and logical network structure.
- Maintain a library of reference documentation, including:
  - User and installation manuals.

- Links to Internet and web-based resources.
- Training materials.
- Document incidents through the use of standardized incident reports.
- Create and maintain organizational policies. This should include:
  - Personnel management policies.
  - Policy on how to handle confidential information.
  - Acceptable use policies.

Topic D

Use Basic Change Management Best Practices

EXAM OBJECTIVES COVERED
1002-4.2 Given a scenario, implement basic change management best practices.

Practically every technical deployment will face unforeseen issues. The IT project team members should address unexpected changes by using a process that keeps stakeholders informed and that minimizes impact on the overall project, especially the project's timelines and goals.

CHANGE MANAGEMENT

Configuration management means identifying all components of the information and communications technology (ICT) infrastructure (hardware, software, and procedures) and their properties. **Change management** means putting policies in place to reduce the risk that changes to these components could cause service disruption (network downtime).

ITIL CONFIGURATION MANAGEMENT MODEL

IT Infrastructure Library (ITIL®) is a popular documentation of good and best practice activities and processes for delivering IT services. Under ITIL, configuration management is implemented using the following elements:

- Service assets are things, processes, or people that contribute to the delivery of an IT service.
- A **Configuration Item (CI)** is an asset that requires specific management procedures for it to be used to deliver the service. Each CI must be identified by some sort of label. CIs are defined by their attributes, which are stored in a **Configuration Management Database (CMDB)**.
- **Baseline** is a fundamental concept in configuration management. The baseline represents "the way it was." A baseline can be a configuration baseline (the ACL applied to a firewall, for instance) or a performance baseline (such as the throughput achieved by a server).
- A **Configuration Management System (CMS)** is the tools and databases that collect, store, manage, update, and present information about CIs. A small network might capture this information in spreadsheets and diagrams; there are dedicated applications for enterprise CMS.

One of the goals of the CMS is to understand the relationships between CIs. Another is to track changes to CI attributes (and therefore variance from the baseline) over time. The purpose of documentation in terms of change and configuration management is as follows:

- Identify each component (CI) and label it.
- Capture each CI and its (relevant) attributes in a CMDB.
- Capture relationships between CIs. This is best done using diagrams.
- Capture changes to a CI as a job log and update the CMDB.

DOCUMENTING CHANGES

Each individual system, server, and network component should have a separate document that describes its initial state and all subsequent changes. This document includes configuration information, a list of patches applied, backup records, and even details about suspected breaches. Printouts of hash results, last modification dates of critical system files, and contents of log files may be pasted into this book. System maintenance can be made much smoother with a comprehensive change document. For instance, when a patch is available for an operating system, it typically applies in only certain situations. Manually investigating the applicability of a patch on every possible target system can be very time consuming; however, if logs are available for reference, the process is much faster and more accurate.

 Note: An example of change management documentation that you can use as a starting point when creating this document for your organization can be found at https:// www.sans.org/summit-archives/file/summit-archive-1493830822.pdf.

DOCUMENTED BUSINESS PROCESSES

Depending on the needs of your organization, you might need general business processes to be documented, or you might need every single thing that happens throughout the workday documented. The latter usually applies to businesses that need FDA or other governmental approval to produce and sell goods and services. At the minimum, you should document changes made to systems such as when a new employee comes on board or when an employee leaves and what happens to their hardware and software when those events occur. You will also want to document how various tasks are completed throughout the organization, including how systems are configured, how the network is configured, what criteria is required for making changes to any equipment that is deployed, how and when to replace equipment, and many other aspects of having an organization filled with computing devices.

SOPs AND WORK INSTRUCTIONS

The main difficulty in implementing a workable configuration management system is in determining the level of detail that must be preserved. This is not only evident in capturing the asset database and configuration baseline in the first place, but also in managing **Moves, Adds, and Changes (MACs)** within the organization's computing infrastructure. In terms of computing tasks, a CMS will require that configuration changes be made only when there is a valid job ticket authorizing the change. This means that the activity of all computer support personnel, whether it be installing new devices or troubleshooting, is recorded in job logs. In a fully documented environment, each task will be governed by some sort of procedure. Formal configuration management models often distinguish between two types of procedural documentation:

- A **Standard Operating Procedure (SOP)** sets out the principal goals and considerations (such as budget, security, or customer contact standards) for performing a task and identifies lines of responsibility and authorization for performing it.
- A **Work instruction** is step-by-step instructions for performing an installation or configuration task using a specific product or technology and credentials.

CHANGE MANAGEMENT DOCUMENTATION

To reduce the risk that changes to configuration items will cause service disruption, a documented management process can be used to **plan for change** in a planned and controlled way. Change requests are usually generated when something needs to be corrected, new business needs or processes are identified, or there is room for improvement in a process or system currently in place. The need to change is often described either as reactive, where the change is forced on the organization, or as proactive, where the need for change is initiated internally. Changes can also be categorized according to their potential impact and level of risk (major, significant, minor, or normal, for instance).

In a formal change management process, the need or reasons for change and the procedure for implementing the change is captured in a **Request for Change (RFC)** document and submitted for approval.

Change request documentation should include:

- The purpose of the change.
- The scope of the change.
- A risk analysis of both performing the change and not performing the requested change.
- A documented plan for carrying out the change.
- A method to acquire end-user acceptance that the change was performed to their satisfaction and that the change was properly implemented.
- A **backout plan** in case unforeseen problems arise when the change is made.
- Document all changes that were made.

CHANGE BOARD APPROVAL

The RFC will then be considered at the appropriate level and affected stakeholders will be notified. This might be a supervisor or department manager if the change is normal or minor. Major or significant changes might be managed as a separate project and require approval through a **Change Advisory Board (CAB)**.

PROCESS FOR INSTITUTING CHANGE TO OPERATIONAL POLICIES AND PROCEDURES

Regardless of whether an organization is large enough to require formal change management procedures and staff, the implementation of changes should be carefully planned, with consideration for how the change will affect dependent components. For most significant or major changes, organizations should attempt a trial implementation of the change first. Every change should be accompanied by a rollback (or backout) plan, so that the change can be reversed if it has harmful or unforeseen consequences. Changes should also be scheduled sensitively if they are likely to cause system downtime or other negative impact on the workflow of the business units that depend on the IT system being modified. Most organizations have a scheduled maintenance window period for authorized downtime.

When the change has been implemented, its impact should be assessed and the process reviewed and documented to identify any outcomes that could help future change management projects.

GUIDELINES FOR USING CHANGE MANAGEMENT BEST PRACTICES

Here are some best practices to follow regarding change management.

USE CHANGE MANAGEMENT BEST PRACTICES

Consider these best practices guidelines for using change management.

- Create a separate document for each individual system, server, and network component that describes its initial state and all subsequent changes. This document includes:
  - Configuration information
  - Applied patch list

- Record of backups
- Details about suspected security breaches
- Configuration management using ITIL should be implemented using:
  - Service assets
  - Configuration items
  - Configuration Management Database (CMDB)
  - Baselines
  - Configuration Management System
- Document the need or desire for a change using an RFC document.
- RFCs should be considered at the appropriate level and affected stakeholders notified.
- Major or significant changes might be managed as a separate project and require approval through a Change Advisory Board (CAB).
- Follow documented SOPs and Work Instructions when performing moves, adds, and changes.
- Implementation of changes should be carefully planned, with consideration for how the change will affect dependent components.
- For most significant or major changes, organizations should attempt to trial the change first.
- Every change should be accompanied by a rollback (or remediation) plan.
- Changes should also be scheduled sensitively if they are likely to cause system downtime or other negative impact on workflow.
- When the change has been implemented, its impact should be assessed and the process reviewed and documented to identify any outcomes that could help future change management projects.

Topic E

Implement Disaster Prevention and Recovery Methods

EXAM OBJECTIVES COVERED
1002-4.3 Given a scenario, implement basic disaster prevention and recovery methods.

Ensuring that data, applications, client computers, servers, and other network resources are available to users is part of a computer technician's responsibilities. This can be challenging when hardware fails or a natural disaster strikes. In this topic, you will see how to implement measures related to disaster prevention and recovery.

DISASTER PREVENTION AND RECOVERY

A disaster could be anything from a fairly trivial loss of power or failure of a minor component to man-made or natural disasters, such as fires, earthquakes, or acts of terrorism. An organization sensitive to these risks will develop an effective, documented **Disaster Recovery Plan (DRP)**. This should accomplish the following:

- Identify scenarios for natural and man-made disasters and options for protecting systems.
- Identify tasks, resources, and responsibilities for responding to a disaster.
- Train staff in the disaster planning procedures and how to react well to change.

When a disaster occurs, the failover recovery plan will swing into action to get the failed part of the network operational as soon as possible. If a disk has failed, swap it out. If a network component has failed, remove and replace or repair the component to provide for high reliability as soon as possible. If data becomes corrupted or lost, utilize your restoration plan to recover the data.

DATA BACKUP AND RESTORATION

One of the important tasks you will need to perform as an A+ technician is making sure that users' data and system settings are being backed up in case things go awry.

Data backup is a system maintenance task that enables you to store copies of critical data for safekeeping. Backups protect against loss of data due to disasters such as file corruption or hardware failure. **Data restoration** is a system recovery task that enables you to access the backed-up data. Restored data does not include any changes made to the data after the backup operation. Data backups can be accomplished simply by copying individual files and folders to a local or network location or by using dedicated software and hardware to back up large amounts of data.

Backup operations can be performed at different levels:

- **File level**—this is used to back up user-generated files stored in local profile folders or network shares. Almost all backup software can perform this basic task.
- **Image-level**—this is used to back up an OS and can include third-party software applications, drivers, and custom settings installed under the OS. An image can be used both to restore physical computers and Virtual Machines (VM).

- **Critical applications**—network applications often depend on some sort of database for storage rather than individual file-based storage. Specialist backup software is required to connect to the database. Backups can be made of the whole database or of individual tables and records.

 Note: As well as the application data and settings, make sure you make a backup of product keys and license information. These might be required to restore the application license.

Many devices and user accounts include cloud storage space. If you store your data in a cloud storage site, the onus of performing backups is left to the provider of the cloud space. This data is often also stored on your local storage device, so you have two copies already. Examples include photos and music stored on smart phones being automatically copied to the platform's related cloud storage site such as iCloud® for Apple® devices and Google Drive™ for Android™ devices.

BACKUP MANAGEMENT

The execution and frequency of backups must be carefully planned and guided by policies. Backups are kept back to certain points in time. As backups take up a lot of space, and there is never limitless storage capacity, this introduces the need for storage management routines and techniques to reduce the amount of data occupying backup storage media while giving adequate coverage of the required recovery window. The recovery window is determined by the **Recovery Point Objective (RPO)**, which is determined through business continuity planning.

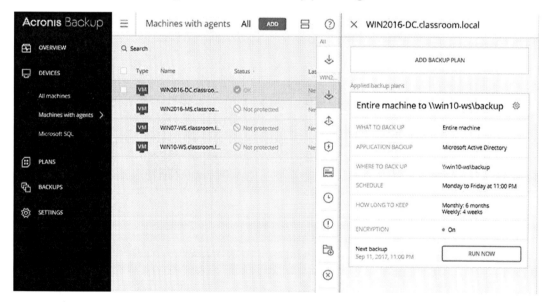

Backing up a domain controller using Acronis backup. The How Long to Keep field specifies the retention period. (Screenshot courtesy of acronis.com.)

Data retention needs to be considered in the short and long term:

- In the short term, files that change frequently might need retaining for version control. Short term retention is also important in recovering from malware infection. Consider the scenario where a backup is made on Monday, a file is infected with a virus on Tuesday, and when that file is backed up later on Tuesday, the copy made on Monday is overwritten. This means that there is no good means of restoring the uninfected file.
- In the long term, data may need to be stored to meet legal requirements or to comply with company policies or industry standards.

A retention policy can either be based on redundancy (the number of copies of each file that should be retained) or on a recovery window (the number of days into the past that should be retained).

BACKUP TYPES

When considering a backup made against an original copy of data, the backup can usually be performed using one of three main types: full, incremental, or differential. In Windows®, a full backup includes all selected files and directories, whereas incremental and differential backups check the status of the archive attribute before including a file. The archive attribute is set whenever a file is modified. This allows backup software to determine which files have been changed and therefore need to be copied.

 Note: *Linux doesn't support a file archive attribute. Instead, a date stamp is used to determine whether the file has changed.*

The following table summarizes the three different backup types.

Type	Data Selection	Backup/Restore Time	Archive Attribute
Full	All selected data regardless of when it was previously backed up	High/low (one tape set)	Cleared
Incremental	New files and files modified since last backup	Low/high (multiple tape sets)	Cleared
Differential	All data modified since the last full backup	Moderate/moderate (no more than 2 sets)	Not Cleared

A typical strategy for a complex network would be a full weekly backup followed by an incremental or differential backup at the end of each day.

- The advantage of using a full daily backup is that one tape set is only required to restore the system.
- The advantage of an incremental backup is that it takes less time to back up, but several tape sets may need to be restored before the system is operational.
- The advantage of a differential backup is the balance of time for both restoring and backing up.

 Caution: *Do not combine differential and incremental backups. Use full backups interspersed with differential backups, or full backups interspersed with incremental backups.*

 Note: *Most software also has the capability to do copy backups. These are made outside the tape rotation system (ad hoc) and do not affect the archive attribute.*

RECOVERY IMAGES

A custom **recovery image** contains the current state of the operating system files, plus all of the desktop applications installed to the boot partition. An image can be used to restore the OS and any critical applications to a workstation or VM in one step. A new image must be created if any additional applications are installed or configuration changes made.

If user account profiles are stored on the same partition or drive as the OS, this user data will be included in the image. As images take a relatively long time to create, it is better to back up user data separately using file level backups. User profiles or home folders might be stored on a network file server to make them easier to back up.

BACKUP TESTING

Before you use a backup to restore data, test it to make sure it's reliable. To test the backup:

- Try restoring some of the backed-up data into a test directory, making sure you don't overwrite any data when doing so.
- Configure the backup software to verify after it writes.
- Verify that the backup contains all the required files.
- Test backup devices and media on a regular basis.

OFF-SITE AND LOCAL STORAGE

Typically, the backups you create are stored off-site. If disaster strikes the facility where your servers are located, you won't lose your backup media as well. You might want to keep a set of backup media on site as well, so that you have instant access to the backups in case files are accidentally deleted or corrupted. For off-site storage, you might use a bank safety deposit box for small organizations, or you might contract with a firm that specializes in securely storing backups. Cloud storage services provide an effective means of storing backed up data off-site. Specialist cloud backup providers allow the scheduling and data transfer all to be managed from the cloud console. For on-site storage, consider using a fireproof safe.

Wherever you decide to keep your backups, environmental considerations must be taken into account. Do not store the backups where there is high heat or humidity, which could damage the backup medium. Be sure not to store the backups near equipment with strong magnets that could erase the data and damage the backup media.

BACKUP STORAGE SECURITY

There are various best practices for ensuring security of backup data. They include:

- Authentication of users and backup clients to the backup server.
- Role based access control lists for all backup and recovery operations.
- Data encryption options for both backup transmission and storage.
- Backup of remote clients to a centralized location behind firewalls.
- Default data storage locations must be standardized.
- Create a policy that defines where documents are backed up from.
- Use segregation of duties enforced by policy for all personnel handling backup data.
- Document all access, testing, backup, and restore cycles.

ACCOUNT RECOVERY

Users are likely to have several different accounts to maintain, each with its own password and login name. Frequently, users will forget the password for an account or there may be some sort of fault preventing use of a smart card or biometric credentials. Usually to recover an account password, you will need to input the answers to one or more **challenge questions** and/or receive a token sent to another trusted device or email account.

If password recovery methods do not work, or if the account profile has been deleted or corrupted, you might need to recreate the account or set up a new account then import any backed up data and settings to the new account. Windows uses an SID to identify each account in file ACLs. If you recreate an account, it will not have the same SID and you will have to reconfigure file permissions and group memberships.

 Note: *If an account profile is corrupted, the key required to decrypt files encrypted using EFS might be lost or damaged. The key is based on the user password. On a domain, you can configure recovery agents with the ability to restore the encryption keys.*

GUIDELINES FOR IMPLEMENTING DISASTER RECOVERY AND PREVENTION METHODS

Here are some guidelines to follow to help you implement disaster recovery and prevention.

IMPLEMENT DISASTER RECOVERY AND PREVENTION METHODS

Consider these guidelines when implementing disaster recovery and prevention methods.

- A disaster recovery plan should:
    - Identify scenarios for natural and man-made disasters and options for protecting systems.
    - Identify tasks, resources, and responsibilities for responding to a disaster.
    - Train staff in the disaster planning procedures and how to react well to change.
- Perform backups of data and configuration files on a regular basis. This might be at the file level or the image level. Critical applications should also be backed up.
- Determine the frequency of backups. This might be hourly, daily, weekly, monthly, or some other interval appropriate for the data and information in your organization.
- Determine data retention needs in both the short and the long term.
- Determine whether you need to perform full, incremental, or differential backups.
- Create a custom recovery image for use in restoring a computer.
- Be aware that when you restore data from a backup, the data is only as current as the backup from which you are restoring, so some data might need to be recreated.
- Test backups after they are created.
- Determine where backups will be stored both locally and offsite.
- Document the account recovery methods that will be needed for any systems, applications, or websites used by the organization.

Topic F
Basic Scripting Concepts

EXAM OBJECTIVES COVERED
1002-4.8 Identify the basics of scripting.

Many IT support tasks are quite straightforward but repetitive. Whenever people are called upon to perform repetitive tasks, there is quite a high chance that they will make mistakes. Developing scripts to automate these repetitive tasks means that they can be performed with greater consistency. Also, if you want to change something about the configuration, it is easier to tweak the script than to adjust a large number of desktops or user accounts manually. As a CompTIA A+ technician, you are highly likely to work in environments that make use of scripting. You should understand the basics of how a script is written and executed.

SCRIPT FILES

A **script file** is a text document containing commands. The commands might be operating system commands that are run in the order they are listed in the script file. In other cases, the script file lists instructions from a particular **scripting language** that are **interpreted** by a **command interpreter** designed for that particular scripting language. When you access a script file, if the appropriate interpreter is installed on the computer, the instructions contained in the file are run or **executed**. You can also open the script file in any text editor, such as Windows **Notepad**.

*Note: You can modify any script in a basic text editor such as **Notepad**, but using a text editor with script support is more productive. Script support means the editor can parse the syntax of the script and highlight elements of it appropriately. For complex scripts, you might use an **Integrated Development Environment (IDE)**. This will provide autocomplete features to help you write and edit code and debugging tools to help identify if the script is executing correctly.*

SCRIPTING LANGUAGES

In computer programming, there are several types of instruction sets.

- One is a **compiled program**, in which the instructions are performed by the computer processor. Examples of compiled language programs are Perl, Java™, C, and C++®.
- The second type is a script, in which the instructions are interpreted and carried out by another program such as the operating system or a command interpreter.
  - Examples of script languages include Visual Basic®, Python®, and JavaScript® scripts. These are general purpose scripting languages.
  - Batch files and PowerShell® in Windows® operating systems and shell scripts in the Linux® operating system are also considered script files. These languages support the automation and configuration of a particular operating system.
- Most languages can call (or "wrap") system commands as part of the code and can therefore also be used for scripting.

File extensions for each of these scripting languages are shown in the following table.

Scripting Language	File Extension
Windows batch file	.bat
PowerShell	.ps1
Linux shell script	.sh
VBScript	.vbs
JavaScript	.js
Python	.py

Whatever language is used to create it, a script is *usually* a smaller piece of code than a program. A script is generally targeted at completing a specific task, whether that task is based within a web-based application or is used by a network administrator to perform a repetitive administrative task. Although a program usually provides some sort of unique functionality, anything a script does could usually be performed manually by a user.

Writing scripts is a good place to learn the basics about programming. They are usually simpler to learn, require no compiling, and are well documented on the Internet should you require guidance or samples.

BATCH FILES

Batch files are a collection of command-line instructions that you store in a .BAT file. You can run the file by calling its name from the command-line, or double-clicking the file in File Explorer. Generally, batch file scripts run from end to end, and are limited in terms of branching and user input.

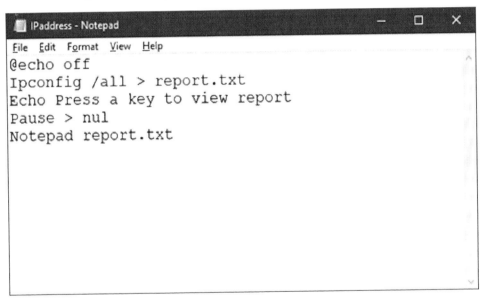

An example of a Windows batch file. (Screenshot used with permission from Microsoft.)

WINDOWS POWERSHELL

Windows PowerShell enables you to perform management and administrative tasks in Windows 7 and later. It is fully integrated with the operating system and supports both remote execution and scripting. To help create and manage your Windows PowerShell scripts, Microsoft provides the Windows PowerShell Integrated Scripting Environment (ISE).

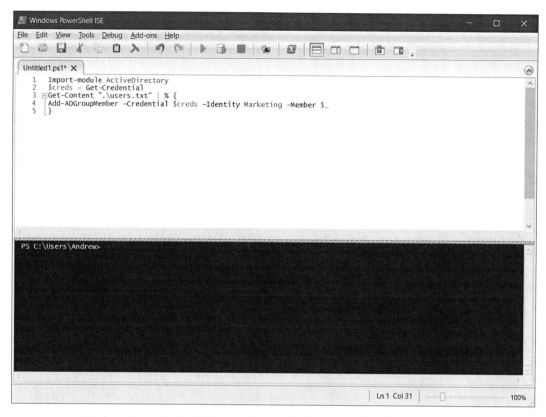

Windows PowerShell ISE. (Screenshot used with permission from Microsoft.)

LINUX SHELL SCRIPT

In Linux, a **shell script** is the equivalent of a Windows batch file. A shell script is a file that contains a list of commands to be read and executed by the shell. Frequently used commands can be stored in a shell script for repeated use. Every shell script starts with a line that designates the interpreter. This line instructs the operating system to execute the script. Shell scripts allow you to perform various functions. These functions include automation of commands and tasks of system administration and troubleshooting, creation of simple applications, and manipulation of text or files.

An example of a Linux shell script open in a text editor.

VBScript

VBScript is a scripting language based on Microsoft's Visual Basic programming language. VBScript is often used by network administrators to perform repetitive administrative tasks. With VBScript, you can run your scripts from either the command-line or from the Windows graphical interface. Scripts that you write must be run within a host environment. Windows 10 provides Internet Explorer, IIS, and Windows Script Host (WSH) for this purpose.

```
highnumber = 50
lownumber = 10
count = 0
Title = "Number count"
for i = 1 to 10
    randomize
    displaynumber = int((highnumber - lownumber + 1) * rnd + lownumber)
wscript.echo displaynumber
if displaynumber > 25 then
    count = count+1
End If
Next
Msg = Cstr(Count) + " numbers are greater than 25"
msgbox Msg,vbok,Title
```

Visual Basic Script in Windows 10. (Screenshot used with permission from Microsoft.)

Note: You would now normally use PowerShell for Windows automation tasks. You might need to support legacy VBScripts, though.

JavaScript

JavaScript is a scripting language that is designed to create interactive web-based content and web apps. The scripts are executed automatically by placing the script in the HTML code for a web page, so that when the HTML code for the page loads, the script is run.

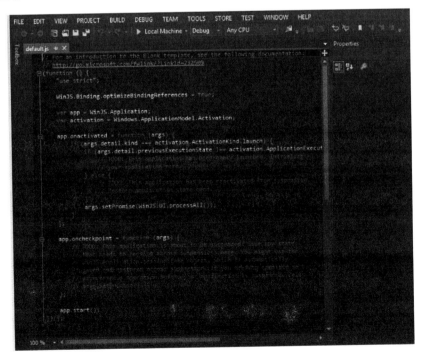

An example of JavaScript code.

PYTHON

Python is a general-purpose programming language that can be used to develop many different kinds of applications. It is designed to be easy to read and program using much fewer lines of code when compared to other programming languages. The code runs in an interpreter. In Windows, a default interpreter called CPython is installed with the Python development tools supplied by the Python Software Foundation (**python.org**). Python is preinstalled on many Linux distributions.

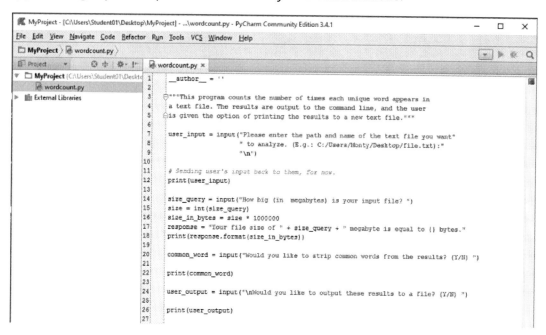

An example of Python code.

BASIC SCRIPT CONSTRUCTS

In order to write a script in a particular language, you must first understand the structure and syntax of the language. Most scripting languages share similarities in their structure and syntax, but it is important to use the specific syntax correctly as any errors will cause the code to not run.

COMMENT SYNTAX

It is important to use comments in code to assist with maintaining it. A comment line is ignored by the compiler or interpreter. A comment line is indicated by a special delimiter, such as double forward slash (//), hash (#), or apostrophe ('). The following table identifies the syntax used to add comments to various languages.

Scripting Language	Comment Syntax
Windows batch file	Rem Comment text is added here
	or
	:: Comment text is added here
PowerShell script	# Comment text is added here
Bash shell script	# Comment text is added here
VBScript	' Comment text is added here
JavaScript	// Comment text is added here
Python	# Comment text is added here

IDENTIFIERS

An **identifier** is used in a program to access a program element, such as a **stored value**. For example, you might assign the identifier FirstName to a stored value that contains a user's first name. In essence, an identifier is a label for something within your program. If your identifier stores data, then it will be either a **variable** or a **constant**.

Type	Description
Variable	A variable contains a value that can change during the execution of the program. This value might be a text string, a number, or any other data type.
	Variables are usually **declared**, defined as a particular **data type**, and given an initial value at the start of the **routine** in which they are used. It is often possible to use **undeclared variables**, but this can make code harder to read and more prone to errors.
	Using the example of a first name, it's important to understand that although a person's name might not change, if you use a programmatic technique to reference a user's name without knowing which user you're referring to, then, as far as the program is concerned, that is a variable. You can assign a value to a variable using fairly simple code. For example, the following **pseudocode** declares the FirstName variable to store a string value with an initial value Andy, then sets it to a value from a data store:

	<pre>declare FirstName as String = "Andy"
	
	FirstName = find LastLoggedOnUser and get Forename
	
	print FirstName</pre>

	Running this code might produce the following output:
	James
Constants	A constant is a specific identifier that contains a value that cannot be changed within the program. For example, you might want to reference the numerical value for the screen dimensions or resolution.

ENVIRONMENT VARIABLES

An **environment variable** is a storage location in the environment of the operating system's command shell. For example, when you are entering directory paths as arguments in a script automating some task in Windows, you may not know exactly which locations were chosen for installation. The shell recognizes some system variables and replaces the correct path when one of these is used. Some of the common variables include:

- %SystemDrive%—for example, "C:"
- %SystemRoot%—for example, "C:\Windows"
- %UserName%—for example, "George"
- %HomeDrive%—for example, "C:"
- %HomePath%—for example, "\Users\George"

In Windows, you can view the full list of variables by using the `set` command (without switches) at the command prompt. `set` also lets you create and modify new variables. You can also view variables through the **Advanced** page of the **System Properties** dialog box by selecting the **Environment Variables** button.

In Linux, you use the `printenv` or `env` commands to view and change environment variables. However, in Linux, each shell can use additional variables, configured by using the `set` command.

 Note: *If you need to use environment variables outside of a batch file or shell script, each language will have a different syntax for reading them.*

BRANCHES AND LOOPS

A script contains one or more statements. In the normal scheme of execution, each statement is processed in turn from top to bottom. Scripts are used for tasks that are too complex to be completed as a simple series of statements, though. In this case, you can change the order in which statements are executed based on logical conditions evaluated within the script. There are two main types of conditional execution: branches and loops.

BRANCHES

A script runs from the start to the end unless you instruct it to deviate from this path. One way of doing so is to create a **branch**, which is an instruction to your computer to execute a different sequence of instructions. You use branches to control the flow within your program.

For example, you might create a branch based on a condition; you might verify that a number has been entered correctly. If it has, then one thing happens, and if it has not, then something else happens. This is a conditional branch.

For example, in the following pseudocode, the value of a variable called `DisplayNumber` is compared to 25. If `DisplayNumber` is greater than 25, then a variable called Count is incremented by 1. If `DisplayNumber` is less than 25, no action occurs and the variable `Count` remains the same.

```
If DisplayNumber > 25 Then
        Count = Count+1
End If
```

LOOPS

Loops are similar to branches in as much as they deviate from a linear sequence of statements according to some sort of logic condition. However, with a loop, you instruct your computer to perform, or repeat, a task until a condition is met. For example, you might create a loop that continues until a certain amount of time has elapsed or until a counter reaches a certain level. Then, a predetermined action might occur, depending upon what you want. In the following example, the program loops around until the value of `i` is 5. Then the program proceeds to the next statement.

```
For i = 1 to 5
      print i
Next
```

As well as "For" structures, loops can also be implemented by "While" statements:

```
Do While i <= 100
      i = i + 1
      print i
Loop
```

Note: *Make sure your code does not contain unintended or infinite loops. Without the statement to increment i in the Do loop example, the loop would continue forever. An infinite loop will make the process hang.*

OPERATORS

Looping and branching structures depend on logical tests to determine whether to continue the loop or the branch to follow. A logical test is one that resolves to a TRUE or FALSE value. You need to be familiar with basic **comparison operators**:

- **==**—is equal to (returns TRUE if both conditions are the same).
- **!=**—is not equal to.
- **<**—less than.
- **>**—greater than.
- **<=** and **>=**—less than or equal to and greater than or equal to.

You might also want to test more than one condition at the same time. The **logical operators** are as follows:

- **AND**—if both conditions are TRUE, then the whole statement is TRUE.
- **OR**—if either condition is TRUE, then the whole statement is TRUE.
- **XOR**—if either condition is TRUE but not both, then the whole statement is TRUE.

You can also use the negation operator NOT to reverse the truth value of any statement.

BASIC DATA TYPES

It is important to understand the different data types that a script can use. The CPU and storage devices in a computer only process data as ones and zeros. These hardware components have no conception of what the data mean. When it comes to writing scripts, though, **data types** are very important because they determine what sort of operations can be performed. For example, the characters "51" can be treated as a number value, in which case you can use the data in addition and subtraction, or they can be treated as a text string (representing a house number, for instance). If "51" is stored as a string, it must be converted before it can be used in a mathematical operation.

There are different types of number values and a variety of text forms. These include:

Data Type	Description
Integers	These are whole numbers. For example: 5, 21, or 65536. An integer data type consumes 1 to 8 bytes of computer storage.
Floating point numbers	This type can support decimal fractions such as 4.1, 26.4, or 5.62. A floating point number (or just "float") consumes between 4 and 8 bytes of storage. Note that the floating point type could store a whole number too (4.0, for instance).
Boolean values	These are a special numeric data type indicating that something is either TRUE or FALSE (with a 1 or 0). They consume a single bit of storage.

Data Type	Description
Characters	A character (or char) is a single textual character, and can be a letter of the alphabet, a symbol, or, indeed, a numerical character. For example: a, D, 7, $, @, #. These consume one byte of storage. Note that when a number is entered as a character data type, you cannot perform any mathematical operations on it.
Strings	A string is a collection of text characters. For example: XYZ, Hello world. There is no real limit on the amount of storage that can be used by a string. Generally, you define the string length when you define the data type.

When single or double quotes can be used to delimit a string ("Hello World"), the quotes are NOT part of the string itself. If you want to represent a quote character (or other delimiter) within a string, you have to use an **escape character**. For example, the string "John said \'Hello World\' then left again." contains two single quotes, escaped using the backslash character (\).

Note: *Different languages have different escape characters, but the backslash is often the syntax used.*

Scripting Language	Escape Character
Windows batch file	%%
PowerShell	There are different escape characters for different circumstances.
	--%
	`
	\
Linux Bash shell script	\
VBScript	To escape a single quote, enter two single quotes: "
	To escape a double quote, enter two double quotes: ""
	Use the `Escape(charString)` function to encode a string so that the string contains only ASCII characters. Any other characters are replaced with %##, where ## is the hexadecimal equivalent to the character.
JavaScript	\
Python	\

Topic G
Professionalism and Communication

 EXAM OBJECTIVES COVERED
1002-4.7 Given a scenario, use proper communication techniques and professionalism.

On almost every service call, you will need to interact with users who are experiencing problems. In this topic, you will identify best practices for PC technicians to use to communicate appropriately with clients and colleagues and to conduct business in a professional manner.

You are a representative of your profession, as well as your company. Working with customers is a fundamental job duty for every A+ technician. How you conduct yourself will have a direct and significant impact on the satisfaction of your customers, and your level of professionalism and communication skills can directly affect whether or not you will do business with them again.

CUSTOMER SERVICE ATTITUDE

A service technician should not only understand technical issues but must also be a good communicator. It is easy to pick up facts and information but it can be much harder to use this information in a troubleshooting scenario requiring customer interaction, whether face-to-face or over the telephone.

Learning how to deal with customers, interpret the information they give you, and respond to their queries can be difficult but logical problem diagnosis and successful techniques for working with customers go hand-in-hand. A person with poor customer contact ability is not likely to impress as a professional customer service technician, even if he or she is competent at technical problem solving.

Remember that "customer" need not refer to someone who buys something; it can include any users or clients of a support service.

Three golden rules can be applied to good customer service:

- Be positive—project confidence, be in control, and drive the issue towards resolution.
- Be clear, concise, and direct.
- Be consistent, fair, and respectful.

COMMUNICATION SKILLS

There are many things that contribute to the art of communication: the words you use, listening effectively, and giving feedback are particularly important.

USING PROPER LANGUAGE

When you greet someone, you should be conscious of making a good first impression. When you arrive onsite, make eye contact, introduce yourself and your company, and shake hands. When you answer the phone, introduce yourself and your department and offer assistance.

When you speak to a customer, you need to make sense. Obviously, you must be factually accurate, but it is equally important that the customer understands what you are saying. Not only does this show the customer that you are competent, but it also proves that you are in control of the situation and gives the customer confidence in your abilities. You need to use clear and concise statements that avoid jargon, abbreviations, acronyms, and other technical language that a user might not understand. For example, compare the following scenarios:

Scenario 1	Scenario 2
"Looking at the TFT, can you tell me whether the driver is signed?"	"Is a green check mark displayed on the icon?"

The first question depends on the user understanding what a TFT is, what a signed driver might be, and knowing that a green check mark indicates one. The second question gives you the same information without having to rely on the user's understanding.

While you do not have to speak very formally, avoid being over-familiar with customers. Try not to use very informal language (slang) and do not use any language that may cause any sort of offense. For example, you should greet a customer by saying "Hello" or "Good morning," rather than "Whassup?" or "Hey!"

LISTENING AND QUESTIONING

You must listen carefully to what is being said to you; it will give you clues to the customer's technical level, enabling you to pace and adapt your replies accordingly. **Active listening** is the skill of listening to an individual so that you give them your full attention and are not trying to argue with, comment on, or misinterpret what they have said.

With active listening, you make a conscious effort to keep your attention focused on what the other person is saying, as opposed to being distracted by thinking what your reply is going to be or by some background noise or interruption. Some of the other techniques of active listening are to reflect phrases used by the other person or to restate the issue and summarize what they have said. This helps to reassure the other person that you have attended to what they have to say. You should also try to take notes of what the customer says so that you have an accurate record.

Listening carefully will help you to get the most information from what a customer tells you. (Image by goodluz © 123RF.com.)

It is important to understand that you must not interrupt customers when they are speaking. Also, do not ignore what they have said. If you are rude in this sort of way, the customer will form a poor opinion of you and may become less willing to help with troubleshooting.

There will inevitably be a need to establish some technical facts with the customer. This means questioning (or probing) the customer for information. There are two broad types of questioning:

- **Open**—a question that invites the other person to compose a response, such as "What seems to be the problem?"
- **Closed**—a question that can only be answered with a "Yes" or "No" or that requires some other fixed response ("What error number is displayed on the panel?" for instance).

The basic technique is start with **open questions**. You may try to guide the customer towards what information will be most helpful. For example, "When you say your printer is not working, what problem are you having—will it not switch on?" However, be careful about assuming what the problem is and leading the customer to simply affirming a guess. As the customer explains what they know, you may be able to perceive what the problem is. If so, do not assume anything too early. Ask pertinent closed questions that prove or disprove your perception. The customer may give you information that is vague or ambiguous. Clarify what they mean by asking questions like "What did the error message say?," or "When you say the printout is dark, is there a faint image or is it completely black?," or "Is the power LED on the printer lit?" If a customer is not getting to the point or if you want to follow some specific steps, take charge of the conversation at the earliest opportunity by asking closed questions. For example, compare the following scenarios:

Scenario 1	Scenario 2
"It's been like this for ages now, and I've tried pressing a key and moving the mouse, but nothing happens."	"It's been like this for ages now, and I've tried pressing a key and moving the mouse, but nothing happens."
"What does the screen look like?"	"OK, pressing a key should work normally, but as it isn't I'd like to investigate something else first. Can you tell me whether the light on the monitor is green?"
"It's dark. I thought the computer was just resting and I know in that circumstance I need to press a key, but that's not working and I really need to get on with..."	"No, there's a yellow light though."

In the first example, the technician asks an open question, which just lets the user focus on what they perceive as the problem, but which isn't producing any valuable troubleshooting information. Using a closed question, as in the second example, allows the technician to start working through a series of symptoms to try to diagnose the problem.

Do note that a long sequence of closed questions fired off rapidly may overwhelm and confuse a customer. Do not try to force the pace. Establish the customer's technical level and target the conversation accordingly. A customer with little technical knowledge will be confused by technical information; conversely, a knowledgeable customer may know exactly what the problem is and will not appreciate being treated like a novice. On the other hand, don't assume that the customer has diagnosed the problem correctly. Sometimes a little knowledge is worse than no knowledge at all.

GIVING FEEDBACK

When you give the customer instructions—for example, if you want them to try to complete a series of troubleshooting steps—be clear and concise. This is where having a good "mental map" of the sequence of steps to any particular configuration option demonstrates its value. Always confirm that the customer has taken the correct step.

Also, you must be patient; remember that the customer probably has little idea of what they are doing and will proceed quite slowly.

Firing question after question at a customer can be off-putting, especially if the customer does not understand what he or she is being asked to do or check.

Technical support depends on good customer relationships. A good understanding between you and a customer also makes troubleshooting that much easier. This sort of understanding is often referred to as rapport.

React to what you learn about the customer's technical ability, and develop the conversation in a positive manner to help resolve the issue. Try and form a partnership with the customer. Avoid using the pronoun "you," as it can imply blame and push the customer away from you. Consider the following:

Scenario 1	Scenario 2
"Have you checked that the printer is turned on?"	"Let's make sure the printer's turned on."

The first statement implies blame and signals that you are not prepared to accept responsibility for troubleshooting the problem. The second emphasizes you are willing to share responsibility for solving the problem and provide assistance at every step.

PROFESSIONALISM

Professionalism means taking pride in one's work and in treating people fairly. Several techniques and procedures can be used to develop an effective support service. You should understand these and the personal qualities that you should develop.

PROPER DOCUMENTATION

One of the key points of providing an effective support service is making it easy for customers to contact it. Most support takes place either over the telephone or through an email/web contact form. More advanced options include text messaging and Remote Assistance-style desktop sharing.

Whatever the method used, the contact information and hours of operation should be well advertised, so that the customer knows what to do. The service should have **proper documentation**, so that the customer knows what to expect in terms of items that are supported, how long incidents may take to resolve, when they can expect an item to be replaced instead of repaired, and so on.

PROBLEM MANAGEMENT

Problem management means tracking and auditing support requests. Whatever the tools and resources used to implement problem management, the basic process of receiving a support request, resolving the problem, and verifying the solution remains much the same.

On receiving the request (whether it is a call, email, or face-to-face contact), acknowledge the request and set expectations. For example, repeat the request back to the customer, then state the next steps, such as "I have assigned this problem to David Martin. If you don't hear from us by 3pm, please call me." The customer may have a complaint, a problem with some equipment, or simply a request for information. It is important to clarify the nature of these factors:

- The customer's expectations of what will be done and when to fix the problem.
- The customer's concerns about cost or the impact on business processes.
- Your constraints—time, parts, costs, contractual obligations, and so on.

It is important not to allow the customer to form unrealistic expectations of how long the problem will take to solve. On the other hand, you should focus your attention on resolving the customer's concerns (if they are valid). Consider this exchange for example:

Customer	A+ Technician
"I have to get a job application printed today—you must send a technician around immediately."	"Do you have another print device that you could use?"
"No, I only have one printer and it's not working."	"Do you have email? You should be able to send the job application to a copy shop and they'll print it for you for a small fee."
"Yes, but I'm sure I don't know about any stores like that."	"There's actually a location a short distance from your house. If you have a pen and paper ready, I can give you the details and arrange an appointment for a technician to come and inspect your printer..."

The course of action that you agree on must be realistic and achievable.

Acknowledge the request and set expectations. (Image by goodluz © 123RF.com.)

Each request must be logged as an **incident** or **ticket** so that progress on resolving it can be documented. Most support departments use a Call Management or Problem Management System for this.

As with any communications, job tickets should be completed professionally, with due regard for spelling, grammar, and clarity. Remember that other people may need to take action using just the information in the ticket and that analysis of tickets will take place as part of quality assurance procedures. It is also possible that tickets will be forwarded to customers as a record of the jobs performed.

If possible, the request should be resolved in one call. If this is not possible, the call should be dealt with as quickly as possible, and escalated to a senior support team if a solution cannot be found promptly. What is important is that you drive problem acceptance and resolution, either by working on a solution yourself or ensuring that the problem is accepted by the assigned person or department.

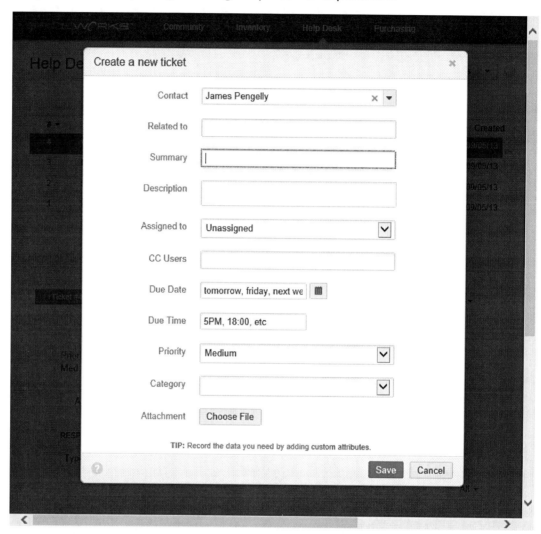

Creating a ticket in the Spiceworks IT Support management tool. (Screenshot courtesy of spiceworks.com.)

If a problem cannot be resolved within the course of a single call, it is imperative to manage the customer's expectations of when the problem will be resolved. Customers should not feel the need to call you to find out what's happening. This is irritating for them to do and means time is wasted dealing with an unnecessary call.

If have resolved the problem, and tested that the system is operating normally again, you should give the customer a general indication of what caused the problem and what you did to fix it plus assurance that the problem is now fixed and unlikely to reoccur. On leaving or on ending the call, thank the customer for their time and assistance and show that you have appreciated the chance to help them.

When the solution has been tested and verified and the customer has expressed satisfaction with the resolution of the problem, log the problem as closed. Record the solution and send verification to the customer via email or phone call.

PRIORITIZING WORK

Time is an invaluable factor in the service industry because workload usually outweighs staff resources. Time management practices impact the level of service you are able to provide to your customers.

Anybody who requests support will hope that their problem can be resolved immediately. However, this is not always possible for a number of reasons, and the customer's idea of an acceptable response time may vary greatly from your own. A formal call management system will usually allow a priority code to be assigned to a call. Open tickets can be monitored and re-prioritized to ensure that they do not fail to meet the agreed on service and performance levels.

PUNCTUALITY AND ACCOUNTABILITY

If a customer expects a visit—or call or email—from a service technician at a certain time, it is reasonable to assume that the technician will respond as promised. If it becomes obvious that the technician is not going to be on time, then the customer should be informed as soon as possible. A customer may make special arrangements to be with the technician at the allotted time and changes can be very annoying.

Be accountable for your actions, both before you arrive on site and while on site. This usually means being honest and direct about issues, but make sure this is done in a positive manner. For example:

- "I'm sorry I'm late—show me this faulty PC and I'll start work right away."
- "The printer needs a new fuser—and I'm afraid that I don't have this type with me. What I will do is call the office and find out how quickly we can get one..."
- "I've not seen this problem before, but I have taken some notes and I'll check this out as soon as I get back to the office. I'll give you a call this afternoon—will that be OK?"

FLEXIBILITY AND COMPROMISE

As a service technician, you want to ensure your customer receives the best possible attention at all times but, unfortunately, saying no is sometimes inevitable:

- The customer may ask that you do something beyond your control or perhaps beyond the terms of the service contract.
- The customer may ask you to confirm a fact or detail beyond your control.
- The customer may demand a replacement when a repair option is the only one merited by your company's procedures.

Consider the following examples; which approach is better?

Customer	A+ Technician
"My printer is broken again—I want a replacement."	1. "I'm sorry, we can't do that..." 2: "I can arrange for a technician to be with you first thing tomorrow, and I'll mention to my supervisor that this is the second time this has occurred."
"Can you guarantee that the technician will be with me before 3 pm?"	1: "Sorry, I can't guarantee a specific time." 2: "I'll ask the technician to try and visit before 3 pm if possible, and I'll call you around 2 pm if it looks like the technician will be later than that—is this OK?"

Note: The key to saying "no" in a positive way is to offer an alternative.

RESPECT

Respect means that you treat others (and their property) as you would like to be treated. Respect is one of the hallmarks of professionalism. At a bare minimum, respect means not being rude or offensive. Some of the other elements are listed below.

- **Avoid Distractions**. Do not allow interruptions when you are working at a customer's site. Do not take calls from colleagues unless they are work related, urgent, and important. Do not take personal calls or respond to texts or posts on social media.

  If you are speaking with a customer on the telephone, always ask their permission before putting them on hold or transferring their call.

- **Respect for Property and Confidentiality**.
  - Do not treat customers' property carelessly. Do not use equipment or services such as PCs, printers, web access, or phones without permission and never for personal use.
  - If you are visiting someone's home or office do not help yourself to food or drink, ask before using the bathroom, and do not attempt to snoop around other areas. Do not be tempted to snoop around data files on someone else's PC either!
  - If you find printed copies of confidential materials while performing some support task (bank statements or personal letters for instance), do not look at them, make the customer aware of them, and allow time for them to be put away.
  - If you are making a site visit, keep the area in which you are working clean and tidy and leave it as you found it.

- **Cultural Sensitivity**.
  - **Cultural sensitivity** means being aware of customs and habits used by other people. It is easy to associate culture simply with national elements, such as the difference between the way Americans and Japanese greet one another. Within each nation, there are many different cultures, however, created by things such as social class, business opportunities, leisure pursuits, and so on. For example, a person may expect to be addressed using a professional title, such as a doctor or a judge; other people may be more comfortable speaking on a first name basis. It is safer to start on a formal basis and use more informal language if the customer signals that they are happier speaking that way.
  - You need to realize that though a person may be influenced by several cultures, their behavior is not determined by culture. Customer service and support requires consideration for other people. You cannot show this if you make assumptions about their cultural background without treating them as an individual (stereotyping).
  - Accent, dialect, and language are some of the crucial elements of cultural sensitivity. These can make it hard for you to understand a customer and perhaps difficult for a customer to understand you. When dealing with a language barrier, use questions, summaries, and restatements to clarify customer statements. Consider using visual aids or demonstrations rather than trying to explain something in words.
  - Also, different cultures define personal space differently, so be aware of how close or far you are from the customer.

CUSTOMER COMPLAINTS

All customer complaints, whether they are valid or not, should be treated with equal seriousness.

MAINTAIN A POSITIVE ATTITUDE

Understand that an angry customer is usually frustrated that things are not working properly or feels let down (perhaps the technician arrived late). Empathizing with the customer is a good way of developing a positive relationship towards resolving their problem. Saying you are sorry does not necessarily mean you agree with what the customer is saying, just that you can understand their point of view.

"I'm sorry you're having a problem with your new PC. Let's see what we can do to sort things out..."

Arguing with the customer, denying that a problem exists, or being judgmental (assuming that the problem is of the customer's making because they do not understand the system properly) will only tend to lower the customer's impression of the service you offer. Do not try to dismiss a problem out of hand or minimize its importance. If the customer has taken it to the point of complaining, then clearly they feel that it is important; whether you consider the matter trivial is not the issue.

Listen while the customer explains the problem and let them know that you are listening. On the phone, use confirmatory phrases such as "Yes," "I see," and "Uh-huh" from time to time to make sure the customer knows you are paying attention. Do not just repeat the same phrase every few seconds—the customer may think you are mocking them.

If you are face-to-face with the customer, maintain eye contact and nod your head frequently but watch your body language. Do not fold your arms as this puts up a barrier.

BE ACCURATE AND HONEST

A common problem when dealing with customer complaints is feeling that you have to defend every action of your company or department. If the customer makes a true statement about your levels of service (or that of other employees), do not try and think of a clever excuse or mitigating circumstance for the failing; you will sound as though you do not care.

If you have let a customer down, it is probably best to empathize while including some positive actions:

"You're right—I'm sorry the technician didn't turn up. I guarantee that a technician will be with you by 3pm and I'll let my supervisor know that you have had to call us. Shall I call you back just after 3 to make sure that things are OK?"

On the other hand, if the customer is incorrect in their understanding of the situation, empathy and correction is in order:

"I'm sorry the replacement disk hasn't arrived, but I know it was put in the mail. Would you be happy to wait to see whether it arrives tomorrow or should I mail another one to you?"

If the customer had a valid cause to complain about levels of service or any aspect of your company's operation, resolve the problem and then investigate what can be done to ensure this type of problem never occurs again.

DEALING WITH A DIFFICULT CUSTOMER

It is never easy to talk to someone who is being unreasonable, abusive, or shouting down the telephone but it is important to be able to deal with these situations professionally.

1. Identify signs that a customer is becoming angry early (for example, raised voice, speaking too quickly, interrupting, and so on). Try to calm the situation down by using a low voice, soothing language, and focusing on positive actions.

2. Do not take complaints personally—provided that you haven't deliberately caused the problem about which the customer is complaining, they are using you as a representative of your organization and any anger expressed in your direction is not personal but a symptom of their frustration.

3. Listen and let the customer explain the problem—draw out the facts and use them as a positive action plan to drive the conversation forward.

4. Hang up—if a customer is persistently abusive or threatening, issue a caution, then warn them about their behavior, then end the call or contact if they do not act reasonably.

Let the customer vent. (Image by Wang Tom © 123RF.com.)

BE PROFESSIONAL

Everyone has bad days when they feel the need to get some difficult situation off their chest. Perhaps a customer has been particularly obtuse or foolish or perhaps someone has treated you unpleasantly. Find a colleague for a private face-to-face chat but under no circumstances should you ever disclose these types of experiences via social media outlets. Remember that anything posted to social media is very hard to withdraw and can cause unpredictable reactions. Tweeting some mistake made by someone you have supported is a sure way to get yourself and your company in trouble.

GUIDELINES FOR COMMUNICATING WITH CUSTOMERS

Here are some guidelines to follow to help you communicate effectively with your customers.

INTERACT WITH CUSTOMERS

Consider these guidelines for interacting with customers.

- Use proper language and avoid jargon, acronyms, and slang whenever possible.
- Maintain a positive attitude and project confidence.
- Actively listen, take notes, and avoid interrupting the customer.
- Be culturally sensitive.
- Use appropriate professional titles, when applicable.
- Be on time, and if you will be late, be sure to contact the customer.

- Avoid distractions, including:
  - Personal calls
  - Texting
  - Accessing social media sites
  - Talking to coworkers while interacting with customers
  - Personal interruptions
- When dealing with difficult customers or situations:
  - Do not argue with customers or be defensive.
  - Avoid dismissing customer problems.
  - Avoid being judgmental.
  - Clarify customer statements by asking open-ended questions to narrow the scope of the problem, restating the issue, or asking questions to verify understanding.
  - Do not disclose experiences via social media outlets.
- Set and meet expectations, adhere to the prescribed timeline, and communicate status with the customer.
  - If necessary, offer different repair or replacement options.
  - Provide proper documentation on the services provided.
  - Follow up with customers and users at a later date to verify satisfaction.
- Deal appropriately with customers' confidential and private materials. This includes items located on a computer, desktop, printer, and in their workspace.

Activity 10-1

Implementing Operational Procedures Review

SCENARIO
Answer the following review questions.

1. **Which of the best practices discussed in this lesson apply in your workplace?**

2. **How do you think the scripting concepts discussed in this lesson will help you at your workplace?**

Summary

In this lesson, you implemented operational procedures, including dealing with environmental impacts and controls, documentation, change management, disaster prevention and recovery, scripting, and communication skills. With the proper tools, awareness of safety and environmental issues, basic communication skills, and a solid method to use when troubleshooting, you are prepared to do your job in a safe, effective, and professional manner.

What's Next?

Become a CompTIA A+ Certified Professional!

CompTIA A+ certified professionals are proven problem solvers. They support today's core technologies from security to cloud to data management and more. CompTIA A+ is the industry standard for launching IT careers into today's digital world. It is the only industry recognized credential with performance-based items to prove pros can think on their feet to perform critical IT support tasks in the moment. It is trusted by employers around the world to identify the go-to person in end point management and technical support roles. CompTIA A+ is regularly re-invented by IT experts to ensure that it validates core skills and abilities demanded in the workplace.

In order to become a CompTIA A+ Certified Professional, you must successfully pass both the A+ Core 1 exam (Exam Code 220-1001) and A+ Core 2 exam (Exam Code 220-1002). Therefore, your first next step might be completing *The Official CompTIA® A+® Core 1 (Exam 220-1001)* course.

In order to help you prepare for the exams, you may also want to invest in CompTIA's practice lab product, CertMaster Labs, and exam prep product, CertMaster Practice for A+.

CertMaster Labs provides learners with the necessary platform to gain critical hands on skills in IT using industry standard technologies and develop a deeper understanding of the subject matter. The labs address the practical aspects of CompTIA certification exam objectives and complement a training program that includes coverage of the theoretical aspects of objectives (ideally through the use of CertMaster Learn).

From the browser, learners gain administrative access to real equipment and software environments, giving them complete control to either carry out their own configurations or follow the lab guides to configure specific technologies that are required for the relevant CompTIA exams.

CertMaster Practice is an online knowledge assessment and certification training companion tool specifically designed for those who have completed The Official CompTIA A+ Core 1 and Core 2 course. It helps reinforce and test what you know and close knowledge gaps prior to taking the exam.

CertMaster Practice features:

- Adaptive knowledge assessments with feedback, covering all domains of the A+ Core 1 or Core 2 exams.
- Practice tests with performance-based questions.
- Question-first design and smart refreshers to get feedback on the questions you get wrong.
- Learning analytics that track real-time knowledge gain and topic difficulty to help you learn intelligently.

Taking the Exams

When you think you have learned and practiced the material sufficiently, you can book a time to take the test.

Preparing for the Exams

We've tried to balance this course to reflect the percentages in the exam so that you have learned the appropriate level of detail about each topic to comfortably answer the exam questions. Read the following notes to find out what you need to do to register for the exam and get some tips on what to expect during the exam and how to prepare for it.

Questions in the exam are weighted by domain area as follows:

CompTIA A+ Core 2 (Exam 220-1002) Certification Domain Areas	Weighting
1.0 Operating Systems	27%
2.0 Security	24%
3.0 Software Troubleshooting	26%
4.0 Operational Procedures	23%

For more information about how to register for and take your exam, please visit the CompTIA website: **https://certification.comptia.org/testing**.

Mapping Course Content to CompTIA® A+® Core 2 (Exam 220-1002)

Achieving CompTIA A+ certification requires candidates to pass exams 220-1001 and 220-1002. This table describes where the exam objectives for Core 2 (Exam 220-1002) are covered in this course.

Domain and Objective	Covered in
Domain 1.0 Operating Systems	
1.1 Compare and contrast common operating system types and their purposes.	
• 32-bit vs 64-bit	Topic 1A
• RAM limitations	Topic 1A
• Software compatibility	Topic 1A
• Workstation operating systems	Topic 1A
• Microsoft Windows	Topic 1A
• Apple Macintosh OS	Topic 1A
• Linux	Topic 1A
• Cell phone/tablet operating systems	Topic 1A
• Microsoft Windows	Topic 1A
• Android	Topic 1A
• iOS	Topic 1A
• Chrome OS	Topic 1A
• Vendor-specific limitations	Topic 1A
• End-of-life	Topic 1A
• Update limitations	Topic 1A
• Compatibility concerns between operating systems	Topic 1A
1.2 Compare and contrast features of Microsoft Windows versions.	
• Windows 7	Topic 1A
• Windows 8	Topic 1A
• Windows 8.1	Topic 1A
• Windows 10	Topic 1A
• Corporate vs. personal needs	Topic 1A
• Domain access	Topic 1A
• BitLocker	Topic 1A
• Media center	Topic 1A
• BranchCache	Topic 1A
• EFS	Topic 1A
• Desktop styles/user interface	Topic 1A
1.3 Summarize general OS installation considerations and upgrade methods.	
• Boot methods	Topic 2C
• Optical disc (CD-ROM, DVD, Blu-ray)	Topic 2C
• External drive/flash drive (USB/eSATA)	Topic 2C
• Network boot (PXE)	Topic 2C
• Internal fixed disk (HDD/SSD)	Topic 2C

Domain and Objective	Covered in
• Internal hard drive (partition)	Topic 2C
• Types of installations	Topic 2C
• Unattended installation	Topic 2C
• In-place upgrade	Topic 2C
• Clean install	Topic 2C
• Repair installation	Topic 2C
• Multiboot	Topic 2C
• Remote network installation	Topic 2C
• Image deployment	Topic 2C
• Recovery partition	Topic 2C
• Refresh/restore	Topic 2C
• Partitioning	Topic 1D
• Dynamic	Topic 1D
• Basic	Topic 1D
• Primary	Topic 1D
• Extended	Topic 1D
• Logical	Topic 1D
• GPT	Topic 1D
• File system types/formatting	Topic 1D, 2A, 2B
• ExFAT	Topic 1D
• FAT32	Topic 1D
• NTFS	Topic 1D
• CDFS	Topic 1D
• NFS	Topic 2A
• ext3, ext4	Topic 2A
• HFS	Topic 2B
• Swap partition	Topic 2A
• Quick format vs full format	Topic 1D
• Load alternate third-party drivers when necessary	Topic 2D
• Workgroup vs. Domain setup	Topic 2C
• Time/date/region/language settings	Topic 2C
• Driver installation, software, and Windows updates	Topic 2C
• Factory recovery partition	Topic 2C
• Properly formatted boot drive with the correct partitions/format	Topic 2C
• Prerequisites/hardware compatibility	Topic 2C
• Application compatibility	Topic 2C
• OS compatibility/upgrade path	Topic 2C

1.4 Given a scenario, use appropriate Microsoft command line tools.

• Navigation	Topic 1C
• dir	Topic 1C
• cd	Topic 1C
• ..	Topic 1C

Domain and Objective	Covered in
• ipconfig	Topic 4E
• ping	Topic 4E
• tracert	Topic 4E
• netstat	Topic 4E
• nslookup	Topic 4E
• shutdown	Topic 1B
• dism	Topic 2C
• sfc	Topic 3C
• chkdsk	Topic 2D
• diskpart	Topic 1D
• taskkill	Topic 3A
• gpupdate	Topic 5C
• gpresult	Topic 5C
• format	Topic 1D
• copy	Topic 1C
• xcopy	Topic 1C
• robocopy	Topic 1C
• net use	Topic 5B
• net user	Topic 5A
• [command name]/?	Topic 1B
• Commands available with standard privileges vs. administrative privileges	Topic 1B

1.5 Given a scenario, use Microsoft operating system features and tools.

• Administrative	Topic 1B, 1E, 3A, 3B, 3C, 4C, 4D, 5A
• Computer Management	Topic 1B
• Device Manager	Topic 1E
• Local Users and Groups	Topic 5A
• Local Security Policy	Topic 5A
• Performance Monitor	Topic 3B
• Services	Topic 3A
• System Configuration	Topic 3C
• Task Scheduler	Topic 2D
• Component Services	Topic 3A
• Data Sources	Topic 3A
• Print Management	Topic 3A
• Windows Memory Diagnostics	Topic 3C
• Windows Firewall	Topic 4C
• Advanced Security	Topic 4C
• Event Viewer	Topic 3C
• User Account Management	Topic 1B
• MSConfig	Topic 3C
• General	Topic 3C
• Boot	Topic 3C

Domain and Objective	Covered in
• Services	Topic 3C
• Startup	Topic 3C
• Tools	Topic 3C
• Task Manager	Topic 3A
• Applications	Topic 3A
• Processes	Topic 3A
• Performance	Topic 3A
• Networking	Topic 3A
• Users	Topic 3A
• Disk Management	Topic 1D
• Drive status	Topic 1D
• Mounting	Topic 1D
• Initializing	Topic 1D
• Extending partitions	Topic 1D
• Splitting partitions	Topic 1D
• Shrink partitions	Topic 1D
• Assigning/changing drive letters	Topic 1D
• Adding drives	Topic 1D
• Adding arrays	Topic 1D
• Storage spaces	Topic 1D
• System utilities	Topic 1B, 1C, 1E, 2D, 3A, 3C
• Regedit	Topic 1B
• Command	Topic 1B
• Services.msc	Topic 3A
• MMC	Topic 1B
• MSTSC	Topic 4D
• Notepad	Topic 1B
• Explorer	Topic 1C
• Msinfo32	Topic 1E
• DxDiag	Topic 1E
• Disk Defragmenter	Topic 2D
• System Restore	Topic 3C
• Windows Update	Topic 2D

1.6 Given a scenario, use Microsoft Windows Control Panel utilities.

Domain and Objective	Covered in
• Internet Options	Topic 4C
• Connections	Topic 4C
• Security	Topic 4C
• General	Topic 4C
• Privacy	Topic 4C
• Programs	Topic 4C
• Advanced	Topic 4C
• Display/Display Settings	Topic 1E

Domain and Objective	Covered in
• Resolution	Topic 1E
• Color depth	Topic 1E
• Refresh rate	Topic 1E
• User Accounts	Topic 1B
• Folder Options	Topic 1C
• View hidden files	Topic 1C
• Hide extensions	Topic 1C
• General options	Topic 1C
• View options	Topic 1C
• System	Topic 3B
• Performance (virtual memory)	Topic 3B
• Remote settings	Topic 3B
• System protection	Topic 3B
• Windows Firewall	Topic 4C
• Power Options	Topic 1E
• Hibernate	Topic 1E
• Power plans	Topic 1E
• Sleep/suspend	Topic 1E
• Standby	Topic 1E
• Credential Manager	Topic 5A
• Programs and features	Topic 3A
• HomeGroup	Topic 5B
• Devices and Printers	Topic 1E
• Sound	Topic 1E
• Troubleshooting	Topic 1E
• Network and Sharing Center	Topic 4A
• Device Manager	Topic 1E
• BitLocker	Topic 7B
• Sync Center	Topic 5B

1.7 Summarize application installation and configuration concepts.

• System requirements	Topic 3A
• Drive space	Topic 3A
• RAM	Topic 3A
• OS requirements	Topic 3A
• Compatibility	Topic 3A
• Methods of installation and deployment	Topic 3A
• Local (CD/USB)	Topic 3A
• Network-based	Topic 3A
• Local user permissions	Topic 3A
• Folder/file access for installation	Topic 3A
• Security considerations	Topic 3A
• Impact to device	Topic 3A
• Impact to network	Topic 3A

Domain and Objective	Covered in
1.8 Given a scenario, configure Microsoft Windows networking on a client/desktop.	
• HomeGroup vs. Workgroup	Topic 5B
• Domain setup	Topic 5C
• Network shares/administrative shares/mapping drives	Topic 5B
• Printer sharing vs. network printer mapping	Topic 5B
• Establish networking connections	Topic 4A
• VPN	Topic 4A
• Dial-ups	Topic 4A
• Wireless	Topic 4A
• Wired	Topic 4A
• WWAN (Cellular)	Topic 4A
• Proxy settings	Topic 4C
• Remote Desktop Connection	Topic 4D
• Remote Assistance	Topic 4D
• Home vs. Work vs. Public network settings	Topic 4C
• Firewall settings	Topic 4C
• Exceptions	Topic 4C
• Configuration	Topic 4C
• Enabling/disabling Windows Firewall	Topic 4C
• Configuring an alternative IP address in Windows	Topic 4A
• IP addressing	Topic 4A
• Subnet mask	Topic 4A
• DNS	Topic 4A
• Gateway	Topic 4A
• Network card properties	Topic 4A
• Half duplex/full duplex/auto	Topic 4A
• Speed	Topic 4A
• Wake-on-LAN	Topic 4A
• QoS	Topic 4A
• BIOS (on-board NIC)	Topic 4A
1.9 Given a scenario, use features and tools of the Mac OS and Linux client/desktop operating systems.	
• Best practices	Topic 2D
• Scheduled backups	Topic 2D
• Scheduled disk maintenance	Topic 2D
• System updates/App Store	Topic 2D
• Patch management	Topic 2D
• Driver/firmware updates	Topic 2D
• Antivirus/Anti-malware updates	Topic 2D
• Tools	Topic 2B, 2D
• Backup/Time Machine	Topic 2D
• Restore/Snapshot	Topic 2D
• Image recovery	Topic 2B

Domain and Objective	Covered in
• Disk maintenance utilities	Topic 2D
• Shell/Terminal	Topic 2B
• Screen sharing	Topic 2B
• Force Quit	Topic 2B
• Features	Topic 2B
• Multiple desktops/Mission Control	Topic 2B
• Key Chain	Topic 2B
• Spot Light	Topic 2B
• iCloud	Topic 2B
• Gestures	Topic 2B
• Finder	Topic 2B
• Remote Disc	Topic 2B
• Dock	Topic 2B
• Boot Camp	Topic 2B
• Basic Linux commands	Topic 2A
• ls	Topic 2A
• grep	Topic 2A
• cd	Topic 2A
• shutdown	Topic 2A
• pwd vs. passwd	Topic 2A
• mv	Topic 2A
• cp	Topic 2A
• rm	Topic 2A
• chmod	Topic 2A
• chown	Topic 2A
• iwconfig/ifconfig	Topic 2A
• ps	Topic 2A
• su/sudo	Topic 2A
• apt-get	Topic 2A
• vi	Topic 2A
• dd	Topic 2A
• kill	Topic 2A

Domain 2.0 Security

2.1 Summarize the importance of physical security measures.

• Mantrap	Topic 6C
• Badge reader	Topic 6C
• Smart card	Topic 6C
• Security guard	Topic 6C
• Door lock	Topic 6C
• Biometric locks	Topic 6C
• Hardware tokens	Topic 6C
• Cable locks	Topic 6C
• Server locks	Topic 6C

Domain and Objective	Covered in
• USB locks	Topic 6C
• Privacy screen	Topic 6C
• Key fobs	Topic 6C
• Entry control roster	Topic 6C
2.2 Explain logical security concepts.	
• Active Directory	Topic 5C
• Login script	Topic 5C
• Domain	Topic 5C
• Group Policy/Updates	Topic 5C
• Organizational Units	Topic 5C
• Home Folder	Topic 5C
• Folder redirection	Topic 5C
• Software tokens	Topic 7A
• MDM policies	Topic 6A
• Port security	Topic 6A
• MAC address filtering	Topic 6A
• Certificates	Topic 6A
• Antivirus/Anti-malware	Topic 6A
• Firewalls	Topic 6A
• User authentication/strong passwords	Topic 7A
• Multifactor authentication	Topic 7A
• Directory permissions	Topic 7B
• VPN	Topic 6A
• DLP	Topic 7B
• Access control lists	Topic 6A
• Smart card	Topic 6C
• Email filtering	Topic 8B
• Trusted/untrusted software sources	Topic 6A
• Principle of least privilege	Topic 6A
2.3 Compare and contrast wireless security protocols and authentication methods.	
• Protocols and encryption	Topic 4B
• WEP	Topic 4B
• WPA	Topic 4B
• WPA2	Topic 4B
• TKIP	Topic 4B
• AES	Topic 4B
• Authentication	Topic 7A
• Single-factor	Topic 7A
• Multifactor	Topic 7A
• RADIUS	Topic 7A
• TACACS	Topic 7A
2.4 Given a scenario, detect, remove, and prevent malware using appropriate tools and methods.	

Domain and Objective	Covered in
• Malware	Topic 8A
• Ransomware	Topic 8A
• Trojan	Topic 8A
• Keylogger	Topic 8A
• Rootkit	Topic 8A
• Virus	Topic 8A
• Botnet	Topic 8A
• Worm	Topic 8A
• Spyware	Topic 8A
• Tools and methods	Topic 8A
• Antivirus	Topic 8A
• Anti-malware	Topic 8A
• Recovery console	Topic 8A
• Backup/restore	Topic 8A
• End user education	Topic 8A
• Software firewalls	Topic 8A
• DNS configuration	Topic 8A

2.5 Compare and contrast social engineering, threats, and vulnerabilities.

• Social engineering	Topic 6B
• Phishing	Topic 6B
• Spear-phishing	Topic 6B
• Impersonation	Topic 6B
• Shoulder surfing	Topic 6B
• Tailgating	Topic 6B
• Dumpster diving	Topic 6B
• DDoS	Topic 6B
• DoS	Topic 6B
• Zero-day	Topic 6B
• Man-in-the-middle	Topic 6B
• Brute force	Topic 6B
• Dictionary	Topic 6B
• Rainbow table	Topic 6B
• Spoofing	Topic 6B
• Non-compliant systems	Topic 6B
• Zombie	Topic 6B

2.6 Compare and contrast the differences of basic Microsoft Windows OS security settings.

• User and groups	Topic 5A
• Administrator	Topic 5A
• Power user	Topic 5A
• Guest	Topic 5A
• Standard user	Topic 5A
• NTFS vs. share permissions	Topic 1C, 5B

Domain and Objective	Covered in
• Allow vs. deny	Topic 5B
• Moving vs. copying folders and files	Topic 5B
• File attributes	Topic 1C
• Shared files and folders	Topic 5B
• Administrative shares vs. local shares	Topic 5B
• Permission propagation	Topic 5B
• Inheritance	Topic 5B
• System files and folders	Topic 1C
• User authentication	Topic 5A
• Single sign-on	Topic 5A
• Run as administrator vs. standard user	Topic 1B
• BitLocker	Topic 7B
• BitLocker To Go	Topic 7B
• EFS	Topic 7B

2.7 Given a scenario, implement security best practices to secure a workstation.

• Password best practices	Topic 7A
• Setting strong passwords	Topic 7A
• Password expiration	Topic 7A
• Screensaver required password	Topic 7A
• BIOS/UEFI passwords	Topic 7A
• Requiring passwords	Topic 7A
• Account management	Topic 7A
• Restricting user permissions	Topic 7A
• Logon time restrictions	Topic 7A
• Disabling guest account	Topic 7A
• Failed attempts lockout	Topic 7A
• Timeout/screen lock	Topic 7A
• Change default admin user account/password	Topic 7A
• Basic Active Directory functions	Topic 5C
• Account creation	Topic 5C
• Account deletion	Topic 5C
• Password reset/unlock account	Topic 5C
• Disable account	Topic 5C
• Disable autorun	Topic 6A
• Data encryption	Topic 7B
• Patch/update management	Topic 6A

2.8 Given a scenario, implement methods for securing mobile devices.

• Screen locks	Topic 9A
• Fingerprint lock	Topic 9A
• Face lock	Topic 9A
• Swipe lock	Topic 9A
• Passcode lock	Topic 9A

Domain and Objective	Covered in
• Remote wipes	Topic 9A
• Locator applications	Topic 9A
• Remote backup applications	Topic 9A
• Failed login attempts restrictions	Topic 9A
• Antivirus/Anti-malware	Topic 9A
• Patching/OS updates	Topic 9A
• Biometric authentication	Topic 9A
• Full device encryption	Topic 9A
• Multifactor authentication	Topic 9A
• Authenticator applications	Topic 9A
• Trusted sources vs. untrusted sources	Topic 9A
• Firewalls	Topic 9A
• Policies and procedures	Topic 9A
• BYOD vs. corporate-owned	Topic 9A
• Profile security requirements	Topic 9A

2.9 Given a scenario, implement appropriate data destruction and disposal methods.

• Physical destruction	Topic 6C
• Shredder	Topic 6C
• Drill/hammer	Topic 6C
• Electromagnetic (Degaussing)	Topic 6C
• Incineration	Topic 6C
• Certificate of destruction	Topic 6C
• Recycling or repurposing best practices	Topic 6C
• Low-level format vs. standard format	Topic 6C
• Overwrite	Topic 6C
• Drive wipe	Topic 6C

2.10 Given a scenario, configure security on SOHO wireless and wired networks.

• Wireless-specific	Topic 4B
• Changing default SSID	Topic 4B
• Setting encryption	Topic 4B
• Disabling SSID broadcast	Topic 4B
• Antenna and access point placement	Topic 4B
• Radio power levels	Topic 4B
• WPS	Topic 4B
• Change default usernames and passwords	Topic 4B
• Enable MAC filtering	Topic 6A
• Assign static IP addresses	Topic 4B
• Firewall settings	Topic 4C
• Port forwarding/mapping	Topic 4C
• Disabling ports	Topic 4C
• Content filtering/parental controls	Topic 4C
• Update firmware	Topic 4B

Domain and Objective	Covered in
• Physical security	Topic 4B
Domain 3.0 Software Troubleshooting	
3.1 Given a scenario, troubleshoot Microsoft Windows OS problems.	
• Common symptoms	Topic 3C
• Slow performance	Topic 3C
• Limited connectivity	Topic 4E
• Failure to boot	Topic 3C
• No OS found	Topic 3C
• Application crashes	Topic 3C
• Blue screens	Topic 3C
• Black screens	Topic 3C
• Printing issues	Topic 3C
• Services fail to start	Topic 3C
• Slow bootup	Topic 3C
• Slow profile load	Topic 3C
• Common solutions	Topic 3C
• Defragment the hard drive	Topic 3C
• Reboot	Topic 3C
• Kill tasks	Topic 3C
• Restart services	Topic 3C
• Update network settings	Topic 4E
• Reimage/reload OS	Topic 3C
• Roll back updates	Topic 3C
• Roll back devices drivers	Topic 3C
• Apply updates	Topic 3C
• Repair application	Topic 3C
• Update boot order	Topic 3C
• Disable Windows services/applications	Topic 3C
• Disable application startup	Topic 3C
• Safe boot	Topic 3C
• Rebuild Windows profiles	Topic 3C
3.2 Given a scenario, troubleshoot and resolve PC security issues.	
• Common symptoms	Topic 8B
• Pop-ups	Topic 8B
• Browser redirection	Topic 8B
• Security alerts	Topic 8B
• Slow performance	Topic 8B
• Internet connectivity issues	Topic 8B
• PC/OS lockup	Topic 8B
• Application crash	Topic 8B
• OS updates failures	Topic 8B
• Rogue antivirus	Topic 8B

Domain and Objective	Covered in
• Spam	Topic 8B
• Renamed system files	Topic 8B
• Disappearing files	Topic 8B
• File permission changes	Topic 8B
• Hijacked email	Topic 8B
• Responses from users regarding email	Topic 8B
• Automated replies from unknown send email	Topic 8B
• Access denied	Topic 8B
• Invalid certificate (trusted root CA)	Topic 8B
• System/application log errors	Topic 8B

3.3 Given a scenario, use best practice procedures for malware removal.

• 1. Identify and research malware symptoms.	Topic 8A
• 2. Quarantine the infected systems.	Topic 8A
• 3. Disable System Restore (in Windows).	Topic 8A
• 4. Remediate the infected systems.	Topic 8A
• a. Update the anti-malware software.	Topic 8A
• b. Scan and use removal techniques (safe mode, pre-installation environment).	Topic 8A
• 5. Schedule scans and run updates.	Topic 8A
• 6. Enable System Restore and create a restore point (in Windows).	Topic 8A
• 7. Educate the end user.	Topic 8A

3.4 Given a scenario, troubleshoot mobile OS and application issues.

• Common symptoms	Topic 9B
• Dim display	Topic 9B
• Intermittent wireless	Topic 9B
• No wireless connectivity	Topic 9B
• No Bluetooth connectivity	Topic 9B
• Cannot broadcast to external monitor	Topic 9B
• Touchscreen non-responsive	Topic 9B
• Apps not loading	Topic 9B
• Slow performance	Topic 9B
• Unable to decrypt email	Topic 9B
• Extremely short battery life	Topic 9B
• Overheating	Topic 9B
• Frozen system	Topic 9B
• No sound from speakers	Topic 9B
• Inaccurate touch screen response	Topic 9B
• System lockout	Topic 9B
• App log errors	Topic 9B

3.5 Given a scenario, troubleshoot mobile OS and application security issues.

• Common symptoms	Topic 9B

Domain and Objective	Covered in
• Signal drop/weak signal	Topic 9B
• Power drain	Topic 9B
• Slow data speeds	Topic 9B
• Unintended WiFi connection	Topic 9B
• Unintended Bluetooth pairing	Topic 9B
• Leaked personal files/data	Topic 9B
• Data transmission over limit	Topic 9B
• Unauthorized account access	Topic 9B
• Unauthorized location tracking	Topic 9B
• Unauthorized camera/microphone activation	Topic 9B
• High resource utilization	Topic 9B

Domain 4.0 Operational Procedures

4.1 Compare and contrast best practices associated with types of documentation.

• Network topology diagrams	Topic 10C
• Knowledge base/articles	Topic 10C
• Incident documentation	Topic 10C
• Regulatory and compliance policy	Topic 10C
• Acceptable use policy	Topic 10C
• Password policy	Topic 10C
• Inventory management	Topic 10C
• Asset tags	Topic 10C
• Barcodes	Topic 10C

4.2 Given a scenario, implement basic change management best practices.

• Documented business processes	Topic 10D
• Purpose of the change	Topic 10D
• Scope of the change	Topic 10D
• Risk analysis	Topic 10D
• Plan for change	Topic 10D
• End-user acceptance	Topic 10D
• Change board	Topic 10D
• Approvals	Topic 10D
• Backout plan	Topic 10D
• Documentation changes	Topic 10D

4.3 Given a scenario, implement basic disaster prevention and recovery methods.

• Backup and recovery	Topic 10E
• Image level	Topic 10E
• File level	Topic 10E
• Critical applications	Topic 10E
• Backup testing	Topic 10E
• UPS	Topic 10B
• Surge protector	Topic 10B
• Cloud storage vs. local storage backups	Topic 10E

Domain and Objective	Covered in
• Account recovery options	Topic 10E
4.4 Explain common safety procedures.	
• Equipment grounding	Topic 10A
• Proper component handling and storage	Topic 10A
• Antistatic bags	Topic 10A
• ESD straps	Topic 10A
• ESD mats	Topic 10A
• Self-grounding	Topic 10A
• Toxic waste handling	Topic 10A
• Batteries	Topic 10A
• Toner	Topic 10A
• CRT	Topic 10A
• Cell phones	Topic 10A
• Tablets	Topic 10A
• Personal safety	Topic 10A
• Disconnect power before repairing PC	Topic 10A
• Remove jewelry	Topic 10A
• Lifting techniques	Topic 10A
• Weight limitations	Topic 10A
• Electrical fire safety	Topic 10A
• Cable management	Topic 10A
• Safety goggles	Topic 10A
• Air filter mask	Topic 10A
• Compliance with government regulations	Topic 10A
4.5 Explain environmental impacts and appropriate controls.	
• MSDS documentation for handling and disposal	Topic 10B
• Temperature, humidity level awareness, and proper ventilation	Topic 10B
• Power surges, brownouts, and blackouts	Topic 10B
• Battery backup	Topic 10B
• Surge suppressor	Topic 10B
• Protection from airborne particles	Topic 10B
• Enclosures	Topic 10B
• Air filters/mask	Topic 10B
• Dust and debris	Topic 10B
• Compressed air	Topic 10B
• Vacuums	Topic 10B
• Compliance to government regulations	Topic 10B
4.6 Explain the processes for addressing prohibited content/activity, and privacy, licensing, and policy concepts.	
• Incident response	Topic 7C
• First response	Topic 7C
• Identify	Topic 7C

Domain and Objective	Covered in
• Report through proper channels	Topic 7C
• Data/device preservation	Topic 7C
• Use of documentation/documentation changes	Topic 7B
• Chain of custody	Topic 7C
• Tracking of evidence/documenting process	Topic 7C
• Licensing/DRM/EULA	Topic 7B
• Open-source vs. commercial license	Topic 7B
• Personal license vs. enterprise licenses	Topic 7B
• Regulated data	Topic 7B
• PII	Topic 7B
• PCI	Topic 7B
• GDPR	Topic 7B
• PHI	Topic 7B
• Follow all policies and security best practices	Topic 7B

4.7 Given a scenario, use proper communication techniques and professionalism.

Domain and Objective	Covered in
• Use proper language and avoid jargon, acronyms, and slang, when applicable	Topic 10G
• Maintain a positive attitude/ project confidence	Topic 10G
• Actively listen (taking notes) and avoid interrupting the customer	Topic 10G
• Be culturally sensitive	Topic 10G
• Use appropriate professional titles, when applicable	Topic 10G
• Be on time (if late, contact the customer)	Topic 10G
• Avoid distractions	Topic 10G
• Personal calls	Topic 10G
• Texting/social media sites	Topic 10G
• Talking to coworkers while interacting with customers	Topic 10G
• Personal interruptions	Topic 10G
• Dealing with difficult customers or situations	Topic 10G
• Do not argue with customers and/or be defensive	Topic 10G
• Avoid dismissing customer problems	Topic 10G
• Avoid being judgmental	Topic 10G
• Clarify customer statements (ask open-ended questions to narrow the scope of the problem, restate the issue, or question to verify understanding)	Topic 10G
• Do not disclose experiences via social media outlets	Topic 10G
• Set and meet expectations/timeline and communicate status with the customer	Topic 10G
• Offer different repair/replacement options, if applicable	Topic 10G
• Provide proper documentation on the services provided	Topic 10G
• Follow up with customer/user at a later date to verify satisfaction	Topic 10G
• Deal appropriately with customers' confidential and private materials	Topic 10G
• Located on a computer, desktop, printer, etc.	Topic 10G

Domain and Objective	Covered in
4.8 Identify the basics of scripting.	
• Script file types	Topic 10F
• .bat	Topic 10F
• .ps1	Topic 10F
• .vbs	Topic 10F
• .sh	Topic 10F
• .py	Topic 10F
• .js	Topic 10F
• Environment variables	Topic 10F
• Comment syntax	Topic 10F
• Basic script constructs	Topic 10F
• Basic loops	Topic 10F
• Variables	Topic 10F
• Basic data types	Topic 10F
• Integers	Topic 10F
• Strings	Topic 10F
4.9 Given a scenario, use remote access technologies.	
• RDP	Topic 4D
• Telnet	Topic 4D
• SSH	Topic 4D
• Third-party tools	Topic 4D
• Screen share feature	Topic 4D
• File share	Topic 4D
• Security considerations of each access method	Topic 4D

Solutions

Activity 1-1: Supporting Operating Systems Review

1. **Which versions of Windows do you expect to support?**

   Answers will vary, but might include a mixture of Windows 7 and Windows 10.

2. **Which Windows features and tools do you think you will use most often and why?**

   Answers will vary, but might include configuring users and systems through Windows Settings and Control Panel, using GUI-based administrative tools, using command line tools, working with registry files, and creating custom MMCs.

Activity 2-1: Installing, Configuring, and Maintaining Operating Systems Review

1. **Do you have experience installing operating systems? Do you feel you will be able to perform installations more efficiently as a result of the information presented in this lesson?**

   Answers will vary, but might include upgrading an OS on a home PC, or installing an OS on a spare PC or notebook, or upgrading a work computer.

2. **How often do you expect to be able to perform in-place upgrades instead of clean installs at your workplace?**

   Answers will vary depending on the operating systems involved. If an environment has a propensity of Windows XP or Windows Vista computers that need to be upgraded to Windows 7 or Windows 8, more clean installs will be required, but if the environment has many Windows Vista computers that need to be upgraded to Windows 7, or Windows 7 computers that need to be upgraded to Windows 8, more in-place upgrades might be possible.

Activity 3-1: Maintaining and Troubleshooting Microsoft Windows Review

1. **Which Windows performance management tools would you expect to use most in your workplace?**

   Answers will vary, but might include Task Manager and Performance Monitor.

2. **Have you ever recovered a severely compromised Windows system? If so, then describe your experience.**

   Answers will vary, but may include having to use Last Known Good Configuration or Safe Mode to identify issues and recover systems. You might need to resort to performing a factory reset if the damage is too severe.

Activity 4-1: Configuring and Troubleshooting Networks Review

1. **What experiences do you have in working with the networking technologies discussed in this lesson?**

   Answers will vary according to the backgrounds of different individuals. Possible experiences include: how do you access library card catalogs from the library, from home, or from the office? How do you troubleshoot your own Internet connectivity problems? Have you ever set up a home network using a router or switch?

2. **Do you have any experience working with SOHO networks? What do you expect to support in future job functions?**

   Answers will vary, but will likely include connecting and setting up a small home wireless network. Most technicians will be installing and supporting SOHO wireless networks within their job role.

Activity 5-1: Managing Users, Workstations, and Shared Resources Review

1. **What experiences do you have in working with any of the technologies discussed in this lesson?**

   Answers will vary according to the backgrounds of different individuals. Possible experiences include: managing local user accounts on a home PC, configuring network shares, and joining a computer to an AD domain.

2. **Which AD configuration task do you expect to perform most often in your workplace?**

   Answers will vary, but might include creating and disabling accounts, joining computers to domains, or configuring home folders and folder redirection.

Activity 6-1: Security Concepts Review

1. **What physical security controls have been employed at organizations where you have worked?**

   Answers will vary, but may include door access controls such as keypad or proximity card reader, video monitoring such as video cameras, emergency procedures in case of fire.

2. **What steps has your organization taken to ensure the security of mobile devices? Have you planned ahead in case the devices are lost or stolen? If so, how?**

   Answers will vary, but may include installing anti-malware apps, ensuring users enable screen lock and passcode settings, configuring device encryption, requiring remote wipe capability in case of loss, enabling location services and applications, requiring that users back up their data, and ensuring that all patches and updates are applied.

Activity 7-1: Securing Workstations and Data Review

1. **Which security best practices do you feel are the most important? Which are the minimum measures that should be taken? Does your organization implement good security practices?**

   Answers will vary, but may include following a company's security policy, entering a password that meets strong password requirements, and installing antivirus software on workstations.

2. **Have you had experience with security incidents such as data breaches? What might have been done differently to further protect the data that was put at risk?**

   Answers will vary, but may include establishing clear incident response policies, appointing key personnel to act as first responders, and training IT personnel in basic data and device preservation techniques.

Activity 8-1: Troubleshooting Workstation Security Issues Review

1. **Which best practice for minimizing the effect of malware do you think is most important?**

   Answers will vary, but might include keeping antivirus software and signature files updated, or user awareness training.

2. **How might you recognize a possible spyware or adware infection on a workstation?**

   Answers will vary, but might include the appearance of pop-ups or additional toolbars, or unexpectedly being redirected to a different web page.

Activity 9-1: Supporting and Troubleshooting Mobile Devices Review

1. **In your professional experience, have you supported mobile devices? If not, what kind of experience do you have with them?**

   Answers will vary, and experience levels can range from no experience at all to power users that are very comfortable with mobile devices.

2. **What type of technical support do you think will be expected of an A+ technician as mobile devices become even more prominent within the workplace?**

   Answers will vary, but will most likely include implementing security methods and synchronizing organizational data with mobile devices.

Activity 10-1: Implementing Operational Procedures Review

1. **Which of the best practices discussed in this lesson apply in your workplace?**

   Answers will vary, but may include silencing phones and pagers, using active listening techniques, and treating clients with respect.

2. **How do you think the scripting concepts discussed in this lesson will help you at your workplace?**

   Answers will vary, but may include the ability to automate repetitive, tedious tasks.

Glossary

2-step verification
When a user connects to a service using a device that was not previously registered with the service, the authenticator application sends a **one time password** to a smartphone or alternate email address that the user then enters to complete the authentication process.

absolute path
The specific location, including the domain name, irrespective of the working directory or combined paths.

accident
Any instance where a person is injured or computer equipment is damaged.

accounting
In security terms, the process of tracking and recording system activities and resource access. Also known as auditing.

ACE
(access control entry) Within an ACL, a record of subjects and the permissions they hold on the resource.

ACL
(Access Control List) The permissions attached to or configured on a network resource, such as folder, file, or firewall. The ACL specifies which subjects (user accounts, host IP addresses, and so on) are allowed or denied access and the privileges given over the object (read only, read/write, and so on).

ACPI
(Advanced Configuration and Power Management Interface) An open standard to communicate between the operating system and hardware to enable power management features.

active listening
The skill of listening to an individual so that you give them your full attention and are not trying to argue with, comment on, or misinterpret what they have said.

ActiveX
Microsoft's software framework for browser plug-ins that allow users to run software components accessed from the Internet.

AD DS
(Active Directory Domain Services) The database that contains the users, groups, and computer accounts in a Windows Server domain.

Administrative Templates
Group Policy files for registry-based policy management. The files have the .ADM file extension.

Administrator account
A Microsoft Windows user account that can perform all tasks on the computer, including installing and uninstalling apps, setting up other users, and configuring hardware and software.

Adult account
Any Microsoft Windows user account that is not configured as a **Child account**.

AES
(Advanced Encryption Standard) Modern encryption suite providing symmetric encryption (the same key is used to encrypt and decrypt). AES is a very strong cipher with many applications, including being part of the WPA2 Wi-Fi encryption scheme.

air or dust filters
Polyester sheets that cover fan inlets to trap dust on their surface, preventing

the dust from getting into a computer or other device.

airborne particles
Dust and other small items that can be blown about and carried on air currents, that if they get inside computers, can prevent effective heat dissipation.

Android
An open-source operating system supported by a wide range of hardware and software vendors.

answer file
An XML text file that contains all of the instructions that the Windows Setup program will need to install and configure the OS without any administrator intervention, including the product key.

anti-malware software
A software program that scans a device or network for known viruses, Trojans, worms, and other malicious software.

anti-virus
Software capable of detecting and removing virus infections and (in most cases) other types of malware, such as worms, Trojans, rootkits, adware, spyware, password crackers, network mappers, DoS tools, and so on. Anti-virus software works on the basis of both identifying malware code (signatures) and detecting suspicious behavior (heuristics). Anti-virus software must be kept up to date with the latest malware definitions and protect itself against tampering.

antistatic bag
A packaging material containing anti-ESD shielding or dissipative materials to protect components from ESD damage.

app scanner
A class of security software designed to monitor the permissions allocated to apps and how they are using (or abusing) them.

Apple ID
A user account on an Apple device based on the sign-in email address that is used to sign-in to the App Store,

access iCloud, and other Apple features and functions.

apps
Installable programs that extend the functionality of a mobile device. An app must be written and compiled for the particular operating system used by the mobile device.

apt
A tool for maintaining packages on Debian-based Linux systems.

arguments
Values supplied to the command for it to operate on, supplied in the correct order required for the command's syntax.

ARP
(Address Resolution Protocol) When two systems communicate using IP, an IP address is used to identify the destination machine. The IP address must be mapped to a device (the network adapter's MAC address). ARP performs the task of resolving an IP address to a hardware address. Each host caches known mappings in an ARP table for a few minutes. It is also a utility used to manage the ARP cache.

ARP poisoning
(Address Resolution Protocol poisoning) Injecting a false IP:MAC lookup into the victim's ARP cache. This can be used to perform a variety of attacks, including DoS, spoofing, and Man-in-the-Middle.

array
See **RAID**.

asset
A thing of economic value. For accounting purposes, assets are classified in different ways, such as tangible and intangible or short term and long term.

asset management
Asset management means identifying each asset and recording its location, attributes, and value in a database.

attended installation
A software or operating system installation where the installer inputs

the configuration information in response to prompts from a setup program.

auditing
See **accounting**.

AUP
(Acceptable Use Policy) A policy that governs employees' use of company equipment and Internet services. ISPs may also apply AUPs to their customers.

authentication
A means for a user to prove their identity to a computer system. Authentication is implemented as either something you know (a username and password), something you have (a smart card or key fob), or something you are (biometric information). Often, more than one method is employed (2-factor authentication).

authentication factor
Information used to identify a user from one of several categories (something the user knows, has, or "is," or the user's location).

authenticator application
An app that requires, when using a new computer or device to access a service, a code to be sent in the form of a **one time password**.

authorization
In security terms, the process of determining what rights and privileges a particular entity has.

availability
The fundamental security goal of ensuring that systems operate continuously and that authorized individuals can access data that they need.

backdoor
A remote administration utility providing a means of configuring a computer. Remote admin software may be installed intentionally, in which case it must be properly secured. Backdoors may also be installed by malware.

background
A process that runs without a window and does not require any sort of user interaction.

backlight
Fluorescent lamp illuminating the image on a flat panel (LCD) screen. If the backlight or inverter fails, the screen image will go very, very dark.

backout plan
A plan defined ahead of making any moves, adds, or changes so that in case unforeseen problems arise when the change is made, there is a plan to put things back as they were before making the change.

backup
Recovery of data can be provided through the use of a backup system. Most backup systems provide support for tape devices. This provides a reasonably reliable and quick mechanism for copying critical data. Different backup types (full, incremental, or differential) balance media capacity, time required to backup, and time required to restore.

backup power generator
A Standby Power Supply fueled by diesel or propane. In the event of a power outage, a UPS must provide transitionary power, as a backup generator cannot be cut-in fast enough.

barcode label
A label containing a UPC code. Can be affixed to tangible assets for identification in an **asset management** system.

baseline
The point from which something varies. A configuration baseline is the original or recommended settings for a device, while a performance baseline is the originally measured throughput.

battery backup
See **UPS**.

BCD
(Boot Configuration Data) Windows stores information about operating systems installed on the computer in a boot configuration data store, located in \boot

\bcd on the system partition. The BCD can be modified using the bcedit command-line tool or MSCONFIG.

biometric devices
Peripherals used to gather biometric data for comparison to data stored in a database.

biometrics
Identifying features stored as digital data can be used to authenticate a user. Typical features used include facial pattern, iris, retina, or fingerprint pattern, and signature recognition. This requires the relevant scanning device, such as a fingerprint reader, and a database of biometric information (template).

blacklisting
An address added to the black list is prohibited from connecting to any port.

blackout
A complete loss of electrical power.

Boolean values
Data type supporting 1-bit storage, representing FALSE and TRUE. Boolean logic is a statement that resolves to a true or false condition and underpins the branching and looping features of computer code.

boot partition
In Microsoft terminology, the partition that contains the operating system (that is, the \WINDOWS folder) is referred to as the boot partition. This is typically a different partition to the system partition (the partition containing the boot files).

boot sector
See **Volume Boot Record (VBR)**.

botnet
A network of computers that have been compromised by Trojan, rootkit, or worm malware. Providing the botnet can also subvert any firewalls between the controller (or herder) and the compromised computers (zombies), so that they can be remotely controlled and monitored using covert channels.

branch
Used to control the flow within a computer program or script, usually based on some type of logic condition. Often implemented with If or Goto statements.

brownout
A brownout occurs when the power that is supplied by the electrical wall socket is insufficient to allow the computer to function correctly. Brownouts are long sags in power output that are often caused by overloaded or faulty mains distribution circuits or by a failure in the supply route from electrical power station to a building.

BSOD
(Blue Screen of Death) A condition that indicates an error from which the system cannot recover (also called a stop error). Blue screens are usually caused by bad driver software or hardware faults (memory or disk).

BYOD
(Bring Your Own Device) Security framework and tools to facilitate use of personally owned devices to access corporate networks and data.

CA
(Certificate Authority) A server that can issue digital certificates and the associated public/private key pairs.

CAB
(Change Advisory Board) In change management, the team responsible for approving or denying RFCs.

CAC
(Common Access Card) An identity and authentication smart card produced for Department of Defense employees and contractors in response to a Homeland Security Directive.

CAL
(Client Access Licenses) Licenses required for clients accessing software services from a server, purchased per server (with a limited number of simultaneous users) or per seat (specifying each unique device or user).

CAM
(Content Addressable Memory) See **MAC address table**.

capacity
The amount of space available on storage media.

chain of custody
Documentation attached to evidence from a crime scene detailing when, where, and how it was collected, where it has been stored, and who has handled it subsequently to collection.

challenge question
Questions asked, usually through software but sometimes from a help desk staff member, that only the end-user can answer. A feature of multifactor authentication or for account recovery.

change management
A means of putting policies in place to reduce the risk that changes to information and communications technology infrastructure components could cause service disruption.

character
Data type supporting storage of a single character.

charms
Commands displayed in a vertical bar on the right side of a Windows 8 Start Screen. The commands are Search, Share, Start, Devices, and Settings.

Child account
A Microsoft Windows user account that is a standard user account with the **Family Safety Settings** enabled.

Chrome OS
Chrome OS is derived from Linux, via an open source OS called Chromium. Chrome OS itself is proprietary. Chrome OS is developed by Google to run on specific laptop (chromebooks) and PC (chromeboxes) hardware.

CI
(configuration item) In change management, an asset that requires specific management procedures for it to be used to deliver the service. Each CI is identified with a label and defined by its attributes and stored in a **CMDB**.

CIRT/CSIRT
(Cyber Incident Response Team/Computer Security Incident Response Team) Team with responsibility for incident response. The CIRT must have expertise across a number of business domains (IT, HR, legal, and marketing, for instance).

clean install
Installing the OS to a new computer or completely replacing the OS software on an existing computer, and in the process, deleting existing applications, user settings, and data files.

CLI
(Command Line Interface) A textual interface based on the operating system, where a user typically enters commands at the command prompt to instruct the computer to perform a specific task.

clusters
Disk sectors are grouped in clusters of 2, 4, 6, 8, or more. The smaller the cluster size, the lower the data overhead in terms of wasted space, but larger clusters can improve performance.

CMDB
(Configuration Management Database) In change management, the database in which **configuration items** are stored, identified using a label and defined by their attributes.

CMS
(Configuration Management System) The tools and databases that collect, store, manage, update, and present information about **CIs**.

coaxial cable
Cable type using two separate conductors that share a common axis (hence the term co-axial). Coax cables are categorized using the Radio Grade (RG) "standard". Coax is considered obsolete in terms of LAN applications but is still widely used for CCTV networks and as drop cables for cable TV (CATV).

COM+
(Component Object Model) Microsoft's object-oriented programming architecture and operating system services for developing applications. See also **Component Services**.

command interpreter
The portion of an operating system or script language that is able to read and implement commands entered by a user or from a **script file**.

command mode
In Linux vi editor, the mode that allows users to perform different editing actions using single keystrokes.

comparison operator
A relationship evaluation between two variables to determine whether they are equal, not equal, less than, greater than, less than or equal to, or greater than or equal to each other.

compiled program
An instruction set in which the programming instructions are performed by the computer processor.

Component Object Model
(COM) Microsoft's object-oriented programming model specification.

Component Services
Windows applications use various component (COM) models and APIs to share data. Component Services in Administrative Tools allows configuration of component servers.

compressed air blaster
A can of air packaged under pressure that is used to remove dust and debris from inside printers and other computing devices.

confidentiality
The fundamental security goal of keeping information and communications private and protecting them from unauthorized access.

configuration baseline
The original or recommended settings for a device.

configuration management
A means of identifying all components of the information and communications technology infrastructure, including hardware, software, and procedures, and the properties of those items.

constant
Identifier for a value that is fixed before program execution and does not change.

Control Panel
Management interface for configuring Windows settings. In Windows 8 and later, the touch-enabled app PC Settings/ Windows Settings is used for many options previously configured via Control Panel.

counter logs
Windows log files that allow you to collect statistics about resources and can be used to determine system health and performance.

cron
A Linux/Unix daemon that runs in the background and executes specified tasks at a designated time or date.

cron table
The file (crontab) in Linux that contains instructions defining the tasks to be executed by a cron.

cryptographic hash
A hashed value from which it is impossible to recover the original data.

cultural sensitivity
Being aware of customs and habits used by other people.

current working directory
In Linux, the location on the file system that you are accessing at any point in time.

cyber warfare
The use of IT services and devices to disrupt national, state, or organization activities, especially when used for military purposes.

cylinder
The aggregate of all tracks that reside in the same location on every disk surface.

data backup
A system maintenance task that enables you to store copies of critical data for safekeeping as protection against loss of data due to disasters such as file corruption or hardware failure.

Data Collector Sets
Windows log files that record information for viewing in real time or at a later date.

data restoration
A system recovery task that enables you to access and restore the backed-up data.

Data Sources
Windows applications can import data from various data sources. The links to different data files and database drivers can be configured from Administrative Tools.

data transmission overlimit
When apps, especially malware or rogue apps, trying to collect data in the background use excessive amounts of data on a mobile device.

data type
The way the data is intended to be used in a program such as character or string, integer, real number, logical, or Boolean.

DCOM
(Distributed COM) Microsoft's interface that allows a client program object to request services from server program objects.

DDoS
(Distributed Denial of Service) A **DoS** attack that uses multiple compromised computers (a "botnet" of "zombies") to launch the attack.

declared variable
A variable for which the data type, possibly the size, and optionally an initial value have been specified within the script or program file.

defense in depth
Configuring security controls on hosts (endpoints) as well as providing network (perimeter) security, physical security, and administrative controls.

defragmentation
See **disk defragmentation**.

degaussing
Exposing the disk to a powerful electromagnet to disrupt the magnetic pattern that stores data on the disk surface.

desktop
The desktop is at the top of the object hierarchy in Explorer, containing the Computer, Documents, Network, and Recycle Bin objects. The desktop also stores shortcuts to programs, files, and system objects.

desktop style
Computers designed for stationary use come in various styles including tower, slimline, and all-in-one.

device driver
A small piece of code that is loaded during the boot sequence of an operating system. This code, usually provided by the hardware vendor, provides access to a device, or hardware, from the OS kernel. Under Windows, a signing system is in place for drivers to ensure that they do not make the OS unstable.

diagram
A drawing that captures the relationships between network elements and identifying the location of items on the network.

dial-up
A remote network access method that utilizes the local telephone line (Plain Old Telephone System [POTS]) to establish a connection between two computers fitted with modems. Dial-up is a legacy method of Internet access. It may still be deployed for special administrative purposes or as an emergency backup connection method. Configuration is generally a case of setting the telephone number, username, and password.

digital certificate
An X.509 digital certificate is issued by a Certificate Authority (CA) as a guarantee that a public key it has issued to an organization to encrypt messages sent to it genuinely belongs to that organization. Both parties must trust the CA. The public

key can be used to encrypt messages but not to decrypt them. A message can only be decrypted by the private key, which is mathematically linked to the public key but not derivable from it. This is referred to as asymmetric encryption. Part of the CA's responsibility is ensuring that this private key is known only to the organization owning the certificate. This arrangement is referred to a Public Key Infrastructure (PKI).

dim display
When a mobile device has the **backlight**set to its lowest setting and the automatic light adjustment is disabled, or the phone is set to conserve power by auto-dimming the light.

Disaster Recovery Plan
A documented and resourced plan showing actions and responsibilities to be used in response to critical incidents. The recovery plan may also provide for practice exercises or drills for testing and to familiarize staff with procedures. As well as facilitating a smooth transition in the event of disaster, plans must stress the importance of maintaining secure systems.

disk defragmentation
Fragmentation occurs when a data file is not saved to contiguous sectors on a disk. This decreases performance by making the disk read/write heads move between fragments. Defragmentation is a software routine that compacts files back into contiguous areas of the disk. The process can be run from a command-line using the defrag utility, but it is more often run from Windows.

disk wiping
Using software to ensure that old data is destroyed by writing to each location on the media, either using zeroes or in a random pattern. This leaves the disk in a "clean" state ready to be passed to the new owner.

distribution
A complete Linux implementation, including kernel, shell, applications, and utilities, that is packaged, distributed, and supported by a software vendor.

distro
See **distribution**.

DLP (loss prevention)
(Data Loss/Leakage Prevention) Software that can identify data that has been classified and apply "fine-grained" user privileges to it (preventing copying it or forwarding by email, for instance).

DMZ
(Demilitarized Zone) A private network connected to the Internet must be protected against intrusion from the Internet. However, certain services may need to be made publicly accessible from the Internet (web and email, for instance). One solution is to put such servers in a DMZ. The idea of a DMZ is that traffic cannot pass through it. If communication is required between hosts on either side of a DMZ, a host within the DMZ acts as a proxy. It takes the request and checks it. If the request is valid, it re-transmits it to the destination. External hosts have no idea about what (if anything) is behind the DMZ. A DMZ is implemented using either two firewalls (screened subnet) or a single three-legged firewall (one with three network ports).

dock
macOS feature for managing applications from the desktop, similar to the Windows taskbar.

domain controller
Any Windows-based server that provides domain authentication services (logon services) is referred to as a domain controller (DC). Domain controllers maintain a master copy of the database of network resources.

domain network
A group of computers which share a common accounts database, referred to as the directory.

domain user account
In a corporate environment, an account that is part of a domain, so the user account settings are controlled by the domain administrator.

DoS
(Denial of Service) A network attack that aims to disrupt a service, usually by overloading it.

driver
Software that creates an interface between a device and the operating system. It may also include tools for configuring and optimizing the device.

DRM
(Digital Rights Management) Copyright protection technologies for digital media. DRM solutions usually try to restrict the number of devices allowed for playback of a licensed digital file, such as a music track or ebook.

dumpster diving
A social engineering technique of discovering things about an organization (or person) based on what it throws away.

EAP
(Extensible Authentication Protocol) Framework for negotiating authentication methods, supporting a range of authentication devices. EAP-TLS uses PKI certificates, Protected EAP (PEAP) creates a TLS-protected tunnel between the supplicant and authenticator to secure the user authentication method, and Lightweight EAP (LEAP) is a password-based mechanism used by Cisco.

EAPoL
(Extensible Authentication Protocol over LAN) Another term for EAP. See **EAP**.

eavesdropping
Some transmission media are susceptible to eavesdropping (listening in to communications sent over the media). To secure transmissions, they must be encrypted.

effective group ID
In Linux, the group ID used by the kernel in determining the group permissions a process has when accessing files and shared resources.

EFS
(Encrypting File System) Under NTFS, files and folders can be encrypted to ensure privacy of the data. Only the user who

encrypted the file can subsequently open it.

Electrostatic discharge
See **ESD**.

email filtering
Techniques to prevent a user being overwhelmed with spam (junk email). Spam can be blocked from reaching an organization using a mail gateway to filter messages. At the user level, software can redirect spam to a junk folder (or similar). Anti-spam filtering needs to balance blocking illegitimate traffic with permitting legitimate messages. Anti-spam techniques can also use lists of known spam servers (blacklists).

enclosure
A container with its own air filters and fans to protect computers or other devices in dirty or dusty environments.

encryption
Scrambling the characters used in a message so that the message can be seen but not understood or modified unless it can be deciphered. Encryption provides for a secure means of transmitting data and authenticating users. It is also used to store data securely. Encryption uses different types of cipher and one or more keys. The size of the key is one factor in determining the strength of the encryption product.

end of life system
A system that is no longer supported by the developer or vendor.

entry control roster
Sign-in sheet for managing access to premises.

environment variable
A storage location in the environment of the operating system's command shell.

environmental power problems
Issues affecting power including **surges**, **brownouts**, and **blackouts** caused by failures in the building power supply.

eSATA
(external Serial Advanced Technology Attachment) An external interface for SATA

connections, enabling you to connect external SATA drives to PCs.

eSATAp
A non-standard powered port used by some vendors that is compatible with both USB and SATA (with an eSATAp cable).

escape character
A character used to allow alternate use of a reserved character within a particular programming language. The escape characters vary between programming languages. Often used to allow use of a reserved character within a string.

ESD
(electrostatic discharge) The release of a charge from a metal or plastic surface that occurs when a potential difference is formed between the charged object and an oppositely charged conductive object. This electrical discharge can damage silicon chips and computer components if they are exposed to it.

EULA
(End User License Agreement) The agreement governing the installation and use of proprietary software.

evil twin
In an evil twin attack, the attacker creates a malicious wireless access point masquerading as a genuine one, enabling the attacker to harvest confidential information as users connect via the AP.

execute
Carry out the command entered by a user or as read from a script file.

execution control
Logical security technologies designed to prevent malicious software from running on a host and establish a security system that does not entirely depend on the good behavior of individual users.

exFAT
A file system designed for flash memory cards and memory sticks.

expansion cards
A printed circuit board that is installed in a slot on a system board to provide special functions for customizing or extending a computer's capabilities. Also referred to as adapter card, I/O card, add-in, add-on, or board.

Explorer
See **File Explorer**.

Face ID
The Apple device feature that uses face lock to grant access to the device.

face lock
A biometric authentication mechanism in which the hash is computed from a picture of the user's face.

factory default reset
Setting a mobile device back to the original factor settings, creating a clean OS, removing all data and apps, and resetting any configuration done by the user.

Factory Recovery Partition
Disk partition accessible via the startup sequence that contains an image of the system partition as produced by the PC vendor. This can be used to recover the PC to its factory state by performing a repair install, but will erase any user data or installed programs.

failed login attempts
A configurable value that specifies how many incorrect login attempts can be used before the device is locked for a specified length of time.

Fair Use Policy
See **AUP**.

false negative
A condition where a system denies entry when it should have granted it.

false positive
A condition where a system grants entry when it should have denied it.

Family Safety Settings
A Microsoft Windows setting that helps protect children by limiting their access to functions and features.

FAT
(File Allocation Table) A basic disk format allowing the OS to write data as files on a disk. The original 16-bit version (FAT16, but

often simply called FAT) was replaced by a 32-bit version that is almost universally supported by different operating systems and devices. A 64-bit version (exFAT) was introduced with Windows 7 and is also supported by XP SP3 and Vista SP1 and some versions of Linux and macOS. There is also a 12-bit version used to format floppy disks.

FAT16
(File Allocation Table, 16-bit) The 16-bit file system used in the Windows 3.1 and DOS operating systems with 128 K sectors that only allowed very small partitions (about 32 MB) with later Windows versions employing 512 K sectors allowing for 2 GB partitions.

FAT32
(File Allocation Table, 32-bit) The 32-bit file system that allows approximately 4 GB partitions.

FDE
(full disk encryption) Encryption of all data on a disk (including system files, temporary files, and the pagefile) can be accomplished via a supported OS, third-party software, or at the controller level by the disk device itself. Used with a strong authentication method, this mitigates against data theft in the event that the device is lost or stolen. The key used to encrypt the disk can either be stored on a USB stick or smart card or in a Trusted Platform Module.

feature updates
Semi-annual updates to the Windows operating system that include enhanced features that are installed in multiple phases, requiring a reboot after each phase of the update installation. Compare with quality updates.

file attribute
A characteristic that can be associated with a file or folder that provides the operating system with important information about the file or folder and how it is intended to be used by system users.

File Explorer
A Microsoft Windows tool that offers a single view of all the resources and information that you can access from a computer.

file extension
A series of characters at the end of a file name; used by an OS to identify the software application that is associated with a file.

file system hierarchy
In Linux, the directory structure starting with the root directory (/) with directories and subdirectories below it to store files.

Finder
The file management GUI in macOS.

fingerprint sensor
A device, usually integrated into a mobile device, that reads the user's fingerprint to determine whether to grant access to the device.

firewall
Hardware or software that filters traffic passing into or out of a network. A basic packet-filtering firewall works at Layer 3 (Network). Packets can be filtered depending on several criteria (inbound or outbound, IP address, and port number). More advanced firewalls (proxy and stateful inspection) can examine higher layer information, to provide enhanced security.

firewall apps
Mobile device firewall app that can monitor app activity and prevent connections to particular ports or IP addresses.

floating point numbers
Data type supporting storage of floating point numbers (decimal fractions).

folder redirection
A Microsoft Windows technology that allows an administrative user to redirect the path of a local folder (such as the user's home folder) to a folder on a network share, making the data available to the user when they log into any computer on the network where the network share is located.

footprinting
An information gathering threat, in which the attacker attempts to learn about the configuration of the network and security systems through social engineering attacks or software-based tools.

force stop
An Android option to close an unresponsive app.

forensics
The process of gathering and submitting computer evidence to trial. Digital evidence is latent, meaning that it must be interpreted. This means that great care must be taken to prove that the evidence has not been tampered with or falsified. The key points in collecting evidence are to record every step and action, to gather appropriate evidence, and to bag evidence. To preserve evidence correctly, it should be stored securely. Any investigation should be done on a copy of the digital files, not the originals. Each piece of evidence must be accompanied by a chain of custody form, detailing when, where, and how it was collected, where it has been stored, and who has handled it subsequently to collection.

fragmentation
Occurs when a data file is not saved to contiguous sectors on a disk. This decreases performance by making the disk read/write heads move between fragments.

freeware
Software that is available for download and use free of charge.

FRU
(field replaceable unit) An adapter or other component that can be replaced by a technician on-site. Most PC and laptop components are FRUs, while the components of smartphones are not.

fuse
A circuit breaker designed to protect the device and users of the device from faulty wiring or supply of power (overcurrent protection).

generator
See **backup power generator**.

geotagging
The process of adding geographic location metadata to captured media such as pictures or videos.

geotracking
Determining the location of a person or object using the GPS data from a GPS-enabled device.

gestures
Finger movements on a trackpad or mouse that enable a user to scroll, zoom, and navigate desktop, document, and application content.

gloves
Latex hand coverings to protect the technician when they are working around a toner spill.

Gnome
A popular Linux GUI desktop.

GNU
A recursive acronym standing for "GNU is Not UNIX."

GPO
(Group Policy Object) On a Windows domain, per-user and per-computer settings can be deployed through Group Policy Objects attached to Active Directory containers, such as domains and Organization Units. Group policy can be used to configure security settings such as password policy, account restrictions, firewall status, and so on.

gpresult
A command line tool that displays the **RSoP** for a computer and user account.

GPT
(GUID Partition Table) A modern disk partitioning system allowing large numbers of partitions and very large partition sizes.

gpupdate
A command line tool to apply a new or changed **policy** immediately. When used with the /force option, it causes all policies (new and old) to be reapplied.

grounded
An equipment ground provides a safe path for electrical current to flow away in the event that a device or cable is faulty. Self-grounding removes any static potential difference between a technician's clothes and body and a device they are handling, reducing the risk of damaging the component through Electrostatic Discharge (ESD).

Guest account
A Microsoft Windows user account with limited capabilities, no privacy, and is disabled by default.

GUI
(Graphical User Interface) An easy to use, intuitive interface for a computer operating system. Most GUIs require a pointing device, such as a mouse, to operate efficiently. One of the world's first GUI-based operating systems was the Apple Mac OS, released in 1984. Thereafter, Microsoft produced their Windows family of products based around their GUI. In fact, recognizing that GUI covers a whole range of designs, the Windows interface is better described as a WIMP (Windows, Icons, Menus, Pointing [device]) interface.

guideline
Used for areas of policy where there are no procedures either because the situation has not been fully assessed or because the decision making process is too complex and subject to variables to capture it in a procedure.

hacker collective
A group of hackers, working together, to target an organization as part of a cyber warfare campaign.

hardening
A security technique in which the default configuration of a system is altered to protect the system against attacks.

hash
The value that results from hashing encryption as a short representation of data. Also called a hash value or message digest.

hash function
A variable length string (text) is taken as input to produce a fixed length value as output.

HCL
(Hardware Compatibility List) Before installing an OS, it is vital to check that all the PC components have been tested for compatibility with the OS (that they are on the Hardware Compatibility List [HCL] or Windows Logo'd Product List). Incompatible hardware may not work or may even prevent the installation from completing successfully.

health policy
Policies or profiles describing a minimum security configuration that devices must meet to be granted network access.

heuristic
Monitoring technique that allows dynamic pattern matching based on past experience rather than relying on pre-loaded signatures.

HFS+
(Extended Hierarchical File System) The file system used by Apple Mac workstations and laptops.

high resource utilization
When apps, especially malware or rogue apps, use excessive processor cycles (often trying to collect data in the background) and overwhelm a mobile device.

hives
The Windows Registry is made up of hives. Each hive contains a discrete body of configuration data corresponding to an aspect of the system; for example; the SOFTWARE hive contains all the software configuration information. The files comprising the hives are stored in the %SystemRoot%\System32\Config folder.

home directory
A directory where you are placed when you log in to a Linux system. It is typically represented by the ~ symbol.

home folder
A private network storage area located in a shared network server folder in which users can store personal files.

homegroup
Windows networking feature designed to allow Windows 7 and later home networks to share files and printers easily through a simple password protection mechanism. Earlier versions of Windows are not supported. Support for homegroups was discontinued in later versions of Windows 10.

host firewall
See **personal firewall**.

hotfix
A hotfix is a software update designed and released to particular customers only, though they may be included in later Service Packs.

HVAC
(Heating, Ventilation, and Air Conditioning) The building environmental heating and cooling services and the control of those systems.

I/O addresses
(Input/Output addresses) Input/output peripherals have a special area of memory in the range 0000-FFFF set aside to allow data reading and writing functions. This is normally configured by Plug-and-Play but can be set manually using Device Manager.

I/O port
A device connection through which data can be sent and received.

iCloud
Cloud storage service operated by Apple and closely integrated with macOS and iOS.

iCloud Keychain
A **Keychain** feature that makes the same passwords securely available across all macOS and iOS devices.

ICM
(information content management) The process of managing information over its lifecycle, from creation to destruction.

ICMP
(Internet Control Message Protocol) IP-level protocol for reporting errors and status information supporting the function of troubleshooting utilities such as ping.

IDE
(Integrated Development Environment) A programming environment that typically includes a code editor containing an autocomplete feature to help you write code, a debugger to help you find coding errors, and an **interpreter** that translates the **script file** code into machine readable code the computer can **execute**.

identifier
A computer programming component used to access program elements such as a stored value, class, method, or interface.

image
A duplicate of an operating system installation (including installed software, settings, and user data) stored on removable media. Windows makes use of image-based backups and they are also used for deploying Windows to multiple PCs rapidly.

image level backup
Backup of a virtual machine which captures all of the information required to run the VM.

impersonation
An approach in which an attacker pretends to be someone they are not, typically an average user in distress, or a help-desk representative.

implicit deny
Implicit deny is a basic principle of security stating that unless something has explicitly been granted access it should be denied access. An example of this is firewall rule processing, where the last (default) rule is to deny all connections not allowed by a previous rule.

in-place upgrade
Installing the OS on top of an existing version of the OS, retaining applications, user settings, and data files.

incident
Something that is not normal and disrupts regular operations in the computing environment.

incident management
A set of practices and procedures that govern how an organization will respond to an incident in progress.

Incident Response Policy
Procedures and guidelines covering appropriate priorities, actions, and responsibilities in the event of security incidents. The stages will generally be notification, investigation, remediation, and follow-up. Incident response is often handled by a special group—the Computer Security Incident Response Team—made up of staff with both technical skills and decision-making authority.

incineration
Exposing the disk to high heat to melt its components.

insert mode
In Linux vi editor, the mode that allows users to insert text by typing.

installation boot method
The way in which the installation program and settings are loaded onto the PC.

integer
Data type supporting storage of whole numbers.

integrity
The fundamental security goal of ensuring that electronic data is not altered or tampered with.

interface
The point at which two devices connect and communicate with each other.

interpreted
A command language in which the commands in a **script file** are performed without being compiled into a machine-level set of instructions. In interpreted languages, the code must be read and evaluated each time the script is run, making it slower than compiled instructions.

iOS
Mobile OS developed by Apple for its iPhone and iPad devices.

IPS
(Indoor Positioning Systems) A system that works out a device's location by triangulating its proximity to other radio sources, such as Wi-Fi access points or Bluetooth beacons.

IPSec
(Internet Protocol Security) Layer 3 protocol suite providing security for TCP/IP. It can be used in two modes (transport, where only the data payload is encrypted, and tunnel, where the entire IP packet is encrypted and a new IP header added). IPsec can provide confidentiality and/or integrity. Encryption can be applied using a number of hash (MD5 or SHA) and symmetric (DES or AES) algorithms. Key exchange and security associations are handled by the Internet Key Exchange Protocol. Hosts can be authenticated by a shared secret, PKI, or Kerberos.

IRQ
(Interrupt Request) A communications channel between a hardware device and the system processor. Originally, when hardware was added to the computer it had to be manually configured with a unique interrupt number (between 0 and 15). Plug-and-Play compatible systems configure resources automatically. The PCI bus introduced IRQ steering, which allowed IRQs to be shared. Modern computers use programmable interrupt controllers, allowing for hundreds of interrupts.

ISO file
A file that contains all of the contents from an optical disc in a single file which can be mounted to the file system as though it were a physical optical drive.

ITIL
(IT Infrastructure Library) An IT best practice framework, emphasizing the alignment of IT Service Management (ITSM) with business needs. ITIL was first developed in 1989 by the UK government and the ITIL v3 2011 edition is now marketed by AXELOS.

jamming
In wireless networking, the phenomenon by which radio waves from other devices interfere with the 802.11 wireless signals

used by computing devices and other network devices.

jitter
A variation in the time it takes for a signal to reach the recipient. Jitter manifests itself as an inconsistent rate of packet delivery. If packet loss or delay is excessive, then noticeable audio or video problems (artifacts) are experienced by users.

KB
(Knowledge Base) A searchable database of product FAQs (Frequently Asked Questions), advice, and known troubleshooting issues. The Microsoft KB is found at support.microsoft.com.

kernel
A low-level piece of code responsible for controlling the rest of the operating system.

key exchange
Two hosts need to know the same symmetric encryption key without any other host finding out what it is.

key fob
A chip implanted in a plastic fob. The chip can store authentication data (such as a digital certificate) that can be read when put in proximity to a suitable scanner. Another use for fobs is to generate a One Time Password, valid for a couple of minutes only and mathematically linked to a code generated on a server.

keyboard
The oldest PC input device and still fundamental to operating a computer. There are many different designs and layouts for different countries. Some keyboards feature special keys.

Keychain
macOS app for managing passwords cached by the OS and supported browser/web applications.

kill switch
Another term for **remote wipe**.

latency
The time it takes for a signal to reach the recipient. A video application can support a latency of about 80 ms, while typical

latency on the Internet can reach 1000 ms at peak times. Latency is a particular problem for 2-way applications, such as VoIP (telephone) and online conferencing.

latent
Evidence that cannot be seen with the naked eye and instead must be interpreted using a machine or process.

least privilege
Least privilege is a basic principle of security stating that something should be allocated the minimum necessary rights, privileges, or information to perform its role.

legacy system
A computer system that is no longer supported by its vendor and so no longer provided with security updates and patches.

light sensors
Sensors in a mobile device used to dim and brighten the display based on ambient conditions.

line conditioner
A device that adjusts voltages in under-voltage and over-voltage conditions to maintain a normal output.

Linux
An open-source operating system supported by a wide range of hardware and software vendors.

Linux processes
An instance of a running program that performs a data processing task.

literal
A match to the exact string.

local account
An account that is only associated with the computer on which it was created.

Local Security Accounts database
A local (non-network) database where local system account information is stored. In Windows systems, this is the **SAM** database, and in Linux systems the information is stored in the /etc/passwd or /etc/shadow file.

Local Security Policy
A set of policies relating to log on, passwords, and other security issues that can be enforced or disabled on the local machine. On domains, security policy is configured centrally using Group Policy Objects (GPO).

locator applications
An app installed on mobile devices that identifies the device location to help locate a lost or stolen device.

locked out
When a user is unable to access a device because the device has been disabled either by means of the user forgetting the passcode too many times or remotely using an app that locks the device if it is reported lost or stolen.

lockout policy
A policy designed to restrict failed login attempts.

logical operator
A comparison of more than one condition at the same time by using AND, OR, or XOR.

logical security
Controls implemented in software to create an access control system.

logon script
A text file that runs when the user logs on. The file contains commands and settings to configure a user's environment.

loop
Like a **branch**, a loop deviates from the initial program path to some sort of logic condition. In a loop, the computer repeats the task until a condition is met. Often implemented with For or While statements.

low level format
A "proper" low level format creates cylinders and sectors on the disk. This can generally only be done at the factory. The disk utilities just clean data from each sector; they don't re-create the sector layout.

MAC address table
The table on a switch keeping track of MAC addresses associated with each port. As the switch uses a type of memory called Content Addressable Memory (CAM), this is sometimes called the CAM table.

MAC filtering
(media access control filtering) Applying an access control list to a switch or access point so that only clients with approved MAC addresses can connect to it.

MAC flooding
Overloading the switch's MAC cache using a tool such as Dsniff or Ettercap to prevent genuine devices from connecting and potentially forcing the switch into hub or flooding mode.

Mac OS
The name of the Apple operating system from launch to 2001.

macOS
Operating system designed by Apple for their range of iMac computers, Mac workstations, and MacBook portables. macOS (previously called OS X) is based on the BSD version of UNIX. macOS is well supported by application vendors, especially in the design industry.

MACs
(Moves, adds, changes) A record of any requested moves, adds, or changes to computers, devices, users, or related policies.

Magic Mouse
An Apple mouse with a touchpad surface that supports **gestures**.

Magic Trackpad
An Apple trackpad with a larger work surface than the Magic Mouse.

mantrap
A secure entry system with two gateways, only one of which is open at any one time.

mask
A face covering, usually made of cloth, plastic, or rubber, that fits over your mouth and nose should be worn when you are using a compressed air canister, working around toner spills, or working in

an otherwise dusty environment. A mask minimizes the risk of inhaling damaging airborne particles.

MBR
(Master Boot Record) A sector on a hard disk storing information about partitions configured on the disk.

MD5
(Message Digest Algorithm v5) The Message Digest Algorithm was designed in 1990 by Ronald Rivest, one of the "fathers" of modern cryptography. The most widely used version is MD5, released in 1991, which uses a 128-bit hash value.

MDM
(Mobile Device Management) Software suites designed to manage use of smartphones and tablets within an enterprise.

member server
Any Windows-based server computer configured into a domain but not maintaining the Active Directory database (authenticating users) is referred to as a member server. Servers in a workgroup are referred to as standalone servers.

message digest
See **MD5**.

metadata
Data about data, typically one set of data summarizes information about the original set of data.

Microsoft account
The type of account required to get apps from the Microsoft Store, to sync data between devices, access OneDrive, and work with parental controls for a Child account.

Microsoft Windows
Windows started as version 3.1 for 16-bit computers. A workgroup version provided rudimentary network facilities. Windows NT 4 workstations and servers (introduced in 1993) provided reliable 32-bit operation and secure network facilities, based around domains. The Windows 9x clients (Windows 95, 98, and Me) had far lower reliability and only support for workgroups, but were still hugely popular

as home and business machines. Windows 2000 and Windows XP workstations married the hardware flexibility and user interface of Windows 9x to the reliability and security of Windows NT, while the server versions saw the introduction of Active Directory for managing network objects. The subsequent client releases of Windows (Vista and Windows 7) featured a substantially different interface (Aero) with 3D features as well as security improvements. The latest client versions—Windows 8 and Windows 10—are designed for use with touchscreen devices.

Mission Control
App facilitating multiple desktops in macOS.

MitM
(Man-in-the-Middle) Where the attacker intercepts communications between two hosts.

mount point
A partition or volume mapped to a folder in another file system rather than allocated a drive letter.

mouse
The essential device to implement a WIMP GUI, a mouse simply controls the movement of a cursor that can be used to select objects from the screen. All Windows mice feature two click buttons, which are configured to perform different actions. Many mice also feature a scroll wheel.

MSDS
(Materials Safety Data Sheet) Information sheet accompanying hazardous products or substances explaining the proper procedures for handling and disposal.

MTBF
(Mean Time Between Failures) The rating on a device or component that predicts the expected time between failures.

multiboot system
Installing multiple operating systems on a single computer. Each OS must normally be installed to a separate partition.

multifactor authentication
Strong authentication is multifactor. Authentication schemes work on the basis of something you know, something you have, or something you are. These schemes can be made stronger by combining them (for example, protecting use of a smart card certification [something you have] with a PIN [something you know]).

multiple desktops
A feature that enables users to set up one or more desktops with different sets of apps, backgrounds, and so on. See **Mission Control**.

mutual authentication
Typically a client authenticates to a server. In many circumstances, it may be necessary for the server to authenticate to the client also (to prevent Man-in-the-Middle attacks, for instance). This is referred to as mutual authentication.

NAC
(Network Access Control) A means of ensuring endpoint security—ensuring that all devices connecting to the network conform to a "health" policy (patch level, anti-virus/firewall configuration, and so on). NAC can work on the basis of pre- or post-admission control. The core components are an agent running on the client, policy enforcers (network connection devices such as switches and access points), and policy decision points (NAC policy server and AAA/RADIUS server).

NAPT
(Network Address Port Translation) Similar to NAT, it (or PAT or NAT overloading) maps private host IP addresses onto a single public IP address. Each host is tracked by assigning it a random high TCP port for communications.

NAT
(Network Address Translation) A network service provided by router or proxy server to map private local addresses to one or more publicly accessible IP addresses. NAT can use static mappings but is most commonly implemented as Network Address Port Translation (NAPT) or NAT overloading, where a few public IP addresses are mapped to multiple LAN hosts using port allocations.

network drive
A local share that has been assigned a drive letter.

network firewall
A firewall placed inline in the network that inspects all traffic that passes through it.

network mapping
Tools used to gather information about the way the network is built and configured and the current status of hosts.

network topology
The shape or structure of a network is commonly described as its topology. Topologies may be either physical (the actual appearance of the network layout) or logical (the flow of data across the network). In a star topology, nodes are connected to a single point while in a hub topology, all nodes connect to the same media and share bandwidth. A ring topology means that communications travel from node-to-node in a loop. In a full mesh network, each node is linked to every other node, but partial meshes are far more common. A hybrid topology uses elements of different topologies, such as a logical bus but physical star.

NFC
(Near Field Communications) A Standard for peer-to-peer (2-way) radio communications over very short (around 4") distances, facilitating contactless payment and similar technologies. NFC is based on RFID.

NFS
(Network File System) A remote file access protocol used principally on UNIX and Linux networks.

NLA
(Network Level Authentication) An RDP technology requiring users to authenticate before a server session is created.

NTFS
(NT File System) A Windows file system that supports a 64-bit address space and is able to provide extra features such as file-by-file compression and RAID support as

well as advanced file attribute management tools, encryption, and disk quotas.

objects
A data structure in Windows that represents system resources.

ODBC Data Sources
See **Data Sources**.

offline files
Files (or folders) from a network share that are cached locally. The Offline Folders tool handles synchronization between the local and remote copies.

on-access
A type of antivirus scan where the AV software intercepts OS calls to open files, so that it can scan the file before allowing or preventing the file from being opened.

onboarding
The process in which MDM software logs use of a device on the network and determines whether to allow it to connect or not, based on administrator-set parameters.

open questions
Questions that guide the customer to telling you what will be most helpful in resolving their issue.

open source
Open source means that the programming code used to design the software is freely available.

operating system
A software package that enables a computer to function. It performs basic tasks, such as recognizing the input from a keyboard, sending the output to a display screen or monitor, and controlling peripheral devices such as disk drives and printers.

options
The modifiers used with Linux commands to make a command more versatile.

OS X
The name of the Apple operating system from 2001 through 2016.

OTP
(one time password) A password that is generated for use in one specific session and becomes invalid after the session ends.

OU
(Organizational Unit) In Windows Active Directory, a way of dividing the domain up into different administrative realms.

packet filtering
A type of firewall that inspects the headers of IP packets and can perform filtering on IP address, protocol type, and port numbers.

pagefile
See **virtual memory**.

parent directory
A directory that is one level above your current working directory.

partitioning
The act of dividing a physical disk into logically separate storage areas, often referred to as drives.

password policy
A weakness of password-based authentication systems is when users demonstrate poor password practice. Examples include choosing a password that is too simple, reusing passwords for different tasks, writing a password down, and not changing a password regularly. Some of these poor practices can be addressed by system policies; others are better approached by education.

PAT
(portable appliance testing) In the UK, Australia, and New Zealand, the process for inspecting and testing electrical equipment to ensure its safety.

PAT
(port address translation) Another term for NAT overloading or **NAPT**.

patch
A fix or update for a software program or application, designed to eliminate known bugs or vulnerabilities and improve performance.

Patch Management
Identifying, testing, and deploying OS and application updates. Patches are often classified as critical, security-critical, recommended, and optional.

Patch Tuesday
The second Tuesday of every month when Microsoft releases updates.

pattern lock
To access a locked device, the user must trace a predetermined pattern on screen, or join the dots.

PCI DSS
(Payment Card Industry Data Security Standard) Information security standard for organizations that process credit or bank card payments.

PDU
(power distribution unit) A device designed to provide power to devices that require power, and may or may not support remote monitoring and access.

peer-to-peer network
In peer-to-peer networks there is no dedicated server, but instead, each computer connected to the network acts as both a server and client (each computer is a peer of the other computers). These types of networks were originally developed as a low-cost alternative to server-based systems for use in smaller companies and organizations where there are up to about ten users. A major drawback to this type of network is a comparative lack of security whereby each user must control access to resources on his/her machine.

permissions
To access files and folders on a volume, the administrator of the computer will need to grant file permissions to the user (or a group to which the user belongs). File permissions are supported by NTFS-based Windows systems.

personal firewall
A firewall implemented as applications software running on the host. Personal software firewalls can provide sophisticated filtering of network traffic and also block processes at the application level. However, as a user-mode application they are more vulnerable to attack and evasion than kernel mode firewalls or network firewall appliances.

pharming
Similar to phishing, this type of social engineering attack redirects a request for a website, typically an e-commerce site, to a similar-looking, but fake, website. The attacker uses DNS spoofing to redirect the user to the fake site.

PHI
(Protected Health Information) Information that identifies someone as the subject of medical and insurance records, plus associated hospital and laboratory test results.

phishing
Obtaining user authentication or financial information through a fraudulent request for information. Phishing is specifically associated with emailing users with a link to a faked site (or some other malware that steals the information they use to try to authenticate). Pharming is a related technique where the attacker uses DNS spoofing to redirect the user to the fake site. Vishing refers to phishing attacks conducted over voice channels (VoIP), while spear phishing or whaling refers to attacks specifically directed at managers or senior executives.

PID
See **Process ID**.

PII
(Personally Identifiable Information) Data that can be used to identify or contact an individual (or in the case of identity theft, to impersonate them). A Social Security number is a good example of PII. Others include names, date of birth, email address, telephone number, street address, biometric data, and so on.

pipe symbol
A vertical bar typed between commands to pipe or redirect the results or output of one command as the input to another command.

PIV Card
(Personal Identification Verification card) Smart card standard for access control to US Federal government premises and computer networks.

PKI
(Public Key Infrastructure) Asymmetric encryption provides a solution to the problem of secure key distribution for symmetric encryption. The main problem is making a link between a particular public-private key pair and a specific user. One way of solving this problem is through PKI. Under this system, keys are issued as digital certificates by a Certificate Authority (CA). The CA acts as a guarantor that the user is who he or she says he or she is. Under this model, it is necessary to establish trust relationships between users and CAs. In order to build trust, CAs must publish and comply with Certificate Policies and Certificate Practice Statements.

Plug and Play
See **UPnP**.

PNAC
(Port-based Network Access Control) An IEEE 802.1X standard in which the switch (or router) performs some sort of authentication of the attached device before activating the port.

pointing device
A peripheral used to move a cursor to select and manipulate objects on the screen.

policy
A subset of a security profile, and a document that outlines the specific requirements and rules everyone must meet.

port (logical)
In TCP and UDP applications, a port is a unique number assigned to a particular application protocol (such as HTTP or SMTP). The port number (with the IP address) forms a socket between client and server. A socket is a bi-directional pipe for the exchange of data. For security, it is important to allow only the ports required to be open (ports can be blocked using a firewall).

port (physical)
A hardware connection interface on a personal computer that enables devices to be connected to the computer.

port forwarding
Port forwarding means that a router takes requests from the Internet for a particular application (say, HTTP/port 80) and sends them to a designated host on the LAN.

port scanning
Software that enumerates the status of TCP and UDP ports on a target system. Port scanning can be blocked by some firewalls and IDS.

port triggering
Port triggering is used to configure access through a firewall for applications that require more than one port. Basically, when the firewall detects activity on outbound port A destined for a given external IP address, it opens inbound access for the external IP address on port B for a set period.

POST
(Power-On Self-Test) A hardware checking routine built into the PC firmware. This test sequentially monitors the state of the memory chips, the processor, system clock, display, and firmware itself. Errors that occur within vital components such as these are signified by beep codes emitted by the internal speaker of the computer. Further tests are then performed and any errors displayed as on-screen error codes and messages.

power drain
When apps, especially malware or rogue apps, use excessive power and quickly drain the battery of a mobile device.

power redundancy
A duplicate power source to be used in case one power source is unavailable.

primary group
In Linux, users can be members of one primary group and multiple supplemental groups.

privacy screen
A filter to fit over a display screen so that it can only be viewed straight-on.

problem management
A method of identifying, prioritizing, and establishing ownership of **incidents**.

procedure
An inflexible, step-by-step listing of the actions that must be completed for any given task.

Process ID
Also PID. The number assigned to a process.

professionalism
Taking pride in one's work and in treating people fairly.

profile of security requirements
A set of policies to apply for different employees and different site areas within a site.

program
Software that provides functionality such as word processing, graphics creation, database management, or other productivity or entertainment uses.

proper documentation
A record of what will be done so that the customer knows what to expect in terms of items that are supported, how long incidents may take to resolve, when they can expect an item to be replaced instead of repaired, and so on.

protocol suite
A collection of several protocols used for networking are designed to work together.

pseudocode
Writing out a program sequence using code blocks but without using the specific syntax of a particular programming language.

PSK
(Pre-shared Key) Symmetric encryption technologies, such as those used for WEP, require both parties to use the same private key. This key must be kept a secret known only to those authorized to use the network. A pre-shared key is normally generated from a passphrase.

PXE
(Preboot Execution Environment) A feature of a network adapter that allows the computer to boot by contacting a suitably configured server over the network (rather than using a local hard disk).

QoS
(Quality of Service) Systems that differentiate data passing over the network that can reserve bandwidth for particular applications. A system that cannot guarantee a level of available bandwidth is often described as Class of Service (CoS).

quality updates
Windows updates that are typically released each Tuesday designed to address security vulnerabilities, usually installed in one group of patches and requiring a single reboot. Compare with feature updates.

RADIUS
(Remote Authentication Dial-in User Service) Used to manage remote and wireless authentication infrastructure. Users supply authentication information to RADIUS client devices, such as wireless access points. The client device then passes the authentication data to an AAA (Authentication, Authorization, and Accounting) server, which processes the request.

RAID
(Redundant Array of Independent/ Inexpensive Disks) A set of vendor-independent specifications for fault-tolerant configurations on multiple-disk systems.

rainbow table
Tool for speeding up attacks against Windows passwords by precomputing possible hashes.

ransomware
A type of malware that tries to extort money from the victim, by appearing to lock their computer or by encrypting their files, for instance.

RDPRA Mode
(RDP Restricted Admin Mode) A method of mitigating the risk of using Remote Desktop.

recovery disc
OEM recovery media enabling the user to reset the system to its factory configuration.

recovery image
A custom image that contains the current state of the operating system files, plus all of the desktop applications installed to the boot partition.

redirection
When the user tries to open a web page but is sent to another page (which may or may not look like the page the user was attempting to access).

reference machine
The process of Windows deployment to multiple computers by using disk imaging software to clone an installation from one PC to the rest.

regex
(regular expressions) Strings of characters that denote a word, a set of words, or a sentence.

relational operators
See **comparison operator**.

relative path
The path relative to the current working directory.

remnant removal
Data that has nominally been deleted from a disk by the user can often be recovered using special tools. The best way to shred data without physically destroying a disk is to ensure that each writable location has been overwritten in a random pattern.

Remote Assistance
A Windows remote support feature allowing a user to invite a technical support professional to help them over a network using chat. The user can also grant the support professional control over their desktop. Remote Assistance uses the same RDP protocol as Remote Desktop.

Remote Credential Guard
A method of mitigating the risk of using Remote Desktop.

Remote Desktop
The Windows feature that allows a remote user to initiate a connection at any time and sign on to the local machine using an authorized account.

remote wipe
Software that allows deletion of data and settings on a mobile device to be initiated from a remote server.

replay attack
Where the attacker intercepts some authentication data and reuses it to try to re-establish a session.

rescue disk
See **recovery disc**.

respect
Treating others and their property as you would like to be treated.

restore points
System Restore takes a snapshot of the system configuration and enables rollbacks to these restore points.

RF
(Radio Frequency) Radio waves propagate at different frequencies and wavelengths. Wi-Fi network products work at 2.4 GHz or 5 GHz.

RFC
(Request for Change) In change management, the formal document submitted to the **CAB** that has the details of the proposed alteration.

RFID
(Radio Frequency Identification) A chip allowing data to be read wirelessly. RFID tags are used in barcodes and smart cards.

RFID badge
(Radio Frequency Identification badge) An ID badge containing a chip allowing data to be read wirelessly.

RFID tag
A tag containing an RFID chip programmed with asset data.

risk
The likelihood and impact (or consequence) of a threat actor exercising a vulnerability.

RJ connector
(Registered Jack connector) A connector used for twisted pair cabling. 4-pair network cabling uses the larger RJ-45 connector. Modem/telephone 2-pair cabling uses the RJ-11 connector.

RJ-11 connector
A six-position connector that uses just one pair of wires. It is used in telephone system connections.

roaming profile
A Microsoft Windows technology that redirects user profiles to a network share so that the information is available when the user logs into any computer on the network where the network share is located.

rogue access point
An unauthorized wireless access point on a corporate or private network, which allows unauthorized individuals to connect to the network.

root directory
Top of the file directory structure on a drive.

root user
A user who has access rights to all files and resources on the system and is the default administrative account on a Linux system.

rootkit
A class of malware that modifies system files, often at the kernel level, to conceal its presence.

routine
A section of code within a program to be used repeatedly for a specific task and is usually independent from the rest of the code within the program.

rpm
(Red Hat Package Manager) A tool for maintaining packages in Red Hat Linux systems.

RPO
(Recovery Point Objective) The amount of data loss that a system can sustain, measured in time. See also **recovery time objective**.

RSA
(Rivest Shamir Adelman) The first successful algorithm to be designed for public key encryption. It is named for its designers.

RSoP
(Resultant Set of Policies) In Windows systems, a Group Policy report showing all of the GPO settings and how they affect the network. It can also be used to show how GPOs affect user and computer combinations with the local security policy in effect.

RSSI
(Received Signal Strength Indicator) For a wireless signal, an index level calculated from the signal strength level.

RTO
(Recovery Time Objective) The period following a disaster that a system may remain offline. See also **recovery point objective**.

sag
A sag can occur when the power supply entering a computer's components dips briefly below that which is required. Sags are commonly caused when heavy machinery or other high power appliances are started.

SAM
(Security Account Manager) The Windows local security account database where local system account information is stored.

schematic
A schematic is a simplified representation of a system. Physical network diagrams or schematics can show the general location of components and their identification. Logical network diagrams show the organization of the network into subnets and zones.

screen lock
A way to prevent unauthorized access to a computer or mobile device. Configuring a

screen lock requires the user to enter a passphrase, complete a pattern, or enter a PIN to access the device.

script file
A text file containing commands or instructions that are performed by a program on the computer rather than by the computer itself.

scripting language
A programming language that is **interpreted** rather than compiled.

sector
A sector is the term given to the regularly sized subdivision of a drive track. During low-level formatting, the size and position of the sectors are written to the disk so that the data can be placed into uniform spots that the drive head can easily access.

secure boot
A security system offered by UEFI that is designed to prevent a computer from being hijacked by malware.

security control
A technology or procedure put in place to mitigate vulnerabilities and risk and to ensure the Confidentiality, Integrity, and Availability (CIA) of information. Control types are often classed in different ways, such as technical, operational, and management.

security group
A collection of user accounts that can be assigned permissions in the same way as a single user object.

security template
Settings for services and policy configuration for a server operating in a particular application role (web server, mail server, file/print server, and so on). In Windows, the current configuration can be compared to the baseline defined in a security template using the Security Configuration and Analysis tool.

self-grounding
Manual dissipation of static buildup by touching a grounded object prior to touching any electronic equipment.

service
Windows machines run services to provide functions; for example, Plug-and-Play, the print spooler, DHCP client, and so on. These services can be viewed, configured, and started/stopped via the Services console. You can also configure which services run at startup using msconfig. You can view background services (as well as applications) using the Processes tab in Task Manager.

SHA
(Secure Hash Algorithm) A cryptographic hashing algorithm created to address possible weaknesses in MDA. The earlier SHA-1 has been superseded by SHA-2.

shareware
Software that you can install free of charge usually for a limited time of use or with limited functionality. To continue using it or to access additional features, the user will need to register and often pay for the software.

shell
An OS component that interacts directly with users and functions as the command interpreter for operating systems.

shell script
A Linux file that contains a list of commands to be read and executed by the shell.

shoulder surfing
A human-based attack where the goal is to look over the shoulder of an individual as he or she enters password information or a PIN.

shredding
Grinding a disk into little pieces.

slipstreamed media
A disc-based installation that has all of the various updates, patches, and drivers included along with the original installation files.

smart card
A card with a chip containing data on it. Smart cards are typically used for authentication, with the chip storing authentication data such as a digital certificate.

smart card reader
A device, either built-in or attached as a peripheral, that uses a slot or NFC to interact with a smart card.

social engineering
A hacking technique, widely publicized by Kevin Mitnick in his book "The Art of Deception," whereby the hacker gains useful information about an organization by deceiving its users or by exploiting their unsecure working practices. Typical social engineering methods include impersonation, domination, and charm.

soft reset
Power cycling a mobile device in an attempt to resolve issues the user is experiencing.

SOHO network
(small office/home office network) A small network that provides connectivity and resource sharing for a small office or home office.

SOP
(Standard Operating Procedure) See **procedure**.

spam
Junk messages sent over email (or instant messaging [SPIM]). Filters and blacklists are available to block spam and known spam servers. It is also important to ensure that any mail servers you operate are not open relays, allowing a spammer to leverage your server to distribute spam and making it likely that it will be blacklisted.

spear phishing
See **whaling**.

spike
A spike can occur when electrical devices are turned off or when electrical storms are happening. Normally, spikes and surges are not sufficient to cause problems but occasionally big fluctuations may lead to the system crashing or hanging.

spoofing
Where the attacker disguises their identity. Some examples include IP spoofing, where the attacker changes their IP address, or

phishing, where the attacker sets up a false website.

Spotlight
File system search feature in macOS.

spyware
Software that records information about a PC and its user. Spyware is used to describe malicious software installed without the user's content. Aggressive spyware is used to gather passwords or financial information such as credit card details.

SSH
(Secure Shell) A remote administration and file copy program that is flexible enough to support VPNs too (using port forwarding). SSH runs on TCP port 22.

SSID
(Service Set ID) Identifies a particular Wireless LAN (WLAN). This "network name" can be used to connect to the correct network. When multiple APs are configured with the same SSID, this is referred to as an E(xtended)SSID.

SSO
(Single Sign-on) Any authentication technology that allows a user to authenticate once and receive authorizations for multiple services. Kerberos is a typical example of an authentication technology providing SSO.

standard
A measure by which to evaluate compliance with a policy.

Standard User account
A Microsoft Windows user account recommended for day-to-day operations, which has much more limited capabilities than the Administrator account, and is able to run installed programs.

stored value
The area where programs keep variable and constant values while the program is running.

string
Data type supporting storage of a variable length series of characters.

superuser
Another term for the root user.

supplicant
Under 802.1X, the device requesting access.

surge
An abrupt but brief change in the value of the voltage, lasting from a few billionths of a second (a transient) to a few thousandths of a second.

surge protector
A simple device intended to protect electrical devices against the damaging effects of a power spike.

swap partition
A portion of the hard disk that is formatted with a minimal kind of file system and used in situations when Linux runs out of physical memory and needs more of it. It can only be used by the memory manager and not for storage of ordinary data files.

swipe lock
Another term for unlocking a device by tracing a predetermined on screen pattern or joining dots on screen.

switches
See **options**.

system files
The files necessary for the operating system to function properly.

system partition
In Microsoft terminology, the system partition is the bootable partition on the hard disk. This is usually, but not always, separate to the boot partition, which contains the operating system. The system partition is usually hidden from File Explorer (no drive letter is assigned to it).

system resources
Settings that enable a device to communicate with the CPU and memory without the device conflicting with other devices.

system restore
See **restore points**.

tab completion
A feature in Linux that facilitates auto completion of commands and file names by pressing Tab.

TACACS+
(Terminal Access Controller Access Control System) An alternative to **RADIUS** developed by Cisco. The version in current use is TACACS+; TACACS and XTACACS are legacy protocols.

tailgating
Social engineering technique to gain access to a building by following someone else (or persuading them to "hold the door").

Task Scheduler
The Task Scheduler is a Windows program that enables the user to perform an action (such as running a program or a script) automatically at a pre-set time or in response to some sort of trigger.

TB
(Thunderbolt) It can be used as a display interface (like DisplayPort) and as a general peripheral interface (like USB 3). The latest version uses USB-C connectors.

telnet
TCP/IP application protocol supporting remote command-line administration of a host (terminal emulation). Telnet is unauthenticated and has therefore been superseded by SSH or graphical remote configuration utilities. Telnet runs over TCP port 23.

terminal window
In Linux, a computer interface for text entry and display, where information is displayed as an array of preselected characters.

threat
Any potential violation of security policies or procedures.

threat actor
See **threat agent**.

threat agent
A person or event that triggers a vulnerability accidentally or exploits it intentionally.

three-factor authentication
An authentication scheme that requires validation of three authentication factors.

ticket
A record created when an incident occurs, or move, add, or change is requested, so that progress on resolving or completing the task can be documented.

Time Machine
App facilitating backup operations in macOS.

TKIP
(Temporal Key Integrity Protocol) Mechanism used in the first version of WPA to improve the security of wireless encryption mechanisms, compared to the flawed WEP standard.

Touch ID
The Apple device feature that uses fingerprint biometric information to grant access to the device.

touchpad
Input device used on most laptops to replace the mouse. The touchpad allows the user to control the cursor by moving a finger over the pad's surface. There are usually buttons too but the pad may also recognize "tap" events and have scroll areas.

TPM
(Trusted Platform Module) A specification for hardware-based storage of digital certificates, keys, hashed passwords, and other user and platform identification information. Essentially, it functions as a smart card embedded on a motherboard.

trace logs
Windows log files that allow you to collect statistics about services, including extensions to Event Viewer to log data that would otherwise be inaccessible.

trip hazard
Any object placed in pathways where people walk.

Trojan Horse
A malicious software program hidden within an innocuous-seeming piece of software. Usually the Trojan is used to try to compromise the security of the target computer.

trusted app source
A source for apps that is managed by a service provider.

two-factor authentication
An authentication scheme that requires validation of two authentication factors.

UAC
(User Account Control) A security system in Windows designed to restrict abuse of accounts with administrator privileges. Actions such as installing hardware and software can be performed without changing accounts but the user must authorize the use of administrative rights by clicking a prompt or re-entering user credentials.

UEFI
(Unified Extensible Firmware Interface) A type of system firmware providing support for 64-bit CPU operation at boot, full GUI and mouse operation at boot, and better boot security.

unattended installation
A software or operating system installation where the configuration information is derived from an input file.

unauthorized account access
When someone other than an authorized user gains access to an online account.

unauthorized camera and microphone usage
When an attacker gains access to the camera and microphone on a mobile device and uses it to cause a security breach of sensitive data.

unauthorized location tracking
Giving away too much sensitive information to third parties.

unauthorized root access
When an attacker gains root access which allows the attacker to have system-level access to every process running in the OS.

undeclared variable
A variable that is used without first identifying the data type.

undocumented feature
A software feature or function that is not included in the official documentation and is typically unsupported, and can be removed or modified without users' knowledge. Also used as a derogatory term for a software bug.

unified file system
Everything available to the Linux OS is represented as a file in the file system, including devices.

UNIX
UNIX is a family of more than 20 related operating systems that are produced by various companies. It can run on a wide variety of platforms. UNIX offers a multitude of file systems in addition to its native system. UNIX remains widely deployed in enterprise data centers to run mission critical applications and infrastructure.

updates
Updates are made freely available by the software manufacturer to fix problems in a particular software version, including any security vulnerabilities. Updates can be classified as hotfixes (available only to selected customers and for a limited problem), patches (generally available), and service packs (installable collections of patches and software improvements).

UPnP
(Universal Plug-and-Play) A protocol framework allowing network devices to autoconfigure services, such as allowing a games console to request appropriate settings from a firewall.

UPS
(Uninterruptible Power Supply) An alternative AC power supply in the event of power failure. A UPS requires an array of batteries, a charging circuit, an inverter to convert DC to AC current, a circuit to allow the system to take over from a failing power supply, and some degree of spike, surge, or brownout protection (possibly including a line conditioner).

UPS sizing
The process of determining the appropriate size UPS to protect the load from a given system.

USB
(Universal Serial Bus) The main type of connection interface used on PCs. A larger Type A connector attaches to a port on the host; Type B and Mini- or Micro-Type B connectors are used for devices. USB 1.1 supports 12 Mbps while USB 2.0 supports 480 Mbps and is backward compatible with 1.1 devices (which run at the slower speed). USB devices are hot swappable. A device can draw up to 2.5 W of power. USB 3.0 and 3.1 define 5 Gbps (SuperSpeed) and 10 Gbps (SuperSpeed+) rates and can deliver 4.5 W of power.

user account
Each user who wishes to access a Windows computer will need a logon ID, referred to as a user account. Each user will normally have a local profile, containing settings and user-created files. Profiles are stored in the "Users" folder or can be redirected to a network folder.

variable
Identifier for a value that can change during program execution. Variables are usually declared with a particular data type.

VBR
(Volume Boot Record) Loads the boot manager, which for Windows is **bootmgr.exe**.

VDI
(Virtual Desktop Infrastructure) Hosting user desktops as virtual machines on a centralized server or cloud infrastructure. The desktop OS plus applications software is delivered to the client device (often a thin client) over the network as an image.

virtual file system
A layer that sits between the actual file system and the kernel. It identifies the location of the persistent root partition from the appropriate storage device and loads the file system stored on the disk.

virtual memory
An area on the hard disk allocated to contain pages of memory. When the operating system doesn't have sufficient physical memory (RAM) to perform a task, pages of memory are swapped to the paging file. This frees physical RAM to

enable the task to be completed. When the paged RAM is needed again, it is re-read into memory.

virtualization
Software allowing a single computer (the host) to run multiple "guest" operating systems (or Virtual Machines [VMs]). The VMs are configured via a hypervisor or VM Monitor (VMM). VMs can be connected using virtual networks (vSwitch) or leverage the host's network interface(s). It is also possible for the VMs to share data with the host (via shared folders or the clipboard, for instance). VT is now used as major infrastructure in data centers as well as for testing and training.

virus
Code designed to infect computer files (or disks) when it is activated. A virus may also be programmed to carry out other malicious actions, such as deleting files or changing system settings.

VNC
(Virtual Network Computing) Remote access tool and protocol. VNC is the basis of macOS screen sharing.

vulnerability
Any weakness that could be triggered accidentally or exploited intentionally to cause a security breach.

WEP
(Wired Equivalent Privacy) A mechanism for encrypting data sent over a wireless connection. WEP is considered flawed (that is, a determined and well-resourced attack could probably break the encryption). Apart from problems with the cipher, the use and distribution of a pre-shared key (effectively a password) depends on good user practice. WEP has been replaced by WPA.

whaling
A form of phishing that targets individuals who are known or are believed to be wealthy.

whitelisting
An address added to the white list is permitted to connect to any port.

Wi-Fi analyzer
A Wi-Fi spectrum analyzer used to detect devices and points of interference, as well as analyze and troubleshoot network issues on a WLAN or other wireless networks.

wiki
A website that is configured so users can view, enter, and share information about a subject.

wildcard
A special character that is used to substitute characters in a string.

Windows Certified Products List
A searchable database of hardware devices that have been tested to ensure they are compatible with the Windows 10 operating system.

Windows Explorer
See **File Explorer**.

Windows LPL catalog
(Windows Logo'd Product List catalog) A catalog of devices and drivers that have been tested to ensure they are compatible with the Windows 7 operating system.

Windows Media Center
An obsolete program included with Windows Vista and Windows 7 that included a broadcast TV schedule that allowed computers equipped with a TV tuner card to view and record TV programs. It also acted as a playback interface for optical discs.

Windows Resource Protection
A Windows feature that prevents essential system files, folders, and registry keys from being replaced to help prevent application and operating system failure.

Windows Server
A network operating system typically used for private network servers and Internet servers running web, email, and social networking apps.

Windows Settings
Windows 10 app for configuring and managing the Windows 10 computer.

WoL

(Wake on LAN) Where a host has a compatible network card, a network server can be configured to transmit a "magic packet" that causes the host to power up.

work instruction

Detailed documents that contain step-by-step tasks needed to perform a specific task.

workgroup

A small group of computers on a network that share resources in a peer-to-peer fashion. No one computer provides a centralized directory.

working directory

See **current working directory**.

worm

A type of virus that spreads through memory and network connections rather than infecting files.

WoWLAN

(Wake-on-Wireless LAN) A wireless version of WoL that is not widely implemented.

WPA

(Wi-Fi Protected Access) An improved encryption scheme for protecting Wi-Fi communications, designed to replace WEP. The original version of WPA was subsequently updated (to WPA2) following the completion of the 802.11i security standard. WPA features an improved method of key distribution and authentication for enterprise networks, though the pre-shared key method is still available for home and small office networks. WPA2 uses the improved AES cipher, replacing TKIP and RC4.

WPS

(Wi-Fi Protected Setup) Mechanism for auto-configuring a WLAN securely for home users. On compatible equipment, users just have to push a button on the access point and connecting adapters to associate them securely.

WWAN

(Wireless Wide Area Network) A large wireless network, such as a cellular data network or line-of-sight microwave transmission.

XML

(eXtensible Markup Language) A system for structuring documents so that they are human- and machine-readable. Information within the document is placed within tags, which describe how information within the document is structured.

yum

A tool for maintaining packages on Fedora-based Linux systems.

zero day exploit

An attack that exploits a vulnerability in software that is unknown to the software vendor and users. Most vulnerabilities are discovered by security researchers and the vendor will have time to create a patch and distribute it to users before exploits can be developed, so zero day exploits have the potential to be very destructive.

zombie

Unauthorized software that directs the devices to launch a DDoS attack.

Index

ISBN-13 978-1-6427-4145-2
ISBN-10 1-6427-4145-0